San Francisco

timeout.com/sanfrancisco

Published by Time Out Guides Ltd, a wholly owned subsidiary of Time Out Group Ltd.
Time Out and the Time Out logo are trademarks of Time Out Group Ltd.

© **Time Out Group Ltd 2008**
Previous editions 1996, 1998, 2000, 2002, 2004, 2006

10 9 8 7 6 5 4 3 2 1

This edition first published in Great Britain in 2008 by Ebury Publishing
A Random House Group Company
20 Vauxhall Bridge Road, London SW1V 2SA

Random House Australia Pty Limited 20 Alfred Street, Milsons Point, Sydney, New South Wales 2061, Australia
Random House New Zealand Limited 18 Poland Road, Glenfield, Auckland 10, New Zealand
Random House South Africa (Pty) Limited Isle of Houghton, Corner Boundary
Road & Carse O'Gowrie, Houghton 2198, South Africa

Random House UK Limited Reg. No. 954009

For further distribution details, see www.timeout.com

ISBN: 9781846700545

A CIP catalogue record for this book is available from the British Library

Printed and bound by Firmengruppe APPL, aprinta druck, Wemding, Germany

The Random House Group Limited supports The Forest Stewardship Council (FSC), the leading international forest
certification organisation. All our titles that are printed on Greenpeace approved FSC certified paper carry the FSC
logo. Our paper procurement policy can be found at http://www.rbooks.co.uk/environment

Time Out Guides Limited
Universal House
251 Tottenham Court Road
London W1T 7AB
Tel + 44 (0)20 7813 3000
Fax + 44 (0)20 7813 6001
Email guides@timeout.com
www.timeout.com

Contributors

History Michael Ansaldo (*Man with a mission* Edoardo Albert; *Write on: Mark Twain* Jonathan Derbyshire; '*We hold the island*' Matt Markovich). **San Francisco Today** Bonnie Wach. **Architecture** Matt Markovich. **Oakland Rising** Matt Markovich. **The Politics of Progress** Matt Markovich. **Where to Stay** Jeanne Cooper. **Sightseeing: Introduction** Will Fulford-Jones. **Downtown** Matt Markovich (*The cable guys* Will Fulford-Jones; *City noir* Elise Proulx). **SoMa & South Beach** Matt Markovich. **Nob Hill & Chinatown** Matt Markovich. **North Beach & Fisherman's Wharf** Matt Markovich (*Walk: North Beach Beat* Jake Bumgardner; *Write on: Armistead Maupin* Jonathan Derbyshire). **Mission & Castro** Matt Markovich (*Streets of San Francisco: Castro* Matt Markovich; *Walk: Murals & Latino life* Matt Markovich). **Haight & Around** Matt Markovich (*Streets of San Francisco: Haight* Matt Markovich). **Sunset, Golden Gate Park & Richmond** Matt Markovich (*Hidden 'hoods* Elise Proulx). **Pacific Heights** Matt Markovich. **The East Bay** Elise Proulx (*Streets of San Francisco: Telegraph Avenue, Berkeley* Matt Markovich; *Write on: Jack Spicer* Jonathan Derbyshire). **Restaurants & Cafés** Robert Farmer (*Viva la tortilla!* Matt Markovich; *On the sunny side of the street* Elise Proulx). **Bars** Matt Markovich. **Shops & Services** Kimberly Chun. **Festivals & Events** Tony Hayes (*Burn, baby, burn* Miranda Morton). **Children** Bonnie Wach. **Film** Elise Proulx. **Galleries** Mark Taylor. **Gay & Lesbian** Marke Bieschke. **Music** Kimberly Chun. **Nightclubs** Marke Bieschke. **Theatre & Dance** Robert Avila (*Dancing outside the box* Miranda Morton). Trips **Out of Town: Heading North** Elise Proulx. **Wine Country** Lesley McCave. **Heading East** Ann Marie Brown, Ruth Jarvis. **Heading South** Lesley McCave, Will Fulford-Jones, Grace Krilanovich. **Directory** Miranda Morton.

Maps john@jsgraphics.co.uk.

Photography All photography by Hans Kwiotek, except: page 10 CORBIS; 15 Private Collection/The Bridgeman Art Library; 16 Library of Congress Prints and Photographs Division; 19 Time Life Pictures/Getty Images; 21, 22 Bettmann/CORBIS; 38 Roger Ressmeyer/CORBIS; 39 Associated Press; 40 Ted Streshinsky/CORBIS; 48 Kimpton Hotels; 70 Warner Bros/First National/The Kobal Collection; 92 Christopher Turner; 143 2008 Drew Altizer; 201 AFP/Getty Images; 219 Leo Herrera; 253 Luiza Silva; 259, 261 Elan Fleisher; 264, 275, 279 Getty Images; 269 Martin Daly; 271, 274 Heloise Bergman; 276 Photolibrary Group.

The following images were provided by the featured establishments/artists: pages 198, 199

The Editor would like to thank all contributors to previous editions of *Time Out San Francisco*, whose work forms the basis for parts of this book.

Contents

Introduction

San Francisco is a small city with a big reputation. Sitting within seven square miles on a peninsula in the Pacific Ocean are dramatic cityscapes and stupendous views that are known the world over. But much as plunging hills, cable cars, and – perhaps most iconic of all – the Golden Gate Bridge, represent the city, it is the energetic, free-thinking, can-do populace that really makes the place what it is.

Money-making and radicalism may seem odd bedfellows, but both have been crucial in forming this city. It was the discovery of gold that transformed a sleepy trading post into a lawless boom town; silver that turned it into a cash-rich, freewheeling market place, with a small number of silver barons making huge fortunes and immigrants from all around the world vying to make a living.

Trailblazers of a different order made their mark on San Francisco in the post World War II era. In the 1950s Jack Kerouac, Allen Ginsberg and other writers of the Beat Generation issued their vision of a different America. Their '60s successors were a new generation of rebels, the hippies, and San Francisco was the site of the epoch-making Summer of Love in 1967. A continued unwillingness to accept the status quo saw gay rights and feminist movements burgeon in the '70s. At the same time, the area's technical brains were hard at work on the radical technology of the future – the computer.

This city has never been afraid of new ideas. It has also been willing and able to reinvent itself – and has done so several times. No one could have predicted that the dotcom crash of the late '90s would be followed by a tech industry revival in the noughties. Yet once again San Francisco is booming, with big construction projects such as the One Rincon Hill condominium tower and the Transbay Transit Center in progress, and regeneration in areas like Mission Bay and China Basin.

San Francisco's energy is infectious. The city punches way above its weight with vigorous arts, culture, restaurant and nightlife scenes. Its size makes it easy to explore; an efficient public transport system helps. This is one US city where a car could be considered an encumbrance. We hope you enjoy exploring the City on the Bay as much as its residents enjoy living here.

ABOUT TIME OUT CITY GUIDES

This is the seventh edition of *Time Out San Francisco*, one of an expanding series of more than 50 guides produced by the people behind the successful listings magazines in London, New York, Chicago, Sydney and many more cities around the world. Our guides are all written and updated by resident experts who have striven to provide you with all the most up-to-date information you'll need to explore San Francisco, whether you're a local or a first-time visitor.

THE LOWDOWN ON THE LISTINGS

Above all, we've tried to make this book as useful as possible. Telephone numbers, websites, transport information, opening times, admission prices and credit card details have all been included in the listings, all checked and correct at press time. However, owners and managers can change their arrangements at any time. Before you go out of your way, we strongly advise you to call and check opening times and other particulars. While every effort has been made to ensure the accuracy of the information contained in this guide, the publishers cannot accept responsibility for any errors it may contain.

PRICES AND PAYMENT

Our listings detail the major credit cards – American Express (AmEx), Diners Club (DC), Discover (Disc), MasterCard (MC) and Visa (V) – accepted by each venue. Many businesses will also accept other cards, such as Maestro and Carte Blanche, as well as travellers' cheques issued by a major financial institution.

The prices we've supplied should be treated as guidelines, not gospel. Fluctuating exchange rates and inflation can cause charges, particularly in shops and restaurants, to change rapidly. If prices vary wildly from those we've quoted, ask whether there's a good reason, then please email to let us know. We aim to give the best and most up-to-date advice, and we always want to know if you've been badly treated or overcharged.

THE LIE OF THE LAND

San Francisco's various neighbourhoods have very distinct characters, but the boundaries that separate them are occasionally fuzzy.

We have used the most commonly accepted deamrcations; see page 308 for an overview map that defines these areas.

In addition to this overview map, the back of this book includes street maps of much of San Francisco, along with a comprehensive street index. The street maps start on p312, and pinpont specific locations of hotels (**❶**), restaurants (**❶**) and bars (**❶**); for all addresses we've given both a cross-street and a map reference, so finding your way around should be simple. The map section also includes a Muni metro map.

TELEPHONE NUMBERS
There are various telephone area codes that serve the Bay Area: 415 for San Francisco and Marin County; 510 for Berkeley and Oakland; 650 for peninsula cities, and 707 for Napa and Sonoma counties. Phone numbers throughout the guide are listed as if you're dialling from San Francisco. If you're dialling from outside our area code, you'll have to add an initial 1 (1-415, 1-510 and so on). Numbers beginning 1-800, 1-866, 1-877 and 1-888 can be dialled free of charge within the US. For more on telephones and codes, *see p293*.

ESSENTIAL INFORMATION
For all the practical information you might need for visiting the city, including customs and immigration information, disabled access, emergency telephone numbers, the lowdown on the local transport network and a list of useful websites, turn to the Directory at the back of this guide. It starts on page 283.

LET US KNOW WHAT YOU THINK
We hope you enjoy *Time Out San Francisco*, and we'd like to know what you think of it. We welcome tips for places that you consider we should include in future editions, and take notice of your criticism of our choices. You can email us at guides@timeout.com.

There is an online version of this guide, along with guides to more than 50 other international cities, at **www.timeout.com**.

Great Value car hire

▶ Explore with Alamo

Time Out readers renting with Alamo across the USA enjoy up to 20% discount off our fully inclusive rates.

Plus, we're offering free additional driver cover, saving you up to $70 per week, per driver.

With a great choice of cars including convertibles and SUVs, at locations throughout the USA, we've got it covered.

Click on the latest Alamo deals at
www.alamo.co.uk/offer/timeout
or call **0870 400 4565** quoting TIMEOUT

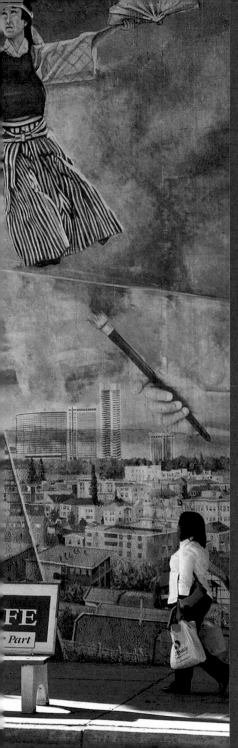

In Context

Features

Chinatown, c1898.

History

Built on gold, nourished on non-conformity.

When excavation began in 1969 for BART's Civic Center station, workers uncovered the body of a young woman. Experts dated the remains to approximately 2,950 BC, the city's earliest known burial. It was a glimpse into the rich indigenous culture of the Bay Area.

During the last Ice Age, 15,000 years ago, nomadic tribes migrated across the Bering Strait from Asia and eventually settled along the shores of the Bay. Ringed by reeds and hills covered with pastures, the Bay Area sustained more than 10,000 Northern Californian natives of different tribes, later collectively dubbed Costanoans ('coast dwellers') by the Spanish.

Despite its current name, the San Francisco Bay is an estuary, mixing the cold Pacific Ocean with the San Joaquin and Sacramento rivers, which originate from the fresh snowmelt of the Sierra Nevada. The Bay reached its present size about 100,000 years ago, when melting glaciers flooded

the world's oceans. Rising sea water flowed inland through the Golden Gate, the point where prominent coastal hills jostling around two peninsulas almost meet. This estuary protects three natural islands, Alcatraz, Angel and Yerba Buena, and the artificial Treasure Island.

At first, the Ohlone people lived here in harmony both with their Miwok neighbours and the land, which provided them with rich pickings of game, fish, shellfish, fruit and nuts (it was, in the words of a later French explorer, a land of 'inexpressible fertility'). They lived a successful hunter-gatherer existence until the arrival of Spanish missionaries. Their previous contacts with Europeans had been friendly, but the Spanish brought with them the dubious gifts of Christianity, hard labour and diseases such as smallpox, which eventually annihilated half the native population of California in 75 years.

THEY CAME, THEY SAW

Looking at the Golden Gate today, it's not hard to imagine how early navigators missed the mile-wide opening. The Bay and its native peoples were hidden by 'stynkinge fogges' (as Francis Drake later complained), which prevented numerous explorers over a period of 200 years from discovering the harbour entrance.

An early series of Spanish missions sent up the coast by Hernán Cortés, notorious conqueror of Mexico and the Aztecs, never got as far as Upper California. In 1542, under the flag of Cortés's successor, Antonio de Mendoza, Portuguese explorer Juan Rodríguez Cabrillo became the first European to visit the area. Inspired by a popular 16th-century novel, the Spanish named their new-found land California. Cabrillo passed the Bay's entrance on his way north and on his way back again, but failed to discover its large natural harbour.

An Englishman got even closer, yet still managed to miss it. In 1579, during a foraging and spoiling mission in the name of the Virgin Queen, Elizabeth I, the then-unknighted Francis Drake landed in Miwok Indian territory just north of the Bay. With one ship, the *Golden Hind*, and a crew in dire need of rest and recreation, he put in for a six-week berth on the Marin coastline, probably near Point Reyes. Long before the Pilgrims landed at Plymouth Rock or the English settled Cupid's Cove at Newfoundland, Drake claimed California for Elizabeth I as 'Nova Albion' or 'New Britain'.

'The *San Carlos*, a Spanish supply vessel, became the first ship to sail into the Bay.'

It would be 190 years before another white man set eyes on the Bay. Spurred on by the pressure of British colonial ambitions in America, the Spanish sent northbound missions to stake out their own territories, intent on converting the *bestias* and claiming land for the Spanish crown. Sailing under the Spanish flag in 1595, Portuguese explorer Sebastian Rodríguez Cermeno was shipwrecked just north of the Golden Gate at what is now known as Drake's Bay. Before he made his way back to Mexico in a small boat saved from the ship, he named the protected cove Bahia de San Francisco.

In 1769 came the 'sacred expedition' of Gaspar de Pórtola, a Spanish aristocrat who would later become the first governor of California, and the Franciscan priest Father Junipero Serra, who set off with 60 men on a gruelling march across the Mexican desert with the aim to establish a mission at San Diego. Once they'd done so, the party worked its way

north to Monterey, building missions and baptising Indians as they went. During the expedition, an advance party discovered an unexpectedly long bay 100 miles further up the coast. They mistook it for Cermeno's Bahia de San Francisco and, since the expedition's brief was only to claim Monterey, returned to San Diego. See also p15 Man with a mission.

It was not until August 1775 that the *San Carlos*, a Spanish supply vessel, became the first ship to sail into the Bay. Meanwhile, a mission set off to establish a safer land route to what would eventually become San Francisco. Roughly concurrent with the signing of the American Declaration of Independence, Captain Juan Bautista de Anza led an advance party to the southern point of the Golden Gate, which he declared a perfect location for a Spanish military garrison, or *presidio*. Three miles inland to the south-east, a suitable site was found for a mission. Before the year was out, the *presidio* was erected, and the mission – named Misión San Francisco de Asís after the holy order operating in Upper California, but popularly known as Mission Dolores – was established by the indefatigable Serra.

FOLLOW THE BEAR

A mix of favouritism, authoritarianism and religious fervour eventually helped sow the seeds of resentment and resistance in territories colonised by Spain. The country's hold on its American empires first began to crumble in Mexico, which declared itself a republic in 1821. The Mexican annexation of California in the same year opened up the area to foreign settlers; among them were American pioneers such as fur trapper Jedediah Smith, who in 1828 became the first white American to reach California over the Sierra Nevada mountain range. His feat was impressive, but the more sedate arrival by whaler ship of an Englishman had more lasting impact. Captain William Richardson, who in 1835 built the first dwelling on the site of the future San Francisco, is credited with giving the city its first name: Yerba Buena, named after the sweet mint (literally 'good herb') the Spanish used for tea.

That same year, the US tried unsuccessfully to buy the whole of the Bay Area from the Mexicans. In the long run, however, they got California for free: the declaration of independence of the territory of Texas, and its subsequent annexation by the US, triggered the Mexican-American war in June 1846. The resulting Guadalupe-Hidalgo Treaty of 1848 officially granted the Union all the land from Texas to California and from the Rio Grande to Oregon. But before the treaty could be nailed down, a few hotheads decided to 'liberate' the territory from Mexico themselves.

The short-lived Mexican rule of California coincided with the era of idealistic frontiersmen such as Kit Carson and Captain John Fremont, who, in June 1846, convinced a motley crew to take over the abandoned *presidio* to the north of Yerba Buena in Sonoma. Fremont proclaimed his new state the 'Bear Flag Republic', after the ragged banner he raised over Sonoma's square (the design was eventually adopted as the state flag), and he named the mouth of San Francisco Bay the 'Golden Gate' after Istanbul's Golden Horn. A few weeks after the Bear Flaggers annexed Sonoma, the US Navy captured Yerba Buena without a struggle and the whole of California became US territory.

The infant Yerba Buena was a sleepy trading post of 500 people. The newly appointed mayor, Lieutenant Washington A Bartlett, officially renamed it San Francisco on 30 January 1847. But unknown to its residents, the tiny settlement was about to change dramatically.

ALL THAT GLITTERS

Californians have the eagle eye of one James Marshall to thank for their current prosperity. Marshall it was who, while building a mill on the American River near Sacramento in January 1848, spotted what he thought was gold in a sawmill ditch. Along with John Sutter, the Swiss-born rancher who was Marshall's landlord, he attempted to keep his findings secret, but when newspaper publisher Sam Brannan dramatically waved a bottle of gold dust in San Francisco's town square, gold fever went global. The Gold Rush was on.

The news brought droves of drifters and fortune-seekers to the Bay Area, their fever fanned by people like Brannan, whose *California Star* newspaper told of men digging up a fortune in an hour. (Brannan eventually became California's first millionaire by selling goods to prospectors. Pure coincidence.) Many never made it: by land, the journey meant months of exposure to blizzards, mountains, deserts and hostile tribes; by sea, they faced disease, starvation or brutal weather. Still, more than 90,000 prospectors appeared in California in the first two years after gold was discovered, and 300,000 had arrived in the state by 1854, one out of every 90 people then living in the US. Though they called themselves the Argonauts, after the mythical sailors who accompanied Jason in search of the Golden Fleece, locals named them after the year the Rush began: the Forty-Niners.

The port town in which they arrived was one without structure, government or even a name (to many, it was still Yerba Buena). They found more hardship than gold: on their way to the mines, predatory merchants fleeced them; when they returned, broke, they were left to grub mean

existences from the city streets, seeking refuge in brothels, gambling dens and bars. Within two years of Marshall's discovery, nearly 100,000 men had passed through the city; the population grew from 600 in 1848 to 25,000 in 1849, swelling the tiny community into a giant, muddy campsite. Despite a fire that levelled the settlement on Christmas Eve 1849, a new town rose up to take its place and the population exploded. Still, this brave new boomtown was not a place for the faint-hearted. Lawlessness and arson ruled; frontier justice was common.

The opening of a post office marked the city's first optimistic stab at improving links with the rest of the continent. John White Geary, appointed postmaster by President James Knox Polk, rented a room at the corner of Montgomery and Washington Streets, where he marked out a series of squares for each letter of the alphabet and began filing letters. This crude set-up was San Francisco's first postal system. In April 1850, the year California became the Union's 31st state, San Francisco's city charter was approved; the city elected Geary its first mayor.

Geary's council later bought the ship *Euphemia* to serve as San Francisco's first jail. It proved a sound investment. Gangs of hoodlums controlled certain districts: the Ducks, led by Australian convicts, lived at a spot known as Sydney Town, and, together with New York toughs the Hounds, roamed Telegraph Hill, raping and pillaging the orderly community of Chilean merchants who occupied Little Chile. Eventually, right-minded citizens decided to take the law into their own hands. Whipped into a fury by rabble-rouser Brannan, vigilantes lynched their first victim, John Jenkins, at Portsmouth Square in June 1851. They strung up three more thieves during the following weeks; the other Ducks and Hounds wisely cut out for the Sierras.

Though their frontier justice temporarily curbed the area's excesses, the vigilantes were viewed by Mayor Geary as part of the problem, not the solution. But his crusade was hardly helped when the riverbed gold started running dry. Boom had turned to bust by 1853, and the resulting depression set a cyclical pattern oft-repeated through the city's history.

And sure enough, a second boom arrived. Henry Comstock's 1859 discovery of a rich blue vein of silver (the 'Comstock Lode') in western Nevada triggered a second invasion by fortune-seekers, nicknamed the Silver Rush. This time, though, the ore's nature demanded more elaborate methods of extraction, with high yields going to a small number of companies and tycoons rather than individual prospectors. Before the supply had been exhausted, silver barons had made enough money to transform

Man with a mission

California is a state of contradictory perceptions: the golden land of opportunity on one hand, the diseased home of the tarnished American dream on the other. So it's no surprise that the man who could be called the founder of California should attract a similar range of views. But who was Junipero Serra and how did he earn such differing evaluations?

The facts are straightforward enough. He was born in 1713 in Majorca and entered the Franciscan order at the age of 16. For 20 years he followed the usual path for a bright Franciscan: study, ordination, teaching. If he had continued in that vein Serra would have merited no more than a footnote in obscure textbooks of theology. But the man wanted something more and, inspired by the missionary example of St Francis, set off to Mexico to... do more of the same for the next nine years. But a hint that that would not remain the case forever was given by the fact that he walked from the port all the way to Mexico City, some 200 miles. Another was his unusual practice, when preaching on repentance, of pulling his habit down from his shoulders and whipping himself. Apparently this was done not only to mortify himself but to encourage contrition in his congregation.

And sure enough, things did change for Serra. Spain, worried about a Russian claim on the Pacific coast (remember that at this time the Tsar still owned Alaska), wanted to establish priority in Alta (upper) California and to this end the governor agreed to fund

missions there. Serra was placed in charge, heading north at the age of 56 to convert the locals. He established nine new missions, dying 14 years later at the Mission San Carlos Borromeo. The missions he founded, including San Francisco de Asis (or Dolores), were linked by El Camino Real, a dirt road that eventually stretched some 600 miles, along the length of present-day California.

And here's the controversy. Was Serra the ecclesiastical face of Spanish hegemony, pulling the free-spirited Native Americans of the coast into a life of stifling monastic discipline in the missions, unwittingly transmitting exotic diseases that killed them by the thousands, and marshalling the forces of cultural genocide? Or was he a man burning with an ideal of love that we find hard to comprehend today, a priest who continually fought with the secular authorities to protect the Indians, who travelled hundreds of miles despite ill health, and who – according to his world view – was offering up his life and labours for their salvation? Pope John Paul II obviously believed the latter, beatifying him in 1988. Some Indian groups opposed this, pointing to an increasing debate about maltreatment in the missions, as well as to the general question of colonisation. Junipero Serra's legacy is inextricably bound up with notions of imperialism, secularism and religion. And because of that it is likely to remain a matter of controversy and uncertainty for many years to come.

San Francisco, establishing a neighbourhood of nouveaux riches atop Nob Hill (the name was adapted from the word 'nabob').

If the nabobs took the geographical and moral high ground, those on the waterfront were busy legitimising their reputation as occupants of the 'Barbary Coast'. Naïve newcomers and drunken sailors were seen as fair game by gamblers and hoods waiting to 'shanghai' them (shanghai, like 'hoodlum', is a San Francisco expression), as were the immigrant women who found themselves trapped into lives of prostitution or slavery. At one low point, the female population numbered just 22; many a madam made fortune enough to buy her way on to Nob Hill.

COME ONE, COME ALL

The seeds of San Francisco's present-day multiculturalism were sown during this period, when a deluge of immigrants poured in from all over the world. French immigrants vying with Italians to make the best bread started baking sourdough in North Beach. A young German garment-maker named Levi Strauss started using rivets to strengthen the jeans he made for miners. In Chinatown, *tongs* (Mafia-like gangs) controlled the opium dens and other rackets; a Chinese immigrant, Wah Lee, opened the city's first laundry. The building in the 1860s of the transcontinental railroad, which employed thousands of Chinese labourers at low pay rates, led to further expansion of Chinatown. Still, despite their usefulness as cheap labour, the Chinese became the targets of racist anti-immigrant activity; indeed, proscriptive anti-Chinese legislation persisted until 1938.

Even in those days, entertainment was high on the agenda for San Franciscans. By 1853, the city boasted five theatres and some 600 saloons and taverns serving 42,000 customers. Locals downed seven bottles of champagne for every bottle swallowed in Boston (San Francisco still leads the US in alcohol consumption per capita). Lola Montez, entertainer to European monarchs and thieves, arrived on a paddle-steamer from Panama in 1853; her 'spider dance' became an instant hit at the American Theater.

Write on Mark Twain

When Samuel Clemens arrived in San Francisco in May 1864, he'd been 'Mark Twain' for a little over a year. He first adopted the pseudonym in Virginia City, Nevada, where he worked as city editor on the local newspaper. But it wasn't until he settled in San Francisco that Twain began to treat that name as if it were his own.

Twain found a room in California Street and a job as a reporter on the *Call*. He was dazzled by the city, which was then in the grip of an extraordinary share-dealing boom. San Francisco was a 'gambling carnival', Twain wrote, simply the 'liveliest, heartiest community on our continent' – compensation, it seems, for the frequent earthquakes, which he never got used to. He complained that when he 'contracted to report for this newspaper, the important matter of two earthquakes a month was not considered in the salary'.

He needn't have worried: the job on the *Call* didn't last long. But in any event, Twain was soon contributing essays, criticism and society gossip to a number of other publications. Indeed, it was in San Francisco that Twain first properly acknowledged that his vocation was writing. And it wasn't long before he was at the centre of a literary circle known as the 'Bohemians'.

Twain wrote vividly about the city, not least about earthquakes. The most powerful struck on October 8, 1865; Twain noted that 'such another destruction of mantel ornaments and toilet bottles as the earthquake created, San Francisco never saw before'.

He left San Francisco in December 1866. In the last piece he ever wrote in the city, Twain looked into the future. 'This straggling town shall be a vast metropolis: this sparsely populated land shall become a crowded hive of busy men. Its estate will be brighter, happier and prouder a hundred fold than it is this day. This is its destiny, and in all sincerity I can say, So mote it be!'

San Francisco's relative isolation from the rest of the continent meant the city was hardly affected by the Civil War that devastated the American South in the early 1860s. The rest of the country seemed remote; mail sometimes took six months to arrive. However, communications were slowly improving. Telegraph wires were being strung across the continent; where telegraph poles ran out, the Pony Express picked up messages, relaying up to 75 riders across the West to the Pacific coast. Even so, when the telegraph pole had all but rendered the Pony Express obsolete, the transcontinental railroad was its coup de grâce.

The completion of the Central Pacific Railroad in 1869 was the signal for runaway consumption in the city. The biggest spenders were the 'Big Four', Charles Crocker, Collis P Huntington, Mark Hopkins and Leland Stanford, brutally competitive millionaires who were the powerful principal investors behind the Central Pacific. Their eagerness to impress the West with their flamboyantly successful business practices manifested itself in the mansions they built on Nob Hill. By 1871, 121 businessmen controlled $146 million, according to one newspaper – but others got in on the act. In particular, four Irishmen – the 'Bonanza Kings': James Flood, William O'Brien, James Fair and John Mackay – made the ascent to Nob Hill, having started out as rough-hewn miners and bartenders chipping out their fortunes from the Comstock Lode.

'The earthquake and three-day inferno probably killed several thousand.'

A Scottish-Irish banker, William Ralston, opened the Bank of California on Sansome Street in 1864. Partnered by Prussian engineer Adolph Sutro, later famous for building the first Cliff House and the Sutro Baths, Ralston was determined to extract every last ounce of silver from the Comstock's Sun Mountain. Unfortunately, he did so too quickly: the ore ran out before he could recoup his investment, and his bank collapsed. Ralston drowned himself, leaving behind the luxurious Palace Hotel and a lasting contribution towards San Francisco's new civic pride: Golden Gate Park. Ralston's company provided the water for William Hammond Hall's audacious project, which transformed a barren area of sand dunes into a magnificent expanse of trees, flowers and lakes.

THE BIG ONE
The city continued to grow, and by 1900 its population had reached more than a third of a million, making it the ninth-largest city in the

Union. But shortly after 5am on 18 April 1906, dogs began howling and horses whinnying – noises that, along with glasses tinkling and windows rattling, marked the unnerving moments before an earthquake.

When the quake hit – a rending in the tectonic plates 25 miles beneath the ocean bed that triggered the shifting of billions of tons of rock – it generated more energy than all the explosives used in World War II. The rip snaked inland, tearing a gash now known as the San Andreas Fault down the coastline. Cliffs appeared from nowhere, cracks yawned, ancient redwoods toppled and part of the newly built City Hall tumbled down. A second tremor struck, ripping the walls out of buildings, destroying the city alarms and disrupting the water pipes that fed the fire hydrants, leaving the city's firefighters helpless. The blaze that followed compounded the damage; it only ceased when, in desperation, Mayor Eugene Schmitz and General Frederick Funston blew up the mansions along Van Ness Avenue, creating a firebreak.

The earthquake and three-day inferno probably killed several thousand. Around 250,000 people were left homeless and thousands of acres of buildings were destroyed; on Schmitz's orders, anyone suspected of looting in the ensuing chaos was shot dead. On the third day of the catastrophe, the wind changed direction, bringing rain. By 21 April the fire was out.

ONWARDS AND UPWARDS
Before the ashes cooled, citizens set about rebuilding; within ten years, San Francisco had risen from the ruins. Some claimed that in the rush to rebuild, planners passed up the chance to replace the city's grid street system with a more sensible one that followed the area's natural contours. But there's no doubt San Francisco was reborn as a cleaner, more attractive city – within three years of the fire, it could boast half of the nation's concrete and steel buildings. Such statistical pride was not out of keeping with the boosterism that accelerated San Francisco's post-Gold Rush growth into a large, modern city. The most potent symbol of restored civic pride was the new City Hall, the construction of which was secured by an $8-million city bond. Completed in 1915, it rose some 16 feet higher than its model, the Capitol building in Washington, DC.

In the years following the catastrophe, two waterways opened that would prove critical to California's economic vitality. The Los Angeles aqueduct was completed in 1913, beginning the transformation of a sleepy Southern California cowtown into the urban sprawl of modern LA. Then, in 1915, the opening of the Panama Canal considerably shortened shipping times between

'We hold the rock'

'We invite the United States to acknowledge the justice of our claim. The choice now lies with the leaders of the American government – to use violence upon us as before to remove us from our Great Spirit's land, or to institute a real change in its dealing with the American Indian.'
Richard Oakes, in a statement to the US Department of the Interior during the occupation of Alcatraz, 1968.

According to Indian oral tradition, Alcatraz has always been a prison island: a place of exile and ostracism for those who had transgressed tribal laws. Among those incarcerated during its infamous years as a US penetentiary were men from the Modoc tribe, imprisoned in 1873 for battling American forces, and 19 Hopi Indians found guilty of – among other offences – refusing to send their children to US government boarding schools (a key part of the government's assimilation policies). It was largely because of this history that the island became a symbol of the oppression and subjugation of native peoples.

Native American groups occupied Alcatraz three times in the 1960s, but it was the final occupation that really hit the headlines. On 20 November 1968 a group of 79 Indians arrived on the island and claimed it in the name of 'Indians of All Tribes'. The cited the 1868 Fort Laramie treaty between the US and the Sioux, which conceded all unused federal land to the Native people from whom it had been acquired – the US government had abandoned the Alcatraz prison in 1963.

The 19-month occupation that followed brought national attention to the grievances of Native Americans. Charismatic figures emerged, including leaders such as Richard Oakes, a former iron worker who was a student at San Francisco State University. Twenty-three-year-old John Trudell became the voice of Radio Free Alcatraz, his broadcast bringing widespread attention to a cause that resonated with many non-Native people in the political atmosphere of the 1960s: the Grateful Dead and Creedence Clearwater Revival played a concert on a boat just off the island; celebrities such as Marlon Brando and Jane Fonda spoke out on the occupiers behalf.

As the movement grew and others came to the island to participate, the group, once tight-knit and well-organised, fell prey to dissent and jealousy. Eventually the government cut off the electricity and fresh water shipments, and there was a fire at the warden's house (blamed by the occupiers on outside forces). The occupation began to disinegrate. The last 15 occupiers – five children, four women and six men – were

the Atlantic and Pacific coasts, an achievement celebrated in San Francisco by the Panama-Pacific Exposition. Not even the outbreak of World War I in Europe could dampen the city's high spirits. Its optimism was well founded: the war provided a boost to California's mining and manufacturing industries. But, as elsewhere in America, the good times were quickly swallowed up in the world depression signalled by the Wall Street Crash of 1929.

The crisis hit the port of San Francisco especially badly; half the workforce was laid off. On 9 May 1934, under the leadership of Harry Bridges, the International Longshoremen's Association declared a coast-wide strike. Other unions, including the powerful Teamsters, came out in sympathy, shutting down West Coast ports for three months. Blackleg workers managed to break through the picket on 5 July – Bloody Thursday – but with disastrous results. As violence escalated, police opened fire, killing two strikers and wounding 30. A general strike was called for 14 July, when 150,000 people

stopped work and brought San Francisco to a standstill for three days. The strike fizzled out when its leaders couldn't agree on how to end the stalemate, but the action wasn't completely futile: the longshoremen won a wage increase and control of the hiring halls.

At the same time, San Francisco managed an amazing amount of construction. The Opera House was completed in 1932; the following year, the island of Alcatraz was transferred from the army to the Federal Bureau of Prisons, which set about building a high-security lock-up. The San Francisco Museum of Modern Art, the first West Coast museum to feature exclusively 20th-century works, opened in 1935. The same decade saw the completion of the San Francisco–Oakland Bay Bridge – six months before work started on the Golden Gate Bridge's revolutionary design. In 1939, on man-made Treasure Island, the city hosted another fair: the Golden Gate International Exposition, described as a 'pageant of the Pacific'. Those who attended were dubbed 'the Thirty-Niners' by local wits.

'escorted' off the island by Federal marshals, Coast Guard and FBI on 11 June 1971, 18 months after the occupation had begun.

It may have seemed like a defeat, or at least an anti-climax, but historians assert that the occupation actually played a real role in raising awareness, leading to the development of a larger Indian movement and persuading the government to act on Oakes' request that it 'institute a real change in its dealing with the American Indian'.

Even as the occupation was in progress, in 1970, President Richard Nixon established a new policy of 'self-determination without termination' – a reversal of the so-called 'termination policies' that aimed at assimilation by terminating the special trusts in which Indian reservations where held. He increased the budget for the Bureau of Indian Affairs by more than 225 per cent, doubled funding for Indian health care, increased college scholarship and economic development funding. Congress passed 52 pieces of legislation supporting Indian tribal self-rule during the period of the occupation.

Alcatraz is still a symbol for Indian people today. Signs of the occupation are still visible on the island, in the form of graffiti. And Indians gather on the island every November for a sunrise 'Un-Thanksgiving Day' ceremony, celebrating their identity and struggle.

It was to be San Francisco's last big celebration for a while: in 1941 the Japanese attacked Pearl Harbor, and America entered World War II.

The war changed the city almost as much as the Gold Rush or the Great Quake. More than 1.5 million men and thousands of tons of material were shipped to the Pacific from the Presidio, Travis Air Force Base and Treasure Island. Between 1941 and 1945, almost the entire Pacific war effort passed under the Golden Gate. The massed ranks of troops, not to mention some half a million civilian workers who flooded into San Francisco, turned the city into a milling party town hell-bent on sending its boys into battle with smiles on their faces.

Towards the end of the war in Europe, in April 1945, representatives of 50 nations met at the San Francisco Opera House to draft the United Nations Charter. It was signed on 26 June 1945 and formally ratified in October at the General Organisation of the United Nations in London. Many people felt that San Francisco would be the ideal location for the UN's headquarters, but the British and French thought it too far to travel. To the city's great disappointment, the UN moved to New York.

BEATNIK BLUES AND HIPPIE HIGHS

The immediate post-war period was coloured by the return of the demobilised GIs, among them Lawrence Ferlinghetti. While studying at the Sorbonne in the early 1950s, the poet had discovered Penguin paperbacks, which inspired him to open his tiny, wedge-shaped bookshop at 261 Columbus Avenue. Called City Lights, the shop became a mecca for the bohemians later dubbed the Beat Generation by Jack Kerouac.

The Beats reflected the angst and ambition of a post-war generation attempting to escape both the shadow of the Bomb and the rampant consumerism of ultra-conformist 1950s America. In Kerouac's definition, Beat could stand for either beatific or beat – exhausted. The condition is best explained in his novel

On the Road, which charts the coast-to-coast odysseys of San Francisco-based Beat saint Neal Cassady (thinly disguised as Dean Moriarty), poet Allen Ginsberg and Kerouac himself (named Sal Paradise).

'The emergence of the Beat Generation made North Beach the literary centre of San Francisco and nurtured a new vision that would spread far beyond its bounds,' reflected Ferlinghetti 40 years on. 'The Beats prefigured the New Left evolution and the impulse for change that swept eastward from San Francisco.' The attention of the world might have been on the beret-clad artists and poets populating North Beach cafés, but an event in Anaheim, 500 miles to the south, was more reflective of mainstream America. In 1955, Disneyland opened its gates.

Despite the imaginary perfect world portrayed by Disney, the media exposure received by Kerouac and Ginsberg established the Bay Area as a centre for the burgeoning counterculture, generating mainstream America's suspicions that San Francisco was the fruit-and-nut capital of the US. Its fears were about to be confirmed by the hippie explosion of the 1960s. The Beats and hippies might have shared a love of marijuana and a common distaste for 'the system', but Kerouac – now an embittered alcoholic – abhorred what he saw as the hippies' anti-Americanism. (It was, in fact, the Beats who coined the term 'hippie' to refer to those they saw as second-rate, lightweight hipsters.) Kerouac's distaste for these new bohemians was shared by John Steinbeck, who shied away from the recognition he received in the streets.

The original Beats had no interest in political action, but the newer generation embraced it. A sit-in protest against a closed session of the House of Representatives Un-American Activities Committee (HUAC) at the City Hall in 1961 drew protesters from San Francisco State University and the University of California's Berkeley campus. It quickly degenerated into a riot, establishing the pattern for later protests and police responses. In 1964 Berkeley students, returning from a summer of civil rights protests in the South, butted heads with university officials over the right to use campus facilities for their campaigns. The conflict signalled the beginning of the 'free speech movement', led by student activist Mario Savio; it marked the split between the politically conscious and those who chose to opt out of the system altogether. America's escalating involvement in the Vietnam War added urgency to the voices of dissent; Berkeley students remained at the forefront of protests on campuses around the country.

The availability of LSD, its popularity boosted in San Francisco by such events as the Human Be-In and the Acid Tests overseen by Owsley Stanley and the Grateful Dead, drew an estimated 8,000 hippies from across America. Over half stayed, occupying cheap Victorian houses around the Haight-Ashbury district (dubbed 'the Hashbury'). Combined with the sun, drugs and acid-induced psychedelic music explosion, the local laissez-faire attitude give rise to the famous Summer of Love. By 1968, however, the spread of hard drugs, notably heroin, had taken the shine off the hippie movement; the fatal stabbing by Hell's Angels of a Rolling Stones fan at the Altamont Speedway during the band's 1969 concert there seemed to confirm darker times were ahead.

'The enduring memory of 1960s San Francisco is as the host city to the Summer of Love.'

Like its drugs, the city's politics were getting harder. Members of the Black Panther movement, a radical black organisation founded across the Bay in Oakland by Huey Newton and Bobby Seale, asked themselves why they should ship out to shoot the Vietnamese when the real enemy was at home. Around Oakland, the Panthers took to exercising the American right to bear arms. Gunfights inevitably followed: Panther leader Eldridge Cleaver was wounded and 17-year-old Bobby Hutton killed in a shoot-out with Oakland police in April 1968. The Black Panther movement had petered out by the early 1970s, its leaders either dead, imprisoned or, like Cleaver, on the run. The kidnapping in 1974 of Patty Hearst, heir to the Hearst newspaper fortune, was the point at which the 1960s revolution turned into deadly farce. When she was captured, along with the other members of the tiny Symbionese Liberation Army, Hearst seemed to have been brainwashed into joining the cause.

Despite the violence that characterised the student and anti-war protests, however, black radicalism and failed revolutions, the enduring memory of 1960s San Francisco is as the host city to the Summer of Love. The psychedelic blasts of the Grateful Dead, Janis Joplin, Country Joe and the Fish and Jefferson Airplane defined both the San Francisco sound and its countercultural attitude. Berkeley student Jann Wenner founded *Rolling Stone* magazine in 1967 to explain and advance the cause, helping to invent New Journalism in the process.

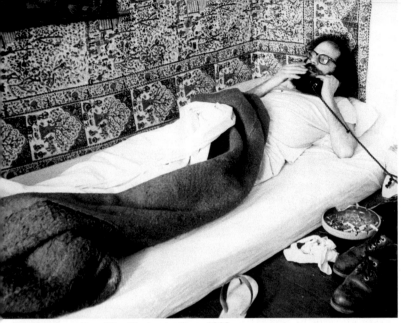

The Beat generation: **Allen Ginsberg** relaxes, 1966.

THE RAINBOW REVOLUTION

San Francisco's radical baton was taken up in the 1970s by the gay liberation movement. Local activists insisted that gay traditions had always existed in the city, first among the Ohlone and later during the 1849 Gold Rush, when women in the West were more scarce than gold. Early groups such as the Daughters of Bilitis, the Mattachine Society and the Society for Individual Rights (SIR) paved the way for more radical new political movements. Gay activists made successful forays into mainstream politics in 1977: SIR's Jim Foster became the first openly gay delegate at a Democratic Convention, and Harvey Milk was elected to the city's Board of Supervisors.

Then Dan White changed everything. A former policeman, White had run for supervisor as an angry, young, blue-collar populist – and won. He suffered poor mental health and had to resign under the strain of office, but quickly changed his mind and asked Mayor Moscone to reinstate him. His refusal led to his assassination of Moscone and Harvey Milk. The killings stunned the city; the verdict outraged it, and rioting ensued, known as the White Night Riot. *See p100* **Streets of San Francisco**. White committed suicide not long after his release.

Gay life and politics changed radically and irrevocably with the onset of the HIV virus, which tore the gay community apart and caused controversy when the city's bathhouses, a symbol of gay liberation and promiscuity,

were closed in panic over the spread of the disease. Gay radicals branded *Chronicle* writer Randy Shilts a 'fascist Nazi, traitor and homophobe' when he criticised bathhouse owners who refused to post safe-sex warnings, but his book *And the Band Played On* is still the definitive account of the period.

Since its identification, AIDS has claimed the lives of some 18,000 San Franciscans. The levelling-out of numbers of new cases in the US and the dangerous misperception that the epidemic is ebbing have endangered fundraising efforts, but the city remains home to the most efficient volunteers in the country.

COLLAPSE AND RECOVERY

Because of its location on the San Andreas Fault, San Francisco has always lived in anticipation of a major earthquake to rival the 1906 disaster. It came in October 1989: the Loma Prieta quake, named after the ridge of mountains at its epicentre, registered 7.1 on the Richter scale (the 1906 quake was an estimated 7.8). Part of the West Oakland Freeway collapsed, crushing drivers; the Marina district was devastated by fires; and 50 feet (15 metres) of the Bay Bridge's upper deck collapsed. In just 15 seconds, more than 19,000 homes were damaged or destroyed; 62 people were killed and 12,000 were displaced.

As the 1990s progressed, changes in the city reflected those in the world beyond. The end of the Cold War meant cuts in military spending,

Salutes at a **Black Panther** liberation school, 1969.

and the Presidio – which operated as a US military base for almost 150 years – was closed in 1994. As part of the Base Closure and Realignment Act, the land was transferred to the National Park Service. The collapse of the Soviet Union also brought in a wave of Russian immigrants, many of them settling in the ethnically diverse Richmond district.

San Francisco also experienced a remarkable renaissance. Its proximity to Silicon Valley's economic boom rejuvenated the city's business structure and reshaped the skyline. In the wake of the Loma Prieta earthquake, the Embarcadero Freeway was torn down and the city's historic bayside boulevard turned into a palm-tree-lined haven for walkers, joggers, in-line skaters and cyclists. Numerous major projects were brought to completion and others begun: in 1995, the San Francisco Museum of Modern Art moved into a new building in burgeoning SoMa, and voters passed a bond allowing for the restoration of City Hall. Five years later, Pac Bell Park (now SBC Park), the first privately funded Major League Baseball park in nearly 40 years, opened its gates. The Yerba Buena Center and Zeum children's museum also opened their doors during this time.

As the 20th century rolled into the 21st, San Francisco suffered from many of the same social problems that plagued other major US cities. Homelessness was particularly severe, with up to 14,000 destitute men and women sleeping without nightly shelter. The late '90s internet boom brought workers from around the world into an increasingly tight housing market and gentrified working-class neighbourhoods.

But by the end of the decade, fortunes had turned and rents had started to drop: the dotcom bubble had burst. What no one could have predicted was that within a few years there would be another tech boom. By 2008 technology companies were on the move again; only this time round there's no manic boomtown atmosphere. A collection of new – and high – buildings, many in mid construction at the time of writing, are perhaps the most obvious manifestation of the booming economy. For more on One Rincon Hill and the Transbay Transit Center, *see p25*.

San Francisco maintains its best-of-the-West-Coast reputation for magnificent food, stylish design, charming architecture and a multicultural, ideas-driven population. In 1889, Rudyard Kipling described San Francisco as a 'mad city inhabited for the most part by perfectly insane people'. His conclusion is one shared by many residents even today: ''Tis hard to leave.'

Key events

c10,000 BC The Ohlone and Miwok Indians begin to settle the Bay Area.
1542 Juan Cabrillo sails up the California coastline.
1579 Francis Drake lands north of the San Francisco Bay, claiming the land for Elizabeth I and calling it 'Nova Albion'.
1769 Gaspar de Pórtola and Father Junípero Serra lead an overland expedition to establish a mission at San Diego. An advance party is sent to scout the coast; they become the first white men to see the San Francisco Bay.
1775 The *San Carlos* is the first ship to sail into the bay.
1776 On 4 July, 13 American colonies declare their independence from Great Britain. In the autumn, a Spanish military fort is founded by Fort Point; Serra establishes Mission Dolores.
1821 Mexico declares its independence from Spain and annexes California.
1828 Fur trapper Jebediah Smith becomes the first white man to reach California across the Sierra Nevada mountain range.
1835 English-born sailor William Richardson sets up a trading post he calls 'Yerba Buena'.
1846 The Bear Flag Revolt takes place against Mexican rule in California. Captain John B Montgomery takes possession of Yerba Buena and claims it for the US.
1847 Yerba Buena is renamed San Francisco.
1848 A US–Mexican treaty confirms American dominion over California. James Marshall finds gold in the low Sierras near Sacramento.
1849 The Gold Rush swells the city's population from 800 to 25,000 in less than a year. A fire levels the city on Christmas Eve.
1850 California becomes the 31st state of the Union.
1859 The Comstock Lode is discovered in western Nevada, triggering the Silver Rush.
1861 The Civil War breaks out between the Union and the Confederacy. California remains largely untouched by hostilities.
1868 The University of California is established at Berkeley.
1869 The transcontinental railroad connects San Francisco with the rest of the US.
1873 Andrew Hallidie builds the first cable car.
1906 A massive earthquake hits the city; a fire follows. Thousands die, and 28,000 buildings are destroyed.
1915 San Francisco celebrates the opening of the Panama Canal with the Panama-Pacific Exposition.

1932 San Francisco Opera House opens.
1934 On 5 July (Bloody Thursday), police open fire on striking longshoremen, leaving two dead and prompting a three-day general strike that brings the Bay Area to a standstill. Also this year, Alcatraz opens as a federal prison.
1936 The Bay Bridge is completed.
1937 The Golden Gate Bridge is completed.
1941 The Japanese attack Pearl Harbor, and the US enters World War II.
1945 Fifty nations meet at the San Francisco Opera House to sign the UN Charter.
1955 Allen Ginsberg reads 'Howl' at the Six Gallery.
1961 UC Berkeley students stage a sit-in protest against a closed session of the House of Representatives Un-American Activities Committee at City Hall.
1964 Student sit-ins and mass arrests grow as the civil rights, free-speech and anti-Vietnam War movements gain momentum.
1967 The Human Be-In pre-empts the Summer of Love.
1968 Teenager Bobby Hutton is killed in a Black Panther shoot-out with Oakland police.
1972 The Bay Area Rapid Transit system (BART) opens.
1978 Mayor George Moscone and Harvey Milk, a gay member of the Board of Supervisors, are shot and killed by former official Dan White.
1981 The city's first known cases of AIDS.
1989 Another major earthquake hits the city.
1992 Fire sweeps through the Oakland hills, killing dozens and destroying 3,000 homes.
1994 After 220 years with the military, the Presidio transfers to the National Park Service.
1995 The San Francisco 49ers win the Super Bowl for the fifth time. Willie Brown Jr becomes the city's first African-American mayor.
1997 Damaged in the 1989 quake, the San Francisco Opera House finally reopens.
2000 Pacific Bell Park (now AT&T Park), the new home of the San Francisco Giants baseball team, opens to great acclaim.
2003 Establishment Democrat Gavin Newsom pips progressive Green Party member Matt Gonzalez in the city's mayoral elections.
2004 Newsom grants the first same-sex marriage licenses in the US, setting off a storm of controversy.
2005 The De Young Museum reopens in a dramatic building in Golden Gate Park.
2008 California Academy of Sciences reopens in Golden Gate Park.

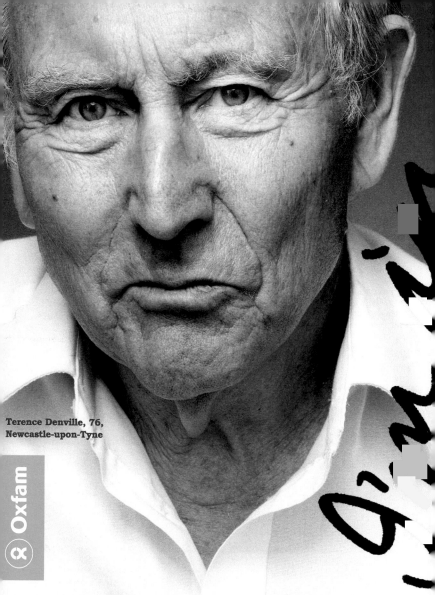

Terence Denville, 76,
Newcastle-upon-Tyne

Oxfam

Hundreds of thousands of people have said *I'm in* to fight the injustice of poverty. And this kind of pressure has already made a huge difference. In Ghana, for example, most of the country's debt has been wiped out. But there's so much more to do: every day, extreme poverty kills 30,000 children. That's unacceptable. Text 'TIMEOUT' and your name to 87099. We'll let you know how to help. We can do this. We *can* end poverty. Are you in?

I give my support to help end poverty. and you know what? things actually get done

Let's end poverty together. Text 'TIMEOUT' and your name to 87099.

San Francisco Today

A city that's always in the vanguard.

Perhaps the only thing that's truly predictable about San Francisco is that things here are never predictable. Contrary, trend-bucking, stubborn and improbably optimistic, the City by the Bay is constantly making fools out of those who try to anticipate the rise and fall of its fortunes.

Just half a dozen years ago, for instance, there wasn't an oddsmaker alive who would have placed bets on a comeback from the dotcom economic debacle. But everywhere you look these days, internet and multimedia companies are blossoming again – albeit with more realistic business plans and more modest spending habits. The phenomenon that is Google continues to defy the doomsday prognosticators of Wall Street, while ubiquitous newcomers YouTube and Wikipedia compete to see who will be the first to become its own verb.

The most obvious indicator that money and ideas are again flowing South of Market Street – where the original dotcom boom transformed deserted warehouses and factories into high-end lofts and trendy bars – is the rapidly changing landscape. The Transamerica Pyramid, once the definitive exclamation point on the city's skyline, is quickly being eclipsed by a series of larger, more imposing structures. The obelisk-like One Rincon Hill condominium tower – the first of two skyscrapers currently under construction next to the Bay Bridge – looms some 641 feet (195 metres) above the Bay. The recently approved plans for the Transbay Transit Center, a combination office/residential/retail complex and train/bus terminal, include a rooftop park the length of five football fields and an 80-storey high-rise tower, which will give San Francisco the dubious distinction of having the tallest

The only way is up: **One Rincon Hill.**

building on the West Coast. The Millennium Tower, a 645-foot (197-metre) blue-glass homage to luxury living, will offer penthouses with showstopping views and amenities that include a residents-only dining room serviced by celebrity chef Michael Mina.

Further south, the sprawling Mission Bay area, which includes 303 acres (123 hectares) of research, retail, office, residential and recreation space, as well as a new biotech and research campus for the University of California, is at long last reaching critical mass. With some 13 housing projects, a community centre, upscale grocers, shops, restaurants and a library all completed or well under way, the industrial wasteland formerly known as China Basin has taken shape as San Francisco's hottest new neighbourhood – no small feat for a city where real estate growth is almost exclusively confined to the vertical.

The opening of the Third Street light-rail line and the neighbourhood's proximity to AT&T baseball park and the Embarcadero waterfront have sparked a renaissance in surrounding areas as well. In the scruffy quadrant known as Dogpatch (off 3rd Street, roughly between Pennsylvania and 22nd Street), whose claim to fame used to be a commuter train stop and a hard-drinking saloon, you'll now find lovingly restored Victorian houses, homey cafés and restaurants, and even an all-organic wine bar.

At Mint Plaza, a side street abutting the historic Old Mint and across from the Westfield Shopping Centre, a new enclave is being refashioned from a former wino alley. Large paving stones signal the first phase of what will be a pedestrian-only plaza that will eventually incorporate restaurants, cafés and a farmers' market, and will serve as a community gathering place for music, outdoor cinema and public art.

POLITICS AS UNUSUAL

The winds of political fortunes have been equally unpredictable in the last couple of years. No one could have guessed that Arnold Schwarzenegger, the actor-governor who just two years ago looked as if he was going down in flames following a disastrous special election in which every one of his initiatives was shot down, would rise like a phoenix from the ashes to enjoy unprecedented popularity again. Sailing into a second term, the Governator has support in both political parties this time around – due in no small part to his groundbreaking 'green' initiatives (*see box right* **Going Green**), and his progressive stance on healthcare reform. To the delight of famously liberal San Franciscans and the chagrin of conservatives, Schwarzenegger is looking more and more like a Democrat with a Republican's haircut these days.

The Republicans' fall from grace in the national political landscape brought about another unlikely victory. Only a modern-day Nostradamus could have foreseen that a woman from San Francisco, long excoriated for her nebulous 'San Francisco values', would break America's glass ceiling to become the nation's first female Speaker of the House of Representatives. Nancy Pelosi, a longtime San Francisco 'bleeding-heart liberal', now reigns over the halls of Congress – by some accounts with an iron fist.

As for San Francisco's other heir apparent, Gavin Newsom, the bloom may not be entirely off the rose, but it certainly doesn't smell as sweet these days. Though the dashing boy-mayor ran for a second term virtually unopposed, his re-election was not without controversy. Newsom is still suffering from the fallout of a sex scandal involving the wife of his campaign manager and a stint in alcohol rehab. That, combined with his failure to fully deliver on promises to cure the chronic homeless problem and supply free citywide wireless internet access, has given his political enemies a lot of salt to rub into his wounds. At his inaugural address in 2008, a more subdued and sober-looking Newsom returned to many of the themes that brought him acclaim the

first time around: a call for universal healthcare, support for same-sex marriage and a vow to make city government carbon-neutral by 2020.

MONEY CHANGES EVERYTHING

The fall of the dollar has been something of a mixed blessing for San Francisco. Prices have risen steeply in a city that already suffers from a painfully high cost of living. But so has the influx of free-spending foreign tourists. Nearly 16 million visitors left their hearts and wallets in San Francisco in 2006, injecting $7.8 billion into the local economy. Among the benefactors has been the retail market. Stores are booming,

Going green

San Francisco has long had a reputation as a land of tree huggers and whale savers, but in the fat, comfortable 1990s, that image got a bit muddied in the stampede for the almighty dotcom dollar. Now green – the leafy kind – is back with a vengeance and is once again putting the city at the forefront of the save-the-earth movement. These days, you can't swing a dead polar bear without hitting an environmental initiative. In restaurants, the terms 'sustainable', 'local' and 'organic' are as commonplace as 'roasted' or 'grilled' were 20 years ago and school children know the 'reduce, re-use, recycle' song as well as 'The Wheels on the Bus'.

But San Francisco is doing far more than just tossing $200 bottles of wine into the recycling bin, or driving a hybrid SUV. It's putting its money where its politics are. From river and creek restoration, to bans on smoking, water bottles, plastic bags, and a sweeping proposal to curb greenhouse gas emissions, California – and the Bay Area in particular – has become, as one newspaper editorial put it, 'the world's last, best hope against climate change'. Small wonder that Nobel Prize winner Al 'An Inconvenient Truth' Gore owns a home in the city and has based his latest venture, CurrentTV, here.

To get a sense of how committed San Francisco is to conservation, consider that in 2007 the city recycled 69 per cent of its waste – more than double the national average – with a goal to reach 75 per cent by 2010. A staggering number of initiatives were also passed in 2007. Among the more controversial:

• A ban on plastic shopping bags in large supermarkets and drugstores, the first city in the US to impose one.

• A ban on the use of Styrofoam in local restaurants.

• A ban on city departments and agencies buying single-serving bottled water.

• A commitment to make all city buses emission-free by 2020, and to convert all taxis to alternative fuels by 2011.

• A state initiative to reduce greenhouse gases by 25 per cent by 2020.

• A number of bans on smoking, including one that prohibits smoking in cars with passengers under the age of 18.

Restaurants all over town continue to ride the momentum of the 'locavore' movement, betting that the way to the public's heart is through its stomach. At Fish & Farm (*see p139*), a new Downtown restaurant, not only are the majority of ingredients sourced from within a 100-mile radius, but staff grow their own herbs in an organic garden on the roof. They also recycle all the kitchen's cooking oil (the city recently began free pick-up of used vegetable oil for conversion to biodiesel). Nearby Mixt Greens, a popular made-to-order salad eatery, composts 80 per cent of its daily waste, and packages its take-out orders in biodegradeable containers.

Hotels, too, have jumped on the bandwagon, increasingly building to LEED (Leadership in Energy and Environmental Design) specs, and using environmentally friendly products. Currently, 60 building projects in San Francisco are registered with the US Green Building Council for LEED certification – an astounding figure for a city this size.

And while some industry bigwigs are fighting these changes, most are happily embracing the wave, banking on the idea that being green will eventually translate into seeing green – the dollar kind – in the not-too-distant future.

especially in the Downtown area, where the grand reopening of the Westfield San Francisco Centre in 2006 brought with it a glut of blue-chip tenants, including Bloomingdale's, Juicy Couture, Lucky Brand Jeans and H&M. Nearby Union Square quickly followed suit with the opening in 2007 of Barney's New York, a Ben Sherman store and a big, splashy new home for Prada. And still to arrive at press time were a De Beers jewellery shop and a Helmut Lang boutique.

The picture hasn't been entirely rosy, however. The bottoming out of the housing market around the country hasn't really affected San Francisco's already stratospheric home prices and rents, which continue to climb, though at a less frenzied pace than a few years ago. Couple this with a law forcing businesses to offer paid sick leave to employees, another one that will require them to provide healthcare for the uninsured, a raising of the minimum wage (now second-highest in the nation) and petrol prices that are approaching $4 a gallon – and it's small wonder the middle classes are fleeing in droves for cheaper pastures.

'It's this unique ability to reinvent itself that keeps the city relevant.'

Probably no sector has been hit harder by these measures than the city's dining establishments. A town of fanatical foodies, San Francisco has felt the restaurateur's pain in its pocketbooks, with rising prices forcing some to curb their voracious appetites. Still, on a Saturday night in the Mission or South of Market Street, you'd be hard-pressed to spot people hesitating as they throw $55 at an organic dry-aged grass-fed porterhouse steak. It might help to explain, though, why the latest food craze in town isn't food at all, but beverage. Wine bars are popping up around the city as fast as Starbucks a few years back. The good news is that with the famed wine valleys of Napa and Sonoma a stone's throw away, it's unlikely there will be a shortage of tasty varietals any time soon.

The restaurant scene suffered an emotional blow as well last year. In 2006, the famed Michelin Guide rendered its first judgement upon the Bay Area and found only one restaurant (French Laundry in Napa Valley) worthy of a three-star rating, while legendary icons such as Chez Panisse were snubbed with only a single star. Happily, it hasn't affected business one bit; the revered House of Alice Waters continues to sell out night after night, with diners patiently waiting up to a month to secure a reservation.

COMINGS AND GOINGS

If ever there was a microcosm for the ups and downs of life in the Bay Area it has to be in the saga of baseball slugger Barry Bonds. The notoriously aloof home-run king, who played for the San Francisco Giants for 15 years, breaking major league and fan attendance records along the way, was both idolised and vilified by fans. In 2007, Bonds cemented his spot in baseball history when he hit his 756th home run, surpassing the legendary Hank Aaron's all-time record. His glory was short-lived. Already under suspicion for using performance-enhancing drugs during his career, he was indicted two months later on perjury charges for lying about his steroid use. San Franciscans, famously loyal to their hometown heroes, have been understandably conflicted. Bonds' record-breaking ball did fetch more than $756,000 at auction, but, following a vote among fans as to its final fate, it will be sent to the baseball Hall of Fame branded with an asterisk.

Fortunately, residents' devotion to other cultural pastimes isn't fraught with such controversy. Art-lovers have embraced the modern, new de Young Museum in Golden Gate Park in all its perforated-copper glory, and are now eagerly awaiting the arrival of the state-of-the-art California Academy of Sciences in autumn 2008. The natural science museum, aquarium and planetarium, designed by Italian architect Renzo Piano, will be housed in what is to be the world's 'greenest' museum – an environmentally sustainable building that boasts a rainforest, a coral reef and a living roof that supports some 1.7 million plants.

The de Young and the Academy are part of a wave of new arts institutions set to open in San Francisco over the next few years. In Yerba Buena, the Museum of the African Diaspora and the Museum of Craft and Folk Art recently joined the Museum of Modern Art and the Center for the Arts in the rapidly expanding arts district. Following them in 2008 will be the über-modern Contemporary Jewish Museum, designed by famed New York architect Daniel Libeskind – which will put the crowning touches on the metamorphosis of a walkway that used to be known as a hangout for indigents and drunks.

While most would agree that these changes are for the better, it seems to be the perennial complaint of old-timers that the city is just not what it used to be. To be fair, that's as true as it's ever been. San Francisco has never strived to be what it once was. And it's this unique ability to constantly reinvent itself that keeps the city relevant, vital and, above all, interesting.

Architecture

Booms, busts and the built environment.

Building in San Francisco has always been a challenge. At times, due to technological constraints, it has been literally impossible, and even when possible, it has been unadvisable. Why? Three words: quakes, borders and hills. Packed into San Francisco's tiny 47-mile area are more than 70 hills, ranging in height from 100 feet to 927 feet (30 to 283 metres). Added to this is the fact that it is located in one of the nation's most populous and seismically active regions. As a result, it has traditionally proved difficult to build up or out and, apparently, without the real possibility that the city will periodically burst into flames. Consequently, San Francisco has been compelled to build and rebuild itself many times over. But these challenges haven't prevented architects the world over from wanting to claim a part of the city. The risks, it seems, are worth it.

A MISSIONARY POSITION

It was the establishment of **Mission Dolores** (*see p98*), an adobe chapel built on swampland, that initially drew settlers to the city; the first Mass was celebrated on 29 June 1776. The simple chapel, with its thick adobe walls, sits north of a cemetery where Native Americans, outlaws and the city's first Irish and Hispanic mayors are buried. The mission was one of 21 built in California by the Spanish; only Carmel and Monterey, rival it for authentic atmosphere. Along with a portion of the walls of the Officers' Club in the Presidio, the mission is the sole piece of colonial architecture to have outlived the city's progress from hamlet to metropolis.

The town inhabited by the Forty-Niners – or 'Argonauts', as the Gold Rush immigrants dubbed themselves – suffered a series of fires. The heart of the outpost was **Portsmouth Square** (*see p87*), located in present-day Chinatown. It was incinerated by two blazes; the surrounding streets perished in the fire following the 1906 earthquake. The most impressive buildings from the Gold Rush era are in the **Jackson Square Historical District** (*see p72*; best viewed on Jackson between Montgomery and Sansome Streets).

THE BOOM YEARS: PART ONE

Although precious metals flooded the town, the big money of the Gold Rush actually came from outfitting the legions of fortune-seekers. A burst of prosperity in the 19th century quickly filled San Francisco's once-empty sloping streets with what have become its signature Victorian terraced houses. Built by middle-class tradesmen in the Mission, Castro and Haight districts, and by rich merchants in Presidio Heights and around **Alamo Square**, these famous 'Painted Ladies' provide San Francisco's most characteristic architectural face. One of the most popular views of the city is framed by a row of six painted Victorians along Steiner Street between Hayes and Grove Streets ('**Postcard Row**'), but there are more than 14,000 examples of this eye-catching vernacular, some even more fanciful.

The wooden frames and elaborate woodwork of San Francisco's Victorians come in four distinct styles: Gothic Revival, Italianate,

Two of the city's many, varied and often-elaborate Victorians.

Stick-Eastlake and Queen Anne. The earliest Gothic Revival houses have pointed arches over their windows and were often painted white, rather than in the bright colours of the later styles. The Italianate style, with tall cornices, neo-classical elements and add-on porches, are best exemplified in the Lower Haight, notably on Grove Street near Webster Street, but there are other examples at **1900 Sacramento Street** (near Lafayette Park) and at 1818 California Street in the shape of the **Lilienthal-Pratt House**, built in 1876.

The Italianate was succeeded by the Stick-Eastlake style, named after furniture designer Charles Eastlake and characterised by square bay windows framed with angular, carved ornamentation. The 'Sticks' are the most common of the Victorian houses left in the city; a shining example is the over-the-top extravaganza at **1057 Steiner Street**, on the corner of Golden Gate Avenue.

With its turrets, towers and curvaceous corner bay windows, the Queen Anne style is amply demonstrated by the **Wormser-Coleman House** in Pacific Heights (1834 California Street, at Franklin Street). However, the most extravagant example is the **Haas-Lilienthal House** (*see p118*); it was built in 1886 by Bavarian grocer William Haas, who treated himself to a home with 28 rooms and six bathrooms. Now a museum, the house is one of the few such examples of Victorian architecture open to the public.

TRIAL BY FIRE (AND EARTHQUAKE)

As wealth flooded the city, it attracted the attention of developers and hoteliers with grand visions for the Bay Area. In 1873, San Francisco financier William Ralston set out to build the crown jewel of his project to make San Francisco a world-class metropolis: the **Palace Hotel** (*see p47*). As founder of the Bank of California, and with massive mining and real-estate holdings, Ralston spared no expense in its construction. At the time, it was the largest, most lavish and most expensive hotel in the world, and incorporated modern innovations including plumbing and private toilets, and the first hydraulic elevators in the West. The hotel continued to reign until the 1906 earthquake and fire. As the post-quake blaze threatened to completely destroy Market Street, firemen tapped the Palace's massive reservoir system in an attempt to fight the flames. After exhausting the hotel's emergency tanks, the 'Grande Dame of the West' was left defenceless. Following the disaster, the building was demolished – a Herculean task that took 18 months – and three years later a very different Palace Hotel rose in its place. The hotel suffered the effects of another earthquake in 1989 when the Loma Prieta temblor shook the Bay Area. Although the damage wasn't extensive, the owners took the opportunity to close for restoration, and, following a $150 million renovation, the Palace was reopened in 1991. Many had feared that the spectacular features of the 1909 design would be lost, but the Garden Court was lovingly restored, the 70,000 pieces of glass in its arched atrium having been removed, cleaned and/or replaced, along with the ten 700-pound (320-kilogram) Venetian crystal chandeliers.

TAKING A BATH
Engineer Adolph Sutro was Ralston's friend and his equal in ambition. He eventually came to own most of the western side of the city, including the sandy wasteland on its westerly edge, which he bought in 1881 for his **Sutro Baths**. Annexed by the new Golden Gate Park, the therapeutic baths were the most elaborate in the western world. Much in need of repair by the 1960s, and badly burned in a fire, they were sold to developers for high-rise apartments that remained unbuilt, and are now San Franciscan's favourite ruins. The adjoining **Cliff House** (see p115) burned twice: the rebuilt eight-storey 'castle' was destroyed again in 1907, then went through further incarnations before reopening in 2004 as a bar and restaurant.

Closer to Downtown, San Francisco's 'Big Four' railroad barons – Mark Hopkins, Leland Stanford, Collis P Huntington and Charles Crocker – made their architectural mark in the late 19th century by building grand edifices. Their mining investments funded railroads, banks and businesses, but also paid for their baronial mansions on Nob Hill. Many were destroyed in the 1906 fire, but their sites have since been filled in suitably grand fashion. Two old mansions have been replaced by hotels: the **Stouffer Renaissance Court** (905 California Street, at Powell Street) and the **Mark Hopkins Inter-Continental** (1 Nob Hill, at California & Mason Streets; see pxxx), while the site of the former **Crocker Mansion**, a Queen Anne manor built in 1888, is now occupied by **Grace Cathedral** (see p83), itself a stunning addition to San Francisco's architectural heritage.

'Flood Mansion survived the 1906 fire and remains a brilliant example of Nob Hill's grandeur.'

However, the nearby **Flood Mansion** (1000 California Street, at Mason Street) survived the blaze and remains a brilliant example of the grandeur of the homes that once perched on Nob Hill. The 42-room sandstone marvel was built in 1886 by silver baron James C Flood and now houses a private club. Another grand old survivor, albeit one that post-dates the quake, is the **Spreckels Mansion**, an impressive Beaux Arts building in Pacific Heights (2080 Washington Street, at Octavia Street). Built in

1912 for sugar baron Adolph Spreckels, it's now owned by mega-selling novelist Danielle Steel.

Unsurprisingly, this most curious of cities boasts many architectural curiosities. Perhaps chief among them is the **Octagon House** (see p118). Built in 1861 during a city-wide craze for eight-sided buildings (they were considered healthier because they let in more light), it's one of just two octagonal buildings left in the city. Furnished in early colonial style, the upper floors have now been fully restored, with a central staircase leading to a domed skylight.

Another oddity is the **Columbarium** (see p115), a neo-classical temple built in 1898 that holds the ashes of thousands of residents. Its interior is decorated with mosaic tiling and elaborate urns in imaginatively bedecked niches. Oriental promise meets occidental vulgarity at the **Vedanta Temple** (see p118), an eccentricity built in 1905 for the Hindu Vedanta Society. Its bizarre mix of styles includes a Russian Orthodox onion-shaped dome, a Hindu cupola, castle-like crenellations and Moorish arches. The building is open to the public for Friday night services.

FROM BOOMTOWN TO METROPOLIS
When the growing city began to burst at its peninsula seams, a ferry network evolved to carry passengers to and from the Bay Area cities. Intended as a symbol of civic pride for the young city, with a clock tower inspired by the Moorish campanile of Seville Cathedral, the **Ferry Building** was built on the Embarcadero in 1896. Its impeccably restored Great Nave, a 660-foot-long (200-metre) steel-framed, two-storey interior now houses everything from office space to a farmers' market (see p73).

After the 1906 earthquake, a passion for engineering spurred an interest in Chicago architect Daniel Burnham's 'City Beautiful' project. Arising from it was a proposal for a heroic new Civic Center planted below a terraced Telegraph Hill, laced with tree-lined boulevards that would trace the city's contours. The plan was the result of Burnham's two-year consultations with leading city architects Bernard Maybeck and Willis Polk (the latter the designer of the wonderful **Hobart Building** at Market and Montgomery Streets, the former responsible for the city's Palace of Fine Arts), and countered the city's impractical grid street pattern. However, it never came to fruition.

Under Mayor 'Sunny Jim' Rolph, the thrust of the 1915 Civic Center complex eventually came from public contests; many were won by Arthur Brown, architect of the mighty domed **City Hall** (see p76). Several other Civic Center buildings date back to this era, among them Brown's **War Memorial Opera House** (see p227), completed in 1932, and the **Bill Graham Civic Auditorium** (see p232). All reflect the Imperial, Parisian Beaux Arts style, sometimes described as French Renaissance or classical baroque, with grandiose proportions and ornamentation, as well as theatrical halls and stairways. The former main library, built by George Kelham in 1915, was redesigned by Italian architect Gae Aulenti, best known for her transformation of Paris's Musée d'Orsay; it now offers a spectacularly modern experience as the **Asian Art Museum** (see p76).

It was largely Rolph's idea to host the huge Panama-Pacific Exposition in 1915, for which he commissioned Bernard Maybeck to build the **Palace of Fine Arts** (see p120) and its myriad pavilions. Originally made of wood and plaster (but rebuilt using reinforced concrete in the 1960s and currently undergoing a $23-millon restoration), it's the only building left from the Exposition. Around this time, Julia Morgan, another Arts and Crafts architect, was designing buildings around the East Bay, at least when she wasn't working for San Francisco newspaper magnate William Randolph Hearst on the extravagant Hearst Castle. In San Francisco, she designed the old Chinese YMCA building, now home to the **Chinese American National Museum & Learning Center** (see p85).

Passionate rebuilding continued during the Depression, with two staggering landmarks leading the way. The **Golden Gate Bridge** (see p123) opened to traffic in 1937, a year after the completion of the **San Francisco-Oakland Bay Bridge**; the latter is currently undergoing extensive seismic retrofitting and the construction of a new span that will offer amazing views, work that is scheduled to be completed in 2012.

The Works Progress Administration (WPA), part of President Roosevelt's New Deal job-creation scheme, was responsible for many structures, such as **Coit Tower** (see p91), designed by Arthur Brown in 1932, and the prison buildings on **Alcatraz** island (see p93). Other examples from this period include the 1932 **Herbst Theatre** (with murals by Frank Brangwyn; see p252), the 1930 **Pacific Coast Stock Exchange** (complete with mural by Diego Rivera; see p71) and the Rincon Annex Post Office Building, built in 1940 to include Anton Refregier's murals and now part of the **Rincon Center** (see p73).

While Frank Lloyd Wright's **Marin Civic Center**, located further north in San Rafael and completed after his death in 1972, is his most stunning civic work, there is one other Lloyd Wright building in the city, at 140 Maiden Lane. Wright designed the edifice in 1948, originally

The controversial **de Young Museum**.

a gift store, as a prototype Guggenheim (notice the winding, circular stair). It now houses a tribal- and folk-art gallery, and is open to the public as the **Xanadu Gallery** (see p69).

CONTEMPORARY CLASSICS

The 1970s saw a small wave of construction that had a big impact on the city's image. Pietro Belluschi and Pier Luigi Nervi completed the **Cathedral of St Mary of the Assumption** (see p107) in 1972; a 255-foot (78-metre) concrete structure supporting a cross-shaped, stained-glass ceiling, it's a 1970s symbol of anti-quake defiance, nicknamed St Maytag because it resembles a giant washing-machine agitator. The same year saw the completion of the 853-foot (260-metre) **Transamerica Pyramid** (see p69), one of San Francisco's most iconic buildings. The $34-million, seismic-proofed structure has an internal suspension system, which served to protect its 48 storeys and 212-foot (65-metre) spire in the 1989 quake. At first unpopular, the pyramid now has few detractors: for many it's become a symbol for the city itself.

Following a relatively restrained period, the last decade has seen a flurry of construction. Unlike Los Angeles, whose development ethic suits its general ethos – too much space, too much money and slavishly fashionable – San Francisco has always taken a quiet approach to construction, zealously protecting its past and begrudgingly embracing its future. However, more recently San Francisco has begun to introduce bold new works into the cityscape. Increasingly, world-renowned architects are being selected for some of its defining projects.

In Context

THE BOOM YEARS: PART TWO

During the second Bay Area boom of the mid to late 1990s, there was not only a renewed interest in development, but deeper pockets to fund it. Designed by architects James Ingo Freed of Pei Cobb Freed and Cathy Simon of Simon Martin-Vegue Winkelstein Moris, the **San Francisco Main Library** (see p76) is a marriage of Beaux Arts and more recent styles. One side links the building to the more contemporary Marshall Plaza; the other echoes the old library to the north, with grandiose, neo-classical columns. The dramatic interior centres around a five-storey atrium below a domed skylight designed to let natural light filter throughout the building.

However, it's SoMa that has really been transformed. Most dramatic, at least for now, is the **San Francisco Museum of Modern Art** (see p81): designed by Mario Botta and opened in 1995, it features a series of stepped boxes and a signature squared circle facing west. Just west of SFMOMA is a great triumph of recent urban planning: **Yerba Buena's Esplanade Gardens** (see p78) is a beautiful urban park, framed by museums, theatres and shops and replete with lush greenery, fountains, sculptures, cafés and the **Metreon** (see p78), a hyper-modern urban mall. Directly opposite is Moscone West, the latest addition to the **Moscone Convention Centre** (see p78). The stunning glass structure incorporates a graphic display screen designed by New York artists/architects Elizabeth Diller and Ricardo Scofidio. Perhaps the most dramatic of the new SoMa projects is the **San Francisco Federal Building** at 7th and Mission Streets. Designed by Thom Mayne, the architect of LA's new Caltrans District 7 Headquarters Building, the structure rises a full 18 storeys; its innovative, energy-efficient sunscreen façade promises to reduce overall energy use. Set to open in 2008 after a delay of several years is architect Daniel Libeskind's strikingly modern update of a 1907 Willis Polk substation, which will house the **Contemporary Jewish Museum** (see p81). Inside, the quixotic design calls for gold-toned extensions clad in stainless steel that will jut out of the original power station.

Nearby, in Mission Bay, is Ricardo Legorreta's **UCSF Community Center** at the UC San Francisco campus, a building that echoes the architect's Mexican roots with its brilliant-red clay and fuchsia-toned palette.

There has been plenty of activity across town at Golden Gate Park too. The **de Young Museum** (see p113) opened its doors in October 2005, after structural damage suffered during the Loma Prieta earthquake rendered it unsound. The ultra-modern design by Swiss architects Herzog & de Meuron caused huge controversy when it was first unveiled. Angular in shape, the museum's helix-like viewing tower rises high above the park; the dappled, copper façade, which will develop a patina over time, offers a burst of colour in the otherwise mild-mannered park setting.

Across from the de Young, a new building is near completion on the site of the **California Academy of Sciences** (see p112). The work of Renzo Piano, it will turn the 155-year-old institution into a world-class planetarium, aquarium and rainforest with a 'living' roof that will undulate according to the building's shape. The park's oldest building, the whimsical **San Francisco Conservatory of Flowers**, was fully restored following the 1989 quake.

The Presidio has also seen plenty of action over the last few years, as work continues on converting and upgrading the old army properties on the site for public habitation. The decision to allow filmmaker George Lucas to build the $350-million **Letterman Digital Arts Center** (see p120 Spatial effects) on a plot at the eastern edge of the park has not been without its controversy, however sympathetic the buildings might be to their surroundings.

The 2005 unveiling of the **St Regis Hotel** (see p52) announced the city's first new luxury hotel in four years. Designed by Skidmore, Owings & Merrill architect Craig Hartman, who also lent his touch to the sparkling International Terminal at **San Francisco International Airport**, the building is also home to the three-storey, non-profit **Museum of the African Diaspora** (see p81).

FUTURE SHOCK

The most notable signs of new development in the city are the high-rise 'multi-use' and luxury condominium buildings increasingly taking up sky space in the **SoMa** and **Rincon Hill** area. One of the few parts of the city suitable for tall buildings because of its bedrock foundation, the area is slated to become home to around a dozen buildings in the next few years, with new One Rincon Hill towering at 641 feet, making it the city's fourth tallest building. To many San Franciscans, the prospect of towering structures that seem so antithetical to the city's overall vibe is, to put it mildly, unwelcome. Then, in late 2007, the city gave the green light to fast-track the development of a structure to replace the admittedly dilapidated **Transbay Terminal**. Hines and Pelli Clarke Pelli Architects, the team that offered $350 million for the land alone, plans to construct a 1,200-foot office tower – the tallest building on the West Coast – smack in the middle of the most earthquake-prone region in the country.

Time Out
Travel Guides

USA

Time Out Boston

Time Out California

Time Out Chicago

Time Out Las Vegas

Time Out Los Angeles

Time Out Miami & the Florida Keys

Time Out New Orleans

Time Out New York

Time Out San Francisco

Time Out Washington, DC

Written by local experts

**Available at all good bookshops
and at timeout.com/shop**

Time Out
Guides

Oakland Rising

There's 'there' there.

Ask people what Berkeley is famous for and they'll say UC Berkeley or Chez Panisse. And Oakland? Probably crime, and perhaps the Black Panthers. Then there's the (in)famous quote by Gertrude Stein, who, along with a list that also includes Jack London, Isadora Duncan and Clint Eastwood, was raised in Oakland. Returning to her childhood home only to find it no longer existed, Stein proclaimed: 'There's no "there" there.' It was probably not even intended as a slight against Oakland itself, but the remark obviously hit a nerve. It has taken on such a life of its own that the *Oakland Tribune* newspaper flies a green and white 'There' flag atop its downtown office in protest.

Oakland has always been San Francisco's gritty alter ego. Over the years, it has had a reputation as a grim, crime-ridden city of industry that has more in common with a metropolis like Detroit than with, say, Pacific Heights, which is visible across the Bay. Like any city, Oakland does have tough areas – maybe more than most for a city of its size

– but what many people have never heard about are the breathtaking, three-bridge vistas from its verdant hills or the enchanting, twinkling Necklace of Lights encircling Lake Merritt viewed from a gondola.

MAKING A NAME FOR ITSELF

It was during the area of rapid growth following the Gold Rush that Oakland began to come into its own as something other than a destination for San Francisco picnickers. In 1864 Frederick Law Olmsted, designer of New York's Central Park, created the beautiful 200-acre **Mountain View Cemetery** (5000 Piedmont Avenue, www.mountainview cemetery.org), whose rolling hills contain the remains of some of the Bay Area's most prominent historical figures, including renowned Californian architect Julia Morgan.

Oakland continued to make its mark on the national map five years later, when it became the terminus of the Transcontinental Railroad. The 1906 earthquake gave the city its biggest population boost, as many of those fleeing the devastation in San Francisco became permanent residents. By 1910 the population had more than doubled from a pre-quake total of 66,960 to over 150,000.

At the same time, Oakland finally wrested control of its waterfront from private hands, and its port would grow to become its most valuable asset. During World War II it produced 35 per cent of the Pacific Coast's cargo ship output, with its canneries supplying 60 per cent of all canned foods for the war effort. Today, the Port of Oakland is the nation's fourth largest port and is the trans-shipment hub for over 60 per cent of the nation's computer equipment. The towering cranes resembling massive iron horses that line the port have virtually become landmarks in themselves.

'Oakland may be known as a majority black city, but it is notably diverse.'

An African-American identity is central to Oakland, and no discussion of the city would be complete without paying tribute to its rich African-American heritage, perhaps best personified by both current Oakland mayor Ron Dellums and his uncle, CL Dellums. A labour and civil rights leader, CL Dellums organised the Brotherhood of Sleeping Car Porters in the 1920s, the first international trade union to be founded and led by African-Americans. Today, Oakland's CL Dellums Station is the primary rail hub of the region.

Oakland is also the home of the Black Panther Party, the oft-maligned civil rights and self-defence organisation. When it was founded in 1966, the Panthers' openly socialist doctrine was more devoted to uniting disenfranchised minorities than the black nationalism for which it became known. Among other things, the group offered a free breakfast programme for children, medical clinics, drug and alcohol rehabilitation programmes and transportation for families of the incarcerated to enable visits. In 1968 J Edgar Hoover called the Black Panthers 'the greatest threat to the internal security of the country' and the FBI set about infiltrating and destabilising it. Today, the **Black Panther Legacy Tour** (1-510 884 4860, www.blackpanthertours.com) traces the history of the Panthers by visiting various landmarks.

NEW OAKLANDERS

Recent years have seen demographic shifts, with a new group of Oaklanders coming to the city – from San Francisco. Sky-high property

prices and expensive living costs there are pricing out many would-be residents, and a good proportion of them have rolled up in Oakland. Some who have made the move across the Bay are edgy creatives and bohemians, but not all: younger families and first-time homebuyers are also realising that the $650,000 that buys a tiny flat in San Francisco fetches a charming house and garden in some of the better neighbourhoods of Oakland. As a result, Oakland is getting an infusion of cash and new blood, bohemian and otherwise.

In July 2007, an article in *The Economist* noted: 'Talented people are not always rich, and San Francisco is in danger of losing those who are not to less fashionable places. Alameda County, which includes scruffy Oakland, attracted 40,000 people with bachelors degrees between 2000 and 2005, according to the census – three times as many as San Francisco.'

But Oakland today is looking a lot less 'scruffy' than it used to. Gentrification means that Oakland is now home to chic boutiques like Drift (815 Washington Street, 1-501 444 8815, www.driftdenim.com), design gallery Fiveten Studio (831 Broadway, 1-510 451 9900, www.fivetenstudio.com), and upscale restaurants such as Tamarindo (468 8th Street, 1-510 444 1944, www.tamarindoantojeria.com), B (499 9th Street, 1-510 251 8770, www.boakland.com), and Levende (827 Washington St, 1-510 835 5585, www.levendeeast.com). Beer lovers' dreams come true at the Pacific Coast Brewing Company (906 Washington Street, 1-510 836 2739, www.pacificcoast brewing.com) and the Trappist (*see p172*), where the selections of beers are boggling. The two bars are less than a block from each other. Each Friday morning one of the city's best farmers' markets takes over the streets of old Oakland, selling the freshest organic produce, cheeses, locally roasted coffee and a host of artisanal foods.

In the late 1990s, the Oaksterdam district began to take shape. So named because of the Amsterdam-style coffee shops that sprung up here, taking advantage of California's legalisation of medical cannabis as well as Oakland's further decriminalisation of marijuana possession and consumption, the once-blighted downtown area has recently enjoyed a renaissance. Tours of the O'dam area are available via the Oaksterdam news.com website and the new Oaksterdam University (410 15th Street, 1-510 251 1544, www.oaksterdamuniversity.com). The area is also host to a vibrant local arts scene, including the growing confederacy of galleries that are included in the Oakland Art Murmur (www.oaklandartmurmur.com), an open gallery walk that takes place on the first Friday of every month. Eleven of the galleries are located within blocks of each other near the convergence of Broadway, Telegraph Avenue and Grand Avenue. The raucous affairs can include everything from art installations to pyrotechnics, burlesque acts to ukulele jams.

But Oakland is not a city that has thrown out the old to make room for the new. Here too is GB Ratto's (821 Washington Street, 1-510 832 6503), a gourmet grocery established in 1897 that's still family run; Ratto's sells fresh-made deli sandwiches, exotic foodstuffs and chocolates. The best of old Oakland is also on view a bit further up Broadway at one of the city's three landmark theatres, the Paramount Theatre (2025 Broadway, between 20th & 21st Streets, *see p125*), which hosts the renowned Oakland Symphony, movie screenings and live music. The exquisitely preserved art deco interior alone is worth a look. From the 'fountain of light', a 35-foot high, illuminated composition of carved glass, to bas-relief structural panels to murals, hand-carved decorative highlights and multiple sculptural elements it is no wonder that the building has been on the National Register of Historic Places for over 30 years. Just blocks away and currently under renovation is the amazingly elaborate Fox Theater (1912 Telegraph Avenue, 1-510 869 3519, www.foxoakland.org), a 3,800-seater 1920s movie theatre set to reopen in October of 2008.

A DIVERSE CITY

Oakland may be known as a majority black city, but it is notably diverse. While San Francisco prides itself on diversity and tolerance, it is actually highly self-segregated. In contrast, Oakland ties with Long Beach for the most diverse population in the country. Over 150 languages are spoken. In 2007, the largest segments of Oakland's population broke down to 31 per cent African American, 26 per cent white, 25 per cent Hispanic and Latino, and 16.4 per cent Asian American. What these figures don't show, however, is the degree to which all of these ethnicities interact on a day-to-day basis and how all the major groups are represented throughout the majority of the city's neighbourhoods.

The question for Oakland's future is whether this kind of diversity will continue, and whether the population influx will bring improvements for all Oaklanders. In 2007 the *San Francisco Chronicle* estimated that Oakland had lost between 18,000 and 34,000 African-Americans since 2000. Newcomers certainly bring in tax dollars, but this will not automatically result in better schools and social services, and at the same time inflated property prices can squeeze long-term residents out of the housing market.

So is Oakland a depressed, crime-ridden city being rescued by enlightened gentrification, skyrocketing tax revenues and the shopping habits of San Francisco refugees fleeing astronomical real-estate costs? Or is its fundamental character as one of America's most famous 'chocolate cities' being steadily extinguished by vampiric developers and dotcom neobohemians? Both sides of the argument have their adherents, and like so many issues in Oakland, the question is one framed by a local political culture of struggle.

What is certain is that change is afoot. With its considerable pool of talent and pride in identity, a rapidly growing population and a thriving arts community, many residents are cautiously optimistic that the city is poised for a real renaissance. This time, it may just be Oakland's turn.

Street art in Oakland.

Gay Freedom Day parade, 1979.

The Politics of Progress

How San Francisco earned its radical reputation.

In some senses, San Francisco has always been a liberal city. Witness, for example, how its early inhabitants were left to go about their boozing, gambling and whoring largely undisturbed by the city authorities during the Gold Rush. However, the city's current status as an oasis of liberal – as in left of centre – political values has been more recently acquired. It was only during the 20th century that this powerhouse of military-industrial expansionism and the home to media outlets that served as a bullhorn of imperial avarice became the epicentre of an American counterculture that stands in direct and vociferous opposition to US foreign policy and corporate dominance.

During the previous century, San Francisco, as the western beachhead of the growing American nation, had come to symbolise what

became known as 'Manifest Destiny', the belief that America deserved – nay, had an obligation and a quasi-divine right – to conquer the North American continent. And beyond that conquest, San Francisco was pinned as a gateway to an all-encompassing imperial vision that, to some, stretched west to the Philippines, Japan and, ultimately, China.

During the 19th century, liberal writers such as Mark Twain openly opposed this drive for conquest. In the same era, John Muir established the modern environmental movement, challenging the city's massive mining and water interests. However, these voices came up against stiff opposition from the city's power base, which colluded with the press – personified in this era by the ultimate press baron, William Randolph Hearst – to get its message across.

The years around World War II saw some of the most egregious examples of racism, human abuse and environmental debasement in the history of the US. During World War II, Japanese-American citizens were dragged from their homes and sent to internment camps. During the same period, the natural riches of northern California and Nevada were wrecked by environmentally catastrophic deforestation, mining and damming operations from which they're still recovering.

BLOWIN' IN THE WIND

San Francisco's political shift did not begin in earnest until the 1950s and early 1960s. After World War II, ethnically diverse populations in urban areas began to gain political strength after 'white flight' sent more affluent families to the suburbs. At the same time many gays and lesbians left the armed forces and settled here. These developments, along with the city's hedonistic reputation, began to draw a bohemian element that flowered with the ascendancy of the Beats.

The early 1960s ushered in more widespread political awareness. The bohemian subculture of San Francisco began to gain strength and voice in literature, art and music. The growth of the civil-rights movement and the start of the Vietnam War in 1965 caused more turbulence. A considerable number of baby boomers came to question the wisdom of the country's political and social leadership, and many embraced full-bore rebellion.

Marijuana had been a staple in the art, literature and music worlds for some time, since the days of the city's early opium dens. But it was the consciousness-altering properties of new and powerful psychedelic compounds such as LSD that led many to question traditional western mores, religions and political theories. The culture of experimentation not only made its way into the work of the area's artists, writers and musicians, but also into the pursuits of academics, technologists, physicians and citizens of the Bay Area in general. The free and easy atmosphere enabled social, personal and sexual experiences without traditional boundaries, contributing to the lore of the 1960s and, in turn, coming to inform the politics of modern-day San Francisco. To many in today's America, the rise of the hippie culture marked the beginning of the decay of so-called 'American values'.

THE AMAZING INTERNET

As the 1960s came to a close, a group of researchers funded by the US military were labouring at Stanford University, just south of San Francisco, to make computing more powerful. At the same time, in nearby Los Altos, pioneering LSD guru and psychologist Dr Timothy Leary and author Ken Kesey were spreading a gospel of psychedelics through the intellectual and research community surrounding the college. A number of technology researchers, influenced by the political movements surging through the Bay Area, began to conceive alternative uses for the military and business computers they were designing.

John Markoff's *What the Dormouse Said: How the '60s Counterculture Shaped the Personal Computer* (the title refers to the

'Turn on, tune in, drop out': **Timothy Leary** at the Human Be-In, 1967.

Campus demonstration: Berkeley women say no to war.

acid-rock lyric of Jefferson Airplane's 'White Rabbit') relates how the development of home computers and the internet is directly attributable to the desire of those Bay Area designers to help people communicate and organise more effectively, both politically and socially. It was an unrivalled power-to-the-people coup that fundamentally reconfigured the daily lives of millions worldwide and resulted in what one Silicon Valley venture capitalist called 'the largest legal accumulation of wealth in the history of the world'. Counterculture researchers and electronics-club geeks took the cream of the US Defense Department's Advanced Research Projects Agency's top-secret work and put it in homes, schools, libraries and businesses around the world. Global communications, collaboration and information-sharing inconceivable just ten years ago are now the stuff of daily life, largely thanks to the efforts of those Bay Area hippies.

THE GAY THING

Like the researchers behind the PC, San Francisco's gay community arose from the Bay Area's military past to become a thriving subculture by the early 1970s, and eventually grew into something far greater. According to a 2001 article in *American Demographics* magazine, the 94114 zip code – San Francisco's Castro neighbourhood – has more gay residents than any other in the country. The 2000 census determined that the city holds six of the top ten densest concentrations of self-identified same-sex couples; in four of those six areas, same-sex couples represent over 40 per cent of the total population. With numbers like these, it's difficult to overstate the impact that San Francisco's gay and lesbian population has had on the culture – and politics – of the city.

San Francisco has virtually always had some sort of queer scene; there were well-known drag bars here in the 1920s and '30s. But it was during the 1950s and '60s, when gay and lesbian servicemen and -women returned to live in the city, that San Francisco became known as a haven in an otherwise intolerant country. When the social movements of the 1960s geared up, so did gay pride. The queer population began to organise, realising that the surest way to gain power was at the ballot box. The setback of the assassination of Harvey Milk (*see p100* **Streets of San Francisco**), galvanised the community into becoming a formidable political force. Through the establishment of many political organisations, voter registration and education campaigns, San Francisco's gay voters have undoubtedly become among some of the most mobilised in the world. Today, they wield substantial political clout across the Bay Area.

UNIQUELY SAN FRANCISCO

The city's footprint may be small, but the impact of San Franciscan politics and innovation is undisputedly global. Since the 1960s, both the city of San Francisco and the state of California have been at the forefront of progressive politics locally, nationally and internationally. The Bay Area has played a major role in advancing worker protection, the minimum-wage, environmental regulation, workplace safety, curbing emissions and other green issues, not to mention civil rights, the GLBT communities, women, undocumented workers and illegal aliens. The northern California chapter of the American Civil Liberties Union is the nation's largest, and Congressional leaders from the Bay Area are among the most outspoken liberal voices in US government.

Where to Stay

Features

Hotel Diva. *See p44*.

Where to Stay

Budget, boutique or blow-out, San Francisco's hotels cover all bases.

The post-9/11 tourism slump is officially over, but let's take a minute to thank that downturn for forcing the city's hotels to stop resting on their laurels and to start earning a fresh batch, through extensive renovations and innovations. Plenty of affordable options still exist, especially if you're smart about where and when you stay, but you won't have to overlook quite so many flaws.

The Castro's rainbow icon of diversity applies citywide to lodgings: there's something for every taste and bank account. The **Union Square** area and **Financial District** are home to most of the city's large hotels. In addition, there are a number of smaller, more charming boutique properties run by operators who don't forsake comfort or style in the name of economy; many are on the fringes of **Union Square**, on **Nob Hill** or in the dicier **Tenderloin**. Indeed, the city is home to three chains, each of which has established mini-empires of chic hotels. Both **Joie de Vivre** (www.jdvhospitality.com),

which has 15 properties in San Francisco, and **Kimpton** (www.kimptonhotels.com), which operates nine hotels here, have garnered a reputation for attention to customer care and unexpected luxury at reasonable prices. The more budget-oriented **Personality Hotels** (www.personalityhotels.com), with seven sites, has made a name for itself with clever makeovers of vintage properties near Union Square. Some of the big players have added boutique appeal thanks to artful makeovers, like the Eurasian aesthetic at the Hilton San Francisco Financial District (*see p57*), formerly a Holiday Inn . The eco-friendly Orchard Garden Hotel (*see p57*), meanwhile, is the city's first hotel built to exacting 'green' specifications. The latest newcomer on the city's hotel scene is the sleek, 32-storey InterContinental Hotel San Francisco, near the convention centre, expected to open in the spring of 2008 with 550 rooms, the largest addition since the earthquake year of 1989.

INFORMATION & PRICES

Accommodation prices vary wildly in San Francisco. From hotel to hotel, sure, but also for the same room within a single property, which might double in price from a dreary midwinter Tuesday to a July weekend or even during a big convention. The Financial District hotels tend to offer the best deals on Friday and Saturday nights, when the suits have gone home. The rates we've given here reflect this disparity: always shop around. Bear in mind, too, that quoted rates exclude a gasp-inducing 14.05 per cent room tax. Parking fees can be exorbitant, too ($20-$55), and in-room internet charges can also add up (although there are plenty of other sites in the city with free wireless access). While occupancy rates (and prices) are rising, savvy travellers can find bargain prices even for peak travel times and dates. Many hotels offer internet-only deals and special packages, but if those prices aren't low enough, check reservation systems such as hotels.com, expedia.com and priceline.com. Always ask about cancellation policies when booking, so you don't get stuck paying for a room you can't use. Most hotels require notice of cancellations at least 24 hours in advance; however, this may not be the case if you booked via an outside

---

The best Hotels

For all-out luxury
Four Seasons (*see p43*), **Huntington Hotel** (*see p53*), **Mandarin Oriental** (*see p45*), **Ritz-Carlton** (*see p53*) and the **St Regis Hotel** (*see p52*).

For eco friendliness
Hotel Triton (*see p45*) and the **Orchard Garden Hotel** (*see p57*).

For wallet friendliness
Edwardian Inn (*see p52*), **HI-Downtown** (*see p62*), **Hotel Metropolis** (*see p51*) and the **Seal Rock Inn** (*see p61*).

For on-site entertainment
Hotel Bijou (*see p49*) and the **Hotel Rex** (*see p44*).

For views with a room
Argonaut Hotel (*see p58*), **Hotel Metropolis** (*see p51*), **Hotel Vitale** (*see p47*), **Huntington Hotel** (*see p53*) and the **Mandarin Oriental** (*see p45*).

JW Marriott San Francisco. See p44.

website, or with a service such as **San Francisco Reservations** (1-800 677 1570, 1-510 628 4440, www.hotelres.com).

Note: if you're a light sleeper, look for recently constructed or substantially renovated hotels – the city's older buildings generally have single-paned windows that can't filter out the busy street scene. And while San Francisco's temperate climate makes air-conditioning less of a concern, be aware that the few hot days of the year may force you to open a window, letting in the sounds of traffic along with fresh air.

'Wireless' denotes a hotel that has a wireless connection throughout; 'DSL' is used for hotels where a high-speed connection is available only via a cable; and 'shared terminal' refers to a computer in the hotel's lobby or business centre that offers high-speed net access. All hotels are required by law to provide accommodation for disabled visitors and, thanks to California's strict anti-smoking policies, all hotels have no-smoking rooms. Indeed, many hotels are now completely non-smoking, so we've made special note of hotels that still offer rooms for smokers.

Downtown

Union Square & around

Expensive

Campton Place Hotel

340 Stockton Street, between Post & Sutter Streets, CA 94108 (1-866 332 1670/781 5555/www. camptonplace.com). BART & Metro to Montgomery/ bus 2, 3, 4, 15, 30, 38, 45, 76 & Market Street routes/cable car Powell-Hyde or Powell-Mason. **Rates** $390-$665 double. **Credit** AmEx, DC, Disc, MC, V. **Map** p315 M5 **1**

Although it sits just half a block from Union Square, this refined hotel attracts a very discreet and wealthy following. Neatly tucked into a small space on Stockton Street, it offers exceptional service, including valet-assisted packing and unpacking. Dogs are allowed to stay with their owners; staff will even walk them. Room amenities are excellent, and there's an elegant restaurant downstairs, plus a handsome cocktail lounge. Luxury brand Taj Hotels, which acquired the property in 2007, plans to reno-vate rooms and public areas as early as 2008.
Bar. Business centre. Concierge. Gym. Internet (free wireless in lobby, $10 high-speed in rooms, free shared terminal). Parking ($51). Restaurant. Room service. Smoking rooms. TV: pay movies.

Four Seasons

757 Market Street, between 3rd & 4th Streets, CA 94103 (1-800 819 5053/633 3000/www.four seasons.com). BART & Metro to Powell/bus 27, 30, 45 & Market Street routes/cable car Powell-Hyde or Powell-Mason. **Rates** $395-$590 double. **Credit** AmEx, DC, Disc, MC, V. **Map** p315 M6 **2**

The sleek 36-storey Four Seasons is situated nicely on the south side of Market Street, conve-nient for both Union Square and SoMa. Its 277 rooms and suites, 142 residential condos, high-end shops and upscale restaurant create the feeling of a city unto itself. The general design and ambience are pretty similar to other Four Seasons around the world: as you might expect, the amply sized rooms (the smallest are 460sq ft/43sq m) are sump-tuously appointed, with no corner-cutting. The list of on-site amenities is lengthy and all-encompass-ing; perhaps the jewel is the health club, with spa, pool and jacuzzi.
Bar. Business centre. Concierge. Gym. Internet ($12.99 wireless & high-speed, $10/15 mins shared terminal). Parking ($56). Pool (indoor). Restaurant. Room service. Smoking rooms. Spa. TV: pay movies.

Hotel Nikko

222 Mason Street, between Ellis & O'Farrell Streets, CA 94102 (1-800 248 3308/394 1111/www.hotel nikkosf.com). BART & Metro to Powell/bus 2, 3, 4, 15, 30, 38, 45, 76 & Market Street routes/cable car Powell-Hyde or Powell-Mason. **Rates** $270-$595 double. **Credit** AmEx, DC, MC, V. **Map** p315 M6 **3**

Part of the Japan Airlines hotel chain, the 25-storey Nikko is incredibly popular with Japanese visitors but welcoming to all. The rooms and suites are large, bright and reasonably attractive, furnished with Frette linens, pillow-top beds and pale furniture. Elsewhere, the design is clean with Asian touches throughout – some subtle, some obvious. There's an indoor pool that lets in light through a glass ceiling, plus a gym and a kamaburo (dry Japanese sauna). The Anzu sushi bar and steakhouse isn't a bad place to eat; its Sunday jazz brunch buffet is a favourite.

Bar. Business centre. Concierge. Gym. Internet ($12.95 wireless). Parking ($45). Pool (indoor). Restaurant. Room service. Smoking rooms. Spa. TV: pay movies.

JW Marriott San Francisco

500 Post Street, at Mason Street, CA 94102 (1-800 605 6568/771 8600/www.marriott.com). Bus 2, 3, 4, 27, 38, 76/cable car Powell-Hyde or Powell-Mason. **Rates** $229-$429 double. **Credit** AmEx, DC, Disc, MC, V. **Map** p314 L5 ④

Rebranded in 2006, the former Pan Pacific hotel is far enough from Union Square that guests can avoid the crush, but close enough that the shops are mere steps away. The dazzling third-floor lobby, with its soaring 18-storey ceiling, is morphing in early 2008 into a 'great room' with coffee kiosk, bar and American restaurant. But Marriott is keeping the brass-railed hallways that circle the atrium and lead to the guest rooms, which, thanks to a $20 million renovation, now include bigger flat-screen TVs, sophisticated lighting and a gold and sage palette with rich red accents. *Photo p43.*

Bar. Business centre. Concierge. Gym. Internet ($12.95 wireless & high-speed, $0.35/min shared terminal). Parking ($51). Restaurant. Room service. TV: pay movies.

Moderate

Hotel des Arts

447 Bush Street, between Grant & Kearny Streets, CA 94108 (1-800 956 4322/956 3232/www.sfhoteldesarts.com). Bus 2, 3, 4, 9X, 30, 45/cable car California. **Rates** $99-$119 double. **Credit** AmEx, DC, MC, V. **Map** p315 M5 ⑤

Once a Victorian boarding house, this small hotel has been dramatically altered by local cutting-edge artists over the last few years. An aggressive, urban aesthetic dominates (spray paint is popular), while furnishings are in the minimalist IKEA vein. Bathrooms are on the small side, like the guest rooms – but then a two-room suite isn't much more expensive than the regular rate. Stairs are steep, and opening the windows will let in street noise, but pluses at this price range include flat-panel cable TV, mini-fridge, a basic but free breakfast and complimentary wireless internet access. Since art is subjective, it pays to peruse the differing decors online first.

Concierge. Internet (free wireless). TV.

Hotel Diva

440 Geary Street, between Mason & Taylor Streets, CA 94102 (1-800 553 1900/885 0200/www.hotel diva.com). Bus 2, 3, 4, 27, 38, 76/cable car Powell-Hyde or Powell-Mason. **Rates** $109-$349 double. **Credit** AmEx, DC, Disc, MC, V. **Map** p314 L5 ⑥

Located in the heart of the city's Theater District, just a block from Union Square, the Diva has a dressier look these days, with new deluxe bedding, as well as designer lounges by top local artists. High tech complements the high style: there are CD players and 36in flat-screen TVs in the rooms, while the Little Divas suite for children comes with a loaned iPod Shuffle, a karaoke machine and a costume trunk. It's part of the local Personality Hotels chain, which includes the Hotel Metropolis (*see p51*), Hotel Union Square (*see p45*) and the Hotel Vertigo (*see p57*).

Business centre. Concierge. Gym. Internet (free wireless). Parking ($35). TV: pay movies.

Hotel Milano

55 5th Street, between Market & Mission Streets, CA 94103 (543 8555/www.hotelmilanosf.com). BART & Metro to Powell/bus 27, 30, 45 & Market Street routes. **Rates** $99-$199 double. **Credit** AmEx, DC, Disc, MC, V. **Map** p315 M6 ⑦

The Milano boasts some of the best-value rooms in Downtown, and one of the best locations: right next door to the San Francisco Shopping Centre, a block from Yerba Buena and five minutes' walk from Union Square. The neo-classical façade dates from 1913, while the guest rooms are modern, featuring Italian decor (blond wood, black accents). A two-storey fitness centre with a steam room, a sauna and a jacuzzi, plus a well-priced Thai restaurant with a bar that stays open late put this a cut above the average business hotel.

Gym. Internet ($9.95 wireless). Parking ($33). Restaurant. Smoking rooms. TV: pay movies.

Hotel Rex

562 Sutter Street, between Powell & Mason Streets, CA 94102 (1-800 433 4434/www.thehotelrex.com). Bus 2, 3, 4, 27, 38, 76/cable car Powell-Hyde or Powell-Mason. **Rates** $149-$349 double. **Credit** AmEx, DC, Disc, MC, V. **Map** p315 M5 ⑧

Named after Kenneth Rexroth, MC for the fabled Six Gallery reading that provided a launchpad for the Beat Generation, the Rex is one of the city's most appealing small hotels, taking 20th-century literary salons for inspiration. There are books scattered throughout, and the walls are adorned with caricatures of writers with local ties. Literary events are often held in the back salon, and the modern business centre even has a few antique typewriters. Local artists' work decorates the guest rooms, and guests have access to a spacious gym near the hotel. The tiny Café Andrée serves seasonal cuisine; hotel guests receive a free glass of wine at cocktail hour.

Bar. Business centre. Concierge. Internet (free wireless). Parking ($34). Restaurant. Room service. TV: pay movies.

Hotel Triton

*342 Grant Avenue, between Bush & Sutter Streets,
CA 94108 (1-800 800 1299/394 0500/www.hotel
triton.com). Bus 2, 3, 4, 9X, 30, 38, 45, 76.* **Rates**
$209-$399 double. **Credit** AmEx, DC, Disc, MC, V.
Map p315 M5
Created by nine artists, this colourful hotel, across
from the ornate Chinatown gate, succeeds in being
both fun and funky. Now part of the Kimpton chain,
it's a leader in 'green hotel' practices. Rooms offer
organic cotton bed linens and 'Earthly Beds' made
entirely of recycled materials; the seventh-storey
'Eco-Floor' has special water- and air-filtration systems and water-saving devices. Also on the hotel's
eclectic menu are nightly tarot readings, fresh cookies and free drinks in the lobby. Much of the joy,
though, is in the design quirks: the small 'Zen Dens'
have incense, books on Buddhism and daybeds, and
there are celebrity suites designed by Jerry Garcia,
Carlos Santana and even comedienne Kathy Griffin.
*Business centre. Concierge. Gym. Internet (free
wireless & shared terminal). Parking ($38).
Restaurant. Room service. TV: pay movies.*

Sir Francis Drake Hotel

*450 Powell Street, between Post & Sutter Streets, CA
94102 (1-800 795 7129/392 7755/www.sirfrancis
drake.com). Bus 1, 2, 3, 4, 30, 31, 38. 45, 76/cable
car Powell & Mason, Powell & Hyde.* **Rates** $119-
$179 double. **Credit** AmEx, DC, Disc, MC, V
See p48 **Drake's progress***.
*Bar. Business centre. Concierge. Gym. Internet
(free wireless & shared terminal). Parking ($44).
Restaurants (2). Room service. Spa. TV: DVD
& pay movies.*

Also recommended

The stylish **Hotel Union Square** (114 Powell
Street, CA 94102, 1-800 553 1900, 397 3000,
www.hotelunionsquare.com, $99-$199 double)
and the modern **Orchard Hotel**, with spacious
rooms (665 Bush Street, CA 94108, 1-888 717
2881, 362 8878, www.theorchardhotel.com,
$139-$299 double).

The Financial District

Expensive

Mandarin Oriental

*222 Sansome Street, between Pine & California
Streets, CA 94104 (1-800 622 0404/276 9888/
www.mandarinoriental.com). Bus 1, 10, 12, 15,
41/cable car California.* **Rates** $605-$920 double.
Credit AmEx, DC, Disc, MC, V. **Map** p315 N4
Few hotels in the world can boast such extraordi-
nary views, or such decadent means of enjoying
them, as the Mandarin Oriental. Its lobby is on the
ground floor of the 48-storey First Interstate
Building, but all of the rooms and suites are on the
top 11 floors, affording breathtaking vistas of the
city and the Bay. Rooms contain Asian artwork and
plush furnishings in sumptuous, bold red and blue

Garden Court at the **Palace Hotel**. *See p47.*

fabrics, courtesy of a recent renovation that also added iPod docking stations and big flat-screen plasma TVs. All have binoculars, and some have glass-walled bathtubs beside the windows. Service is exemplary, while the lobby-level Silks Asian fusion restaurant continues to receive high acclaim.
Bar. Business centre. Concierge. Gym. Internet (free wireless in lobby, $12.95 high-speed in rooms, free shared terminal). Parking ($51). Restaurant. Room service. Smoking rooms. TV: DVD.

Omni San Francisco

500 California Street, at Montgomery Street, CA 94104 (1-888 444 6664/677 9494/www.omni hotels.com). BART & Metro to Montgomery/ bus 1, 9X, 10, 12, 41/cable car California. **Rates** $169-$519 double. **Credit** AmEx, DC, Disc, MC, V. **Map** p315 N4 ⓬
With a great central location right on the cable car line, this business-friendly hotel is relatively new, but feels as though it's been part of the landscape for years. That's partly because it has been built into a historic structure, with decor inspired by the 1920s and '30s, but it's also due to the exceptional service. The rooms are larger than you might expect and are appointed with comfortable amenities, including upscale bath accessories, plush robes and large work desks. The ground-floor restaurant, Bob's Steaks & Chops, is one of the better steakhouses in town.
Bar. Business centre. Concierge. Gym. Internet (free wireless in lobby, $9.95 high-speed in rooms, $5.95/ 15 mins shared terminal). Parking ($51). Restaurant. Room service. Smoking rooms. TV: pay movies.

Palace Hotel

2 New Montgomery Street, at Market Street, CA 94105 (1-800 325 3589/512 1111/www.sf palace.com). BART & Metro to Montgomery/bus 2, 3, 4, 30, 45 & Market Street routes. **Rates** $179-$449 double. **Credit** AmEx, DC, Disc, MC, V. **Map** p315 N5 ⓭
Famous guests are nothing new to the Palace, which witnessed the death of Hawaii's last king in 1891 and hosted Enrico Caruso the night of the great 1906 earthquake. But unfortunate events like those are happily a rarity at the hotel, which was rebuilt to magnificent effect after the 1906 quake and thoughtfully renovated in 1991. Part of the Starwood Collection, it maintains its unique identity with only a few key nods to the 21st century. The elegantly furnished rooms and modern bathrooms are small, but ceilings are high – and none higher than the soaring glass of the Garden Court restaurant, a popular breakfast destination. The large, fourth-floor lap pool, next to the modern fitness centre and spa, benefits from a skylight roof. The Pied Piper Bar and Maxfield's restaurant ooze vintage charm, while the Kyo-ya Japanese restaurant offers serenely classic fare. *Photo p45.*
Bar. Business centre. Concierge. Gym. Internet (free wireless in lobby, $16.99 high-speed in rooms, $7.50/15 mins shared terminal). Parking ($48). Pool (indoor). Restaurants (3). Room service. Smoking rooms. Spa. TV: pay movies.

Moderate

Galleria Park Hotel

191 Sutter Street, at Kearny Street, CA 94104 (1-800 792 9639/781 3060/www.jdvhotels.com/ galleria_park). Bus 1, 9X, 30, 31, 38, 45. **Rates** $159-$219 double. **Credit** AmEx, DC, Disc, MC, V. **Map** p315 M5 ⓮
Next to the Crocker Galleria mall, this boutique hotel built in 1911 was looking a bit frayed until the Joie de Vivre chain recently snapped it up and poured in $7 million of updates. Now its rooms provide pillow-top bedding with Frette linens, flat-panel TVs and DVD players, and free internet access and office supplies. The endearingly snug hotel, with its elegant art nouveau fireplace and evening wine reception, is the hotel's showcase of charm. A serviceable American restaurant is next door.
Concierge. Gym. Internet (free wireless & high-speed). Parking ($35). Room service. TV: pay movies.

Also recommended

A pair of businessfolks' favourites: the immense **Hyatt Regency** (5 Embarcadero Center, CA 94111, 1-866 716 8145, 788 1234, http://san franciscoregency.hyatt.com, $199-$339 double) and the polished **Le Méridien**, formerly the Park Hyatt (333 Battery Street, CA 94111, 1-888 591 1234, 296 2900, www.lemeridien.com. $289-$499 double).

The Embarcadero

Expensive

Hotel Vitale

8 Mission Street, at Embarcadero, CA 94105 (1-888 890 8688/278 3700/www.hotelvitale.com). BART & Metro to Montgomery/bus 2, 3, 4, 31 & Market Street routes. **Rates** $319-$419 double. **Credit** AmEx, DC, Disc, MC, V. **Map** p315 O4 ⓯
Blessed with a truly dramatic location on the Embarcadero (many of the rooms have great views of the Bay Bridge, and the spa is atop a penthouse suite), Joie de Vivre's Hotel Vitale is otherwise discreet in its stylishness. The capacious rooms are done out in pale colours, all the better to reflect the light, with super-comfortable beds and excellent amenities – including wall-mounted LCD flat-screen TVs. The huge but inviting bathrooms have a sliding door that allows some sounds to waft through; you can also soak in the spa's deep tubs on the rooftop. Downstairs is a bar and restaurant (the Americano; *see p136*) that conforms immaculately to the comfortably chic ambience. Highly recommended.
Bar. Business centre. Concierge. Gym. Internet (free wireless & shared terminal, $9.95 high-speed). Parking ($45). Restaurant. Room service. Spa. TV: pay movies.

Drake's progress

Older European travellers. Younger gay couples. Briefcase-toting professionals with child-toting spouses in tow. Airline crews in for a night. Singles looking for fun. Stereotypical shorts-wearing tourists in search of sun. In its prestigious Powell Street perch just above Union Square, the venerable **Sir Francis Drake Hotel** (*see p45*), built in 1928, has something for just about everyone – and at busy times it can seem like everyone has taken up the offer. That's because, like the city itself, it's not afraid to be a little bit cheesy, a little bit racy, proud of its colourful past but also quick to bring the future into the present.

This wasn't always the case. When Kimpton Hotels took over management of the 416-room hotel a few years ago, it spent nearly $20 million and two years putting the bloom back on this pseudo-English rose, named for the Elizabethan explorer whose near-discovery of San Francisco is celebrated in vintage murals in the lobby. The hoteliers wisely decided to keep the iconic if somewhat silly Beefeater-costumed doormen – one of whom, Tom Sweeney, has served more than three

decades in the bright red get-up – but quickly set about updating the rooms into little jewel boxes of plush green, gold and cream, with smart baths done in black tile and stainless steel. Animal-print robes add a frisky touch, while the emblem of the puffy, flower-bedecked Beefeater hat appears on doors and shower curtains, as if to say 'In for a penny, in for a pound'. The new flat-screen TVs and DVD players, not to mention free Wi-Fi access, reflect more modern tastes.

Gone are the 'Servidors', special door panels that made it easy for hotel valets to pick up laundry or deliver room service – perhaps including a clandestine drink or two during the Prohibition era. But the ornate lobby has been rejigged to accommodate a delightfully inviting bar with a luxurious 1930s design, enjoyed by both guests and residents, and in 2008 the hotel managers expect to offer packages that include tours of another Prohibition feature: a hidden room between floors served by only one of four lifts – sort of like a Hogwarts Express for boozers. There's still a peephole hidden in the room's floor, which allowed occupants to see who had pressed the buzzer for entry from the foyer below.

That same foyer fills with young and beautiful people on Wednesday nights, queuing up for the long-running Indulgences dance party in the penthouse nightclub, Harry Denton's Starlight Room (*see p239*. On other nights, the slightly less young will enjoy beautiful city and Bay views, along with dancing. And it wouldn't be a truly San Franciscan experience without a drag show; Harry Denton's conveniently has two seatings during Sunday brunch, so you can take in painted ladies of all sorts on high.

Other staples of the city – sourdough, strong coffee and Cali-Franco-Italian cuisine – are provided by Caffè Espresso and Scala's Bistro on the hotel's ground floor. After enjoying a night at the newly indulgent Sir Francis Drake, you may not feel like heading up Nob Hill or hitting the revamped gym, but you can play explorer in Union Square or simply let your golden hind lounge in style at Bar Drake.

Moderate

Harbor Court Hotel

165 Steuart Street, between Mission & Howard Streets, CA 94105 (1-866 792 6283/882 1300/ www.harborcourthotel.com). BART & Metro to Embarcadero/bus 1, 12, 20, 41 & Market Street routes. **Rates** $159-$309 double. **Credit** AmEx, DC, Disc, MC, V. **Map** p315 O5 ⑯

On the Embarcadero waterfront, Harbor Court is something of an undiscovered treat. The stylishly cosy rooms look out to San Francisco Bay and the bridge; in addition to niceties such as bathrobes and a top-notch Japanese restaurant and saké bar, guests enjoy freebies such as wireless internet access, a weekday morning in-town car service and use of the adjacent YMCA, a top-quality facility with pool, sauna and steam room.

Business centre. Concierge. Internet (free wireless & shared terminal). Parking ($40). Restaurant. Room service. Smoking rooms. TV: DVD & pay movies.

The Tenderloin

Expensive

Clift Hotel

495 Geary Street, at Taylor Street, CA 94102 (1-800 697 1791/775 4700/www.clifthotel.com). Bus 2, 3, 4, 27, 38, 76/cable car Powell-Hyde or Powell-Mason. **Rates** $245-$395 double. **Credit** AmEx, DC, Disc, MC, V. **Map** p314 L6 ⑰

This Schrager-Starck property is still the hippest hotel in town, and doesn't it know it. Staff range from cooler-than-thou to ultra-friendly (thankfully, there's more of the latter). There's no denying the beauty of the public spaces – from the striking lobby with oversized bronze chair to the gorgeous Redwood Room bar and classy Asia de Cuba restaurant – but as a place to stay it does feel, whisper it, just a touch overrated. Sure, the minimalist rooms are on the right side of comfortable, with easy-on-the eye grey, tangerine and lavender decor, but standard rooms lack the 'wow' factor, and the bathrooms are poky. Snag a heavily discounted rate on the website and it'll feel like value for money.

Bar. Business centre. Concierge. Gym. Internet ($10 wireless, free shared terminal). Parking ($45). Restaurant. Room service. Smoking rooms. Spa. TV: pay movies.

Hotel Monaco

501 Geary Street, at Taylor Street, CA 94102 (1-866 622 5284/292 0100/www.monaco-sf.com). Bus 2, 3, 4, 27, 38, 76/cable car Powell-Hyde or Powell-Mason. **Rates** $219-$349 double. **Credit** AmEx, DC, Disc, MC, V. **Map** p314 L6 ⑱

Part of the Kimpton group, the Monaco is much more down to earth than its swanky neighbour, the Clift. But that doesn't mean it's boring: rooms feature striped wallpaper, huge mirrors and beds with

silk canopies, and there are funky touches such as animal-print robes, iHomes and flat-screen TVs. Thoughtful extras include complimentary wi-fi, and free wine and cheese receptions every night. It's also a pet-friendly hotel: you can even request a goldfish for your room. The location is great, right near Union Square and the entertainment district, but with the Grand Café and Spa Equilibrium within the hotel, you need never set foot outside the door.

Bar. Business centre. Concierge. Gym. Internet (free wireless, high-speed, shared terminal). Parking ($45). Restaurants. Room service. Smoking rooms. Spa. TV: pay movies & DVD.

Moderate

Hotel Adagio

550 Geary Street, between Taylor & Jones Streets, CA 94102 (1-800 228 8830/775 5000/www.the hoteladagio.com). Bus 2, 3, 4, 27, 38, 76. **Rates** $159-$359 double. **Credit** AmEx, DC, Disc, MC, V. **Map** p314 L6 ⑲

Now owned by Joie de Vivre, the Adagio has been in town in one incarnation or another since 1929. Its current version is the best yet: the casual, mellow decor combines deserty muted colours and arty photos, making the 171-room hotel feel comfortable as well as chic and smart without ever giving too businessy a feel. Lather bathroom products, high-definition TVs and on-the-spot room service help guests feel pampered. Having the attractive, Mediterranean-flavoured Cortez (*see p137*) as the bar-restaurant and breakfast room is another major boon. *Photo p51.*

Bar. Business centre. Concierge. Gym. Internet (free wireless in lobby & high-speed in rooms). Parking ($33). Restaurant. Room service. TV: pay movies.

Hotel Bijou

111 Mason Street, at Eddy Street, CA 94102 (771 1200/www.hotelbijou.com). BART & Metro to Powell/bus 27, 30, 38, 45 & Market Street routes/cable car Powell-Hyde or Powell-Mason. **Rates** $99-$159 double. **Credit** AmEx, DC, Disc, MC, V. **Map** p315 M6 ⑳

If you're happy in this slightly edgy pocket of the Tenderloin, you'll appreciate this Joie de Vivre hotel's proximity to Market Street. Cinephiles will love the cleverly executed homage to 1930s movie houses: walls are covered in black and white images of old cinema marquees and local film schedules are posted on a board. Best of all, there's a mini-theatre, with real vintage cinema seating, in which guests can enjoy nightly viewings (albeit on a TV). All of the comfortably stylish rooms (with bijou-like amethyst and gold tones) are named after a movie shot in the city, but there's nothing to distinguish *Vertigo* from *Mrs Doubtfire* besides a film still on the wall. Free pastries, coffee and tea in the morning will help you face the all-too-real world outside.

Concierge. Internet ($8 wireless, $12/60 mins shared terminal). Parking ($28). TV.

Airline flights are one of the biggest producers of the global warming gas CO_2. But with **The CarbonNeutral Company** you can make your travel a little greener.

Go to **www.carbonneutral.com** to calculate your flight emissions then 'neutralise' them through international projects which save exactly the same amount of carbon dioxide.

Contact us at **shop@carbonneutral.com** or call into the office on **0870 199 99 88** for more details.

CarbonNeutral®flights

Hotel Metropolis

25 Mason Street, at Turk Street, CA 94102 (1-800 553 1900/775 4600 /www.hotelmetropolis.com). BART & Metro to Powell/bus 27, 31 & Market Street routes/cable car Powell-Hyde. **Rates** *$99-$289 double.* **Credit** *AmEx, DC, Disc, MC, V.* **Map** *p315 M6* ㉑

An oasis where Market Street turns dodgy (especially at night), the Metropolis is eco-friendly yin meets mid-priced yang, with each floor colour-coded in shades of olive green (earth), taupe (wind), yellow (fire) and aquamarine (water). The compact rooms have nicely understated furnishings: one of the suites, specially designed for kids, has bunk beds, a blackboard and toys. Cable TV and better-than-average toiletries complete the comforts. From the tenth floor, where some rooms have balconies, there are splendid views over Potrero Hill to the Oakland hills beyond. Facilities include a small library, tiny workout room (ask for the discounted passes to a nearby gym) and small meditation space. You can expect some street noise at night, but bargain hunters will be happy. *Photo p53.*

Business centre. Concierge. Gym. Internet (free wireless, high-speed & shared terminal). Parking ($30). Smoking rooms. TV: pay movies.

Hotel Serrano

405 Taylor Street, at O'Farrell Street, CA 94102 (1-866 289 6561/885 2500/www.serranohotel.com). Bus 2, 3, 4, 27, 38, 76/cable car Powell-Hyde. **Rates** *$179-$259 double.* **Credit** *AmEx, DC, Disc, MC, V.* **Map** *p314 L6* ㉒

Right next door to the more lavish and expensive Monaco (*see p48*), this 17-storey Spanish Revival building is no less decoratively daring. The lobby is in a Moorish style – jewel tones, rich dark woods and high, elaborately painted ceilings – but the rooms are cosier, with buttery yellow damask walls, cherrywood furniture and warm red striped curtains. The upper floors have good city views. Pet- and kid-friendly, the Serrano has a games library; guests are invited, at check-in, to play a round of blackjack for prizes. Ponzu, the hotel's hip Asian-fusion restaurant, is a great place for dinner.

Bar. Business centre. Concierge. Gym. Internet (free wireless & shared terminal). Parking ($40). Restaurant. Room service. Smoking rooms. Spa. TV: DVD & pay movies.

Phoenix Hotel

601 Eddy Street, at Larkin Street, CA 94109 (1-800 248 9466/776 1380/www.thephoenixhotel.com). BART & Metro to Civic Center/bus 19, 31 & Market Street routes. **Rates** *$99-$189 double.* **Credit** *AmEx, DC, Disc, MC, V.* **Map** *p314 K6* ㉓

Add funky styling to affordable rates and parking for tour buses in a 'gritty' neighbourhood, then sit back and watch the hipsters roll in. That's certainly the way things have worked at the Phoenix, which has housed a who's who of upcoming musical talent on tour – everyone from Red Hot Chili Peppers to the Killers. Rooms are bright and casual, but they're not the main draw. The adjoining

Hotel Adagio. *See p49.*

Bambuddha restaurant and cocktail lounge, which serves exotic cocktails and Asian tapas, and the hotel's heated pool are both popular places to lounge (and be seen lounging); the free continental breakfast is also served poolside.

Bar. Concierge. Internet (free wireless). Parking (free). Pool. Restaurant.

Also recommended

The old-fashioned **Best Western Hotel California**, formerly the Savoy Hotel (580 Geary Street, CA 94102, 1-800 227 4223, 441 2700, www.thesavoyhotel.com, $149-$219 double) is good value.

Budget

The **Adelaide Hostel** (*see p62*) also has 20 private rooms, some with en suite bathrooms.

Touchstone Hotel

480 Geary Street, between Mason & Taylor Streets, CA 94102 (1-800 620 5889/771 1600/www.the touchstone.com). BART & Metro to Powell/bus 2, 3, 4, 27, 38, 76 & Market Street routes/cable car Powell-Hyde or Powell-Mason. **Rates** *$69-$129 double.* **Credit** *AmEx, MC, V.* **Map** *p314 L5* ㉔

This family-run hotel offers good-value basic accommodation in an excellent location (it's two blocks from Union Square and virtually next door to the pricier Clift). Rooms come with few frills, but they're all clean and nicely appointed. The Jewish deli downstairs is a local institution, popular with theatregoers for the pastrami on rye, and with guests for the free, made-to-order breakfasts with organic coffee.

Internet (free wireless & shared terminal). Parking ($28). Restaurant. Smoking rooms. TV.

Civic Center

Moderate

Inn at the Opera

333 Fulton Street, between Gough & Franklin Streets, CA 94102 (1-800 325 2708/863 8400/ www.innattheopera.com). BART & Metro to Civic Center/bus 5, 21, 47, 49 & Market Street routes. **Rates** $159-$179 double. **Credit** AmEx, DC, Disc, MC, V. **Map** p318 J7 ㉖

Tagged by crooner Tony Bennett as the 'best romantic hotel I know', this charmer is popular with a culturally motivated older crowd, thanks to its handy location near the Opera House, Davies Symphony Hall and the shops of Hayes Valley. Framed portraits of composers hang on the walls, and the sound systems in every room are tuned to classical stations. Rooms are fairly handsome and spacious, and most have kitchenettes (a continental breakfast buffet is complimentary). The restaurant, Ovation, gets busy before and after performances.

Bar. Concierge. Internet ($10 wireless, $4/15 mins shared terminal). Parking ($25). Restaurant. Room service. TV.

Budget

Edwardian Inn

1668 Market Street, between Rose & Haight Streets, CA 94102 (1-888 864 8070/864 1271/www. edwardiansfhotel.com). Metro to Van Ness/bus 6, 7, 71. **Rates** $89-$169 double. **Credit** AmEx, MC, V. **Map** p318 K8 ㉘

This European-style hotel is one of the best bargains in the area, offering charm and tidiness for a relative song. The location is a plus: it's close to various performing arts venues and with easy access to Market Street transportation. Some rooms are small, but most offer private bathrooms (some with jetted tubs), and all are warmly appointed with good-quality bedlinens and nice touches such as freshly cut flowers.

Bar. Concierge. Internet ($2.99 wireless & shared terminal). Parking ($12). TV.

SoMa & South Beach

SoMa

Expensive

St Regis Hotel

125 3rd Street, at Mission Street, CA 94103 (1-877 787 3447/284 4000/www.stregis.com). BART & Metro to Montgomery/bus 9, 9X, 12, 30, 45, 76 & Market Street routes. **Rates** $589-$739 double. **Credit** AmEx, DC, Disc, MC, V. **Map** p315 N6 ㉗

The pinnacle of SoMa's museum district and a worthy rival to the nearby Four Seasons, this 40-storey hotel and condominium tower seemed to take forever to open, but now that it's here it has redefined luxury (and how much people are willing to pay for it). Guest rooms come with butler service, limestone baths, high-end finishings and high-tech fixtures; rooms on the sixth floor and above have the best city views. A combination of new and old construction, the property includes sprawling spa facilities with a heated indoor lap pool, the new Museum of the African Diaspora and two restaurants patronised by the city's elite, Aim and Vitrine.

Bar. Business centre. Concierge. Gym. Internet ($14.95 wireless, free shared terminal). Parking ($40). Restaurant. Room service. Smoking rooms. Spa.

W Hotel

181 3rd Street, at Howard Street, CA 94103 (1-888 625 5144/777 5300/www.whotels.com). BART & Metro to Montgomery/bus 9X, 12, 30, 45, 76 & Market Street routes. **Rates** $189-$429 double. **Credit** AmEx, DC, Disc, MC, V. **Map** p315 N6 ㉘

This trailblazing, chic and ever-so-slightly snooty urban hotel chain continues to expand around the country, but it hasn't yet reached the point at which hip and fashionable turns to yesterday's thing. For that, full credit goes to the design, which eschews grand flourishes in favour of a simple and unobtrusive stylishness in both the rooms and the public spaces. Immediately on entering the hotel, you'll find yourself in a buzzing lobby bar, crowded with visitors and after-work locals making the scene. The rooms are modern and loaded up with indulgences:

Where to Stay

Metropolis. *See p51.*

CD players, wireless keyboards, goose-down duvets. The Bliss Spa includes manicures with movies, and men's and women's lounges.
Bar. Business centre. Concierge. Gym. Internet (free wireless in lobby, $16 high-speed, $6/15 mins shared terminal). Parking ($49). Pool (indoor). Restaurant. Room service. Smoking rooms. Spa. TV: DVD & pay movies.

Moderate

Courtyard San Francisco Downtown
229 2nd Street, between Howard & Folsom Streets, CA 94105 (1-800 321 2211/947 0700/www. marriott.com/courtyard). BART & Metro to Montgomery/bus 9X, 12, 30, 45, 76 & Market Street routes. **Rates** $129-$269 double. **Credit** AmEx, DC, Disc, MC, V. **Map** p315 N6 ㉕
Although it's run by a large chain, this comfortable, modern hotel with artful touches feels like a one-off. The service is friendly and professional, and amenities are far nicer than those of most hotels of this calibre. The recently upgraded rooms and suites include 37in flat-screen TVs, and plenty of accessories (big desks, free internet) designed to cater to business travellers. The location, close to the ballpark and within walking distance of Yerba Buena and the Financial District, is also a selling point. Coffee addicts will appreciate the on-site Starbucks.
Bar. Business centre. Concierge. Gym. Internet (free wireless in lobby, high-speed in rooms & shared terminal). Parking ($45). Pool (indoor). Restaurant. Room service. TV: pay movies.

Mosser
54 4th Street, between Market & Mission Streets (1-800 227 3804/986 4400/www.themosser.com). BART & Metro to Powell/bus 9X, 14, 30, 45, 76 and Market Street routes/cable car Powell-Hyde & Powell-Mason. **Rates** $59-$279. **Credit** AmEx, DC, Disc, MC, V. **Map** p315 M6 ㉚
A gem of a newly renovated hotel. A distinguished-looking Victorian lobby leads up to spruced-up, modern rooms that are not large, but chic and comfortable, with clever use of space. Palettes are fuschia and brown with bright white walls: simple but effective. All rooms come with CD players. A few rooms are available without bath, hence the very reasonable charges at the lower end of the price scale. The Mosser has the distinction of being the only hotel in San Francisco to have a recording studio on the premises. *Photo p54.*
Bar. Concierge. Internet ($10 wireless). Parking ($29). Restaurant. TV: pay movies.

Nob Hill & Chinatown

Nob Hill

Expensive

Huntington Hotel
1075 California Street, at Taylor Street, CA 94108 (1-800 227 4683/474 5400/www.huntington hotel.com). Bus 1/cable car California, Powell-Hyde or Powell-Mason. **Rates** $339-$399 double. **Credit** AmEx, DC, Disc, MC, V. **Map** p314 L5 ㉛
One of the truly iconic San Francisco hotels, this old-world, family-owned and -operated property exemplifies understated luxury. The hotel is perched high on Nob Hill, and features lovely, well-appointed rooms and suites, offering Irish linens, iPod clock radios and eye-popping views of the city. What could be better than a swimming pool overlooking Union Square or indulgent treatments at the lush Nob Hill Spa (345 2888)? Of course, you'll pay for the privilege: if you have to check the rates before booking, you're probably in the wrong place. The California cable car line rattles past the front door. *Photo p55.*
Bar. Business centre. Concierge. Gym. Internet ($9.95 wireless, free shared terminal). Parking ($29). Pool (indoor). Restaurant. Room service. Spa. TV: DVD & pay movies.

Ritz-Carlton
600 Stockton Street, at California Street, CA 94108 (1-800 241 3333/296 7465/www.ritzcarlton.com). Bus 1, 9X, 30, 45/cable car California, Powell-Hyde or Powell-Mason. **Rates** $429-$649 double. **Credit** AmEx, DC, Disc, MC, V. **Map** p315 M4 ㉜
The Ritz-Carlton has been the de facto choice for dignitaries and heads of state for years. As you might expect, then, the rooms and suites are sumptuously

Mosser. *See p53.*

appointed, immaculately clean, stocked with luxurious treats and new gadgets like 32in LCD flat-panel TVs and iPod docking stations. Amenities include an indoor spa with gym, swimming pool, whirlpool and sauna; the Dining Room, a top-class French restaurant; daily piano performances in the Lobby Lounge; and an armada of valets to meet your every need. Mere mortals can pop in for the Sunday Jazz Brunch, held on a sunken roof terrace.

Bars (3). Business centre. Concierge. Gym. Internet ($14.95 wireless & high speed). Parking ($59). Pool. Restaurants (3). Room service. Spa. TV: DVD, pay movies.

Also recommended

The imposingly swanky **Fairmont Hotel & Tower** (950 Mason Street, CA 94108, 1-800 527 4727, 772 5000, www.fairmont.com, $399-$519 double); the similarly moneyed **Mark Hopkins InterContinental** (1 Nob Hill, CA 94108, 1-800 662 4455, 392 3434, www.san-francisco. intercontinental.com, $259-$379 double); the **Renaissance Stanford Court Hotel** (905 California Street, CA 94108, 1-800 236 2427, 989 3500, www.marriott.com, $179-$299 double).

Moderate

Executive Hotel Vintage Court

650 Bush Street, at Powell Street, CA 94108 (1-800 654 1100/392 4666/www.executivehotels.net/vintage court). Bus 2, 3, 4, 27, 38, 76/cable car Powell-Hyde or Powell-Mason. **Rates** $109-$309 double. **Credit** AmEx, DC, Disc, MC, V. **Map** p315 M5 ③③

Despite the deeply uninspiring name, this elegant, relaxed hotel gives guests a taste of Wine Country within a stroll of both Union Square and Chinatown. Every room is named after a Californian winery, and there are daily tastings beside the grand marble fireplace in the lobby. Rooms have bay windows with venetian blinds, handsome writing desks and green-striped, padded headboards. The penthouse Niebaum-Coppola Suite boasts views of the Bay, a jacuzzi, a wood-burning fireplace and a 1912 stained-glass window. But the best reason to bunk here is that guests get guaranteed reservations at Masa's (*see p133*), the hotel's notoriously hard-to-access French restaurant.

Concierge. Gym. Internet ($9 wireless, $0.15/1 min shared terminal). Parking ($36). Restaurant. TV: pay movies.

White Swan Inn

845 Bush Street, between Taylor & Mason Streets, CA 94108 (1-800 999 9570/775 1755/www.white swaninnsf.com). Bus 2, 3, 4, 27, 38, 76/cable car Powell-Hyde or Powell-Mason. **Rates** $169-$249 double. **Credit** AmEx, DC, Disc, MC, V. **Map** p314 L5 ③④

Essentially, California's version of an English B&B, and how you just reacted to that sentence will be pretty much how you react to the inn itself. Some will find its lodgings quaint and delightful, while others will take one look, throw both hands in the air, holler 'Chintz!' and run screaming from the premises. Either way, the early-evening wine receptions and the breakfast buffet with freshly baked bread are a nice touch (as are fireplaces in all the rooms) and the staff are charmers. Next door, the Petite Auberge (www. petiteaubergesf.com) is a cheaper, country-French

version of the Swan, with many of the same amenities; both are Joie de Vivre properties.
Concierge. Gym. Internet ($7.95 wireless, $5/20 mins shared terminal). Parking ($32). TV.

Also recommended

The century-old, 21-room **Nob Hill Inn** (1000 Pine Street, CA 94109, 673 6080, www.nobhillinn.com, $125-$165 double).

Budget

Andrews Hotel

624 Post Street, between Jones & Taylor Streets, CA 94109 (1-800 926 3739/563 6877/www.andrewshotel. com). BART & Metro to Powell/bus 2, 3, 4, 27, 38, 76/cable car Powell-Hyde or Powell-Mason. **Rates** $89-$169 double. **Credit** AmEx, MC, V. **Map** p314 L5 ㉟
It's something of a mystery as to why American hotels continue to describe themselves as 'European-style'; seasoned travellers are aware that, in Europe itself, that often means creaky bedsprings, rude staff and a toilet several miles down the corridor. Still, this handsome old Queen Anne structure, formerly the opulent Sultan Turkish Baths, isn't on that particular radar. Guest rooms are well kept, if hardly stylish; the public spaces are considerably more charming; and Fino, the hotel's restaurant, is a decent spot. The main drawback: walls are on the thin side – but that's true of many vintage buildings.
Bar. Concierge. Internet (free wireless). Parking ($28). Restaurant. Room service (evenings). TV: DVD.

Cornell Hotel de France

715 Bush Street, between Powell & Mason Streets, CA 94108 (1-800 232 9698/421 3154/www. cornellhotel.com). Bus 2, 3, 4, 9X, 30, 45, 76/ cable car Powell-Hyde or Powell-Mason. **Rates** $80-$170 double. **Credit** AmEx, DC, Disc, MC, V. **Map** p315 M5 ㊱
One of a number of small hotels and B&Bs along Bush Street, the Cornell makes no secret of its origins: the Lamberts, who've run the Cornell for decades, are French imports. Downstairs is a restaurant, Jeanne d'Arc, serving complimentary breakfast and non-complimentary dinners; the place is a blast on Bastille Day. Rooms are attractive; the smallest ones have just a shower in the bath, but lower rates to match. Note that the whole property is non-smoking.
Internet (wireless: free in lobby, $6 in rooms, $1/15 mins shared terminal). Parking ($20). Restaurant. TV.

Golden Gate Hotel

775 Bush Street, between Powell & Mason Streets, CA 94108 (1-800 835 1118/392 3702/www.gold engatehotel.com). Bus 2, 3, 4, 9X, 30, 45, 76/ cable car Powell-Hyde or Powell-Mason. **Rates** $80-$150 double. **Credit** AmEx, DC, MC, V. **Map** p315 M5 ㊲
This 1913 Edwardian hotel is a real charmer; a little creaky in places, certainly, but generally delightful. Rooms vary in style a fair bit, thanks to the presence throughout of one-of-a-kind antiques, but the majority are cosy and easy on the eye; many have claw-foot tubs. The welcome from owners John and Renate Kenaston, not to mention the hotel dog and cat, couldn't be warmer (or the oatmeal cookies fresher). Wireless internet is free. The traffic noise from busy Bush Street isn't as bad as you might expect, but light sleepers should ask for a room in the back.
Internet (free wireless & shared terminal). Parking ($20). TV.

Old-world comfort and understated luxury at the **Huntington Hotel**. *See p53.*

Hotel Vertigo

940 Sutter Street, between Leavenworth & Hyde Streets, CA 94109 (1-800 553 1900/885 6800/ www.personalityhotels.com). Bus 2, 3, 4, 27, 38, 76. **Rates** *$169-$269 double; $350-$495.* **Credit** *AmEx, DC, Disc, MC, V.* **Map** *p314 K5* ㊳

Part of the Personality Hotels mini chain, this striking property was undergoing a transformation at the time of writing. LA designer Thomas Schoos is responsible for its identity shift from the York to become the Hotel Vertigo, going for a bold effect with plenty of colour and bold patterns. Rooms here are larger than many in the city. The new restaurant will have chef Tyler Florence at the helm.
Bar. Business centre. Concierge. Internet (free wireless). Parking ($25). Restaurant. Room service.

Also recommended

The affordable, wheelchair-friendly **Grant Hotel** (753 Bush Street, CA 94108, 1-800 522 0979, 421 7540, www.granthotel.net, $65-$100 double); the cheap but nicely located **Hotel Astoria** (510 Bush Street, CA 94108, 1-800 666 6696, 545 8889, www.hotelastoria-sf.com, $59-$125 double), the no-frills but good-value **Dakota Hotel** (606 Post Street, at Taylor Street, CA 94109, 931 7475, www.hotelsan francisco.com, $55-$89 double). **USA Hostels** has private rooms, some with en suite baths (711 Post Street, CA 94109, 1-877-483-2950, 440-5600, www.usahostels.com, $62-$73 double).

Chinatown

Moderate

Orchard Garden Hotel

466 Bush Street, between Grant & Kearny Streets, CA 94108 (1-888 717 2881/399 9807/www.the orchardgardenhotel.com). Bus 1, 2, 3, 4, 9X, 30, 31, 38, 45, 76/cable car Powell-Hyde or Powell-Market. **Rates** *$149-$339 double.* **Credit** *AmEx, DC, Disc, MC, V.* **Map** *p315 M5* ㊴

Opened in 2007, the Orchard Garden was only the fourth hotel in the world to win LEED (Leadership in Energy & Environmental Design) certification, meaning it was designed according to strict environmental standards. Chemical-free cleaning products are used in its energy-saving rooms, which are large by boutique hotel standards (and surprisingly quiet); furnishings sport a pale green and light wood palette. The lobby-level restaurant relies on organic, seasonal ingredients. The fitness centre is petite, but discounted day passes are available to larger gyms nearby; the rooftop garden beckons in fair weather. A few blocks away on Bush Street, between Stockton and Powell, is its sister operation, the similarly pleasant and modern – though not as 'green' – Orchard Hotel (*see p44*).
Bar. Business centre. Concierge. Gym. Internet (free wireless, high-speed & shared terminal). Parking ($34). Restaurant. Room service. TV: DVD & pay movies.

Budget

Grant Plaza Hotel

465 Grant Avenue, at Pine Street, CA 94108 (1-800 472 6899/434 3883/www.grantplaza.com). BART & Metro to Montgomery/bus 1, 2, 3, 4, 9X, 30, 45, 76/cable car California. **Rates** *$59-$129 double.* **Credit** *AmEx, DC, Disc, MC, V.* **Map** *p315 M5* ㊵

As long as you don't need to find somewhere to park, the Grant Plaza Hotel, located right in the middle of busy Chinatown, is an excellent deal. The immaculately clean (if rather small) rooms are hardly stacked with amenities (basically a bath, a TV, a clock radio and a phone), but it's all about the location, location, location for most people who stay here. *Internet ($8.95 wireless, $5-$12 shared terminal). TV.*

Also recommended

The sweepingly remodelled, choicely located **Hilton San Francisco Financial District** (750 Kearny Street, CA 94108, 1-800 445 8667, 483 1498, www.sanfranciscohilton.com, $119-$269 double).

North Beach to Fisherman's Wharf

North Beach

Moderate

Hotel Bohème

444 Columbus Avenue, between Vallejo & Green Streets, CA 94133 (433 9111/www.hotel boheme.com). Bus 9X, 12, 30, 39, 41, 45. **Rates** *$164-$184 double.* **Credit** *AmEx, DC, Disc, MC, V.* **Map** *p315 M3* ㊶

First set up after the 1906 earthquake by an Italian immigrant family and reopened as the Hotel Bohème in 1995, this hotel positively brims with North Beach Beat-era history. The walls are lined with smoky black and white photos of 1950s jazz luminaries, fragments of poetry turn up everywhere and you may even sleep in Allen Ginsberg's room (no.204): in his last years he was often seen here, looking out of the bay window, tapping away on his laptop (Wi-Fi access is free). The rooms are pretty tiny, on the whole, but at least you're surrounded by cafés and restaurants, with City Lights (*see p176*) just across the street. For quieter nights, request a room not facing bustling Columbus Avenue. *Photo p59.*
Concierge. Internet (free wireless). TV.

Washington Square Inn

1660 Stockton Street, between Union & Filbert Streets, CA 94133 (1-800 388 0220/981 4220/ www.wsisf.com). Bus 9X, 12, 30, 39, 41, 45. **Rates** *$169-$309 double.* **Credit** *AmEx, Disc, MC, V.* **Map** *p315 M3* ㊷

Close to one of San Francisco's prettiest urban parks, in a quiet part of North Beach, this is a convivial little inn, beautifully decorated with large gilt mirrors, pots of exotic orchids and lots of character. Each of the smallish rooms is furnished with antiques and luxurious fabrics, and the modern touch of free wireless internet access. A couple of rooms' private baths are across the hall. The service is excellent: guests are provided with tea, wine and hors d'oeuvres every afternoon. The rates also include a decent continental breakfast, though it's a foolish soul who forgoes getting in line early for the outstanding breakfasts served at Mama's (see p146) across the square.
Concierge. Internet (wireless, DSL, shared terminal). Parking ($20-$35). Room service. TV

Budget

San Remo Hotel

2337 Mason Street, at Bay Street, CA 94133 (1-800 352 7366/776 8688/www.sanremohotel.com). Bus 9X, 10, 30, 39, 47/cable car Powell-Mason. **Rates** $65-$90 double. **Credit** AmEx, MC, V. **Map** p314 L2 ㊸

It's difficult to imagine this meticulously restored Italianate Edwardian serving time as a boarding house for dockworkers displaced by the Great Fire. Although the rooms are on the small side and the spotless shower rooms are shared (there's also one bath), you would be hard-pressed to find a finer hotel in San Francisco at this price. The rooms have either brass or cast-iron beds, wicker furniture and antique armoires, but otherwise are fairly basic. Ask for a room on the upper floor facing Mason Street or, if the penthouse is free, book it: it's so lovely you'll never want to leave.
Bar. Concierge. Internet ($5/30 mins shared terminal). Parking ($15). Restaurant.

Fisherman's Wharf

Moderate

Argonaut Hotel

495 Jefferson Street, at Hyde Street, CA 94109 (1-866 415 0704/563 0800/www.argonauthotel.com). Streetcar F/bus 10, 19, 20, 30, 47/cable car Powell-Hyde. **Rates** $239-$379 double. **Credit** AmEx, DC, Disc, MC, V. **Map** p314 K2 ㊹

Built into a historic fruit-packing warehouse, this beautiful luxury hotel is the best in the area by far. Located directly opposite Hyde Street Pier, the property celebrates the city's seafaring past, evidenced in the blue and yellow maritime decor and the abundant nautical props. The carefully furnished regular rooms have all the mod cons you might need (flat-screen TVs, Aveda bath products), but it's in the suites that the hotel excels itself: hot tub with a view of the ocean, tripod telescope in the lounge by the dining table. Breakfast is served in the Blue Mermaid (see p148) on the ground floor.

If you want a sea view, ask for a north-facing room on the third floor or above. There's a small nautical museum off the lobby.
Bar. Business centre. Concierge. Gym. Internet (free wireless & shared terminal). Parking ($39). Restaurant. Room service. TV: DVD & pay movies.

Wharf Inn

2601 Mason Street, at Beach Street, CA 94133 (1-800 548 9918/673 7411/www.wharfinn.com). Streetcar F/bus 9X, 10, 30, 39, 47/cable car Powell-Mason. **Rates** $99-$155 double; $155-$389. **Credit** AmEx, DC, Disc, MC, V. **Map** p314 L2 ㊺

This little hotel doesn't look like much from the outside. And, if we're being totally honest, it doesn't look like much from the inside, either. However, the location is perfect for those travelling with children, the rates are decent (the free parking is a real bonus). The service is friendly, and most of the rooms – which are done out with a playful retro beach motel theme – have balconies, some overlooking Pier 39.
Concierge. Internet (free wireless). Parking (free). TV.

Also recommended

Two big-chain favourites of tour groups and meeting planners: the lively, brightly renovated 529-room **Sheraton Fisherman's Wharf** (2500 Mason Street, CA 94133, 1-877 271 2018, 362 5500, www.sheratonatthewharf.com) and the 313-room, family-friendly **Hyatt Fisherman's Wharf** (555 North Point Street, CA 94133, 1-888 591 1234, 563 1234, http://fishermanswharf.hyatt.com).

The Mission & the Castro

The Mission

Moderate

Inn San Francisco

943 S Van Ness Avenue, between 20th & 21st Streets, CA 94110 (1-800 359 0913/641 0188/www.innsf.com). BART to 24th Street Mission/bus 12, 14, 49. **Rates** $105-$325 double. **Credit** AmEx, DC, Disc, MC, V. **Map** p318 K11 ㊻

This friendly Italianate Victorian, built in 1872, invites you to sprawl about in its beautifully restored sitting rooms, rather than just admire them. You can also take advantage of the garden hot tub or the panoramic city views from its rooftop if your antiques-bedecked room starts to feel a bit too cosy. All but two rooms have private baths; thick rugs and carpets help dampen the noise common to older hotels. In any case, you'll probably use this location to explore the still-gentrifying neighbourhood. The ample breakfast buffet is

Beat vibes at **Hotel Bohème**. *See p57.*

served until 11am, allowing late sleepers a chance to restore themselves completely before hitting the streets of the Mission again.
Internet (free wireless). Parking ($15). TV.

Parker House

520 Church Street, between 17th & 18th Streets, CA 94114 (1-888 520 7275/www.parkerguesthouse .com). Metro to Castro & Church & 18th Street/bus 22, 33. **Rates** *$139-$249 double.* **Credit** AmEx, Disc, MC, V. **Map** p318 J10 ⑰
A couple of blocks from the heart of the Castro, this smartly renovated Victorian (with an Edwardian annex) caters to gay and lesbian travellers, but everyone is welcome. Most rooms have private baths, and all have homey, contemporary decor. There are slight variations in amenities (dataports, desk sizes, shower versus bath), so let the hotel know if you have special requests. On sunny days the English gardens provide a nice respite from the bustling street scene, which also spills over into nearby Dolores Park (best avoided at night). Continental breakfast, free internet access and a wine social are included.
Concierge. Internet (free wireless & shared terminal). Parking ($20). TV.

The Haight & Around

Haight-Ashbury

Moderate

Stanyan Park Hotel

750 Stanyan Street, at Waller Street, CA 94117 (751 1000/www.stanyanpark.com). Metro to Cole & Carl/bus 7, 33, 37, 43, 71. **Rates** *$130-$185 double.* **Credit** AmEx, Disc, MC, V. **Map** p317 E9 ㊽
This beautifully maintained, three-storey Victorian building on the edge of Golden Gate Park has been accommodating travellers in fine style since 1904; it's even listed on the National Register of Historic Places. The handsome rooms, of varying sizes and views, are filled with authentic Victorian antiques, right down to the drapes and quilts. Large groups may be attracted to the six big suites with full kitchens, dining rooms and living spaces. Rates include free Wi-Fi, breakfast and afternoon tea.
Internet (free wireless & shared terminal). TV.

Budget

Red Victorian

1665 Haight Street, between Belvedere & Cole Streets, CA 94117 (864 1978/www.redvic.com). Metro to Cole & Carl/bus 7, 33, 37, 43, 71. **Rates** *$86-$149 double.* **Credit** AmEx, DC, Disc, MC, V. **Map** p317 E9 ㊾
Still basking in the Summer of Love, the hotel – a red Victorian, funnily enough – wears its hippie heart on its sleeve: wildly colourful rooms revel in names such as Flower Child and Rainbow, there's a Peace Café downstairs, and the eccentric, septuagenarian artist-owner goes by the name Sami Sunchild. Rooms have no TVs; only six have private baths; some of the furnishings are looking rather tatty, but neatness wasn't exactly what the '60s were about. A continental breakfast is included. No smoking – tobacco or grass – throughout the hotel, despite what the decor may lead you to believe.
Internet (shared terminal). Parking ($12). Restaurant.

Lower Haight

Budget

Metro Hotel

319 Divisadero Street, between Oak & Page Streets, CA 94117 (861 5364/www.metrohotelsf.com). Bus 6, 7, 22, 24, 66, 71. **Rates** *$76-$130 double.* **Credit** AmEx, Disc, MC, V. **Map** p317 G8 ㊿
The 24-room Metro is cheap, convenient and a good base for exploring neighbourhoods somewhat off the tourist track. The decor is bare-bones, the walls

are a little thin, and the street-side rooms are noisy at night; all rooms have shower stalls only. Still, at these prices, complaining seems a little churlish. Request a room overlooking the back garden, which the hotel shares with an excellent French bistro. Around the corner, and under the same ownership, is a two-room apartment, which is available for about $100 a night.

Concierge. Internet (free wireless). TV.

The Western Addition

Moderate

Hotel Kabuki

1625 Post Street, at Laguna Street, CA 94115 (1-800 533 4567/922 3200/www.hotelkabuki.com). Bus 2, 3, 4, 38. **Rates** $159-$199 double. **Credit** AmEx, DC, Disc, MC, V. **Map** p314 J6 ⑤

As the Radisson Miyako, this efficient Japantown hotel was a favourite of Japanese business travellers. Its new incarnation, unveiled in late 2007, should appeal to both eastern and western sensibilities, with its sophisticated, modern Japanese design and plush American comforts. (For a budget, postmod version, inspired by the Japanese comic book art of anime, stay at the nearby Best Western Hotel Tomo, also managed by Joie de Vivre). The rooms include 26in flat-panel TVs, iPod docking stations, and new marble and tile baths (some with Japanese-style soaking tubs). Other oriental touches: Asian tea kettles in the rooms, traditional welcome tea service and Japanese cultural programmes. Overlooking the Peace Pagoda, the Miyako is just steps from dozens of sushi restaurants, shops and a Japanese bathhouse (hotel guests receive a free pass).

Bar. Business centre. Gym. Internet (free wireless & high-speed, $5/20 mins shared terminal). Parking ($28). Restaurant. Room service. TV: pay movies.

Hotel Majestic

1500 Sutter Street, at Gough Street, CA 94109 (1-800 869 8966/441 1100/www.thehotel majestic.com). Bus 2, 3, 4, 38. **Rates** $110-$160 double. **Credit** AmEx, DC, Disc, MC, V. **Map** p310 F4 ⑤

The Majestic is the oldest hotel in the city to have remained in continuous operation: it welcomed its first guests in 1904, only two years after it was completed as a railroad magnate's private residence. Living up to the hotel's name, every room in this white five-storey Edwardian has canopied four-poster beds with quilts, French Imperial and English antiques, and Gilchrist & Soames goodies. Ask to stay on an upper-floor room to avoid street noise. Free hors d'oeuvres and wine are served in the evening. Café Majestic, the hotel bar and restaurant, features an extensive butterfly collection, in keeping with the haute-Victorian decor. On weekday mornings there's a free car service to Union Square or the Financial District.

Bar. Concierge. Internet (free wireless & shared terminal). Parking ($20). Restaurant. Room service. TV.

Queen Anne Hotel

1590 Sutter Street, at Octavia Street, CA 94109 (1-800 227 3970/441 2828/www.queenanne.com). Bus 2, 3, 4, 38. **Rates** $100-$300 double. **Credit** AmEx, Disc, MC, V. **Map** p314 J6 ⑤

One of the more successful olde-worlde hotel operations in San Francisco, the Queen Anne is, as its name suggests, housed in an extremely handsome old Victorian property. Having begun life as a finishing school for the city's posh young debs (the headmistress, Mary Lake, is rumoured to haunt her former office, now Room 410), it was converted into a hotel in the 1980s. Each of the individually decorated rooms contains Victorian antiques, and the lobby area is a splendid space. Continental breakfast, afternoon tea and sherry, and a weekday morning car service to Downtown are included in the rate; guests receive a discounted rate on day passes to the posh Plaza Athletic Club two blocks away.

Business centre. Concierge. Internet (free wireless, high speed). Parking ($14). Room service. TV: pay movies.

Hotel del Sol.

Sunset, Golden Gate Park & Richmond

Richmond

Budget

Seal Rock Inn

*545 Point Lobos Avenue, at 48th Avenue, CA 94121
(1-888 732 5762/752 8000/www.sealrockinn.com).
Bus 18, 38.* **Rates** $124-$167 double. **Credit** AmEx,
DC, MC, V

San Francisco doesn't really do beach motels, but
this 1960s motor lodge comes pretty close. Most of
the large and spotless rooms have at least partial
ocean views and, at night you can fall asleep to the
sound of distant foghorns. Furnishings won't win
any awards, but most third-floor rooms have wood-
burning fireplaces (in this foggy part of town, these
book up early). Family-sized rooms come with a folding vinyl wall for visual privacy; some rooms have
kitchenettes, the rest have mini-fridges and
microwaves. Seal Rock is next to Sutro Heights Park
and has free covered parking, a patio and, for the
thick of skin, a heated outdoor pool.
*Internet (free high-speed). Parking (free). Pool
(outdoor). Restaurant. TV.*

Pacific Heights to the Golden Gate Bridge

Pacific Heights

Moderate

Hotel Drisco

*2901 Pacific Avenue, at Broderick Street, CA 94115
(1-800 634 7277/346 2880/www.hoteldrisco.com).
Bus 3, 24, 43.* **Rates** $169-$269 double. **Credit**
AmEx, DC, Disc, MC, V. **Map** p313 F5 ⬛54

It might be yet another in the seemingly endless list
of Joie de Vivre properties around town, but this
hotel has actually been in business for over a century.
These days, the rooms pay a kind of gentle homage
to the hotel's history: the decor is a crisp, modern
update of past fashions, the various fittings as handsome and refined as the environs. (Note that a few
rooms have private but detached baths down a hall.)
Business travellers will be grateful for the morning
towncar service to the Financial District (weekdays
only). The complimentary breakfast buffet includes

espresso drinks, while evenings bring free wine and
cheese. (You can work off indulgences with a free
pass to the Presidio YMCA.)
*Business centre. Concierge. Internet (free high-speed,
$5/20 mins shared terminal). Gym. Room service.
TV: DVD.*

Jackson Court

*2198 Jackson Street, at Buchanan Street, CA 94115
(929 7670/www.jacksoncourt.com). Bus 3, 12, 24.*
Rates $160-$225 double. **Credit** AmEx, MC, V.
Map p314 H4 ⬛55

This fantastic neighbourhood B&B is still, happily,
flying under most visitors' radar. Located on a calm
residential stretch of Pacific Heights, Jackson Court
is built into a beautiful 19th-century brownstone
mansion and is as quiet as a church. Each of the
eight rooms and two suites is furnished with a soothing combination of antiques and tasteful contemporary pieces; all have private baths. Some have
working fireplaces; ask for the Library Room, which
boasts a hearth and a brass bed. Rates include continental breakfast and afternoon tea.
Internet (free wireless). TV.

Laurel Inn

*444 Presidio Avenue, between California &
Sacramento Streets, CA 94115 (1-800 552
8735/567 8467/www.thelaurelinn.com). Bus 1,
2, 3, 4, 43.* **Rates** $139-$239 double. **Credit**
AmEx, DC, Disc, MC, V. **Map** p313 F5 ⬛56

A motor inn renovated in mid-century modern style
a few years ago, this neighbourhood gem (now run
by Joie de Vivre) packs plenty of hip into a modest
shell. The rooms are chicly appointed, with great
bathroom amenities and modern accessories; some
have kitchenettes and city views. Located well off
the Downtown path, the Laurel nonetheless has easy
transport options just out front. The lobby level is
home to the popular G Bar (*see p172*), which brings
in the scenesters on weekend nights. Service is excellent, continental breakfast is included, and there are
great restaurants close at hand.
*Bar. CD. Concierge. DVD. Internet (wireless, DSL,
shared terminal). Parking (free).*

Cow Hollow

Moderate

Hotel Del Sol

*3100 Webster Street, at Greenwich Street, CA 94123
(1-877 433 5765/921 5520/www.thehoteldelsol.com).
Bus 28, 30, 43, 76.* **Rates** $119-$189 double. **Credit**
AmEx, Disc, MC, V. **Map** p313 H3 ⬛57

While Joie de Vivre took a subtle approach at the
Laurel Inn (*see above*), it gave this 1950s motel a
splashy tropical palette. The 47 rooms and ten suites
(three with kitchenettes, two with fireplaces) are decorated with bright crayon colours; cool details include
clock radios that wake guests to the sound of rain or
waves. The family suite has bunk beds, toys, books
and games, and guests can go to the quirky Pillow

Library to choose their own headrests. Complimentary coffee, tea and muffins are served by the heated outdoor pool each morning, and the free parking is a valuable commodity in these parts. *Photo p60.*
Concierge. Internet (wireless). Parking (free). Pool (outdoor).

Union Street Inn

2229 Union Street, between Fillmore & Steiner Streets, CA 94123 (346 0424/www.unionstreet inn.com). Bus 22, 41, 45. **Rates** $189-$329 double. **Credit** AmEx, Disc, MC, V. **Map** p313 G4 ⑤⑧
Rooms at this B&B are furnished in traditional style, with canopied or brass beds, feather duvets and fresh flowers. All have private bathrooms, some of them with jacuzzi tubs. The English Garden room has a private deck, while the Carriage House behind the inn has its own garden. An extended continental breakfast can be taken in the parlour, in your room or on a terrace overlooking the hotel garden. Evening pampering is available in the form of hors d'oeuvres and cocktails, included in the room price.
Concierge. Internet (wireless). Parking ($15).

Budget

Edward II Inn & Pub

3155 Scott Street, between Greenwich & Lombard Streets, CA 94123 (1-800 473 2846/922 3000/fax 931 5784/www.edwardii.com). Bus 28, 30, 43, 76. **Rates** $69-$199 double. **Credit** AmEx, Disc, MC, V. **Map** p313 G3 ⑤⑨
There's a wide array of room styles at the Edward II, catering to almost every whim and budget and, in the main, really quite pleasant with it. You can choose from 26 rooms – some with shared baths – or three suites, with living rooms and whirlpool baths. Most have 'traditional British' (country house) decor; complimentary continental breakfast and evening drinks are served in the adjoining pub. The new fitness centre costs $10 per day to use. The inn's location is a little traffic-heavy, but it's near the shops and restaurants of Chestnut and Union Streets.
Bar. Gym. Internet (wireless, DSL). Parking ($12). Room service.

Also recommended

The **Cow Hollow Motor Inn** (2190 Lombard Street, CA 94123, 921 5800, www.cowhollow motorinn.com, $79-$145 double) is good value.

The Marina & the waterfront

Budget

The **HI-Fisherman's Wharf hostel** (*see below*) has some private rooms.

Marina Inn

3110 Octavia Street, at Lombard Street, CA 94123 (1-800 274 1420/928 1000/www.marinainn.com). Bus 28, 30, 76. **Rates** $75-$125 double. **Credit** AmEx, DC, Disc, MC, V. **Map** p314 H3 ⑥⓪

The rooms at the Marina Inn are surprisingly quiet. Spread over the four storeys of this Victorian-style inn (it actually dates to 1924), they are all furnished with floral wallpaper, pine fittings and four-poster beds. Continental breakfast is included.
Internet (free wireless). TV.

Also recommended

The basic, affordable **Marina Motel** (2576 Lombard Street, CA 94123, 1-800 346 6118, 921 9406, www.marinamotel.com, $75-$145 double).

Hostels

Budget-conscious travellers have around 20 hostels to choose from in San Francisco. Go to www.hostels.com/us.ca.sf.html for a full listing.

Adelaide Hostel

5 Isadora Duncan Lane, off Taylor Street, between Post & Geary Streets, Tenderloin, CA 94102 (1-877 359 1915/359 1915/www.adelaidehostel.com). BART & Metro to Powell/bus 2, 3, 4, 27, 38, 76/cable car Powell-Hyde or Powell-Mason. **Rates** $20 dorm bed; $70-$110 private room. **Credit** AmEx, DC, MC, V. **Map** p314 L5 ⑥①
Until 2003, the Adelaide was a friendly, old-fashioned pension, but the following year the owners expanded the 18 rooms to add six en suites and two 12-bed dormitories. The rooms have TVs but no phones, but on the plus side, continental breakfast and internet/computer use are free to guests. The hostel is tucked into a quiet alley.
Internet (free shared terminal & wireless). Parking ($16).

HI-Downtown

312 Mason Street, at O'Farrell Street, Union Square & around, CA 94102 (1-888 464 4872/788 5604/ www.sfhostels.com). BART & Metro to Powell/bus 2, 3, 4, 9X, 30, 38, 45, 76 & Market Street routes/cable car Powell-Hyde or Powell-Mason. **Rates** $23-$29.75 dorm bed; $60-$100 private room. **Credit** MC, V. **Map** p315 M6 ⑥②
Make your reservation at least five weeks in advance during high season to stay at this popular 260-bed hostel. It prides itself on its privacy and security, with guests accommodated in small single-sex rooms; some larger rooms also have their own bathroom. Beds for walk-ins are available on a first-come, first-served basis: bring ID or you'll be turned away. Free breakfast and wireless internet access.
Hostelling International also runs two other hostels in San Francisco. The 75-room HI-City Centre (685 Ellis Street, between Larkin & Hyde Streets, Tenderloin, 474 5721) was refurbished to a decent standard a few years ago, while HI-Fisherman's Wharf (Building 240, Fort Mason, at Bay & Franklin Streets, Marina, 771 7277) offers a wide variety of rooms (some private), free parking and astonishing views of the Bay. As with HI-Downtown, both provide free breakfast and Wi-Fi, and are bookable via 1-888 464 4872 or www.sfhostels.com.
Internet (free wireless).

Sightseeing

Haight Street. *See p102.*

Introduction

Your key to the city.

Every city worth its salt can be said to offer something for everyone. The astonishing thing about San Francisco is that it does so within such a small area, just seven miles long by seven miles wide. The city feels squeezed together at times, as well it might: the streets around Union Square are packed with both buildings and people, the latter a mix of workaday commuters and curious tourists. But you don't have to travel far from the centre to encounter a variety of different worlds: buzzing ethnic 'hoods, chi-chi shopping corridors, eye-catching new buildings, expansive old parks... The variety here is virtually endless.

Getting around San Francisco is relatively simple. As befits a city its size, it's pedestrian-friendly; indeed, the best way to see the place is on foot. If the hills get a little too much, worry not: there's an excellent public transportation network in place, a mix of buses, streetcars, trains and the world-famous cable cars. For more on getting around town, *see pp283-86.*

THE NEIGHBOURHOODS

Arranged by area, our sightseeing chapters start at **Union Square**, where visitors are most likely to have procured a hotel or emerged from public transport. From here, we explore the rest of Downtown north of Market Street: the high-rise **Financial District**, the lovely **Embarcadero**, the run-down **Tenderloin** and the grand **Civic Center**. Then we go south of Market into **SoMa**: centre of the dot-com boom and bust, but now up and coming again. From Downtown, we move north towards the water, through posh **Nob Hill**, vibrant **Chinatown**, espresso-scented **North Beach** and on to the tourist heaven of **Fisherman's Wharf**.

We then go south to the Latino-meets-hipster **Mission**, its neighbour **Potrero Hill**, the city's gay heartland in the **Castro** and pretty **Noe Valley**. From here, it's to the still-lively **Haight**, the sprawling **Western Addition** (including **Japantown**) and smart **Hayes Valley**. West of here are the largely residential areas of the **Richmond** and the **Sunset**, with **Golden Gate Park** in between. North from the Western Addition, meanwhile, lie the upmarket trio of **Pacific Heights**, **Cow Hollow** and the **Marina**, the former military base of the **Presidio** and the **Golden Gate Bridge**. Finally, we cross the Bay Bridge to

the **East Bay**, to ethnically diverse **Oakland** and the People's Republic of **Berkeley**.

A few things about the city never change: its relative safety and its topography. Lace up your boots, and remember: for every uphill climb, there's a downslope to follow.

BASIC NAVIGATION

As a rule of thumb, blocks in San Francisco work in units of 100 heading north or south away from **Market Street**, west from the **Embarcadero** or (for the numbered avenues) south from the **Presidio**. Thus 250 24th Avenue is the third block south of the Presidio; 375 Mason on the fourth block north of Market. Most street signs indicate whether you're heading towards larger or smaller numbers.

Tours

Vehicle tours

Fire Engine Tours & Adventures

333 7077/www.fireenginetours.com. **Tours** 1pm Mon, Wed-Sun; call for details of additional tours. **Cost** $45; $25-$35 reductions. **Credit** MC, V.
A shiny red 1955 Mack fire engine whisks you from Beach Street, behind the Cannery, through the Presidio across the Golden Gate Bridge and back in 75 minutes. Wearing a fireman's coat. Well, why ever not? Book ahead.

San Francisco Helicopter Tours

1-800 400 2404/1-650 635 4500/www.sfhelicopter tours.com. **Tours** 10am, 12.30pm, 3pm, 5.30pm daily. **Cost** $130-$275. **Credit** AmEx, MC, V.
See San Francisco from the skies. Helicopter tours the Vista ($140, $100 children; 15-20mins) and Vista Grande ($185, $130 children; 25-30mins) soar up from SFO over San Francisco; the latter also takes in the Marin Headlands and Sausalito. The views, predictably, are truly stunning, especially when the fog holds off. Other options include a helicopter ride followed by dinner on a yacht ($285). Booking is essential for all tours; ground transportation to and from your hotel is included.

San Francisco Seaplane Tours

332 4843/www.seaplane.com. **Tours** 10.30am, noon, 1.30pm, 3pm daily. **Cost** $139; $99 reductions; $189 Sunset Champagne flight (summer). **Credit** MC, V.
Starting from Pier 39, this de Havilland Beaver zooms round the Bay for half an hour.

Shopping and hanging out in **Haight Street**. *See p103.*

Rendezvous Charters

543 7333/www.rendezvouscharters.com. **Tours**
Sunset from 2hrs before sunset Fri, Sat. *Brunch*
11am-2pm Sun. *Afternoon* 3-5pm Sun. **Cost** *Sunset,*
Afternoon $25; $20 reductions. *Brunch* $40; $35
reductions. **Credit** AmEx, MC, V.
A variety of boat trips, leaving from Pier 40 in South
Beach Harbor. Book well in advance.

Walking tours

All About Chinatown

982 8839/www.allaboutchinatown.com. **Tours** 10am
daily. **Cost** $28; $15 reductions. *With lunch* $40; $27
reductions. **No credit cards**.
Everything you need to know about what is perhaps the city's most fascinating neighbourhood,
told from a genuine insider's perspective: chief
guide Linda Lee was raised here. Tours last two
hours, or three if you stay for a dim sum lunch.
Reservations are essential; when you've booked,
you'll be told the meeting point.

Cruisin' the Castro

255 1821/www.webcastro.com/castrotour. **Tours**
10am Sat. **Cost** $35; $25 reductions. **Credit** *booking
on website only* AmEx, DC, MC, V.
The Castro's most entertaining tour points out historic queer landmarks and traces the origins of the
gay community. The tour lasts four hours and starts
at the corner of Castro and Market Street above
Castro Metro station. Reservations are required.

Dashiell Hammett Walking Tour

www.donherron.com. **Tours** *May, Sept* noon Sun;
check website for others. **Cost** $10. **No credit cards**.
For four hours, you can walk in the footsteps of the
city's most famous thriller writer and see the places
about which he wrote in his novels. Meet by the
Main Library, at Fulton and Larkin Streets; reservations aren't necessary.

Flower Power Walking Tour

863 1621/www.haightashburytour.com **Tours**
9.30am Tue, Sat; 2pm Thur; 11am Fri. **Cost** $20;
free under-9s. **No credit cards**.
A two and a half hour walk that relives 1967's
Summer of Love. Meet at the corner of Stanyan and
Waller Streets. Tours for groups of four or more can
be arranged at other times; booking ahead is necessary for all tours.

San Francisco Architectural Heritage Tours

441 3000/www.sfheritage.org. **Tours** 1.30pm
Sat. **Cost** $8; $5 reductions. **No credit cards**.
SF Architectural Heritage runs a number of different
tours on different Saturday: 'A Walk Along Broadway',
covering the area north and west of the Haas Lilienthal
house; 'Beyond Union Street: a Walk Through Cow
Hollow'; and 'Walk the Line: Van Ness Avenue. There
is also a walking tour of Pacific Heights. Call or check
the website for details of what's on.

San Francisco Literary Tours

441 0140/www.sfliterarytours.com. **Tours** noon Sat.
Cost $25. **No credit cards**.
A two-hour jaunt around North Beach and
Chinatown in the company of local writer Scott
Lettieri. Keeping in the Beat spirit, the admission
price includes a free drink: a Jack Kerouac cocktail.
The tour meets in front of the City Lights bookstore
(*see p178*) at noon every Saturday, though other tour
times can be arranged.

Victorian Home Walk

252 9485/www.victorianwalk.com. **Tours** 11am
daily. **Cost** $20 **No credit cards**.
Experienced guides lead these terrific tours of some
of the city's loveliest Victorian houses. Meet in the
lobby of the Westin St Francis on Union Square, and
bring a camera. Transport from the Westin to the
Victorians is included in the tour price. Reservations
aren't necessary.

Downtown

Head to the compact city centre for shopping, museums – and cable cars.

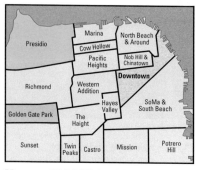

Maps pp314-315 & p318

San Francisco's Downtown area may be the hub that saves the city from being seen simply as a series of villages. The city isn't even close to being one of the ten largest in the country: by population, Phoenix, Arizona, is twice its size and Jacksonville, Florida, beats it by 50,000. But cultural attractions and Downtown's stellar shopping, with outposts representing virtually every significant international luxury brand, give the city a cosmopolitanism that exceeds its modest size. Luckily, Downtown's compactness means it's a breeze to navigate on foot. And if you want to climb its daunting hills, there are always the famous cable cars.

The centre of the action is **Union Square**, a handsome space ringed with shops and hotels. East of here sits the **Financial District**, one of the few places where one can see northern Californians in business attire; beyond it is the elegant **Embarcadero**, which meanders towards the Pacific Coast. To the west of Union Square, it's all very different: after the **Tenderloin**, a gritty area defined by dive bars, ethnic restaurants and panhandlers, comes **Civic Center**, the city's seat of government.

Union Square & around

The best place to begin an exploration of Union Square is at the corner of **Post** and **Stockton Streets**, where a timeline of its history is etched into the granite. This little patch of the city was destined to be common ground from an early date. In 1839, Jean Vioget laid out a park in the location when designing Yerba Buena, the city that would become San Francisco. In 1850,

Colonel John Geary (who would give his name to Geary Boulevard, west of the square) deeded the land to the city for use as a public space.

The square's name harkens back to its use in 1861 as a pro-Union rallying point on the eve of the Civil War. The 97-foot (30-metre) Corinthian column that rises from the middle of the square was designed by Robert Aitken to commemorate Admiral Dewey's 1898 victory at Manila during the Spanish-American War. This monument to militarism and imperialism stands in contrast to the mindset of most San Franciscans today.

In 1941, the square was rebuilt according to a somewhat severe design by Timothy Pflueger. Pflueger's vision can still be seen in the early Francis Ford Coppola film *The Conversation*, and it acts as a counterpoint to some of his more characteristic art deco designs – notably the stunning Castro Theatre (*see p209*). In 1997, a competition was held to create a new Union Square. After much wrangling, April Phillips and Michael Fotheringham's winning design was unveiled in 2002. Conceived to encourage use by shoppers and lunchtime throngs, yet maintaining its vast central area, the new layout altered the character of the area overnight, with a more open design and plenty of benches.

Once a major hangout of San Francisco's homeless, Union Square was transformed into a lively gathering place in the centre of Downtown. Located in one of the few areas of the city with a paucity of parks, what little green space was added went a long way. Although critics and sceptics had initially feared that the $25 million renovation would be a bust, one need only take a seat on the grass on a sunny afternoon to see what a success it has become. Tourists and locals sprawl on the strips of lawn along the southern edge of the square, taking a break from the shops, connecting to the square's free Wi-Fi network on their laptops, or simply enjoying a bit of sun and some live music.

At the south-west corner of the square is a kiosk that serves as the TIX Bay Area outlet, offering 50 per cent off tickets for shows, tours and events throughout the city. Diagonally across the square is a branch of Emporio Rulli café, with sandwiches, strong espressos and frosty-mugged beers. However, the real commerce is around the outside: the square is ringed by upscale stores and hotels. At no.335, facing right on the square, the once-glamorous

Westin St Francis Hotel is where silent-era film star Fatty Arbuckle's lethal libido ignited Hollywood's first sex scandal in 1921.

Once you've maxed out the credit cards, head to the Rotunda restaurant at **Neiman Marcus** (150 Stockton Street, between Geary & O'Farrell Streets, 362 4777, www.neiman marcus.com) for a lobster club sandwich and a glass of California chardonnay beneath the breathtaking stained-glass dome. Built in 1909 for the City of Paris department store that first occupied this site, the dome was shipped across the country for repair when Neiman Marcus took over the building; each of its 26,000 pieces was individually cleaned and restored. There's more history at nearby jeweller **Shreve & Co** (200 Post Street, at Grant Avenue, 421 2600, www.shreve.com): founded in 1852, four years after the discovery of gold in California, it remains the city's oldest retail store.

The stretch of **Powell Street** that links Union Square to Market Street is among the city's busiest thoroughfares. Watching the cable cars clatter past, only to realise that the cables are still humming under your feet, is a quintessential San Francisco experience. At the foot of Powell, where it joins **Market Street**, huge queues of tourists hang around and wait to catch a cable car at the roundabout where conductors manually rotate the cars on a giant turntable for the return journey back up the hill.

The once-grand Market Street has not aged well, though recent revitalisation efforts leave

San Franciscans still living in hope. Lined with office blocks at its northern end and dilapidated storefronts further south, the crowds are here for the big chain stores: Old Navy looms large on the south side of Market at 4th Street, with a capacious Virgin Megastore also doing swift business. The most handsome building in the area is arguably the triangular **Phelan Building**, on the north side of Market Street, between Stockton and O'Farrell Streets. Built in 1908 as part of Mayor James Phelan's post-quake reconstruction programme, it's the largest of San Francisco's 'flat-iron' structures, similar to the notable **Flood Building** just down the street (870 Market Street, between 4th & 5th Streets). How Phelan would have felt about the cavernous CompUSA store on the bottom floor is not a matter of public record. Across the street, levity is provided at the historic **Mechanics' Institute** (57 Post Street, between Kearny & Montgomery Streets, 393 0101, www.milibrary. org), home to the nation's oldest chess club and a 150-year-old library that contains more than 160,000 books. Free tours are offered every Wednesday at noon and author events, monthly film series and special exhibitions are ongoing.

The streets north of Market Street and east of Union Square are home to several handsome little alleyways, missed by most tourists but treasured by locals for the relative peace and quiet they afford. **Maiden Lane**, adjoining the square to the east, was once one of the city's most notorious thoroughfares, where randy

Hanging out in **Union Square**: a unique city gathering place.

Sightseeing

residents headed to pick up the town's cheapest prostitutes. Now gated by day, it's considerably more handsome, awash with chic boutiques and one-off stores such as **Xanadu Gallery** (no.140, 392 9999, www.folkartintl.com). The swooping circular interior of the building, designed in 1948 by Frank Lloyd Wright, is filled with wonderful and exotic merchandise – everything from coffee-table books on South Seas art to *nandi* masks from 17th-century India.

Further north sit two more notable alleys. **Belden Place**, a small street between Kearny and Montgomery Streets, is the main artery of Downtown's increasingly established (though unofficial) French Quarter, offering dining both fine and casual plus the most enthusiastic Bastille Day celebrations (14 July) in the city. Nearby **Mark Lane**, another tiny road just off Bush Street, forgoes the red, blue and white in favour of green: it's home to the Irish Bank, an old-school Irish pub. Post-work revellers spill out into the alley clutching pints of the black, and the annual St Patrick's Day celebrations (17 March) are the stuff of legend.

The other streets surrounding Union Square are dominated by shops and hotels, although there are a handful of landmarks that may please literary buffs. Head two blocks north of Union Square on Stockton Street, take a left down Bush Street, and you'll come to Burritt Street; it is in this alley that the byzantine plot of Dashiell Hammett's *The Maltese Falcon* begins with the murder of Sam Spade's partner, Miles Archer. The street opposite is even named after the author, who, like his fictional alter ego Sam Spade, used to regularly visit the century-old **John's Grill** (63 Ellis Street, between Market & Powell Streets, 986 0069, www.johnsgrill.com). *See also p70* **City noir**.

San Francisco Museum of Craft & Design

550 Sutter Street, between Powell & Mason Streets (773 0303/www.sfmcd.org). Bus 2, 3, 4, 76/cable car Powell-Mason & Powell-Hyde. **Open** 10am-5pm Tue, Wed, Fri, Sat; 10am-7pm Thur; noon-5pm Sun. **Admission** *Suggested donation* $3; $2 discounts. **Credit** AmEx, MC, V. **Map** p315 M5.

This modest, three-room museum, opened in 2004, highlights how contemporary craft and design enrich everyday life. Exhibitions have included contemporary studio furniture from Tanzania and the United States, and the confluence of art and wine label design.

The Financial District

Bounded by Market, Kearny and Jackson Streets, plus the Embarcadero to the east, the Financial District has been the business and banking hub of San Francisco, and the West at large, since the Gold Rush of the mid 19th

Bank of America Center. *See p71.*

century. Its northern edge is overlooked by the **Transamerica Pyramid**, (600 Montgomery Street, between Washington & Clay Streets). Built on the site of the Montgomery Block, a four-storey office building that formerly housed writers, artists and radicals including Rudyard Kipling and Mark Twain, the structure provoked public outrage when William Pereira's design was unveiled. However, since its completion in 1972, the 853-foot (260-metre) building has become an iconic spike that defines the city's skyline. The pyramid sits on giant rollers that allow it to rock safely in the event of an earthquake. It sounds a little wacky, but it must work: the building wasn't damaged by the 1989 Loma Prieta tremor, which measured 7.1 on the Richter Scale. Sadly, the only people who get to access the vertiginous observation deck are those who work in the building.

On the pyramid's east side, tiny **Redwood Park** is a cool refuge that lunching workers share with majestic trees and bronze sculptures of frogs that are frozen mid-leap in the pond. The redwood tree is thought to be the longest-living organism on the planet; some specimens exceed 2,200 years in age. (Just up the California coast in Humboldt County's Redwood National Park stands the world's tallest known tree, a redwood standing at 379 feet/116 metres).

City noir

Was it the steep hills, the foggy nights or a certain brand of louche cosmopolitan glamour that drew 1930s crime novelists and 1940s Hollywood directors to San Francisco as a location? From author Dashiell Hammett's *The Maltese Falcon* (pictured) and Orson Welles's *The Lady from Shanghai* to Alfred Hitchcock's *Vertigo*, the hills, the fog and the views provided backdrops for shady dealings. Whether it was the exoticism of Chinatown or the dark secrets of the wealthy denizens of Nob Hill, here was a city where things might not be quite what they seemed.

This shadowy history is still celebrated in today's San Francisco, where there's even an alley named after noir writer and erstwhile San Franciscan Hammett, who in addition to introducing private dick Sam Spade in *The Maltese Falcon* also penned such classics as *The Thin Man* and *Red Harvest* – in between a lifelong series of liquid lunches. If you want to see where the writer lived and worked as well as the locations where he set his tales, take the Dashiell Hammett Tour, led by the trench-coated noir aficionado Don Herron ($10, May & Sept only, www.donherron.com). Four hours long and covering three miles, the tour makes its way through Downtown, the Tenderloin, Nob Hill and Chinatown.

Highlights include Burritt Alley, where a bronze plaque celebrates a fictional event – the murder of Spade's business partner – and also the location of John's Grill, opened in 1908, where the fictional Spade (and Hammett himself) stopped in for a meal. Upstairs, the restaurant has a dining room filled with Hammett memorabilia, although one of the original falcon figurines used in the classic 1941 film flew the coop in 2007 – stolen along with signed copies of books by Hammett and noted San Francisco columnist Herb Caen. A replica has been made and fans continue to check out the spot where Sam Spade had his pork chops and potatoes.

Contemporary local authors help keep the noir tradition alive. A recent collection, *San Francisco Noir* (www.akashicbooks.com/sfnoir.htm), features stories by the likes of 'Czar of Noir' Eddie Muller, long-time Mission District squatter Peter Plate and man-about-town Robert Mailer Anderson, putting a modern spin on the city's hard-boiled tradition. The book was edited by City Lights Bookstore's Peter Maravelis and each story is set in a different neighbourhood, from Chinatown's back alleys to the faded Victorians of Haight-Ashbury.

Muller also uses his cred to bring forth the noir faithful for the annual Noir City film festival (www.noircity.com; motto: 'if you want fresh air, don't look for it in this town'), featuring a week of celebrated classics and little-known noir gems early in the new year, complete with live appearances by actors and others involved in the original films. Be sure to wear your fedora.

Across from the Transamerica, in front of the California Pacific Bank, a plaque marks another classic piece of vanished Americana: the Western Headquarters of **Russell, Majors & Waddell**, founders and operators of the Pony Express (1860-61), whose riders tore across the West at breakneck speeds delivering messages over the 1,966 miles from St Joseph, Missouri, to Sacramento, California. The fastest run on record took seven days and 17 hours, with riders averaging 10.6mph over some of the world's most rugged and dangerous terrain and carrying packages of real import – not least among them, President Abraham Lincoln's first inaugural address. Further south, on nearby Commercial Street, in the city's former mint, the modest **Pacific Heritage Museum** holds an art collection that's small but worth a peek.

Continuing south from the Transamerica, the area's history as the financial heart of the American West reveals itself further in its architecture. The **Omni Hotel** (500 California Street, at Montgomery Street) was built in 1926 as a bank and wears its origins proudly; just up the road is the small but nonetheless enjoyable **Wells Fargo History Museum**. However, both are dwarfed by the nearby **Bank of America Center**, now officially known as 555 California Street (555 California Street, at Kearny Street; *photo p69*), which towers over the Financial District. The skyscraper is 75 feet (23 metres) shorter than the Transamerica, but feels more massive thanks to its larger girth and its carnelian granite zigzag frame, often seen disappearing into the clouds. On the 52nd floor sits the **Carnelian Room** (433 7500, www.carnelianroom.com), a cocktail lounge, upscale restaurant and favourite dating spot among locals, not all of whom remember its role in the 1974 star-studded disaster epic *The Towering Inferno*.

A block east of the Bank of America Center sits the **Merchant's Exchange** (465 California Street, between Sansome & Montgomery Streets, 421 7730). The building is no longer used by share traders, but its historic spaces illustrate the important role it once played in the financial life of the city. The lavish trading hall, designed by Julia Morgan, is now the lobby of the California Bank & Trust offices and home to a rather impressive collection of William Coulter seascapes.

There's further financial heritage close by at the Union Bank of California's **Museum of the Money of the American West** (400 California Street, at Sansome Street, no phone). The bank's doors and imposing columns may seem massive next to the museum's modest Wild West collection, but the collection actually includes a variety of fascinating artefacts.

Among them is a hyper-rare three-dollar bill signed by the founder of Mormonism, Joseph Smith, and a pair of duelling pistols used in a fateful 1859 duel between a former Chief Justice of the California Supreme Court and a US Senator, which came to be known as 'the duel that ended duels'. The museum also reveals a little about William Chapman Ralston, the bank's founder, a major figure in the development of the city and the man responsible for the lavish Palace Hotel (*see p48*). To learn more about these posh lodgings, take one of the thrice-weekly tours of the hotel run by San Francisco City Guides (10am Tue & Sat, 2pm Thur, www.sfcityguides.org). If you've not got time, a visit to its **Pied Piper Bar** (512 1111, www.maxfields-restaurant.com) is a must, to wet one's whistle with a fine cocktail and to see the expansive (and expensive) Maxfield Parrish painting *The Pied Piper of Hamelin*, valued at over $2 million, which hangs behind the bar. Just across the street – and, strictly speaking, in SoMa – stands the venerable bar **House of Shields** (39 New Montgomery Street, between Stevenson & Jessie Streets, 975 8651, www.houseofshields.com). Its mahogany bar was originally meant to go in the Palace Hotel's Piper Bar, but a careless carpenter made it to dimensions that meant the room couldn't hold both the bar and the Parrish painting.

A block east, at the intersection of Market, Kearny and Geary Streets, a uniquely San Franciscan ritual is played out every year. At 5.13am on 18 April, the last survivors of the 1906 earthquake gather around the ornate, lion-headed **Lotta's Fountain** (named after the popular vaudevillian Lotta Crabtree, who donated it to the city), just as they did a century ago when families separated by the huge quake used the fountain as a meeting point. On the 101st anniversary in 2007 a single survivor made the commemoration, 104-year-old Herbert Hamrol who, at the time of writing, still works stocking shelves at the Albertson's supermarket in San Francisco's Sunset district.

Pacific Coast Stock Exchange

155 Sansome Street, at Pine Street (421 9939/ tours 202 9700 ext 72). Bus 1, 10, 12, 15, 41/ cable car California. **Open** tours by appointment. **Admission** $5 donation. **Map** p315 N5.

The Exchange was modernised in 1928 by architect Timothy Pflueger, who believed art should be an integral part of architecture. He commissioned sculptor Ralph Stackpole to create the two granite statues outside, which represent Agriculture and Industry (the twin sources of wealth), while above the entrance is a figure called *Progress of Man* with arms outstretched. The building's main attraction is on the tenth floor: Diego Rivera's 1930 mural *Allegory of California*. It is richly ironic that Rivera,

Sightseeing

a committed communist, should have been allowed to create such a magnificent work within the heart of capitalism; Stackpole, an old friend of Rivera, had recommended him for the job. The mural shows Bay Area industries, including aviation and oil, with Mother Earth in the centre and the emphasis firmly on workers rather than bosses, highlighting Rivera's socialist penchant for sticking it to the authorities. The building is not open to the public, but tours can be arranged by appointment through the City Club, (www.cityclubsf.com), a members-only club, on the tenth floor.

Pacific Heritage Museum

608 Commercial Street, at Montgomery Street (399 1124/www.ibankunited.com/phm). Bus 1, 10, 12, 15, 41/cable car California. **Open** 10am-4pm Tue-Sat. **Admission** free. **Map** p315 N4.

Once the city's mint, this structure is now a Bank of Canton and also a museum. Emphasising San Francisco's connections with the Pacific Rim, the museum features changing exhibits of contemporary artists from countries such as China, Taiwan, Japan and Thailand. Much of what is displayed here is on loan from private collections rarely seen elsewhere.

Wells Fargo History Museum

420 Montgomery Street, at California Street (396 2619/www.wellsfargohistory.com/museums/museum_sf.htm). Bus 1, 10, 30, 41/cable car California. **Open** 9am-5pm Mon-Fri. **Admission** free. **Map** p315 N4.

Ferry Building: a port of call for foodies.

Wells Fargo is California's oldest bank, and this collection of Gold Rush memorabilia gives a good history of banking in California. You'll find gold nuggets, an old telegraph machine and a Concord stagecoach, built in 1867, plus historical photos.

Jackson Square

The northern edge of the Financial District is marked by the **Jackson Square Historical District** (bounded by Washington, Kearny and Sansome Streets and Pacific Avenue).

It's the last vestige of San Francisco's notorious Barbary Coast, once a seething mass of low-life bars and 19th-century sex clubs, the floor shows of which made modern-day Tijuana seem like an ice-cream social. Today, its few blocks of 1850s-era brick buildings – housing upmarket antiques shops and lovingly restored offices – stand far from the waterfront, though they once stood on the shoreline itself. Indeed, their foundations are made from the hulls of ships abandoned by eager gold-seekers.

Stroll along Jackson Street (between Sansome & Montgomery Streets) and Hotaling Street to see the only neighbourhood left in San Francisco that pre-dates the ubiquitous Victorian style. It was spared during the 1906 quake and the subsequent fire, not least because several of the buildings were liquor warehouses that had been built of stone to protect the precious booze. By the 1930s, Jackson Square was popular with a number of bohemian artists and writers; John Steinbeck and William Saroyan, among others, used to drink at the now long-vanished Black Cat Café (710 Montgomery Street). For a bit of the maritime history of these few blocks, duck into the **Old Ship Saloon** (298 Pacific Avenue, at Battery Street, 788 2222, www.old shipsaloon.com). A ship that ran aground on Alcatraz Island, the *Arkansas,* was towed to the corner where the bar now resides – the original proprietor simply cut a door in the hull to allow access. Over the past century the boat has morphed into a fairly conventional bar, but the story holds water: the remains of ships are still regularly unearthed in the area as crews excavate for new constructions.

The Embarcadero

For decades, San Franciscans old enough to recall the majesty of the original Embarcadero became misty-eyed for the old days when it was a palm-lined thoroughfare as opposed to a double-decker freeway with all the charm of Chicago's Lower Wacker Drive. Then came the devastating 1989 Loma Prieta earthquake. Although the quake wreaked havoc throughout the region, it also felled the Embarcadero's ill-considered upper deck, returning it to its former glory. Today, refurbished antique streetcars from around the world – Moscow, Milan, Oporto, Japan, and even a roofless number from the English resort town of Blackpool – ply the ribbon of road that unfurls along the Bay.

At the foot of Market Street stands the centrepiece of the Embarcadero: the beautifully restored **Ferry Building**, which divides even-numbered piers (to the south) from odd (to the north). Major renovations to this California landmark, originally completed in 1898, were unveiled in 2003; the building now bustles with the unmatched **Ferry Plaza Farmers' Market** (*see p189*), where stallholders sell organic produce, artisan breads, cheeses and other gourmet delicacies. The 660-foot (201-metre) Grand Nave gets packed with foodies as daytrippers pile out of the back, laden with picnic supplies, to hop on ferries to Sausalito, Tiburon or the East Bay.

Opposite the Ferry Building is Justin Herman Plaza, where you'll be confronted by Benicia-born artist Robert Arneson's bronze sculpture *Yin and Yang*. Looming behind it is a mysteriously dry series of square pipes that together make up a fountain by French-Canadian artist Armand Vaillancourt; at the foot of the Hyatt Regency hotel is Jean Dubuffet's *La Chiffonière*, a stainless steel sculpture of a larger-than-life figure.

The phalanx of wafer-thin towers behind the plaza, at the foot of Sacramento Street, comprises the **Embarcadero Center** (*see p176*), a labyrinthine shopping, dining and theatre complex. The **Embarcadero Cinema** (*see p208*) screens art house movies.

Walk south from the Ferry Building along the Embarcadero to Howard Street, and you'll see low cement walls where bronze starfish, turtles and octopi have been 'washed up' on the shore. Nearby, and easy to miss, is the small sign that marks **Herb Caen Way**, named after the late and ever-popular *San Francisco Chronicle* columnist. Lovers who come down this way may feel they've walked into their destiny when they spy an immense Cupid's bow in gold, complete with a silver and red arrow. This is Claes Oldenburg and Coosje van Bruggen's *Cupid's Span*, installed in 2002 in a field of native grass.

After taking in the wonderful views of the Bay Bridge, and perhaps also stopping for a spot of lunch at the Hotel Vitale's **Americano** restaurant (*see p136*), continue south to **Red's Java House** (Pier 30, 777 5626), a small and quirky snack shack that has been a favourite for coffee and burgers since it opened in 1912, when workers constructing the original Bay Bridge would drop in for meals. Sadly, the future of Red's was looking uncertain at the time of writing thanks to a huge rent increase.

Between Brannan and Townsend Streets, you'll see a cement marker reading 'Great Seawall'. This is exactly what the Embarcadero was built to be. It is entirely man-made, neatly rounding off the treacherous crags and coves that had been the end of many ships plying the San Francisco shores. Work on the sea wall started in 1878 and continued for nearly five decades, adding another 800 acres to the city and an additional 18 miles of useable dock space. Today, a push to revitalise the vacant waterfront areas sees new stores, restaurants and public spaces emerging from the timber skeletons of the old docks.

Once you've had your fill of the waterside views, head inland to the **Rincon Center**, at the intersection of Mission and Spear Streets. This former main post office, now containing a number of impressive art pieces and historic murals, is clear of San Franciscans at weekends, except for the dim sum crowd at **Yank Sing** (49 Stevenson Street, between 1st & 2nd Streets).

Alternatively, head north. From the Ferry Building, the Embarcadero evolves into a long, gently curving promenade along the waterfront, extending all the way to the confounding tourist magnet of **Fisherman's Wharf**. Skaters meet at 9pm each Friday for the Midnight Rollers, a 12-mile skate through the city (www.cora.org). Pier 7, a wide-open public pier jutting out into the Bay, offers lovely views of **Treasure Island** (*see p74*). North and a little inland, where Green and Sansome Streets meet, you'll find the former laboratory of boy-genius Philo T Farnsworth. Here, in 1927, Farnsworth invented the current system of TV transmission; a small plaque marks the achievement.

Rincon Center

101 Spear Street, at Mission Street (243 0473). *BART & Metro to Embarcadero/bus 1, 12, 20, 30, 41 & Market Street routes.* **Open** 24hrs daily. **Admission** free. Map p315 O4.

The lobby (facing Mission Street) of this art deco post office-cum-residential and office tower has intriguing WPA-style murals. Painted in 1941 by the Russian Social Realist painter Anton Refregier, this luscious historical panorama was hugely controversial at the time of its unveiling, not only because it was the most expensive of the WPA mural projects, but also because it included many dark moments from California's past. The central atrium has a unique all-water sculpture by Doug Hollis, dubbed *Rain Column*. The sculpture's 50-plus gallons of recycled water fall 85ft (26m) into a central pool every minute.

Treasure Island

Bus 108.

Flat-as-a-griddle Treasure Island, built on the shoals of neighbouring Yerba Buena Island, is entirely man-made from boulders and sand. Originally constructed as a site for 1939's Golden Gate International Exposition, the island was seized by the US Navy in 1942. It served as a troop deployment staging area for many years, until it was returned to the city in 1997. At around this time it was determined that the entire island sinks a bit deeper into the Bay each year. Despite this, it now functions as a sort of mid-Bay suburb, with some lucky San Franciscans moving into the former military housing. Why lucky? The views are spectacular, as many Hollywood location scouts have realised: parts of *The Caine Mutiny* and two of the Indiana Jones movies were filmed here. In 2007, the island hosted the first Treasure Island Music Festival (www.treasureislandfestival.com).

Yerba Buena Island – literally, 'Good Herb Island' (the Yerba Buena referred to is actually an aromatic perennial from the mint family used in medicinal tea by Native Americans) – is an important Coast Guard station. You can drive on the island's one road, but there's nowhere to stop.

The Tenderloin

There are two competing stories as to how the Tenderloin got its name. The first is that police who worked the beat here in the 19th century were paid extra for taking on such a tough neighbourhood, and could therefore afford to buy better cuts of meat. The second is similar, but with one key change: the cops got their extra cash not from police chiefs in the form of wages, but from local hoods in the form of bribes. No one is sure which tale is correct, but neither reflects especially well on an area that's always lived on the wild side.

The Tenderloin is a far cry from the retail mecca of Union Square a few blocks to the east. The area is home to a spirited community and its reputation shouldn't put people off visiting the local theatres, staying in one of its stylish hotels or checking out its myriad terrific bars. That said, there's not much reason to visit the area during the day, when the only streetlife comes courtesy of the panhandlers and drug addicts who cluster on corners. Depending on where you're planning to walk (Geary Street and points north are usually safe; streets south of it can get a bit sketchy), it may be best to hail a cab at night.

While the city struggles with the question of how best to care for the Tenderloin's dissolute souls (it's been a key issue in every mayoral contest for at least two decades), soup kitchens provide a partial solution. In particular, one pair of churches share a long and compassionate history. **St Boniface Catholic Church** (*see below*) hosts dozens of benefit programmes and has a dining room that serves food to the needy, while the Free Meals programme at **Glide Memorial Church** (330 Ellis Street, at Taylor Street), started back in 1969, offers similar sustenance. Both, of course, also cater to the religious: St Boniface offers Mass in English, Spanish, Tagalog and Vietnamese, while at Glide on Sundays, ecstatic gospel singing drags an amazingly diverse congregation to its feet. Glide runs services at 9am and 11am; get there early, as the place is usually packed.

Outside of Sundays, the main attractions in the Tenderloin are nocturnal. Dinner (as well as lunch) is served by aspiring chefs at the California Culinary Academy's **Carême Room** (625 Polk Street, at Turk Street, 292 8229, www.baychef.com/restaurants.asp). The area is also known as the Tandoor-loin because of the surprising profusion of good and affordable Indian restaurants on or near O'Farrell Street: try **Shalimar** (532 Jones Street, at O'Farrell Street, 928 0333, www.shalimarsf.com), which serves up inexpensive Pakistani and Indian food, or **Naan 'n' Curry** (690 Van Ness Avenue, at Turk Street, 775 1349, or 336 O'Farrell Street, near Mason Street, 346 1443). Wherever you eat, wash your dinner down with a beer or a cocktail at one of countless bars in the locale, which range from spit 'n' sawdust dives to wannabe-swank lounges. However, the joint most characteristic of the area's reputation is the landmark **Mitchell Brothers O'Farrell Theatre** (895 O'Farrell Street), a huge strip club that started life as a porn cinema, with a colourful and murderous history (in 1991 one brother, Jim, shot the other, Artie). Just down the street is the **Great American Music Hall** (859 O'Farrell Street, between Polk & Larkin Streets; *see p232*), said to be the oldest nightclub in San Francisco and now a beautiful music venue whose interior evokes Versailles' Hall of Mirrors. However, even this grand space is not as virtuous as it looks: although it's now unimpeachably respectable, it spent a number of its tender years as a bordello.

St Boniface Catholic Church

133 Golden Gate Avenue, at Leavenworth Street (863 7515). BART & Metro to Civic Center/bus 19, 31 & Market Street routes. **Open** hours vary. **Map** p318 L7.

St Boniface's Romanesque interior, restored in the 1980s, has some impeccable stencilling and a beautifully gilded apse topped by a four-storey cupola. Outside Mass times, you'll find the church is gated, so ring the buzzer to get in. Be sure to get there before 1.30pm during the week, when the church closes for cleaning until the next morning.

San Francisco's **City Hall** is an impressive Beaux Arts monument to democracy.

Civic Center

South-west of the Tenderloin and north of Market Street, San Francisco's Civic Center is a complex of imposing government buildings and immense performance halls centred on the Civic Center Plaza, an expansive and well-tended lawn. By day, it's populated by an extreme spread of locals, from smartly turned-out officials and dignitaries who work within the buildings, to the homeless folk who hang around outside them. At night, the worker bees are replaced by culture vultures, here to take in a concert, ballet, lecture or opera at one of the area's several venues.

Facing the plaza, and dominating the area, is the stunning Beaux Arts **City Hall**, a glory both inside and out. Across the four lanes of traffic on Van Ness Avenue is a trio of grand edifices. The multi-storey, curved-glass façade of the **Louise M Davies Symphony Hall** (201 Van Ness Avenue, at Hayes Street; *see p228*) would be unforgettable even without the reclining Henry Moore bronzes in front, while just north of Grove Street sits the **War Memorial Opera House** (301 Van Ness Avenue, at Grove Street; *see p227*), directly behind City Hall. In many ways the City Hall's companion piece, the Opera House was also designed by architect Arthur Brown.

The last of the triumvirate of buildings is the **Veterans' Memorial Building** (Van Ness Avenue, at McAllister Street), a venerable workhorse the various spaces of which hold offices, performance theatres and even galleries. On its main floor sits the

tiny **San Francisco Art Commission Gallery** (*see p216*), which specialises in politically or sociologically driven art. Take the lift to the fourth floor and you'll find the **Museum of Performance and Design** (*see p76*); also here is the beautiful **Herbst Theatre** (*see p252*). It is a little-known but proud part of San Francisco history that the UN Charter was drafted and signed by 51 nations in what is now the Herbst Theatre on 26 June 1945.

In the south-east corner of Civic Center Plaza are two further landmark buildings. Named after the promoter who almost single-handedly created the musical juggernaut that was San Francisco in the 1960s, the 7,000-capacity **Bill Graham Civic Auditorium** (99 Grove Street, at Polk Street) now stages gigs by big names. The nearby **Main Library** (*see p76*) is a six-storey building mixing Beaux Arts elements with modernism; the old library is now home to the world-class collections of art and antiquities at the **Asian Art Museum** (*see p76*).

On the edge of the Civic Center is **United Nations Plaza**. A farmers' market operates here on Wednesday and Sunday mornings, with arts and crafts stalls moving in on Mondays, Thursdays and Fridays. The action takes place under the approving gaze of a mounted statue of Simón Bolívar, the great liberator of Central America. The plaza, created to honour San Francisco's role as host of the signing of the original UN Charter, has in recent years become a veritable campground for the city's disenfranchised. Attempts at redevelopment have – so far – faltered.

There's not much in the way of restaurants, bars or shops in this corner of the city. One of the few good bets for eating is the great little café-restaurant in the Asian Art Museum. Alternatively, if you can successfully negotiate the legions of homeless, head across Market Street to **Tu Lan** (8 6th Street, at Market Street; *see p140*). While this hole-in-the-wall diner may look like nothing to write home about (and there really are holes in its walls), it's widely considered to serve some of the best Vietnamese cuisine in the city.

Asian Art Museum

200 Larkin Street, at Fulton Street (581 3500/ www.asianart.org). BART & Metro to Civic Center/ streetcar F/bus 5, 19, 21, 47, 49 & Market Street routes. **Open** 10am-5pm Tue, Wed, Fri-Sun; 10am-9pm Thur. **Admission** $12; $7-$8 reductions. **Credit** AmEx, Disc, MC, V. **Map** p318 K7.

This popular museum has one of the world's most comprehensive collections of Asian art, spanning 6,000 years of Asian history and with more than 15,000 objects on display. Artefacts range from Japanese Buddhas and sacred texts to items from the Ming Dynasty. The outdoor café is a great place to enjoy American- and Asian-inspired dishes on sunny days, and the gift shop is well stocked with high-quality stationery, decorative items and a handsome selection of coffee-table books. The museum once resided in Golden Gate Park, but in 2003 it reopened in this building, former home of the San Francisco Public Library. Extensively and beautifully redesigned by Gae Aulenti, the architect responsible for the heralded Musée d'Orsay conversion in Paris, the museum retains remnants of its previous role, including bookish quotes etched into the fabric of the building.

City Hall

1 Dr Carlton B Goodlett Place (Polk Street), between McAllister & Grove Streets (554 4933/tours 554 6023). BART & Metro to Civic Center/streetcar F/bus 19, 21, 47, 49 & Market Street routes. **Open** 8am-8pm daily. *Tours* 10am, noon, 2pm Mon-Fri. **Admission** free. **Map** p318 K7.

Built in 1915 to designs by Arthur Brown and John Bakewell, City Hall is the epitome of the Beaux Arts style visible across the whole Civic Center. The building has lots of ornamental ironwork, elaborate plasterwork and a dome – modelled on the one at St Peter's in Rome – that is higher than the one on the nation's Capitol (sources vary as to just how much higher). The central rotunda, with its sweeping staircase, is a magnificent space and the dome overlooks a five-storey colonnade, limestone and granite masonry, regal lighting and majestic marble floors. Dubbed 'the most significant interior space in the United States' by a New York architectural critic, City Hall inspires a marked feeling of municipal awe. The city capitalises on this by renting it out for private functions, with one night's rental ranging from $12,000 up to $30,000.

Beneath its neo-classical exterior, the building hums with modern technology. After it was damaged in the 1989 earthquake, city planners spent $300 million protecting it against future shocks and restoring it to its original grandeur. A system of rubber-and-steel 'base isolators' now allows the structure to move a metre in any direction. Its 600 rooms have seen plenty of history: Joe DiMaggio got hitched to Marilyn Monroe on the third floor in 1954, although nobody knows in which office; on a more sombre note, it was here that Dan White assassinated Mayor George Moscone and City Supervisor Harvey Milk in 1978. Today, the building houses the legislative and executive branches of both city and county government. Free tours offering behind the scenes views of the Board of Supervisors' chambers (panelled in hand-carved Manchurian oak) are available Monday to Friday at 10am, noon and 2pm.

With the exception of a number of impossibly intricate handmade wooden models of San Francisco landmarks – among them a cross-section of the building's dome – the Museum of the City of San Francisco in South Light Court isn't that impressive. There's a small café for the weary of feet, and the basement contains exhibits sponsored by the San Francisco Arts Commission.

San Francisco Main Library

100 Larkin Street, between Grove & Fulton Streets (library 557 4400/history room 557 4567/www. sfpl.org). BART & Metro to Civic Center/bus 5, 21, 47, 49 & Market Street routes. **Library** 10am-6pm Mon, Sat; 9am-8pm Tue-Thur; noon-6pm Fri; noon-5pm Sun. **History room** 10am-6pm Tue-Thur, Sat; noon-6pm Fri; noon-5pm Sun. **Tours** 2.30pm Wed, Fri. **Admission** free; 3mth visitor's card $10. **Map** p318 L7.

Built in 1996 by the architectural firm Pei Cobb Freed & Partners, San Francisco's public library is beautifully designed, though locals still complain about the number of missing and lost books. On the top floor, the San Francisco History Room hosts changing exhibitions, a large photo archive and knowledgeable, friendly staff. The basement café is mediocre, but the small shop on the main floor has bargains on local titles. Readings by big-name and up and coming authors are held here on a regular basis.

Museum of Performance & Design

4th floor, Veterans' Memorial Building, 401 Van Ness Avenue, at McAllister Street (255 4800/www. sfpalm.org). BART & Metro to Civic Center/bus 21, 47, 49 & Market Street routes. **Map** p318 K7.

The former San Francisco Performing Arts Library & Museum was closed for renovation at the time of writing, due to reopen in March 2008 as the Museum of Performance and Design. Exhibitions at this enjoyable museum relate to every one of the performing arts, from puppet shows to operas, but the principal attraction for scholars is the prodigious amount of resource material: thousands of books on design, fashion, music, theatre, opera and other art forms.

The cable guys

Installed in 1873 by wily Scotsman Andrew Hallidie, cable cars were an ingenious solution to San Francisco's eternal problem: how to get up the damn hills. Nob Hill and Russian Hill in particular were tempting morsels of real estate, yet remained mostly undeveloped. Horse-drawn carriages could barely make the climb, and Victorian gentlefolk were unwilling to exhaust themselves by slogging up and down on foot.

Enter Hallidie and his idea of introducing cable-drawn transport to the city streets, a method he had first used hauling ore carts in California's gold mines. When, to everyone's amazement, his first cars worked flawlessly, imitators sprang up overnight. Soon, more than 100 miles of tracks criss-crossed the city, operated by seven cable-car companies.

It didn't last. Earthquakes, fires and the advent of automobiles and electric trolleys spelled doom for most of the cable-car lines; by 1947, the city had proposed tearing up the last lines and replacing them with buses. Happily, the outraged citizenry stopped the plan going ahead. Since then, the government has declared the system a National Historic Landmark, which means the cars are here to stay. Three lines survive, covering a total of eight miles: the Powell-Mason and Powell-Hyde lines, both of which depart from Powell Street turnaround (where Powell meets Market Street) and run to, respectively, North Beach and Fisherman's Wharf; and the California line, which runs along California Street between Market Street and Van Ness Avenue.

If you're expecting to see a network of cable cars dangling in the air above the city, think again. San Francisco cable cars remain firmly grounded. First-timers are often surprised to learn that cable cars have no engine or other means of propulsion. All they need is a 'grip', a steel clamp that grabs on to a subterranean cable, running under the streets at a constant 9.5mph. The cables never stop moving: you can hear them humming even when there are no cable cars in sight. Every car has two operators: a gripman, who works the cranks and levers that grab on to and release the underground cable; and a conductor, who takes fares and somehow manages to cram 90-plus passengers, many of them hanging off the running boards, on to a single vehicle. Visit the **Cable Car Museum** (*see p83*) to inspect the system's inner workings: as well as Hallidie's original 1873 car, you'll get to see the immense winding turbines that power the cables. From the balcony you can watch the ten-foot (three-metre) wheels spinning, as gears and pulleys whirr.

While the cable cars are a legendary part of San Francisco history, so is the hassle of waiting for one at Powell Street turnaround. So don't. Instead, walk up Powell a few blocks and board the car at O'Farrell or Union Square. Or, if you aren't going anywhere in particular, take the rarely crowded California line. The views aren't as good as on the Powell lines, but it's still a cable car. If you are tired of forking over the $5 fare, cable-car rides are included in the price of various travel passes. Cars run every 12-15 minutes from 6.30am to midnight; the Powell Street ticket booth is open from 8.30am until 8pm.

Sightseeing

Soma & South Beach

It boomed, it burned, now it's soaring again: SoMa is the phoenix of 'Frisco.

Maps p315 & pp318-319

For much of the 20th century, the streets south of Market Street and east of 10th Street were an industrial wasteland, filled with warehouses and sweatshops. The dotcom boom brought rapid regeneration: warehouses were converted into high-end loft apartments, bars opened to serve the new locals, and SoMa ('South of Market', a nod to SoHo in New York City) took off.

The dotcom boom burst in a hurry, and 2002 to 2006 were fairly lean years for the neighbourhood as San Francisco's commercial real estate market tanked (vacancy rates hit a high of 21per cent in 2003). But steadily, as cooler heads prevailed and new technologies began to emerge, San Francisco in general and SoMa in particular were well suited to take advantage of the long-term benefits.

With the construction of a new satellite campus for the University of California San Francisco in the **Mission Bay** area of SoMa, the former industrial zone has not only bounced back, but is on the verge of explosive growth. UCSF was recently awarded a $100-million grant from the National Institute of Health for biotechnology research. In addition, the SoMa/Mission Bay area was selected as the site for the headquarters of the California Institute for Regenerative Medicine, a $3-billion project dedicated to stem cell research. The 3rd Street light rail line opened in April 2007, linking what were once hinterlands and housing projects to the heart of the city. The first new public library branch in 40 years opened in the area in 2006, and the city's Mission Bay plan calls for a further 48 acres of parks, an elementary school and a hotel.

But the primary draw remains the **San Francisco Giants** baseball team. Their stadium, **AT&T Park**, draws huge crowds for its 81 home games each spring and summer, and surrounding streets also turn festive as supporters pack the bars and restaurants.

Yerba Buena Gardens & around

Bounded by Mission, 3rd, Folsom and 4th Streets, the Yerba Buena Gardens complex was renovated as part of a city-funded project in the 1980s and '90s. Attractions and businesses are housed in a purpose-built series of structures that is half above ground and half below it. **Esplanade** within the Gardens is an urban park with sculpture walks, shady trees and the *Revelations* waterfall, constructed in 1993 in memory of Martin Luther King Jr. A selection of Dr King's quotes is inscribed beneath the waterfall in various languages. On one side of the block sits the **Yerba Buena Center for the Arts**, an architectural beauty in itself. Filling the other half of the block (4th Street, from Howard to Mission Streets) is the **Metreon**, a four-storey futuristic mall where 16 cinema screens (including a giant-screen IMAX) are backed up by high-tech shops, restaurants, video-game rooms and the country's only official Sony PlayStation store. The 270-foot (86-metre) lobby, which exits out to the Esplanade Gardens, contains amenities such as ATM machines and public restrooms.

Across 3rd Street from Yerba Buena Gardens sits the **San Francisco Museum of Modern Art**, where the permanent collection and temporary exhibits are supplemented by a top-quality shop and a somewhat pricey café. Next door is the staggering **St Regis Museum Tower**, a luxury hotel that also houses the **Museum of the African Diaspora**. The **Moscone Convention Center** (747 Howard Street, between 3rd & 4th Streets), named after assassinated mayor George Moscone, is a similarly daunting building. Most of it is of little interest to casual visitors, but the Rooftop at Yerba Buena Gardens, ingeniously covering the top of the Moscone Center on the south side of Howard Street, offers the child-friendly attractions of **Zeum** (221 4th Street, at Howard Street, 820 3320, www.zeum.org). Also here are

Art vesus nature: at **Yerba Buena Gardens** you can enjoy the best of both.

a delightful carousel, hand-carved by Charles Looff in 1906 (a $3 ticket is good for two rides), an ice rink, a bowling alley and an ultra-cool interactive sculpture by Chico Macmurtrie: sit on the middle pink bench and your weight moves the metal figure up and down on top of its globe. Attempt this only before lunch.

Contrasting with all this modernity is the high-ceilinged **St Patrick's Church** (756 Mission Street, between 3rd & 4th Streets, 421 3730, www.stpatricksf.org). Built in 1851, the church ministered to the growing Irish population brought to the city by the Gold Rush. It was destroyed by the 1872 earthquake but subsequently restored to its original state; it now hosts both services and concerts (*see p228*). Nearby is a trio of other museums: the **Cartoon Art Museum**, the free **California Historical Society** and the **Society of California Pioneers**. Also here are the new sites for the **Contemporary Jewish Museum** and the **Mexican Museum**. While the new Jewish Museum is scheduled to open in spring 2008, construction on the Mexican Museum is unlikely to begin until 2008-09.

Several blocks south-west of Yerba Buena, **Folsom Street** savours its kinky reputation each autumn during the annual Folsom Street Fair, but the Cake Gallery (290 9th Street, at Folsom Street, 861 2253, www.thecakegallery sf.com) is a year-round thrill: with a nod to the legendary Magnolia Thunderpussy, it's the only bakery in the city that sells pornographic-style cakes. Nearby is the **BrainWash Café** (1122 Folsom Street, between 7th & 8th Streets, www.brainwash.com), a spot about which weary travellers have fantasised for generations: a combo bar/musicvenue/restaurant/laundromat, where you can sip some suds while your duds get their suds.

California Historical Society

678 Mission Street, between 3rd & New Montgomery Streets (357 1848/www.calhist.org). BART & Metro to Montgomery/bus 9, 9X, 10, 14, 30, 45, 71. **Open** noon-4.30pm Wed-Sat. **Admission** $3; $1 reductions. **Credit** (bookstore only) AmEx, DC, Disc, MC, V. **Map** p315 N6.

The state's official historical group has focused its efforts on assembling this impressive collection of Californiana. The vaults hold half a million photographs and thousands of books, magazines and paintings, as well as an extensive Gold Rush collection; selections are presented as changing displays on the state's history. The gift shop has an excellent little bookshop and a selection of souvenirs, including one of the best: the California Republic T-shirt.

Cartoon Art Museum

655 Mission Street, between 3rd & New Montgomery Streets (227 8666/www.cartoonart.org). BART & Metro to Montgomery/bus 9, 10, 14, 30, 45, 71. **Open** 11am-5pm Tue-Sun. **Admission** $6; $4 reductions; $2 6-12s. **Credit** DC, MC, V. **Map** p315 N6.

The camera that was used to create the first animation for television (called *Crusader Rabbit* and produced from 1949 to 1951) graces the lobby of this museum. Boasting over 5,000 pieces of cartoon and

SFMOMA. See p81.

animation art, as well as a research library, this is the only museum in the western US dedicated to the form. The bookstore contains a large and eclectic selection of books, 'zines, periodicals and coffee-table tomes covering everything from erotic photography to Asterix books. The first Tuesday of each month is 'Pay What You Wish Day'.

Contemporary Jewish Museum

736 Mission Street, between 3rd & 4th Streets (655 7800/www.thecjm.org). BART & Metro to Montgomery/bus 9, 9X, 10, 14, 30, 45, 71. **Open** 11am-5.30pm Mon, Tue, Fri-Sun; 1-8.30pm Thur. **Admission** $8; $6 reductions. **Credit** AmEx, DC, Disc, MC, V. **Map** p315 M6.

Slated to reopen in its new Yerba Buena Gardens location in late spring 2008, the Contemporary Jewish Museum is devoted to linking the art of the Jewish community with the community at large. The museum runs educational programmes and shows works by students and established artists, many of them political or controversial in nature. Its new home, in a Willis Polk power substation that dates to 1907, has been in the planning stage for the better part of a decade. Architect Daniel Libeskind – in the news for his part in the controversy over the structure to replace the Twin Towers in New York – is responsible for the black box design.

Museum of the African Diaspora

685 Mission Street, at 3rd Street (358 7200/www. moadsf.org). BART & Metro to Montgomery/bus 9, 9X, 10, 14, 30, 45, 71. **Open** 11am-6pm Wed-Sat; noon-5pm Sun. **Admission** $10; $5 reductions; free under-12s. **Credit** AmEx, DC, MC, V. **Map** p315 N5.

Opened in November 2005, in an $11-million centre on the first three floors of the St Regis Museum Tower, the Museum of the African Diaspora (MoAD) is the world's first museum dedicated to exploring the international impact of the diaspora of African peoples across the globe. Rotating exhibitions highlight the art and culture of the continent, with multimedia exhibits and moving first-person accounts.

San Francisco Museum of Modern Art (SFMOMA)

151 3rd Street, between Mission & Howard Streets (357 4000/www.sfmoma.org). BART & Metro to Montgomery/bus 9, 9X, 10, 14, 30, 45, 71. **Open** *Memorial Day-Labor Day* 10am-5.45pm Mon, Tue, Fri-Sun; 10am-8.45pm Thur. *Labor Day-Memorial Day* 11am-5.45pm Mon, Tue, Fri-Sun; 11am-8.45pm Thur. **Admission** $12.50; $7-$8 reductions; free under-12s. Half price 6-8.45pm Thur; free 1st Tue of mth. **Credit** AmEx, DC, Disc, MC, V. **Map** p315 N6.

The second-largest US museum devoted to modern art, SFMOMA moved here from Civic Center in 1995, reaping enthusiastic approval as much for its $60-million design as for the improvement to the collections. Swiss architect Mario Botta's red-brick building, with its huge, circular skylight, is as dramatic from the outside as within, and still feels brand new. Don't miss the spectacular catwalk beneath the skylight, accessible from the top-floor galleries: though not recommended if you suffer vertigo, it offers a stunning view of the striped marble below.

The four floors of galleries that rise above the stark black-marble reception area house a solid permanent collection, with some 15,000 paintings, sculptures and works on paper, as well as thousands of photographs and a range of works related to the media arts. The collection includes works by artists as varied as René Magritte, Jeff Koons, Piet Mondrian (characteristically geometric) and Marcel Duchamp (a urinal). However, the special exhibits are the real draw. A Bay Area native, gallery director Neal Benezra returned to San Francisco in 2002 following a distinguished career at the Smithsonian and the Art Insititute of Chicago to bring a steady managerial hand and broad creative vision to the museum. His efforts can be seen in the continuing growth (both in physical size and the stature of its collections) and general renown of SFMOMA.

Society of California Pioneers Seymour Pioneer Museum

300 4th Street, at Folsom Street (957 1849/ www.californiapioneers.org). BART & Metro to Montgomery/bus 9X, 12, 27, 30, 45. **Open** 10am-4pm Wed-Fri, 1st Sat of mth. *Library* by appointment. **Admission** $5; $2.50 reductions. **Credit** (bookstore only) DC, MC, V. **Map** p319 N7.
Operated by descendants of the state's first settlers, this small museum, a treasure trove for the historically inclined, has occasional intriguing displays on California's past, alongside 10,000 books, 50,000 prints and all kinds of other ephemera, such as 19th-century paintings, sculpture and furniture.

Yerba Buena Center for the Arts

701 Mission Street, at 3rd Street (978 2787/ www.ybca.org). BART & Metro to Montgomery/ bus 9, 9X, 10, 14, 30, 45, 71. **Open** noon-5pm Tue, Wed, Fri-Sun; noon-8pm Thur. **Admission** $7; $5 reductions. Free 1st Tue of mth. **Credit** AmEx, DC, MC, V. **Map** p315 N6.
Yerba Buena Center stands opposite SFMOMA and is somewhat in its shadow, yet it seems unintimidated, tugging at the modern art scene's shirt-tails with a scrappy itinerary and great attitude. Housed in Fumihiko Maki's futuristic-looking building, it contains four changing galleries and a 96-seat theatre. The focus here is on the contemporary and the challenging (installation and video art,

SF Giant Willie Mays outside **AT&T Park**.

outsider art); past exhibitions have included work by such diverse names as Henry Darger, Fred Thomaselli, Anna Halprin and Kumi Yamashita.

South Park & South Beach

If any one area in San Francisco embodies the dotcom rollercoaster ride, it's this one. A few years ago, finding a clear space in the green oval of **South Park** took more time and moxie than snagging one of the coveted parking spaces. Techies would duck out to grab a burrito and end up never returning to the office: they'd been poached by a rival offering an extra 20k a year. Today, though, it has returned to being an oasis of green in the middle of the bustle.
South Park was San Francisco's first gated community, until it suffered from a string of misfortunes. Getting burned to the ground early in the 20th century may have been careless, but it was pure bad luck that the invention of the cable car caused the local millionaires to abscond to Nob Hill. The area then became an African-American enclave after World War II, but was otherwise neglected until a tornado of young men both fuelled by and fluent in Java arrived in the 1990s.
The madness of Multimedia Gulch has pretty much mellowed, but some remnants of those days remain. No single establishment is as representative of the new South Park as **Tres Agaves Mexican Kitchen & Tequila Lounge** (130 Townsend Street, between 2nd & 3rd Streets; *see p144*), which serves upscale cuisine, premium cocktails made with fresh fruit and a staggering selection of tequilas.
A few blocks south, **AT&T Park** (24 Willie Mays Plaza, at 3rd & King Streets) is home to the San Francisco Giants baseball team. Instantly hailed as a classic when it opened in 2000, the Bayside ballpark is a wonderful place to catch a game: with striking views of the Bay and good sightlines of the field, there's not a bad seat in the house.
Close by stands an intriguing architectural gem: the **Francis 'Lefty' O'Doul Bridge** (3rd Street, near Berry Street), the only working drawbridge in the city. A charming antique, it was designed by JB Strauss, better known for designing the Golden Gate Bridge. Born in San Francisco, 'Lefty' started out as a pitcher but made his name as a hitter in New York and Philadelphia, before eventually returning home to manage the minor league San Francisco Seals. The eponymous restaurant and bar he opened just steps from Downtown's Union Square in 1958 (333 Geary Street, at Powell Street, 982 8900, www.leftyodouls.biz) remains in business to this day.

Nob Hill & Chinatown

Cable cars and Taoist temples.

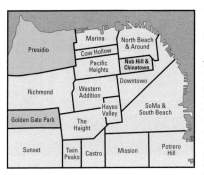

Map pp314-315

Nob Hill & Polk Gulch

Overlooking the Tenderloin and Union Square, the Nob Hill neighbourhood was named after the wealthy nabobs – as they were known – who built their mansions in the area; Robert Louis Stevenson, who lived briefly on its lower flank, described it as 'the hill of palaces'. A short but incredibly steep walk up from Union Square, the summit stands 338 feet (103 metres) above the bay. Both the houses and their residents retain an appropriately haughty grandeur.

After a cable car started running up the hill in the 1870s, the area began to attract wealthy folk, among them the 'Big Four' railroad tycoons: Charles Crocker, Mark Hopkins, Leland Stanford and Collis P Huntington. Their grand mansions were to perish in the fire that followed the 1906 earthquake – in fact, only the 1886 mansion belonging to millionaire silver baron James C Flood survived. Later remodelled by Willis Polk, the brownstone is now the site of the private **Pacific-Union Club** (1000 California Street, at Mason Street). Next to it, at the corner of California and Taylor Streets, is the public but prissy **Huntington Park**, with its fountain modelled on Rome's Fontana delle Tartarughe. Across the park, **Grace Cathedral** is another lovely landmark. Midnight Mass here, sung by the celebrated boys' choir, is a marvellous Christmas tradition; evensong with the choir is at 3pm most Sundays.

Elegant hotels surround the park and the club. The **Fairmont Hotel** (950 Mason Street, at California Street; see p54) has a plush marble lobby and the fabulously tacky Tonga Room (see p166), complete with regularly scheduled monsoons. The quieter **Huntington Hotel** (1075 California Street, at Taylor Street; see p53) is known as a royals' hideaway, but you don't have to stay there to use its luxurious **Nob Hill Spa** (345 2888) or cosy up next to the fireplace with a cognac at the wood-panelled bar of its restaurant, the **Big Four**. Nearby, the **Top of the Mark** bar (see p166), on the 19th floor of the **Mark Hopkins Inter-Continental Hotel**, offers terrific views of the city. Moving down the hill, the free **Cable Car Museum** (see below) displays antique cable cars and the mighty turbines that power the cables beneath the city's streets.

At the base of Nob Hill's western slopes, the stretch of Polk Street between Geary and Washington Streets comprises a small, block-wide neighbourhood known as **Polk Gulch**. Before the Castro, this was the city's gay mecca, home to bold bars, adult bookshops and street-corner encounters. It fell on hard times in the 1970s, and developed an unsavoury reputation as the last resort for runaway teenage boys selling sex. The ambience has mellowed, with shops and restaurants crowding every block. But many of the teenage boys seem to have grown up into sad-eyed transvestites, and the area seems to be searching for a new identity.

Cable Car Museum

1201 Mason Street, at Washington Street (474 1887/www.cablecarmuseum.org). Bus 1, 9, 12, 30, 45/cable car Powell-Hyde or Powell-Mason. **Open** *Oct-Mar* 10am-5pm daily. *Apr-Sept* 10am-6pm daily. **Admission** free. **Map** p314 L4.

The sight most often associated with San Francisco is its cable cars. The best way to study them is to ride one, but at this entertaining museum you can find out how the cars work, as well as view the cable-winding machinery that actually powers them. You'll also learn about emergency procedures, bell-ringing competitions and the workmanship that goes into each car. Vintage cable cars, associated artefacts and dozens of old photos complete matters.

Grace Cathedral

1100 California Street, at Taylor Street (749 6300/ www.gracecathedral.org). Bus 1, 2, 3, 4, 27/cable car California. **Open** *Cathedral* 7am-6pm Mon-Fri, Sun; 8am-6pm Sat. *Tours* 1-3pm Mon-Fri; 11.30am-1.30pm Sat; 12.30-2pm Sun. **Admission** donation requested. **Map** p314 L5.

View from **Nob Hill**. See p83.

Begun in 1928, this Episcopalian cathedral was once a private mansion. It was later taken over by the church and is, by the standards of most cathedrals in the US, an architectural extravaganza, with a façade modelled on Paris's Notre Dame. Its other features include a fine rose window, a magnificent organ and gilded bronze portals made from casts of the Doors of Paradise in Florence's Baptistery. Murals depict the founding of the United Nations and the burning of Grace's predecessor; the AIDS Interfaith Chapel has an altarpiece by Keith Haring. Popular features within the cathedral include two massive labyrinths, based on the 13th-century example at Chartres, that allow visitors to wander in a contemplative manner.

Chinatown

The 1849 Gold Rush and its promise of untold prosperity drew shiploads of Cantonese to California. The excitement didn't last, but many immigrants decided to stay, finding work on the railroads or the farms of the San Joaquin Valley. Californians both feared and loathed the Chinese, and were enthusiastic about the federal Chinese Exclusion Act of 1882, which halted the immigration of anyone of Chinese origin. Only officially repealed in 1943, the act also effectively made existing Chinese immigrants permanent aliens, with no hope of gaining citizenship. However, famine and unrest across China gave the immigrants little incentive to return home, and their understandable need for a strong community led to a 20-block area of central San Francisco becoming a focal point for Chinese immigrants of every stripe.

The **Chinatown** that arose in San Francisco soon developed a reputation for vice; curious Caucasians were lured here round the clock

by cheap hookers, well-stocked opium dens and all-hours gambling. After the 1906 earthquake and fire, which devastated the district, the city fathers tried to clean up the neighbourhood and, crucially, appropriate what had become prime real estate. However, not only did the illicit activity continue, but the Chinese held fast and rebuilt their community.

The crowded streets and dark alleys of Chinatown – bordered today by **Bush Street** to the south, **Broadway** to the north, and **Powell** and **Kearny Streets** from west to east – evoke an earlier era. There are nearly 100 restaurants, some serving exotic specialities. Elsewhere, herbalists prepare natural remedies and laundry flutters from windows above the streets. Many wealthier Chinese immigrants have moved out to Richmond, Sunset and even other Bay Area towns, but some 10,000 Chinese still live in Chinatown, lending it one of the largest Asian populations outside Asia itself.

Today, Chinatown also feels like two distinct neighbourhoods. Along **Grant Avenue**, one of the two main north–south drags, store owners target tourists with plastic Buddhas and bright fabrics; conversely, little English is spoken at the ornate temples and food stalls on and near **Stockton Street**. In fact, this contradiction is nothing new. Chinatown has been a thriving, tightly knit community for 150 years, but, since the 1920s, it's also been one of the most visited attractions on the West Coast.

Stockton Street & around

You'll see very few tourists among the throngs of customers that pack the grocery stores of **Stockton Street**. It's easy to understand why, especially if you contrast it with the shops on adjacent Grant Avenue (*see below*), which offer an anaesthetised version of Chinese culture, and fill daily with gift-hunting visitors. However, whether selling medicines or turtles (many of the markets here are 'live', with fish and animals on display in tanks and cages), the enterprises on Stockton cater to locals, who conduct their business in a range of dialects. In much the same way, the restaurants on Stockton have a more authentic feel than those on Grant; indeed, for many, Stockton Street constitutes the 'real' Chinatown.

One of the oldest religious structures in San Francisco, the **Kong Chow Temple**, stands on Stockton Street (no.855, between Sacramento & Clay Streets). Established in 1857, it was moved to its present home on the fourth floor of the Chinatown Post Office in 1977. Divination sticks, red satin banners and flowers flank a fabulous altar from which a statue of the god Kuan Ti has a keen view of the Bay. Nearby, the façade of the photogenic **Chinese Six Companies Building** (no.843) sports stone lions, ceramic carp and coloured tiles.

Perhaps the truest taste of Chinatown can be found in the alleys a half-block east of Stockton Street, sprouting off Jackson and Washington Streets. In cosy **Ross Alley**, you can watch cookies being made by hand at the **Golden Gate Fortune Cookie Factory** (no.56, 781 3956; *photo p87*), or have a trim at **Jun Yu's Barber Shop** (no.32), which, since opening in 1966, has reputedly sheared celebrities including Michael Douglas and Clint Eastwood. Sweet **Waverly Place**, just to the south, was the scene of a famous 1879 battle between two *tongs* (local organised crime gangs that ran gambling and prostitution) over the owners hip of a prostitute – at least four men are believed to have been hacked to death by cleavers during the skirmish. These days, it's best visited for the historic **Tien Hau Temple** (no.125). Another kind of history was made in adjacent **Spofford Street**, where between 1904 and 1910 Sun Yat-sen launched a revolution against the Manchu Dynasty from the **Ghee Kung Tong Building** (no.36).

An intriguing landmark stands just south of here, at 920 Sacramento Street. Named after Donaldina Cameron, the New Zealand crusader who devoted her life to saving San Francisco's Chinese girls from prostitution and slavery, **Cameron House** today provides help to low-income Asian immigrants and residents. However, it's also just about the only place in the city where you can still see traces of the great 1906 fire: misshapen 'clinker' bricks, melted by the intense heat, protrude from the walls.

Chinese American National Museum & Learning Center

965 Clay Street, between Stockton & Powell Streets (391 1188/www.chsa.org). Bus 1, 9, 12, 30, 45/ cable car Powell-Hyde or Powell-Mason. **Open** noon-5pm Tue-Fri; noon-4pm Sat. **Admission** $3; $2 reductions; $1 6-17s; free 1st Thur of mth. **Credit** DC, MC, V. **Map** p315 M4.

Formerly the Chinese Historical Society Museum, this facility opened in 2001 in the historic Chinese YWCA building, which was designed by renowned local architect Julia Morgan and completed in 1932. The move enabled the museum to continue and expand its mission of promoting the understanding of Chinese history. Displays in English and Chinese follow California's Chinese population from the frontier years to the Gold Rush, through the building of the railroads and the Barbary Coast opium dens.

Grant Avenue & around

A few blocks from Union Square, at Grant Avenue and Bush Street, the dragon-topped **Chinatown Gate** (*photo p87*) heralds the southern entrance to Chinatown. A gift from Taiwan in 1970, the green-tiled portal is made to a traditional design, and comes complete with a quotation from Confucius that urges passers-by to work for the common good.

Grant Avenue itself is Chinatown's main thoroughfare and arguably the oldest street in the city. In the 1870s and '80s, when it was called Dupont Street (it was later renamed in honour of President Ulysses Grant after the 1906 earthquake), it was controlled by *tongs*. These days, however, the cash-grabbing is more obvious; almost as far as the eye can see, souvenir shops sell T-shirts, toys, ceramics and jewellery, the genuine mixed with the junk.

Although most buildings on Grant have been built in undistinguished American styles, a few structures stand out. The **Ying On Labor Association** building (nos.745-747) is a gaudy study in chinoiserie; across the street, the **Sai Gai Yat Bo Company** building (no.736) features ornate balconies and a pagoda-style roof. Slightly more kitsch – check the circular gold entrance – is the **Li Po** dive bar (no.916, 982 0072), named after the great drunken poet of the T'ang Dynasty. Even the street lamps are sculpted in the likeness of golden dragons, created during the tourist boom of the 1920s at the behest of the Chinese Chamber of Commerce. The shops are a mixed bunch, but one popular stop is the **Ten Ren Tea Company** (no.949, 362 0656, www.tenren.com), which offers free samples to help its patrons choose. On the corner of Grant and California Streets, meanwhile, is the Roman Catholic **Old St Mary's Cathedral**, a sturdy 1854 edifice made of granite imported from China.

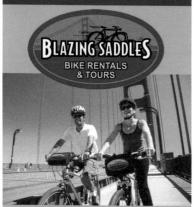

Old St Mary's Cathedral

660 California Street, at Grant Avenue (288 3800/ www.oldsaintmarys.org). Bus 1, 9X, 30, 45/ cable car California. **Open** *7am-4.30pm Mon-Fri; 10am-6pm Sat; 7.30am-3pm Sun.* **Admission** *free.* **Map** *p315 M5.*

Much early missionary work, and the city's first English lessons for Chinese immigrants, took place under this 19th-century building's foreboding clock tower: 'Son, observe the time and fly from evil', it warns. Observe your time at lunchtime concerts staged in the cathedral's dainty yet glorious interior.

Portsmouth Square

Many people consider **Portsmouth Square**, which sits on the corner of Clay and Kearny Streets a half-block east of Grant Avenue, as the true birthplace of the city. It was here that Captain John B Montgomery first hoisted the US flag, having captured the city – then known as Yerba Buena – from the Mexicans on 9 July 1846; the plaza is now named after his ship, the USS *Portsmouth*. Two years later, newspaper boss Sam Brannan stood here and announced to the public that gold had been discovered at Sutter's Mill, sparking the Gold Rush. It is also the site of the first public school in California.

Within a few years of Brannan's declaration, Chinese immigrants had settled in the area for good. Today, the elderly congregate to practise t'ai chi, argue politics and play games of cards or the Chinese board game 'go'. Among the monuments is one shaped like the galleon *Hispaniola* from *Treasure Island* and dedicated to Robert Louis Stevenson, who used to sit here in 1879 when he lived briefly at 608 Bush Street (a plaque marks the spot). The monument was designed by architect Willis Polk and artist Bruce Porter, who sketched their initial ideas on a tablecloth during lunch at the Palace Hotel (*see p47*). Stevenson is believed to have based the setting of *Treasure Island* on stunning Point Lobos, south of Monterey.

The buildings here, meanwhile, include the **Bank of Canton** (743 Washington Street), one of the most photographed spots in Chinatown. The pagoda-like structure was built in 1909 for the Chinese American Telephone Exchange; for four decades, multilingual phone operators routed calls throughout Chinatown by memory alone, since there was no area phone directory.

Chinese Culture Center

3rd floor, Hilton Hotel, 750 Kearny Street, at Washington Street (986 1822/www.c-c-c.org). Bus 1, 9X, 12, 20, 41/cable car California. **Open** *10am-4pm Tue-Sat.* **Admission** *free.* **Map** *p315 M4.*

Linked to Portsmouth Square by a footbridge and located on the third floor of a Hilton hotel, the Center hosts a variety of events, including Asian-themed art exhibitions and performances, as well as workshops and walking tours. There's also an annual festival to celebrate Chinese New Year.

Two Chinas: the **Golden Gate Fortune Cookie Factory** and **Chinatown Gate**. *See p84.*

North Beach to Fisherman's Wharf

The Beat goes on.

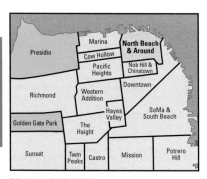

Map pp314-315

Among San Francisco's many notable neighbourhoods, **North Beach** is one of the best known, a popular destination for tourists, beloved by locals and an integral part of the old Barbary Coast. Grant Avenue, which runs through the middle of the area, is San Francisco's oldest street; along with the North Point docks, the century-old ethnic neighbourhoods of Chinatown (just south of North Beach; *see p84*) and Little Italy are reminders that San Francisco once served as the gateway to the west. With the legendary City Lights bookstore and a variety of cafés, the area is also bound to the Beat movement of the 1950s (*see p89* **Walk**).

To the north of North Beach is an area that's treasured by tourists but looked upon by locals with something approaching despair. Once a genuine fishing port, **Fisherman's Wharf** is now a dreary tourist trap, whose theme park vibe is fed by identical T-shirt stalls, tacky museums and overpriced restaurants. It could be anywhere in America that has a waterfront; it's just a crying shame that it has to be here, in a city whose citizenry is fiercely proud (to the point of being smug) of their city's beauty and independent spirit. Looking down on all this tomfoolery are the residents of **Russian Hill**, one of the city's richest neighbourhoods and also, it stands to reason, among its nicest. By contrast, it draws tourists for its most unique feature: zigzagging Lombard Street.

North Beach

North Beach, north and east of Columbus Avenue, was the place that turned San Francisco into the counterculture capital of the US. Originally, it was home to the city's Italian community, who rebuilt it after the 1906 earthquake and liked it so much they stayed. Eventually, it came to attract leagues of writers and artists, drawn not only by the European aura but also by the low rents.

Even after the Beat Generation had come and gone the area maintained its reputation for individualism and artistic endeavour. In the early 1960s, nightclubs such as the Purple Onion and the Hungry i showcased an array of boundary-pushing comedians such as Woody Allen and Lenny Bruce; later, punk venues solidified the indelible stamp of hipness. Today, North Beach has avoided falling victim to homogeny. The mellow streets, with their famously lambent light on sunny days, are still home to elderly Italians playing *bocce*, reading Neapolitan newspapers and nibbling cannoli.

The brash strip joints along Broadway are another tourist draw, whether locals like it or not; indeed, North Beach has long been as famous for its sex shows as for its literary heritage and its lasagne. But time hasn't stood still here. Amid the long-standing strip clubs, the vintage cafés, the cultured dive bars and the Old World delicatessens sit shops offering handmade and imported goods, restaurants serving all manner of classic, contemporary and international cuisine, and a slew of lively – or, if you prefer, noisy – bars and nightclubs. North Beach's secret, it seems, is that it has figured out that with a little effort, it is possible to be all things to all people.

City Lights & around

Much of North Beach's history and many of its treasures lie along **Columbus Avenue**, and especially close to the three-way junction of Columbus, Broadway and Grant Avenue that represents North Beach's beating heart.

To get up to speed on the Beats and their legacy, check out the **Beat Museum** (540 Broadway, at Columbus Avenue, 399 9626, www.thebeatmuseum.org) before heading over to what was both the head and the heart of the Beat movement, **City Lights** bookstore (261 Columbus Avenue, at Broadway; *see p176*). Still run by the original owner, 89-year-old poet Lawrence Ferlinghetti, City Lights has grown to occupy an entire building. Ferlinghetti began his shop with the then-radical concept of selling only paperbacks, believing that the best books should be available to as many people as possible, in an economical and portable form. To this day, City Lights stocks not only books published in-house, but a variety of the finest world literature, political thinking and small-circulation periodicals. The upper floor houses the shop's considerable Beat collection.

Step across Jack Kerouac Alley just next door to **Vesuvio** (255 Columbus Avenue, at Broadway; *see p167*), which welcomes mad

Walk The North Beach beat

Our walk starts on **Columbus Avenue** and **Broadway**, where the literary spirits are packed so tightly you practically have to step into the road to avoid them. First, have a peek into **Vesuvio** (no.255; *see p167*); the jaunty multicoloured sign has welcomed poets and artists since it opened in 1948. Neither Dylan Thomas nor Jack Kerouac could resist when they were in town, nor can the dipsomaniacal poets and poetical dipsomaniacs of today. To the right of Vesuvio is Jack Kerouac Alley, renamed by the city in 1988, and the world-famous City Lights bookstore (no.261; *see p176*).

Cross Columbus heading east along Broadway. **Tosca** (no.242; *see p167* can lay proud claim to having ejected Bob Dylan one boisterous evening, and it was at **Spec's** (12 William Saroyan Place; *see p167*) that famed *Chronicle* columnist Herb Caen coined the derogatory term 'Beatnik' to describe the increasingly large numbers of youths heading to North Beach in search of jazz, sex and poetry. They found the former, at least, just away from City Lights along the right-hand side of Broadway: at nos.471-3, the **Jazz Workshop** once hosted the likes of Miles Davis, John Coltrane, Sonny Rollins and Ornette Coleman; it was also here that Lenny Bruce was first arrested for obscenity in 1961.

Head up to Montgomery Street for a great view of the Bay Bridge, then cross Broadway. Allen Ginsberg lived at **1010 Montgomery** with Peter Orlovsky, and probably conceived his epochal poem *Howl* here. The site is now an old folks' home. Heading back along Broadway you will pass the Green Tortoise Hostel at no.494. It may not look like much now, but this was once the chic **El Matador**, where Frank Sinatra and Duke Ellington performed for Marlon Brando's Hollywood set.

Turn right on to Kearny and you're facing more than 100 pretty steps. Locals call them the Kearny Steps, but the official title is the Macchiarini Steps; it's named for a local family that still makes jewellery in the area. From the top, it's downhill again (you'll be pleased to hear) for a break at **Caffe Trieste** (601 Vallejo Street; *see p146*), the coffee house where Francis Ford Coppola is said to have penned *The Godfather*.

Turn right down Green Street. If it's sunny, turn left and head up to **Washington Square** for a glorious mix of tatty old bohemians, wannabe alternative types and discreet Chinese ladies doing t'ai chi. Otherwise, zigzag across the intersection between Green, Columbus and Stockton. Stick on Green Street, passing Caffè Sport at no.574. When this was the **Cellar**, Kenneth Rexroth and Ruth Weiss read to improvised accompaniment here, a first foray into jazz poetry. Turn right on to Grant Avenue and head past the Grant & Green Saloon (no.1371) and the Lost & Found Saloon (no.1361), until you reach the plain old **Saloon** (no.1232; *see p231*). This is San Francisco's oldest bar, open since 1861. There's no smoky jazz, but there is live blues.

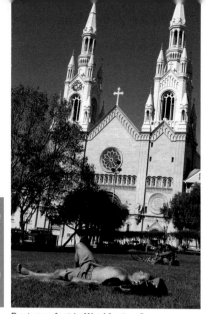

Rest your feet in **Washington Square**.

poets and tourists in equal measure, much as it did when Kerouac and crew drank here in the 1950s. **Tosca** (242 Columbus Avenue, between Broadway Street & Pacific Avenue, 986 9651) was another favourite watering hole of the Beats, and today attracts actors and filmmakers.

The copper-sheathed **Columbus Tower** at the corner of Columbus and Kearny Streets, purchased by film director Francis Ford Coppola following the resounding success of *The Godfather*, houses his Zoetrope Studios as well as office space for a number of independent film producers. Coppola himself occupies the penthouse office. On the ground floor is elegant **Café Zoetrope** (916 Kearny Street, at Jackson Street, 291 1700, www. cafecoppola.com), which sells wines from the director's own Napa Valley vineyard.

East of here is **Broadway**, which, between Columbus Avenue and Montgomery Street, is lined with nightclubs featuring strippers and sexy floorshows. History was made at the **Condor Club** (300 Columbus Avenue, at Broadway, 781 8222, www.condorsf.com) in 1964 when a buxom waitress named Carol Doda went topless for the first time. Just down the street, the **Hungry i** (546 Broadway, at Columbus Avenue, 362 7763), once a nightclub that launched the careers of luminaries such as Barbra Streisand and Woody Allen, is a strip club. A new culture of a slightly different stripe was forged in the **Mabuhay Gardens** at 443 Broadway (now the Velvet Lounge

restaurant-nightclub), a punk mecca where the Dead Kennedys got their start.

Just down on Kearny Street are two newer adult hangouts, which represent a pair of contradictory extremes. Larry Flynt's **Hustler Club** (no.1031, 434 1301, www.hustlerclubsf. com) is about as crude and modern as they come, every bit the reflection of its famous owner's proudly crass image. Next door sits the **Lusty Lady** (no.1033, 391 3126, www.lustyladysf.com), a pretty scruffy-looking peep show notable for being the first unionised strip joint in the US, and, since 2003, for being the only place of its type to be owned and operated by the women who work in it. The club was the subject of a 2000 documentary, *Live Nude Girls Unite*.

Washington Square & around

The **Molinari Delicatessen** (373 Columbus Avenue, at Vallejo Street; *see p189*), one of San Francisco's most beloved institutions, boasts a cameo role in *Babycakes*, one of Armistead Maupin's *Tales of the City* series. Pick up a sopressata sandwich on a hard roll and take it just up the road to Washington Square, a lovely patch of greenery that really comes into its own at the height of summer. Alternatively, walk up **Grant Avenue** and browse blocks of one-of-a-kind boutiques, antiques and curiosity shops. From luxury lingerie to Asian antiquities, Grant Avenue is entertaining in itself, but perhaps the best place to stop for a bit of history is **Schein and Schein** (no.1435, 339 8882, www.schein andschein.com), a miscellany of antique maps and prints, and also home to a fascinating collection of vintage photographs. Just down the street is **Savoy Tivoli** (no.1434, 362 7023), a bar that has been in operation since 1907, and a great place to stop for a drink on the patio.

Washington Square is overlooked by the white stucco Romanesque **Church of St Peter and St Paul**, where Marilyn Monroe and local hero Joe DiMaggio had their wedding photos taken. Since both were divorced and Joe was a Catholic, the couple were married in a civil ceremony at City Hall. An 1879 statue of Benjamin Franklin stands in the park on a granite-encased time capsule – it's scheduled to be reopened in 2079.

At **Caffe Roma** (526 Columbus Avenue; *see p146*), coffee is freshly roasted on the premises, while at **Liguria** (1700 Stockton Street, at Filbert Street, 421 3786), the locals stand in line for foccacia made in-house, baked by members of the same family since 1911.

The district of **Telegraph Hill**, bordered by Grant Avenue and Green, Bay and Sansome Streets, was so named as the site of the West Coast's first telegraph. The landmark

Coit Tower sits on top. Two nearby hotels neatly sum up the area. The **Hotel Bohème** (444 Columbus Avenue, between Vallejo & Green Streets; *see p57*) celebrates Beat heritage with framed snapshots of life in bohemian North Beach in the 1950s and '60s, while the *pensione*-like **San Remo Hotel** (2337 Mason Street, at Chestnut Street; *see p58*), a pretty Italianate Victorian, is an ideal base for soaking up the area's Italian ambience.

Coit Tower

Peak of Telegraph Hill, at the end of Telegraph Hill Boulevard (362 0808). Bus 39. **Open** 10am-5pm daily. **Admission** *Elevator* $4.50. **No credit cards.** **Map** p315 M3.

This 210ft (64m) concrete turret, built by City Hall architect Arthur Brown in 1933, was a gift to the city from the eccentric Lillie Hitchcock Coit, famed for her love of firemen. Legend has it that as a school-girl, Coit happened upon the Knickerbocker #5 Volunteer Fire Company attempting to haul their fire engine up steep Telegraph Hill. As their energy flagged, she grabbed the rope and exhorted the men to pull on. From that day on, she became the mascot of the #5s. Upon her death, she bequeathed a massive sum to the city. A memorial to her beloved Knickerbockers was erected in Washington Square, and Coit Tower was built to fulfil her wish to 'add to the beauty of the city I have always loved'. While most assume that the tower represents the nozzle of a fire hose, the architects always denied it.

The spectacular views from the top aren't the tower's only attraction. Under the supervision of Diego Rivera, some wonderful murals were created here, a series of socialist-realist images so subversive that, when they were completed in 1934, delayed the opening so that an errant hammer and sickle could be erased.

Fisherman's Wharf

Fisherman's Wharf dates back to the Gold Rush, when Italian and Chinese immigrants plied the Bay for crab and other seafood and sold it right off their boats. Famous families included Joe DiMaggio's and the Alioto clan (who own an eponymous restaurant on the Wharf; *see p148*). Alas, there is little evidence of that historic past today: the wharf, roughly bounded by Jefferson, North Point and Kearny Streets and Fort Mason, is little more than a conglomeration of novelty attractions, tacky shops and heavy pedestrian traffic. In surveys, Fisherman's Wharf routinely ranks as the No.1 destination for visitors, despite the fact that its main attractions were built in the late 1960s and '70s. Still, those with a few hours to kill can find some inexpensive entertainment here, along with unrivalled views of the Bay.

Jefferson Street, the wharf's main drag, is a fairly undignified spectacle. The **Wax Museum** (no.145, 1-800 439 4305, www.waxmuseum.com) and **Ripley's Believe It Or Not! Museum** (no.175, 771 6188, www.ripleys.com) are clichéd dockside diversions; elsewhere, sidewalk crab stalls and seafood restaurants thrive. For the only remaining glimpse of Fisherman's Wharf as it once was, turn towards the water off Jefferson and on to Leavenworth Street, then slip into **Fish Alley**. There, you will find real fishing boats and real fishermen. Although it's within shouting distance of Jefferson, it feels like miles away. Another nipper of the fishing life can be hooked at **Frank's Fisherman** (366 Jefferson Street, between Leavenworth Street & Al Scoma Way, 775 1165, www.franksfisherman.com), which sells everything from silk yachting shirts to antique scrimshaw tusks.

At the eastern end, **Pier 39** is a sprawling prefab array of seafront shops, attractions and arcade games patently designed to separate you from your money. Luckily, crowds of sea lions barking and belching on nearby pontoons provide a natural respite. Offshore from H Dock on Pier 39, **Forbes Island** (951 4900, www.forbesisland.com) is 700 tons of man-made, engine-propelled, floating lighthouse and restaurant. Further west, at Pier 45, a World War II submarine, the **USS Pampanito** (*see p94*), is open to the public for self-guided tours.

Sea lions at **Fisherman's Wharf**.

Sightseeing

A reminder of the area's former industrial life is the **Cannery** (2801 Leavenworth Street, enter on Jefferson or Beach Streets, 771 3112, www.delmontesquare.com). Built in 1907 as a fruit-canning factory, it's now another twee mall modelled on London's Covent Garden Piazza, complete with street performers. The red-brick **Ghirardelli Square** (at North Point & Larkin Streets, www.ghirardellisq.com) dates to the 19th century and housed a famous chocolate factory until the 1960s; the namesake chocolate is still sold, but the building itself is now a complex of shops and restaurants. The newest addition (beyond the free Wi-Fi access on the square) is the conversion of part of the structure into luxury condominiums in partnership with the Fairmont hotel that isslated to open in 2008. Despite all this, the **Ghirardelli Ice Cream & Chocolate Shop** (900 North Point Street, 474 1414, www.ghirardelli.com) on the southern edge of the square is the place to get some of the best hot fudge sundaes on earth. You can sort through any tourist monstrosities that you may have acquired in the central plaza, alongside the lovely *Mermaid Fountain* sculpted by local artist Ruth Asawa.

There's more to enjoy to the west. The shores of **Aquatic Park** (between Hyde Street & Van Ness Avenue) offer one of the best strolls in the city, with a panorama of the Golden Gate Bridge, Alcatraz, windsurfers, sailing boats, wildly coloured kites and dogs catching frisbees. Along the **Municipal Pier** (access from the northern end of Van Ness), fishermen try their luck; at **Hyde Street Pier** (*see p93*), a fleet of carefully restored historic ships is docked permanently and open to the public. The **San Francisco Maritime Museum** (*see p94*), opposite Ghirardelli Square, recaptures West Coast whaling, steamboating and perilous journeys 'around the Horn'.

The **Golden Gate Promenade** begins here, continuing for three miles along the shoreline to **Fort Point** (*see p122*). The entire stretch of waterfront from Aquatic Park to Ocean Beach was incorporated into the Golden Gate National Recreation Area in 1972, with the authorities thankfully arresting Fisherman's Wharf-style

Write on Armistead Maupin

Armistead Maupin likes to tell visitors a story about how Mark Twain met a fireman named Tom Sawyer in a Turkish bath on the site of what is now the Transamerica Pyramid.

Like Twain, Maupin arrived in the Bay Area as a reporter – he was a stringer in the Associated Press's San Francisco bureau when he settled in the city in 1972. He was also a Vietnam veteran, a conservative son of the South (he was born and raised in North Carolina) and 'frightened to death' of his own homosexuality. Like thousands of others in

the early 1970s, Maupin had come to San Francisco to learn, as the writer Edmund White once put it, how to live a gay life.

It was in learning how to live as a gay man, in bathhouses like the one in which Twain had met Tom Sawyer, that Maupin found his subject as a novelist. *Tales of the City* is a series of six books that began life as a serial in the *San Francisco Chronicle*. Each week, in the manner of the great social novelists of the 19th century, Maupin would chronicle the social and sexual revolution in which he was also a participant.

The focal point of the novels is a rooming house at 28 Barbary Lane (a fictional address not unlike the real-life Macondray Lane, in a neighbourhood very much like Russian Hill), owned by the mysterious and flamboyant Anna Madrigal. Among Anna's tenants are Mary Ann Singleton, an ingénue newly arrived from the Midwest, and Michael Tolliver, a gay man from the Deep South. An extravagant parade of characters, drawn with Dickensian dash and vigour, passes through the house and through the lives of Michael and Mary Ann. *Tales of the City* stands as a record of an extraordinary cultural experiment and, above all, a hymn to a city that, as Maupin proudly recalls, was described by the *New York Post* in 1849 as 'mad, stark mad'.

tourist kitsch spreading any further along one of the most scenic bits of coast in the region.

Alcatraz

Alcatraz Island, San Francisco Bay (www.nps.gov/alcatraz). Alcatraz Cruises ferry from Pier 33, Embarcadero (981 7625/www.alcatrazcruises.com). Streetcar F/bus 9X, 10, 39, 47. **Tickets** (incl audio guide) $24.50-$31.50; $15.75-$29.25 reductions. **Credit** AmEx, DC, Disc, MC, V. **Map** p315 M1.

'Alcatraz' is Spanish for pelican, but to its inmates it was simply known as 'the Rock'. The West Coast's first lighthouse was built here in 1854, but it was soon decided that the island's isolated setting made it perfect for a prison. It became a military jail in the 1870s, but it wasn't until it was converted into a high-security federal penitentiary in 1934 that the name Alcatraz became an international symbol of punishment. Despite being in operation for less than 30 years, Alcatraz remains fixed in the popular imagination as the ultimate penal colony. Today, its ominous prison buildings are no longer used (its last inmates left in 1963), but the craggy outcrop, now a National Park, lures over a million visitors each year.

Despite what you might expect, Alcatraz is far from being from a tourist trap. The audio tour of the facility, which features actual interviews from a variety of former prisoners and guards, is powerful, chilling and evocative, and the buildings retain an eerie and fascinating appeal. Departure times for both the day tours and the far less frequent (and wildly oversubscribed) evening jaunts vary by season: check the website for details. One word of warning: capacity on the tours is limited, and those who don't book ahead of time may find the only views they get of the island are from the shore.

Angel Island

Angel Island State Park, San Francisco Bay (435 1915/www.angelisland.org). Blue & Gold ferry from Pier 41, Embarcadero (705 5555/www.blueandgold fleet.com). Streetcar F/bus 9X, 10, 39, 47. **Tickets** $14.50; $8.50 reductions. **Credit** AmEx, DC, Disc, MC, V. **Map** p314 L1.

Blue & Gold runs a ferry service to Angel Island; times vary with the season, so check online or call ahead before setting out. Boats arrive at the Ayala Cove visitors' centre, where there are maps, bikes to rent and all-important picnic tables. Views from the island are unrivalled. At its peak, one has 360-degree views of the entire Bay Area – one of the primary reasons the top was sheared off and replaced with a gun bunker as a part of the Bay's coastal artillery defences. Luckily, they replaced the top but the bunkers are still scattered around the island, whose history dates back before the Civil War. Author Richard Henry Dana recounts in his *Two Years Before the Mast* (1840) how he collected a year's supply of wood for his ship *Alert* when it stopped here in the winter of 1835-36. Later it acted as 'the Ellis Island of the West' serving as one of America's busiest immigration ports. Later, in its darkest chapter, it served as an internment camp for Japanese-Americans dur-

Hyde Street Pier: Ships ahoy!

ing WWII. Now, it's a great place to hike, tour by bicycle and have a picnic with time enough to get back to the city for a night on the town.

Hyde Street Pier

At the foot of Hyde Street (561 7000/www.maritime.org). Streetcar F/bus 10, 19, 20, 30, 47/cable car Powell-Hyde. **Open** 9.30am-4.30pm daily. **Admission** free ($5 for vessels). **No credit cards. Map** p314 K1.

Maritime fans, students of history and children will love the historic vessels permanently docked here. Typical of the ships that would have been common here in the 19th and early 20th centuries, they include the 1886 full-rigged *Balclutha*, built to carry grain from California to Europe; the *CA Thayer*, an 1895 sailing ship that carried timber along the West Coast; the *Alma*, an 1891 scow schooner that hauled cargo throughout the Bay Area; *Hercules*, a 1907 ocean tugboat; and the 1890 commuter ferry *Eureka*.

Along with the San Francisco Maritime Museum (*see p94*), the set-up is the highlight of what is officially designated as the San Francisco Maritime National Historic Park. The park's lovely visitors' centre, at the corner of Jefferson and Hyde Streets (June-Sept 9.30am-7pm daily; Oct-May 9.30am-5pm daily), contains a fascinating series of displays on the area's seafaring history, which makes for a welcome contrast to the variety of miserable tourist traps just a few blocks down the street. For more on the park and its various services and attractions, call 447 5000 or visit www.nps.gov/safr.

Musée Mécanique

Pier 45, at the end of Taylor Street (346 2000/www.
museemecanique.org). Streetcar F/bus 10, 19, 30, 47/
cable car Powell-Mason. **Open** 11am-7pm Mon-Fri;
10am-8pm Sat, Sun. **Admission** free. **Map** p314 K1.

Pack a pocketful of quarters before you visit this wonderful museum, a vintage arcade housing more than
170 old-fashioned coin-operated gizmos dating from
the 1880s, ranging from fortune-telling machines to
player pianos. Best of all is Laughing Sal, a somewhat
scary relic from Whitney's Playland at the Beach, San
Francisco's long-defunct coastside amusement park.
It's an enormous mechanical figure with a crazy laugh
that sends little kids running for their parents.

San Francisco Maritime Museum

900 Beach Street, at Polk Street (561 7100/www.
maritime.org). Streetcar F/bus 10, 19, 20, 30,
47/cable car Powell-Hyde. **Open** 10am-5pm daily.
Admission free. **Map** p314 J2.

Such is the art deco beauty of this building, closed
for restoration until 2009, that you almost fail to
notice its resemblance to a cruiseliner marooned on
shore. Those with a yen for maritime lore will enjoy
the cache of models, interactive displays, oral histories and exhibits, which offer something for even the
saltiest swabbie. The renovation also promises to
restore the fantastic Atlantis murals by Hilaire Hiler.

USS Pampanito

Pier 45 (775 1943/www.maritime.org). Streetcar F/
bus 10, 19, 30, 47/cable car Powell-Hyde. **Open** *Mid*
Oct-late May 9am-6pm Mon-Thur, Sun; 9am-8pm Fri,
Sat. *Late May-mid Oct* 9am-8pm Mon, Tue, Thur-Sun;
9am-6pm Wed. **Admission** $9; $3-$5 reductions; $20
family. **Credit** AmEx, DC, MC, V. **Map** p314 K1.

The *Pampanito* is a World War II, Balao-class Fleet
submarine with an impressive record: it made six
patrols in the Pacific at the height of the war, sink-
ing six Japanese ships and damaging four others.
The vessel has been restored to look much as it
would have in its prime in 1945. The sub is still sea-
worthy: in 1995 it sailed under the Golden Gate
Bridge for the first time in 50 years.

Russian Hill

Russian Hill got its name when several Cyrillic-
inscribed gravestones were discovered here
during the Gold Rush. Local lore has it that
a Russian warship put into the harbour of San
Francisco in the early 1840s, and a number
of the disease-stricken crew died while ashore.
As they belonged to the Orthodox Church,
they couldn't be buried in any of the existing
Protestant or Catholic cemeteries, so one was
created for them in this area. By the late 1800s,
the gravestones had disappeared; along with
them went any trace of Russian influence.

Today, Russian Hill is a quiet, residential
and pricey neighbourhood roughly bordered
by Larkin and North Point Streets, Columbus

Avenue, Powell Street and Pacific Avenue.
Its most notorious landmark is the world's
'crookedest' (and no doubt most photographed)
thoroughfare: **Lombard Street**, which snakes
steeply down from Hyde Street to Leavenworth,
packing nine hairpin bends into one brick-
paved and over-landscaped block. In summer,
tourists queue for the thrill of driving down its
hazardous 27 per cent gradient at 5mph, much
to the annoyance of local residents. Arrive early
or late to avoid the throng. For further thrills,
test your skills behind the wheel on the steepest
street in the city: Filbert Street between Hyde
and Leavenworth descends at a whopping 31.5
per cent gradient. Also up on Russian Hill is
the **San Francisco Art Institute** (*see below*),
housed in an attractive 1920s Spanish Revival
building on Chestnut Street and containing a
wonderful Diego Rivera mural.

Struggle up Vallejo Street to Taylor Street
to take in the views from **Ina Coolbrith Park**,
little more than a narrow ledge with benches.
Arrive early in the morning, and you'll catch
elderly Chinese practising t'ai chi. Up from the
park, the top of the **Vallejo Street Stairway**,
designed by Willis Polk and surrounded on
each side by landscaped gardens, is the apex
of the neighbourhood. Laura Ingalls Wilder,
author of *Little House on the Prairie*, lived here
(at 1019 Vallejo). Indeed, Russian Hill is riven
with quaint stairs and alleyways: if you don't
mind the ups and downs, it can be fun to prowl
the neighbourhood for secret passages.

Other landmark addresses in the district
include **29 Russell Street**, off Hyde Street,
where Jack Kerouac lived with Neal and
Carolyn Cassady during his most creative
period in the 1950s; and the **Feusier Octagon
House**, one of the city's oldest dwellings, at
1067 Green Street, near Leavenworth. Best
viewed from across the street to appreciate its
odd shape, the pastel structure is one of only
two survivors of the 19th-century octagonal-
house craze (the other is in Pacific Heights).

San Francisco Art Institute

800 Chestnut Street, between Leavenworth & Jones
Streets (771 7020/www.sanfranciscoart.edu). Bus 10,
20, 30, 47/cable car Powell-Hyde or Powell-Mason.
Open *Diego Rivera Gallery* 8am-7pm daily. *Walter*
McBean Gallery 11am-6pm Tue-Sat. **Admission**
free. **No credit cards.** **Map** p314 K2.

This hip and prestigious art school offers the full
spectrum of fine arts, including painting, film, photography, sculpture and new media. Its student
shows are legendary. Most people visit to see Diego
Rivera's mural *The Making of a Fresco*, one of various works he completed in San Francisco in the
1930s. If you're worn out from climbing all those hills,
have a rest in the pretty open-air courtyard, or grab
a cheap snack in the cafeteria and soak up the views.

The Mission & the Castro

A very San Franciscan melting pot.

Maps p317 & pp318-319

The heady cultural mix of the Mission, the Castro and Noe Valley makes for a unique kind of melting pot. Here, rainbow-swathed muscle shirt boutiques rub shoulders with beautifully renovated Victorian homes; temples to pristine gastronomy give way to burritos the size of babies' arms. These close-knit enclaves of all things queer, yuppie, hip and Latino provide a colourful snapshot of the city's remarkably diverse charm.

The Mission

First settled by the Spanish in the 1770s and later home to Irish, German, Italian and Asian immigrants, the Mission today is the centre of Latin culture in San Francisco. A steady influx of families and workers from Mexico and South and Central America lends the neighbourhood its distinctive character, especially on **Mission Street** between 14th and Cesar Chavez Streets, the area's main drag. Along here, the scents and sights are plentiful: the mix of sidewalk sausage stands, bootleg DVD vendors, dollar stores and *taquerías* colourfully paints the strip of one of the city's tightest ethnic communities.

However, walk a couple of blocks west to **Valencia Street** and you'll see evidence of the area's other main occupants: San Francisco's creative classes. The invasion of *nouveau riche* techies during the dotcom boom drove some rents sky-high, sending many locals on a

scramble to find cheaper quarters, but the musicians and artists who colonised the area in the 1990s remain in situ, and despite fears that the area would gentrify beyond recognition, it seems to have regained its equilibrium. Trendy Valencia Street hasn't yet overwhelmed the throbbing pulse of blue-collar Mission Street, and the two co-exist in relative harmony: gone are the days when a group calling itself the Yuppie Eradication Project would vandalise pricey SUVs or leave dog-waste calling cards on the doorsteps of wealthy homeowners.

A quick practical note: unlike Downtown and SoMa, the street numbering along Mission and Valencia Streets doesn't correspond to the numbered streets that cross them. For example, 2000 Mission Street is not at the junction of 20th Street, as you might expect, but of 16th Street; similarly, 2800 Mission is actually at 24th Street. It's a similar story two blocks away: 500 Valencia Street sits at the junction with 16th Street, while 1300 Valencia is at 24th Street. Still, while the numbering doesn't match the streets, it does at least increase at the standard rate of 100 per block, which makes it easy to figure out how far you have to walk.

Mission Street & East

Mission Street is the main thoroughfare of the Latino quarter. Cheque-cashing operations, bargain shops, taco stands and grocery stores (selling such exotica as sugar cane and prickly pears – the fruit borne by the cactus of the same name) conduct brisk business, while Banda (the Mexican music descended from the oompah bands of German immigrants) drifts out of open doors and windows. In a few places, the narrow, crowded sidewalks are a scene straight out of Guadalajara; it's especially eye-catching in autumn, when Mexican-run shops and art galleries fill with traditional ghoulish items in advance of Dia de los Muertos (Day of the Dead) in November.

The neighbourhood can feel a little shady east of Mission Street itself in the inner Mission, particularly north of 19th Street and its environs. The *barrio* has its share of prostitutes,

Walk Murals and Latino life

East of Mission Street, **24th Street** is booming, with new restaurants, shops and coffeehouses breathing life into the 12-block stretch from **Mission** to **Potrero Streets**. Mexican, Cuban, Salvadoran, Guatemalan and American: this part of 24th Street is the Mission District in microcosm. Street names like Treat and Balmy may make the neighbourhood seem rather quaint, but nearby Shotwell Street was once the more aptly named in an area known for gang violence. Although this stretch of 24th can still be gritty late at night, sunny daytime strolls are perfectly safe, and with a profusion of murals and tasty places to stop for a snack, it deserves attention.

Head west from Mission Street to begin your 24th Street cultural immersion. **Casa Bonampak** (3321 24th Street, 642 4079, www.casabonampak.com) is a must-see shop where you can pick up all your Día de los Muertos (Day of the Dead) supplies. It also sells excellent compilation CDs and fair trade apparel, as well as postcards of such figures as Che Guevara and Mexico's masked revolutionary, Subcomandante Marcos.

Heading back east across Mission you'll spy **Carlos' Club** (no.3278, 285 1512) a real Mexican dive bar – true to the tradition of such places in Mexico – is mainly the territory of men. You may feel more like a coffee. If so, you can sample what some say is the best in the city at **Philz Coffee** (no.3101, at Folsom Street, 282 9155, www.philzcoffee.com): over 20 secret blends known only to the founder and his son are filter brewed here.

In this part of the Mission, vibrant murals are everywhere. Even the local McDonald's on the corner of Mission and 24th has a technicolour coat. The vivid public art that graces the area's alleys is here largely thanks to the vision of one woman, Susan Cervantes, founder of **Precita Eyes Mural Arts & Visitors Center** (no.2981, at Harrison Street, 285 2287, www.precitaeyes.org), which celebrated its 30th birthday in 2007. The

drug addicts and gangs, and doorway drug-deals around the scruffy junction of 16th and Mission Streets are usually enough to scare off the timid. However, it's safer than it once was, and 24th Street is undergoing a transformation that celebrates the personality of the Mission with a more business-savvy outlook.

Tourist buses tend to limit their explorations to the admittedly fascinating Mission Dolores, but there are other worthwhile stops. On Mission Street, the **Mission Cultural Center** (no.2868, at 25th Street, 821 1155, www.missionculturalcenter.org) hosts a theatre and a gallery displaying works by under-the-radar artists. It's also a terrific

resource for the area's wealth of public art, as is the **Precita Eyes Mural Arts & Visitor Center** on 24th Street (*see p96* **Walk**).

At this juncture it's important to acknowledge the centrality of food to the Mission experience. It's one of the area's main attractions, and no discussion of Mission food would be complete without mentioning the mythical creation that is the Mission Burrito: a glory to behold, this steamed tortilla is an object of fanatical devotion. Packed with meat, cheese, rice, beans, guacamole and spicy, peppery salsa, it is perhaps the ultimate food for the new millennium. It's fast, cheap and portable, takes under five minutes to prepare centre has a shop that carries mural T-shirts, mural maps and mural postcards as well as general art supplies. For the best overview, Precita Eyes runs walking tours: the Mission Trail Mural Walk runs every Saturday and Sunday at 1.30pm ($12); other slightly shorter walks are held at 11am on weekends; private tours are available by appointment.

If you can't take the tour, be sure to double back to check out the murals along **Balmy Alley**. Back on 24th Street, at the corner of Florida Street, **St Peter's Church** is similarly adorned. And don't miss the hilarious mural on the Mr Burbujas (Mr Bubbles) laundromat, just across the street.

By now it's probably lunchtime, and food is a big part of what's good about this part of the Mission. Don't let the humble appearance of many of the restaurants put you off. There's some great Mexican food to be had, at **Resturente El Delphin** (no.3066, 643 7955) or **Tortas Los Picudos** (no.2969, 824 4199), for example, both within easy reach of Balmy Alley and St Peter's Church.

To follow your burrito with something sweet, check out one of the many Mexican bakeries or *panaderías*. At **La Victoria** (no.2937, 642 7120), customers can pick up a tray and tongs and choose from a selection of crazy-coloured sugar cookies, quivering flan and *pan de muerto*, the Bread of the Dead, a traditional sweet bun made for the Día de los Muertos festivals in late October and early November. The other unmissable place along this stretch comes with a dose of full-on Americana and dates from another age of the Mission entirely. The **St Francis Fountain** (no.2801, at York Street; *see p152*) is a century-old soda fountain that is reputedly the birthplace of the San Francisco 49ers football team – what more perfect place for a classic ice-cream soda or a traditional savoury dish like mac and cheese?

By now you are approaching Potrero Avenue and the end of this stretch of 24th. You may not have walked far, but rest assured you've seen some unique San Francisco street art and tasted some of the city's best food.

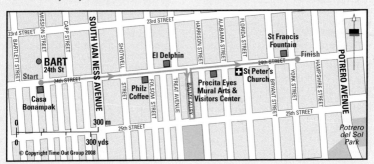

and costs $5. Needless to say, competition is fierce. A quick course in the fundamentals of what makes a good burrito can be found at www.burritoeater.com. Some of the area's best are **Taqueria San Francisco** (2794 24th Street, at York Street, 641 1770), **La Taqueria** (2889 Mission Street, 285 7117), **Taqueria Cancun** (2288 Mission Street, 252 9560) and the place that lays claim to creating the original Mission burrito, **Taqueria La Cumbre** (515 Valencia Street, 863 8205). **Casa Sanchez** (2278 24th Street, 695 0700), which makes and sells its own line of salsas, once offered free burritos for life to anyone who would get a tattoo of its logo; it had to

cancel the offer after several regulars took up the challenge. At **Pancho Villa** (3071 16th Street, at Valencia Street, 864 8840) rocker Beck has been spotted sitting in for the regular serenading mariachi.

Valencia Street & west

While Mission Street retains a headily Latino feel, Valencia Street, parallel to Mission and just two blocks west, is an altogether different kettle of fish. The occasional Mexican business remains, but many of the storefronts have been taken over by boho types, who occupy bar stools and fill seats at the **Roxie Theater**

(3117 16th Street, 863 1087, www.roxie.com), the neighbourhood movie house and one of five independent cinemas left in San Francisco.

Lined with boutiques, with nary a chain store to be seen, Valencia Street is a shopaholics' paradise. Within a four-block stretch, book-lovers get to sift through the shelves of **Dog-Eared Books**, **Modern Times Bookstore**, **Valencia Street Books** and **Abandoned Planet** (*see p176*), a trove of new and second-hand literary treasures that comes in handy for students of the über-liberal New College of California, just blocks away, and the City College of San Francisco. **Aquarius Records** (1055 Valencia Street, between 21st & 22nd Streets, 647 2272, www.aquariusrecords.org) satisfies the area's vinyl junkies.

Local designers also have a presence here, at shops such as **House of Hengst** (924 Valencia Street, at 20th Street, 642 0841, www.houseofhengst.com) and **Dema** (no.1038, at 21st Street, 206 0500, www.godemago.com). At **Paxton Gate** (no.824, between 19th & 20th Streets; *see p192*), a cadre of creative landscapers and taxidermists sells gardening equipment and stuffed vampire mice. However, the most notable commercial landmark is the pirate supply store at 826 Valencia (642 5905). It's said that owner Dave Eggers, bestselling author and the brains behind publishing house McSweeny's, opened the shop to meet a commercial storefront zoning code: in reality, its main purpose is as a support for the centre for young writers located inside.

The Mission's reputation as a kind of art colony-cum-neighbourhood is evident in the numerous galleries and performance stages in the area, the majority either on Valencia Street or just off it. The Women's Building (3543 18th Street, between Valencia & Guerrero Streets, 431 1180, www.womensbuilding.org) is home to a dozen feminist non-profit groups. Meanwhile, three groups on Valencia Street – Artists' Television Access (no.992, 824 3890, www.atasite.org), the Marsh (no.1062, 826 5750, www.themarsh.org) and Intersection for the Arts (no.446, 626 2787, www.theintersection.org) – offer a forum for genre-smashing filmmakers, actors, playwrights, artists and musicians.

The three-block stretch of 16th Street between Mission and Dolores Streets is packed with colourful hangouts, although most are a bit heavier on bohemian atmosphere than they are on taste. Still, a walk along 16th will lead you to the building that gave the city its name: the 225-year-old Misión San Francisco de Asis, better known as **Mission Dolores** (*see below*).

Just south of here, bordered by Dolores, Church, 18th and 20th Streets, is **Mission Dolores Park**. There's great people- and dog-watching during the day; when it's warm, sunbathers line the park's upper end, earning it the nickname Dolores Beach. Summer evenings offer free film screenings (www.sfneighborhood theater.org; *see also p209* **Films alfresco**), often of classic, SF-centric flicks, but bring a sensible coat and blanket: contrary to Eric Burdon of the Animals' experience, there's no such thing as 'a warm San Franciscan night'.

Mission Dolores

3321 16th Street, at Dolores Street (621 8203/ www.missiondolores.org). BART 16th Street/ Metro J to Church/bus 22. **Open** 9am-5pm daily. **Admission** $3-$5. **Credit** (groups only) AmEx, DC, MC, V. **Map** p318 J10.

Founded by a tiny band of Spanish missionaries and soldiers in 1776, and completed 15 years later, Mission Dolores is the oldest structure in the city and San Francisco's Registered Landmark No.1. The building was originally called the Misión San Francisco de Asis (after St Francis of Assisi), and provided the town with its name. However, it takes its common name from Laguna de los Dolores, the swampy lagoon on the shores of which it was built. Although the original mission became an expansive outpost, housing over 4,000 monks and converts, today only the tiny old church remains. The adobe structure, constructed from 16,000 earthen bricks and 4ft (1.2m) thick, survived the 1906 and 1989 earthquakes unscathed, while the new church next door crumbled. Small wonder that the cool, dim interior looks and feels authentic: almost everything about it is unreconstructed and original, from the redwood logs holding up the roof to the ornate altars brought from Mexico centuries ago. (The modern-day church next door is a 20th-century basilica with no real architectural significance; it does, however, handle all the mission's religious services.) A small museum on the mission premises offers volunteer-led tours. The picturesque, flower-filled cemetery containing the remains of California's first governor and the city's first mayor, as well as assorted Spanish settlers and the mass grave of 5,000 Costanoan Indians who died in their service, backs up on to a grade-school playground. Film buffs may recall that in Hitchcock's *Vertigo*, an entranced Kim Novak led Jimmy Stewart to the gravestone of the mysterious Carlotta Valdes in this very cemetery. You won't find Carlotta's stone, though: it was merely a prop and was removed after filming.

Potrero Hill & Bernal Heights

On the outskirts of the Mission, the quiet neighbourhoods of **Potrero Hill** (loosely bordered by 16th Street, I-280, Cesar Chavez Avenue and Potrero Avenue) and **Bernal Heights** (south of the Mission) are often sunny, even when the rest of San Francisco is shrouded in fog. Home to a mix of young families, dog-walking lesbians and hipsters who've fled the Mission, both areas are a little off the beaten track, but boast compact, lively commercial districts.

On 18th Street at the peak of Potrero Hill is one of San Francisco's many pockets of French cuisine. Here, upscale **Chez Papa** (no.1401, 824 8210, www.chezpapasf.com) and its more casual spouse **Chez Maman** (no.1453, 824 7166, www.chezmamansf.com) cradle their *bébé*, organic bakery **Petite Patisserie** (no.1415, 821 9378, www.petite patisserie.com), between them. Meanwhile, local bar **Bloom's Saloon**, (no.1318, 552 6707) is a low-key place to knock back a drink while drinking in the panoramic views from its back deck. Heading down the hill, the aptly named **Bottom of the Hill** (1233 17th Street, at Missouri Street; *see p234*) is the place to go for punk, metal and rockabilly bands and/or a seat on the patio, while the beautiful **Anchor Brewery** (1705 Mariposa Street, between Carolina & De Haro Streets, 863 8350, www. anchorbrewing.com) has an illustrious history as a pioneer of the American craft brewing movement. It created its first brew in 1896, and bottled its first 200 cases of Anchor Steam beer in 1971. Today, it produces various beers and spirits, including the much-admired Junipero Gin and Old Potrero Whiskey. Informative

tours (ending in the tasting room, of course) take place twice a day, by reservation only (call four to six weeks in advance).

Bernal Heights, meanwhile, boasts an eclectic mix of bars, restaurants and shops on and around Cortland Avenue, including attitude-free lesbian spot **Wild Side West** (no.424, at Bennington Street, 647 3099), which welcomes patrons of all genders and proclivities. Those with energy to burn can hike up the hill to Bernal Park, a car-free stretch that affords spectacular 360° views of the city and Bay.

The Castro

Bordered by Market, Diamond, 20th and Church Streets, the Castro is an international gay mecca. Being gay is the norm here; straights are welcome, but, for once, they're in the minority. Along this rainbow-flag-festooned stretch of trendy shops and see-and-be-seen cafés and bars, most of them gay-owned, a predominantly male populace enjoys a hard-won social and political influence.

A steadfastly working-class Irish-Catholic stronghold for nearly a century, the Castro changed rapidly in the 1970s, when gay residents began buying businesses and battered Victorian and Edwardian properties at rock-bottom prices, renovating them into what's now some of the city's prettiest and priciest real estate. No place exemplifies the

Sightseeing

At the end of the rainbow you'll find **Castro Street**.

change more than the landmark **Twin Peaks Tavern** (401 Castro Street, at Market Street, 864 9470, www.twinpeakstavern.com): its 1973 metamorphosis from traditional pub to gathering place for a mostly male and conspicuously gay clientele began just as the Castro was, so to speak, coming out. The bar's location on what was fast becoming the gayest corner of the gayest street in the country drew an ever-larger crowd, and socialising unashamedly behind its daring, pavement-fronting windows became more of a political act than a mere evening's entertainment. So strong was the sense of community in the area that the AIDS crisis of the 1980s and '90s proved to be a force as socially galvanising as it was locally disastrous.

During the week, the Castro is a relatively quiet, cheerful neighbourhood. However, on weekends (and, of course, during Pride Week), the area around Castro and 18th Streets is overrun with visitors and locals who come to mix it up at **Harvey's** (500 Castro Street, at 18th Street, 431 4278), **Moby Dick's** (4049 18th Street, at Harford Street, 861 1199, www.mobydicksf.com) and the **Bar on Castro** (456 Castro Street, between 17th & 18th Streets, 626 7220, www.thebarsf.com), and revel in the exuberantly queer party atmosphere.

A huge rainbow flag flies over **Harvey Milk Plaza** (the Muni stop at the corner of Market and Castro Streets), named after the camera-shop owner and activist who, in 1977, became San Francisco's city supervisor and the first openly gay elected official in the US, but was assassinated the following year. A small plaque in the pavement and a modest mural mark the site of Milk's former shop and campaign headquarters at 575 Castro Street, considered to be as significant in the history of gay politics as New York's Stonewall bar. He is also remembered around the area in the names of a school, a library and a community centre. *See also* *p101* **Streets of San Francisco**.

The other must-see local landmark is the dazzling art deco **Castro Theatre** (*see* *p209*). Constructed in 1922, it is one of the few American movie palaces that has remained in constant operation. It was designed by noted Bay Area architect Timothy L Pflueger, and became the 100th structure to be designated a US National Historic Landmark, 55 years after its completion. The theatre (motto: an acre of seats in a palace of dreams) has retained its original vibe, with an organist hunched over the mighty Wurlitzer pipe organ and banging out show tunes before each night's screening. Programming includes large-scale film festivals, premières, themed film series and new prints of classic movies.

For a great view of the Castro from above, get lunch to go and wander up to **Corona Heights** – walk all the way up 16th Street to Flint Street, then take a right; the bare red rock of Corona will loom overhead. Along with beautiful vistas, you'll see plenty of Castro pooches out with their humans. If you've got tinies in tow, you can also check out the animal exhibits and miniature railroad at the **Randall Museum** (199 Museum Way, 554 9600, www.randallmuseum.org).

Noe Valley

Quaint **Noe Valley**, roughly bordered by 20th, Dolores, 30th and Douglass Streets, is a self-contained village cut off from the rest of the city by steep hills on every side. In the 1970s it housed a fairly bohemian mix of straight, gay, working-class and white-collar residents, before growing more family-oriented in the 1980s and '90s – a place to which well-paid young couples could retreat to raise a family away from the chaos of the rest of the city. **Twin Peaks** overlooks the area from the west and its flanks offer attractive views of the East Bay.

Noe's main shopping strip, 24th Street, is substantially different from its funky brother that stretches east of Mission Street. This part of 24th is outfitted with all the amenities you might expect: streetside cafés, romantic restaurants and boutiques where owners and regulars are on first-name terms. The **24th Street Cheese Company** (no.3893, 821 6658) has a massive selection of cheeses, both local and international, along with a variety of snacks and charcuterie. For mystery buffs, a stop at the **San Francisco Mystery Book Store** (no.4175, at Castro, 282 7444, www.sfmysterybooks.com) is a must. Selling nothing but mystery and true crime books for 30 years, the staff have an encyclopaedic grasp of titles on the shelves. Even if you don't know what you want, they'll triangulate your tastes and send you off with something to make you shiver. Just across the street is the cosy **Firefly** (no.4288, at Douglass Street, 821 7652, www.fireflyrestaurant.com), whose warm atmosphere, carefully chosen wine list and amazingly affordable three-course prix fixe menu make it the perfect place for a romantic end to the day. A few blocks off the main drag, **Lovejoy's Antiques & Tea Room** (1351 Church Street, at Clipper Street, 648 5895, www.lovejoystearoom.com) seems to think it's in the Lake District, complete with Victorian high teas. It's a little bit out of the way, but **Mitchell's Ice Cream** (688 San José Street, at 29th Street, 648 2300, www.mitchellsicecream.com) arguably serves the city's best.

Streets of San Francisco Castro

If everyone didn't know that San Francisco was the capital of the gay world, and that Castro Street was the capital of gay San Francisco, they'd take the hint when they saw the massive rainbow flag – symbol of gay pride – cracking in the breeze above the corner of Market and Castro Streets. It was here, on 25 June 1978, that the prototype of the flag, hand-dyed by San Francisco artist Gilbert Baker, was first flown. It marked not only the heart of the neighbourhood, but the centre of a community that has given San Francisco a large part of its identity.

Castro's transformation into a gay hub, begun in the 1960s, really became visible in the '70s. Among those buying homes and businesses in the area was Harvey Milk, who moved to San Francisco in 1972 with his partner, Scott Smith, and opened a camera store in Castro Street. Over the next few years Milk became active in the gay rights movement and in local politics, running for the San Francisco Board of Supervisors. Despite being defeated twice, Milk became a prominent voice of the gay community, known as the 'Mayor of Castro Street'. It was at his third attempt, in 1977, that Milk finally became what *Time* magazine referred to as 'the first openly gay man elected to any substantial political office in the history of the planet'. Castro Street politics were now mainstream politics.

Tragically, the victory was short-lived. Dan White, a former member of the Board, approached San Francisco mayor George Moscone on 27 November 1978 with a plea to be reinstated. When his request was denied, White shot and killed the mayor. He reloaded, went to Milk's office and shot him five times. At trial, White's lawyers contended that his severe depression – as evidenced by increased consumption of Twinkies and Coca-Cola (he had formerly been a health-food zealot) – meant he had diminished responsibility for his actions. And the sugar, it was argued, could have exacerbated his mood swings. The 'Twinkie defense', as the press went on to dub it, appeared to work. White was found guilty of manslaughter rather than murder, and sentenced to just seven years.

Outraged, members of the gay community marched on City Hall, and the ensuing White Night Riots caused damage to the premises. Later that same evening, the police came to Castro Street to carry on the fight, storming the Elephant Walk bar at Castro and 18th Streets (now Harvey's) and beating up patrons.

Milk's shop premises at 575 Castro Street have recently been restored and now house **Given** (865 0353, www.givenonline.com), an art- and design-themed gift boutique. Proprietor Nick Romero commissioned painter John Baden to design a mural to honour Milk, which was completed in September 2007. Fearful of assassination, Milk had recorded audiotapes outlining his political stance and how he wished to be remembered if he met a violent death. In the mural, a pistol is aimed at Milk's head and appears to fire the words of his eerily prescient statement: 'If a bullet should enter my brain, let the bullet destroy every closet door.'

Sightseeing

The Haight & Around

Just a few hippie traces remain in what was once Counterculture Central.

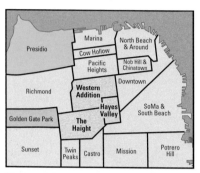

Maps p313, p314, p317 & p318

Mention the words 'Haight-Ashbury', or even just 'the Haight', and members of a certain generation will either sigh with a nostalgic longing or groan in exasperation, depending on their political persuasion and/or their psychological or physical proximity to 1967's legendary Summer of Love. However, once the crowds had tuned out, turned off and dropped back in again, the neighbourhood resumed duty as one of the most liveable and vibrant areas of San Francisco. Bordering the Haight, the Western Addition has alternately been the heart of the West Coast jazz scene and the centre of its Japanese community, while Hayes Valley has emerged as an enclave of considerable hipness.

The Haight

The Haight's history is written in its Victorian buildings, many of them painstakingly restored and elaborately painted. Despite being three miles from the ocean, the neighbourhood was considered a beach town in the mid 19th century and many wealthy families from Nob Hill kept vacation homes here. In 1870, the first San Francisco Park Commission was appointed. As development began on Golden Gate Park, the neighbouring Haight began to expand, and it was to thrive still further in the years following the 1906 earthquake, from which it emerged relatively unscathed.

As the 1950s phenomenon of 'white flight' swept through American urban areas, families left for the suburbs, and the Victorian houses of the Haight were increasingly left both vacant

and affordable. Inevitably, the city's students and post-war bohemian culture kids moved in. An offshoot of the North Beach beat scene of the late 1950s, the Haight went on to become the epicentre of hippie culture, the most famous youth movement in history. The beats, however, were scornful of the monied, pleasure-seeking hippies, considering them a kind of 'beatnik-lite': the word 'hippie' is itself said to have derived from a derogatory beatnik term meaning 'little hipster'.

In Berkeley and Oakland, the Free Speech and Black Power movements were already bringing a new political consciousness to the Bay Area. Duly inspired, the hippies were the driving force behind the anti-Vietnam War protests in San Francisco in the 1960s, and a new counterculture emerged. In January 1967, 25,000 gathered for the Human Be-In, a proto-hippie get-together that was the precursor to the Summer of Love. Yet after speed and heroin replaced marijuana and LSD as the drugs of choice, and free love turned into grim disaffection, unsavoury sorts such as Charles Manson (who lived at 636 Cole Street) emerged as gurus to the impressionable youth, counteracting the work of idealistic political groups such as the Diggers and guerrilla theatre pioneers the San Francisco Mime Troupe, who still perform today and whose anti-war message has regained its currency with the conflict in Iraq.

Just as the bold and the beautiful still flock to Hollywood from all over the world hoping to be 'discovered', so teenage runaways still gravitate to **Haight Street** looking for peace, love and understanding. Traces of the radical past linger at anarchist-run bookshop Bound Together (1369 Haight Street, at Masonic Avenue, 431 8355) and the Haight-Ashbury Free Clinic (558 Clayton Street, at Haight Street), while mellow coffeehouses hark back decades. The branch of Gap that was at the corner of Haight and Ashbury Streets has finally given up the ghost – its windows were usually either spray-painted with graffiti or smashed by the large local contingent of anti-corporate types – and has been replaced by the clothing store RVCA (1485 Haight Street, 701 7822, www.rvca clothing.com), noted for its promotion of contemporary and underground artists and its steady clientele of skateboarders and surfers.

Haight-Ashbury

The stretch of Haight Street that sits between **Masonic** and **Stanyan Streets**, known both as Haight-Ashbury and Upper Haight, makes for a lively scene on weekends and warm-weather days. Stores hawk new age and Eastern esoterica, elaborate hand-blown glass smoking paraphernalia, edgy clothing, high-fashion shoes and mountains of records and CDs, not least at the vast **Amoeba Music** (1855 Haight Street, between Shrader & Stanyan Streets, 831 1200, www.amoeba.com). Shoppers also have to duck the buskers and bums, who add more local flavour than some tourists were expecting. Just west of Amoeba, across Stanyan Street, is Golden Gate Park. A couple of blocks north is the Panhandle, the park's grand entrance; at the height of the hippie era, local bands that went on to fill stadiums (the Grateful Dead, Janis Joplin et al) played free shows here.

More evidence of the neighbourhood's past can be found at the charming **Red Victorian B&B** (1665 Haight Street, between Clayton & Cole Streets, 864 1978, www.redvic.com), which recently added a new coffee shop and retail space; the independent **Red Vic Movie House** (1727 Haight Street, at Cole Street, 668 3994, www.redvicmoviehouse.com); and the **Magnolia** brewpub (1398 Haight Street, at Masonic Avenue, 864 7468). This former pharmacy served as a hippie haven called the Drogstore Café [sic] back in the 1960s, before becoming the base for Magnolia Thunderpussy and her erotically themed desserts. The new owners have named their brewpub in her honour and covered the walls in psychedelic 1960s murals.

At the corner of Haight Street and Central Avenue is the aptly named, beautifully wooded **Buena Vista Park**, the oldest designated park in the city and the unofficial eastern terminus of Upper Haight. In 1867, when the land was still known as Hill Park, the city paid squatters $88,250 (equivalent to around $1.1 million today) to gain rights to the park. It was a wise investment, not only for the city, but in terms of the example it set for the zealous culture of land preservation that still flourishes today across northern California. The paths on the west side of the park are lined with marble gutters and a retaining wall built by WPA workers using Victorian headstones, some laid face up with their inscriptions visible. The walk to the park's 589-foot (180-metre) peak is worth the effort: the views over the city and (on clear days) out to the Golden Gate Bridge and Marin Headlands are commanding.

Life on **Haight Street**.

Sightseeing

Relaxing in **Buena Vista Park**. *See p103.*

Cole Valley

It's only a few blocks from the bustle of Haight-Ashbury, but the cosy enclave of Cole Valley is a different world altogether: low-key, smart and upscale. The businesses here are all clustered around a two-block area of **Cole** and **Carl Streets**. **Zazie** (941 Cole Street, at Carl Street, 564 5332, www.zaziesf.com) is a great spot for brunch or lunch; **Le Boulange de Cole** (1000 Cole Street, at Parnassus Street, 242 2442) serves own-made pastries, breads and small baguette sandwiches.

Alternatively, you can pick up supplies from **Say Cheese** (856 Cole Street, at Carl Street, 665 5020), which sells vast selections of gourmet cheeses, meats and wines, and enjoy a picnic on Tank Hill. Head one block west from Cole Street to Shrader Street and continue south up the hill until you reach Belgrave Street; turn left (east) on to Belgrave and take the rustic stairway at the end of the street to the top of the hill. It's a bit of a slog, but worth the effort. Once home to a water tank (hence the name), the 650-foot (200-metre) peak offers some of the city's best views, yet remains relatively unknown; it's literally overshadowed by nearby Twin Peaks.

LOWER HAIGHT

While Upper Haight still clings dreamily to its political past, the young, the disenchanted and the progressive have migrated down the hill to Lower Haight, on and around Haight Street between **Divisadero** and **Octavia Streets**. The area's main intersection is at Haight and Fillmore Streets, from which fashion shops, tattoo parlours, funky bars, ethnic eateries and pile-on-the-pancakes cafés radiate in all directions. Beer-lovers would do well to try **Toronado** (547 Haight Street, between Fillmore & Steiner Streets, 863 2276). It doesn't serve food, but you can get gourmet sausages next door at the **Rosamunde Sausage Grill** (545 Haight Street, 437 6851) and take them to the bar.

The Western Addition was not only the city's first suburb, but also its first multicultural neighbourhood. Mapped out in the 1860s to accommodate the post-Gold Rush population boom, the area was home to a thriving Jewish community from the 1890s. After the 1906 earthquake, the **Fillmore District**, the area's heart, sprang to life as displaced residents, many of them Japanese, began arriving.

After the Japanese had been removed to internment camps following Pearl Harbor, thousands of black Southerners, who had come west for work, moved into their houses. Because the area didn't observe the racial covenant laws that prevented African-Americans from owning land elsewhere in the city, the Western Addition soon developed into what became known as the 'Harlem of the West'.

Today it still has a very distinct character, with a mix of African-Americans, Russian seniors, immigrants from other countries and UCSF students who live in everything from amazing Victorians – some of the oldest in the city – to bland high-rises. Gentrification is creeping in, but slowly, and the area's shopping remains mostly chain-free. The stretch of Divisadero Street between Page and Fulton Streets holds a number of notable stops, including the **Independent** club (no.628, at Hayes Street) and the bar-restaurant **Club Waziema** (no.543, at Fell Street, 346 6641), which offers honey wine, Harar beer and Ethiopian food. The most notable addition to the area, meanwhile, is **Nopa** (no.560, 864 8643, www.nopasf.com), shorthand for North of the Panhandle and arguably the hottest restaurant in town right now, with a cuisine and a clientele that embodies a whole new neighbourhood aesthetic.

At the corner of Divisadero and Fulton, past the incense emporiums and African-American barbershops, sit yet more notable businesses, including **Café Abir** (no.1300, 567 6503; beers and magazines),**Tsunami** (no.1306, 567 7664; sushi and saké) and, serving some of the best pizza in the city, **Little Star Pizza** (846 Divisadero Street, 441 1118, www.littlestarpizza.com).

Alamo Square

San Francisco is crammed full of handsome Victorian-era houses (commonly known as 'Victorians'). However, most tourists choose not to roam the city and discover them at random; instead, they head to the 'Postcard Row' of tidy pastel Victorians on the east side of Alamo Square, which are juxtaposed wonderfully with the sweeping view of Downtown behind them. Many visitors are so taken with the homes that they wish they could stay in one; the **Alamo Square Inn** (719 Scott Street, 922 2055) offers just such an opportunity. And there are many fine Victorians nearby simply to visit; chiefly, perhaps, the ornate Italianate **Westerfield**

Streets of San Francisco Haight

For most people, the Haight-Ashbury didn't exist before the Summer of Love. But in reality, it was in the years prior to that vaunted summer of '67 that the Haight truly shone – a magnet for many talents that combined to produce an unprecedented explosion in virtually all forms of art, political discourse and even healthcare. The trouble was that as word spread about the new world of the Haight, people started to pour in – mainly to drop out – and Haight Street and the area surrounding it, arguably the world's most fecund artists' colony, turned into a kind of hippie refugee camp virtually overnight.

To hear it told by the people who lived through it, being a part of the Haight scene prior to the invasion was the closest thing to bathing in the primordial ooze of creativity (not to mention LSD). What really made the time and place unique, though, was how those many strands of creativity were fused together by a shared pursuit – re-imagining what society could be.

Legions of people who are now household names lived in close proximity. Walking down Haight Street, one might encounter the likes of the Grateful Dead, Jefferson Airplane or Janis Joplin. And that was just the beginning. The father of underground comics, Robert Crumb, might be scribbling away somewhere, while visionary musician Frank Zappa was hunched over a score with collaborator Captain Beefheart. *Howl* poet Allen Ginsberg (who once lived at 1360 Fell Street) might be found wandering the park in a trance. One might bump into Steve Miller (in his pre-Steve Miller Band days), or Jimi Hendrix (he lived

at 1524A Haight Street), or Sly and the Family Stone, or Carlos Santana, or Crosby, Stills and Nash.

Those strapped for cash could visit the Free Store run by the Diggers, a semi-anarchic group dedicated to turning the Haight into a barter society, or get medical help at the Haight-Ashbury Free Clinic. The Hell's Angels' clubhouse, meanwhile, was located across the street from the Grateful Dead's residence. (Although the Angels no longer own the building, the gang still starts its annual Thanksgiving run from the People's Café on Haight Street).

In his seminal *Fear and Loathing in Las Vegas*, Hunter S Thompson, who lived at 318 Parnassus Street, delivered a eulogy to the San Francisco of the '60s: 'There was a fantastic universal sense that whatever we were doing was right, that we were winning', he wrote. 'And that, I think, was the handle – that sense of inevitable victory over the forces of Old and Evil... Our energy would simply prevail... We had all the momentum; we were riding on the crest of a high and beautiful wave...'

The unique **Cathedral of St Mary of the Assumption**.

House, located at the corner of Fulton and Scott Streets, which dates back to 1882.

The Fillmore District

The Fillmore neighbourhood was a mecca for jazz and blues musicians in the 1940s and '50s. Several albums, among them Miles Davis's 1961 *In Person* recordings at the Blackhawk club, are testament to its pedigree. However, the locale was declared a slum by the San Francisco Redevelopment Agency in the 1960s and torn apart under the guise of urban renewal.

Luckily, new life is being slowly and steadily breathed into the area. New from November 2007 is the San Francisco branch of the much-loved Oakland-based **Yoshi's Jazz Club**. Yoshi's at Fillmore Heritage Center (1330 Fillmore Street, at Eddy Street, 665 5600, www.yoshis.com) will include a sushi restaurant and a purpose-built 400-seat venue. If the track record established at its Oakland location is any indication, guests will have access to truly world-class concerts.

The legendary **Fillmore Auditorium** (1805 Geary Boulevard, at Fillmore Street, 346 6000, www.thefillmore.com) is still going strong, booking top-flight rock and independent acts. So close you can almost hear the ghosts is the now-defunct Winterland (formerly at the north-west corner of Post and Steiner Streets), where The Band filmed *The Last Waltz* and Johnny Rotten asked the audience 'Ever get the feeling you've been cheated?' at the final Sex Pistols show in 1978 (Sid Vicious endured a non-fatal overdose at the Haight's 32 Delmar Street following the show).

Yards away, on the wall of the Hamilton Recreation Center at the corner of Post and Steiner, is a huge musical mural, created by local musician and painter Santie Huckaby over a two-year span. The mural features dozens of musicians with an SF connection: some lived here, some simply played here, and one, John Lee Hooker, even opened his own club here. Hooker died in 2001, but the **Boom Boom Room** (1601 Fillmore Street, at Geary Boulevard; *see p230*) is still open for business. Next to the Fillmore Auditorium, at 1849 Geary Boulevard, is an eerier landmark. A post office has stood here in recent years, but from 1971 to 1977 this site was the home of the notorious Jim Jones and his People's Temple. Despite running his own legendarily cultish church, Jones was a respectable citizen. However, when reports emerged of physical and sexual abuse within the church, he moved it from here to a settlement he named Jonestown located in French Guyana. The following year, Jones and almost 1,000 disciples, the majority former Fillmorites, committed mass suicide or were murdered in the now-infamous Jonestown Massacre.

Japantown

Three commercial blocks and a compound-like shopping mall are all that remains of what once may have been the US's largest Japanese community. Devastated by the forced relocation of Japanese-Americans during World War II, sent by the government to internment camps after the surprise attack by the Japanese on Hawaii's Pearl Harbor, the community is now

Cathedral of St Mary of the Assumption

1111 Gough Street, at Geary Boulevard (567 2020/ www.stmarycathedralsf.org). Bus 2, 3, 4, 38. **Open** 6.45am-4pm Mon-Fri, Sun; 6.45am-5.30pm Sat. **Admission** free.

Dominating the skyline, the exterior of this 1970 cathedral is stark, a flowing, sculptural structure (some say it resembles the blades of a washing machine) reaching 198ft (60m) into the sky. The four corner pylons were designed to support millions of pounds of pressure and extend 90ft (27m) down to the bedrock beneath the church. Inside, the staggering structure of the cupola is revealed in 1,500 triangular coffers, in over 128 sizes, meant to distribute the weight of the roof. The trumpets of the huge organ, on a raised pedestal that floats above the congregation, appear capable of blasting down the walls of Jericho. Large corner windows allow views of the city.

HAYES VALLEY

Hayes Valley, just west of the Civic Center, was literally overshadowed by the Central Freeway for years. However, when the 1989 earthquake all but destroyed the roadway, it also hurried the transformation of the area from drug- and prostitution-riddled slum to perhaps the hippest urban shopping area in town. Streets that once sat under a tangle of concrete overpasses now have sidewalk cafés, boutiques, galleries and even **True Sake** (560 Hayes Street, at Laguna Street; *see p190*), a specialist saké shop.

The locals know how good they've got it. The community association is active here, and gets results: it has fought to keep out the chains (current score: Hayes Valley 1, Starbucks 0), won the battle to close the major Fell Street highway off-ramp, and established a little tree-lined boulevard along Octavia Street, home to great soul-food eaterie **J's Pots of Soul** (no.203, at Page Street; 861 3230). During the day, Hayes Street gets busy with well-dressed couples shopping for modernist furniture and Italian shoes, and brunching on champagne and oysters at **Absinthe** (no.388, at Gough Street, 551 1590, www.absinthe.com), a belle époque French restaurant with tables spilling on to the pavement. Don't miss the stretch of Market Street between Gough Street and Van Ness Avenue, a shopping hub for deco antiques and upmarket accessories. But be wary of walking west of Laguna Street at night: the area changes abruptly and can occasionally feel a bit dicey.

Based in the city for three decades, the **African Orthodox Church of St John Coltrane** at 1286 Fillmore Street (at Eddy Street, 673 7144, www.coltranechurch.org), where it continues to hold jazz-driven services – Coltrane's seminal invocation of the divine, 'A Love Supreme', is the key work – every Sunday at noon.

home to only a tiny percentage of the city's 12,000 Japanese-Americans. But the locale still provides support for the elderly, history lessons for the young and a banquet of aesthetic and pop-cultural delights for anyone interested.

At the heart of Japantown is the Japan Center, a mostly underground maze of shops, restaurants and unique businesses that cater to Japanese residents. The **Kinokuniya Bookstore** (1581 Webster Street, 567 7625) is a fascinating clearing-house of J-pop culture, comics and Japanese-language books, while **Paper Tree** (1743 Buchanan Mall, 921 7100, www.paper-tree.com) specialises in origami supplies. Set to open in early 2008 is another hugely anticipated tenant: the **Sundance Kabuki Theater** (1881 Post Street, at Fillmore Street, 929 4650, www.sundancecinemas.com), which takes over the current mainstream cinema on this site. The Sundance Kabuki complex will be the flagship cinema of actor/activist Robert Redford's film company. Seven screens with stadium seating will feature the latest independent films and the winners of Redford's renowned Sundance Film Festival. There will also be two bars and an upscale bistro.

To gain a bit of cultural context on the area, visit the **National Japanese American Historical Society** (684 Post Street, between Buchanan & Laguna Streets, 921 5007, www. nikkeiheritage.org) or the nearby **Japanese American Community Center** (1840 Sutter Street, at Webster Street, 567 5505, www. jcccnc.org), which hosts exhibitions on the Japanese-American way of life. To the east of the Japan Center, meanwhile, is the impressively modern **Cathedral of St Mary of the Assumption**.

Sightseeing

Sunset, Golden Gate Park & Richmond

Head west until you hit the ocean – unless you get sidetracked on the way.

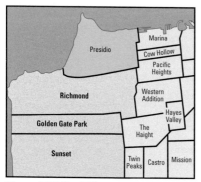

Map p312 & p316

To many visitors, and some San Franciscans, the **Richmond** and **Sunset** districts are largely unexplored areas that sandwich the verdant expanse of **Golden Gate Park**, one of San Francisco's greatest attractions. And that's fine with the locals, who tend to be a bit more unassuming, a bit less concerned with appearances and a bit more welcoming than those in other neighbourhoods. This happy melange of active immigrant communities, students, families, working-class folk and, by the ocean, surfers, also enjoys the city's very best coastal trails. Less crowded, less touristy, less flashy and more foggy: for some, this is the real San Francisco.

Sunset & further south

This large southern neighbourhood, west of the Haight and south of Golden Gate Park, usually belies its own name. The sunsets in the Sunset are more often than not swathed in fog from June to September, and often in other months too, but if you do catch a fair day, they can be spectacular.

The stretch of **Irving Street** between 5th and 10th Avenues, in an area informally known as the **Inner Sunset**, is the area's shopping corridor. Just off Irving on 9th Avenue sit two fine eateries: sushi stop **Ebisu** (no.1283, 566 1770, www.ebisusushi.com), and **Park Chow**

(no.1240, 665 9912, www.chowrestaurant.com). However, the Sunset's main attractions are way west, out where the land meets the water. Perhaps chief among them is thin, sandy **Ocean Beach** (*see p117* **Beach life**), which runs for roughly three and a half miles south from the **Cliff House** (*see p115*). It's a good spot for a contemplative wander, to spend time watching the surfers (who sometimes count Sunset homeowner and rocker Chris Isaak among their number) battling strong rip tides and chilly water. Take a warming break either over coffee at the **Java Beach Café** (*see p157*) or with a garlic whole-roasted crab at Vietnamese restaurant **Thanh Long** (4101 Judah Street, at 46th Avenue, 665 1146, www.anfamily.com).

The southernmost point of Ocean Beach is marked by **Fort Funston**, a large natural area in the far south-west of the city. The reservation is criss-crossed with hiking trails, dramatic promontories and jagged beaches, and is both a favourite place for local dog-walkers and a point from which hang-gliders launch themselves above the waves.

Just over a mile north of Fort Funston is **San Francisco Zoo** (*see p205*), one of very few zoos to house koalas. Beyond the zoo is the recently refurbished **Harding Municipal Park & Golf Course** (*see p247*). Cradled by picturesque Lake Merced and encircled by lovely biking and jogging trails, the new design of the public course is so admired that it played host to the 2005 World Golf Championships, although anyone can play there provided they've reserved a tee time. North of the lake is Stern Grove, just over 60 acres of eucalyptus and redwood that hosts the annual **Stern Grove Festival** (*see p231*). And slightly further inland is **Mount Davidson**, which, at 927 feet (283 metres) is the highest point in San Francisco. If you can ignore the enormous cross that sits at its apex, the views are terrific. If you can't, you are not alone: the cross has been a source of controversy – and a victim of several arson attacks – since it was first erected in 1923. In 1991, several organisations sued the city, claiming that such an overt religious display on public land was illegal under US law. The

Ocean Beach.

city then auctioned the parcel of land on which the cross stood to the highest bidder and the Council of Armenian-American Organizations of Northern California won, dedicating it to the victims of the 1915 Armenian genocide and thus keeping the cross in place for future generations to variously love and loathe.

Golden Gate Park

Roughly three miles in length and half a mile wide, **Golden Gate Park** is one of the largest man-made parks in the world and a testament to human dominion over nature – or, put another way, a gargantuan project that introduced non-native species and used vast resources in ways that would never have been approved in modern-day San Francisco. The ambitious task of creating this pastoral loveliness – a thousand acres of landscaped gardens, forests and meadows – from barren sand dunes began in 1870 in an attempt to solidify San Francisco's position as a modern urban centre, to meet the growing public demand for a city park, and, on the part of the wealthy land speculators in the area, to stimulate property values.

William Ralston, founder of the Bank of California and builder of the Palace Hotel, first approached Frederick Law Olmsted, the visionary behind Manhattan's Central Park, to design the project. Believing that the arid landscape of the Outside Lands, as the virtually uninhabited area was then known, was a barren wasteland that could never support a park,

Olmsted's original design instead proposed a green stretch that would take advantage of the large natural valley that ran through the city. However, once Olmsted left town, his plan was shelved; the valley he planned to utilise is now Van Ness Avenue.

The project was next awarded to a young civil engineer named William Hammond Hall. The park's wealthy patrons, whose motives were more fiscal- than civic-minded, saw Hall as a sympathetic individual who would accede to their plans for the land development, and they were right. Hall's family was hooked into every level of government and industry, and many felt that he had been handed an impossible task. Olmsted even wrote to Hall, telling him that he 'did not believe it practicable to meet the natural but senseless demand of unreflecting people bred in the Atlantic states and the North of Europe for what is technically termed a park under the climatic conditions of San Francisco'.

Work continued, however, and while it cost the surrounding environment dearly, the result was clearly a marvel. Still, it wasn't until eccentric Scottish-born John McLaren took over stewardship in 1890 that the park finally came together (*see p110* **Walk**). McLaren spent more than 50 years as park superintendent, expanding on Hall's innovations and planting by stages, to allow what are now the lakes, meadows and forests of the park to evolve in ways that would allow the substrate to sustain them. In the process, he was responsible for planting more than a million trees.

Walk Golden wander

Start your tour of Golden Gate Park at the **McLaren Lodge** (John F Kennedy Drive, 831 2700). Once the residence of John McLaren, the lodge is now the site of the park offices and visitors' centre (open 8am-5pm Mon-Fri). Strike out south from the lodge down the tree-lined path running parallel to Stanyan Street, bearing right until you come to **Alvord Lake**. Keep right by the lake and pass under Alvord Lake Bridge, which dates to 1889. It was the first reinforced concrete bridge built in the US and one of few bridges to survive the 1906 earthquake, vindicating its builder's then-controversial faith in concrete construction.

Head through to Mothers' Meadow until you reach a fork. The left branch brings you to the recently (and inventively) restored **Children's Playground**, the oldest municipal playground in the nation and home to the 62 hand-painted animals of the wonderful 1912 Herschel-Spillman Carousel. North, past the Sharon Art Building, is Sharon Meadow. You'll hear **Hippie Hill**, in the middle of the meadow, before you see it. The hill became the heart of the Summer of Love; the never-ending pick-up drum jams on the hill are still going strong.

Follow the path north to the tennis courts and continue round their right-hand side. Cross John F Kennedy Drive after you emerge from the trees to take in the gleaming, white-domed **Conservatory of Flowers** up to your left. Badly damaged by a storm in 1995, it reopened to considerable excitement in 2003 after an eight-year, $25-million restoration.

It's the oldest glass-and-wood Victorian greenhouse in the western hemisphere, and is home to more than 10,000 plants.

Take the stairs up to JFK Drive and head along Middle East Drive. On your left is the 7.5-acre **National AIDS Memorial Grove**. It bears the names of some of the city's nearly 20,000 dead engraved in stone amid redwoods, oaks and maples. (For a guided tour, call 750 8340.) Opposite, a path leads north to the lovely **Lily Pond**. Follow it round the west side to the crossroads. On the right, a grove of ferns dates to 1898. Head straight on, taking the footpath to your left that parallels JFK Drive, to another botanical delight: the **John McLaren Rhododendron Dell**. Lovingly restored following the same storm that damaged the Conservatory of Flowers, it holds a statue of McLaren himself. Further on stands a memorial to another Scotsman, Robert Burns.

Here you have a choice: carry on west towards the **De Young Museum** (see p113) before heading south, or amble south along the leafy walkways to the **California Academy of Sciences** complex (see p112). From either venue, press on across the Music Concourse through the arch in the Temple of Music to reach the **Japanese Tea Garden** (752 1171, $3.50). Built in 1893 for the Exposition, the landmark garden – ironically, the spot where the Chinese fortune cookie is said to have been invented – still delights visitors with its steep bridges, bonsai, huge bronze Buddha

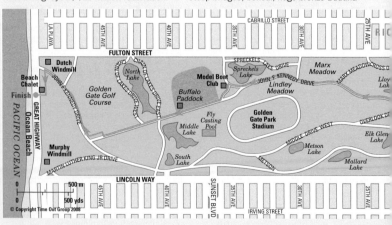

and outdoor tearoom with kimono-clad servers. Another nice stopping-off point is the **Strybing Arboretum & Botanical Gardens** (661 1316), which house some 7,000 species from diverse climates. There's a fragrant garden designed for the visually impaired and a particularly appealing moon-viewing garden. The John Muir Nature Trail focuses on local flora.

Return to MLK Drive, head west up the hill and take the stairs to Stow Lake. Wandering along the broad path on the south side of the lake, you'll come to the **Rustic Bridge**: cross here to explore Strawberry Hill island and its Chinese pavilion. A gift from the people of Taipei, it was shipped in 6,000 pieces and reassembled here in 1981. Head round the lake to the **Boathouse**, where paddle boats, canoes and bicycles are available for rent.

From the Boathouse walk north. Pick up the path to the left of the restrooms across the parking lot, and you'll come out opposite **Rainbow Falls** and the **Prayer Book Cross**, which commemorates Sir Francis Drake's chaplain offering up prayers during their brief holiday in the Bay Area in 1579. Follow the little waterway west under Cross Over Drive Bridge and across Transverse Drive to Lloyd Lake and the **Portals of the Past**, the only memorial in the city devoted to the 1906 earthquake and fire. The ornate marble archway that now stands here was once the front entrance to the Towne Mansion at 1101 California Street, home of Alban Towne; it was

the last structure left standing atop Nob Hill following the great fire. From there JFK Drive takes you through meadows offering plenty of picnicking opportunities. After about half a mile, you'll come to **Spreckels Lake**, with its ducks and model sailing boats.

When you're ready, get back on to JFK (passing the San Francisco Model Yacht Club on your right) and press ever west. Almost immediately, on your right, you'll pass the large **Buffalo Paddock**, where a small herd of bison roams on a 'prairie'. Pass Chain of Lakes Drive West on your right and keep going for about five minutes. Just past the golf course (watch for stray balls), you'll find a pleasant tree-lined pedestrian path that will take you round to the north, and soon to **Queen Wilhelmina's Tulip Gardens**. A gift from the eponymous Dutch monarch in 1902, the garden is shaded by the commanding **Dutch Windmill**, aka the North Windmill, which boasts the world's largest windmill wings. It functioned as a huge pump, feeding water to the verdant urban wonderland that is now Golden Gate Park but which was once only sand dunes. The windmill recently underwent a $6.4-million restoration, and was turning once more for a while, though at the time of writing it seemed to have stopped again.

Head through the tunnel or across the road on one of the wooded paths and you'll shortly be at journey's end: the 80-year-old **Beach Chalet** and the new **Park Chalet** (*see p112*). Bus 5 will take you back to civilisation.

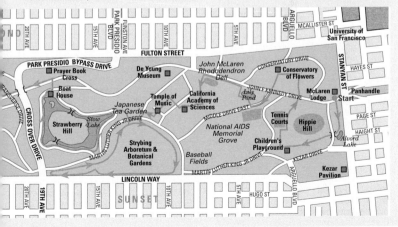

Golden Gate Park. *See p109.*

The park's public debut occurred in 1894, when more than 1.3 million people visited for the Midwinter International Exposition. Covering around 200 acres, the six-month fair filled more than 100 temporary buildings. Two still remain: the **Japanese Tea Garden** and the **Music Concourse**. As the park's fame spread in the wake of the exposition, horticulturalists from all over the world sent in seeds and cuttings. Today, a rose garden, a Shakespeare garden, a rhododendron dell and a tulip garden are among hundreds of living delights; the colours dazzle on a sunny day and console on a foggy one. Among all the soaring eucalyptus and pine trees, the city is so rarely in view that it is easily forgotten.

Sampling all that the park has to offer, from the assorted natural attractions to the violently modern new **De Young Museum** (*see p113*), would take days. The prospect is even more daunting when one adds in a new natural history museum, the **California Academy of Sciences** (*see below*), due to open in autumn 2008. Its design is a marvel of green engineering.

However, one great way to see it over the course of a single afternoon is to stroll all the way from the entrance of the park along the pedestrian footpaths beside John F Kennedy

Drive, the park's main east–west artery, to the ocean. It takes a few hours if you stop along the way, but your reward will be the crashing waves of the Pacific. If you prefer to travel on wheels, then bikes and in-line skates can be hired from various locations. Indeed, if you join the throngs of locals biking, walking, jogging and in-line skating along JFK Drive on a Sunday afternoon, when the road is closed to traffic, you'll soon understand why the park is known as San Francisco's collective backyard.

If you're planning on entering Golden Gate Park from Haight-Ashbury, you can do so at the west end of Haight Street by crossing Stanyan Street. Otherwise, come in via the Panhandle, a couple of blocks north. This was once the grand entrance to the park, designed with paths wide enough to accommodate carriages. It brings you out next to the park headquarters in McLaren Lodge, where you can pick up information. For a self-guided tour of the park, *see p110* **Walk**.

Beach Chalet & Park Chalet

1000 Great Highway (visitor centre 751 2766/ restaurant 386 8439/www.beachchalet.com). Bus 5, 18. **Open** *Visitor centre & Beach Chalet 9am-10.30pm daily. Park Chalet noon-10.30pm daily.* **Credit** AmEx, DC, MC, V.

A perfect spot for sunset cocktails, the Beach Chalet, a historic Willis Polk-designed building on the coast, is home to a fine restaurant and brewpub. The ground-floor walls are awash in WPA (Works Progress Administration) frescoes by Lucien Labaudt depicting notable San Franciscans, among them sculptor Benny Bufano and John McLaren. The views of the ocean from upstairs are stupendous.

The newer Park Chalet, which faces Golden Gate Park, doesn't have the views of the Beach Chalet. However, the more mellow atmosphere makes it ideal for whiling away a sunny afternoon in one of the Adirondack chairs arrayed around the beautifully landscaped lawns, or cooling off with a beer after a walk along Ocean Beach.

California Academy of Sciences

55 Concourse Drive (321 8000/www.calacademy. org). Bus 5, 44. **Map** *p316 C9.*
Note: Details of opening hours and admission prices had not been made available as this guide went to press. Phone or visit the website for information.
How has life on earth evolved? How do we foster the respect needed to preserve and protect its future? These are the themes the California Academy of Sciences will tackle when it opens in new – and architecturally stunning – premises in autumn 2008. The $484-million facility will house an extraordinary wealth of exhibits; luckily, the 20 million research specimens and 38,000 live animals already in the collections of this 152-year-old institution have given the authorities something of a head start on the project. It was always hoped that the

building would be a masterpiece of green architecture, and Renzo Piano's design, clearly inspired by
the natural world, doesn't disappoint. The organically shaped living roof – a vast expanse of green,
undulating domes – will eventually accommodate
1.7 million native flowers and plants.

Inside, exhibits cover a huge spectrum of life on
our planet – and worlds beyond. They include the
country's largest planetarium; its 90ft-tall (27m)
domed screen allows visitors to watch real-time
NASA feeds. Elsewhere, the 212,000-gallon tank of
the Steinhart Aquarium will be home to 4,000 fish
and 1,500 colonies of living coral. The four-storey
rainforest exhibit takes visitors along a spiral walkway that takes them from ground level to above the
tree canopy, where birds and butterflies fly free.
Visitors can also take an elevator to an underground
tropical habitat beneath the forest that includes a
water tunnel, home to anacondas, piranhas and
giant catfish. Another exhibit recreates the environment of an American subtropical swamp, with
inhabitants including a rare white alligator. Other
displays showcase the zoological landscape of
Africa by means of traditional dioramas, explore
biodiversity and the effect of climate change on natural habitats in California, recreate the California
coast, and examine insights gained by expeditions
and the latest scientific discoveries.

De Young Museum

50 Hagiwara Tea Garden Drive (863 3330/www.
deyoungmuseum.org). Bus 5, 44. **Open** 9.30am-
5.15pm Tue-Thur, Sat, Sun; 9.30am-8.45pm Fri.
Admission $10; $6-$7 reductions; free under-12s.
Credit AmEx, DC, MC, V. **Map** p316 B9.
The most prominent feature of this controversial new
future-primitive building, designed by Herzog & de
Meuron, is the massive tower that emerges from the
surrounding canopy of trees, making all those who
approach from the 10th Avenue entrance to Golden
Gate Park feel like the vanguard of an expedition
that's just stumbled across an ancient lost city – or
an abandoned mothership. Most peole would agree
that the design – seemingly a combination of extra-
terrestrial metals wedded to sharp angles and
organic forms found in ancient structures (like a surreal interpretation of the temples of Machu Picchu)
– is at once overwhelming and electrifying. The exterior walls are all made from patterned copper
designed to take on the colour of the surrounding
greenery as they oxidise. While the jury is still out
about the building's exterior, the quality of its con-
tents is not in doubt. Along with its vast collections
of American art from the 17th to 20th centuries, the
museum showcases an extensive collection from
New Guinea and the Oceania, as well as contemporary crafts and textiles. There's also an excellent
store and café with outdoor seating areas. However,
with commanding views over the park, the soaring
observation tower is worth the trip alone. The courtyard, café, store, sculpture garden and tower can be
entered without paying the admission fee.

Richmond

Bordering the northern edge of Golden Gate
Park, from beyond Arguello Boulevard to the
Pacific Ocean, and from Fulton to California
Streets, the largely residential neighbourhood
of Richmond is a highly flavoured cultural mix,
predominantly but not exclusively made up of
Russian, Chinese and Irish immigrants. Once
a sandy waterfront wasteland, the region was
developed after the construction of the Geary
Boulevard tramway in 1906. Eastern European
Jews formed a strong community after World
War I, and many of their synagogues and
delicatessens still thrive.

The **University of San Francisco** and
the peculiar **Columbarium** (*see p115*) hover
at the easterly edge of the area, but **Clement
Street** is the district's primary commercial
centre. Stretching from 2nd Avenue all the
way to 34th Avenue, the stretch of Clement
Street between Arguello and Park Presidio
Boulevards arguably offers a more accessible
Chinatown than the more famous one in the
centre of the city. It's also more pleasant:
the wider streets and lack of tourists make
browsing the stores for Asian groceries and
kitchenware a pleasure.

Literary types have long been enamoured
of **Green Apple Books** (506 Clement Street,
at 6th Avenue; *see p178*). Just a block north is
the **Antique Traders** (4300 California Street,
at 5th Avenue, 668 4444, www.theantique
traders.com), whose breathtaking collection of
stained-glass windows, salvaged from the city's
many Victorians, has countless out-of-town
shoppers calculating shipping costs. Tucked
away behind the misleadingly tiny shopfront,
6th Ave Flowers & Aquarium (425
Clement Street, between 5th & 6th Avenues,
668 7190, www.6thaveaquarium.com) is a
store that rivals many municipal aquariums
in its selection of sea creatures, among them
dwarf jellyfish and bioluminescent shrimp,
which swim through the cumulative 13,000
gallons of water in their tanks.

Speaking of shrimp, the takeout dumplings
from **Good Luck Dim Sum** (no.736, at 8th
Avenue, 386 3388) are authentic and cheap
(you can get stuffed for under $5). Super-funky
Q Restaurant (no.225, at 3rd Avenue; *see
p157*) serves up American comfort food in a
mildly surreal setting; the Burmese specialities
at **Burma Superstar** (no.309, at 4th Avenue,
387 2147, www.burmasuperstar.com) are
inspired; and **Chapeau!** (no.1408, at 15th
Avenue, 750 9787) offers more upscale ambience,
highlighting Provençal cuisine. One block south
of Clement is **Geary Boulevard**, Richmond's
main thoroughfare. Fine home-made ice-cream

Hidden 'hoods

San Francisco is a city of neighbourhoods, each one a walkable universe in its own right; ignore these local microcosms in favour of tourist hotspots like Fisherman's Wharf and you'll be in danger of missing San Francisco as the locals live and live it. Read on, however, to discover some of the more multifaceted, lesser-known 'hoods that city dwellers call home.

Tucked into the hillside to the south of San Francisco's vibrant Mission District, **Bernal Heights** is a funky and family-friendly area. It's home to biannual soap box derbies (held on Sunday afternoons before Halloween and Mother's Day), which see local residents racing home-made three- and four-wheeled contraptions down a steep road in Bernal Heights Park. The area's tiny shopping strip is Cortland Avenue, which extends between Mission Street and the industrial Bay Shore Boulevard, and where rollicking lesbian bar **Wild Side West** (424 Cortland Avenue, between Bennington & Wool Streets; *see p225*) welcomes patrons of all sexual persuasions, and the **Liberty Café** (410 Cortland Avenue, between Bennington & Wool Streets, 695 8777, www.thelibertycafe. com) serves up homestyle American fare. Nearby, the café **Progressive Grounds** (400 Cortland Avenue, between Bennington & Wool Streets, 282 6233) offers top-notch coffee and sandwiches, and boasts a lovely back patio for fair weather refreshment.

Another locale worth hunting down is **Glen Park**, south of Noe Valley, which boasts its own BART station as well as a good range of mom 'n' pop shops and a plethora of homey restaurants. Tiny **Gialina** (2842 Diamond Street, between Bosworth & Chenery Streets, 239 8500) serves up

authentic thin-crust Neapolitan pizzas and regional Italian specialities, while **Le P'tit Laurent** (699 Chenery Street, at Diamond Street, 334 3235) is a short hop over the road and a local favourite for unpretentious French food and wine. The neighbourhood itself is named after **Glen Canyon Park**, a 70-acre refuge for urban wildlife including possums, skunks, raccoons, red-tailed hawks, great-horned owls and alligator lizards, not to mention a romping ground for local dogs and a good spot to practise low-level, rope-free rock climbing.

Foggy **Outer Richmond**, meanwhile, is home to a small shopping district on Balboa Street, a neighbourhood within a neighbourhood that lays claim to a great local cinema, the **Balboa** (3630 Balboa Street, at 38th Avenue, 221 8184, www.balboamovies.com), which screens a mixture of new releases and indie gems. Grab a pre-show dinner of Shanghai-style soup at the nearby **Shanghai Dumpling Shop** (3319 Balboa Street, at 35th Avenue, 387 2088), and indulge in a nightcap afterwards at the rough-and-ready **Hockey Haven** (3625 Balboa Street, at 38th Avenue, 752 4413), or the **Simple Pleasures Café** (3434 Balboa Sreet, at 36th Avenue, 387 4022), which hosts live jazz in the evenings.

Finally, the hyper-affluent **Sea Cliff** neighbourhood, along the Pacific Ocean just west of the Golden Gate Bridge, has played home to some of San Francisco's most famous inhabitants over the years – Robin Williams and Sharon Stone are two of the most notable – and is a great spot for the shameless ogling of mansions. It's also home to tiny **China Beach**, where in-the-know locals head to both sunbathe and stargaze in the summer months.

can be found at **Joe's** (no.5351, between 17th & 18th Avenues, 751 1950). Heading deeper into the avenues you will stumble across **Tommy's Mexican Restaurant** (no.5929, at 23rd Avenue), with 250 pure agave tequilas on offer. The much-admired 'free wine while you wait' policy is an added bonus at **Pacific Café** (no.7000, at 34th Avenue, 387 7091), which serves fresh seafood.

Out at 34th Avenue, turn north back over Clement into Lincoln Park and you'll find the **California Palace of the Legion of Honor** (*see p115*), built by George Applegarth to pay homage to the Palais de la Legion d'Honneur in

Paris. Just north of the car park is the haunting **Jewish Holocaust Memorial**, created by George Segal. The surrounding wooded and hilly park contains the 18-hole **Lincoln Park Golf Course** (*see p247*) and a number of well-maintained hiking trails, shaded by twisted cypresses that meander along the spectacular cliffs of Land's End.

At the westerly end of the Richmond, **Sutro Heights Park** is a tiny idyll, virtually empty except for a few Russians walking their dogs or playing chess. A statue of the goddess Diana is often decorated with flowers by local pagans. In the nearby garden, enjoy a secluded picnic and marvel at the captivating panoramic view of the Pacific. If the weather's not good enough, head across the street below Sutro Heights Park to **Louis' Restaurant** (902 Point Lobos Avenue, 387 6330), a 70-year-old 'greasy spoon' that serves milkshakes and ham steaks at Formica counters. The views of the ocean rival those from the somewhat touristy and pricey **Cliff House** (*see below*) down the road; both perch on the very edge of the city.

The Cliff House was the brainchild of silver baron and former mayor Adolph Sutro, who owned most of the land on the western side of the city. The remains of Sutro's own mansion are at the western edge of Sutro Heights Park; below the Cliff House to the north are the ruins of Sutro Baths, built by the man himself in 1896 and once the world's biggest swimming baths. Fed by the Pacific, seven pools holding more than one and a half million gallons of water could be filled by the tides in one hour. The baths were destroyed by fire in 1966, but the ruins are strangely photogenic. A windswept three-mile coastal path winds north towards the Golden Gate Bridge.

California Palace of the Legion of Honor

Lincoln Park, at 34th Avenue & Clement Street (750 3600/www.thinker.org). Bus 1, 2, 18, 38. **Open** 9.30am-5.15pm Tue-Sun. **Admission** $10; $6-$7 reductions; free under-12s. Free 1st Tue of mth. **Credit** AmEx, DC, MC, V.

Built as a memorial to the Californians who died in World War I, and set in a wooded spot overlooking the Pacific Ocean, the Palace of the Legion of Honor is San Francisco's most beautiful museum, its neo-classical façade and Beaux Arts interior virtually unchanged since it was completed in 1924. A cast of Rodin's *The Thinker* dominates the entrance; the French sculptor was the personal passion of Alma Spreckels, the museum's founder, and the collection of his work here is second only to that of the Musée Rodin in Paris. A glass pyramid acts as a skylight for galleries containing more than 87,000 works of art, spanning 4,000 years but with the emphasis on European painting and decorative art (El Greco, Rembrandt, Monet). An expanded garden level houses temporary exhibitions, the Achenbach Foundation for Graphic Arts and the Bowles Collection of porcelain.

Cliff House

1090 Point Lobos Avenue, at the Great Highway (386 3330/www.cliffhouse.com). Bus 18, 38. **Open** *Bar/restaurant* 11.30am-3.30pm, 5-9.30pm daily. *Bistro* 9am-9.30pm Mon-Sat; 8.30am-9.30pm Sun. *Walkways* 24hrs daily. **Credit** AmEx, DC, MC, V.

After a fire in 1894, a magnificent, eight-storey Victorian turreted palace replaced the original 1860s house on this site. However, only a year after surviving the 1906 earthquake, the second building

also burned. Its subsequent 'restorations' involved more demolition and rebuilding; the current, contemporary structure, completed in 2004, includes an upscale restaurant and bar with floor-to-ceiling glass walls that make the most of its breathtaking Pacific views. Public walkways allow the less well-heeled to amble around the building. The whimsical camera obscura, a 19th-century optical marvel, was saved after a public outcry halted its demolition and is still accessible on the walkway; it projects an image of the outside world, including a large stretch of Ocean Beach, on to a giant parabolic screen using mirrors and lenses.

Columbarium

1 Loraine Court, off Anza Street (752 7891). Bus 31, 33, 38. **Open** 9am-5pm Mon-Fri; 10am-3pm Sat, Sun. **Admission** free. **Map** p316 D7.

This round, domed neo-classical rotunda is honeycombed with hundreds of niches, all filled with lavishly and individualistically decorated cremation urns. Among them are the remains of many of the city's first families, such as the Folgers (of coffee fame), the Magnins and the Kaisers. With the exception of the Presidio's military cemetery, it's the only active burial site in the city: a 1901 law made burial illegal within San Francisco, and all graves were moved south to the town of Colma. Indeed, most Richmond residents are unaware that their homes were built on a massive 167-acre cemetery now known as the Richmond district, which centred around the Columbarium.

Columbarium.

Sightseeing

Pacific Heights to the Golden Gate Bridge

There's a lot to see en route to that iconic San Francisco landmark.

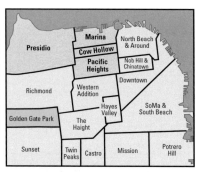

Maps pp312-313 & p314

If there's one classic San Francisco view – in a city with a multitude – it is the vista across the Bay from Pacific Heights and the northern waterfront. What sets this view apart from all the others is the presence of the iconic Golden Gate Bridge. It's hard to imagine the view without the bridge, but the very wealthy had already staked their claim to these hills well before its construction began in 1933.

The area covered in this chapter spans Bush Street to the Bay and from Van Ness Avenue to the Presidio, and it has much to offer beyond the engineering marvel that grabs all the attention. The Pacific Heights mansions overlook some of the most beautiful coastline in the United States, while the vast expanses of wooded trails and cliffs in the former military base of the Presidio run up against the well-scrubbed opulence of the Marina.

Pacific Heights

True to its name, **Pacific Heights** peers over the Pacific from on high, its mansions home to the cream of San Francisco's high society for generations. The Casebolt house at 2727 Pierce Street was built in 1866, the Burr mansion at 1772 Vallejo Street in 1878 and the Flood mansion (which now operates as a school) at 2222 Broadway was completed in 1901. One of the newest mansions in the neighbourhood is a little way down the road at 2845 Broadway:

construction on this Frankenstein's monster of a home was only 40 per cent complete when it sold in 2002 for $32 million – the most ever paid for a home in San Francisco at the time. The new owner spent the next five years pumping an additional $18 million into the house and, at the time of writing, no one has ever lived in the building, although it was recently put on the market for $65 million. You need to be a millionaire to buy around here; normal people, meanwhile, can get a taste of the Heights life at the recently opened **Hotel Drisco** (2901 Pacific Avenue, 346 2880, www.jdvhotels.com/drisco), housed in a grand building constructed in 1903.

As if anyone needed further proof of the neighbourhood's cup running over, billionaire socialites Gordon and Ann Getty and Oracle billionaire Larry Ellison have houses here, as do many of the famous 'old' families of San Francisco (the Floods, the Bechtels and others).

The eastern edge of the neighbourhood contains some beautiful Victorian houses. The blue-and-white **Octagon House** (*see p118*) is perhaps the most famous, but there are also rich pickings to the south: the **Haas-Lilienthal House** (*see p118*), for example, which offers visitors a rare chance to see inside a grand old Queen Anne. Nearby is the ornate **Spreckels Mansion**, which spans the entire block between Jackson, Gough, Washington and Octavia Streets. Built by sugar heir Adolph Spreckels for his young wife Alma (the model for the statue that adorns the top of the Dewey Monument in Union Square), the 'Parthenon of the West' has been used as a location in several films, most notably Steve McQueen's *Bullitt*. It's now home to the novelist Danielle Steel.

Wander west from here, perhaps stopping in **Lafayette Park** (Washington & Gough Streets) to watch pedigree dogs walking their pedigree owners, to the stretch of **Fillmore Street** between Bush and Jackson Streets. This is the main shopping hub of the area, lined with smart shops and restaurants. A few blocks west, elegant antiques shops, ateliers and boutiques sit on **Sacramento Street** between Presidio Avenue and Spruce Street; **George** (2411 California Street, at Fillmore

Beach life

Unlike in Southern California, the majority of beaches in and around San Francisco aren't great for swimming. As if the locals care: between the cavorting families, the picnicking couples, the idle promenaders and, on one or two beaches, clothes-free pick-up artists, visitors to beaches in San Francisco aren't short of activities.

Most visitors start with the **East Beach**, up close to the Marina in the Presidio. During the week, it can be very pleasant, with dog-walking women, jogging men and cyclists of both sexes (including many tourists bound for the Golden Gate Bridge; *see p123*) passing the time of day along the edge. However, on weekends, it gets a little busier, and space is at a premium. Many people head further west to **Crissy Field** (*pictured*), where there's a lagoon popular with kiddies, and a lovely (if unofficial) beach that's part of the protected shoreline along Golden Gate Promenade.

Running for almost a mile along the craggy western Presidio shoreline, **Baker Beach** is a better bet. It's accessible, for one thing, and offers both great views and easy access to the city's most popular nude beach, the north end of the same stretch. In 1905 the US Army decided to use Baker as the hiding place for a huge 95,000-pound (43,000-kilogramme) cannon. The naval invasion it was built to repel never came, but a replica of the original has been installed for the curious.

Hidden between Baker Beach and Lincoln Park, in the exclusive Seacliff neighbourhood, you'll find the exquisitely sheltered James D Phelan Beach. Better known as **China Beach** (Seacliff Avenue, off 26th Avenue), it takes its nickname from the settlement of Chinese fishermen who camped here in the 19th century. There's plenty of parking and a pleasant hike down to the sand, then a free sundeck, showers and changing rooms once you get there. It's the favourite beach of many locals; should you be around at sunset, with Marin Headlands opposite, the Golden Gate Bridge to your right and sea lions in the ocean ahead of you, it will be your favourite too.

Extending from Cliff House (*see p115*) south towards the city limits, **Ocean Beach** (Great Highway, between Balboa Street & Sloat Boulevard) is by far San Francisco's biggest beach: a three-mile sandy strip along the Pacific. Widening into dunes and plateaux at the end of the fog-bound Sunset District, it's a fine place for strolling, dog-walking and the odd illicit midnight ritual and bonfire. But look, don't taste: tremendous waves come thundering ashore when the weather's up, and even on seemingly calm days the tides and currents can be lethal.

Sightseeing

Street, 441 0564, www.georgesf.com) sells gourmet confections and couture canine sweaters to what must be the most spoiled dogs on the West Coast; and nearby charity shops stock the cast-offs of the rich and famous.

It may come as some surprise to learn that it was from this now-highfalutin neighbourhood that poet Allen Ginsberg launched a cultural renaissance in 1955, when he gave the first public reading of *Howl* at the long-vanished Six Gallery, the site of which is now home to furniture store **Liv** (3115 Fillmore Street, at Filbert Street, www.livfurniture.com). North-west of here, past **Alta Plaza Park** (at Jackson and Steiner Streets), things grow even more handsome: the stretch of **Broadway** between Divisadero Street and the Presidio holds some of the best architecture in the city.

Haas-Lilienthal House

2007 Franklin Street, between Washington & Jackson Streets (441 3000/www.sfheritage.org/ house.html). Bus 1, 12, 27, 47, 49, 76. **Open** noon-3pm Wed, Sat; 11am-4pm Sun. **Admission** $8; $5 reductions. **Credit** AmEx, DC, MC, V. **Map** p314 J4.
Built in 1886 by Bavarian immigrant William Haas, this 28-room house has elaborate wooden gables and a circular tower, clearly marking it as being in the Queen Anne style. Fully restored and filled with period furniture, it also has photos documenting its history and that of the family that lived in it until 1972. It's maintained by San Francisco Architectural Heritage, which also organises walking tours.

Cutting corners: the **Octagon House**.

Octagon House

2645 Gough Street, at Union Street (441 7512). Bus 41, 45. **Open** noon-3pm 2nd & 4th Thur, 2nd Sun of mth. **Admission** free. **Map** p314 J4.
The 1861 Octagon House is home to the small Museum of Colonial and Federal Decorative Arts, but is most notable as one of two surviving examples of eight-sided homes in the city. Across the nation, 700 such houses were built in the belief that they improved their occupants' health by letting in more natural light. Once owned by a wealthy dairyman named Charles Gough (back when nearby Cow Hollow still contained cows), the Octagon House stands on the street to which he magnanimously gave his name while on the city's naming commission; he also named an adjacent street 'Octavia' in honour of his sister.

Cow Hollow

From Pacific Heights, it's only a few blocks downhill towards the Bay to Cow Hollow. Once a dairy pasture, the area is still serene, but its grazers are now of the well-heeled, two-legged kind. The activity is centred on **Union Street** between Broderick and Buchanan Streets, a chic and bijou stretch of bars, restaurants (among them **Betelnut** at no.2030, 929 8855, www.betelnutrestaurant.com) and boutiques (including wonderful antiques store **Past Perfect** at no.2224, 929 7651). Hiding in an alleyway is **Carol Doda's Champagne & Lace Lingerie Boutique** (no.1850, 776 6900); Doda, who owns the store, found fame in the mid 1960s when, while as a waitress at the Condor Club in North Beach, she became the city's first-ever topless dancer.

Perhaps even more impressive than Carol's fabled domes are those atop the nearby **Vedanta Temple** (2963 Webster Street, at Filbert Street), former headquarters of the Vedanta Society. Dating back to 1905, the temple is dedicated to an ancient strain of Hinduism that holds all religions to be viable paths to spiritual awareness. Accordingly, each of its six domes represents a different architectural style, with elaborate Moorish arches, a Saracenic crescent, a Russian onion-style dome and a Victorian gingerbread trim.

The Marina & the waterfront

Built on soft rubble from the 1906 earthquake, the Marina, between the Fort Mason Center and the Presidio, shook harder than any other part of San Francisco in 1989's Loma Prieta quake. Buildings collapsed hither and thither, but the only reminders of the damage are the renovated pavements and suspiciously new structures among the otherwise staid townhouses.

Get active in **Marina Green** – or just sit back and enjoy the spectacular views.

In a city justifiably famous for its gay scene, the pastel-painted Marina is conspicuously straight. It's also one big pick-up joint. By night, its bars fill with twentysomethings sipping cocktails and making eye contact; for decades, even the local **Safeway** (15 Marina Boulevard, at Laguna Street) was a pulling spot, and featured in Armistead Maupin's *Tales of the City*. The main commercial drag is **Chestnut Street**. The stretch between Fillmore and Divisadero Streets is a shrine to self-indulgence, with clothing boutiques and beauty salons seeming to occupy half the shopfronts. The recently renovated **Presidio Cinema** (no.2340, at Scott Street, 776 2388) lends the place a little culture. The **Grove** (no.2250, at Avila Street) is a woodsy café where it is said that San Francisco resident and author of the *Tapestry* series, Henry Neff, wrote much of the first installment (there is even a café called the Grove in the book). It's also a good stopping point to watch the preened denizens of the area 'fabu-lapping'.

A little more levity is provided at the eastern edge of the Marina waterfront. The **Fort Mason Center** (*see p120*) started out as a US Army command post in the 1850s, and its reconditioned military buildings retain a forbidding mien, but these days they house some fine little museums and exhibitions. For the 1915 Panama-Pacific Exposition, a mile-long swathe of temporary structures was erected all the way from here to **Fort Point** (*see p122*).

This fantastical city-within-a-city was torn down to make way for the houses we see today, but a small part of the fantasy-scape survived in the shape of the **Palace of Fine Arts** (*see p120*). The original plaster edifice, set in a little park at the western edge of the Marina, was expensively converted to concrete just in time for the opening of the adjacent **Exploratorium** (*see p205*) in 1969. Still actively and brilliantly curated, it was one of the world's first hands-on science museums and remains deservedly popular across the generations.

The vast, sloping lawns of the **Marina Green** (Marina Boulevard, between Scott and Webster Streets) are the locals' favourite place to fly kites, jog or picnic, offering dizzying views of the Golden Gate Bridge and the Bay. At the far west side of the green, a path leads past the **Cavern on the Green**, a small stone snack hut perched above a large pool just past the boat marina but before Crissy Field. Stop in for an It's It (a delicious Bay Area-made ice-cream treat) on a warm afternoon.

From here, head west along the edge of Marina Boulevard and around the harbour. Either continue west to the fascinating **Crissy Field** to explore a model of wetlands restoration, or follow the signs to the **Golden Gate Yacht Club**, along a kind of expansive promontory. Keep going past the boats and the boaters and, when you can go no further, you'll get to Peter Richards's amazing **Wave Organ**. Part artwork, part musical instrument, this mostly

Spatial effects

Fans of *Star Trek* will recognise the Presidio as the headquarters of Starfleet Command, so it's somewhat ironic that the company responsible for that other great sci-fi franchise, *Star Wars*, has chosen the spot as the real-world home of its special effects arm, Industrial Light & Magic (ILM). Nonetheless, fans of both will probably be interested in a quick stroll around the publicly accessible areas of the **Letterman Digital Arts Center** (located just inside the Presidio's Lombard Gate), which houses the facility, in a bid to spot a few familiar faces.

The complex contains LucasArts and LucasFilm, as well as ILM. Much to the surprise of employees, the Yoda Fountain (as it has become known) is now one of the prime attractions in the Presidio: located at the entrance to Building B, the likeness of the diminutive Jedi Master is one of the only hints to what lies within the otherwise low-key structure, which houses what is arguably the world's most advanced digital production facility. The miniature for the house in *A Series of Unfortunate Events* occupies one corner and stands some six feet tall; elsewhere are busts and animatronic heads of characters such as the Ghostbusters' sidekick Slimer, and the tentacled face of Davy Jones from *Pirates of the Caribbean II: Dead Man's Chest* (a film that garnered ILM an Academy Award for Best Visual Effects). Incidentally, the ghostbusters could well find employment at the studio that created them: the LDAC complex is thought to stand on the site of a former military hospital in the Presidio, and some employees claim to have seen the ghosts of nurses and soldiers roaming the grounds as they did while alive.

Past the security checkpoints, the inner sanctum consists of screening rooms, offices and enough computing power to run several nations, its hushed hallways peppered with posters for films the studio has made over the years. At the time of writing, the ILM team was entering post-production on the next instalment of the *Indiana Jones* series. Not that you'll get a peep out of them: almost the entire facility is inaccessible to anyone but those with security badges (even official visitors must sign a non-disclosure agreement that forbids filming or otherwise revealing what happens inside).

However, with a bit of luck, you can duck into the lobby of Building B, butter up the security guard and get a quick snapshot with full-size replicas of two of the most evil dudes in the universe: Darth Vader and Boba Fett.

underwater structure is made up of pipes and benches built from San Francisco's dismantled cemeteries; the tubes make eerie music with the ebb and flow of the Bay. From here the views of the Golden Gate Bridge, the city skyline and Alcatraz are excellent and unobstructed.

Fort Mason Center

Marina Boulevard, at Buchanan Street (441 3400/ www.fortmason.org). Bus 10, 22, 28, 30, 47, 49. **Map** p314 H2.

This collection of ex-military buildings features various cultural institutions, including the Museo ItaloAmericano (Building C, 673 2200, www.museo italoamericano.org) and the airy SFMOMA Artists' Gallery (Building A, 441 4777, www.sfmoma.org), the latter selling and renting out contemporary works by northern Californians. Both museums are closed on Mondays and offer free admission the first Wednesday of the month.

Other enterprises here include the Book Bay Bookstore (Building C, 771 1076, www.friendsand-foundation.org/bookstores.cfm), which sells rejected stock from the public library, as well as LPs and art. Over in Building D is the Magic Theatre (441 8822, www.magictheatre.org), which stages works by a mix of emerging and established playwrights in its two performance spaces. Before the performance, have dinner at Greens (Building A, 771 6222, www.greensrestaurant.com): one of the city's favourite vegetarian eateries, it is run by the San Francisco Zen Center and boasts high ceilings that frame a wide view of the Marina and the Bay. A constant array of changing displays is on view at two waterside pavilions (actually reconstituted shipbuilding bays); concerts, gardening competitions and even the local pagan community's major Halloween fête are held here. Also based on site are the administrative offices for the Golden Gate National Recreation Area (GGNRA), responsible for the 75,398 acres that comprise one of the largest urban park areas in the world.

Palace of Fine Arts

Lyon Street, at Bay Street (563 6504/www.palaceof finearts.org). Bus 28, 30, 43, 76. **Map** p313 F2.

Local architect Bernard Maybeck's pièce de résistance, the Palace is a neo-classical domed rotunda supported by a curved colonnade topped with friezes and statues of weeping women, and flanked by a pond alive with ducks, swans and lily pads. Initially designed only as a temporary structure,

Sightseeing

it's been repeatedly saved by generations of San Franciscans, and has served as everything from a tennis centre to a motor pool for dignitaries assisting in the creation of the United Nations after World War II – as it fell into neglect and disrepair, it even served as a telephone-book distribution centre and the Fire Department headquarters. The original building was demolished in 1964 – only the shell of the rotunda remained – then reconstructed at ten times the original cost. The Palace is currently in the final phases of a $21 million renovation that aims to create an aeration system for the lagoon and restore the surrounding landscape, with work due for completion in 2009.

The Presidio

The Presidio is sometimes called 'the prettiest piece of real estate in America'; it's certainly among the most valuable. At the northern tip of the city, overlooking the Bay, the Pacific and the Golden Gate Bridge, its location could hardly be more stunning, but for centuries it endured a workaday existence as a military base, closed to the public. Now completely demilitarised and amazingly revitalised, it has become a national park, complete with 11 miles of hiking trails, 14 miles of bicycle routes and three miles of beaches, and with the more recent addition of several fine restaurants.

The tip of the San Francisco Peninsula was first established as a military outpost in 1776, when a group led by Captain Juan Bautista de Anza planted the Spanish flag here to protect the newly discovered San Francisco Bay. The site was claimed as a garrison first for Spain (*presidio* means fortress in Spanish) and then for Mexico, but the US took it over, along with the rest of California, in 1848. The US military embarked on a huge landscaping project that converted hundreds of acres of windswept, sandy moors into a tree-lined garden. However, by 1994 they'd had enough. After 220 years, the US Army handed the Presidio over to the Park Service, claiming it could no longer afford the upkeep. The dramatic changeover, from army base to national park, followed soon after.

So far, so good, but the switch hasn't been without its controversies. Among the handful of organisations charged with looking after the immense site is the Presidio Trust; it has also been charged with the unenviable task of making the Presidio self-sustaining by 2013, which it aims to accomplish by renting some buildings as private residences, renting others to businesses, and even allowing some new construction. A plot near the Lombard Gate, formerly home to the Letterman Hospital, has been given over to George Lucas's Industrial Light & Magic film company, which spent $350

million developing the 24-acre plot into the **Letterman Digital Arts Center** (*see p120* **Spatial effects**), a state-of-the-art complex of offices and studios that opened in 2005. The $5.6 million annual rent that Lucas will pay to the Presidio Trust constitutes around one-sixth of the trust's budget. Conservationists have cried foul, but development appears likely to continue and even accelerate.

Both the Letterman complex and nearby park now boast a variety of dining options to suit all tastes and budgets. **Dish Café** (San Francisco Film Center, 39 Mesa Street, 561 2336) offers good picnicking fare, while the alfresco tables at **La Terrasse** (215 Lincoln Boulevard, 922 3463, www.laterrassepresidio.com) boast views of the bridge and a casual atmosphere. **Pres a Vi** (Building D, 1 Letterman Drive, 409 3000, www.presavi.com) offers small plates and wine flights, while the upscale **Presidio Social Club** (563 Ruger Street, 885 1888, www.presidiosocialclub.com), housed in a beautifully restored barracks, serves up gourmet versions of American favourites from the requisite mac and cheese to sloppy joes.

The sheer size of the park, not to mention its inevitably hilly nature, makes exploring it purely on foot something of an adventure,

A reminder of the **Presido**'s military past.

and it's definitely worth considering hiring a bike from one of the rental firms at Fisherman's Wharf. While getting lost in this curious environment is something of a pleasure, maps are available at several information points: the **Crissy Field Center** on Mason Boulevard (enter the Presidio at Marina Boulevard, in its north-east corner, and carry on down the road for around half a mile); the **Visitor Center** in the old Officers' Club at the Main Post, close to the centre of the park (easily accessible from any entrance, but coming in via the Presidio Boulevard Gate at Presidio and Pacific Avenues will take you through fairytale woods, often shrouded in mist); and at the **Battery East Overlook** close to the Golden Gate Bridge.

The large expanse of lawn and bucolic wetlands on the northern Presidio shoreline has a military past as an army airfield. It was returned to the city in the 1990s, and restored to its original state, planted with over 100,000 native plants: a pristine tidal marshland home for hundreds of migrating bird species. Its shoreline promenade lures walkers and joggers, daredevil kiteboarders and windsurfers who challenge the notorious waters.

The centre of the Presidio is the **Main Post**, a complex of old buildings arrayed along parallel streets on the site of the original Spanish fort. Aside from the main visitors' centre – now temporarily located in the Officers' Club while its original home is refitted (Building 50 Moraga Avenue, 561 4323) and home to a well-stocked shop selling maps, books and gifts – you'll also find two 17th-century Spanish cannons on Pershing Square, plus rows of Victorian-era military homes along Funston Avenue.

Follow Sheridan Avenue west from the Main Post and you'll soon arrive at the **San Francisco National Cemetery**. Among the army officers (and their family members) laid here in hauntingly straightforward fashion are more than 450 'Buffalo Soldiers'. African-American servicemen known to many simply as the subject of the eponymous Bob Marley song, they served not only alongside future president Theodore Roosevelt at the Battle of San Juan Hill (the battle namechecked by Marley), but also throughout the Civil War, the Indian Wars, the Spanish-American War and virtually every conflict up to the Korean War, after which the US armed services became officially integrated.

Continuing along Lincoln and taking the first right (McDowell Avenue), you'll soon stumble upon the **Pet Cemetery**. While its human counterpart sits high on a hill, its gravestones gleaming and its grass immaculately tidy, the cemetery in which servicemen buried their beloved animals sits directly under the Route

101 overpass, its markers made by hand and its grass unkempt. Still, there's something touching about these crumbling memorials, some of which – complete with poems and drawings – almost constitute folk art.

Much of the rest of the Presidio is a jumble of former servicemen's quarters, now converted into private homes. Around 500 structures from the former military base remain, ranging from Civil War mansions to simple barracks. Some are utilitarian, but others, such as **Pilot's Row** on Lincoln Boulevard near the Golden Gate Bridge toll plaza, are truly delightful. In between these sometimes melancholic clusters run numerous hiking and cycling paths, all marked on the maps available from the visitors' centres. Taking one – or more – is the best way to really get a feel for the Presidio. The easiest is the flat, paved **Golden Gate Promenade**, which follows the shoreline up to the foot of the Golden Gate Bridge. However, the rewards are greater with more effort. The hilly, unpaved **Coastal Trail** runs out past the Golden Gate Bridge to the beginning of the Pacific, with spectacular views of the Marin Headlands. And the **Ecology Trail** begins directly behind the Officers' Club and follows a pastoral path on to **Inspiration Point**, which affords terrific views, and picturesque **El Polin Spring**.

That said, there are other landmarks. A number of haunting old coastal batteries that once held guns capable of shooting 15 miles out to sea – although thankfully never fired in anything other than practice – sit along the western edge of the park. **Batteries Godfrey** and **Crosby** are both easily accessible on foot. The last pictures taken by photographer Ansel Adams were of these concrete bunkers and they offer stunning views of the Golden Gate Bridge, making them the perfect place for couples to enjoy a romantic bottle of wine at sunset. Below them is **Baker Beach** (*see also p117* **Beach life**), a favourite getaway among locals where, in 1986, the first 'burning man' was the spark that began one of the biggest festivals in the country. To the south of the Presidio sits the relaxing idyll of **Mountain Lake Park** (access at Lake Street and Funston Avenue). Just next to it is the public **Presidio Golf Course**, formerly a private club favoured by presidents and generals.

Fort Point

Marine Drive, beneath Golden Gate Bridge (556 1693/www.nps.gov/fopo). Bus 28, 29. **Open** 10am-5pm Fri-Sun. **Admission** free. **Map** p312 A1.
The spectacular brick-built Fort Point was built between 1853 and 1861 to protect the city from a sea attack. The assault never came; the 126 cannons remained idle, and the fort was closed in 1900. Today the four-storey, open-roofed building houses

various military exhibitions; children love to scamper among the battlements and passageways. Climb on to the roof for a fabulous view of the underbelly of the Golden Gate Bridge, which was built more than seven decades after the fort was completed.

The fort's pier is famous as the spot where Kim Novak's character attempts suicide in Hitchcock's *Vertigo*. While Novak was only pretending, onlookers might think the surfers plying the point break as it wraps around the fort are actually suicidal. They're certainly daredevils, but they're not dumb: many wear helmets to guard against the hazards of a wipeout on the jagged, rocky shoreline.

The Golden Gate Bridge

Few cities need bridges like this one. Without the **Golden Gate Bridge** connecting it to the northern half of the state and the **Bay Bridge** linking it to the rest of the country, the city would be isolated at the tip of a mountainous peninsula. Sure, it thrived that way for almost a century, but the rise of the automobile meant that ferries and ocean liners were no longer sufficient. Bridges were built, and now, for $5 (charged only on southbound journeys), motorists can exult in crossing one of the greatest bridges in the world.

Luminous symbol of San Francisco and of California itself, the Golden Gate Bridge (linking the Presidio to Marin County, 921 5858, www.goldengatebridge.org) may not be the longest bridge in the world, but it's among the most beautiful and may well be the most famous. Completed in 1937, it's truly immense: the towers are 746 feet (227 metres) high, the roadway runs for 1.75 miles, and enough cable was used in its construction to encircle the globe three times. However, raw statistics can't convey the sense of awe the bridge inspires, and no trip to the city is complete without walking across it. Drive, walk, ride a bike or take a bus to the toll plaza, and head out on foot along the walkway. Once you feel it thrumming beneath your feet, you'll understand even more why people feel such a strong connection to the span.

The person mainly responsible for making the bridge a reality was one Joseph Strauss, a pugnacious Chicagoan engineer. Strauss spent over a decade lobbying to build a bridge, circumventing innumerable financial and legal hurdles in the process. But it was a little-known freelance architect named Irwin F Morrow who eventually designed it, his brilliantly simple pitch selected in preference to Strauss's hideous and complicated cantilever plans.

The bridge's name has nothing to do with its colour, and everything to do with the name of the strait it spans. The Golden Gate strait was named by Captain John Fremont – not after

the Gold Rush (Fremont christened the strait in 1846, more than two years before gold was discovered in the California foothills), as many believe, but after the Golden Horn, the geologically similar channel that links the Black Sea to the Mediterranean. The bridge's stroke-of-genius orange colour was also an accident of fate: San Franciscans were so delighted by the reddish tint of the bridge's primer paint that the builders decided to stick with it, rather than paint the whole bridge in the traditional grey or silver. The bridge has been totally repainted only once, a project completed in 1995 using 2,206 gallons (8,350 litres) of primer and topcoat designed to withstand the corrosive salt and fog that continually bathe it, though it's constantly being repaired and touched up by a 55-strong team of ironworkers and painters.

Reputedly five times stronger than it needs to be, the bridge has survived hurricane-force winds, earthquakes and over 65 years of abuse without the slightest sign of damage. Built to flex under pressure, it can sway 21 feet (6.4 metres) and sag ten feet while withstanding 100mph winds, and can support the weight of bumper-to-bumper traffic across all six lanes at the same time as shoulder-to-shoulder pedestrians covering the walkways. Although large portions of the Marina were totally devastated by the 1989 earthquake, the bridge survived unscathed. But the virtual certainty of another earthquake of a similar (if not greater) magnitude prompted officials to undertake a seismic refitting project. Vehicle tolls were hiked from $3 to $5 to help pay for the reinforcements, which will require around 22 million pounds (10 million kilograms) of structural steel and 24,000 cubic yards (18,000 cubic metres) of concrete.

It's estimated that around 1,200 people have committed suicide by plunging the 250 feet (76 metres) or more into the water below, although countless more are never found, swept out to sea by the Gate's intense currents. For years debate has raged about erecting a suicide barrier beneath the bridge, but opponents fear that such an addition would ruin its aesthetic appeal. City newspapers stopped publishing a running tally of suicide figures years ago at the request of the authorities, leaving it a topic rarely discussed by locals, albeit one that was recently brought back into the spotlight when filmmaker Eric Steel released *The Bridge*, a documentary highlighting bridge suicides and including actual footage of jumpers plunging to their deaths. Although many San Franciscans are reluctant to discuss the bridge's status as the world's most popular suicide spot, it nevertheless engenders a solemn respect as both a monument to the triumph of the human spirit and a memorial to its fragility.

Sightseeing

The East Bay

Eastern promise.

There's so much to see and do in San Francisco that many visitors miss the less well-known opportunities lying just half an hour away by either BART or car. They're making a mistake. Oakland and Berkeley, the best-known East Bay cities, are between them home to fine museums, a world-renowned university, miles of parkland, numerous great restaurants, some decent nightlife, tons of shops and even two professional sports teams. Need another reason to visit? The temperatures in East Bay run an average 10°F higher than at the Golden Gate.

Oakland

Named after its now-vanished oak forests, San Francisco's stepsister was once the western terminus of the 3,000-mile transcontinental railway. The slow bells of passing freight trains are still strangely evocative of the city's working heritage. However, Oakland faded in the bright light of San Francisco's fame and came to be seen as merely the working-class city across the Bay. Going back there to her childhood home only to discover it no longer existed, modernist author Gertrude Stein wrote: 'What was the use of my having come from Oakland… there is no there there.'

The 1960s ushered in an era of both violence and social change, with the once-notorious Black Panthers characterising the Oakland scene along with hippies, yippies, Merry Pranksters and mob-handed, crystal-meth-snorting Hell's Angels. Today, parts of Oakland (specifically West Oakland) still have a high crime rate, but much of the city is on the rise, with luxurious hillside mansions, swanky live-work lofts and hip shopping districts. Check out the city with eight free walking tours during the months of May to October (1-510 238 3234, www.oakland net.com/government/cmo/walkingtours), covering everything from churches to the spiffed-up 1930s shopping district.

Oakland is easily accessible from San Francisco. It's a short drive over the Bay Bridge or a BART ride to City Center/12th Street or 19th Street, both handy for central Oakland. There's also a regular ferry service from the Ferry Building (see p71) and Pier 41 in San Francisco to Oakland's Clay Street Ferry Terminal, near Jack London Square (1-510 522 3300, www.eastbayferry.com).

On the waterfront lies one of Oakland's main tourist hives: **Jack London Square** (at Broadway & Embarcadero), named after the noted local author who used to carouse at **Heinold's First & Last Chance** (see p172), a funky bar in a little wooden shack. The square also offers a lovely farmers' market, held from 10am to 2pm on Sundays. Franklin Delano Roosevelt's 'floating White House', the USS *Potomac*, is docked to the west; its visitors' centre (540 Water Street, 1-510 627 1215, www.uss potomac.org) arranges tours and Bay cruises.

Having undergone huge redevelopment, downtown Oakland is now much more inviting than in years gone by. **Chinatown**, which covers the few blocks south of Broadway around 7th, 8th and 9th Streets, is less tourist-focused than its San Francisco counterpart, but still packed with places to eat and shop. Grab a Vietnamese sandwich, dim sum or Thai barbecue while you're there: all can be found within a few steps of the corner of 9th and Franklin Streets, along with all manner of Chinese trinkets. Across Broadway, check out **Swan's Marketplace** (907 Washington Street, at 9th Street, 1-510 444 1935), a renovated 1917 brick building filled with food and wine vendors, and the adjoining **Oakland Museum of Children's Art** (538 9th Street, at Washington Street, 1-510 465 8770, www.mocha.org, closed Mon), which has a wealth of hands-on activities for kids.

Your next stop should be the **Oakland Museum of California**, a great place to learn about the state; it's also well worth negotiating the rather unpleasant road that separates it from the lovely **Lake Merritt**, where you can catch a ride in a Venetian-style gondola at the end of Bellevue Avenue (1-510 737 8494, www.gondolaservizio.com). Down the road is the charming **Children's Fairyland** (699 Bellevue Avenue, at Grand Avenue, 1-510 452 2259, www.fairyland.org), full of sets and characters from classic nursery rhymes. Nearby, the **Parkway Theater** (1834 Park Boulevard, between East 18th & East 19th Streets, 1-510 814 2400, www.picturepub pizza.com) offers pizza and beer along with your favourite indie flicks , and shopping opportunities await on **Lakeshore Boulevard**, including chic retail boutique **Maribel** (no.3251, 1-510 419 0677) and trendy girls' shop **Glow** (61 Lakeshore Avenue, 1-510 832 4132). Other notable attractions, a short ride away in East Oakland, include the **Chabot Space & Science Center**, **Oakland Zoo** and **Redwood Regional Park** (7867 Redwood Road, 1-510 562 7275, www.ebparks.org), the latter being almost three square miles of partially wild parkland, with horse riding, 150-foot (45-metre) redwoods and hiking trails.

With the dotcom boom pricing musicians and artists out of San Francisco, Oakland developed strong theatre, dance, ballet, classical and rock music scenes, and now boasts one of the West Coast's best jazz venues in the form of **Yoshi's at Jack London Square** (*see p231*). West of Lake Merritt is the **Paramount Theatre** (2025 Broadway, between 20th & 21st Streets, 1-510 465 6400, www.paramounttheatre.com),

Streets of San Francisco
Telegraph Avenue, Berkeley

As the student activism and radical politics of the 1960s heated up, many believed that revolution was imminent. And if there was going to be a revolution, it was probably just to happen at Berkeley. Young people on the campus were in the vanguard of the student movement. Always focused on opposition to the Vietnam War, the movement had become increasingly radicalised until, for many, the ultimate aim was nothing less than the bringing down of the state.

By 1969, demonstrations, many against the war, and frequently involving clashes with police, took place regularly along Telegraph Avenue. But the most violent and notorious in the avenue's history didn't involve the war, but a piece of unused university property that had been claimed by students and local residents, planted with trees and turned into a People's Park. Governor Ronald Reagan, hardly a friend of the students (he called Berkeley 'a haven for communist sympathisers, protesters and sex deviants'), decided to make an issue of it. He sent in the police to reclaim the park on 15 May 1969. Plants were destroyed and a fence put up to keep people out. Later that day a huge crowd gathered on Sproul Plaza, on campus at the north end of Telegraph Avenue. Angry

demonstrators set off down the avenue shouting 'We want the park'. After local police failed to quell the demonstration, officers from other districts entered the fray. They chased the crowd down Telegraph Avenue, firing buckshot that caused serious injuries and one death. Reagan declared a state of emergency and sent in the National Guard – it would remain for two weeks. During a peaceful memorial for the slain student at Sproul Plaza, National Guardsmen surrounded the plaza, put on gas masks and then CS gas was let loose from helicopters. Many were injured in the ensuing panic. For a while it seemed as if war had been declared and the battle lines firmly drawn between old and young, left and right.

There never was a war, of course, and today street vendors and hippie clothes are the most obvious references to Telegraph's past. The park survived, though. Hardly the beating heart of a radical community as the '60s idealists had envisaged, it's a rather forlorn space, used mainly by the homeless. But it may be due for a new lease of life: the University of California, which still owns the park, is considering some 21st century solutions in a bid to boost the use of this symbolic space.

Berkeley

a fabulous art deco movie house built by renowned Bay Area architect Timothy L Pflueger in 1931. Complete with a Mighty Wurlitzer organ and full bar in the lobby, the theatre is home to the **Oakland East Bay Symphony** (1-510 444 0801, www.oebs.org), and also features rock, blues, soul and comedy shows. For punk and hardcore rock, try the **Stork Club** (2330 Telegraph Avenue, at 23rd Street, 1-510 444 6174, www.storkcluboakland. com), where you can hear local favourites letting rip in a suitably grubby corner of the neighbourhood.

The best corner for shoppers is the stretch of College Avenue in the ritzy **Rockridge** district to the north (served by its own BART station). As well as high-end home accessories, pricey children's boutiques and French bistros, you'll find the **Market Hall** (5665 College Avenue, 1-510 652 4680, www.rockridgemarkethall.com), which caters to local yuppies with a butcher, fishmonger, wine shop, bakery, pasta shop, cheese shop, florist and café. A relatively new shopping destination is the **Temescal** district, along Telegraph Avenue at 51st Street. An upscale yarn shop, good bakery and weekly farmers' market (5300 Claremont Avenue, at Telegraph Avenue, 1-510 745 7100, www. urbanvillageonline.com, 9am-1pm Sun) are major draws. Just a bit further down Telegraph is Oakland's **Koreatown**, well known for its restaurants. A favourite with local critics is **Koryo Wooden Charcoal BBQ** (Suite J, 4390 Telegraph Avenue, at 44th Street,

1-510 652 6007), where barbecue feasts are cooked at your own tabletop *hibachi*.

The nearby city of **Alameda**, accessible by car from downtown Oakland through the Webster Street Tube or by ferry from San Francisco's Ferry Building or Pier 41, is a charming blast from the past. Once the railroads' Western Terminus (before Oakland took away that honour), then home to a naval air station, Alameda – along its main drags of Webster Street and Park Street – is now a good destination for shopping, eating and…pinball. Visit **Lucky Ju Ju** (713 Santa Clara Avenue, at Webster Street, 1-510 205 9793, www.ujuju. com) for hours of fun with vintage pinball games from the 1960s through to the 1980s. You can also catch some rays or learn to windsurf at Alameda's **Crown Memorial Beach** (Boardsports School, Westline Drive, at Otis Drive, 385 1224, www.boardsportsschool.com).

Chabot Space & Science Center

10000 Skyline Boulevard (1-510 336 7300/www. chabotspace.org). **Open** 10am-5pm Wed, Thur; 10am-10pm Fri, Sat; 11am-5pm Sun. **Admission** (incl Planetarium) $13; $10 reductions; $9 3-12s. *MegaDome Theater* $8; $7 3-12s, seniors. **Credit** DC, MC, V.

High in the Oakland Hills, the Chabot combines a superbly equipped, state-of-the-art planetarium with an observatory and film theatre; the latter runs 70mm projections of the internal workings of the human body or the cosmos, seen at both the largest scale and the submolecular level. The three telescopes here include a 36in reflector telescope that is housed in the rotating roof observatory; you can look through all three most Fridays and Saturdays, depending on the weather conditions.

Oakland Museum of California

1000 Oak Street, at 10th Street (1-510 238 2200/ www.museumca.org). **Open** 10am-5pm Wed-Sat; noon-5pm Sun. **Admission** $8; $5 reductions; free under-6s. Free 2nd Sun of mth. **Credit** AmEx, DC, MC, V.

The art collection includes sketches by early explorers and genre pictures from the Gold Rush, along with sculpture, landscapes and Bay Area figurative, pop and funk works. The Hall of California Ecology uses stuffed animals to show the local range of habitats, while the Cowell Hall of California History houses curiosities going back to the Spanish incursion. The collection of priceless Chinese artefacts includes some stunning pieces. In March, the museum hosts a huge White Elephant Sale, renowned for unbelievable bargains, in a warehouse near the Oakland estuary.

Oakland Zoo

9777 Golf Links Road, off I-580 (1-510 632 9525/www.oaklandzoo.org). **Open** 10am-4pm daily. **Admission** $9.50; $6 2-12s, reductions; free under-2s. **Credit** DC, MC, V.

Over the last few years the formerly cramped Oakland Zoo, in Knowland Park, has put effort into creating decent-sized naturalistic habitats for its 400-plus species, including lions and tigers, chimps, elephants, tarantulas and snakes, ibis and toucans. Other zoo attractions include the CP Huntington miniature train, a carousel and the Sky Ride, a children's petting zoo and a chair lift that takes you over the bison and elk on the 'North American Range'.

Berkeley

Berkeley worked hard to earn a reputation for its avant-garde arts, leftist politics and marvellous food. Over the decades, it has shown proper dedication to maintaining all three. It remains a fascinating and wonderfully contradictory place, where gourmet eating is accepted as a form of radical liberalism and Noam Chomsky always attracts standing-room-only crowds. Relying on public transport? Downtown Berkeley BART station is convenient for all attractions.

University of California

To suggest that Berkeley is slightly in thrall to its university is like hinting that San Francisco gets a little foggy from time to time – the **University of California** campus here, known locally just as 'Cal', is the straw that stirs the Berkeley drink, and it has lent the place a countrywide reputation for its erudite, progressive liberalism. The university was the birthplace of America's youth revolution 40 years ago, with student protests against campus rules and the Vietnam War inspiring a nation of youthful rebels. For more on those heady days, check out Mark Kitchell's documentary *Berkeley in the '60s*.

It's very easy to idle away a few hours just wandering the campus. However, it's worth heading first to the **Sather Tower** (known simply as 'the Campanile'); for great views of the campus and the surrounding area, take the lift to the 200-foot (60-metre) level observation deck (open 10am-4pm Mon-Fri, 10am-5pm Sat, 10am-1.30pm, 3-5pm Sun, $2). Elsewhere on the campus are museums dedicated to art, anthropology, palaeontology and plenty of other disciplines. Some operate set hours, while others are open by appointment only; there's a list of all the collections, along with details of ongoing temporary exhibitions at www.berkeley.edu/libraries. However, at the head of the pack are the **Berkeley Art Museum** (*see p128*) and, across the street, the **Pacific Film Archive** (2575 Bancroft Way, between Telegraph Avenue & Bowditch Street, 1-510 642 1412). On the peak above the campus, but still run by the university, is the **Lawrence Hall of Science** (*see p129*), a fascinating

science museum aimed at children and with the additional attraction of commanding views over the entire Bay Area. Cal also operates a handful of excellent outdoor swimming pools, lovely on summer days, including two pools (one a wading pool for the kids) at **Strawberry Canyon Recreation Area** (Centennial Drive, at Memorial Stadium, 1-510 642 6400).

For more information on Cal, drop in on the campus **Visitors' Center** (University Hall, 2200 University Avenue, at Oxford Street, 1-510 642 5215, www.berkeley.edu/visitors) for maps and information. If you've got time, take one of the free 90-minute campus tours, which leave from the Visitors' Center at 10am from Monday to Saturday and from the Campanile at 10am on Saturday and at 1pm on Sunday. Bookings are only required for groups of ten or more.

Beyond the college

Even outside the campus, a liberal collegiate vibe dominates Berkeley. Spiking southwards from the university, **Telegraph Avenue** provides a home for street-vendor jewellery, crafts stands and hippyish clothes shops. Woefully, the world-famous Cody's Books has shut down, citing increasing rents in the area, but bibliophiles can still check out **Moe's** for a huge selection of both new and used books (no.2476, between Dwight Way & Haste Street, 1-510 849 2087). Further south along Telegraph are two huge record stores: **Rasputin** (no.2401, at Channing Way, 1-800 350 8700, www.rasputinmusic.com) and the superior **Amoeba Records** (no.2455, at Haste Street, 1-510 549 1125, www.amoebamusic.com). Cafés line the university's southern limit, among them the mainly outdoor **Café Strada** (2300 College Avenue, at Bancroft Way, 1-510 843 5282) and **Café Milano** (2522 Bancroft Way, at Telegraph Avenue, 1-510 644 3100). At weekends, students and others loiter around on the corner of Ashby Avenue and Martin Luther King Jr Way for the **Berkeley Flea Market**.

North-west of campus sits the culinary hot zone known as the **Gourmet Ghetto**, which runs along Shattuck Avenue between Delaware and Rose Streets. It's more popular with professors and tutors than with their students, on the whole, but the restaurants are still very egalitarian. The star of the show is undeniably **Chez Panisse** (*see p160*), set up back in the 1970s by Alice Waters, the elfin leader of the revolution in California cuisine. It's hardly the only option, though. Next door is **César** (*see p161*), which serves an enticing array of cultured tapas; more or less opposite is **Cheeseboard Pizza** (no.1512, 1-510 549 3055, www.cheeseboardcollective.coop), an

Write on Jack Spicer

The poet Jack Spicer was born and raised in LA, but the Bay Area was his spiritual home. He always said his life didn't really start until 1946 when, as a student at UC Berkeley, he met fellow poets Robert Duncan and Robin Blaser. Blaser recalls what an extraordinary figure the gay, bohemian Spicer cut when they met for the first time: 'He arrived at my door in trenchcoat, Hollywood dark glasses [and] sandals. His feet were purple with treatment for athlete's foot.' Spicer and Duncan met a year later on the F train, returning from an anarchist meeting across the Bay in San Francisco.

The three young poets soon established themselves as the prime movers in what became known as the 'Berkeley Renaissance'. If Duncan was the movement's self-proclaimed leader, Spicer was its theoretician. Indeed, some of his best-known writings aren't poems at all but public lectures in which he elaborates a decidedly

idiosyncratic theory of poetic creation. Spicer saw poetry not as a form of lyrical self-expression but rather as a kind of 'dictation', in which the poet receives his metaphors from some mysterious 'Outside'. Poems, he wrote, are 'delivered very much like a message that's delivered over a radio and the poet is the radio.'

In northern California, it seems, the signal was especially clear. Spicer imagined this 'seacoast of Bohemia' to be like one end of a 'rabbit hole', a portal to the Outside. He left the area only once, for a brief sojourn in New York and then Boston in 1955.

Spicer's last ever lecture was delivered at the Berkeley Poetry Conference in July 1965. Chastened and now ruined by drink, Spicer warned an audience from the Berkeley Free Speech Movement that it was a delusion to suppose that poetry could 'influence Lyndon Johnson'. He died shortly afterwards of alcohol poisoning. He was 40 years old.

employee-owned collective that offers a single type of vegetarian pizza to crowds that inevitably begin to gather before opening time each day. Two doors down, the original **Cheeseboard** (no.1504, 1-510 549 3183) sells a plethora of cheese. **Juice Bar Collective**, another co-operative featuring inexpensive organic comfort food, is just around the corner (2114 Vine Street, between Shattuck Avenue & Walnut Street, 1-510 548 8473, www.the juicebar.org), with **Peet's Coffee & Tea** (2124 Vine Street, at Walnut Street, 1-510 841 0564, www.peets.com) a few doors away. Opened in 1966, this branch of the coffee chain was where the founder of Starbucks got his training. So now you know who to blame.

Other areas of Berkeley hold different fascinations. Trendy **4th Street**, between Hearst Avenue and Virginia Street, near the waterfront, is home to numerous exclusive and stylish shops, as well as the last surviving location of legendary Berkeley bookstore **Cody's** (no.1730, between Cedar Street & University Avenue, 1-510 559 9500, www.codysbooks.com). If you're in the mood for some creepy crawlies, check out the **East Bay Vivarium** (1827C 5th Street, between Hearst Avenue and Delaware Street, 1-510 841 1400, www.eastbayvivarium.com), which is stuffed to the gills with glass cases of lizards, snakes, turtles and spiders. On the food front, there's great fish at century-old **Spenger's**

(1919 4th Street, at University Avenue, 1-510 845 7771) and hearty fare at **Brennan's** (4th Street & University Avenue, 1-510 841 0960), a cavernous, old-fashioned Irish pub and cafeteria.

Residential South Berkeley, meanwhile, has many California Craftsman-style homes, plus the **Judah L Magnes Museum** (2911 Russell Street, between Claremont & College Avenues, 1-510 549 6950, www.magnes.org), a large mansion that bursts at the seams with Jewish history and culture.

Many people visit the area just for its hills. The lovely and magnificently wild **Tilden Regional Park** (1-510 562 7275) offers hiking, nature trails and pony rides, a botanical garden containing the world's most complete collection of native California plants, a children's carousel, a steam train and Lake Anza, a great spot for taking a dip on hot days. Those who manage the trek up to **Inspiration Point** or **Wildcat Peak** are rewarded with 180° views. For a more leisurely take on nature, the **UC Berkeley Botanical Garden** (200 Centennial Drive, 1-510 643 2755, www.botanicalgarden.berkeley.edu), below Tilden Park, has cacti, orchids and an abundance of native California flora.

Berkeley Art Museum

2626 Bancroft Way, at Telegraph Avenue (1-510 642 0808/www.bampfa.berkeley.edu). **Open** 11am-5pm Wed, Fri-Sun; 11am-7pm Thur. **Admission** $8; $5 reductions; free under-12s. Free 1st Thur of mth. **Credit** AmEx, DC, MC, V.

Opened in 1970, this dramatic exhibition space is arranged in terraces so visitors can see the works from various vantage points. The collection's strength is 20th-century art, be it sculpture, painting, photography or conceptual work, and there's also a good collection of Asian pieces.

Lawrence Hall of Science

Centennial Drive, nr Grizzly Peak Boulevard (1-510 642 5132/www.lhs.berkeley.edu). **Open** 10am-5pm daily. **Admission** $10; $5.50-$8 reductions; free under-3s. **Credit** DC, Disc, MC, V.
Perched on the hills facing the Bay, this kids' science museum has computers to explore the inside of your brain, a Young Explorers Area and a huge DNA model to scramble over. Fascinating temporary exhibits appeal to all ages. It's also a great spot for daytime views and evening stargazing. Don't miss the telescope and wind-driven organ pipes at the back.

North of Berkeley

On Berkeley's north side, the tiny city of **Albany** may now be famous for excellent schools and a tidy Downtown, but it was once renowned for seedy strip joints along San Pablo Avenue. The clubs have vanished, but some legendary dive bars remain, including **Club Mallard** (no.752, between Portland & Washington Avenues, 1-510 524 8450) and **Tierney's Sports Bar** at the Albany Bowl (no.540, between Garfield & Brighton Avenues, 1-510 526 8818, www.albanybowl.biz), where you can knock back a few cold ones before hitting some pins. Or head to **Schmidt's Tobacco Trading & Pub** (1492 Solano Avenue, between Santa Fe & Curtis Avenues, 1-510 525 1900), a small bar in a converted home.

Albany Mudflats, between the Bay shore and Buchanan Street, is a paradise for wading birds. Go further north, however, and you enter an industrial zone. **Richmond**'s shipbuilding industry is long gone, and the town is now sustained by an oil refinery: the route into Marin County via the Richmond-San Rafael Bridge passes through it. To the north-east are the Carquinez Straits and **Rodeo**, a tiny town dwarfed by the neighbouring oil refinery.

The former C&H Sugar company town **Crockett** has kept firm hold of the charms of small-town life – its population hovers at around 3,000 people – despite being only a 15-minute drive north of Berkeley. The town nestles in the hillside over the **Alfred Zampa Memorial Bridge**, the gateway to the neighbouring wine country (*see p265*) and also the first major US bridge to have been named after a blue-collar worker. Al Zampa worked on all the major Bay bridges, including the one that stood on this site before his namesake bridge.

From here, signs mark a meandering road east to tiny **Port Costa**, once thriving as a gateway town for the Sacramento River delta. Go on a sunny day to grab some beer at the waterside **Warehouse Café** – a bar and barbecue joint with a resident stuffed polar bear that attracts a gaggle of leather-clad bikers. Also of note is the gallery-cum-workshop **Theatre of Dreams** (11 Canyon Lake Drive, 1-510 787 2164), where Wendy Addison concocts modern-day Victoriana from old paper dolls, sheet music, birds' nests and glitter. The studio is open by appointment only, but the window display is a treat in itself.

Livermore

It's all a bit suburban, but if you want a wine-tasting experience that is closer to the big city and actually quieter than either Napa or Sonoma, you could try Livermore, home to some 38 wineries. Good picks include the low-key and friendly **Fenestra Winery** (83 Vallecitas Road, 1-925 447 5246, www. fenestrawinery.com) and **Concannon Vineyard** (4590 Tesla Road, at Buena Vista Avenue, 1-925 456 2505, www.concannon vineyard.com), founded in 1883 and one of the oldest winemakers in the country.

Sightseeing

Berkeley Campus.

FINANCE TODAY

Eat, Drink, Shop

Features

Brown Eyed Girl. *See p182.*

Restaurants & Cafés

Sense and sensibility make a comeback.

Café Claude.

There's little to say about San Francisco's food culture that hasn't been said before. The city's culinary reputation is well established, and well deserved. From harnessing the globe's many flavours to setting the latest trends, San Francisco kitchens are known worldwide as an epicentre of vitality.

Lately, however, it seems that the trend has been to buck the trend. Perhaps because of a renewed need to be conscientious about conspicuous consumption, there has been a rethinking of priorities. The most obvious sign of this has been the return to simplicity. Big, glamorous and expensive nights on the town can still be had with little effort, but it's easier still to find a great meal you can enjoy while wearing jeans and trainers. Comfort food might be out, but comfort is definitely in. Restaurants are eager to make money-conscious patrons feel welcome by offering an unfussy atmosphere and friendly service without forsaking quality in the kitchen. The come-as-you-are attitude prevails in restaurants throughout town. Group dining at large noisy tables has supplanted the romantic dinner for two by quiet candlelight. Great food

> ▶ ❶ Purple numbers given in this chapter correspond to the location of each restaurant and café as marked on the street maps. See pp312-319.

for great food's sake is the order of the day – less fussy, less stuffy and definitely less pretentious.

Happily, all the things that solidified San Francisco's food reputation are still intact. The fresh ingredients, inventive recipes and big-name chefs are all present and accounted for. The mild weather and rich soil of the Bay Area create great growing conditions for foods of all kinds, and bring excellent fish and meat into easy reach. The rich panoply of the world's cuisine is all still here. It's just a lot easier – in most cases – to experience it. It's a return to what matters: the food.

Price ranges for main courses in this chapter refer to dinner; lunch tends to be cheaper.

Downtown

Union Square & around

Union Square is known for its high-glitz dining rooms where tourists congregate in large numbers and high-profile chefs have reputations above what they deserve. **Farallon** (450 Post Street, between Powell & Mason Streets, 956 6969, www.farallonrestaurant.com) and **Postrio** (545 Post Street, between Taylor & Mason Streets, 776 7825, www.postrio.com) have cachet, but the food doesn't always match the hype, and it can come with a hefty price tab.

Cafés, delis & diners

Caffe Kuleto's

Villa Florence Hotel, 221 Powell Street, at Geary Street (397 7720/www.kuletos.com). BART & Metro to Powell/bus 2, 3, 4, 9X, 30, 38, 45, 76 & Market Street routes/cable car Powell-Hyde or Powell-Mason. **Open** 7-10.30am, 11.30am-10.30pm Mon-Thur; 7-10.30am, 11.30am-11pm Fri; 8-10.30am, 11.30am-11pm Sat; 8-10.30am, 11.30am-10.30pm Sun. **Main courses** $5-$15. **Credit** AmEx, DC, Disc, MC, V. **Map** p315 M6 ❶

Located near Union Square, this is a nice, sophisticated spot for recharging the shopping batteries. An annex of the popular Kuleto's Italian Restaurant (same phone), the café features fresh-prepared Italian pastries, as well as just-squeezed juices and excellent lattes and espresso. For lunch, choose from pizza by the slice, panini, antipasti and rich desserts.

French

Café Claude

7 Claude Lane, off Sutter Street, between Kearny Street & Grant Avenue (392 3505/www.cafeclaude. com). BART & Metro to Montgomery/bus 2, 3, 4, 9X, 30, 38, 45, 76 & Market Street routes/cable car Powell-Hyde or Powell-Mason. **Open** 11.30am-4.30pm, 5.30-10.30pm Mon-Sat; 5.30-10.30pm Sun. **Main courses** $9-$23. **Credit** AmEx, DC, Disc, MC, V. **Map** p315 M5 ❷

Owner Stephen Decker purchased Le Barbizon café in Paris and shipped it to San Francisco one piece at a time. The result, set in an alleyway and resplendent with French style and attitude, is as close to a true French café as can be found in America. Dishes include salad niçoise and steak tartare.

Café de la Presse

352 Grant Avenue, at Bush Street (398 2680/www. cafedelapresse.com). BART & Metro to Montgomery/ bus 2, 3, 4, 9X, 30, 38, 45, 76 & Market Street routes/cable car Powell-Hyde or Powell-Mason. **Open** 7.30-10am, 11.30am-2.30pm, 5.30-9.30pm Mon-Thur; 7.30-10am, 11.30am-2.30pm, 5.30-10pm Fri; 8am-4pm, 5.30-10pm Sat; 8am-4pm, 5.30-9.30pm Sun. **Main courses** $19-$24. **Credit** AmEx, DC, Disc, MC, V. **Map** p315 M5 ❸

Since its transformation into a fully fledged bistro, this bustling spot has become one of the most reliable in the downtown area. The classic French-inspired fare and café-style choices are always winners. It also stocks a bevy of foreign newspapers and magazines for the news hungry.

Fifth Floor

Hotel Palomar, 12 4th Street, at Market Street (348 1555/www.fifthfloorrestaurant.com). BART & Metro to Powell/bus 9X, 27, 30, 45 & Market Street routes/cable car Powell-Hyde or Powell-Mason. **Open** 5.30-10pm Mon-Thur; 5.30-11pm Fri, Sat. **Main courses** $39-$50. **Credit** AmEx, DC, Disc, MC, V. **Map** p315 M6 ❹

Since its start-of-the-century debut, this chic and reliable high-dollar restaurant has become established as one of the best places in the city to find a five-star French experience. The dining room – which was undergoing a renovation at press time – has proven reliably sophisticated and stylish, and the daily changing menu is among the city's best. Preparations are unfussy, and service is top-notch. The wine list, administered by one of the area's top sommeliers, is among the best in the region.

Masa's

648 Bush Street, between Stockton & Powell Streets (989 7154www.masasrestaurant.com). Bus 2, 3, 4, 9X, 30, 38, 45, 76/cable car Powell-Hyde or Powell-Mason. **Open** 5.30-9.30pm Tue-Sat. **Set meal** $100/6 courses; $150/9 courses. **Credit** AmEx, DC, Disc, MC, V. **Map** p315 M5 ❺

Masa's was the first notable restaurant to combine SF haute cuisine with a French dining aesthetic. The kitchen has seen many talented chefs at the stoves, but each has maintained the high level of care taken by his predecessor, ensuring the Masa's experience remains one worth having (and paying for). The French-inspired fare is typically as mouthwatering as it is eye-popping.

International

Michael Mina

Westin-St Francis Hotel, 335 Powell Street, at Geary Street (397 9222/www.michaelmina.net). BART & Metro to Powell/bus 2, 3, 4, 9X, 30, 38, 45, 76 & Market Street routes/cable car Powell-Hyde or

The best Restaurants

For brilliant brunches
Dottie's True Blue Café (*see p139*); Kate's Kitchen (*see p155*); Slow Club (*see p150*); Zazie's (see p154).

For Mexican food with a twist
Colibrí Mexican Bistro (*see p135*); Impala (*see p147*); Tres Agaves (*see p144*).

For sustainable eating
Acme Chop House (*see p141*); Fish & Farm (*see p139*); Incanto (*see p153*).

For Cal-Ital
Americano (*see p136*); Chez Panisse (*see p161*); Zuni Café (*see p139*).

For special occasions
Asia de Cuba (*see p139*); Fifth Floor (*see above*); Frisson (*see p136*); Gary Danko (*see p147*); Jardinière (*see p140*); Masa, Michael Mina (for both, *see above*).

Powell-Mason. **Open** 5.30-10pm Mon-Sat; 5.30-9.30pm Sun. **Set meal** $98/3 courses; $135/6 courses. **Credit** AmEx, DC, Disc, MC, V. **Map** p315 M5 **6**
This spare-no-expense room introduced Union Square to famed chef Mina, who micromanaged the look of the restaurant much like he does his artistic food. Meals are offered in a three-course menu, each with three preparations of a theme, or as a seven-course tasting menu. Quality special-occasion dining.

Italian & pizza

Scala's Bistro
Sir Francis Drake Hotel, 432 Powell Street, between Post & Sutter Streets (395 8555/www.scalasbistro. com). BART & Metro to Powell/bus 2, 3, 4, 9X, 30, 38, 45, 76 & Market Street routes/cable car Powell-Hyde or Powell-Mason. **Open** 8am-midnight daily. **Main courses** $22-$38. **Credit** AmEx, DC, Disc, MC, V. **Map** p315 M5 **7**
Recently refurbished to fine effect, this bustling bistro is frequented by tourists staying in Union Square and locals attracted by robust, reasonably priced Cal-Mediterranean food. Reliable choices range from the daily risotto to fresh-made pasta. Meal-size salads are a hit during lunch. The wine list is well chosen from nearby regions, with occasional surprises from beyond the borders.

Latin American

Colibrí Mexican Bistro
438 Geary Street, between Taylor & Mason Streets (440 2737/www.colibrimexicanbistro.com). BART & Metro to Powell/bus 2, 3, 4, 9X, 30, 38, 45, 76 & Market Street routes/cable car Powell-Hyde or Powell-Mason. **Open** 11.30am-10pm Mon-Thur; 11.30am-11pm Fri; 10am-11pm Sat; 10am-10pm Sun. **Main courses** $12-$18. **Credit** AmEx, DC, MC, V. **Map** p314 L5 **8**
In the heart of Theatre District, this unpretentious tucked-away restaurant serves delicious and atypical Mexican fare. Dishes are presented tapas-style, with unfamiliar regional flavours. The selection includes brilliant tortilla soup, tamarind-sautéed shrimp served with corn cakes, and a fire-roasted *chile relleno* that will have you raving almost before you put down your fork.

The Financial District

American

Sam's Grill
374 Bush Street, between Montgomery & Kearny Streets (421 0594). Bus 15, 45, 76. **Open** 11am-9pm Mon-Fri. **Main courses** $10-$75. **Credit** AmEx, DC, Disc, MC, V. **Map** p315 M5 **9**
Sam's has been satisfying San Franciscan appetites for over 140 years. The restaurant holds fast to history, with a friendly atmosphere and a charming dining room panelled in dark wood and punctuated by

bright-white tablecloths. The American menu is largely driven by seafood, but it's worth opting for such local specialities as the wonderful Hangtown Fry. At lunch, don't pass on the burgers.

Fish & seafood

Aqua
252 California Street, between Battery & Front Streets (956 9662/www.aqua-sf.com). BART & Metro to Embarcadero/bus 1, 10, 12, 15, 41 & Market Street routes/cable car California. **Open** 11.30am-2.30pm, 5.30-10.30pm Mon-Fri; 5.30-11pm Sat; 5.30-9.30pm Sun. **Set meal** $72/3 courses; $125/7 courses. **Main courses** *Lunch* $15-$25. **Credit** AmEx, DC, Disc, MC, V. **Map** p315 N4 **10**
This sleek and handsomely appointed space is enlivened by floral arrangements and good-looking servers. The seasonal menu includes local and imported fish, prepared with brilliant flourishes. The wine list is award-winning and the service is exemplary. Aqua is one of the best choices in town for a power lunch.

French

Jeanty at Jack's
615 Sacramento Street, at Montgomery Street (693 0941/www.jeantyatjacks.com). BART & Metro to Montgomery/bus 1, 9X, 10, 12, 41/cable car California. **Open** 11.30am-10.30pm Mon-Fri; 5-10.30pm Sat, Sun. **Main courses** $16.50-$38. **Credit** AmEx, DC, MC, V. **Map** p315 M4 **11**
The 'Jack's' of the name is a brasserie that opened in 1864; the 'Jeanty' is chef Philippe, who has consolidated his reputation over the last decade by directing proceedings at his excellent bistro in the Napa Valley's Yountville. The two have combined to create one of the city's better and more authentic French restaurants. Don't leave without trying the steak-frites.

Plouf
40 Belden Place, between Bush & Pine Streets (986 6491/www.ploufsf.com). BART & Metro to Montgomery/bus 2, 3, 4, 9X, 30, 38, 45, 76 & Market Street routes/cable car Powell-Hyde or Powell-Mason. **Open** 11.30am-3pm, 5.30-11pm Mon-Thur; 11am-3pm, 5.30-11pm Fri; 5.30-11pm Sat. **Main courses** $16-$26. **Credit** AmEx, DC, MC, V. **Map** p315 M5 **12**
This charming, always-packed restaurant is named after the French word for 'splash'. No dining experience here is complete without a bucket of steamed mussels, but the ever-changing array of fish is also excellent. The fish and chips is a staple.

International

Kokkari Estiatorio
200 Jackson Street, at Front Street (981 0983/ www.kokkari.com). BART & Metro to Embarcadero/ bus 1, 10, 12, 20, 41. **Open** 11.30am-10pm

Mon-Thur; 11.30am-11pm Fri; 5-11pm Sat. **Main courses** $18.50-$39. **Credit** AmEx, DC, Disc, MC, V. **Map** p315 N4 ⑬

Kokkari serves what it describes as 'Hellenic cuisine'. It's quite outstanding, although highly priced, and unlike what most people think of when it comes to Greek food. The *pikilia*, an appetiser plate featuring three traditional Greek dips with fresh pittas, is a good place to start. Grilled lamb chops, pan-roasted fish and traditional dishes like moussaka are the main-course highlights.

The Embarcadero

American

Americano

Hotel Vitale, 8 Mission Street, at the Embarcadero (278 3777/www.americanorestaurant.com). BART & Metro to Embarcadero/streetcar F/bus 2, 14, 12, 20, 21, 31, 41, 71 & Market Street routes. **Open** 6.30-10.30am, 11.30am-2.30pm, 5.30-10pm Mon-Thur; 6.30-10.30am, 11.30am-2.30pm, 5.30-11pm Fri; 7.30am-3pm, 5.30-11pm Sat; 7.30am-3pm, 5.30-10pm Sun. **Main courses** $16-$32. **Credit** AmEx, DC, Disc, MC, V. **Map** p315 O4 ⑭

This sleek, understatedly elegant restaurant in the Hotel Vitale offers seasonally fresh, Italian-inspired food, cooked and served with Californian flair. Chef Paul Arenstam frequently employs seasonal ingredients sourced from the Ferry Plaza Farmers' Market across the street. Try panini at lunch, grilled ribeye at dinner, and the restaurant's own-made gelato for dessert. Much attention is also paid to the breakfasts.

Boulevard

1 Mission Street, at Steuart Street (543 6084/ www.boulevardrestaurant.com). BART & Metro to Embarcadero/streetcar F/bus 2, 14, 12, 20, 21, 31, 41, 71 & Market Street routes. **Open** 11.30am-2pm, 5.30-10pm Mon-Thur; 11.30am-2pm, 5.30-10.30pm Fri; 5.30-10.30pm Sat; 5.30-10pm Sun. **Main courses** $29-$45. **Credit** AmEx, DC, Disc, MC, V. **Map** p315 O4 ⑮

Since 1993, this classic-looking restaurant has been one of San Francisco's most consistently reliable: from the service to the cooking, there's seldom a misstep. Always busy, it attracts locals and visitors with waterfront views and hearty food. Self-taught chef Nancy Oakes specialises in elaborate New American dishes – pork chops, steaks and risottos – although wood-roasted dishes are another strength.

Chaya Brasserie

132 the Embarcadero, at Mission Street (777 8688/www.thechaya.com). BART & Metro to Embarcadero/streetcar F/bus 2, 14, 12, 20, 21, 31, 41, 71 & Market Street routes. **Open** 11.30am-2.30pm, 5.30-10pm Mon-Wed; 11.30am-2.30pm, 5.30-10.30pm Thur, Fri; 5.30-10.30pm Sat; 5-9.30pm Sun. **Main courses** $24-$39. **Credit** AmEx, DC, Disc, MC, V. **Map** p315 O4 ⑯

A southern California transplant (where it was once a be-seen destination among celebs), this large and bustling restaurant offers an extensive menu of Japanese-meets-French specialities and sweeping Bay views to enjoy it by. The toughest decision is deciding which country to lean towards when ordering – the sushi is excellent, but the grilled meat specialities are also always tempting.

Fog City Diner

1300 Battery Street, at Greenwich Street (982 2000/ www.fogcitydiner.com). Streetcar F to Lombard & Embarcadero/bus 10. **Open** 11.30am-10pm Mon-Thur; 11.30am-11pm Fri; 10.30am-11pm Sat; 10.30am-10pm Sun. **Main courses** $12-$20. **Credit** AmEx, DC, MC, V. **Map** p315 ⑰

From outside, this looks like a modern update of a classic 1950s diner. Inside, the decor is swankier, and the menu lurches from burgers and steaks to crab cakes and grilled salmon. The menu is too long for its own good, and prices are higher than they should be, but you can still eat well here.

Frisson

244 Jackson Street, between Battery & Front Streets (956 3004/www.frissonsf.com). Streetcar F/bus 1, 10, 12, 20, 41. **Open** 5.30-10pm Mon-Thur; 5.30-11pm Fri, Sat. **Main courses** $26-$35. **Credit** AmEx, DC, Disc, MC, V. **Map** p315 N4 ⑱

Be prepared to people-watch and to be watched by people: this is a social showcase, from its high-design modern decor to the playful interpretations of French-Californian cuisine. There is a tendency here, both in the kitchen and among the cooler-than-you clientele, to overdo things, but staples such as slow-cooked chicken are outstanding. There's also a good selection of wines by the glass.

Globe Restaurant

290 Pacific Avenue, at Battery Street (391 4132/ www.globerestaurant.com). Bus 1, 10, 12, 41. **Open** 11.30am-3pm, 6pm-1am Mon-Fri; 6pm-1am Sat; 6pm-midnight Sun. **Main courses** $18-$27. **Credit** AmEx, DC, Disc, MC, V. **Map** p315 N3 ⑲

A popular hangout for off-duty chefs, this dining room has an exposed-brick look that imparts an urban, New York feel to it. The menu offers such standards as wood-oven pizzas, braised short ribs and grilled salmon, prepared with fresh ingredients and without complications.

Market Bar

1 Ferry Building, at the Embarcadero (434 1100/ www.marketbar.com). BART & Metro to Embarcadero/streetcar F/bus 2, 14, 12, 20, 21, 31, 41, 71 & Market Street routes. **Open** 11.30am-10pm Mon-Fri; 9am-10pm Sat, Sun. **Main courses** $17-$34. **Credit** AmEx, DC, MC, V. **Map** p315 O4 ⑳

This casual brasserie at the waterfront features hearty California cuisine and some Italian fare. The catch here is the excellent seafood: soul-warming bouillabaisse and *cioppino*. Dinner begins with fresh bread, and typically finishes with a lovely dessert, such as chocolate croissant pudding.

Butterfly: beautiful views, beautiful people and bountiful pan-Asian cuisine.

Taylor's Refresher

1 Ferry Building, at the Embarcadero (1-866 328 3663/www.taylorsrefresher.com). BART & Metro to Embarcadero/streetcar F/bus 2, 14, 12, 20, 21, 31, 41, 71 & Market Street routes. **Open** 10.30am-10pm daily. **Main courses** $7-$14. **Credit** AmEx, DC, MC, V. **Map** p315 O4 ㉑

Over 50 years after the original opened its drive-thru window in the Napa Valley, the second branch of Taylor's Refresher set up shop in the Ferry Building. The decor is rather more modern than at the original, and the menu a little posher in parts, but the basics – burgers, fries, malts and shakes – remain peerless.

Asian

Butterfly

Pier 33, at Bay Street (864 8999/www.butterflysf. com). Streetcar F to Bay & Embarcadero/bus 9X, 10, 39. **Open** 11.30am-10pm Mon-Fri; 11am-10pm Sat, Sun. **Main courses** $18-$39. **Credit** AmEx, DC, Disc, MC, V. **Map** p315 M2 ㉒

Although chef-owner Robert Lam's pan-Asian cuisine is good, it's nearly incidental to the stylish surroundings: beautiful views of the Bay without and a beautiful crowd within. Culinary highlights include the duck confit spring roll appetiser and the *ponzu*-grilled hanger steak main.

Ozumo

161 Steuart Street, at Mission Street (882 1333/ www.ozumo.com). BART & Metro to Embarcadero/ streetcar F/bus 2, 14, 12, 20, 21, 31, 41, 71 & Market Street routes. **Open** 11.30am-2pm, 5.30-10pm Mon-Wed; 11.30am-2pm, 5.30-10.30pm Thur; 11.30am-2.30pm, 5.30-11pm Fri; 5.30-11pm Sat; 5.30-10pm Sun. **Main courses** $21-$38. *Sushi omakase* from $125. **Credit** AmEx, DC, MC, V. **Map** p315 O4 ㉓

A beautiful contemporary Japanese restaurant where some 6,000sq ft (560sq m) of design panache swaddle an equally chic crowd. The front dining room holds a bar and lounge serving an exhaustive menu of sakés and rare teas. Amble past the robata grill – the meat, fish and vegetables from the robata menu are the real attractions – and you'll come to an enormous main dining room, with a sushi bar and Bay Bridge views.

Slanted Door

1 Ferry Building, at the Embarcadero (861 8032/www.slanteddoor.com). BART & Metro to Embarcadero/streetcar F/bus 2, 14, 12, 20, 21, 31, 41, 71 & Market Street routes. **Open** 11am-2.30pm, 5.30-10pm Mon-Thur, Sun; 11am-2.30pm, 5.30-10.30pm Fri, Sat. **Main courses** $16-$32.50. **Credit** AmEx, DC, MC, V. **Map** p315 O4 ㉔

The sleek lines and Bay views of Charles Phan's popular restaurant are alluring, but the attraction remains Phan's incredible, inventive Vietnamese-inspired food. There isn't a bad choice on the menu, although the shaking beef, the spicy short ribs and the shrimp and crab spring rolls continue to stand out. A must.

Yank Sing

Rincon Center, 101 Spear Street, at Mission Street (781 1111/www.yanksing.com). BART & Metro to Montgomery/bus 2, 3, 4, 31 & Market Street routes. **Open** 11am-3pm Mon-Fri; 10am-4pm Sat, Sun. **Main courses** *Dim sum* $3-$8. **Credit** AmEx, DC, MC, V. **Map** p315 O4 ㉕

The quality of Yank Sing's food explains how it manages to thrive in the corner of a massive office complex. Non-English-speaking waitresses roll out an endless array of steaming dumplings; a loyal, on-the-go business crowd snaps them up with speed.
Other locations 29 Stevenson Street, SoMa, 541 4949.

Cafés, delis & diners

Imperial Tea Court
27 Ferry Market Place, Ferry Building, at the Embarcadero (544 9830/www.imperialtea.com). BART & Metro to Embarcadero/streetcar F/ bus 2, 14, 12, 20, 21, 31, 41, 71 & Market Street routes. **Open** 10am-6pm daily. **Main courses** $6-$10. **Credit** AmEx, DC, MC, V. **Map** p315 O4 ❷⑥
There are few better places in the city of San Francisco for tea. This serene tea house, an offshoot of the original Chinatown shop, offers a vast array of teas, served to the accompaniment of birds chirping in cages. Presented in the traditional Chinese *gaiwan* (covered cup), the teas include Fancy Dragon Well, Silver Needle and Snow Water; they're all available to take away too, along with teapots, teacups and

other accessories. Don't expect serious food here, although traditional nibbles are served. The outlet inside Berkeley's Epicurious Garden is open daily.
Other locations Epicurious Garden, 1511 Shattuck Avenue, Berkeley (1-510 540 8888).

International

Café de Stijl
1 Union Street, at Front Street (291 0808/www. destijl.com). Streetcar F/bus 10. **Open** 6.30am-5pm Mon-Fri. **Main courses** $6-$10. **Credit** AmEx, DC, Disc, MC, V. **Map** p315 N3 ❷⑦
Named after the Dutch art movement, de Stijl is a small but lively café with sleek decor, pleasant ambience and a wide-ranging menu. Middle Eastern dishes are a speciality, as are Tuscan-style roast chicken and bowl-sized lattes.

¡Viva la tortilla!

Surpreme evidence of San Francisco's supremacy in the realm of the burrito can be found in New York City, where an Upper West Side Mexican eaterie has a sign in its window boasting that it serves 'San Francisco Mission-District Style' burritos. The reputation is well deserved. There are many imitators flung far and wide, and while the real thing can be found in copious, mouthwatering array throughout SF, ground zero for the glorious steamed tortillas packed with meat (optional), cheese, rice, beans, guacamole and spicy, peppery salsa is without doubt the Mission.

Originally consumed by field workers, the tortilla is essentially an edible-sack lunch: it was called a *burrito* ('little donkey') because it carried everything. On 29 September 1969, the first Mission burrito was sold at the still-extant **La Cumbre Taqueria** (515 Valencia Street, at 16th Street, 863 8205). Today, the Mission is packed with burrito joints, walk-up counters dishing up immense hunks of food for a meagre few bucks. Some of the more accessible ones, among them mega-*taquería* **Pancho Villa** (3071 16th Street, at Valencia Street, 864 8840, www.panchovillasf.com) and the respected **El Toro** (598 Valencia Street, at 17th Street, 431 3351), are both good and authentic. However, the best places are a bit further afield. Consistent champion **Taqueria San Francisco** (2794 24th Street, at York Avenue, 641 1770) slings exquisite *carne asada* (grilled beef) into lightly grilled, warm and flaky tortillas, while **Taqueria Cancun** (2288 Mission Street, near 19th Street, 252 9560) does

a particularly fine vegetarian burrito. Pair the slabs at **El Farolito** (2777 Mission Street, at 24th Street, 826 4870) with the refreshing canteloupe *agua fresca* – 'fresh water' flavoured with fruit juice. At **Papalote** (3409 24th Street, at Valencia Street, 970 8815, www.papalote-sf.com), the ingredients are fresher and the decor is more colourful, but the price is still right.

While the Mission simply means Mexican food to many locals and visitors, there's more to it than that. These days, the neighbourhood is home to eateries covering most of South and Central America, as well as the so-called Nuevo Latino fusion movement, which weds traditional Latin American cuisine with American, Asian and continental food. The **Balompie Café** (3349 18th Street, at Capp Street, 648 9199) and the more upscale **Panchitas #3** (3115 22nd Street, at S Van Ness Avenue, 821 6660) serve Salvadorean favourites such as *pupusas*, thick tortillas stuffed with meat, beans, cheese or *loroco*, a fresh green herb. **San Miguel** (3263 Mission Street, between 29th & Valencia Streets, 641 5866, www.forored.com/sanmiguel) offers choice Guatemalan fare, while at **El Majahual** (1142 Valencia Street, between 22nd & 23rd Streets, 821 7514), a Colombian husband and his Salvadorean wife offer flavourful, inexpensive food. At the other end of the price spectrum, the Nuevo Latino take on Peruvian cuisine served up at **Limón** (*see p162*) has garnered awards, and deservedly so.

The Tenderloin

American

Fish & Farm
339 Taylor Street, at Ellis Street (474 3474/www.
fishandfarmsf.com). BART & Metro to Powell/bus 2,
3, 4, 27, 31, 38, 76/cable car Powell-Hyde or Powell-
Mason. **Open** 5-10pm Tue, Wed, Sun; 5-11pm Thur-
Sat. **Main courses** $17-$28. **Credit** AmEx, DC,
Disc, MC, V. **Map** p314 L6 🢀
Building on the city's claim to embrace sustainability
in all facets of life, this chic, intimate restaurant
endeavours to source items on its menu from no more
than 100 miles away, and creating ingredients for
their all-organic cocktail list in-house. Dishes are simple, tasty and elegantly plated, and include many
familiar American favourites (seafood chowder, pork
chops, pasta), along with more unusual choices such
as sablefish. The well-chosen wine list consists of varietals from small organic and biodynamic producers.

Asian

Asia de Cuba
Clift Hotel, 495 Geary Street, at Taylor Street
(929 2300/www.chinagrillmanagement.com/adecSF).
BART & Metro to Powell/bus 2, 3, 4, 27, 38, 76/
cable car Powell-Hyde or Powell-Mason. **Open** 7am-
2.30pm, 5.30-10.30pm Mon-Wed, Sun; 7am-2.30pm,
5.30-11.30pm Thur-Sat. **Main courses** $32-$79.
Credit AmEx, DC, MC, V. **Map** p314 L6 🢀
Popular with out-of-towners and business travellers
with unlimited expense accounts, this swishy
Starck-designed room at the Clift is worth popping
in to just to see what all the fuss is about. The menu
is good for groups, with many dishes designed to be
shared. Rich, sweet sauces characterise most items
on the intensely flavoured Chino-Latino menu.

Cafés & diners

Dottie's True Blue Café
522 Jones Street, at O'Farrell Street (885 2767).
BART & Metro to Powell/bus 2, 3, 4, 27, 38,
76/cable car Powell-Hyde or Powell-Mason. **Open**
7.30am-3pm Mon, Wed-Sun. **Main courses** $6-$12.
Credit DC, Disc, MC, V. **Map** p314 L6 🢀
Be prepared to wait a little to be seated for your
breakfast: maybe huevos rancheros, perhaps pancakes, possibly a funky omelette or huge scramble
of cheese and veg. However, when it arrives, it may
well be one of the best breakfasts you've ever tasted. A quintessential piece of West Coast Americana.

International

Cortez Restaurant & Bar
550 Geary Street, between Taylor & Jones Streets
(292 6360/www.cortezrestaurant.com). BART &
Metro to Powell/bus 2, 3, 4, 27, 38, 76/cable car
Powell-Hyde or Powell-Mason. **Open** 5.30-10.30pm
daily. **Main courses** $25-$27. **Credit** AmEx, DC,
MC, V. **Map** p314 L6 🢀
This stylish restaurant seems an anomaly on an
unseemly stretch of Geary Street. The room is modern and energetic, filled with well-dressed patrons
eager to experience the assortment of small plates,
which range from the Far East to the American West.
Wash down the maze of tasties with a house cocktail.

Millennium
Hotel California, 580 Geary Street, at Jones Street
(345 3900/www.millenniumrestaurant.com). BART
& Metro to Powell/bus 2, 3, 4, 27, 38, 76/cable car
Powell-Hyde or Powell-Mason. **Open** 5.30-9.30pm Mon-
Thur, Sun; 5.30-10pm Fri, Sat. **Main courses** $21-$24.
Credit AmEx, DC, Disc, MC, V. **Map** p314 L6 🢀
Casual, elegant Millennium is still setting the pace
when it comes to vegetarian and vegan cooking in
San Francisco, doing things with vegetables that
you'd never dream possible. The food, both the
carte and the $65 tasting menu, changes frequent-
ly, driven by the freshest available ingredients; it's
accompanied by one of the best all-organic wine
lists in the US.

Shalimar
532 Jones Street, at O'Farrell Street (928 0333/
www.shalimarsf.com). BART & Metro to Powell/bus
2, 3, 4, 27, 38, 76/cable car Powell-Hyde or Powell-
Mason. **Open** noon-3pm, 5-11.30pm daily. **Main**
courses $5-$10. **No credit cards**. **Map** p314 L6 🢀
Locals have other favourites, but this is perhaps the
best Indian and Pakistan cuisine in this grubby corner of the Tenderloin. The dishes here are fairly
spicy, turned out at speed and at predictably keen
prices. The room's not much to look at, but you'll
only have eyes for the food.
Other locations 1409 Polk Street, Polk Gulch
(776 4642).

Civic Center

American

Indigo
687 McAllister Street, at Gough Street (673 9353/
www.indigorestaurant.com). Bus 5, 21, 47, 49.
Open 5-11pm Tue-Sun. **Main courses** $18-$21.
Credit AmEx, DC, MC, V. **Map** p318 J7 🢀
The key to Indigo's success is good food, well priced
and served in an edgy, chic environment that defies
modishness. The lounge-like setting features a long,
open kitchen, from which emerges a broad mix of
inventive New American dishes. The three-course
evening special prix fixe (5-7pm) is one of the best
deals in town at just $34.

Zuni Café
1658 Market Street, between Franklin & Gough Streets
(552 2522/www.zunicafe.com). Metro to Van Ness/
streetcar F/bus 6, 7, 26, 47, 49 71. **Open** 11.30am-
midnight Tue-Sat; 11am-11pm Sun. **Main courses**
$24-$35. **Credit** AmEx, DC, MC, V. **Map** p318 K8 🢀

Eat, Drink, Shop

After more than 25 years, Zuni has developed a cult following on a par with Berkeley's Chez Panisse. Chef Judy Rodgers's Cal-Ital food manages to be both memorable and transparently simple. The art-filled setting, comprising four separate dining rooms, can be quite a scene before and after cultural events in the vicinity, but the sourdough bread and oysters on an iced platter, the roast chicken for two and the wood-fired pizzettas are attractions in themselves.

Asian

Tu Lan

8 6th Street, at Market Street (626 0927). BART & Metro to Powell/streetcar F/bus 5, 14, 26 & Market Street routes. **Open** 11am-9.30pm Mon-Sat. **Main courses** $5-$9. **No credit cards.** **Map** p318 L7 ❸
Other restaurants around town put a modern American spin on Vietnamese cuisine, serving the food in chic surroundings and upping the charges in the process. Tulan, however, keeps things authentic, scruffy and cheap: the menu sticks to Vietnamese basics, the room hasn't been decorated in decades (in a neighbourhood that could generously be described as downtrodden) and the prices are gloriously low.

Cafés, delis & diners

Saigon Sandwich Café

560 Larkin Street, between Turk & Eddy Streets (474 5698). BART & Metro to Civic Center/bus 5, 19, 31 & Market Street routes. **Open** 6am-6pm Mon-Sat; 7.30am-5pm Sun. **Main courses** $2-$3. **No credit cards.** **Map** p314 K6 ❸
Still the Civic Center's best unsung spot, this tiny, dingy room is typically jammed with foodies and federal workers who file in for huge sandwiches at rock-bottom prices. The bare-bones menu is made up almost entirely of Vietnamese banh mi sandwiches, which are prepared with such ingredients as roast pork with a chilli sauce.

French

Jardinière

300 Grove Street, at Franklin Street (861 5555/ www.jardiniere.com). BART & Metro to Civic Center Metro to Van Ness/bus 5, 21, 47, 49 & Market Street routes. **Open** from 5pm (last reservation 10pm) Mon, Sun; from 5pm (last reservation 10.30pm) Tue-Sat. **Main courses** $25-$40. **Credit** AmEx, DC, Disc, MC, V. **Map** p318 K7 ❸
This beautiful, whimsically shaped (meant to resemble an overturned champagne glass) restaurant is one of the best high-dollar special-occasion eateries in the state. Chef Traci Des Jardins continues to seek out the best and most environmentally friendly local ingredients. Starters can be a meal in themselves, but save room for the stellar mains (or try the $125 tasting menu). The wine list has pages of sparklers.

SoMa & South Beach

American

Public

1489 Folsom Street, at 11th Street (552 3065/www. thepublicsf.com). Bus 9, 12, 27, 47. **Open** 6-9.30pm Tue-Thur; 6-10.30pm Fri, Sat. **Main courses** $18-$25. **Credit** AmEx, DC, MC, V. **Map** p318 L8 ❸
A deft mix of fine-dining sophistication and nightclub energy, Public is built into a historic brick building. American-Italian comfort food is the theme: highlights might include braised duck leg with pappardelle, or pan-roasted ribeye with a balsamic glaze. The stylish bars continue buzzing long after the kitchen closes.

Salt House

545 Mission Street, between 1st & 2nd Streets (543 8900/www.salthousesf.com). BART & Metro to Montgomery/bus 9, 9X, 10, 12, 14, 30, 45, 76. **Open** 11.30am-11pm Monur; 11.30am-midnight Fri; 5.30pm-midnight Sat; 5-10pm Sun. **Main courses** $24-$29. **Credit** AmEx, DC, Disc, MC, V. **Map** p315 N5 ❹
Built into a loft-style space in a small brick building quickly being overshadowed by new neighbouring skyscrapers, this is one of the most vibrant new additions to the SF dining scene (from the people behind Town Hall; *see below*). The restaurant always looks great, especially at night, when soft glowing light illuminates the noisy crowd as they enjoy the inventive contemporary American cuisine. The menu changes seasonally, but standouts among the main courses include roasted lamb loin and dry-aged ribeye grilled to perfection. At lunch, don't miss the Cuban pork sandwich and housemade chips.

Town Hall Restaurant

342 Howard Street, at Fremont Street (908 3900/www.townhallsf.com). BART & Metro to Embarcadero/bus 1, 10, 14, 21, 41, 76. **Open** 11.30am-2.30pm, 5.30-10pm Mon-Thur; 11.30am-2.30pm, 5.30-11pm Fri; 5.30-11pm Sat; 5.30-10pm Sun. **Main courses** $18-$26.50. **Credit** AmEx, DC, MC, V. **Map** p315 O5 ❹
This little slice of New England, a collaboration between Postrio chefs Mitchell and Steven Rosenthal, and legendary front-of-house man Doug Washington, is a great-looking restaurant. The frequently changing menu recalls American classics, often peppered with southern inspiration; highlights might include such treats as sautéed dayboat scallops or Chimay-seasoned short ribs. The bar is known for its speciality cocktails, including an excellent sazerac.

XYZ

*W Hotel, 181 3rd Street, at Howard Street
817 7836/www.xyz-sf.com). BART & Metro to
Montgomery/bus 9X, 12, 30, 45, 76.* **Open** 6.30-
10.30am, 11.30am-2.30pm, 6-10.30pm Mon-Thur;
6.30-10.30am, 11.30am-2.30pm, 6-11pm Fri; 6.30am-
2.30pm, 6-11pm Sat; 6.30am-2.30pm, 6-10.30pm Sun.
Main courses $21-$36. **Credit** AmEx, DC, Disc,
MC, V. **Map** p315 N6 **⓬**

Adjacent to the lobby of the W, XYZ holds fast to its
austere decor and sophisticated clientele. Although the
parade of chefs who have worked here is long, the
kitchen has been re-energised more recently with a
tempting choice of modern California fare with
Provençal touches. The seasonally changing menu
might include the likes of seared Sonoma duck breast
or rabbit ravioli. The wine list is excellent.

Cafés & diners

The café at **SFMOMA** (*see p81*) is also good.

Brainwash

*1122 Folsom Street, between 7th & 8th Streets (861
3663/www.brainwash.com). BART & Metro to Civic
Center/bus 12, 14, 19, 27, 47.* **Open** *Café* 8am-9pm
daily. *Laundromat* 7am-11pm Mon-Thur, Sun; 7am-
midnight Fri, Sat.* **Main courses** $5-$10. **Credit** DC,
MC, V. **Map** p319 M8 **⓭**

Part laundromat, part bar/café and part performance
space, this popular spot remains one of the premier
singles hangouts in town. People bring along their
dirty linens and a wandering eye as they peruse the
array of potential mates and the menu of soups, salads and burgers. On most evenings, the atmosphere
is brightened by live music, poetry readings or
improv comedy (all ages, no cover).

French

Le Charm

*315 5th Street, at Folsom Street (546 6128/www.
lecharm.com). BART & Metro to Powell/bus 9X,
12, 27, 30, 45, 76.* **Open** 11.30am-2pm, 5.30-9.30pm
Tue-Thur; 11.30am-2pm, 5.30-10pm Fri; 5.30-10pm
Sat; 5-8.30pm Sun. **Main courses** $19-$28. **Credit**
AmEx, DC, MC, V. **Map** p319 N7 **⓮**

One of the few places in town where you can enjoy
eating your way through an authentic French bistro
menu without having to make a massive cash out-
lay. Alongside an excellent standard *carte*, Le Charm
has a three-course prix fixe menu ($30) that includes
main courses such as pan-roasted calf's liver and
steak-frites. The pick of the desserts is the tarte tatin.
There's only a tiny wine list, but it is well chosen.

International

Bossa Nova

*139 8th Street, at Minna Street (558 8004/www.
bossanovasf.com). BART & Metro to Civic Center/
bus 12, 14, 19, 26, 27, 47.* **Open** 5.30pm-midnight

Tue-Sat. *Bar* until 2am. **Main courses** $7-$58.
Credit AmEx, DC, MC, V. **Map** p318 L7 **⓯**

Although Bossa Nova is off the beaten track and
lacks a sign, locals have found their way to this
very hip, eclectically appointed and quite tasty bit
of Rio in the city. It's popular for its nightly namesake music as well as for its refreshing take on
Brazilian food. Plantain chips and salsa verde get
things started while you sip a caipirinha and await
the soccer uniform-clad waitstaff to usher out such
delicacies as shellfish stew with coconut milk, seasoned lamb tenderloin, and grilled T-bone big
enough for two.

Ame

*689 Mission Street, at 3rd Street (284 4040/
www.amerestaurant.com). BART & Metro to
Montgomery/bus 9, 9X, 10, 12, 14, 30, 45, 76.*
Open 5.30-10pm daily. **Main courses** $28-$38.
Credit AmEx, DC, MC, V. Map p 319 N6 **⓰**

Hiro Sone and Lissa Doumani, the team behind Terra
in Napa Valley, have brought their Japonesque sensibilities to this stylish and intimate dining room in
the St Regis Hotel. The menu emphasises raw – sashimi, crudo, tartare, carpaccio – and southern France:
grilled duck with a ragout of wild mushrooms, with
a confit of giblets and bok choy, say. Everything is
exquisitely prepared and presented. The bar features
limited-edition sakes and small-lot wines.

Italian & pizza

LuLu

*816 Folsom Street, between 4th & 5th Streets (495
5775/www.restaurantlulu.com). BART & Metro to
Powell/bus 9X, 12, 27, 30, 45, 76.* **Open** 11.30am-
10pm Mon-Thur, Sun; 11.30am-11pm Fri, Sat. **Main
courses** $16-$50. **Credit** AmEx, DC, MC, V.
Map p319 N7 **⓱**

LuLu majors in delicious, rustic, Italian-influenced
cuisine, including specialities from the wood-fired
oven, rotisserie and grill. Pizzas, pasta and shellfish
come on large platters, designed to be shared. LuLu's
wine bar next door offers a more intimate alternative; executive chef Jody Denton also owns nearby
Azie (538 0918) and the LuLu Petite deli in the Ferry
Building (362 7019).

South Park & South Beach

American

Acme Chop House

*24 Willie Mays Plaza, corner of King & 3rd Streets
(644 0240/www.acmechophouse.com). Metro to 2nd
& King/bus 9X, 10, 30, 45, 47.* **Open** 11am-2.30pm,
5.30-10pm Tue-Fri; 5.30-10pm Sat, Sun. **Main
courses** $23-$55. **Credit** AmEx, DC, Disc, MC, V.
Map p319 O7 **⓲**

Traci Des Jardins of Jardinière (*see p140*) oversees
the menu at this large, comfortable restaurant at the
ballpark, and her commitment to sustainability

Eat, Drink, Shop

Bacar.

and organically raised meat sets it apart from most steakhouses. Beef is tender and perfectly prepared, and the raw seafood bar makes a fine start to a meal. Needless to say, it gets crowded on game days.

Bacar

448 Brannan Street, between 3rd & 4th Streets (904 4100/www.bacarsf.com). Metro to 4th & King/bus 9X, 10, 30, 45, 47, 76. **Open** 5.30-10pm Mon-Thur, Sun; 5.30-11pm Fri, Sat. **Main courses** $22-$38. **Credit** AmEx, DC, Disc, MC, V. **Map** p319 O7 ㊾

Bacar is a wine-lover's Valhalla: some 100 of the 1,000 varietals are available by the glass. The 'wine wall' is the most eye-catching aspect of this remarkable three-level converted warehouse, but these days the food is also worth talking about. Wood-fired pizzas are the best bet, although the mesquite-grilled meat, seared diver scallops and the smoked sturgeon are also highlights on the approachable US and Mediterranean menu.

Jack Falstaff

598 2nd Street, at Brannan Street (836 9239/www. plumpjack.com). Metro to 2nd & King/bus 9X, 10, 12, 30, 45, 76. **Open** 11.30am-2pm, 5.30-10pm Mon-Thur; 11.30am-2pm, 5.30-11pm Fri; 5.30-11pm Sat; 5.30-10pm Sun. Also open for lunch on Giants game days Sat, Sun. **Main courses** $22-$32. **Credit** AmEx, DC, Disc, MC, V. **Map** p315 O6 ㊿

This smart-looking restaurant from the folks behind PlumpJack Wines (*see p190*) has an urban appeal that doesn't forsake comfort or hospitality.

The often-changing menu features reassuring dishes, prepared with organic touches and a slow-food approach. Highlights include pan-roasted Liberty Farms duck and prosciutto-wrapped clay-pot baked monkfish. Finish with the fantastic cheese plate.

Paragon

701 2nd Street, at Townsend Street (537 9020/ www.paragonrestaurant.com). Metro to 2nd & King/bus 9X, 10, 12, 30, 45, 76. **Open** 11.30am-2.30pm, 5.30pm-close Mon-Fri; 5.30pm-close Sat. Also open for lunch on Sat, Sun on Giants game days. **Main courses** $17.50-$22. **Credit** AmEx, DC, Disc, MC, V. **Map** p319 P7 ㉛

Before Giants games, fans press shoulder to shoulder at the huge bar here. The attractive dining room is similarly energy-charged. The classic American brasserie fare is rustic and reliable; steaks and seafood come with hearty sides such as mashed potato or vegetable gratin.

Cafés & diners

Butler & the Chef

155 South Park, at 3rd Street (896 2075/www. thebutlerandthechefbistro.com). Metro to 2nd & King/bus 9X, 10, 12, 30, 45, 76. **Open** 8am-3pm Tue-Sat; 10am-3pm Sun. **Main courses** $8-$15. **Credit** AmEx, DC, Disc, MC, V. **Map** p319 O7 ㉜

This très French little café is always crowded with locals who queue for the fresh-made breakfast

Designs on SF dining

San Francisco is a city of appetites – for life, for politics, and above all for food. And perhaps no other person has had more influence on shaping those appetites than Pat Kuleto. Like a restaurant renaissance man, Kuleto has fashioned a reputation as an entrepreneur, a restaurant designer, a vintner and a creator of trends. He has designed and built more than 175 restaurants worldwide, but has his firmest foothold in San Francisco and the Bay Area, where some of the most popular establishments bear his inimitable stamp.

Kuleto is both co-owner and designer of such highly acclaimed restaurants as **Boulevard** (*see p136*), **Jardinière** (*see p140*) in San Francisco, as well as **St Helena's Martini House** in the Napa Valley and **Nick's Cove** on Tomales Bay. He is also the proprietor of the Kuleto Estate Winery in the Napa Valley and had a hand in the design and concept of **Fog City Diner** (*see p136*) and McCormick & Kuleto's on Ghirardhelli Square. But while Kuleto has been an influential force in Bay Area dining over the last 20 years, his reputation has taken a significant upwards turn.

Kuleto has just opened two of the most high-profile new restaurants San Francisco has seen in the past decade: **Waterbar** (399 The Embarcadero, between Folsom & Harrison Streets, 284 9922, www.waterbar sf.com) and **EPIC Roasthouse** (no.369, 369 9955, www.epicroasthousesf.com), side-by-side destination restaurants in Rincon Park. They are the first privately owned buildings to break ground on the San Francisco waterfront in nearly a century. Waterbar is a seafood restaurant, while EPIC offers a menu centred on meats, game and poultry. It's a new approach to surf-and-turf, and another indication that Kuleto remains at the top of this game.

The two restaurants will share an outdoor piazza (with seating) offering panoramic views of the Bay Bridge, Treasure Island and the San Francisco skyline. Both showcase the kind of interior styling for which Kuleto has become known: bold, innovative and eye-popping, but never distracting too much from the food. To that end, Kuleto also has a reputation of partnering with capable kitchen veterans. Waterbar is operated and co-owned by acclaimed chef Mark Franz of Farallon

fame, while EPIC will be headed and co-owned by renowned chef Jan Birnbaum, who enjoyed a rabid following at the highly acclaimed Catahoula restaurant in Calistoga. Kuleto's design for Waterbar includes floor-to-ceiling aquariums and a cascading raw bar. For EPIC, he drew in a custom wood-fired grill and a large wood-burning oven, along with an enormous fireplace.

It's not often that new restaurants generate as much anticipation among jaded, food-savvy locals as this duo of waterfront eateries has done. But when Pat Kuleto is involved, it's usually a safe bet that the hype is worth it. At this guide went to press, the restaurants has just opened, and local mouths were already starting to water.

Eat, Drink, Shop

pastries and wonderful breads. Tuck into pain au chocolat or sip a Pernod while chatting with Pierre, the amiable owner. The Butler & the Chef also runs a warehouse of French antiques (290 Utah Street, at 16th Street, Potrero Hill, 626 9600).

International

Coco 500

500 Brannan Street, at 4th Street (543 2222/ www.coco500.com). Metro to 4th & King/bus 9X, 10, 30, 45, 47, 76. **Open** 11.30am-10pm Mon-Thur; 11.30am-11pm Fri; 5.30-11pm Sat. **Main courses** $10-$26. **Credit** AmEx, DC, Disc, MC, V. **Map** p319 N7 ⑤④
This SoMa restaurant is a reinvention of sorts for its popular proprietor, Loretta Keller, whose penchant for Parisian hospitality has given way to a small plate style. Mediterranean-influenced dishes prepared with organic, today-fresh ingredients range from light pizzas from a wood-fired oven to beef-cheek *mole* and whole fish with fennel saffron sauce. Seafood, steaks and poultry are also cooked *a la plancha*.

South Food & Wine Bar

330 Townsend Street, at 4th Street (974 5599/ www.southfwb.com). Metro to 4th & King/bus 9X, 10, 30, 45, 47, 76. **Open** 11.30am-3pm, 5.30-11pm Mon-Fri; 10am-3pm, 5.30-11pm Sat; 10am-3pm Sun. **Main courses** $18-$25. **Credit** AmEx, DC, MC, V. **Map** p319 O7 ⑤⑤
This is San Francisco's first dining import from Australia, an intimate 50-seat dazzler with an international vibe and a chef (Luke Mangan) who brings with him a global reputation for inventiveness and refreshing simplicity. Most dishes are imbued with Asian influence; highlights include marinated pork belly with scallops and tamarind dressing, fish and chips with wasabi mayo, and pan-fried islands snapper with curried lentils and coriander yogurt. No, there's no kangaroo on the menu, but there is an excellent wine list of Australian and New Zealand vintages.

Italian & pizza

Zuppa

564 4th Street, between Bryant & Brannan Streets (777 5900/www.zuppa-sf.com). Metro to 4th & King/bus 9X, 10, 30, 45, 47, 76. **Open** 11.30am-2.30pm, 5.30-10pm Mon-Thur; 11.30am-2.30pm, 5.30-11pm Fri; 5.30-9pm Sun. **Main courses** $19-$34. **Credit** AmEx, DC, MC, V. **Map** p319 N7 ⑤⑥
Despite the long banquettes that flank the dining room, and the post-work young professionals and adventurous Mission hipsters who sit in them, it's the rustic, fresh-made southern Italian cuisine that really steals the show at Zuppa. Almost everything on the menu is excellent, especially the house-cured meats offered at each table and fresh, seasonal dishes that use ingredients from the rooftop garden. The wine list is all-Italian.

Latin American

Tres Agaves

130 Townsend Street, between 2nd & 3rd Streets, (227 0500/www.tresagaves.com). Metro to 2nd & King/bus 9X, 10, 12, 30, 45, 76. **Open** 11.30am-10pm Mon-Wed; 11.30am-11pm Thur, Fri; 10am-11pm Sat; 10am-10pm Sun. **Main courses** $13-$27. **Credit** AmEx, DC, Disc, MC, V. **Map** p319 O7 ⑤⑦
Tequila expert Julio Bermejo has teamed up with impresario Eric Rubin, chef Joseph Manzare and rocker Sammy Hagar to create this homage to the Mexican state of Jalisco, home to the town of Tequila. The cavernous brick and timber space houses ample bar space for Bermejo to serve a huge variety of artisan, pure-agave tequilas, while the display kitchen turns out gourmet regional Mexican cuisine around the clock.

Nob Hill & Chinatown

Nob Hill & Polk Gulch

Cafés, delis & diners

Café Nook

1500 Hyde Street, at Jackson Street (447 4100/www. cafenook.com). Bus 1, 12, 19, 27/cable car Powell-Hyde. **Open** 7am-10.30pm Mon-Fri; 8am-9pm Sat, Sun. **Main courses** $6-$8. **Credit** DC, Disc, MC, V. **Map** p314 K4 ⑤⑧
This unassuming little café is popular for its easygoing atmosphere, good prices and Monday-Friday free wireless internet access. The menu is an assortment of bagels, soups, salads and sandwiches, plus small-plate-style appetisers. There's a list of sakés and wines in the evening.

Fish & seafood

Swan Oyster Depot

1517 Polk Street, between California & Sacramento Streets (673 1101). Bus 1, 19, 47, 49, 76/cable car California. **Open** 8am-5.30pm Mon-Sat. **Main courses** $14-$35. **No credit cards**. **Map** p314 K5 ⑤⑨
Don't miss this Polk Gulch institution: half fish market, half counter-service hole in the wall, it has been delighting locals since 1912. The best time to visit is between November and June, when the local Dungeness crab is in season. But at any time of year, the selections are straight-from-the-water fresh. Specialities include clam chowder and an obscenely large variety of oysters, best downed with a pint of locally brewed Anchor Steam beer. You can buy shellfish to take away.

tive without being overbearing. One of the best pull-out-all-the-stops restaurant in town.

Tres Agaves: ¡Viva Tequila!

French

Dining Room

Ritz-Carlton Hotel, 600 Stockton Street, at California Street (773 6198/www.ritzcarlton.com). Bus 1, 15, 30, 45/cable car California. **Open** 6-9pm Tue-Thur; 5.30-9.30pm Fri, Sat. **Set meal** $74/3 courses; $110/8 courses. **Credit** AmEx, DC, Disc, MC, V. **Map** p315 M4 ⑥⓪

The Dining Room has a global reputation and a waitstaff-to-diner ratio of almost 1:1. It's opulent without being over the top, although it can feel a little serious. The modern French menu is inventive and artfully executed by chef Ron Siegel (the first non-Japanese to win the Iron Chef contest), as are the famous seasonal speciality menus, such as the annual white truffle festival. Master sommelier Stephane Lacroix will guide you to an appropriate wine; the bar list of single malts is one of the largest in the US.

Fleur de Lys

777 Sutter Street, between Jones & Taylor Streets (673 7779/www.fleurdelyssf.com). Bus 2, 3, 4, 27, 38, 76. **Open** 6-9.30pm Mon-Thur; 5.30-10.30pm Fri; 5-10.30pm Sat. **Set meal** $70/3 courses; $79/4 courses; $92/5 courses. **Credit** AmEx, DC, MC, V. **Map** p314 L5 ⑥①

A fine dining experience so memorable it's been duplicated in Las Vegas. Chef Hubert Keller's cuisine is deserving of a wider audience because of his vast repertoire: his menu is lush, even exorbitant. It all plays out like a symphony, a feast for the eyes as much as the palate, enhanced by service that is atten-

Chinatown

American

Alfred's Steakhouse

659 Merchant Street, between Kearny & Montgomery Streets (781 7058/www.alfreds steakhouse.com). Bus 1, 9X, 10, 12, 20, 30, 41, 45. **Open** 5-9pm Mon, Sat, Sun; 11.30am-9pm Tue-Thur; 11.30am-10pm Fri. **Main courses** $14-$39. **Credit** AmEx, DC, Disc, MC, V. **Map** p315 M4 ⑥②

With decades of experience as one of the city's best steakhouses, Alfred's feels like a bit of San Francisco gone by, but it continues to prove itself worthy of a fiercely loyal fanbase. The chief attractions are giant Chicago ribeyes, tender T-bones and a porterhouse that covers the plate, but the fish and pasta are also from the top drawer. The bar, which mixes superlative martinis, stocks more than 100 single malts.

Asian

San Francisco's best Chinese food is actually found in the Richmond (*see p113*), but there are still worthwhile options in Chinatown. The Chinese crowd at **Dol Ho's** (808 Pacific Avenue, at Stockton Street, 392 2828) speaks volumes about the food's authenticity, and **House of Nanking** (919 Kearny Street, at Jackson Street, 421 1429), while touristy, never disappoints with its food.

R&G Lounge

631 Kearny Street, between Clay & Sacramento Streets (982 7877/www.rnglounge.com). Bus 1, 9X, 10, 12, 20, 30, 41, 45. **Open** 11am-9.30pm daily. **Main courses** $10-$28. **Credit** AmEx, DC, MC, V. **Map** p315 M4 ⑥③

Always busy and often chaotic, R&G Lounge has two levels for dining, neither of them much to look at. The Hong Kong-style food is authentic, emphasising seafood that's taken mainly from the in-house tanks. People come from miles around for the deep-fried salt and pepper crab and barbecue pork.

Yuet Lee

1300 Stockton Street, at Broadway (982 6020). Bus 9X, 12, 20, 30, 41, 45/cable car Powell-Mason. **Open** 11am-3am Mon, Wed-Sun. **Main courses** $5-$27. **Credit** DC, MC, V. **Map** p315 M3 ⑥④

Terrific seafood and the opportunity to indulge in some small-hours dining attract sundry restaurant folk to this tiny, bright-green Chinese eaterie. The roasted squab with fresh coriander and lemon, sautéed clams with black bean sauce, and 'eight precious noodle soup', made with eight kinds of meat, are all worth trying. Lighting is glaringly unflattering and the service matter-of-fact.

North Beach to Fisherman's Wharf

North Beach

American

Moose's
1652 Stockton Street, between Union & Filbert Streets (989 7800/www.mooses.com). Bus 9X, 20, 30, 39, 41, 45/cable car Powell-Mason. **Open** 5.30-10pm Mon-Sat; 10.30am-2.30pm, 5.30-10pm Sun. **Main courses** $18-$37. **Credit** AmEx, DC, MC, V. **Map** p315 M3 ⑥
This Washington Square staple was long the haunt of local politicos and bon vivants, and it's hoped that a recent refurbishment will return is original lustre. The new, comfy-looking design brings with it a new chef and menu, which acknowledges long-established favourites like the Mooseburger, but also updates with such touches as farm-fresh ingredients and locally caught fish. The wine list is still impressive. The lounge area is perfect for drop-in dining.

Asian

House
1230 Grant Avenue, at Columbus Avenue & Vallejo Street (986 8612/www.thehse.com). Bus 9X, 12, 20, 30, 39, 41, 45. **Open** 11.30am-2.30pm, 5.30-10pm Mon-Thur; 11.30am-2.30pm, 5.30-11pm Fri; 11.30am-2.30pm, 5-11pm Sat; 5-10pm Sun. **Main courses** $17-$25. **Credit** AmEx, DC, MC, V. **Map** p315 M3 ⑥
This no-frills (though often ear-shatteringly loud) Chinese fusion dining room works wonders with fresh, seasonal produce and East-meets-West preparations. The Chinese chicken salad with sesame soy illustrates the menu: light, tangy and big enough to be a meal on its own. The menu changes often, resisting trends while remaining decidedly sophisticated.

Cafés & diners

Caffe Puccini
411 Columbus Avenue, at Vallejo Street (989 7033). Bus 9X, 12, 20, 30, 41, 45/cable car Powell-Mason. **Open** 6am-11.30pm Mon-Fri, Sun; 6am-12.30am Sat. **Main courses** $6.50-$9.50. **No credit cards.** **Map** p315 M3 ⑥
Like the composer after whom the café is named, friendly owner Graziano Lucchese is from Lucca in northern Italy. His welcoming café serves vast sandwiches stuffed with salami, prosciutto and mortadella.

Caffe Roma
526 Columbus Avenue, at Union Street (296 7942/ www.cafferoma.com). Bus 9X, 12, 20, 30, 39, 41, 45/ cable car Powell-Mason. **Open** 6am-7pm Mon-Thur; 6am-8pm Fri; 6.30am-11pm Sat; 7am-8pm Sun. **Credit** AmEx, DC, Disc, MC, V. **Map** p314 L3 ⑥
Some say it's the strongest coffee in the city – it's certainly the most coveted, roasted on the premises by three generations of the Azzollini family.. Espressos, other coffees and a range of gelati are served in a large, airy space, perfect for sipping, thinking and explaining your latest conspiracy theory.
Other locations 885 Bryant Street, SOMA (296 7662).

Caffe Trieste
601 Vallejo Street, at Grant Avenue (982 2605/ www.caffetrieste.com). Bus 9X, 12, 20, 30, 39, 41, 45. **Open** 6.30am-11pm Mon-Thur, Sun; 6.30am-midnight Fri, Sat. **Main courses** $5-$10. **No credit cards.** **Map** p315 M3 ⑥
This is one of the city's great cafés, a former hangout for Kerouac and Ginsberg and is where Coppola is said to have written the screenplay for *The Godfather.* The dark walls are plastered with photos of opera singers and famous regulars. There are muffins, pastries and sandwiches to eat, and the lattes are legendary, as are the opera sessions held here on a Saturday afternoon.
Other locations 199 New Montgomery Street, SoMa (538 7999); 1667 Market Street, Civic Center (551 1000); 2500 San Pablo Avenue, Berkeley (1-510 548 5198).

Mama's on Washington Square
1701 Stockton Street, at Filbert Street (362 6421/ www.mamas-sf.com). Bus 9X, 12, 20, 30, 39, 41, 45/cable car Powell-Mason. **Open** 8am-3pm Tue-Sun. **Main courses** $6-$10. **No credit cards.** **Map** p314 L3 ⑩
The weekend queue is part of the fun at this wildly popular North Beach mainstay. Once seated, you'll be faced with such temptations as a giant made-to-order 'm'omelette' or the Monte Cristo sandwich on home-made bread. Service is swift and familiar.

Mario's Bohemian Cigar Store
566 Columbus Avenue, at Union Street (362 0536). Bus 9X, 12, 20, 30, 39, 41, 45/cable car Powell-Mason. **Open** 10am-11pm daily. **Main courses** $4-$9. **Credit** DC, MC, V. **Map** p314 L3 ⑪
Despite the name, you can't buy a cigar at Mario's, nor will you be allowed to smoke one. Instead, sip a flavoured Italian soda and watch the neighbourhood while perusing a light menu of focaccia sandwiches and salads, own-made biscotti, beer and coffee. Mario's location means it's always packed, so lunch may be slow in coming, but there's no more essential North Beach café.

International

Iluna Basque
701 Union Street, at Powell Street (402 0011/ www.ilunabasque.com). Bus 9X, 12, 20, 30, 39, 41, 45/cable car Powell-Mason. **Open** 5.30-10.30pm Mon-Thur, Sun; 5.30-11.30pm Fri, Sat. **Main courses** $11-$15. *Tapas* $4-$10. **Credit** AmEx, DC, Disc, MC, V. **Map** p314 L3 ⑫
With views of Washington Square and Coit Tower, this lively restaurant has become a fast favourite among locals, as much for its fun atmosphere as for

Caffe Trieste: sip legendary lattes while listening to opera.

its memorable Basque-influenced tapas. Graze your way through plates of delightful delicacies, from empanadas to Spanish omelettes to a traditional cassoulet of sausage and lamb chop.

Italian & pizza

For North Beach's best Italian cafés, *see p88-91.*

Sodini's

510 Green Street, at Grant Avenue (291 0499). Bus 9X, 12, 20, 30, 39, 41, 45. **Open** 5-10pm Mon-Thur; 5-11pm Fri; 4.45-11pm Sat; 4.45-10pm Sun. **Main courses** $11-$23. **Credit** AmEx, DC, Disc, MC, V. **Map** p315 M3 ⑱
Sodini's is small and darkly romantic, in a Chianti bottle as candle-holder sort of way. Patrons are jammed close together to enable their servers to squeeze past with platters of sloppy pasta and rib-sticking lasagne. The fact that it's off the beaten track doesn't dampen its popularity: be sure to arrive earlier than you intend to eat and sign the list; you can then drop over to a neighbourhood bar while waiting for a table. Once inside, the wine is cheap and in plentiful supply.

Tommaso's Ristorante Italiano

1042 Kearny Street, at Pacific Avenue (398 9696/www.tommasonorthbeach.com). Bus 9X, 10, 12, 20, 30, 41, 45. **Open** 5-10.30pm Tue-Sat; 4-9.30pm Sun. **Main courses** $13-$22. **Credit** AmEx, DC, Disc, MC, V. **Map** p315 M3 ⑭
Tommaso's is known city-wide for its simple Italian food, which has been served family-style in a tiny, boisterous room since 1935. The wood-fired pizzas and calzones deserve their reps and the house red is surprisingly good. No affectations, no frills and no reservations. Join the queue and keep your eyes peeled: you never know who might walk in.

Latin American

Impala

501 Broadway, at Kearny Street (982 5299/www.impalasf.com). Bus 9X, 10, 12, 20, 30, 41, 45. **Open** 5.30-11pm Tue-Sat. **Main courses** $17-$24. **Credit** AmEx, DC, Disc, MC, V. **Map** p315 M3 ⑮
In the otherwise honky-tonk heart of North Beach, this buzzing, popular restaurant is surprisingly chic. It aims to raise Mexican cuisine to a higher level and, in many aspects, it succeeds. Mains focus on fish dishes, slow-roasted meats and Mexican classics; the crowd eats them up with as much enthusiasm as it does the lounge-style atmosphere, a combination of candlelight and DJ-spun music. The bar is open until 2am.

Fisherman's Wharf

American

Gary Danko

800 North Point Street, at Hyde Street (749 2060/www.garydanko.com). Streetcar F to Fisherman's Wharf/bus 10, 19, 20, 30, 47/cable car Powell-Hyde. **Open** 5.30-10pm daily. **Set meal** $65/3 courses; $81/4 courses; $96/5 courses. **Credit** AmEx, DC, Disc, MC, V. **Map** p314 K2 ⑯
Superstar chef Danko's fine-dining restaurant near the wharf is fabulous – and fabulously understated. The best way to experience his dexterity and genius is via the tasting menus, which change seasonally but might include seared foie gras with caramelised red onions as a starter, beef tenderloin with king trumpet mushrooms as a main, and farmhouse cheeses to finish. A more casual adventure can be had at the bar. Reservations are essential and can be hard to come by.

Eat, Drink, Shop

Asian

Ana Mandara
*981 Beach Street, at Polk Street (771 6800/www.
anamandara.com). Streetcar F to Fisherman's
Wharf/bus 10, 19, 20, 30, 47/cable car Powell-
Hyde.* **Open** 11.30am-2pm, 5.30-9.30pm Mon-Thur;
11.30am-2pm, 5.30-10.30pm Fri; 5.30-10.30pm Sat;
5.30-9.30pm Sun. **Main courses** $21-$38. **Credit**
AmEx, DC, Disc, MC, V. **Map** p314 J2 **⑦**
Although located in touristy Ghirardelli Square, this
fabulous French-Vietnamese restaurant could hold
its own in the foodiest of neighbourhoods. The room
is beautiful, with soaring ceilings and a staircase
that sweeps you to a chic lounge. The sumptuous
and beautifully presented specialities are enriched
with the aromas and flavours of Vietnam. The Cham
Bar has live jazz from Thursday to Saturday.

Cafés, delis & diners

Boudin Sourdough Bakery & Café
*2890 Taylor Street, at Jefferson Street (928 1849/
www.boudinbakery.com). Streetcar F to Pier 39/bus 9X,
10, 20, 30, 39, 47/cable car Powell-Mason.* **Open** *Café*
8am-9pm Mon-Thur, Sun; 8am-10pm Fri, Sat. *Bistro*
11.30am-10pm Mon-Thur, Sun; 11.30am-10.30pm Fri,
Sat. **Main courses** *Bistro* $15-$38. *Café* $7-$12.
Credit AmEx, DC, Disc, MC, V. **Map** p314 L1 **⑦**
Locals brag that sourdough bread was invented here,
and the Boudin family is among its founding fathers
– baking their bread from the same mother dough
since 1849. The flagship store, a relaxing alternative
to ear-busting crab and seafood stands along the
Wharf, offers delights as sourdough pizzas and clam
chowder served in a hollowed-out sourdough bowl.
Other locations throughout the Bay Area.

Fish & seafood

Alioto's
*8 Fisherman's Wharf, at Taylor & Jefferson Streets
(673 0183/www.aliotos.com). Streetcar F to Pier 39/
bus 9X, 10, 20, 30, 39, 47/cable car Powell-Mason.*
Open 11am-11pm daily. **Main courses** $22-$48.
Credit AmEx, DC, Disc, MC, V. **Map** p314 K1 **⑦**
Alioto's began as a sidewalk stand serving crab and
shrimp cocktails to passers-by. Now, more than eight
decades later, it's a hugely popular restaurant owned
by a prominent local family. The room offers an amazing view of the Bay, enough to draw in tourists year-
round, but the kitchen still manages to turn out decent
(if pricey) seafood, as well as fish-centred Sicilian specialities. The wine list is outstanding.

Blue Mermaid
*Argonaut Hotel, 471 Jefferson Street, at Hyde Street
(771 2222/www.bluemermaidsf.com). Streetcar F to
Fisherman's Wharf/bus 10, 19, 20, 30, 47/cable car
Powell-Hyde.* **Open** 7am-9pm Mon-Thur, Sun; 7am-
10pm Fri, Sat. **Main courses** $11-$25. **Credit**
AmEx, DC, Disc, MC, V. **Map** p314 K2 **⑧**

Designed to recall the history of the working wharf
(don't miss the excellent on-site museum), this
rustic-looking restaurant is set into the corner of the
Argonaut Hotel. The menu is perfect for San
Francisco's fogged-in days, with hearty chowders
spooned up from large cauldrons – don't miss the
award-winning Dungeness crab and corn. The
Treaasure Chest offers a choice of marine dishes.
There's also a kids' menu: it's a top choice for families.

Russian Hill

Asian

Sushi Groove
*1916 Hyde Street, between Union & Green Streets
(440 1905). Bus 41, 45/cable car Powell-Hyde.* **Open**
5.30-9.30pm daily. **Main courses** *Sushi* $5.50-$15.
Credit AmEx, DC, MC, V. **Map** p314 K3 **⑧**
If you don't mind sitting elbow to elbow in a dining room that's roughly the size of a postage
stamp, join the stylish clientele at this creative and
highly charged Japanese sushi restaurant. The
decor is postmodern, the mood music is loungy
and the original rolls and salads are mostly very
good. Fresh crab, sea urchin and eel join the familiar mackerel, tuna and salmon. The impressive
saké selection is worth the trip alone.

Pesce.

Cafés, delis & diners

La Boulange de Polk

2310 Polk Street, at Green Street (345 1107/www.
baybread.com). Bus 12, 19, 47, 49, 76/cable car
Powell-Hyde. **Open** 7am-6.30pm Tue-Sat; 7am-6pm
Sun. **Main courses** $3-$10. **Credit** AmEx, DC, MC,
V. **Map** p314 K3
In the style of a Parisian boulangerie, this café serves
beautiful pastries and tasty fresh-baked bread. The
best spot to watch a morning unfold is from one of
the inviting pavement tables, but they can be diffi-
cult to acquire, especially at the weekend.
Other locations throughout the city.

Fish & seafood

Pesce

2227 Polk Street, between Green & Vallejo Streets
(928 8025/www.pescesf.com). Bus 12, 19, 47, 49,
76/cable car Powell-Hyde. **Open** 5-10pm Mon-Thur;
5-11pm Fri; noon-4pm, 5-11pm Sat; noon-10pm Sun.
Main courses *Small plates* $6-$13. **Credit** AmEx,
DC, Disc, MC, V. **Map** p314 K4
Modest and comfortable, Pesce is a great place to
make a mess with your local speciality *cioppino*.
This simple restaurant and bar proves that fabulous
seafood doesn't have to be fancy or expensive, making it wildly popular with those lucky enough to live
nearby. Starters include excellent mussels, cod cakes
and calamari; main courses tend to be Italian.

French

La Folie

2316 Polk Street, between Union & Green Streets
(776 5577/www.lafolie.com). Bus 12, 19, 47, 49,
76/cable car Powell-Hyde. **Open** 5.30-10.30pm Mon-
Sat. **Set meal** $70/3 courses; $80/4 courses; $90/5
courses. **Credit** AmEx, DC, Disc, MC, V.
Map p314 K3
If you want to find out why chef Roland Passot
enjoys a passionate following, opt for the five-course
discovery menu ($90) and sample his ever-changing
selection of classic French fare, prepared with seasonally fresh ingredients. The Provençal decor and
attentive staff add to the charm of this delightful
French-Californian eaterie. The adjoining Green
Room is a good option for intimate dining.

Le Petit Robert

2300 Polk Street, at Green Street (922 8100).
Bus 12, 19, 47, 49, 76/cable car Powell-Hyde.
Open 11.30am-10pm Mon-Fri; 10.30am-10pm Sat,
Sun. **Main courses** $11-$22. **Credit** AmEx, DC,
MC, V. **Map** p314 K3
With an air of casual sophistication, this high-ceilinged
room is easily able to accommodate both boisterous
parties and romantically inclined couples. The menu
features above-par French classics, including salad
niçoise and steak tartare. The wine list has many
affordable selections and good choices by the glass.

International

Helmand Palace

2424 Van Ness Avenue, between Union & Green
Streets (345 0072/www.helmandrestaurant
sanfrancisco.com). Bus 19, 41, 45, 47, 49, 76.
Open 5.30-10pm Mon-Thur, Sun; 5.30-11pm Fri,
Sat. **Main courses** $11-$19. **Credit** AmEx, DC,
MC, V. **Map** p314 J3
The Helmand – the city's only Afghan restaurant –
moved from North Beach and added 'Palace' to its
name, but it's still as good as it ever was. Influenced
by the flavours of India, Asia and the Middle East,
the food is deliciously aromatic, with marinades and
fragrant spices. Specialities include leek ravioli and
lamb lawand (leg of lamb sautéed with garlic, onion,
tomatoes, mushrooms, yoghurt and spices).

Zarzuela

2000 Hyde Street, at Union Street (346 0800). Bus 41,
45/cable car Powell-Hyde. **Open** 5.30-10pm Tue-Thur;
5.30-10.30pm Fri, Sat. **Main courses** $14-$19. *Tapas*
$5-$9. **Credit** DC, Disc, MC, V. **Map** p314 K3
The tapas are always a treat at cosy Zarzuela, where
the Spanish cuisine is served amid bullfight posters
and maps of Spain. Old standbys such as grilled
aubergine filled with goat's cheese, sautéed shrimps
in garlic and olive oil, and fried potatoes with garlic
and sherry vinegar never disappoint.

Eat, Drink, Shop

The Mission & the Castro

American

Delfina

3621 18th Street, between Dolores & Guerrero Streets (552 4055/www.delfinasf.com). BART 16th Street Mission/Metro to Church & 18th Street/bus 14, 26, 33, 49. **Open** 5.30-10pm Mon-Thur, Sun; 5.30-11pm Fri, Sat. **Main courses** $18-$27. **Credit** DC, MC, V. **Map** p318 J10 ⓺

Chef/owner Craig Stoll favours simplicity over whimsy, and tradition over fashion. Yet his food is never ordinary: fresh pasta, fish and braised meats all burst with flavour. The menu changes daily, reflecting Stoll's desire to stay on his toes; it's a pity the staff don't always seem to share his ambition. Stoll's casual Pizzeria Delfina (437 6800) is just next door, serving some of the best thin-crust pizzas in town.

Luna Park

694 Valencia Street, at 18th Street (553 8584/www. lunaparksf.com). BART 16th Street Mission/Metro to Church & 18th Street/bus 14, 26, 33, 49. **Open** 11.30am-2.30pm, 5.30-10.30pm Mon-Thur; 11.30am-2.30pm, 5.30-11.30pm Fri; 11.30am-11.30pm Sat; 11.30am-10pm Sun. **Main courses** $12-$29. **Credit** AmEx, DC, MC, V. **Map** p318 K10 ⓺

The notion of serving no-nonsense food at decent prices in a place where people want to linger has been a successful one. That Luna Park is tiny doesn't deter locals from queuing; a vibrant lounge bar catches the spillover. Expect swift, courteous service and a selection of hearty dishes, including flatiron steak and fries, and earthy stomach-fillers such as breaded pork cutlet stuffed with mushrooms and cheese.

Range

842 Valencia Street, at 22nd Street (282 8283/www. rangesf.com). BART 24th Street Mission/Metro to Church & 24th Street/bus 14, 26, 48, 49, 67. **Open** Mon-Thur, Sun; 5.30-11pm Fri, Sat. **Main courses** $18-$24. **Credit** DC, MC, V. **Map** p314 K11 ⓺

Run by husband and wife Phil and Cameron West, Range has been a big hit since it opened in 2005. The concise and constantly changing menu never fails to have something on it that you want to eat – wild-nettle stuffed pasta with lemon and goat cheese, or slow-cooked lamb shoulder with parsnip purée. The meyer lemon pudding cake will make you weep.

Slow Club

2501 Mariposa Street, at Hampshire Street (241 9390/www.slowclub.com). Bus 9, 22, 27, 33, 53. **Open** 8-11am, 11.30am-2.30pm, 6.30-10pm Mon-Thur; 8-11am, 11.30am-2.30pm, 6.30-11pm Fri; 10am-2.30pm, 6.30-11pm Sat; 10am-2.30pm Sun. **Main courses** $8-$23. **Credit** DC, MC, V. **Map** p319 M10 ⓺

With its remote location and hideaway vibe, this is a true locals' hangout. Slow Club's understated charm makes it one of the coolest restaurants in town. Typical mains include pan-roasted chicken and braised beef shank. There are no reservations, but you can wait in the cosy bar area. The weekend brunch is a winner.

Asian

Nihon

1779 Folsom Street, at 14th Street (552 4400/www. nihon-sf.com). BART 16th Street/bus 9, 12, 14, 22, 33, 49, 53. **Open** 5.30pm-midnight Mon-Sat. *Bar* until 2am. **Main courses** $14-$25. **Credit** AmEx, DC, MC, V. **Map** p318 L9 ⓺

With its emphasis on scene and style, this sushi lounge has given this out-of-the-way location a bit of life. The space features edgy design, with conversation-starters in each of three areas: a bar, a lounge and a bottle-service room. The menu has nicely presented renditions of Japanese small plates, as well as fresh sushi and sashimi. At the bar, a menu of more than 120 whiskies is a big plus.

Cafés, delis & diners

Atlas Café

3049 20th Street, at Alabama Street (648 1047/ www.atlascafe.net). Bus 9, 27, 33. **Open** 6.30am-9pm Mon-Wed; 6.30am-10pm Thur; 8am-9pm Sat; 8am-8pm Sun. **Main courses** $4-$8. **No credit cards.** **Map** p317 L11 ⓺

This comfortable, popular café is one of the outer Mission's best hangouts, with people lining up for fresh breakfast pastries in the morning and settling into just-roasted lattes for the afternoon and evening. A daily list of grilled sandwiches includes many vegetarian specialities, and there are also soups and salads. There's music (usually bluegrass or country) on Thursday evenings. On nice days, try for a sunny seat on the patio at the back (where dogs are allowed).

Ritual Roasters

1026 Valencia Street, between 21st & 22nd Streets (641 1024/www.ritualroasters.com). BART to 24th Street Mission/bus 14, 26, 48, 49. **Open** 6am-10pm Mon-Fri; 7am-10pm Sat; 7am-9pm Sun. **Credit** DC, MC, V. **Map** p318 K11 ⓺

In the Bay Area, where coffee is regarded with religious concern, it's not surprising that folks talk about this place with a zealot-like rapture. The beans, formerly from Portland's Stumptown roasters, are now roasted in-house. The room itself is a fairly standard café; some are here to talk, but most to surf.

St Francis Fountain

2801 24th Street, at York Street (826 4200). Bus 9, 27, 33, 48. **Open** 8am-10pm daily. **Main courses** $6-$10. **Credit** DC, MC, V. **Map** p319 M12 ⓺

An almost classical link from old Mission to new, this ancient soda fountain has been given a new lease of life in recent years thanks to the attention lavished on it by its new owners. The menu offers a

On the sunny side of the street

Sunshine in the summer is a rarity in Fog City, but when the rays come out to play, expect hordes of San Franciscans in the know to head to one of a number of alfresco brunch and lunch spots.

Located Bayside in the industrial China Basin neighbourhood, the **Ramp** (855 China Basin Street, at Illinois Street, 621 2378, www.ramprestaurant.com) is a boozy SF brunch institution on sunny days. Head here for eggs Benedict and burgers and fries served up with margaritas and bloody marys. If you don't arrive before noon, expect a long wait, but in the end the ample sun, full bar and water view make fending off the local pigeon population worth it. Closer to the Bay Bridge lies **Red's Java House** (Pier 30, at the Embarcadero & Bryant Street, 777 5626), where the menu makes things easy for you: burgers, fries, and beer are what's on offer. Order lunch in the front of this 1920s-era little shack, and bring your grub back to the pier itself for a leisurely lunch. It's an especially good place to grab something to eat before Giants games at nearby AT&T Park.

A more upscale option for weekend brunch and weekday lunch along the Embarcadero is the funky but white-tableclothed **Pier 23 Café** (Pier 23, at the Embarcadero, 362 5125, www.pier23cafe.com), which serves delicious seafood such as fried oyster po' boy sandwiches, crab and shrimp Louie, along with – a San Francisco speciality – whole cracked crabs. Sunday afternoons (from 3pm) feature live music on a huge patio overlooking the Bay.

If you're in search of a sunny lunch in nearby Downtown, your best bets are the sidewalk seating at tasty French hotspot **Café Claude** (*see p133*) or one of the outdoor restaurants lining the tiny **Belden Place** (between Pine & Bush Streets, www.belden-place.com), also called the French Quarter (although Catalan, Mediterranean, Italian and seafood specialities are also on offer).

At the other end of town, the beachside **Park Chalet** an d **Beach Chalet** (*see p112*) is perfect for both sunny days and the more typically foggy beach weather, featuring big brunches (upstairs) and seafood-heavy lunches next to a roaring fire (downstairs) where Golden Gate Park meets Ocean Beach. House-brewed beers on tap.

In the Castro District, grab a salad or sip a latte while you do some boy-watching at **Café Flore** (*see p220*), where even if you choose to sit inside rather than on the flower-bedecked patio, you'll get a great view of the great outdoors through the floor-to-ceiling windows.

On the south side of the city, Noe Valley dishes up huge omelettes, crêpes, salads and sandwiches at the family-friendly **Savor** (3913 24th Street, at Sanchez Street, 282 0344) while, for those brave enough to face the sometimes surly bar staff, the Mission's divey **Zeitgeist Bar** (*see p169*) serves microbrewed beer and barbecue to tattooed hipsters, bikers and others on its large deck. For a very different, and even more unusual, outdoor Mission dining experience, try dinner with a film at **Foreign Cinema** (*see p152*).

Eat, Drink, Shop

Foreign Cinema.

St Francis Fountain: ice-cream sodas in a retro caff. *See p150.*

few nods to the 21st century, but it's mainly a wonderfully retro experience, from the Formica tabletops to the magnificent mac and cheese and ice-cream sodas.

French

Ti Couz Creperie

3108 16th Street, between Valencia & Guerrero Streets (252 7373). BART 16th Street Mission/ bus 14, 22, 26, 33, 49, 53. **Open** 11am-11pm Mon, Fri; 5-11pm Tue-Thur;10am-11pm Sat, Sun. **Main courses** $4-$12. **Credit** DC, MC, V. **Map** p318 K10 **96**

The classic Breton buckwheat galettes (savoury) and crêpes (sweet) are cooked captivatingly before your eyes. All kinds of urbanites pop in to try more than 100 fillings, from smoked salmon to lemon and brown sugar. Next door, Ti Couz Two has seafood and a full bar.

International

Andalu

3198 16th Street, at Guerrero Street (621 2211/ www.andalusf.com). **BART** 16th Street/bus 14, 26, 33, 49. **Open** 5.30-9.30pm Mon-Tue; 5.30-10.30pm Wed, Thur; 5.30-11.30pm Fri; 10.30am-2.30pm, 5.30-11.30pm Sat; 10.30am-2.30pm, 5.30-9.30pm Sun. **Main courses** *Tapas* $6-$12. **Credit** AmEx, DC, MC, V. **Map** p318 J10 **97**

This spacious and inviting room is anchored by a long bar at the back. It's a great spot when you're waiting for a table. But as soon as you sit down, your attention will shift from crowd to cuisine. Items on the tapas-style menu are given an inventive twist,

with such surprises as miso-glazed sea bass and ricotta-stuffed grilled aubergine. Save room for the fresh doughnuts.

Foreign Cinema

2534 Mission Street, between 21st & 22nd Streets (648 7600/www.foreigncinema.com). BART 24th Street Mission/bus 14, 26, 48, 49, 67. **Open** 6-10pm Mon-Thur; 6-11pm Fri; 11am-11pm Sat; 11am-10pm (until 9pm winter) Sun. *Bar & gallery* until 2am daily. **Main courses** $16-$30. **Credit** AmEx, DC, Disc, MC, V. **Map** p318 K11 **98**

Now one of the stalwarts of Mission dining, this restaurant is dominated by the screen on one side of the outdoor courtyard dining room, on which classic foreign films are projected each night; there are speakers at each table if you want to listen. But the focus is still the food, a frequently updated list of classically rooted Mediterranean favourites and a massive range of stellar oysters. The popular adjacent bar, Laszlo, contributes to the steady stream of customers.

Limón

524 Valencia Street, at 16th Street (252 0918/ www.limon-sf.com). BART 16th Street Mission/ bus 14, 22, 26, 33, 49, 53. **Open** 5.30-10.30pm Mon; 11.30am-3pm, 5.30-10.30pm Tue-Thur; 11.30am-3pm, 5.30-11pm Fri; noon-11pm Sat; noon-10pm Sun. **Main courses** $17-$26. **Credit** AmEx, DC, MC, V. **Map** p318 K10 **99**

One of a handful of SF eateries glamourising Peruvian food, this chic, packed, low-lit hotspot serves the traditional dishes of this South American country inventively infused with Chinese and Japanese influences. There are few misses on the menu. The popular dishes such as *lomo saltado*, beef stir-fried with french fries, tomatoes and onions, and grilled lamb served with crispy plantains are easily paired with zesty sangria and other speciality Latin-inspired cocktails.

Italian & pizza

Pauline's Pizza

260 Valencia Street, between Brosnan & 14th Streets (552 2050/www.paulinespizza.com). BART 16th Street Mission/Metro to Church/bus 14, 22, 26, 33, 49, 53. **Open** 5-10pm Tue-Sat. **Main courses** $13-$25. **Credit** DC, MC, V. **Map** p318 J9 **100**

Pauline's inventive thin-crust pies all come with top-quality ingredients: roasted peppers, perhaps, or goat's cheese, edible flowers or exotic vegetables. The pesto pizza (basil and pesto are baked into the crust) is justly renowned.

The Castro

For other good Castro eateries, *see pp99-100.*

American

Chow

215 Church Street, at Market Street (552 2469/ www.chowfoodbar.com). Metro to Church/streetcar F/bus 22, 37. **Open** 7am-11pm Mon-Thur; 7am-midnight Fri; 8am-midnight Sat; 8am-11pm Sun. **Main courses** $7.50-$25. **Credit** AmEx, DC, Disc, MC, V. **Map** p318 J9 **101**

Chow furthers its reputation by serving hugely popular, well-priced, straight-ahead American fare. The menu ranges widely from roast chicken and burgers to Asian noodles, and the kitchen succeeds at most things it tries. Staff are pally, and the portions huge. **Other locations** Park Chow, 1240 9th Avenue, Sunset (665 9912).

Home

2100 Market Street, at Church Street (503 0333/ www.home-sf.com). Metro to Church/streetcar F/ bus 22, 37. **Open** 5-10pm Mon-Thur; 5-11pm Fri; 10am-2pm, 5-11pm Sat, Sun. **Main courses** $10-$18. **Credit** AmEx, DC, Disc, MC, V. **Map** p318 H9 **102**

One of the Castro's can't-go-wrong options, this sceney restaurant has big-city atmosphere but small-town comfort. The crowd tends to be on the make, but that doesn't interfere with good conversation and generous portions of well-prepared classic American fare. Roast chicken and meatloaf are right at home alongside seafood specialities and vegetable spring rolls. At weekend brunch, there's a make-your-own bloody mary bar.

Mecca

2029 Market Street, at Dolores & 14th Streets (621 7000/www.sfmecca.com). Metro to Church/bus 22, 37. **Open** 5-10pm Tue-Wed; 5pm-midnight Thur-Sat; 11am-3.30pm Sun. **Main courses** $18-$36. **Credit** AmEx, DC, MC, V. **Map** p318 J9 **103**

Always in harmony with the surroundings, the food at this big, bustling and unswervingly fashionable

restaurant remains one of the best bets in the Castro. The menu is world-influenced and ever-changing. Highlights might include such inventions as confit of pork shoulder or prosciutto-wrapped tuna. Back at the bar, the mood gets ever looser as the cocktails flow and the DJ works his platters.

Noe Valley

American

Firefly

4288 24th Street, at Douglass Street (821 7652/ www.fireflyrestaurant.com). Metro to Church & 24th/ bus 24, 35, 48. **Open** 5.30-9.30pm Mon-Thur; 5.30-10pm Fri, Sat; 5.30-9pm Sun. **Main courses** $18-$22. **Credit** AmEx, DC, MC, V. **Map** p317 G12 **104**

White-topped tables aglow with soft lights and a room buzzing with good conversation are hallmarks of this neighbourhood restaurant. The eclectic menu might feature fried chicken (among the best in town), honey-braised lamb shoulder or rib-sticking chicken and dumplings. There are always a number of inventive seasonal vegetarian selections. From Sunday to Thursday, it's also good value: three courses go for just $35. Warm, romantic and utterly charming.

Asian

Alice's

1599 Sanchez Street, at 29th Street (282 8999). Metro to Church & 29th/bus 24, 26. **Open** 11am-9.30pm Mon-Thur; 11am-10pm Fri, Sat; noon-9.30pm Sun. **Main courses** $8-$11. **Credit** DC, MC, V.

Banish any thought of Arlo Guthrie from your mind: it's worth trekking to Alice's restaurant for the spicy Hunan and Mandarin cooking. The clean and spare setting enhances such dishes as asparagus salmon in black bean sauce or delicate orange beef; and the spicy fried string beans will remain in your memory for all the right reasons.

Cafés, delis & diners

Lovejoy's Tea Room

1351 Church Street, at Clipper Street (648 5895/ www.lovejoystearoom.com). Metro to Church & 24th/bus 24, 48. **Open** 11am-6pm Wed-Sun. **Main courses** $6-$13. **Credit** DC, MC, V.

Select from Lovejoy's six different teas, including the Queen's Tea ($22) and the Wee Tea ($13) for children. They're all served in a room furnished with a jumble of antiques and knick-knacks. *Photo p154.*

Italian & pizza

Incanto

1550 Church Street, at Duncan Street (641 4500/ www.incanto.biz). Metro to Church & 24th/bus 24, 48. **Open** 5.30-9.45pm Mon, Wed-Sun. **Main courses** $15-$24. **Credit** DC, MC, V.

Chris Cosentino's highly regarded restaurant is known for championing sustainably harvested produce, meat and seafood, and for the frequent appearance of offal on the daily changing menu (part of Cosentino's commitment to reduce waste). Typically robust dishes might include milk-braised pork with braising greens and polenta. Italian wines are a very big deal here.

The Haight & Around

Cole Valley

Asian

Eos Restaurant
901 Cole Street, at Carl Street (566 3063/www.eos sf.com). Metro to Carl & Cole/bus 6, 37, 43. **Open** 5.30-10pm Mon-Thur, Sun; 5.30-11pm Fri, Sat. **Main courses** $12-$18. **Credit** AmEx, DC, MC, V. **Map** p317 E10 **106**
The best of East-West fusion, served in a comfortably spare, highly designed restaurant. Classically trained chef/owner Arnold Eric Wong produces dishes such as tea-smoked peking duck and tamarind chilli-glazed spare ribs, backed up by one of the Bay Area's best wine lists. The same menu is served in the wine bar next door (101 Carl Street).

French

Zazie
941 Cole Street, at Parnassus Street (564 5332/ www.zaziesf.com). Metro to Carl & Cole/bus 6, 37, 43. **Open** 8am-2.30pm, 5.30-9.30pm Mon-Thur; 8am-2.30pm, 5.30-10pm Fri; 9am-3pm, 5.30-10pm Sat; 9am-3pm, 5.30-9.30pm Sun. **Set meal** $23.50/3 courses. **Main courses** $12-$19. **Credit** DC, MC, V. **Map** p317 E10 **107**
This cosy venue serves gentle breakfasts on a weekday morning, a small variety of lunch dishes (pasta, sandwiches), a more French menu for dinner and a weekend brunch. Some see Zazie as a café, others a bistro, but it manages to pull in easygoing locals throughout the day, whatever they're wanting it to be.

Haight-Ashbury

American

Alembic
1725 Haight Street, between Cole & Shrader Streets (666 0822/www.alembicbar.com). Metro to Cole & Carl/bus 7, 33, 37, 43, 71. **Open** 4pm-midnight Mon-Thur; noon-midnight Fri-Sun. *Bar* until 2am daily. **Main courses** $7-$12. **Credit** AmEx, DC, Disc, MC, V. **Map** p317 E9 **108**

Lovejoy's Tearoom. *See p153.*

The Haight has no shortage of excellent drinking holes, but few possess the panache of this whisky-fuelled destination in the heart of the neighbourhood. The food menu is spare but pretty good, consisting of hits like the housemade saké gravlax, spätzle and spiced lamb burger. Everything is designed as accompaniment to the main attraction: booze. A head-spinning array of boutique beers, Scottish single malts, American whiskies and even rare ryes ensures the trendy clientele is always kept happily buzzing along.

Lower Haight

American

RNM
598 Haight Street, at Steiner Street (551 7900/ www.rnmrestaurant.com). Bus 6, 7, 22, 71. **Open** 5.30-10pm Tue-Thur; 5.30-11pm Fri, Sat. **Main courses** $12-$26. **Credit** DC, MC, V. **Map** p318 H8 **109**

A slice of New York's SoHo translated for a laid-back Californian crowd. The high-style dining room (complete with massive chandelier) belies the food, which is almost entirely without pretension and mostly off-the-chart delicious. Don't miss ahi on roasted garlic crostini or the Maine lobster with white corn risotto. Alongside the regular carte there is a list of small plates.

Asian

Thep Phanom
400 Waller Street, at Fillmore Street (431 2526/ www.thepphanom.com). Bus 6, 7, 22, 66, 71. **Open** 5.30-10.30pm daily. **Main courses** $9-$17. **Credit** AmEx, DC, Disc, MC, V. **Map** p317 H9 ⓾
Be sure to book in advance at Thep Phanom – and once you're there, be sure to order the *tom ka gai* (coconut chicken soup) as a starter. The 'angel wings' – fried chicken wings stuffed with glass noodles – are another universally popular choice. This place is often hailed as the best Thai restaurant in San Francisco.

Cafés, delis & diners

Grind Café
783 Haight Street, at Scott Street (864 0955/www. thegrindcafe.com). Bus 6, 7, 24, 71. **Open** 7am-8pm Mon-Fri; 7am-6pm Sat; 8am-6pm Sun. **Main courses** $5-$8. **Credit** AmEx, DC, Disc, MC, V. **Map** p317 H9 ⓫
This casual café is populated by too-cool-for-school denizens of the Lower Haight, likely to be spending the morning leafing through Sartre or sweating off a hangover, or both. The best eats are the vegetable-packed omelettes and stacks of pancakes. The open-air patio welcomes dog owners and the occasional cigarette.

Kate's Kitchen
471 Haight Street, between Fillmore & Webster Streets (626 3984). Bus 6, 7, 22, 71. **Open** 8am-2.45pm Mon-Fri; 8.30am-3.45pm Sat, Sun. **Main courses** $5-$9. **No credit cards. Map** p317 H8 ⓬
A buzzing spot that's an excellent choice when you've got a mountain of Sunday papers to wade through at your leisure. Ease into the day with the assistance of a giant bowl of granola, a huge omelette or the signature dish of hush puppies (drop pancakes made of cornmeal). Lower Haight's unofficial brunch HQ.

The Western Addition

American

1300 On Fillmore
1300 Fillmore Street, at Eddy Street (771 7100/ www.1300fillmore.com). Bus 22, 31, 38. **Open** 5.30-11pm Mon, Sun; 5.30pm-1am Tue-Sat. *Bar* from 4.30pm daily. **Main courses** $18-$29. **Credit** AmEx, DC, Disc, MC, V. **Map** p317 H7 ⓭

Part of the long-overdue and much-anticipated revitalisation of the historic Fillmore Jazz District, this soul-food eatery is, along with Yoshi's (*see below*), a welcome addition to the area. The Southern-influenced fare is anchored in classics: fried chicken, barbecued shrimp with grits, and mac and cheese. The room has a lounge-club atmosphere, with big leather chairs and endless classic jazz streaming through the air. Don't miss the Heritage Wall in the lounge, with a collection of historic photos and TV screens scrolling through images of jazz greats who once played in the area.

Asian

Yoshi's
1330 Fillmore Street, at Eddy Street (655 5600/ www.yoshis.com/sf). Bus 22, 31, 38. **Open** 5.30-10.30pm Mon-Wed; 5.30-11pm Thur-Sat; 5-10pm Sun. *Bar & lounge* 5pm-1am Mon-Sat; 5pm-midnight Sun. **Main courses** $18-$48. **Credit** AmEx, DC, MC, V. **Map** p317 H7 ⓮
The new San Francisco branch of the legendary East Bay jazz club and sushi restaurant has infused the Fillmore Heritage Center with a vibrancy not seen since the area served as a West Coast jazz mecca. The calendar of jazz performers both well known and up-and-coming is the main attraction here, but the extensive menu of sushi and other Japanese specialities doesn't disappoint. Book in advance and arrive early to enjoy dinner before moving in to the theatre for the show. Alternatively, you can dine before the later show and reserve seats through your server (if available). *See also p231.*
Other locations 510 Embarcadero West, Oakland (1-510 238 9200).

Cafés, delis & diners

Café Abir
1300 Fulton Street, at Divisadero Street (567 6503). Bus 5, 21, 24. **Open** 6am-12.30am daily. **Main courses** $7-$10. **No credit cards. Map** p317 G7 ⓯
This hip, laid-back café is one of the most popular options in the Western Addition area, and the friendly staff and well-chosen house music mean it's as much about nightlife as morning life. An organic grocery store, a bar, a coffee roastery and an international newsstand supplement the large café. Choose from the freshly made sandwiches and deli salads, or just get a bagel to accompany your latte and newspaper.

Italian & pizza

Nopa
560 Divisadero Street , at Hayes Street (864 8643/www.nopasf.com). Bus 5, 21, 24. **Open** 6pm-1am (bar open 5pm) daily. **Mains** $12-$23. **Credit** AmEx, Disc, MC, V. **Map** p313 G8 ⓯ⓐ

Eat, Drink, Shop

One of the hottest restaurants in town, Nopa's attractions include the wood-fired oven, and the late hours – unusual in a city where many kitchens pack up at 10pm. Italian- and Med-inspired ('urban rustic') dishes can show an inventive use of ingredients – like pasta with home-smoked bacon, brussels sprouts and goat's cheese. Others are more classic – the likes of pork chop with cannellini beans, wilted greens and salsa verde. The interior is spacious, with high wood beams, the ambience is pleasantly casual.

Japantown

Asian

Mifune

Japan Center, 1737 Post Street, between Webster & Buchanan Streets (922 0337/www.mifune.com). Bus 2, 3, 4, 22, 38. **Open** 11am-9.30pm daily. **Main courses** $6-$18. **Credit** AmEx, DC, MC, V. **Map** p314 H6 ⑯
Mifune's motto is 'It's okay to slurp your noodles', which gives you an idea of the atmosphere and focus of this place. Good for kids and vegetarians, here you'll find the lowly noodle prepared in at least 30 different ways. Orders come quickly, and the food is that appealing combination: inexpensive and delicious.

O Izakaya Lounge

Hotel Kabuki, 1625 Post Street, at Laguna Street (614 5431/www.jdvhotels.com/dining). Bus 2, 3, 4, 38. **Open** 6.30-10.30am, 5-10pm Mon-Fri; 7am-3pm, 5-10pm Sat, Sun. *Bar* 5pm-1am daily. **Main courses** *Small plates* $9-$15. **Credit** AmEx, DC, Disc, MC, V. **Map** p314 J6 ⑰
Situated in the recently updated Hotel Kabuki in the newly buzzing Japantown, this combination *izakaya* house and Japanese sports bar is a bit bizarre at first glance. But the oddball vibe is all part of the charm, and it has quickly caught on with a hipster crowd and curious onlookers as well as with fans of the very good food from chef Nicolaus Balla. The menu features small plates of traditional Japanese cuisine prepared with fresh local ingredients. Menu specialities include the likes of pork belly braised with house-made kimchee, and seaweed salad with mustard greens and *umeboshi*. There are more than 20 different sakes on offer, which can be sampled by the flight or in one of the signature sake cocktails.

Seoul Garden

22 Peace Plaza, Geary Boulevard, at Laguna Street (563 7664/www.seoulgardenbbq.com). Bus 2, 3, 4, 38. **Open** 11.30am-10.30pm daily. **Main courses** $12-$26. **Credit** AmEx, DC, MC, V. **Map** p314 H6 ⑱
Seoul Garden is a good choice when all the Japanese eateries are too crowded (which is often the case), here you grill marinated beef at your table while nibbling at the myriad little dishes that make up Korean cuisine.

Hayes Valley

Cafés, delis & diners

Citizen Cake

399 Grove Street, at Gough Street (861 2228/ www.citizencake.com). BART & Metro to Civic Center/Metro to Van Ness/bus 5, 21, 47, 49 & Market Street routes. **Open** 8am-10pm Tue-Fri; 10am-10pm Sat; 10am-5pm Sun. **Main courses** $20-$25. **Credit** AmEx, DC, MC, V. **Map** p318 J7 ⑲
Quite possibly the trendiest place for dessert in town, this recently remodelled café sells gorgeous sweet things to a crowd of well-dressed and good-looking patrons. As wonderful as the cakes and pies are, the excellent – if slightly pricey – lunch and dinner menus are also worth exploring. For a small on-the-go bite, try Citizen Cupcake next door.

French

Absinthe

398 Hayes Street, at Gough Street (551 1590/ www.absinthe.com). BART & Metro to Civic Center/Metro to Van Ness/bus 5, 21, 47, 49 & Market Street routes. **Open** 11.30am-midnight Tue-Fri; 11am-midnight Sat; 11am-10.30pm Sun. *Bar* until 2am Fri, Sat. **Main courses** $24-$29. **Credit** AmEx, DC, Disc, MC, V. **Map** p318 J7 ⑳
The spirit of bohemian France is reborn in San Francisco as this boisterous brasserie. The French menu lists reliable favourites, including excellent coq au vin and cassoulet. Try the seafood platter to start. The bar – thanks to a change in the law – now offers genuine absinthe too. See **Mixologist Magic** *p164*.

International

Suppenküche

601 Hayes Street, at Laguna Street (252 9289/ www.suppenkuche.com). Bus 21, 49. **Open** 5-10pm Mon-Sat; 10am-2.30pm, 5-10pm Sun. **Main courses** $10.50-$18.50. **Credit** AmEx, DC, Disc, MC, V. **Map** p318 J8 ㉑
If you're hungry for something that's going to last you all day, Suppenküche is a good bet. Its menu, which covers spätzle, schnitzels and dense, dark breads, is authentically German, and not for the faint of belly. An impressive array of flavoursome German beers is served in tall steins; seating is on benches. Good vegetarian options too.

Latin American

Destino

1815 Market Street, between Guerrero & Valencia Streets (552 4451/www.destinosf.com). Metro to Van Ness/bus 6, 7, 26, 71. **Open** 5-10pm Mon-Thur; 5-11pm Fri-Sat; 5-10pm Sun. **Main courses** $18-$21. **Credit** AmEx, DC, MC, V. **Map** p318 J9 ㉒

This casual, fun restaurant serves specialities from Central and South America in a lively neighbourhood setting. The theme is small plates meant for sharing, but à la carte options are also available. Empanadas, ceviches and other indigenous dishes are all given a robust, flavourful treatment. From seafood to meat, it all works well and is always unique. Try the three-course prix fixe menu ($32) to take the guesswork out of ordering.

EspetuS

1686 Market Street, at Gough Street (552 8792/ www.espetus.com). Metro to Van Ness/bus 6, 7, 26, 47, 49, 71. **Open** 11.30am-3pm, 5-10pm Mon-Thur; 11.30am-3pm, 5-11pm Fri; noon-3pm, 5-11pm Sat; noon-3pm, 4-9pm Sun. **Set meal** $45. **Credit** AmEx, DC, Disc, MC, V. **Map** p318 K8 ⓬③
An impressive, authentic take on the increasingly popular *churrascaria*, this is San Francisco's first Brazilian-style steakhouse. It's a meat-lover's paradise, wherein attendant servers, adorned head-to-toe in white, continuously cruise through the restaurant wielding skewers laden with straight-from-the-fire pork, steak, shrimp and lamb, known as Rodizio style, awaiting your request; this is indicated by displaying a green chip while red indicates a full stop. All the while, the evocative strummings and patterings of Brazilian jazz unfurl in the background.

PJ's Oyster Bed: marine mania.

Sunset, Golden Gate Park & Richmond

Sunset

American

PJ's Oyster Bed

737 Irving Street, between 8th & 9th Avenues (566 7775/www.pjsoysterbed.com). Metro to Judah & 9th/bus 6, 43, 44, 66. **Open** 5-10pm Tue-Thur, Sun; 5-11pm Fri, Sat. **Main courses** $12-$23. **Credit** AmEx, DC, Disc, MC, V. **Map** p316 C10 ⓬④
There's a bit of New Orleans fun in this friendly neighbourhood seafood restaurant, which makes some of San Francisco's freshest and most authentic Cajun food. The seafood is displayed on ice, with oysters shucked to order, and portions are generous. Not surprisingly, it's always packed.

Asian

Ebisu

1283 9th Avenue, between Irving Street & Lincoln Way (566 1770/www.ebisusushi.com). Metro to Judah & 9th/bus 6, 43, 44, 66. **Open** 11.30am-2pm, 5-10pm Mon-Thur; 11.30am-2pm, 5-11pm Thur, Fri; 11.30am-11pm Sat. **Main courses** $10-$19. *Sushi* $3-$12. **Credit** AmEx, DC, MC, V. **Map** p316 C10 ⓬⑤
Many locals agree that this is the best sushi in town – and so there's often a wait for a table. Put your name on the list and get a drink at the bar with a light heart, because you're going to enjoy house specialities like the 'pink Cadillac' (salmon sushi roll) and seafood salad. Good as the sushi is, you can happily forgo it for the traditional Japanese cooked food.

Cafés, delis & diners

Java Beach Café

1396 La Playa Boulevard, at Judah Street (665 5282/ www.javabeachcafe.com). Metro to Ocean Beach/bus 18. **Open** 5.30am-11pm Mon-Fri; 6am-11pm Sat, Sun. **Main courses** $5-$8. **Credit** DC, MC, V.
Java Beach is funky and civilised, with the wetsuits and grand Pacific views making it feel a bit like LA's Hermosa Beach – minus the permatans. Surfers, cyclists and ordinary passers-by pop in for a basic sandwich, some soup or maybe a pastry.

Tart to Tart

641 Irving Street, between 7th & 8th Avenues (504 7068). Metro to Judah & 9th/bus 6, 43, 44, 66. **Open** 6am-1am Mon-Thur, Sun; 6am-2am Fri, Sat. **Main courses** $4-$5. **Credit** DC, MC, V. **Map** p316 C10 ⓬⑥

Eat, Drink, Shop

There are few late-night options in the Inner Sunset, perhaps because residents are mainly families. No matter: at Tart to Tart you can get freshly made cookies and cakes, above-average salads and sandwiches, and more tarts than you could comfortably sample over the course of a month.

Golden Gate Park

Park Chow, sister restaurant to **Chow** (*see p153*), is handy for Golden Gate Park, as are the **Beach Chalet** and **Park Chalet** (*see p112*).

Richmond

American

Q Restaurant

225 Clement Street, at 3rd Avenue (752 2298/www. qrestaurant.com). Bus 1, 2, 4, 38, 44. **Open** 11am-3pm, 5-11pm Mon-Fri; 10am-11pm Sat; 10am-10pm Sun. **Main courses** $9-$16. **Credit** DC, MC, V. **Map** p312 C6 **127**
A delightful restaurant, serving some of the tastiest comfort food in town. The name comes from its earlier ambitions as a barbecue joint, but the kitchen now runs to grilled steaks and seafood, pasta and some of the city's top fried chicken. A good wine list and eclectic decor make Q one of a kind.

Asian

Khan Toke Thai House

5937 Geary Boulevard, between 23rd & 24th Avenues (668 6654). Bus 2, 29, 38. **Open** 5-10pm daily. **Main courses** $7-$12. **Credit** AmEx, DC, MC, V.
Locals often overlook one of the city's most attractive Thai restaurants, Khan Toke. But it should be considered by anyone looking for an authentic experience. Slip off your shoes, sit on a low chair (with a padded back support) and enjoy fiery, colourful curries with excellent noodles and decent wines.

Mayflower

6255 Geary Boulevard, at 27th Avenue (387 8338). Bus 2, 29, 38. **Open** 11am-2.30pm, 5-10pm Mon-Fri; 10am-2.30pm, 5-10pm Sat, Sun. **Main courses** $9-$35. **Dim sum** $2-$6. **Credit** DC, MC, V.
Best known for its terrific mid-morning dim sum, the Mayflower also serves good seafood, fine claypot dishes and superb roast chicken and duck. Alongside the broad range of Cantonese options you'll find Mongolian beef, another favourite. The restaurant is large, noisy and family-oriented; arrive after 8pm if you want to avoid the dinner hordes.

Ton Kiang

5821 Geary Boulevard, between 22nd & 23rd Avenues (387 8273/www.tonkiang.net). Bus 2, 29, 38. **Open** 10am-10pm Mon-Thur; 10am-10.30pm Fri; 9.30am-10.30pm Sat; 9am-10pm Sun. **Main courses** $8.50-$26. **Credit** AmEx, DC, MC, V.

This large restaurant's stock-in-trade is quality *hakka* cuisine, a style of Chinese gypsy cooking. Favourite dishes include the authentic salt-baked chicken served with a ground garlic and ginger paste. Around Chinese New Year there's a delicious seasonal menu, and dim sum is very popular on weekend mornings.

Cafés & diners

Blue Danube Coffee House

306 Clement Street, at 4th Avenue (221 9041). Bus 1, 2, 4, 38, 44. **Open** 7am-10pm Mon-Thur, Sun; 7am-11pm Fri, Sat. **Main courses** $5-$8. **No credit cards. Map** p312 C6 **128**
One of the city's first hip coffee houses, Danube still enjoys a loyal following after a quarter of a century: grab a latte or a pint, and sit watching passers-by from the large streetside windows.

International

Bistro Chapeau!

1408 Clement Street, at 15th Avenue (750 9787). Bus 1, 2, 28, 38. **Open** 5-10pm Tue-Thur, Sun; 5-10.30pm Fri, Sat. **Main courses** $20-$25. **Credit** AmEx, DC, MC, V. **Map** p312 A6 **129**
Bistro Chapeau! is a proper little French charmer, with cosy bistro decor and friendly staff. The Provençal fare is just as comforting, with excellent trad dishes like coq au vin, onion soup and duck à l'orange. There's a fine brunch on Sundays, which makes an ideal opportunity for exploring the bubbly list. 'Hat!', appropriately enough, is more or less French for 'Wow!'.

Pacific Heights to the Golden Gate Bridge

Pacific Heights

American

Harris'

2100 Van Ness Avenue, at Pacific Avenue (673 1888/www.harrisrestaurant.com). Bus 12, 27, 47, 49, 76. **Open** 5.30-9.30pm Mon-Fri; 5-10pm Sat; 5-9pm Sun. **Main courses** $22-$75. **Credit** AmEx, DC, Disc, MC, V. **Map** p314 J4 **130**
One of San Francisco's steakhouse standbys, Harris' offers classy old-style dining, with big steaks, big martinis, and big bills at meal's end. Sink into your booth, start with a strong cocktail, then proceed with a textbook Caesar salad (put together at your table), a prime piece of carefully aged steak and a baked potato with all the trimmings. Hefty desserts follow.

Spruce

3640 Sacramento Street, at Spruce Street (931 5100/www.sprucesf.com). Bus 1, 3, 4, 33, 43. **Open** 11.30am-11pm Mon-Fri; 5-11pm Sat, Sun. **Main courses** $20-$40. **Credit** AmEx, DC, MC, V. **Map** p313 E5 **131**

From its location in an otherwise sleepy but upscale Presidio Heights neighbourhood, this chic, handsome restaurant has managed to set the city abuzz, and the scarcity of available reservations shouldn't put you off trying to experience chef Mark Sullivan's approach to fresh, inventive cooking. Once you're in, you're part of the scene, a locals-only feel where a lounge, a takeout area and a formal dining room all exist peacefully. Specialities of lobster and steak and other extravagances make the point that this is a place of comfort and style.

Cafés, delis & diners

Ella's

500 Presidio Avenue, at California Street (441 5669/ www.ellassanfrancisco.com). Bus 1, 2, 3, 4, 43. **Open** 7am-3pm Mon-Fri; 8.30am-2pm Sat, Sun. **Main courses** $7-$12. **Credit** AmEx, DC, Disc, MC, V. **Map** p313 F5 **132**

This stylish, neighbourly corner restaurant is famed for its weekend brunch. The wait can be long, but it's worth it. Favourites include the chicken hash with eggs and toast, and the potato scramble, prepared with a frequently changing list of fresh ingredients. The thick, perfectly crisped French toast is superb.

French

Florio

1915 Fillmore Street, between Bush & Pine Streets (775 4300/www.floriosf.com). Bus 1, 2, 3, 4, 22. **Open** 5.30-10pm Mon, Tue, Sun; 5.30-11pm Wed-Sat. **Main courses** $15-$25. **Credit** AmEx, DC, MC, V. **Map** p313 H5 **133**

A quintessential local bistro, celebrating 10 years of of service, Florio is warm and welcoming, with just the right degree of refinement. Dark wood and white tablecloths set the tone for the French-inspired rural cooking. The ribeye steak-frites and the Tuscan seafood stew are always soul-warming. Service is swift and friendly.

Italian & pizza

SPQR

1911 Fillmore Street, between Bush & Pine Streets (771 7779/www.spqrsf.com). Bus 1, 2, 3, 4, 22. **Open** 11.30am-2.30pm, 5.30-10pm Mon-Wed, Sun; 10.30am-2.30pm, 5.30-11pm Thur-Sat. **Main courses** $11-$19. **Credit** AmEx, DC, MC, V. **Map** p313 H5 **134**

In this small, spare, one-room dining space, the spirit of Roman cuisine shines through. Dishes are rustic, unadorned and incredibly flavourful, calling up the best in straightforward Italian cooking. Pork saltimbocca with carrots and pickled peppers, calamari with ceci beans, and beef brisket with pancetta, red wine and tomato are among the specialities. So, it's that simple. The toughest part is getting a table – no reservations are accepted, but browsing the excellent by-the-glass wine list will help pass the time.

Latin American

Fresca

2114 Fillmore Street, at California Street (447 2668/ www.frescasf.com). Bus 1, 3, 22. **Open** 11am-3pm, 5-10pm Mon-Thur; 11am-3pm, 5-11pm Fri, Sat; 11am-3pm, 5-9pm Sun. **Main courses** $16-$28. **Credit** AmEx, DC, Disc, MC, V. **Map** p313 H5 **135**

Fresca claims to have SF's only ceviche bar, but has a broader menu than you might expect. Try tangy halibut ceviche or flambéed pisco prawns to start, followed by grilled ribeye with fries and plantains or sweet soy-roasted trout. The space can be very loud and tables are crammed together, but the quality of the Peruvian food makes up for any discomfort. **Other locations** 3945 24th Street (695 0549), Noe Valley (695 0549); 24 West Portal Avenue, Sunset (759 8087).

Cow Hollow

American

PlumpJack Café

3127 Fillmore Street, between Greenwich & Filbert Streets (563 4755/www.plumpjack.com). Bus 22, 28, 41, 43, 45, 76. **Open** 11.30am-2pm, 5.30-10pm Mon-Fri; 5.30-10pm Sat, Sun. **Main courses** $22-$34. **Credit** AmEx, DC, MC, V. **Map** p313 G3 **136**

The success of PlumpJack Wines (*see p190*) inspired the opening of this high-profile, special-occasion eaterie. A blend of new ideas and old money (co-owner Gavin Newsom is the city's mayor), it produces outstanding California cuisine, with a penchant for interesting seafood and Mediterranean recipes. Wines are the main attraction.

Presidio Social Club

563 Ruger Street, Building 563, at Lombard Street (885 1888/www.presidiosocialclub.com). Bus 28, 29, 41, 43, 45, 76. **Open** 5.30-11pm Mon-Sat; 4.30-9.30pm Sun. **Bar** from 5pm Mon-Sat; 4pm Sun. **Main courses** $18-$33. **Credit** AmEx, DC, Disc, MC, V. **Map** p313 F4 **137**

Housed in a historic building in the verdant Presidio, this rambling wooden structure – a former army barracks – is an ideal setting for the charm within. The intimate setting gives way to a lively crowd as the evening progresses and the foghorn moans outside. The menu features unfussy classics of the comforting steaks and chops variety, simply prepared using local ingredients. With its large communal table, the bar is perfect for soaking up the atmosphere on misty evenings.

Asian

Betelnut

2030 Union Street, between Webster & Buchanan Streets (929 8855/www.betelnutrestaurant.com). Bus 22, 41, 45. **Open** 11.30am-11pm Mon-Thur, Sun; 11am-midnight Fri, Sat. **Main courses** $10-$20. **Credit** AmEx, DC, Disc, MC, V. **Map** p313 H4 ⬤

This cool-looking restaurant has managed to retain its popularity by combining a relatively exotic South Pacific concept and consistent execution. Sidestep the sometimes-can't-be-bothered attitude up front, join the crowd at the bar and peruse a menu that's made for grazing. The best bet is to keep ordering small plates (tea-smoked duck, braised short ribs, papaya salad) until either your waistline or your credit card goes pop.

The Marina & the waterfront

American

Bin 38

3232 Scott Street, between Lombard & Chestnut Streets (567 3838/www.bin38.com). Bus 28, 30, 43, 76. **Open** 3pm-midnight Mon-Wed; 3pm-1am Thur-Fri; 2pm-1am Sat; 2pm-midnight Sun. **Main coøurses** $9-$19. **Credit** AmEx, DC, Disc, MC, V. **Map** p313 G3 ⬤

A surprisingly sophisticated find among the collection of after-work destinations, this wine bar and small-plates restaurant is as big on atmosphere as it is on choice of tipple. The menu of Wine Country-inspired American fare is designed to be easily paired with selections from the wine and beer list. Indeed, suggestions are offered on the page – so you needn't worry if your grilled grass-fed beef tenderloin kebabs will go well with the cabernet from Napa's Spring Mountain.

Greens

Building A, Fort Mason Center, Marina Boulevard, at Buchanan Street (771 6222/www.greens restaurant.com). Bus 10, 19, 28, 30, 47, 49. **Open** 5.30-9pm Mon; noon-2.30pm, 5.30-9pm Tue-Sat; 10.30am-2pm Sun. **Main courses** $16-$23. **Credit** AmEx, DC, Disc, MC, V. **Map** p313 H2 ⬤

Vegans and carnivores alike extol the virtues of venerable Greens, with its waterfront views of the Golden Gate Bridge and award-winning, all-vegetarian menu. An extensive wine list complements mesquite-grilled vegetables and wood-fired pizzas topped with wild mushrooms. If you don't fancy queuing, pick up sandwiches or soups from the takeaway counter.

Cafés, delis & diners

Grove

2250 Chestnut Street, at Avila Street (474 4843). Bus 28, 30, 43, 76. **Open** 7am-11pm Mon-Fri; 8am-11pm Sat, Sun. **Main courses** $7-$10. **Credit** AmEx, DC, Disc, MC, V. **Map** p313 G3 ⬤

This happening place is a true outpost of café culture. As well as coffee, beer, wine and comfort food (lasagne,

chicken pot pie), patrons can enjoy chess and backgammon. The Fillmore Street location offers the same kind of woodsy interior and big cappuccinos, but for a less trend-conscious clientele.
Other locations 2016 Fillmore Street, Pacific Heights (474 1419).

International

Isa

3324 Steiner Street, between Chestnut & Lombard Streets (567 9588/www.isarestaurant.com). Bus 22, 28, 30, 43, 76. **Open** 5.30-10pm Mon-Thur; 5.30-10.30pm Fri, Sat. **Main courses** $9-$18. **Credit** DC, MC, V. **Map** p313 G3 ⬤

Expect such interesting fare as roast mussels with shallots and white wine, or hanger steak with tarragon mustard and roast garlic potatoes from the tapas-like menu at Isa. Cosy, with a secluded back patio, it is winningly free of Marina affectations.

Latin American

Los Hermanos

2026 Chestnut Street, at Fillmore Street (921 5790). Bus 22, 28, 30, 43, 76. **Open** 10.30am-9.30pm Mon-Sat. **Main courses** $5-$8. **No credit cards**. **Map** p313 G3 ⬤

Chaotic but friendly, with people shouting orders from three rows back, this nondescript spot thinks it's in the Mission. Expect authentic Mexican food, including enormous, freshly made burritos.

The East Bay

A solid case can be made that the roots of San Francisco's current high culinary standing are grounded across the Bay. **Chez Panisse** (*see below*) is the headline-maker, but there are other dining options that make a jaunt over the bridge a powerful temptation.

Oakland

American

Bay Wolf

3853 Piedmont Avenue, between 40th Street & MacArthur Boulevard (1-510 655 6004/www.bay wolf.com). BART to MacArthur/bus 51, 57, 59, 851. **Open** 11.30am-1.45pm, 5.30-9pm Mon-Thur; 11.30am-1.45pm, 5.30-10pm Fri; 5.30-10pm Sat; 5.30-9pm Sun. **Main courses** $12.50-$28. **Credit** AmEx, DC, MC, V.

Opened by Michael Wild in 1975, this comfortable East Bay staple is housed in a beautifully revamped Craftsman-style house. Wild is renowned for his duck specialities, which form part of a seaonal blend of California and Mediterranean fare. In nice weather, the best seats are on the enclosed redwood deck outfront.

Chez Panisse.

organic and of the very best quality. The excellent wine list combines French and Californian options, but you can also bring your own if you're prepared to pay the $25 corkage fee. You can (and should) book up to one month in advance for both the restaurant and café; a credit card deposit of $25 per person is required for the restaurant.

Italian & pizza

Oliveto

5655 College Avenue, at Shafter Avenue (1-510 547 5356/www.oliveto.com). BART Rockridge/bus 7, 51, 59, 851. **Open** *Café* 7am-9pm Mon; 7am-10pm Tue-Fri; 8am-10pm Sat; 8am-9pm Sun. *Restaurant* 11.30am-2pm, 5.30-9pm Mon; 11.30am-2pm, 5.30-9.30pm Tue, Wed; 11.30am-2pm, 5.30-10pm Thur, Fri; 5.30-10pm Sat, 5-9pm Sun. **Main courses** *Café* $6-$13. *Restaurant* $27-$32. **Credit** AmEx, DC, MC, V.
One of Oakland's true destination restaurants, this Rockridge area hotspot features soul-warming northern Italian fare that is almost entirely handmade, right down to its trademark olive oils and salumi. The speciality is house-cured, grilled and spit-roasted meat, but menus change daily to showcase the freshest available ingredients. The downstairs café features pizzas and baked goods from the wood-fired oven.

Berkeley

American

Chez Panisse

1517 Shattuck Avenue, between Cedar & Vine Streets (restaurant 1-510 548 5525/café 1-510 548 5049/www.chezpanisse.com). BART Downtown Berkeley. **Open** *Restaurant* sittings (reservations required) 6-8.30pm, 8.30-9.30pm Mon-Sat. *Café* 11.30am-3pm, 5-10.30pm Mon-Thur; 11.30am-3.30pm, 5-11.30pm Fri, Sat. **Set meal** *Restaurant* $55-$85. **Main courses** *Café* $18-$24. **Credit** AmEx, DC, Disc, MC, V.
This is where chef/owner Alice Waters created California cuisine more than 35 years ago. Her modest, wood-framed restaurant still reigns supreme, serving impeccable prix fixe dinners downstairs in the restaurant and more casual à la carte meals in the upstairs café. Ingredients are always fresh, local,

Italian

Rivoli

1539 Solano Avenue, between Neilson Street & Peralta Avenue (1-510 526 2542/www.rivoli restaurant.com). Bus 18, G. **Open** 5.30-9.30pm Mon-Thur; 5.30-10pm Fri; 5-10pm Sat; 5-9pm Sun. **Main courses** $19-$26. **Credit** AmEx, DC, Disc, MC, V.
Rivoli is a charming, intimate and neighbourly Italian-inspired restaurant, run by talented chef Wendy Brucker. The menu offers simple versions of classic fare, prepared with seasonal organic produce; although it changes every three weeks, the portobello mushroom fritters (a signature dish), Caesar salad and the excellent hot fudge sundae remain a constant presence.

Spanish

César

1515 Shattuck Avenue, between Cedar & Vine Streets (1-510 883 0222/www.barcesar.com). BART Downtown Berkeley. **Open** noon-11pm Mon-Thur, Sun; noon-11.30pm Fri, Sat. *Bar* until midnight daily. **Main courses** *Tapas* $6-$17. **Credit** AmEx, DC, MC, V.
It was pretty daring to locate César right next door to Chez Panisse (*see above*), but it has more than held its own, despite the competition. It no doubt helps that the ambience here is very different (lively, thanks in part to the presence of a bar area), but the food, a collection of Spanish-influenced tapas made from high-quality ingredients, also impresses.
Other locations 4039 Piedmont Avenue, Oakland (1-510 985 1200).

Walnut Creek

American

Lark Creek Inn

1360 Locust Street, at Diablo Street (1-925 256 1234/www.larkcreek.com). BART to Walnut Creek. **Open** 11.30am-2.30pm, 5-9pm Mon-Thur; 11.30am-2.30pm, 5-10pm Fri; 5-10pm Sat; 10am-3pm, 5-9pm Sun. **Main courses** $13-$32. **Credit** AmEx, DC, Disc, MC, V.
In 1995, chef Bradley Ogden and restaurateur Michael Dellar established a Walnut Creek branch of their Lark Creek empire. The charming dining room has a bustling neighbourhood feel, and the kitchen prepares American fare with considerable imagination. Fish, fowl and grilled meats are all served in huge portions, along with signature Lark Inn dishes, such as the famed clam chowder.

Bars

Raise your glasses to these distinctive drinking spots.

Catalyst Cocktails. *See p165.*

Thanks to San Francisco's proximity to one of the largest wine-growing regions in the world, its residents aren't afraid of a drink. Indeed, California is responsible for over 90 per cent of the wine produced in the US. More likely to be found in a Bacchanalian revel than cowering beneath the sommelier's withering gaze, San Franciscans spend more on booze and books than the citizens of any other American city. As a result, they are educated consumers in every sense. After all, local booze production (and consumption) isn't limited to wine: the region is home to a goodly number of breweries and micro-distilleries, along with many brewpubs and speciality bars dedicated to more exotic tipples. Witness, too, the

> ▶ ❶ Pink numbers given in this chapter correspond to the location of each bar on the street maps. *See pp312-319.*

new trend towards wine bars and high-end cocktailing. More so than any other big city in the state, this is a drinking town.

WHERE TO DRINK
Generalists will delight in the number and variety of drinking holes here, but each locale has bars that fit its personality. The hangouts in the **Financial District** suit the suits that frequent them, while those around the **Tenderloin** and the **Civic Center** tend towards the earthy (and, sometimes, seedy). **North Beach**, the place to drink back in the days of the Beats, is now best avoided on weekends, when the bridge-and-tunnel crowd invades. The scene is smart, sometimes even chi-chi, in **Nob Hill** and **Pacific Heights**. **Haight-Ashbury** draws a down-to-earth, occasionally crunchy crowd; denizens of the **Lower Haight** may have more ink on their skin, but they're a friendly bunch.

The **Mission**, home to artists, musicians and much of the city's Latino population, is powered by a bohemian engine that also drives its nightlife. Choose from Czech-style beer gardens or Moroccan-themed cocktails on roof decks, or Mexican *cervecerias*, chic style bars and a host of dives that are pure Americana. More intrepid drinkers, meanwhile, should make the trek to the **East Bay**, home to some of the region's most historic bars, as well as some of its best brewpubs.

For information on how to navigate between venues by train, check out **www.beerbybart. com**, a blog that lists the best places to drink beer based on their proximity to BART stations. Hop on in San Francisco and you're belly up at the Trappist in Oakland, only 15 minutes later. Note that BART shuts down around midnight, however.

BOOZE AND THE LAW
You have to be aged 21 or over to buy and consume alcohol in the US, and it can only be sold between 6am and 2am. Always bring ID, even if you look older – there are varying levels of enforcement and you don't want to be caught out. Once denied entry as a result of ID, it's virtually impossible to talk your way in (penalties for those selling booze to punters without proper ID are intensely punitive). However, many bars choose to remain closed until late afternoon, and last

call is often around 1.15am-1.30am. Staff are obliged to confiscate unconsumed alcoholic drinks after 2am, and don't take kindly to being messed around.

Smoking is illegal in bars, restaurants and cafés. However, there is a loophole: because the anti-smoking law is based on safety in the workplace, bar-owners who employ no staff can permit smoking on the premises.

Downtown

Union Square & around

Tunnel Top
601 Bush Street, at Stockton Street (986 8900/ www.tunneltop.com). Bus 2, 3, 4, 30, 45, 76/cable car Powell-Hyde or Powell-Mason. **Open** 5pm-2am Mon-Sat. **No credit cards. Map** p315 M5 **❶**
The two-storey Tunnel Top is perched above the Stockton Tunnel, between Chinatown and Union Square, and looks a little shabby from the outside. Inside, however, the decor is urban-decay cool; films are projected against rust-coloured walls, while a DJ soundtracks the conversation. Just outside is the spot where Sam Spade surveys the scene of his partner's murder at the beginning of *The Maltese Falcon*.

The Financial District

Bix
56 Gold Street, between Montgomery & Sansome Streets (433 6300/www.bixrestaurant.com). Bus 9X, 10, 12, 20, 41. **Open** *Bar* 4.30-10pm Mon-Thur; 11.30am-midnight Fri, 5.30pm-midnight Sat; 5.30-10pm Sun. **Credit** AmEx, DC, Disc, MC, V. **Map** p315 N4 **❷**
The secretive locale and supper-club menu of Bix, named for owner Doug 'Bix' Biederbeck ('very vaguely related' to 1920s and '30s jazz cornet legend Bix Beiderbecke, evoke the opulence of the Jazz Age. The room combines the glamour of Harlem's Cotton Club with the splendour of a cruise liner's dining room so effectively that you half expect to spy Rita Hayworth sipping a martini in a booth.

Bubble Lounge
714 Montgomery Street, between Washington & Jackson Streets (434 4204/www.sanfrancisco. bubblelounge.com). Bus 1, 9X, 10, 12, 20, 41. **Open** 5.30pm-1am Tue-Thur; 5pm-2am Fri; 6.30pm-2am Sat. **Credit** AmEx, DC, Disc, MC, V. **Map** p315 N4 **❸**
After the stock market closes, stockbrokers and short-skirted executives tickle their noses with an incredible selection of sparkling wines and champagnes at this upscale hangout. The booze is paired with fine pâté, salads and caviar for a top-drawer taste of the Wall Street of the West.

The Tenderloin

Also here is the **Hemlock Tavern** (*see p234*), best known as a music venue but with a fine bar.

Edinburgh Castle
950 Geary Street, between Larkin & Polk Streets (885 4074/www.castlenews.com). Bus 2, 3, 4, 19, 38, 47. **Open** 5pm-2am daily. **Credit** DC, MC, V. **Map** p314 K6 **❹**
Once through the humble entranceway of what appears to be a small, dark dive, the adventurous are rewarded with a raffish, capacious booze hall with 30ft vaulted ceilings. Upstairs is a small cultural venue, playing host to local bands, DJ nights, literary readings and even the odd play that suit the salty tastes of its Scottish owner. Downstairs, the jukebox cranks favourite obscurities while patrons order fish and chips and settle in with the other unpretentious patrons. The highlight of the drinks selection is a vast and affordable range of single malt whiskies. It may not be on the Spey, but it'll do for a day.

Redwood Room
Clift Hotel, 495 Geary Street, at Taylor Street (929 2372/www.clifthotel.com). BART & metro to Powell/bus 2, 3, 4, 27, 38, 76/cable car Powell-Hyde or Powell-Mason. **Open** 5pm-2am Mon-Thur, Sun; 4pm-2am Fri, Sat. **Credit** AmEx, DC, Disc, MC, V. **Map** p314 L6 **❺**

The best Bars

For outdoor drinking
Make a beeline for **Jupiter**'s al fresco beer garden (*see p173*), the **Medjool Sky Terrace**'s deck (*see p169*) or the **Park Chalet**'s lovely lawn (*see p170*).

For upscale cocktailing
The **Matrix** (*see p172*), the **Redwood Room** (*see p163*), **Tony Nik's** (*see p167*) and **Top of the Mark** (*see p166*) provide plenty of opportunities to splurge. *See also p164* **Mixologist magic**

For downmarket boozing
500 Club (*see p168*), **Mauna Loa** (*see p172*) and **Mr Bing's** (*see p166*) are among the favourite haunts of the city's low-key lushes.

For beer lovers
Specialists include **City Beer Store** (bottled; *see p165*), **Jupiter** (local; *see p173*), **Lucky 13** (German; *see p168*), **Rogue Ale's Public House** (microbrews; *see p166*), **Toronado** (draught; *see p170*), **Trappist** (Belgian; *see p173*).

Eat, Drink, Shop

Mixologist magic

If you think that a mixologist is simply putting on airs and graces when he calls himself a 'bar chef', think again. Throughout the Bay Area, bars and restaurants are making names for themselves by creating speciality cocktail lists that look more like food menus (Mushroom Martini, anyone?). And with bar chefs even having a hand in creating their own bitters, simple syrups, essences and distillates, they're a breed more akin to mad scientists than the ol' barkeep who pulls a pint of ale from the cask.

Often, the purveyors of such potions are attached to restaurants: after all, the recipes revolve around not only top-shelf spirits but extremely fresh, seasonal produce and obscure ingredients that any smaller operation would find difficult to source. And the roster of such ingredients is staggering: herbs such as wild spearmint, lemongrass, clove, coriander, cardamom, basil; fruit including mandarin oranges, pluots, pears, apples, cranberries, blackberries, raspberries; flavourings such as orange blossom honey, harissa, aged balsamic vinegar; infused salts and sugars, and even flowers such as chrysanthemum blossom.

The high-end cocktail menu has become an institution throughout the city, so, regardless of the neighbourhood, you're bound to come across at least one. Bar menus rotate so frequently (again, depending on seasonality and the availability of fresh ingredients) that it's tough to pin down 'the best' at any given time. But here are a few of our favourites.

The Ferry Building's **Slanted Door** (*see p137*) has a cocktail menu that perfectly complements its Vietnamese-fusion cuisine. With a nod to French colonial history, too, cocktails meld ingredients such as lemongrass and elderflower syrup with spirits such as brandy, Chartreuse and Cointreau. The Richmond district's **Aziza** (5800 Geary Boulevard, at 22nd Avenue, 752 2222, www.aziza-sf.com) is a chic Moroccan restaurant, whose flavours into its nuanced creations. Try delicious and refreshing cucumber infusions or a bloody mary spiced up with harissa and – the secret ingredient – a dash of aged balsamic vinegar.

Absinthe (*see p156*) in Hayes Valley can truly live up to its name now that the eponymous spirit has been legalised in the

US. Yet while its remarkable spirits selection and world-class cocktails may incorporate the Green Fairy, the mixmasters here have also culled classic drinks and recreated them with up-to-date, premium ingredients. One example is their 'Uptown' Manhattan, featuring house-selected Eagle Rare Bourbon, Carpano Punt e Mes (vermouth), orange and Angostura bitters, brandied cherries and a twist of orange.

Relative newcomer **Grand Pu Bah** (88 Division Street, at 8th Street, 255 8188, www.grandpubahrestaurant.com), a Thai restaurant bordering SoMa and Portrero Hill, comes on strong with its Thai-themed concoctions. Its Bah Bah Noom cocktail mingles Thai chilli, kaffir lime leaves, lemongrass and fresh lime with cucumber-infused gin to create a spicy yet deeply refreshing chiller. The Tenderloin's **Rye** (668 Geary Street, at Leavenworth Street, 474 4448) is simply a bar, but what it lacks in food it makes up for in fresh fruit and herbs. As the name implies, it offers an excellent selection of rye- and bourbon-based cocktails, but there are also many lighter ones to please any palate.

Haight-Ashbury's **Alembic** (*see p154*) was created by the crew behind the neighbourhood institution that is **Magnolia** brewpub (*see p169*). Alembic keeps true to its commitment to use small, craft-made ingredients that are locally and sustainably sourced whenever possible. Check out the Boutonniere: Glenrothes Special Reserve Scotch with Nocino della Cristina (a digestif made with brandy infused with walnuts), orange bitters and candied kumquat.

No time was wasted in adding a bar to the Clift after the repeal of Prohibition in 1933, and the magnificent result has been a fixture for high-end cocktailing ever since. Although the decor shifted from art deco to postmodern under Schrager, the bar is neither tacky nor too flamboyant, its towering walls still panelled in redwood thought to have come from a single tree. A DJ spins four nights a week for a well-dressed and moneyed crew.

SoMa & South Beach

Close by AT&T Park is the **Hotel Utah** (*see p234*), a good music venue with a great, old bar.

Butter

354 11th Street, between Folsom & Harrison Streets (863 5964/www.smoothasbutter.com). Bus 9, 12, 27, 47. **Open** 6pm-2am Wed-Sun. **Credit** AmEx, DC, Disc, MC, V. **Map** p318 L9 **6**
Butter combines chill-room vibe (complete with DJ) with trailer-trash kitsch and food. After several years on the scene, it still packs people in, and its magic formula repast of a corn dog, Twinkie and can of Pabst Blue Ribbon may just prove to be the elixir of life.

Catalyst Cocktails

312 Harriet Street, between Bryant & Brannan Streets (621 1722/www.catalystcocktails.com). Bus 9X, 12, 19, 27, 47. **Open** 4-11pm Tue-Thur; 4pm-2am Fri, Sat. **Credit** DC, MC, V. **Map** p319 N8 **7**
Sipping cocktails beneath the spires of Catalyst's art deco bar is a bit like making a toast under a miniature Statue of Liberty, but there's much to celebrate here, including a daunting four-page cocktail menu: sup a Ukrainian Quaalude , a Black Dahlia or a Hairy Cherry. Handily located across from the city jail. *Photo p162.*

City Beer Store

1168 Folsom Street, between 7th & 8th Streets (503 1033/www.citybeerstore.com). Bus 9X, 12, 19, 27, 47. **Open** noon-9pm, Tue-Sat; noon-6pm Sun. **Credit** AmEx, DC, Disc, MC, V. **Map** p319 M8 **8**
This modest storefront operation consists of four tables and floor-to-ceiling refrigerators packed with over 300 kinds of bottled beers and six on draught. Grab a beer from the cooler, order a small plate of regional cheeses and salametto and banter with the other beer-o-philes. When it's time to head out, the owners encourage patrons to mix and match a six-pack to take away.

Hi Dive

Pier 28 1/2, Embarcadero, at Bryant Street (977 0170/www.hidive.net). Metro to Folsom/bus 12. **Open** 11.30am-late Mon-Fri; 10am-late Sat, Sun. **Credit** AmEx, DC, Disc, MC, V. **Map** p315 P5 **9**
Once patronised by dock workers and sailors on shore leave, the Hi Dive was renovated a while back, but still draws a low-key crowd. A fine pit stop during a walk down the Embarcadero, it's right on the water, and gets lively – or, depending on your mood, crowded – before and after Giants games.

21st Amendment

563 2nd Street, between Bryant & Brannan Streets (369 0900/www.21st-amendment.com). Metro 2nd & King/bus 9X, 10, 12, 30, 45, 76. **Open** 11.30am-midnight daily. **Credit** AmEx, DC, Disc, MC, V. **Map** p315 O6 **10**
Named in honour of the constitutional diktat repealing Prohibition, this brewpub gets packed with Giants fans looking to load up on good, nicely priced booze (a mix of own-label beers and guests) before getting soaked by the exorbitant beer prices inside the stadium. At other times, it's a standard brewpub, with decent food and a convivial atmosphere.

W Hotel

181 3rd Street, at Howard Street (817 7836/www.starwoodhotels.com). BART & Metro to Montgomery/bus 9X, 12, 30, 45, 76 and Market Street routes. **Open** 7pm-2am Tue-Sat. **Credit** AmEx, DC, Disc, MC, V. **Map** p315 N6 **11**
The two bars at this fashionable hotel (*see p52*) are filled with beautiful people. The first bar is a circular affair in the lobby, while the main room lies behind a beaded curtain above. Some may find the atmosphere a bit competitive, but the scene shifts nightly and banquettes upstairs encourage an intimate vibe.

Nob Hill & Chinatown

Nob Hill & Polk Gulch

Le Colonial

20 Cosmo Place, between Jones & Taylor Streets (931 3600/www.lecolonialsf.com). Bus 2, 3, 4, 27, 38, 76. **Open** 4.30-10pm Mon-Wed, Sun; 4.30-11pm Thur-Sat. **Credit** AmEx, DC, MC, V. **Map** p314 L5 **12**
Designed to approximate Vietnam c1920, when the country was still a French colony, this elegant hideaway has a sizeable dining room, while the stylish upstairs lounge serves tropical drinks, exotic teas and a menu highlighting Vietnamese fusion cuisine. The comfortable couches invite cocktailing and more in a lush environment of palm trees, rattan furniture and shuttered windows.

Hidden Vine

1/2 Cosmo Place, at Taylor & Post Streets (674 3567/www.thehiddenvine.com). Bus 2, 3, 4, 27, 38, 76. **Open** 5pm-midnight Tue-Thur; 5pm-2am Fri, Sat.* **Credit** DC, MC, V. **Map** p314 L5 **13**
Hidden is the operative word for this extremely cosy, husband-and-wife-owned wine bar that offers over 30 wines by the glass and 100 by the bottle. The thoughtfully conceived menu features numerous flights, allowing wine lovers to explore various varietals and regions. It's a great little sitting room atmosphere that encourages hushed conversation; those looking for a snack will be happy to find cheese, crackers and charcuterie to complement their fruit of the vine.

Red Room

827 Sutter Street, between Jones & Leavenworth Streets (346 7666). Bus 2, 3, 4, 27, 38, 76. **Open** 7pm-2am Tue-Thur, Sat; 5pm-2am Fri. **No credit cards. Map** p314 L5 ⓮
Enough to inspire a craving in any vampire, this slick hotel bar is entirely blood red: the walls, the tables, the semicircular bar, even one of the many speciality martinis. It's wildly popular but tiny – an uncomfortable combination at weekends. Come during the week when it's cosier.

Tonga Room & Hurricane Bar

Fairmont, 950 Mason Street, between California & Sacramento Streets (772 5278/www.fairmont.com). Bus 1/cable car California, Powell-Hyde or Powell-Mason. **Open** 5pm-midnight Mon-Thur, Sun; 5pm-1am Fri, Sat. **Credit** AmEx, DC, Disc, MC, V. **Map** p314 L4 ⓯
Despite the all-you-can-eat happy-hour dim sum, the sarong-clad waitresses and the enormous, exotic cocktails, the real attraction at this long-lived tiki bar is the spectacle of house musicians performing off-key covers of cheesy pop songs while afloat on a raft on the Tonga's indoor 'lagoon'. There's even an indoor thunderstorm every 20 minutes, complete with rain.

Top of the Mark

Inter-Continental Hotel Mark Hopkins, 1 Nob Hill, at California & Mason Streets (392 3434/www. topofthemark.com). Bus 1/cable car California, Powell-Hyde or Powell-Mason. **Open** 5pm-midnight Mon-Thur, Sun; 4pm-1am Fri, Sat. **Admission** $10 after 8pm Fri, Sat. **Credit** AmEx, DC, Disc, MC, V. **Map** p314 L5 ⓰
Neatly named for its location at the summit of the InterContinental Mark Hopkins Hotel, Top of the Mark offers spectacular panoramic views of San Francisco. It's worth a quick visit just to check the view and sip a cocktail from the extensive martini menu, but arrive early in the evening to avoid the cover charge and the dress code (look smart or drink elsewhere).

Chinatown

Li Po

916 Grant Avenue, at Washington Street (982 0072). Bus 1, 9X, 12, 20, 30, 41, 45. **Open** 2pm-2am daily. **No credit cards. Map** p315 M4 ⓱
A fun spot for a pick-me-up when you're done with the junk shops on Grant Avenue. Li Po is basically a dive, but the cave façade and giant, tattered Chinese lantern inside set it nicely apart from its neighbours. It'll take you back to Barbary Coast-era San Francisco with no risk of being shanghaied by anything except the potent cocktails.

Mr Bing's

201 Columbus Avenue, at Pacific Avenue (362 1545). Bus 9X, 12, 20, 30, 41, 45. **Open** noon-2am daily. **No credit cards. Map** p315 M4 ⓲

This shambles of a bar doesn't look like much from the outside, and looks like even less once you're through the door. But, thanks partly to its highly conspicuous location, it's a prince among dives, frequented by a mix of idling Chinese, haggard old North Beach bums and those who are simply, plainly desperate for a drink. For dive bar devotees, Mr Bing's is rarely less than entertaining.

North Beach to Fisherman's Wharf

North Beach

Rogue Ale's Public House

673 Union Street, between Powell Street & Columbus Avenue (362 7880/www.rogue.com). Bus 9X, 20, 30, 39, 41, 45. **Open** 3pm-midnight Mon-Thur; noon-2am Fri, Sat; noon-midnight Sun. **Credit** AmEx, DC, Disc, MC, V. **Map** p314 L3 ⓳
Oregon microbrewery Rogue Ale's bold land grab is evidenced by this ale house, devoted to its staggering array of brews. The standard selection of ambers and lagers is supplemented by such gems as chilli-pepper-tinged Chipotle Ale, Smoke Ale (with strong flavours of smokehouse almonds), Coffee Stout and Iron Chef Morimoto's Black Obi Soba Ale.

Rosewood

732 Broadway, between Stockton & Powell Streets (951 4886/www.rosewoodbar.com). Bus 9X, 12, 20, 30, 41, 45. **Open** 5.30pm-2am Tue-Fri; 7pm-2am Sat.* **Credit** DC, MC, V. **Map** p315 M3 ⓴
This stylish bar boasts rosewood panelling and is furnished with low black leather benches. Located on a neglected commercial strip at the edge of North Beach and Chinatown, with no sign outside, it hasn't been overrun, and remains one of the best places in the city to sip a cocktail while DJs spin low-key tunes.

San Francisco Brewing Company

155 Columbus Avenue, at Pacific Avenue (434 3344/ www.sfbrewing.com). Bus 9X, 20, 30, 41, 45. **Open** noon-1.30am daily. **Credit** AmEx, DC, MC, V. **Map** p315 M4 ㉑
Housed in a restored 1907 saloon (it has operated as some form of a bar almost continuously since the late 19th century), this brewpub offers microbrews, pub grub and even free tours. Formerly the Andromeda Saloon, it was here that gangster 'Baby Face' Nelson was allegedly captured. The scene is more staid today, but it's hard to pass up the $1 brews from 4pm to 6pm and midnight to 1am.

Savoy Tivoli

1434 Grant Avenue, between Green & Union Streets (362 7023/www.savoy-tivoli.netfirms.com). Bus 9X, 12, 20, 30, 39, 41, 45. **Open** 6pm-2am Tue-Thur; 5pm-2am Fri; 3pm-2am Sat. **No credit cards. Map** p315 M3 ㉒

Eat, Drink, Shop

Opened in 1906, this long-established bar tends to get packed with Marina-ites on warm, weekend nights due to the expanse of outdoor seating out front, but when things are a bit slower it's a perfect place to grab a beer and enjoy the weather or perhaps play a few games of pool. Cocktails are a bit on the pricey side and not carefully mixed, but they'll do.

Spec's
12 William Saroyan Place, at Broadway & Columbus Avenue (421 4112). Bus 9X, 12, 20, 30, 41, 45. **Open** 4.30pm-2am Mon-Fri; 5pm-2am Sat, Sun. **No credit cards. Map** p315 M3 ㉓
Spec's really is the quintessential old-school San Francisco bar: one part North Beach bohemian and one part Wild West saloon, with a dash of weirdness thrown in for good measure. It's tucked away in a false alley (you'll see what we mean), with nearly every inch covered with dusty detritus from around the world. If you're feeling peckish, a basket of saltines and a wedge of gouda can be had for four bucks. *Photo p168.*

Tony Nik's
1524 Stockton Street, at Green Street (693 0990). Bus 9X, 12, 20, 30, 39, 41, 45. **Open** 4pm-2am daily. **Credit** DC, MC, V. **Map** p315 M3 ㉔
This venerable lounge, which is essentially a long bar with a few extra seats, opened the day after Prohibition was repealed in 1933, and keeps the old-time vibe alive thanks to Atomic Age decor and comfortably hip and friendly environs. Cocktails are a serious business here: there's always a surprise lurking behind the bar if the right mixologist is on duty.

Tosca Café
242 Columbus Avenue, between Broadway & Pacific Avenue (986 9651). Bus 9X, 12, 20, 30, 41, 45. **Open** 5pm-2am Mon-Sat; 7pm-2am Sun. **No credit cards. Map** p315 M3 ㉕
Formica-topped tables, massive copper espresso machines, Caruso warbling from an ancient jukebox… bars with interiors this lush deserve to double as movie sets. The house speciality, a blend of coffee, steamed milk and brandy, really packs a punch. The Bada Bing Italian ambience and Hollywood-connected owner have drawn the likes of Bono and Sean Penn.

Vesuvio
255 Columbus Avenue, between Broadway & Pacific Avenue (362 3370/www.vesuvio.com). Bus 9X, 12, 20, 30, 41, 45. **Open** 6am-2am daily. **Credit** AmEx, DC, MC, V. **Map** p315 M4 ㉖
A funky old saloon with a stained-glass façade, Vesuvio preserves the flavour of the bars of an earlier era. It's next to the famous City Lights bookshop (*see p178*), just across Jack Kerouac Alley (the writer was a regular here), and its walls are covered with Beat memorabilia. Sit on the narrow balcony and check out the scene downstairs and on the street.

The Mission & the Castro

The Mission

Argus Lounge
3187 Mission Street, at Valencia Street (824 1447/ www.arguslounge.com). BART 24th Street Mission/ bus 12, 14, 26, 27, 49, 67. **Open** 4pm-2am daily. **No credit cards. Map** off p318 K12 ㉗
Known by some as the Peacock because of the illuminated feather out front (there's no other sign), the Argus is far enough down Mission to escape the gentrifying masses. A clean, simple hangout, it draws a happy crowd, including local indie-rock heroes. A superlative jukebox and back-room pool table add to quirky touches such as a working 1950s exercise belt. Shake it, baby.

Tonga Room & Hurricane Bar.

Eat, Drink, Shop

Spec's: for the real old-school San Francisco bar experience. *See p167.*

Beauty Bar

*2299 Mission Street, at 19th Street (285 0323/
www.beautybar.com). BART 16th Street/bus
14, 22, 26, 33, 49.* **Open** 5pm-2am Mon-Fri;
7pm-2am Sat, Sun. **Credit** DC, MC, V.
Map p318 K11 ㉘
This little cocktail bar, modelled after its sister bar
in New York (and now four other locations nation-
wide), is decorated with bric-a-brac salvaged from a
Long Island hair salon. Instead of a couch, curl up
on a Naugahyde salon chair, with hairdryer still
attached. On Thursday to Saturday evenings, buy
a $10 cocktail and get a free manicure.

Dalva

*3121 16th Street, between Mission & Guerrero
Streets (252 7740). BART 16th Street/bus 14, 22,
26, 33, 49.* **Open** 4pm-2am daily. **No credit cards.**
Map p318 J10 ㉙
An unspoiled oasis of cool in the manic Mission bar
scene, Dalva worships good music. The jukebox,
named Orpheus, carries a wonderfully diverse array
of sounds, from Cuban music to tiki kitsch. When
it's not on, DJs spin drum 'n' bass, jazz, soul, funk,
salsa and other odds and sods.

Doc's Clock

*2575 Mission Street, at 22nd Street (824 3627).
BART 24th Street Mission/bus 12, 14, 26, 48,
49, 67.* **Open** 6pm-2am Mon-Sat; 8pm-2am Sun.
No credit cards. Map p318 K12 ㉚
This place was formerly a total dive but, in common
with many nearby bars, it had a kindly refit a while
back. The mahogany bar was buffed up, the booze
selection expanded, and the CD changer now spits
out anything from Air to Sufjan Stevens. Just down
the road is the similarly revamped Mission Bar
(2695 Mission Street, 647 2300), which lacks both the
shuffleboard table and the magnificent neon sign of
Doc's Clock, but has a great jukebox and adds some
of the area's strongest drinks.

500 Club

*500 Guerrero Street, at 17th Street (861 2500).
BART 16th Street Mission/bus 14, 22, 26, 33, 49.*
Open 3pm-2am Mon-Fri; 1pm-2am Sat, Sun. **No
credit cards. Map** p318 J10 ㉛
Vying with Doc's Clock for the title of the Mission's
best marquee, the 'Five Hunge' is everybody's
favourite dive. Cavernous booths, a punk jukebox,
a pool table and cheap, stiff drinks keep the place
brimming with an incredibly various crowd. Pull up
a stool at the long, long bar and don't make any
plans to leave.

Kilowatt

*3160 16th Street, between Valencia & Guerrero
Streets (861-2595/www.barbell.com/kilowatt). BART
16th Street/bus 14, 22, 26, 33, 49.* **Open** 4.30pm-
2am Mon-Fri; 1pm-2am Sat, Sun. **No credit cards.**
Map p318 J10 ㉜
Does what a solid bar should. With reasonable
prices, generous drink pours, a good selection of
beers, a top-notch jukebox, pool tables, dartboards
and comfortable booths, this no-nonsense joint is a
great option. Add in an excellent location near
Dalva, the 500 Club and a number of restaurants,
and it just gets better. For a meal of champions,
grab a lamb shawarma from Truly Mediterranean
across the street, return to the bar and order one of
its mean bloody marys.

Knockout

*3223 Mission Street, at Valencia Street (550 6994/
www.theknockoutsf.com). BART 24th Street Mission/
bus 12, 14, 26, 27, 49, 67.* **Open** 5pm-2am daily.
No credit cards.

This divey old hangout takes on all challengers, hosting diverse live acts as well as DJs spinning sounds from reggae to rockabilly. Thursday night bingo sessions are a lot of fun, and happy hour karaoke is a hit too.

Medjool Sky Terrace

2522 Mission Street, between 21st & 22nd Streets (550 9055/www.medjoolsf.com). BART 24th Street Mission/bus 12, 14, 26, 48, 49, 67. **Open** 5-10pm Mon-Wed; 4pm-midnight Thur; 4pm-1.30am Fri; 2pm-1.30am Sat; noon-10pm Sun. **Credit** AmEx, DC, Disc, MC, V. **Map** p318 K11 ㉝
This two-building complex, topped by a massive roof deck, contains a restaurant, a café and an excellent hostel. However, weather permitting, the deck is the primary draw. Sip cocktails, draft beer or wine, and scoff scaled-down, lighter fare from the restaurant's menu while taking in some of the Mission's best views.

Phone Booth

1398 S Van Ness Avenue, at 25th Street (648 4683). BART 24th Street Mission/bus 12, 14, 26, 27, 49, 67. **Open** 1pm-2am Mon-Fri, Sun; 2pm-2am Sat. **No credit cards. Map** p318 K12 ㉞
This place is about the size of an actual phone booth, and its tiny dimensions often make it appear more popular than it is, but most drinkers are too bombed on the cheap booze to notice. Ageing British punks and new wavers will find plenty to like on the jukebox.

Zeitgeist

199 Valencia Street, at Duboce Avenue (255 7505). BART to 16th Street Mission/Metro to Van Ness/streetcar F/bus 26, 49. **Open** 9am-2am daily. **No credit cards. Map** p318 K9 ㉟
Sited on the border between SoMa and the Mission, Zeitgeist is one of the hippest and most mellow bars in town, popular with bikers (Hondas rather than Harleys), bike messengers and people from every walk of alternative life. On sunny evenings, it's hard to find a seat at the benches and tables in the giant beer-garden-meets-junkyard back patio. The jukebox places special emphasis on underground punk.

The Castro

The majority of decent bars in the Castro are gay-oriented, although a number do draw a mixed crowd. For a full list of gay and lesbian hangouts in the area, *see pp221-24*; for the **Café du Nord**, which serves double-duty as both bar and music venue, *see p234*.

Lucky 13

2140 Market Street, between Church & Sanchez Streets (487 1313). Metro to Church/streetcar F/bus 22, 37. **Open** 4pm-2am Mon-Thur; 2pm-2am Fri-Sun. **No credit cards. Map** p318 H9 ㊱
Dark, spacious and always busy, Lucky 13 has long been a favourite with those who crave the aura of a

punk/biker bar without the perceived risk. There's pinball, pool and foosball, but the main entertainments are people-watching and choosing from one of the best German beer selections in the Bay Area.

The Haight & around

Haight-Ashbury

Hobson's Choice

1601 Haight Street, at Clayton Street (621 5859/ www.hobsonschoice.com). Metro to Cole & Carl/bus 6, 7, 33, 37, 43, 71. **Open** 2pm-2am Mon-Fri; noon-2am Sat, Sun. **Credit** DC, MC, V. **Map** p317 E9 ㊲
At this 'Victorian punch bar' (the owners' description), bartenders ladle out tall glasses of tasty rum punch; the menu boasts more than 70 kinds of rum. Fresh, grilled kebabs from the neighbouring Asqew Grill soak up the booze as it settles in the bellies of the collegiate-cum-jam-band set that fills the place.

Madrone Lounge

500 Divisadero Street, at Fell Street (241 0202/ www.madronelounge.com). Bus 21, 24. **Open** 2pm-midnight Mon, Sun; 2pm-2am Tue-Sat. **Credit** DC, MC, V. **Map** p317 G8 ㊳
A funky lounge and gallery whose beautifully restored Victorian exterior brought joy to the neighbours when it was revived from almost total dilapidation. Inside, draught beers, a speciality cocktail list and a bar menu keeps patrons occupied while digging DJs, independent film screenings or live music.

Magnolia

1398 Haight Street, at Masonic Avenue (864 7468/ www.magnoliapub.com). Bus 6, 7, 33, 37, 43, 71. **Open** noon-1am Mon-Thur; noon-1am Fri; 10am-1am Sat; 10am-11pm Sun. **Credit** AmEx, DC, Disc, MC, V. **Map** p317 F9 ㊴
This brewpub's decor plays up to its history: built in 1903, it was a focal point of hippie culture in the 1960s, before being taken over by quasi-legendary local dessert maven Magnolia Thunderpussy, after whom it's now named. A solid bar menu complements the own-brewed beer selection, which includes some cask ales.

Zam Zam

1633 Haight Street, between Clayton & Belvedere Streets (861 2545). Metro to Cole & Carl/bus 6, 7, 33, 37, 43, 71. **Open** 3pm-2am Mon-Fri; 1pm-2am Sat, Sun. **No credit cards. Map** p317 E9 ㊵
This tiny bar became famous under notoriously cantankerous owner Bruno Mooshei, who inherited it from his father and waged a one-man campaign to keep it exactly as it must have been circa World War II. Mooshei died in 2000, but the place was bought by long-time patrons devoted to keeping its *Casablanca* aura intact, and they've done an excellent job. It's a great place for a pre- and/or post-cinema drink when catching a flick at the Red Vic Movie House just up the street.

Lower Haight

Mad Dog in the Fog
*530 Haight Street, between Fillmore & Steiner
Streets (626 7279). Metro to Duboce & Church/
bus 6, 7, 22, 71.* **Open** 3pm-midnight Mon;
11am-2am Tue; 3pm-2am Wed-Fri; 10am-2pm
Sat; 10am-midnight Sun. **No credit cards.**
Map p318 H8 ④
Anglophiles and expats pack the Mad Dog for pub
quizzes and football broadcasts (it opens early at
weekends for English Premiership matches). Strong
selections of 20 beers on tap and another 30 in bottles back up the menu of pub grub, which includes
English breakfasts.

Noc Noc
*557 Haight Street, between Fillmore & Steiner
Streets (861 5811/www.nocnocs.com). Metro
to Duboce & Church/bus 6, 7, 22, 71).* **Open**
5pm-2am daily. **Credit** DC, MC, V. **Map** p318 H8 ④
If Dr Seuss and Trent Reznor had gone into the bar
business together, this is what they'd have come up
with. The decor is described as post-apocalyptic
industrial, and the whole place has a peculiarly
organic Gaudi feel. Always plunged in near dark-
ness and with a mellow chill-room vibe, Noc Noc
attracts a multi-ethnic lot.

Toronado
*547 Haight Street, between Fillmore & Steiner
Streets (863 2276/www.toronado.com). Bus 6, 7,
22, 66, 71.* **Open** 11.30am-2am daily. **No credit
cards.** **Map** p317 H8 ④
This noisy hangout is a beer drinker's delight. A
board posted on the wall shows the massive, ever-
changing selection of draughts (which includes local
brews and Belgian imports), while the blackboard
behind the bar highlights bottled beer and non-alco
options. Patrons are encouraged to bring in fresh
sausages from Rosamunde Sausage Grill next door.

Hayes Valley

Hotel Biron
*45 Rose Street, between Market & Gough Streets
(703 0403/www.hotelbiron.com). Metro to Van Ness/
streetcar F/bus 6, 7, 26, 71.* **Open** 5pm-2am daily.
Credit AmEx, DC, MC, V. **Map** p318 K8 ④
Home to a wine bar and gallery, this stylish yet
unpretentious hotel is named after the Hôtel Biron
in Paris, which houses the Rodin museum. The walls
showcase the work of local artists; the impressive
wine list boasts 80 wines by the bottle and 35 or so
by the glass, plus a selection of beers and a small
but appealing menu of cheeses, caviar and olives. A
great, low-key place for drinkers who like to talk.

Jade Bar
*650 Gough Street, at McAllister Street (869 1900/
www.jadebar.com). Bus 5, 21, 47, 49.* **Open** 5pm-
2am Mon-Sat; 8pm-2am Sun. **Credit** AmEx, DC,
Disc, MC, V. **Map** p318 J7 ④

Restaurateur Greg Medow calls his lounge 'three
bars in one', thanks to the distinct personality of
each of its three modest floors. Signature cocktails
go down easy in the shag-shod loft; the stylish
main- floor bar comes with orchids in highlighted
nooks; and a 20ft (6m)waterfall trickles into the
basement lounge. Male patrons will appreciate
being able to keep an eye on their drink even
while in the gents, thanks to a one-way mirror that
overlooks the bar.

Sunset, Golden Gate Park & Richmond

Richmond
In addition to the bars listed below, the
Richmond and the Sunset are characterised
by a profusion of Irish joints; in the Sunset,
head to the historic **Little Shamrock** (807
Lincoln Way, at 9th Avenue, 661 0060). For
something a bit grander, try the **Beach Chalet**
(*see p112*) for cocktails or the **Cliff House**
(*see p115*) for views.

Park Chalet
*1000 Great Highway, at Fulton Street (386 8439/
www.parkchalet.com). Bus 5, 18, 31, 38.* **Open**
noon-10.30pm daily. **Credit** AmEx, DC, MC, V.
Younger sibling of the well-known Beach Chalet ,
the Park Chalet doesn't have the same views of
Ocean Beach (it backs on to Golden Gate Park),
but it does have a gorgeous expanse of lush lawn
and beautifully landscaped local flora. On sunny
days, it's great to lounge in one of its Adirondack
chairs while enjoying a pint (or several) of the
house-brewed beer.

Tommy's Mexican Restaurant
*5929 Geary Boulevard, between 23rd & 24th
Avenues (387 4747/www.tommysmexican.com). Bus
1, 2, 29, 31, 38.* **Open** noon-11pm Mon, Wed-Sun.
Credit AmEx, DC, MC, V.
Although there is a restaurant attached to the bar,
it's all about the tequila, on which Julio Bermejo,
son of founder Tommy, is a global authority. Ask
him for advice on which of the 240-plus varieties
to sample; then sip, don't shoot. The house mar-
garita, made with fresh Peruvian limes, agave nec-
tar and top-shelf tequila, is a doozy; order it with
rocks but no salt.

Trad'r Sam
*6150 Geary Boulevard, between 25th & 26th
Avenues (221 0773). Bus 1, 2, 29, 31, 38.*
Open 10am-2am daily. **No credit cards.**
A local favourite since 1939, this unabashedly traditional tiki bar serves the kind of cocktails that can
only be described as dangerous. Planter's punch,
mai tais, singapore slings, the ever-popular Volcano
& Goldfish Bowl… there's a guaranteed hangover
under every tiny umbrella.

Drink hard, speak easy

It was on 16 January 1920 – a dark day in American history – that the production, transport and sale of alcohol were prohibited under Federal law. But thanks to the ingenuity and pluck of the foes of temperance, the Prohibition Era (which lasted until 1933) was not entirely dry in San Francisco – if you knew where to look. Luckily, one of the institutions that resulted from the Prohibition Era has recently been revived: the speakeasy.

It's said that the name arose from bartenders advising patrons to order *sotto voce*, or to 'speak easy', lest the law overhear their call for contraband hooch. Needless to say, the romance of throwing down bootleg moonshine in such places captured the imagination of many, and San Francisco, once crowded with actual speakeasies during Prohibition, is now home to several drinking establishments that capitalise on that cachet.

The venerable **Café du Nord** (2170 Market Street, at 15th Street, Castro, 861 5016, www.cafedunord.com) started life as a speakeasy in 1907, and its basement bar and music venue retain their classic Victorian interiors. The **House of Shields** (39 New Montgomery Street, at Market Street, SoMa, 975 8651, www.houseofshields.com), started by one Eddie Shields in 1908, is still said to house a subterranean network of tunnels once frequented by surreptitious tipplers.

While many speakeasies were essentially repurposed basements, storerooms or even secret floors in hotels, their modern-day facsimiles are anything but bare bones. **Bourbon & Branch** (501 Jones Street, at O'Farrell Street, Tenderloin, 346 1735, www.bourbonandbranch.com) may be ultra-stylish (and have a cocktail list to match), but it has somehow managed to rekindle the spirit of the speakeasy. Reservations are required (that's also when you'll learn the password to gain entry) and the only indication that there is anything housed in the dark, corner building is the 'Anti-Saloon League' sign (a nod to an actual organisation) that hangs outside. The interior is dim and the booths are designed to be a bit tight but that's all part of the charm, as is the hidden latch in the bookcase that opens the door to a secret, second bar.

At one of the most notorious speakeasies in San Francisco, Coffee Dan's, patrons would access the basement bar by riding down a 15-foot slide. Featured in the 1927 Al Jolson movie, *The Jazz Singer*, Coffee Dan's was also a gambling den and cabaret, which played host to the likes of clarinettist Artie Shaw. Coffee Dan's location at 430 Mason Street is now home to **Slide** (between Geary & Post Streets, Union Square & around, 421 1916, www.slidesf.com), a swank speakeasy created by the owners of the over-the-top Ruby Skye nightclub. As Slide's name suggests, guests can access the bar via a long slide, which launches them into an elegant interior with plush booths, bottle service (for a hefty premium, starting at $250/bottle), a striking, backlit honey onyx bar, acres of mahogany panelling and a DJ booth housed in a grand piano. Despite Slide's unbeatable provenance, the contemporary crowd is heavily South Bay meets LA in orientation; it's hard to imagine how their truly outlaw forebears would regard them. At the very least, though, it's worth sliding in to sample some of the many martinis or champagne cocktails.

Bourbon & Branch.

Eat, Drink, Shop

Pacific Heights to the Golden Gate Bridge

Pacific Heights

G Bar

Laurel Inn, 488 Presidio Avenue, between Sacramento & California Streets (409 4227/www. gbarsf.com). Bus 1, 2, 3, 4, 43. **Open** 6pm-midnight Mon, Tue; 6pm-2am Wed-Fri; 7pm-2am Sat. **Credit** AmEx, DC, Disc, MC, V. **Map** p313 F5 ⑯

If you're saddened that San Francisco doesn't look like LA, head to the bar at the Laurel Inn. The place was a nondescript motel until the folks behind the Commodore (home to the Red Room; *see p166*) and the Phoenix (where you'll find the Bambuddha Lounge; *see p51*) got hold of it. The bar here now has a neo-1950s look and bachelor-pad atmosphere.

Cow Hollow

For weekend partiers in Cow Hollow and the Marina, life is unchanged since their frat and sorority house days. Located on Fillmore Street around the junction with Greenwich Street, the **City Tavern** (no.3200, 567 0918), the **Balboa Café** (no.3199, 921 3944) and **Eastside West** (no.3154, 885 4000) are collectively known as the Triangle, and get packed on weekends with yuppies performing the mating ritual.

Liverpool Lil's

2942 Lyon Street, between Lombard & Greenwich Streets (921 6664/www.liverpoollils.com). Bus 28, 41, 43, 45, 76. **Open** 11am-1am Mon; 11am-2am Tue-Fri; 10am-2am Sat; 10am-1am Sun. **Credit** AmEx, DC, MC, V. **Map** p313 F3 ⑰

The façade looks like it's made out of driftwood, and the main decorative touches are old sports photos and paintings of jazz greats. No matter: this is the Marina's least pretentious bar. The crowd ranges from old-timers having their morning Scotch to well-heeled newcomers nipping in for a pint. There's a considerable pub menu too.

Matrix

3138 Fillmore Street, between Filbert & Greenwich Streets (563 4180/www.matrixfillmore.com). Bus 22, 28, 43, 76. **Open** 5.30pm-2am daily. **Credit** AmEx, DC, Disc, MC, V. **Map** p313 G3 ⑲

At the original Matrix, you might have seen Hunter S Thompson in the bathroom sucking LSD off a stranger's sleeve, or the Grateful Dead playing an impromptu set. These days, however, the Matrix draws label-conscious fashionistas and financiers who sip from the pricey cocktail menu at what is really a high-style pick-up joint.

Mauna Loa

3009 Fillmore Street, at Union Street (563 5137). Bus 22, 28, 41, 43, 45, 76. **Open** 2pm-2am Mon-Fri; noon-2am Sat, Sun. **No credit cards. Map** p313 G4 ⑲

Originally opened by a Hawaiian in the late 1950s, Mauna Loa has morphed into perhaps the only bar in the Marina that could be considered divey; the crowd, at least, is far more down to earth than you'll find at the Triangle. A pool table, foosball and Pop-A-Shot entertain patrons, but on weekends it's tough to manoeuvre your cue through the crush.

The East Bay

Oakland

Alley

3325 Grand Avenue, between Elwood & Lake Park Avenues (1-510 444 8505). BART 19th Street, then bus 12. **Open** 4.30pm-2am Tue-Sat. **No credit cards.**

The Alley is designed to look like a shanty-town street, complete with knickers strung between building façades and jagged fences separating the booths. At the end of the bar is a piano surrounded by bar stools, each with a mic. Anyone is free to take a seat and join the singalong that takes place every Thursday through Saturday night. Don't worry if you're not sure of the words: neither is the pianist. Business cards stapled to the walls flap like leaves in the breeze of passing patrons.

Heinold's First & Last Chance.

Heinold's First & Last Chance

48 Webster Street, at Jack London Square (1-510 839 6761/www.heinoldsfirstandlastchance.com). BART Oakland City Center/12th Street, then bus 58, 72L, 301. **Open** noon-1am daily. **No credit cards.**

One of California's – if not America's – most historic bars is still going strong, 125 years after it opened. The positively Melvillian structure was built from the salvaged timbers of a whaling ship right on the Oakland docks. It was at these same tables that a young Jack London did his homework. The entire room dips in the middle and the bar (still the original, made in 1883 by a ship's carpenter) is canted at a sharp grade as the foundation settled after the Great Earthquake of 1906. As evening descends the barman ignites the original gaslamps – the only gas lighting still in use in a commercial enterprise in California.

Ruby Room

132 14th Street, between Madison & Oak Streets (1-510 444 7224). BART Lake Merritt. **Open** 5pm-2am daily. **Credit** AmEx, DC, MC, V.

Neither the fantastic jukebox nor the new-wave DJs seem able to entice people on to the tiny dancefloor here, but everyone hums or sings along. The crowd is young, hip, tattooed and pierced, and happy to while away the hours in Ruby Room's dim, womb-like space, all red walls and black ceiling.

Trappist

460 8th Street, between Broadway & Washington Street (1-510 238 8900/www.thetrappist.com). BART Oakland City Center/12th Street. **Open** 4pm-midnight Wed-Fri; 2pm-midnight Sat, Sun. **Credit** DC, MC, V.

Beer-lovers beware: although the Trappist can hold a mere 46 patrons, it's easy to get lost in this place for days. Working with a small group of distributors, proprietors Chuck Stilphen and Aaron Porter have created a fitting tribute to the Belgian beer bars they love so much. There's a staggering selection of Belgian and speciality beers on offer: 15 on draught and more than 120 bottled. Even better, they refuse to stock beer from major breweries. Luckily, their extensive knowledge and encyclopaedic beer menu mean that even neophytes won't be daunted.

Berkeley

Albatross Pub

1822 San Pablo Avenue, between Delaware & Hearst Streets (1-510 843 2473/www.albatrosspub.com). BART North Berkeley or Downtown Berkeley, then bus 51. **Open** 6pm-2am Mon, Tue, Sun; 4.30pm-2am Wed-Sat. **No credit cards.**

The welcoming atmosphere at Berkeley's oldest pub allows its diverse crowd to take part in a range of activities. For the (relatively) active, there's a huge variety of board games, four separate dart stalls, a pool room and regular live music. For the couch potatoes? A fireplace, a large range of beers, free popcorn, reading lamps and a host of quiet corners.

Blake's on Telegraph

2367 Telegraph Avenue, between Durant Avenue & Channing Way (1-510 848 0886/www.blakeson telegraph.com). BART Downtown Berkeley. **Open** 11.30am-2am Mon-Sat; 11.30am-1am Sun. **Credit** AmEx, DC, Disc, MC, V.

A Berkeley institution, Blake's has grown up with the university. Three floors handle overflow crowds on days when Cal teams play, but at other times the space offers something for everyone: you may find a ska band hopping in the basement, a crowd from the local fraternity on the main floor and a mellow vibe upstairs. Each floor has its own bar.

Jupiter

2181 Shattuck Avenue, between Allston Way & Center Street (1-510 843 8277/www.jupiterbeer. com). BART Downtown Berkeley. **Open** 11.30am-1am Mon-Thur; 11.30am-1.30am Fri; noon-1.30am Sat; 1pm-midnight Sun. **Credit** DC, MC, V.

The copper bar, the interior walls clad in patterned tin siding, the pews (rescued from a local church), the two-storey outdoor beer garden… there's much to love about this pub even before you've thought about which of the 34 locally brewed draft beers to drink, and whether to supplement it with a pizza from the wood-fired oven. Jupiter is the dream-bar creation of one of the founders of the hallowed Triple Rock (1920 Shattuck Avenue, at Hearst Avenue, 1-510 843 2739, www.triplerock.com), which claims to be one of the first brewpubs in the US and is still worth a look.

Albany

Club Mallard

752 San Pablo Avenue, between Portland & Washington Avenues (1-510 524 8450/www.club mallard.com). BART El Cerrito Plaza. **Open** 2pm-2am Mon-Fri; noon-2am Sat, Sun. **Credit** DC, MC, V.

The good-natured crowd at the half log-cabin, half tiki-style Mallard are more congenial than the salty folk who frequent the Hotsy Totsy and the Ivy Room just along the street. The two pool tables on the main floor cost only 25¢, with more tables upstairs for hire by the hour. The eclectic jukebox ranges from funk and reggae to campy lounge tunes, heightening the surreal atmosphere.

Schmidt's Tobacco Trading & Pub

1492 Solano Avenue, between Santa Fe & Curtis Avenues (1-510 525 1900). BART El Cerrito Plaza. **Open** noon-midnight Mon-Wed, Sun; noon-1am Thur-Sat. **No credit cards.**

An impressive array of tobaccos and accessories welcomes the weary to this smoker-centric outpost. Rolling machines are made available for patrons to twist up a smoke of their own while quaffing fresh-pulled pints. Pull up an overstuffed chair in front of the living room fireplace and inhale the pungent aromas from your neighbour's leaf, or play one of the house-supplied board games.

Eat, Drink, Shop

Shops & Services

Independent shops for a city with an independent spirit.

San Francisco's famously diverse shopping scene continues to withstand the threat of retail boredom. Impossibly edgy thrift-chic boutiques exist within shouting distance of department store behemoths, international couture and ever-present Gap, and while things do sometimes get prickly in this most independent-minded of cities, where resistance to national chain stores has been fierce over the years, they mostly remain cordial rivals. In recent times, the local fashion scene has also felt the impact of newly arrived out-of-towners such as Barneys New York and Bloomingdale's, as well as trend-driven low-price women's fashion emporiums like H&M, Forever 21 and Zara. But the city continues to rise above it, welcoming a constant stream of new designers and other fun outlets: fun, often Japanese-inspired design stores/ galleries that mix fine art, publications and pop collectibles; and girly gift shops that combine independently designed letterpress paper goods with women's and children's clothing.

When scouring the city for the latest It bag, It coat or It iPod accessory, don't be afraid to travel around town. Along with Union Square, posher neighbourhoods such as Cow Hollow and Pacific Heights are great for high-end designer chic. However, if your tastes extend to (for example) independent designers, two-of-a-kind shoes and vintage tracksuits, head for hipper residential areas such as the Mission, the Haight and emerging 'hood Hayes Valley.

The second-hand scene is mighty here. It's not unusual to find customised clothes amid the racks of jeans and jackets cast asunder by the resolutely trendy, or out-of-print rare books alongside the hot new paperbacks; there are bargains everywhere you look. If you'd rather stick to the new goods, the important thing to keep in mind is that no matter how fabulous the salesperson says your purchase looks, the returns policy probably doesn't care either way. Shop with confident discretion.

TAX & DUTY

Local sales tax, currently 8.5 per cent, will be added to all purchases. You can avoid paying this if you live out of state and either arrange shipment by US mail or courier or get the shop to do it for you. If you are taking goods out of the country, remember you'll be liable for duty and tax on goods worth more than a certain amount (£145 for the UK).

OPENING TIMES

Note that many shops extend their opening hours between Thanksgiving and Christmas.

General

Department stores

Barneys New York

77 O'Farrell Street, at Stockton Street, Union Square & Around (268 3500/www.barneys.com). BART & Metro to Powell/bus 2, 3, 4, 15, 30, 38, 45, 76 & Market Street routes/cable car Powell-Hyde or Powell-Mason. **Open** 10am-7pm Mon-Wed, Fri, Sat; 10am-8pm Thur; 11am-6pm Sun. **Credit** AmEx, DC, MC, V. **Map** p315 M6.

Every fashionista's best friend, Barneys arrived in San Francisco in 2007 in a quiet, low-key manner in keeping with its tasteful style (and perhaps the chain's years of financial turmoil, which may have ended with its recent acquisition by Dubai investment firm Istithmar). But it has already been making its presence known among San Francisco followers of fashion with its spare modernist decor and its laid-back sell. The men's departments are probably the best in the city, while the women's clothing and shoes are equally well edited, with everything from Chloé and Balenciaga to Barneys' own youthful Co-Op separates.

Bloomingdale's

Westfield San Francisco Centre, 845 Market Street, between 4th & 5th Streets, Union Square & Around (856 5300/www.bloomingdales.com). BART & Metro to Powell/bus 27, 30, 45 & Market Street routes/ cable car Powell-Hyde or Powell-Mason. **Open** 9am-9pm Mon-Sat; 10am-7pm Sun. **Credit** AmEx, DC, Disc, MC, V. **Map** p315 M6.

Filling the retail gap between Macy's and Neiman Marcus, the Little Brown Bag's temple to luxe wares has finally touched down in San Francisco, in the cavernous space that once housed the stodgy Emporium department store. Of note are the lavish fragrance section and the sparkling array of fine china and stemware on the ground floor.

Gump's

135 Post Street, between Grant Avenue & Kearny Street, Union Square & Around (984 9439/www.gumps.com). BART & Metro to Montgomery/bus 2, 3, 4, 15, 30, 38, 45, 76 & Market Street routes/cable car Powell-Hyde or Powell-Mason. **Open** 10am-6pm Mon-Sat; noon-5pm Sun. **Credit** AmEx, DC, MC, V. **Map** p315 M5.

Eat, Drink, Shop

Saks Fifth Avenue: mannequins and must-haves at this famous department store.

Established in 1861, Gump's is the place where moneyed San Franciscans buy wedding presents, china and a variety of baubles, from black pearls to custom green peridot necklaces. A thoroughly elegant shopping experience for those who think a silver service for less than 12 is simply out of the question.

Macy's
170 O'Farrell Street, between Powell & Stockton Streets, Union Square & Around (397 3333/www. macys.com). BART & Metro to Powell/bus 2, 3, 4, 15, 30, 38, 45, 76 & Market Street routes/cable car Powell-Hyde or Powell-Mason. **Open** 10am-9pm Mon-Sat; 11am-7pm Sun. **Credit** AmEx, DC, Disc, MC, V. **Map** p315 M6.

The definitive department store: what Macy's lacks in grace, it more than makes up for in discounts. Join the fray and pick up shoes, home furnishings,

and accessibly luxurious women's fashions care of DKNY, Theory, Calvin Klein and Michael Kors.

Neiman Marcus
150 Stockton Street, between Geary & O'Farrell Streets, Union Square & Around (362 3900/www. neimanmarcus.com). BART & Metro to Powell/bus 2, 3, 4, 15, 30, 38, 45, 76 & Market Street routes/cable car Powell-Hyde or Powell-Mason. **Open** 10am-7pm Mon-Wed, Fri, Sat; 10am-8pm Thur; noon-6pm Sun. **Credit** AmEx. **Map** p315 M5.

Now commonly referred to as 'Needless Markup', Neiman Marcus was revered by old San Francisco society back in the day – when labels said 'Exclusively for Neiman Marcus'. Today, luxury of the mink-covered coat-hanger variety can still be yours, along with new designer and diffusion labels (from Prada to Blahnik).

Eat, Drink, Shop

Nordstrom

Westfield San Francisco Centre, 865 Market Street, at 5th Street, Union Square & Around (243 8500/ www.nordstrom.com). BART & Metro to Powell/bus 27, 30, 45 & Market Street routes/cable car Powell-Hyde or Powell-Mason. **Open** 9.30am-9pm Mon-Sat; 10am-7pm Sun. **Credit** AmEx, DC, Disc, MC, V. **Map** p315 M6.

Bourgeois old Nordstrom has something for everyone – there's even a spa on the top floor. The expansive men's section includes Ben Sherman and Ted Baker, while the vast women's department features silk camisoles, designer handbags, swish maternity wear and, most notably, a majestic shoe section.

Saks Fifth Avenue

384 Post Street, at Powell Street, Union Square & Around (986 4300/www.saksfifthavenue.com). BART & Metro to Powell/bus 2, 3, 4, 30, 45, 76 & Market Street routes/cable car Powell-Hyde or Powell-Mason. **Open** 10am-7pm Mon-Wed, Fri, Sat; 10am-8pm Thur; 11am-6pm Sun. **Credit** AmEx, DC, Disc, MC, V. **Map** p315 M5.

The San Francisco branch of this upmarket store is less claustrophobic than most of its ilk. The second floor offers designers such as Marc Jacobs, Moschino and Gucci, but several storeys up you'll find less pricey, but just as trendy, labels like Temperley London, Tory Burch and Diane von Furstenberg. At the menswear store, the more cutting-edge creations are to be found on the fifth floor. *See p175.*

Other locations Menswear, 220 Post Street, Union Square & Around (986 4300).

Malls

If you're after tourist tat, look no further than the inexplicably popular **Fisherman's Wharf** (Jefferson Street, between Hyde & Powell Streets, 674 7503, www.fishermanswharf.org) or nearby **Pier 39** (Beach Street & Embarcadero, 705 5500, www.pier39.com). Note that the opening times for individual shops and restaurants within the malls listed below may vary.

Embarcadero Center

Sacramento Street, between Battery & Drumm Streets, Financial District (772 0700/www. embarcaderocenter.com). BART & Metro to Embarcadero/bus 1, 2, 10, 14, 15, 31 & Market Street routes/cable car California. **Open** 10am-7pm Mon-Fri; 10am-6pm Sat; noon-5pm Sun. **Map** p315 N4.

Major chains (Banana Republic, Gap, Victoria's Secret, Nine West) sit comfortably ensconced in the Embarcadero towers, which also host the bulk of the city's lawyers and financiers.

Ghirardelli Square

Beach Street, between Larkin & Polk Streets, Fisherman's Wharf (775 5500/www.ghirardellisq. com). Metro F to Fisherman's Wharf/bus 10, 15, 30, 39, 47/cable car Powell-Hyde or Powell-Mason. **Open** 10am-6pm Mon-Thur, Sun; 10am-9pm Fri, Sat. **Map** p314 J2.

At the home of the Ghirardelli chocolate company, gorge yourself on ice-cream drizzled with chocolate made on the premises, then wander the square, which is home to outposts like Ghirardelli Ts (souvenirs), Kara's Cupcakes and Lola card shop.

Westfield San Francisco Centre

865 Market Street, at 5th Street, Union Square & Around (512 6776/www.westfield.com). BART & Metro to Powell/bus 27, 30, 45 & Market Street routes/cable car Powell-Hyde or Powell-Mason. **Open** 9.30am-9pm Mon-Sat; 10am-7pm Sun. **Map** p315 M6.

Spiral escalators wind slowly up this vast mall, enticing shoppers with mid-priced chain stores including J Crew, Abercrombie & Fitch and Club Monaco. Nordstrom (*see above*) resides on top like a society matron; express elevators whizz you straight there. The new expansion in the old Emporium features a glittering new Bloomingdale's (*see p174*), a long-awaited addition to the downtown shopping scene. Further draws include H&M, Zara, Juicy Couture, a sizeable Borders bookstore and a nine-theatre cineplex. You won't go hungry here, either, with eateries such as Out the Door, the spin-off of Vietnamese celeb-stop Slanted Door (*see p137*).

Specialist

Books & magazines

San Francisco has such a strong literary history that it's no wonder bookstores are in high demand. Many antiquarian booksellers are clustered at 49 Geary Street, near Union Square, but the heaviest concentration of used bookshops is in the Mission: sci-fi fans should try **Abandoned Planet** (518 Valencia Street, between 16th & 17th Streets, 861 4695), while the politically minded are directed to **Modern Times Bookstore** (888 Valencia Street, between 19th & 20th Streets, 282 9246, www. mtbs.com). Speciality stores include the literary-minded used bookseller **Black Oak Books** (630 Irving Street, between 7th & 8th Avenues, Inner Sunset, 564 0877, www.blackoak books.com), **San Francisco Mystery Bookstore** (4175 24th Street, between Castro & Diamond Streets, Noe Valley, 282 7444, www.sfmysterybooks.com) and **William Stout Architectural Books** (804 Montgomery Street, between Jackson Street & Pacific Avenue, Financial District, 391 6757, www.stoutbooks. com). And don't miss Berkeley's **Telegraph Avenue**, home to several excellent stores.

Adobe Bookshop

3166 16th Street, at Albion Street, Mission (864 3936/http://adobebooksbackroomgallery. blogspot.com). BART 16th Street/bus 14, 26, 33, 49. **Open** 11am-midnight daily. **Credit** DC, MC, V. **Map** p318 J10.

Deal or no deal

Bargains are plentiful and rarities scream out to be fondled and haggled over at the Bay Area flea markets. Come prepared: bring plenty of cash, as well as sturdy bags or a shopping cart (or beg a truck for large finds). The earlier you arrive the better the buys, although at the end of the day, usually mid-afternoon, you just might score an art deco nightstand with Bakelite handles for $5 from that weary peddler who simply doesn't want to pack it up again.

The finest of all local flea markets – showcasing everything from Victorian lace and Depression-era dishware to 1950s Formica kitchen tables and 1970s stacked Superfly boots – is **Alameda Point Antiques & Collectibles Faire**, at the former Alameda Point Naval Air Station (6am-3pm, 1st Sun of mth, 1-510 522 7500, www.antiques bybay.com). Touted as Northern California's largest antiques and collectibles show, with more than 800 dealers, the event takes about half a day to cover and entry costs $5-$15 (it's cheapest after 9am).

No vendors of cheap socks or sellers of fallen-off-the-truck food here (the bane of other massive swap meets in Oakland and San Jose) – everything sold at the Alameda market must be at least 20 years old, and no reproductions are permitted.

Also worth a peek is San Francisco's **Alemany Flea Market** (8am-3pm Wed-Sun, 647 2043), held in the concrete freeway nexus of Highways 101 and 280, at 100 Alemany Boulevard. This smaller market highlights a less refined and varied array of goods but can yield unexpected treasures in used furniture, homewares, paper ephemera and vintage jewellery, as well as random booty culled from estate sales.

For a taste of incense-burning, multiculti Berkeley grit, stop at the **Berkeley Flea Market** (7am-6pm Sat & Sun, 1-510 644 0744), conveniently located at the Ashby BART station parking lot, at Ashby and Martin Luther King Streets. Here you'll find new and used wares, African art, jewellery, handicrafts, books, antiques, clothing and music.

Alemany Flea Market.

Woe is the book buyer hoping to find exactly what he or she is looking for at Adobe. But those itching for a genuine taste of today's SF bohemia must stop by. Survey the hopelessly chaotic shelves, pile into an ancient armchair to talk up a random poet or painter, check out the artwork in the tiny exhibit space, or stay for a free performance by a local musician.

Books Inc

2275 Market Street, at 16th Street, Castro (864 6777/www.booksinc.net). Metro to Church/bus 22, 37. **Open** *9.30am-11pm Mon-Sat; 9.30am-10pm Sun.* **Credit** AmEx, DC, Disc, MC, V. **Map** p317 H10.
A huge selection of fiction and non-fiction, a lively atmosphere and a wide range of authors' readings, discussions and other events.
Other locations Opera Plaza, 601 Van Ness Avenue, Civic Center (776 1111); Laurel Village, 3515 California Street, Presidio Heights (221 3666); 2251 Chestnut Street, Marina (931 3633).

Booksmith

1644 Haight Street, between Clayton & Belvedere Streets, Haight-Ashbury (1-800 493 7323/863 8688/www.booksmith.com). Bus to Carl & Cole/bus 6, 7, 33, 43, 66, 71. **Open** *10am-10pm Mon-Sat; 10am-8pm Sun.* **Credit** AmEx, DC, Disc, MC, V. **Map** p317 E9.
The Haight's best bookshop hosts many authors' readings and events, and stocks a decent selection of magazines, both literary and obscure.

City Lights

261 Columbus Avenue, at Jack Kerouac Alley, between Broadway & Pacific Avenue, North Beach (433 8193/www.citylights.com). Bus 12, 15, 30, 41, 45. **Open** *10am-midnight daily.* **Credit** AmEx, DC, Disc, MC, V. **Map** p315 M3.
The legacy of Beat anti-authoritarianism lives on in this publishing company and bookshop, co-founded by poet Lawrence Ferlinghetti in 1953. Be sure to head upstairs to the Poetry Annex, where books by the Beats sit beside contemporary small-press works and the photocopied ravings of 'shroom-addled hippies, raging punks and DIY indie voices. Readings here are real events.

Cody's Books

1730 4th Street, Berkeley (1-510 559 9500/www.codysbooks.com). BART North Berkeley, then 20mins walk/bus 9, 19, 51. **Open** *10am-7pm Mon-Wed, Sun; 10am-8pm Thur-Sat.* **Credit** AmEx, DC, Disc, MC, V.
Once one of the staunchest and most successful independent bookstores in the US, Cody's sustained a tradition of supporting writers who might not otherwise be heard with regular readings at its Telegraph Avenue store. The closing of that shop in 2006 was a heartbreaker for Bay Area bibliophiles but trade continues at the 4th Street outlet.

Get Lost Travel Books, Maps & Gear

1825 Market Street, at Pearl Street, Hayes Valley (437 0529/www.getlostbooks.com). Metro to Van Ness/bus 26. **Open** *10am-7pm Mon-Fri; 10am-6pm Sat; 11am-5pm Sun.* **Credit** AmEx, DC, Disc, MC, V. **Map** p318 J9.

This excellent enterprise offers a compelling assortment of travel guides and literature, plus various other bits and pieces to help you on your way (maps, accessories and the like).

Green Apple Books & Music

506 Clement Street, at 6th Avenue, Richmond (387 2272/www.greenapplebooks.com). Bus 1, 2, 4, 38, 44. **Open** *10am-10.30pm Mon-Thur, Sun; 10am-11.30pm Fri, Sat.* **Credit** DC, Disc, MC, V. **Map** p312 C6.
This long-standing Inner Richmond store has a staggering selection of new and used titles, crammed together in glorious disarray (don't miss the fiction and music annex, and ask if their 'temporary' clearance-sale outlet down the street is open).

Kayo Books

814 Post Street, between Hyde & Leavenworth Streets, Tenderloin (749 0554/www.kayobooks.com). Bus 2, 3, 4, 19, 38, 47. **Open** *11am-6pm Thur-Sat.* **Credit** AmEx, DC, Disc, MC, V. **Map** p314 L5.
This emporium of pulp delivers the goods for those who like their mysteries hard-boiled, their juveniles delinquent and their porn quaintly smutty. Specialities include vintage paperbacks and dime-store novels from the 1940s to the '70s, and exploitation ephemera of all levels of debasement.

Moe's

2476 Telegraph Avenue, between Dwight Way & Haste Street, Berkeley (1-510 849 2087). BART Downtown Berkeley/bus 7, 40, 51. **Open** *10am-11pm daily.* **Credit** AmEx, DC, Disc, MC, V.
Another Berkeley literary landmark, Moe's has some 100,000 volumes spread over four floors, which means you're nearly as likely to find a 17th-century bible as a first edition of *Naked Lunch*. The fourth floor holds antiquarian, out-of-print and art books. Check out the discounted deleted volumes in the basement.

Smoke Signals

2223 Polk Street, between Vallejo & Green Streets, Polk Gulch (292 6025). Bus 19, 41, 45, 47, 49, 76/cable car Powell-Hyde. **Open** *8am-8pm Mon-Sat; 8am-6pm Sun.* **Credit** AmEx, DC, Disc, MC, V. **Map** p314 K4.
Homesick expats can smooth the process of assimilation with the latest *Le Monde* or Italian *Vogue* from this international newsstand. It also has a comprehensive selection of national and local papers, design annuals and obscure literary journals.

Stacey's

581 Market Street, between 1st & 2nd Streets, Financial District (1-800 926 6511/421 4687/www.staceys.com). BART & Metro to Montgomery/bus 2, 3, 4, 31 & Market Street routes. **Open** *9.30am-7pm Mon-Fri; 11am-6.30pm Sat.* **Credit** AmEx, DC, Disc, MC, V. **Map** p315 N5.
The city's oldest and largest independent bookshop (it was established in 1923), Stacey's offers an impressive selection of signed books, makes excellent staff recommendations, and co-sponsors lectures (from the likes of Gore Vidal) with the Commonwealth Club.

Children

Fashion

Cotton Sheep

*573 Hayes Street, between Laguna & Octavia
Streets, Hayes Valley (621 5546). Bus 16, 21, 47,
49.* **Open** 11am-7pm Mon-Sat; 11am-6pm Sun.
Credit DC, MC, V. **Map** p318 J8.
Organic cotton garments, designed and manufac-
tured in Japan, rule the roost here. Finger the utterly sweet children's hoodies or the truly unusual
toddlers' socks shaped like Godzilla heads.

Fiddlesticks

*508 Hayes Street, between Laguna & Octavia
Streets, Hayes Valley (565 0508/www.shop
fiddlesticks.com). Bus 16, 21, 47, 49.* **Open** 11am-
7pm Mon-Sat; 11am-6pm Sun. **Credit** DC, MC, V.
Map p318 J8.
The prices are steep, but the clothing is astonishing-
ly stylish at this shop helmed by the owners of Lavish,
a few doors down (*see p191*). Look for Livie and Luca
animal motif shoes and Luna pointelle sweaters.

Kids Only

*1608 Haight Street, at Clayton Street, Haight-
Ashbury (552 5445). Metro to Carl & Cole/bus 6,
7, 33, 43, 66, 71.* **Open** 10.30am-6.30pm Mon-Fri;
10am-6pm Sat; 11am-5pm Sun. **Credit** AmEx, DC,
Disc, MC, V. **Map** p317 E9.
Why should adults have all the fun? Here's where to
get the kids tooled up with leopard-print blankets,
handmade caps and tie-dye worthy of the Dead.

Laku

*1089 Valencia Street, between 21st & 22nd Streets,
Mission (695 1462). BART 24th Street/bus 14, 26,
48, 49, 67.* **Open** 11.30am-6.30pm Tue-Sat; noon-
5pm Sun. **Credit** DC, MC, V. **Map** p318 K11.
Exquisite, intricate little slippers and coats, sewn by
Laku's owner from velvet and shantung silk on a
machine in the back of the shop. For baby royalty.

Murik

*73 Geary Street, at Grant Avenue, Union Square &
Around (395 9200/www.murikwebstore.com). BART
& Metro to Powell/bus 2, 3, 4, 15, 30, 38, 45, 76 &
Market routes/cable car Powell-Hyde or Powell-
Mason.* **Open** 10am-6pm daily. **Credit** AmEx, DC,
MC, V. **Map** p315 M5.
Sweet, affordable togs by European makers such as
Joha, Juttum, Filou & Friends and Micro Bulle, using
simple, whimsical motifs and tasteful, muted colours.

Toys

Ambassador Toys

*2 Embarcadero Center, Financial District (345 8697/
www.ambassadortoys.com). BART & Metro to
Embarcadero/bus 1, 2, 10, 14, 15, 31, 66, 71/cable
car California.* **Open** 10am-7pm daily. **Credit**
AmEx, DC, MC, V. **Map** p315 N4.

Does the thought of Toys 'R Us drive you to the
brink of insanity? This straightforward store, which
specialises in toys from outside the US, has a charming selection of dolls, books, games and animals.
Other locations 186 W Portal Avenue, Sunset
(759 8697).

Chinatown Kite Shop

*717 Grant Avenue, at Sacramento Street, Chinatown
(989 5182). Bus 1, 12, 15, 30, 41, 45/cable car
California.* **Open** 10am-9pm daily. **Credit** AmEx,
DC, Disc, MC, V. **Map** p315 M4.
It only stands to reason that hilly, windy SF should
have an excellent kite shop. Stocked with hundreds
of different kites in every imaginable shape and
colour, the shop is perfectly situated for you to get kit-
ted out before heading on to Marina Green. *See p180.*

Electronics & photography

San Francisco remains at the forefront of
technological advancement, and prices here are
keen. Be sure that your item will still work when
you get home, and beware of Downtown stores
advertising cheap cameras and other electronics:
if a deal seems too good to be true, it probably
is. Chains dominate the commercial landscape.
Locals love the low prices at **Circuit City** (1200
Van Ness Avenue, at Post Street, Polk Gulch,
441 1300, www.circuitcity.com) and **Best Buy**
(1717 Harrison Street, at 14th Street, Upper
Market, 626 9682, www.bestbuy.com), but
those stores and the goods they sell are rather
left in the shade by the sleek **Apple Store** (1
Stockton Street, at Ellis Street, Union Square &
Around, 392 0202, www.apple.com). Authentic
geeks will also hanker for a pilgrimage to
superstore **Fry's Electronics** (closest location:
340 Portage Avenue, at Ash Street, Palo Alto,
1-650 496 6000, www.frys.com).

Specialist

Adolph Gasser

*181 2nd Street, between Natoma & Howard Streets,
SoMa (495 3852/www.gassers.com). BART & Metro
to Montgomery/bus 2, 3, 4, 12, 15, 31, 76 & Market
Street routes.* **Open** 9am-6pm Mon-Fri; 10am-5pm
Sat. **Credit** AmEx, DC, Disc, MC, V. **Map** p315 N6.
This justly famous photographic shop has clued-up
staff and the largest inventory of photo and video
equipment in northern California. There's also
a good selection of scanners and digital cameras.

Discount Camera

*33 Kearny Street, between Post & Market Streets,
Union Square & Around (392 1103/www.discount
camera.com). BART & Metro to Montgomery/bus 2,
3, 4, 14, 15, 30, 31, 45 & Market Street routes/cable
car Powell-Hyde or Powell-Mason.* **Open** 8.30am-
6.30pm Mon-Sat; 9.30am-6pm Sun. **Credit** AmEx,
DC, Disc, MC, V. **Map** p315 M5.

Eat, Drink, Shop

Get ready to fly at the **Chinatown Kite Shop**. *See p176.*

More than 45 years old, Discount Camera is recommended by concierges anxious to steer their guests away from Downtown's unscrupulous tourist traps. New and second-hand models are sold, and there's on-site camera repair.

Fashion

Designer

Unsurprisingly, San Francisco is home to branches of pretty much all the major high-end labels, with many ensconced in premises on or near Union Square. Among them are ever-elegant **Prada** (140 Geary Street, between Grant Avenue & Stockton Street, 391 8844, www.prada.com), chi-chi **Chanel** (156 Geary Street, between Grant Avenue & Stockton Street, 981 1550, www.chanel.com), smooth **Armani** (278 Post Street, at Stockton Street, 434 2500, www.armani.com) and extravagant **Gucci** (200 Stockton Street, at Geary Street, 392 2808, www.gucci.com).

For the best home-grown names, *see p184* **Frisco fashionistas**.

AB Fits

1519 Grant Avenue, between Union & Filbert Streets, North Beach (982 5726/www.abfits.com). Bus 15, 30, 39, 41. **Open** 11am-6.30pm Tue-Sat; noon-6pm Sun. **Credit** AmEx, DC, MC, V. **Map** p315 M3.

The jean-ius of Howard Gee and Christopher Louie is to mix the familiar brands (Rag & Bone, Rogan, Nicole Farhi, LAMB, Earnest Sewn, Edun) with ones that are more rarefied (vintage denim by Nudie) or just plain fabulous. You'll also find separates and

accessories by designers like Band of Outsiders. **Other locations** 40 Grant Avenue, Union Square & Around (391 3360).

Diana Slavin

3 Claude Lane, between Sutter & Bush Streets, Union Square & Around (677 9939/www.diana slavin.com). BART & Metro to Montgomery/bus 2, 3, 4, 15, 30, 38, 45, 76/cable car Powell-Hyde or Powell-Mason. **Open** 11am-6pm Tue-Fri; noon-5pm Sat. **Credit** AmEx, DC, MC, V. **Map** p315 M5.

In this haberdasher's for women, Slavin designs and displays her trademark fashions: menswear-inspired clothing in rich, subtle colours and lush fabrics. Vintage Vuarnet shades and Vera Wang shoes complete the look.

Erica Tanov

2408 Fillmore Street, between Jackson & Washington Streets, Pacific Heights (674 1228/www.ericatanov. com). Bus 3, 12, 22, 24. **Open** 11am-6pm Mon-Sat; 11am-5pm Sun. **Credit** AmEx, DC, MC, V. **Map** p313 H5.

Antique fabrics are the highlight at Erica Tanov – and they're multitasking in the form of gossamer party dresses, bed linens, delicate lingerie and imported sweaters.

Other locations 1827 4th Street, Berkeley (1-510 849 3331).

MAC (Modern Appealing Clothing)

387 Grove Street, between Franklin & Gough Streets, Hayes Valley (863 3011). Bus 16, 21, 47, 49. **Open** 11am-7pm Mon-Sat; noon-6pm Sun. **Credit** AmEx, DC, MC, V.

Belgian designers as well as local creatives get the treatment they deserve in this brother and sister owned boutique that resembles a chic pied-à-terre. Men, in particular, who are willing to open their wal-

Eat, Drink, Shop

lets wide will discover great items by Martin Margiela, Dries Van Noten and AF Vandevorst, in addition to Raf Simons for Jil Sander.

Metier

355 Sutter Street, between Stockton Street & Grant Avenue, Union Square & Around (989 5395/www. metiersf.com). BART & Metro to Powell/bus 2, 3, 4, 15, 30, 38, 45, 76/cable car Powell-Hyde or Powell-Mason. **Open** 10am-6pm Mon-Sat. **Credit** AmEx, DC, MC, V. **Map** p315 M5.
Touted as a 'premier Downtown design boutique', Metier is indeed Serious Fashion. From slouchy sophistication care of Cathy Waterman, the glamorous detailing of Vena Cava and the bohemian chic of Mayle, to lingerie by Cosabella and contemporary sterling silver jewellery from Ten Thousand Things, the 'hot mum' set at last has a place to call home.

Susan

3685 Sacramento Street, between Locust & Spruce Streets, Presidio Heights (922 3685). Bus 1, 3, 12, 22, 24. **Open** 10.30am-6.30pm Mon-Fri; 10.30am-6pm Sat. **Credit** AmEx, DC, MC, V. **Map** p313 E5.
This retail legend is renowned for championing fashion's avant-garde aeons before Carolyn Bessette Kennedy took her Yohji Yamamoto out for its first red carpet run. Just read the labels: Comme des Garçons, Balenciaga, Lanvin, Dolce & Gabbana, Marni and Prada. Sister shop the Grocery Store (3625 Sacramento Street, 928 3615) sells diffusion lines.

Discount

The Bay Area has several sizeable outlet malls, but they're well outside town. An hour north on Highway 101, **Petaluma Village Premium Outlets** (2200 Petaluma Boulevard N, 1-707 778 9300, www.premiumoutlets.com) has 60 shops, including Liz Claiborne, Gap Outlet, Off 5th-Saks Fifth Avenue and Brooks Brothers, while **Napa Premium Outlets** (Highway 29 to 1st Street exit, 629 Factory Stores Drive, 1-707 226 9876, www.premiumoutlets.com), about 90 miles from the city, has 50 stores, among them Barneys, Hilfiger, Timberland, J Crew, DKNY Jeans, Calvin Klein, Banana Republic and Kenneth Cole. For a complete list of stores, check the website.

Jeremy's

2 South Park, off 2nd Street, between Bryant & Brannan Streets, SoMa (882 4929/www.jeremys. com). Bus 10, 15. **Open** 11am-6pm Mon-Sat; 11am-5pm Sun. **Credit** AmEx, DC, MC, V. **Map** p315 O6.
Jeremy's sits on a sunny corner of South Park, hawking designer wares at discount store prices. It's a label-whore's dream come true, especially the satchels in front and the shoes at the back: if you're lucky, you just might find Jimmy Choo pumps, Prada slides and Dolce & Gabbana boots. There's also excellent menswear, ties and accessories. The

Berkeley location sells more casual clothing.
Other locations 2967 College Avenue, Berkeley (1-510 849 0701).

Loehmann's

222 Sutter Street, between Grant Avenue & Kearny Street, Union Square & Around (982 3215/www. loehmanns.com). BART & Metro to Montgomery/bus 2, 3, 4, 15, 30, 38, 45, 76/cable car Powell-Hyde or Powell-Mason. **Open** 9am-8pm Mon-Fri; 9.30am-8pm Sat; 11am-7pm Sun. **Credit** AmEx, DC, Disc, MC, V. **Map** p315 M5.
Communal dressing rooms, eh? Don't be put off: the prices make Loehmann's worth a look. Designer clothes (Prada, Marc by Marc Jacobs, Diane von Furstenberg, Philosophy di Alberta Ferretti, Michael Kors, Moschino) hang from the rafters; you can get more than 50% off activewear. Be sure to visit Loehmann's shoe store at 211 Sutter Street (395 0983).

General

San Franciscans love shops with a bit extra – more character, a touch of pzzazz – and it's these of this nature that we list below.
Tourists, however, tend to go with what they know, which is why the monoliths are so keenly represented on and around Union Square. Posh, preppy **Banana Republic** rules almost a full city block (256 Grant Avenue, at Sutter Street, 788 3087, www.bananarepublic. com); cheap and casual **Old Navy** has a vast store on Market Street (No.801, at 4th Street, 344 0375, www.oldnavy.com); and **Gap** is ubiquitous (890 Market Street, at 5th Street, 788 5909, www.gap.com). Other familiar chains include sexy **Bebe** (Westfield San Francisco Centre, 865 Market Street, at 5th Street, 543 2323, www.bebe.com), long-standing **Guess** (90 Grant Avenue, at Geary Street, 781 1589, www.guess.com), Brit import **French Connection** (101 Powell Street, at Ellis Street, 677 4317, www.frenchconnection.com), girly **Betsey Johnson** (160 Geary Street, at Stockton Street, 398 2516, www.betseyjohnson. com) and slick women's label **BCBG Max Azria** (331 Powell Street, at Union Square, 362 7360, www.bcbg.com).

Ambiance

1458 Haight Street, between Masonic Avenue & Ashbury Street, Haight-Ashbury (552 5095/www. ambiancesf.com). Metro to Carl & Cole/bus 6, 7, 33, 43, 66, 71. **Open** 10am-7pm Mon-Sat; 11am-7pm Sun. **Credit** AmEx, DC, MC, V. **Map** p317 F9.
If you've got an occasion, Ambiance has the perfect ensemble for it: its glowing collection of retro-style dresses and saucy skirts is even arranged by colour for your convenience. The sales staff are beyond friendly.
Other locations 1864 & 1858 Union Street, Cow Hollow (923 9797, 932 9796); 3985 & 3989 24th Street, Noe Valley (647 7144, 647 5800).

American Apparel

1615 Haight Street, between Belvedere &
Clayton Streets, Haight-Ashbury (431 4038/
www.americanapparel.net). Bus 6, 7, 33, 43, 71.
Open 11am-9pm Mon-Thur; 11am-10pm Fri, Sat;
noon-7pm Sun. **Credit** AmEx, DC, Disc, MC, V.
Map p317 E9.

This Los Angeles-founded clothing maker boasts
that its T-shirts, jersey minis, hoodies, undies and
bikinis are sweatshop labour-free, which makes it
even harder to resist the designs, in tasty hues and
desirable cuts.
Other locations 2174 Union Street, Cow Hollow
(440 3220); 2315 Telegraph Avenue, Berkeley
(1-510 981 1641).

American Rag

1305 Van Ness Avenue, between Bush & Sutter
Streets, Polk Gulch (474 5214). Bus 2, 3, 4, 47, 49,
76/cable car California. **Open** 10am-9pm Mon-Sat;
noon-7pm Sun. **Credit** AmEx, DC, MC, V.
Map p314 K5.

After an outfit that says casual without suggesting
distressed? American Rag is less daunting than a
used-clothing shop but a cut above chain institutions
such as Diesel. Riffle the racks of used and new
threads safe in the knowledge that the poly-blend
button-down you eventually choose will be a one
and only. The shop also stocks harder-to-find, desirable pieces by APC and Nice Collective and an ultra-
trendy shoe selection.

Anthropologie

880 Market Street, between Powell & Stockton
Streets, Union Square & Around (434 2210/www.
anthropologie.com). BART & Metro to Powell/bus 2,
3, 4, 14, 15, 30, 45 & Market Street routes/cable car
Powell-Hyde or Powell-Mason. **Open** 10am-8pm Mon-
Sat; 11am-7pm Sun. **Credit** AmEx, DC, Disc, MC, V.
Map p315 M6.

Indulge your desire for beaded cardigans, patterned
and floral A-line skirts and romantic, swingy jackets, plus home furnishings, decadent scented candles, cute pyjamas and coquettish lingerie. The sale
racks are at the back.
Other locations 750 Hearst Avenue, Berkeley (1-
510 486 0705).

Behind the Post Office

1510 Haight Street, between Ashbury & Clayton
Streets, Haight-Ashbury (861 2507). Metro to Carl
& Cole/bus 6, 7, 33, 43, 66, 71. **Open** 11am-7pm
Mon-Thur, Sun; 11am-7.30pm Fri, Sat. **Credit**
AmEx, DC, MC, V. **Map** p317 F9.

Space is at a premium here, but this tiny boutique
packs in the style with vibrant T-shirts and edgy
new designers, all at moderate prices. Even better,
the expert opinions of the owners are worth their
weight in (carefully fitted) denim.

Brown Eyed Girl

2999 Washington Street, at Broderick Street, Pacific
Heights (409 0214/www.shopbrowneyedgirl.com).
Bus 1, 3, 22. **Open** 11am-7pm Mon-Sat; noon-5pm
Sun. **Credit** AmEx, DC, MC, V. **Map** p313 F5.

Housed in a renovated Victorian, this pastel-hued
shop for moneyed 20-year-olds has designer denim
and an endless array of pricey clingy tees.

Candystore

3153 16th Street, between Albion & Guerrero
Streets, Mission (863 8143/www.candystore-sf.com).
BART to 16th Street/bus 14, 26, 33, 49. **Open** noon-
7pm Mon-Sat; noon-6pm Sun. **Credit** AmEx, DC,
Disc, MC, V. **Map** p318 J10.

Sweet stuff for trendy young women with an eye for
whimsy: patterned wallets, new-wave slingbacks
and gold danglers brush up against puffed sleeve
hoodie-jackets, airy dresses and striped separates.

Citizen Clothing

536 Castro Street, between 18th & 19th Streets,
Castro (575 3560/www.bodyclothing.com). Metro
to Castro/bus 24, 33, 35, 37. **Open** 10am-8pm Mon-
Sat; 11am-7pm Sun. **Credit** AmEx, DC, Disc, MC, V.
Map p317 H11.

Citizen is all about upscale utilitarian chic, meaning
Scotch & Soda, Ben Sherman and Fred Perry appear
alongside Ted Baker, Jack Spade and Gucci accessories. Boys seeking something a bit more sporty
head up the street to sibling establishment Body
(450 Castro Street, 575 3562).

Diesel

101 Post Street, at Kearny Street, Union Square &
Around (982 7077/www.diesel.com). BART & Metro
to Montgomery/bus 2, 3, 4, 15, 30, 38, 45, 76/cable
car Powell-Hyde or Powell-Mason. **Open** 10am-9pm
Mon-Fri; 10am-7pm Sat; noon-6pm Sun. **Credit**
AmEx, DC, Disc, MC, V. **Map** p315 M5.

Not just a zillion styles of jeans, retro sneakers and
edgy separates, spread over three floors, but also the
StyleLab line for those extra-experimental types
who covet jeans made out of astronaut suits.

Dylan

2146 Chestnut Street, at Pierce Street, Marina (931
8721/www.dylanboutique.com). Bus 30. **Open** 11am-
7.30pm Mon-Sat; 11.30am-5.30pm Sun. **Credit**
AmEx, DC, MC, V. **Map** p314 K4.

This locale showcases a dizzying spread of boutique
designers: expect to find clothing and jewellery by
Alexander Wang, Cacharel, Anna Sui, Charlotte
Ronson, Jill Stuart, Eugenia Kim and J Brand, plus
shoes from Galliano, Stella McCartney, Christian
Lacroix, Chloé and 3.1 by Phillip Lim.

Forever 21

7 Powell Street, at Market Street, Union Square
& Around (984 0380/www.forever21.com).
BART & Metro to Powell/bus 2, 3, 4, 15, 30,
38, 45, 76 & Market Street routes/cable car Powell-
Hyde or Powell-Mason. **Open** 9.30am-9pm Mon-Sat;
10am-7pm Sun. **Credit** AmEx, DC, Disc, MC, V.
Map p315 M6.

Juniors will go knock-off crazy for this rock-bottom
low-priced mecca of flirty dresses, skimpy club-kid
gear and skinny jeans. Larger sizes will have to content themselves with the glitzy jewellery, fun shoes,
heaps of hip hats and adorable bags.

Eat, Drink, Shop

Brown Eyed Girl: heaven for dedicated foilowers of fashion.

Frisco fashionistas

San Francisco may not have a reputation as a fashion capital, but its independent spirit has produced a good crop of home-grown designers.

Foremost among them is SF minimalist maven **Sunhee Moon** (3167 16th Street, at Guerrero Street, Mission, 355 1800, www.sunheemoon.com; other locations in Cow Hollow and Western Addition), known for her way with a sash and subtly retro-tinged modernist separates marked by clean, crisp lines and rich, jewel-like hues.

Also in the Mission District is a slew of designers whose looks evoke a vintage cool and get snapped up by fun-loving area hipsters, club kids and boho creatives: Terri Olson of **Minnie Wilde** (3266 21st Street, at Valencia Street, 642 9453, www.minniewilde.com) dreams up kicky knickerbockers, sexy secretary frocks and particularly adorable outerwear in the form of capelets and 'ca-ponchos'; Dema Grim of **Dema** (1038 Valencia Street, at 21st Street, 206 0500, www.godemago.com) specialises in blouses, skirts and sheaths in gloriously bold prints; and Susan Hengst of **House of Hengst** (924 Valencia Street, at 20th Street, 642 0841, www.houseof hengst.com) delivers disco-era glamour in the form of drawstring tops, beautifully draped tunics and wide-legged sailor slacks.

Stylistically somewhere between Moon and Wilde are Eric and Danette Scheib at **Lemon Twist** (537 Octavia Boulevard, between Grove & Hayes Streets, Hayes Valley, 558 9699, www.lemontwist.net). They have a knack for classic jackets as well as groovy A-line shifts in painterly prints. On the manly front, the designers at **Nice Collective** have been making a splash with their sexy, streamlined, urban-inspired menswear in muted, dusky neutrals; their covetable slim-cut hooded jackets can be picked up at **Barneys New York** (see p174), **American Rag** (see p182) and **Archive** (317 Sutter Street, at Grant Avenue, Union Square & Around, 391 5550).

Lest you imagine San Francisco to be the land of eternal casualwear, seek out the elegantly tailored suits created by Pirya Saraswati of **Saffron Rare Threads** (3579 17th Street, at Dolores Street, Mission, 626 2533, www.saffronrarethreads.com), which are also available at **Mingle** (1815 Union Street, at Octavia Street, Cow Hollow, 674 8811, www.mingleshop.com) and **Ooma** (see p186). For a formal frock or couture gown, turn to **Colleen Quen** (7 Heron Street, at 8th Street, SoMa, 551 0013), who works out of the ivory atelier she shares with her husband, sculptor Rick Lee. Duchess silk and chiffon creations take off soaring with high collars, or are grounded beautifully in fields of hand embroidery.

Relying on textiles as varied as Polartec and satin brocade, Oakland designer **Cari Borja** (2117 4th Street, at Allston Way, Berkeley, 1-510 981 0067, www.cari borja.com) is sure to touch your inner Vincent Minnelli heroine with such Victorian-inspired finery as her extravagantly ruffled jackets and tiered skirts, found also at **Rabat** (see p186). And on the deliriously romantic, dressy side, Berkeley's **Erica Tanov** (see p180) shows off her eye for mixing prints and textures with sweet balloon-sleeved dresses, yoked and seamed skirts, and architectural monk coats.

Minnie Wilde.

H&M

150 Powell Street, at O'Farrell Street, Union Square & Around (986 4215/www.hm.com). BART & Metro to Powell/bus 2, 3, 4, 15, 30, 38, 45, 76 & Market Street routes/cable car Powell-Hyde or Powell-Mason. **Open** 10am-9pm Mon-Sat; 11am-8pm Sun. **Credit** AmEx, DC, Disc, MC, V. **Map** p315 M6.

Dare any fashion follower to not snap up a glossy handbag, a pair of over-the-top earrings or a lacy frock at this trend-driven giant. Stella McCartney and Viktor & Rolf designs have triggered sprees at this flagship jammed with affordable cool for men and women. **Other locations** 150 Post Street, Union Square & Around (986 0156); Westfield San Francisco Centre, 845 Market Street, Union Square & Around (543 1430); Stonestown Galleria, 3251 20th Avenue, Sunset & Further South (242 1459).

Ooma

1422 Grant Avenue, between Green & Union Streets, North Beach (627 6963). Bus 15, 30, 39, 41, 45. **Open** 11am-7pm Tue-Sat; noon-5pm Sun. **Credit** AmEx, DC, Disc, MC, V. **Map** p315 M3.

The name stands for 'Objects of My Affection'; owners Glenda and Jessica have a fine eye for the latest local designer threads, making it all but impossible to leave empty-handed. 'Flirty' pretty much sums up the whimsical fashions on offer.

Rabat

4001 24th Street, at Noe Street, Noe Valley (282 7861/www.rabatshoes.com). Bus 24, 35, 48. **Open** 10am-6.30pm Mon-Fri; 10am-6pm Sat; 11am-5.30pm Sun. **Credit** AmEx, DC, Disc, MC, V. **Map** p317 H12.

Sparkly chic is what Rabat's about. A huge variety of shoes, accessories and women's clothing provides reams of material for you to work with, and the staff are happy to suggest ways to co-ordinate it all. **Other locations** 2080 Chestnut Street, Marina (929 8688).

Urban Outfitters

80 Powell Street, at Ellis Street, Union Square & Around (399 1515/www.urbanoutfitters.com). BART & Metro to Powell/bus 2, 3, 4, 15, 30, 38, 45, 76 & Market Street routes/cable car Powell-Hyde or Powell-Mason. **Open** 9.30am-9.30pm Mon-Sat; 10.30am-9pm Sun. **Credit** AmEx, DC, Disc, MC, V. **Map** p315 M6.

Sturdy Ben Sherman trousers, adorable Free People cardigans, old-school T-shirts, funky jewellery and tons of jeans at seriously affordable prices. Perfect for those just out of college – or those who wish they were. **Other locations** 2590 Bancroft Way, Berkeley (1-510 486 1300).

Villains

1672 Haight Street, between Clayton & Cole Streets, Haight-Ashbury (626 5939). Metro to Carl & Cole/bus 6, 7, 33, 43, 66, 71. **Open** 11am-7pm daily. **Credit** AmEx, DC, Disc, MC, V. **Map** p317 E9.

Villains sells a mix of cropped trousers, experimental fabrics and trendy ensembles for men and women that scream 'I party!' Next door is a great selection of covetable shoes, from Schmoove to spiked heels straight out of a Joan Jett video.

Zara

250 Post Street, at Stockton Street, Union Square & Around (399 6930/www.zara.com). BART & Metro to Powell/bus 2, 3, 4, 15, 30, 38, 45, 76 & Market Street routes/cable car Powell-Hyde or Powell-Mason. **Open** 10am-8pm Mon-Sat; 11am-6pm Sun. **Credit** AmEx, DC, Disc, MC, V. **Map** p315 M5.

Count on this sophisticated, appealing Spanish chain for low-priced, on-trend looks for both men and women. It's just the spot for a classic yet eye-catching coat, silky party halter or tissue-weight T with a deco graphic.

Used & vintage

Also check out **American Rag** (*see p182*) and **Urban Outfitters** (*see p185*) for vintage wear mixed with new and retro-inspired styles.

Buffalo Exchange

1555 Haight Street, at Clayton Street, Haight-Ashbury (431 7733/www.buffaloexchange.com). Metro to Carl & Cole/bus 6, 7, 33, 71. **Open** 11am-7pm Mon-Wed; 11am-8pm Thur-Sun. **Credit** DC, MC, V. **Map** p317 F9.

Buffalo Exchange didn't achieve its lofty station as a national trade-in chain by its gentle touch: locals are used to looks of near-contempt when trying to get rid of those stone-washed Gap reverse-cut jeans. Still, the range is vast. **Other locations** 1210 Valencia Street, Mission (647 8332); 2585 Telegraph Avenue, Berkeley (1-510 644 9202).

Crossroads Trading Co

2123 Market Street, at Church Streets, Castro (552 8740/www.crossroadstrading.com). Metro to Church/bus 22, 37. **Open** 11am-8pm Mon-Sat; noon-7pm Sun. **Credit** DC, MC, V. **Map** p318 H10.

People who still haven't got over that 1980s retro thing should pop into the Market and Haight Street branches of this favourite local chain; the Fillmore location is best for jeans, dresses and designer and vintage pieces. **Other locations** throughout the city.

GoodByes

3483 Sacramento Street, between Laurel & Walnut Streets, Presidio Heights (674 0151). Bus 1, 4. **Open** 10am-6pm Mon-Wed, Fri, Sat; 10am-8pm Thur; 11am-5pm Sun. **Credit** DC, Disc, MC, V. **Map** p313 E5.

For rich pickings, take advantage of this consignment boutique's distance from the less upmarket Haight and Mission scenes. Cast-offs from some of the town's most upscale closets might include a barely worn Miu Miu sweater or a classic Chanel suit. **Other locations** *Menswear* 3464 Sacramento Street, Presidio Heights (346 6388).

Painted Bird

1201A Guerrero Street, at 24th Street, Mission (401 7027/www.paintedbird.org). BART 24th Street/bus 14, 26, 33, 49. **Open** 11am-8pm daily. **Credit** DC, MC, V. **Map** p318 J12.

Cooler than cool and extremely well priced, this brilliantly edited vintage outpost has become a must-shop for hipsters in search of granny sundresses, glam disco bags, flash but cute jewellery and styling shoes and boots from the 1980s, '70s and earlier eras.

Schauplatz

791 Valencia Street, between 18th & 19th Streets, Mission (864 5665). BART 16th Street/bus 14, 26, 33, 49. **Open** 1-7pm daily. **Credit** DC, MC, V. **Map** p318 K11.

The second-hand gear on offer here, mixed with new clothing, is more artfully collated than elsewhere in the Mission. In German, Schauplatz means 'show-place'; the name makes sense when you spy Italian sunglasses, intricately beaded Moroccan mules or a Swedish policeman's leather jacket.

Static

1764 Haight Street, between Shrader & Cole Streets, Haight-Ashbury (422 0046/www.staticvintage.com). **Open** noon-7pm Mon-Thur, Sun; noon-8pm Fri, Sat. **Credit** DC, MC, V. **Map** p317 E9.

'Vintage for the modern' is the hallmark of this boutique with a distinct high-'70s, rocker-tough and California-cool sensibility. Read: used denim and leather, Gucci bags, worn-soft T-shirts and boots.

Ver Unica

437B Hayes Street, between Gough & Octavia Streets, Hayes Valley (431 0688/www.ver-unica.com). Bus 21, 47, 49. **Open** 11am-7pm Mon-Sat; noon-6pm Sun. **Credit** AmEx, DC, MC, V. **Map** p318 J8.

Ver Unica is where people with a proper pay cheque go to buy second-hand: it sells unique retro finds, not cast-offs crammed together on dusty shelves. It now stocks men's clothing too.

Wasteland

1660 Haight Street, between Clayton & Cole Streets, Haight-Ashbury (863 3150). Metro to Carl & Cole/bus 6, 7, 33, 43, 66, 71. **Open** 11am-8pm Mon-Sat; noon-7pm Sun. **Credit** AmEx, DC, MC, V. **Map** p317 E9.

Possibly the most popular used clothier in town, Wasteland sells second-hand clothing with history, including a rich supply of vintage costume jewellery, fancy gowns and worn-in leather jackets.

Fashion accessories & services

Handbags

Coach

190 Post Street, at Grant Avenue, Union Square & Around (392 1772/www.coach.com). BART & Metro to Powell/bus 2, 3, 4, 15, 30, 38, 45, 76 & Market Street routes/cable car Powell-Hyde or Powell-Mason. **Open** 10am-8pm Mon-Sat; 11am-6pm Sun. **Credit** AmEx, DC, Disc, MC, V. **Map** p315 M5.

The logo fabric in the window of this pristine designer outlet gives no sense of the high-quality leather or suede totes, satchels and accessories within. The returns policy is incredible: staff will hand you a new bag if but a single stitch comes out. **Other locations** 1 Embarcadero Center, Financial District (362 2518); Westfield San Francisco Centre, 865 Market Street, Union Square & Around (543 7152).

Kate Spade

227 Grant Avenue, between Post & Sutter Streets, Union Square & Around (216 0880/www.kate spade.com). BART & Metro to Powell/bus 2, 3, 4, 15, 30, 38, 45, 76/cable car Powell-Hyde or Powell-Mason. **Open** 10am-6pm Mon-Sat; noon-5pm Sun. **Credit** AmEx, DC, Disc, MC, V. **Map** p315 M5.

Once a neatly sewn label on a simple black nylon handbag, Kate Spade is now a full-blown lifestyle, selling luggage, shoes, fragrances and jewellery. The bags, of course, remain exemplary.

Marc Jacobs

125 Maiden Lane, between Stockton Street & Grant Avenue, Union Square & Around (362 6500/www. marcjacobs.com). BART & Metro to Powell/bus 2, 3, 4, 15, 30, 38, 45, 76 & Market Street routes/cable car Powell-Hyde or Powell-Mason. **Open** 10am-7pm Mon-Sat; noon-6pm Sun. **Credit** AmEx, DC, Disc, MC, V. **Map** p315 M5.

Terminally cool Marc Jacobs keeps lines fresh and just affordable enough for the under-thirties. The bags sit on glowing shelves, drawing you in with their utilitarian glamour. The Marc by Marc Jacobs branch has cheeky window displays, great low-priced five and dime-style gifts and, of course, cool men's and women's clothing. **Other locations** Marc by Marc Jacobs, 2142 Fillmore Street, Pacific Heights (447 9322).

Jewellery

Metier (*see p181*) also has a divine selection of contemporary and vintage jewellery.

De Vera

29 Maiden Lane, between Grant Avenue & Kearny Street, Union Square & Around (788 0828/www. deveraobjects.com). BART & Metro to Powell/bus 2, 3, 4, 15, 30, 38, 45, 76 & Market Street routes/cable car Powell-Hyde or Powell-Mason. **Open** 10am-6pm Tue-Sat. **Credit** AmEx, DC, MC, V. **Map** p315 M5.

Federico de Vera's covetable jewellery – yellow tourmaline, carnelian, rose-cut diamond – ranges from intricate beadwork to clean-lined intaglios. Don't miss the stunning collection of *objets*, ancient and modern.

Five & Diamond

510 Valencia Street, at 16th Street, Mission (255 9747/www.fiveanddiamond.com). BART 16th Street/ bus 14, 26, 33, 49. **Open** noon-8pm Mon-Thur; noon-9pm Fri-Sun. **Credit** DC, MC, V. **Map** p318 K10.

This could be rocker LA, by way of a *Mad Max* meets *Deadwood* cowboy apocalypse, if it wasn't fixed in the grungy heart of the Mission. Phoebe Minona Durland and Leighton Kelly – 'Nomadic artists', Yard Dogs Road Show burlesque/vaudeville performers, and designers – showcase their upscale piercing line here, along with wild and stunning jewellery. When you've wearied of shopping, you can hop in the chair and acquire some skin art from award-winning tattoo artist Phil Milic.

Gallery of Jewels

2115 Fillmore Street, between California & Sacramento Streets, Pacific Heights (771 5099/ www.galleryofjewels.com). Bus 1, 2, 3, 4, 12, 24. **Open** 10.30am-6.30pm Mon-Sat; 11am-6pm Sun. **Credit** AmEx, DC, Disc, MC, V. **Map** p313 H5.
Peruse local creations of silver and semi-precious stones, as well as funky beads and antique bracelets. Designs run from fresh and modern to mumsy. **Other locations** 4089 24th Street, Noe Valley (285 0626); 2101 Union Street, Cow Hollow (929 0259).

Macchiarini Creative Design

1453 Grant Avenue, between Green & Union Streets, North Beach (982 2229/www.macreativedesign.com). Bus 12, 15, 30, 41, 45. **Open** 10am-6pm Tue-Sat; also by appointment. **Credit** AmEx, DC, MC, V. **Map** p315 M3.
Three generations of the Macchiarini family have been crafting African-inspired jewellery for more than 70 years. They also do custom wedding rings, sculpture and calligraphy. So old-school they even have a set of North Beach steps named after them.

Superior precious stones at **De Vera**.

Launderettes

Don't miss **BrainWash** (*see p141*), SoMa's still-popular café/bar/launderette.

Star Wash

392 Dolores Street, at 17th Street, Mission (431 2443). Metro to Church & 18th/bus 22, 33. **Open** 7am-9pm daily. **No credit cards. Map** p318 J10.
If you don't mind having your knickers scrutinised by Bogey and Bacall (in poster form only, more's the pity), this is the place for your washing chores.

Leather goods & luggage

Edwards Luggage

3 Embarcadero Center, between Davis & Drumm Streets, Financial District (981 7047/www.edwards luggage.com). BART & Metro to Embarcadero/bus 1, 2, 10, 14, 15, 31, 66, 71/cable car California. **Open** 10am-7pm Mon-Fri; 10am-6pm Sat; noon-5pm Sun. **Credit** AmEx, DC, Disc, MC, V. **Map** p315 N4.
Since 1946, Edwards Luggage has been kitting people out with everything they need to hit the road, or the skies, from trim carry-ons to duffle bags and voltage converters.
Other locations throughout the Bay Area.

Flight 001

525 Hayes Street, between Laguna & Octavia Streets, Hayes Valley (487 1001/www.flight001.com). Bus 21, 47, 49. **Open** 11am-7pm Mon-Sat; 11am-6pm Sun. **Credit** AmEx, DC, Disc, MC, V. **Map** p318 J8.
If it's important that you travel in style, Flight 001 is the place to go. Streamlined like a jet airliner, the store sells beautiful modern designs, from Japanese metal suitcases to gorgeous accessories.
Other locations 1774 4th Street, Berkeley (1-510 526 1001).

Hideo Wakamatsu

563 Valencia Street, at 17th Street, Mission (255 3029/www.hideostore.com). BART 16th Street/bus 14, 26, 33, 49. **Open** noon-7pm Mon, Tue, Thur-Sat; noon-6pm Sun. **Credit** DC, MC, V.
The designs are extremely well considered, the construction and materials are impeccable, and the prices are, well, up there in the sky with the planes. Still, considering how passionate its fans are, it's no wonder Hideo Wakamatsu has gone from a cult name at Flight 001 to a stand-alone boutique.

Johnson Leathers

1833 Polk Street, between Jackson & Washington Streets, Polk Gulch (775 7392/www.johnsonleather.com). Bus 12, 19, 27, 47, 49, 76/cable car Powell-Hyde. **Open** 10.30am-6.30pm Mon-Sat; noon-5pm Sun. **Credit** AmEx, DC, Disc, MC, V. **Map** p314 K4.
Both a factory and a shop, Johnson Leathers makes and sells jackets and motorbike racing suits, as well as vests, trousers and chaps, all at very reasonable prices. Alterations can be done while you wait.

Eat, Drink, Shop

Lingerie & underwear

Alla Prima Fine Lingerie
*539 Hayes Street, between Laguna & Octavia Streets,
Hayes Valley (864 8180/www.allaprimalingerie.com).
Bus 21, 47, 49.* **Open** 11am-7pm Mon-Sat; noon-5pm
Sun. **Credit** AmEx, DC, Disc, MC, V. **Map** p318 J8.
Known for its thorough fittings and sky-high designer offerings, Alla Prima specialises in everything
from Dolce & Gabbana bras and La Perla delicacies
to sublime swimsuits and thigh-high fishnets.
Other locations 1420 Grant Avenue, North Beach
(397 4077).

Belle Cose
*2036 Polk Street, between Broadway & Pacific
Avenue, Polk Gulch (474 3494). Bus 12, 27, 49, 76.*
Open 11am-6.30pm Mon-Fri; 11am-6pm Sat; noon-
5pm Sun. **Credit** DC, MC, V. **Map** p314 K4.
'Vintage lingerie' sounds pretty scary, but here it's
all about the 1920s boudoir theming. While there is
the odd second-hand slip, nightie or corset for sale,
the shop majors in new designer lingerie.

Dark Garden
*321 Linden Street, between Octavia & Gough Streets,
Hayes Valley (431 7684/www.darkgarden.net). Bus
21, 47, 49.* **Open** 1-7pm Mon-Sat. **Credit** AmEx,
DC, Disc, MC, V. **Map** p318 J8.
Autumn Carey-Adamme's métier is bespoke corsets.
Select style, fabric and colour and, by the magic of
12 individual measurements, she'll create a custom-
fit garment. The off-the-rack models are seductive,
and the bridal corsets remain hugely popular.

Shoes
For non-specialists with great selections, try
Barneys New York (*see p174*), **American
Rag, Rabat** (*see p186*), **Nordstrom** (*see p177*)
or the cut-price range at **Jeremy's** (*see p181*).

Bulo
*418 Hayes Street, at Gough Street, Hayes Valley
(255 4939/www.buloshoes.com). Bus 21, 47, 49.*
Open 11am-7pm Mon-Sat; noon-6pm Sun. **Credit**
AmEx, DC, Disc, MC, V. **Map** p318 J8.
Two shops in Hayes Valley (the men's store is at at
no.437A, 864 3244) sell a handsome array of shoes
by European designers. On big sale days, expect to
queue for those Cydwoq knee-high boots.

Gimme Shoes
*416 Hayes Street, at Gough Street, Hayes Valley
(864 0691). Bus 21, 47, 49.* **Open** 11am-7pm Mon-
Sat; noon-6pm Sun. **Credit** AmEx, DC, Disc, MC, V.
Map p315 M5.
The richer fare at this fashion-forward, gender-
neutral shoe salon includes Paul Smith, Costume
National and Miu Miu. An impressive cache of train-
ers and casual shoes ranging from Adidas to Prada
tempts locals out of their flip-flops.
Other locations 2358 Fillmore Street, Pacific
Heights (441 3040).

Harputs
*1527 Fillmore Street, at Geary Boulevard, Western
Addition (923 9300/www.harputs.com). Bus 2, 3, 4,
22, 38.* **Open** 11am-7pm Mon-Sat; noon-6pm Sun.
Credit AmEx, DC, MC, V. **Map** p313 H6.
The Harputs family has been supplying the 'hood –
and the rock stars who'd play down the street at the
Fillmore auditorium – with kicks since 1978. These
days you'll still find rare Adidas, Nike, Converse and
Royal Elastics, as well as sportswear. Amble next
door (no.1525) to check out the more upscale designs,
with Martin Margiela footwear, as well as Yohji
Yamamoto's Y-3 line for Adidas, at Harputs Market
(922 9644).

Huf
*516 Hayes Street, between Laguna & Octavia
Streets, Hayes Valley (552 3820/www.hufsf.com).
Bus 21, 47, 49.* **Open** 11am-7pm Mon-Sat; noon-6pm
Sun. **Credit** AmEx, DC, Disc, MC, V. **Map** p315 M5.
Sneaker demons will love the limited-edition Adidas,
Nike and New Balance rarities sold at this stream-
lined, personable shoe shop. Be sure to check out the
skull-bedecked Vans for your budding baby skater.
Other locations 808 Sutter Street, Nob Hill/
Tenderloin (614 9414).

Shoe Biz
*1446 Haight Street, between Ashbury Street &
Masonic Avenue, Haight-Ashbury (864 0990/www.
shoebizsf.com). Metro to Carl & Cole/bus 6, 7, 33,
43, 66, 71.* **Open** 11am-7pm Mon-Sat; noon-6pm
Sun. **Credit** AmEx, DC, Disc, MC, V. **Map** p317 F9.
Whether you need a spike heel or a hot-pink pointy-
toed flat, Shoe Biz adds a bit of punky glamour to
current trends. Trainer addicts should head for Shoe
Biz II at no.1553 for racks of rare Pumas, Adidas and
New Balance.
Other locations throughout the city.

Shoe repair

Anthony's Shoe Service
*30 Geary Street, between Grant Avenue & Kearny
Street, Union Square & Around (781 1338). BART
& Metro to Montgomery/bus 2, 3, 4, 15, 30, 38, 45,
76 & Market Street routes/cable car Powell-Hyde or
Powell-Mason.* **Open** 8.30am-5.30pm Mon-Fri; 9am-
5pm Sat. **Credit** AmEx, DC, Disc, MC, V.
Map p315 M5.
If you're down at heel, let Anthony's minister to you.
Staff will undertake any kind of shoe repair, as well
as handbags and other leather goods, but the work
doesn't come cheap.

Food & drink

Bi-Rite Market
*3639 18th Street, between Guerrero & Dolores
Streets, Mission (241 9773/www.biritemarket.com).
Metro to Church & 18th/bus 33.* **Open** 9am-9pm
Mon-Fri; 9am-8pm Sat, Sun. **Credit** AmEx, DC,
MC, V. **Map** p318 J10.

Ferry Plaza Farmers' Market.

Bi-Rite has been sustaining the hungry locals for more than 60 years, but only became a gourmet deli in 1997. For picnics there are Middle Eastern dips, house-smoked salmon, salads, cakes, an olive bar and more than 100 cheeses; own-made sausages and pasta sauces bring smiles to self-caterers. Also a must for foodies: Bi-Rite's newer creamery/bakery up the street at no. 3692 (626 5600), selling artisan ice-creams, cookies and cakes.

Ferry Plaza Farmers' Market

Ferry Building, Embarcadero, at Market Street. BART & Metro to Montgomery/bus 1, 9, 14, 31 & Market Street routes (291 3276/www.ferrybuilding marketplace.com). **Open** *Farmers' Market* 10am-2pm Tue; 8am-2pm Sat. *Ferry Building Marketplace* 10am-6pm Mon-Fri; 9am-6pm Sat; 11am-5pm Sun. **Credit** (Marketplace only) DC, MC, V. **Map** p315 O4.

Since the restored Ferry Building reopened in 2002, the Ferry Plaza farmers' market has become a sightseeing attraction in its own right. White tents spill out into the open air from both the north and south arcades, with locals and tourists grazing from stalls of aged goat's cheese, freshly baked bread slathered in flavoured olive oil, organic persimmons, pasta and gourmet sausages. There's lots of bustle, especially on a Saturday: agoraphobics should visit on a non-market day to check out the excellent food shops and restaurants inside the Ferry Building. Note that hours for individual shops and eateries within the Ferry Plaza Farmers' Market may vary.

Molinari Delicatessen

373 Columbus Avenue, at Vallejo Street, North Beach (421 2337). Bus 12, 15, 30, 41, 45. **Open** 9am-5.30pm Mon-Sat. **Credit** DC, MC, V. **Map** p315 M3.

Own-made gnocchi, meatballs and sandwiches (try the Joe's Special: mozzarella, just-sliced prosciutto and pesto). So good that it's worth tolerating the huge crowds and chaotic deli-style ordering system.

Rainbow Grocery

1745 Folsom Street, at 14th Street, Mission (863 0621/www.rainbowgrocery.org). BART 16th Street/ bus 14, 26, 33, 49. **Open** 9am-9pm daily. **Credit** DC, MC, V. **Map** p318 L9.

This worker-owned organic co-op qualifies as an SF institution for its comprehensive bulk food bins, vitamin and supplement aisles, and employees – many of whom are notable musicians and artists.

Tartine Bakery

600 Guerrero Street, between 18th & 19th Streets, Mission (487 2600/www.tartinebakery.com). Metro to Church & 18th/bus 33. **Open** 8am-7pm Mon; 7.30am-7pm Tue, Wed; 7.30am-8pm Thur, Fri; 8am-8pm Sat; 9am-8pm Sun. **Credit** DC, MC, V.

Likely the best bakery in San Francisco, Tartine triggers queues and makes foodies swoon over the hot-pressed sandwiches (on housemade French bread), brioche bread pudding, pastries, cakes and croissants.

Trader Joe's

3 Masonic Avenue, at Geary Boulevard, Western Addition (346 9964/www.traderjoes.com). Bus 2, 4, 38, 43. **Open** 8am-9pm daily. **Credit** AmEx, DC, Disc, MC, V. **Map** p313 F6.

With over 2,000 unique grocery items on its label, Trader Joe's is tough to beat for variety, quality and price. Expect organic, veggie and kosher products, cut-rate wines (yes, the $1.99 Charles Shaw Cabernet, aka Two-Buck Chuck, is still available) and affable salespeople.

Other locations 555 9th Street, SoMa (863 1292); 401 Bay Street, Fisherman's Wharf (351 1013).

Whole Foods Market

*1765 California Street, between Franklin Street &
Van Ness Avenue, Pacific Heights (674 0500/www.
wholefoodsmarket.com). Bus 1.* **Open** 8am-10pm
daily. **Credit** DC, MC, V. **Map** p314 J5.
This monolithic organic foods chain can overwhelm:
the cheese, meats, seafood and produce sections are
sumptuous altars to pristine, high-minded consumption. Add in the delightful hot food, deli, salad and
soup takeout bars, and there's no denying the allure.
Other locations 399 4th Street, SoMa (618 0066);
450 Rhode Island Street, Potrero Hill (552 1155).

Alcohol

Arlequin Wine Merchant

*384 Hayes Street, between Franklin & Gough
Streets, Hayes Valley (863 1104). Bus 16, 21, 47,
49.* **Open** 11am-7pm Mon; 11am-8pm Tue-Sat; noon-
6pm Sun. **Credit** AmEx, DC, MC, V. **Map** p318 J8.
The owners of this sister establishment to Absinthe
(*see p156*) are thoroughly unpretentious, yet savvy
enough to satisfy any armchair quaffer. Taste (and
then, most likely, buy) elusive domestic bottles and
coveted imports, ranging from under $10 to
over $200.

K&L Wine Merchants

*638 4th Street, between Brannan & Townsend
Streets, SoMa (896 1734/www.klwines.com). Metro
2nd & King/bus 12, 15, 30, 45, 76.* **Open** 10am-7pm
Mon-Fri; 9am-6pm Sat; 11am-6pm Sun. **Credit**
AmEx, DC, Disc, MC, V. **Map** p319 O7.
The SF branch of California-focused K&L is a modest warehouse, filled with carefully selected wines
and spirits. Most of the staff claim specialisations in
particular regions and/or varietals, and their encyclopaedic knowledge always seems to induce
a spending spree.

PlumpJack Wines

*4011 24th Street, at Noe Street, Noe Valley (282
3841/www.plumpjack.com). Bus 24, 35, 48.* **Open**
11am-9pm Mon-Sat; noon-6pm Sun. **Credit** AmEx,
DC, Disc, MC, V. **Map** p317 H12.
Though PlumpJack only opened in this location in
2001, there has been a wine shop on the site since
Prohibition ended. You'll find a great selection of
world wines for under $10, as well as grower-
produced champagne, premium saké, vintage port,
Madeira and microbrews.
Other locations 3201 Fillmore Street, Cow Hollow
(346 9870).

True Sake

*560 Hayes Street, between Laguna & Octavia
Streets, Hayes Valley (355 9555/www.truesake.com).
Bus 21, 47, 49.* **Open** noon-7pm Mon-Sat; 11am-6pm
Sun. **Credit** AmEx, DC, MC, V. **Map** p318 J8.
A beautiful and elegant place, this is the first US
shop devoted entirely to saké. Owner Beau Timken
is every bit as helpful and knowledgeable about the
rice-fermented beverage as you might hope, even
suggesting food pairings for your purchase.

Tea & coffee

Blue Bottle Coffee Kiosk

*315 Linden Street, at Gough Street, Hayes Valley
(252 7535/www.bluebottlecoffee.net). Bus 21, 47, 49.*
Open 7am-6pm Mon-Fri; 8am-6pm Sat, Sun. **No
credit cards. Map** p318 J8.
Java junkies from all over the area double-park in
this alley and swarm over this seatless stand for

Red Blossom Tea Co: taming the brew.

what many call the best joe in the city. Fans swear by the New Orleans-style iced coffee and rich, multi-faceted blends of hand-roasted beans, delivered with a socially conscious vibe. Look out for the new Blue Bottle Café in 2008 at Mint Plaza (66 Mint Street, between Jessie & Mission Streets, SoMa).

Graffeo Coffee Roasting Company

735 Columbus Avenue, at Filbert Street, North Beach (1-800 222 6250/986 2429). Bus 15, 30, 39, 41, 45/cable car Powell-Mason. **Open** 9am-6pm Mon-Fri; 9am-5pm Sat. **Credit** DC, MC, V. **Map** p314 L3.
If you're awake, you'll smell it. This San Francisco institution stocks fresh coffee from various plantations around the world, roasting its beans right on the premises.

Red Blossom Tea Co

831 Grant Avenue, between Washington & Clay Streets, Chinatown (395 0868/www.redblossomtea. com). Bus 1, 9, 15/cable car California. **Open** 10am-6.30pm Mon-Sat; 10am-6pm Sun. **Credit** AmEx, DC, MC, V. **Map** p315 M4.
Renamed and expanded in 2005, Red Blossom has been in the tea business for more than two decades – and it shows. Not only is there a selection of more than 100 teas (black and green? Pshaw! Get into pu-erh and white), but you can get advice on the art of proper brewing.

Gifts & souvenirs

Museum gift stores are a lovely place to shop. The **California Palace of the Legion of Honor** shop (*see p115*) has rare photography books, prints and offbeat jewellery from local designers, while the **Exploratorium** store (*see p205*) has a bundle of things to spark young imaginations. The warm, welcoming shop on the first floor of the **Asian Art Museum** (*see p76*) has re-creations of artefacts among its unique and pricey mementos, and the wares at the **SFMOMA MuseumStore** (*see p81*) are sometimes more of a draw than the museum.

African Outlet

524 Octavia Street, between Hayes & Grove Streets, Hayes Valley (864 3576). Bus 21, 47, 49. **Open** 10.30am-7pm daily. **Credit** AmEx, DC, MC, V. **Map** p318 J7.
This gorgeous jumble of tribal artefacts and antiques – brilliantly coloured textiles, jewellery and beads, sculpture, fetishes, and ceremonial masks – has been gathered by a Nigerian expat and his wife, who delight in explaining their pieces. to interested customers. You may have trouble hearing them over the blasting reggae.

Alabaster

597 Hayes Street, at Laguna Street, Hayes Valley (558 0482/www.alabastersf.com). Bus 21. **Open** 11am-6pm Mon-Wed; 11am-7pm Thur-Sat; noon-5pm Sun. **Credit** AmEx, DC, Disc, MC, V. **Map** p318 J8.

This elegant shop not only looks beautiful, but sells beautiful things: alabaster, of course, in the form of urns and lamps, but also little boxes, Buddhas, vintage globes and even framed exotic butterflies and beetles.

Curiosity Shoppe

855 Valencia Street, at 20th Street, Mission (839 6404/www.curiosityshoppeonline.com). BART 16th Street/bus 14, 26, 33, 49. **Open** 11am-7pm Wed-Sat; noon-6pm Sun. **Credit** AmEx, DC, Disc, MC, V. **Map** p318 K11.
Owners Lauren Smith and Derek Fagerstrom set up the Curiosity Shoppe to showcase their obsession with the gorgeous and strange. Pick up a kit to make a duct tape wallet or radio receiver for that crafty chum – or simply buy a sweet charm necklace for yourself.

Flax Art & Design

1699 Market Street, between Gough & Valencia Streets, Upper Market (552 2355/www.flaxart.com). Metro F to Valencia Street. **Open** 9.30am-6pm Mon-Sat. **Credit** AmEx, DC, MC, V. **Map** p318 K8.
So much more than an art supply store, this Bay Area landmark teems with papers, fine pens, children's toys, blank books, timepieces, lighting, portfolios – everything you could possibly desire for the boho live/work space of your dreams.

Giant Robot

618 Shrader Street, between Haight & Waller Streets, Haight-Ashbury (876 4773/www.giant robot.com). **Open** 11.30am-8pm Mon-Fri; 11am-8pm Sat; noon-7pm Sun. **Credit** DC, MC, V. **Map** p317 E9.
This innovative retailer, which spun off the 'zine of the same name and has inspired other area boutiques/galleries such as Super 7 (1628 Post Street, Western Addition, 409 4700) and Park Life (220 Clement Street, Richmond, 386 7275), specialises in Asian-American pop in all its incarnations: fine art, toys, illustration, T-shirts, anime artefacts, art books, ephemera and all manner of ultra-covetable and collectable tchotchkes. Be sure to check out the affordable art in the gallery space.

Lavish

540 Hayes Street, at Octavia Street, Hayes Valley (565 0540/www.shoplavish.com). Bus 21, 47, 49. **Open** 11am-7pm Mon-Sat; 11am-6pm Sun. **Credit** DC, MC, V. **Map** p318 J8.
Gorgeous letterpress cards, charming print bags, delicate jewellery and oodles of whimsical baby clothes make this a must-stop on the way to a girlie soirée or baby shower.

Little Otsu

849 Valencia Street, between 19th & 20th Streets, Mission (255 7900/www.littleotsu.com). BART 16th Street/bus 14, 26, 33, 49. **Open** 11.30am-7.30pm Wed-Sun. **Credit** DC, MC, V. **Map** p318 K11.
Vegan principles at this artful, airy space translate as cute, recycled-paper cards (as well as diaries, calendars and books) printed with soy-based inks.

Needles & Pens

3253 16th Street, at Guerrero Street, Mission (255 1534/www.needles-pens.com). BART 16th Street/bus 14, 26, 33, 49. **Open** noon-7pm daily. **Credit** AmEx, DC, Disc, MC, V. **Map** p318 J10.

This epicentre of DIY culture in Mission combined with gallery space trades in 'zines, bric-a-brac and hand-embellished T-shirts. A great place to pick up a polemical print by your local anarchist.

Nest

2300 Fillmore Street, at Clay Street, Pacific Heights (292 6199). Bus 1, 3, 12, 22, 24. **Open** 10.30am-6.30pm Mon-Sat; 11am-6pm Sun. **Credit** AmEx, DC, MC, V. **Map** p313 H5.

A nest in the magpie sense, this Parisian bohemia-inspired shop is a beguiling compilation of tin jack-in-the-boxes, gauzy Chinese lanterns, woodcuts, glassware, French jewellery and some adorable kids' clothes.

Paxton Gate

824 Valencia Street, between 19th & 20th Streets, Mission (824 1872/www.paxtongate.com). BART 16th Street/bus 14, 26, 33, 49. **Open** noon-7pm Mon-Fri; 11am-7pm Sat, Sun. **Credit** AmEx, DC, MC, V. **Map** p318 K11.

That kneeling cushion may be more practical, but the gardener in your life will find something from this deeply bizarre shop rather more fun. Alongside ghoulish pieces of taxidermy – mice in anthropomorphic poses, say – sits an array of traditional, hand-crafted Japanese garden knives.

Sam Bo Trading Co

38 Waverley Place, between Sacramento & Clay Streets, Chinatown (397 2998). Bus 1, 12, 15, 30, 41, 45/cable car Powell-Hyde or Powell-Mason. **Open** 9.30am-6pm daily. **Credit** DC, MC, V. **Map** p315 M4.

The best things in Chinatown are found down side streets, and this tiny shop of Buddhist and Taoist religious items is a prime example. Sam Bo sells Buddhas, ceremonial candles, incense and intriguing paper goods that are to be burned in honour of ancestors or to request a favour of the gods.

Swallowtail

2217 Polk Street, between Vallejo & Green Streets, Polk Gulch (567 1555). Bus 19, 41, 45, 47, 49, 76/cable car Powell-Hyde. **Open** noon-6pm daily. **Credit** AmEx, DC, MC, V. **Map** p314 K4.

Slightly creepy but always engaging, Swallowtail takes you through art into the realm of theatre design, with a vast range of collectibles.

Therapy

545 Valencia Street, between 16th & 17th Streets, Mission (865 0981). BART 16th Street/bus 14, 26, 33, 49. **Open** 11.30am-10pm Mon-Thur; 11am-10.30pm Fri; 10.30am-10.30pm Sat; 10.30am-9pm Sun.* **Credit** AmEx, DC, MC, V. **Map** p318 K10.

This hipster central stocks cute earrings and hair clips, stationery and undefinable gifts, as well as women's and men's clothing. For furniture and home-wares, check out its other shop a few doors down.

Health & beauty

Complementary medicine

Scarlet Sage Herb Co

1173 Valencia Street, between 22nd & 23rd Streets, Mission (821 0997/www.scarletsageherb.com). BART 24th Street/bus 14, 26, 48, 49, 67. **Open** 11am-6.30pm daily. **Credit** AmEx, DC, Disc, MC, V. **Map** p318 K12.

The owners of this Mission apothecary focus on organic Native American and more familiar European herbs, essential oils, tinctures and plant essences, with a section dedicated to homeopathy. There's also a good choice of books for sale on alternative healing.

Vinh Khang Herbs & Ginsengs

512 Clement Street, between 6th & 7th Avenues, Richmond (752 8336). Bus 1, 2, 4, 38, 44. **Open** 10am-7pm Mon, Wed, Thur, Sat, Sun. **No credit cards.** **Map** p312 C6.

Feel the strength of San Francisco Chinese traditions at Vinh Khang, where herbal specialists can create a customised concoction for your ailment while you wait on their premises.

Hairdressers & barbers

Backstage Salon

2134 Polk Street, between Broadway & Vallejo Street, Polk Gulch (775 1440). Bus 12, 27, 49, 76. **Open** 11am-7pm daily. **Credit** DC, MC, V. **Map** p314 K4.

This salon/gallery showcases local art while providing intense colour treatments and innovative haircuts from a rotating fleet of international stylists.

Hair Play

1599 Dolores Street, at 29th Street, Noe Valley (550 1656). Metro to Church & 30th/bus 24, 26. **Open** noon-6pm Mon, Sun; 10am-6pm Tue, Wed, Sat; noon-8pm Thur, Fri.* **Credit** DC, Disc, MC, V.

Hair Play's earthy interior calms, while seasoned stylists whip your hair into shape without the divaish attitude. Lauded as the best salon in San Francisco, and popular with those who suffer the blessing of curly hair.

Opticians

City Optix

2154 Chestnut Street, between Pierce & Steiner Streets, Marina (921 1188/www.cityoptix.com). Bus 22, 28, 30, 43, 76. **Open** 10am-6pm Mon-Wed, Fri, Sat; 10am-8pm Thur; noon-5pm Sun. **Credit** AmEx, DC, MC, V. **Map** p313 G3.

Alain Mikli, Oliver Peoples and LA Eyeworks frames are all sold here, and helpful staff will sift through the entire collection to find you the ideal pair. **Other locations** 1685 Haight Street, Haight-Ashbury (626 1188).

Pharmacies

Walgreens Drugstore
3201 Divisadero Street, at Lombard Street, Marina (931 6417/www.walgreens.com). Bus 28, 30, 43, 76. **Open** 24hrs daily. **Credit** AmEx, DC, Disc, MC, V. **Map** p313 F3.
Prescriptions and general drugstore purchases are available at this pharmacy around the clock. **Other 24hr locations** 459 Powell Street, Union Square & Around (984 0793); 498 Castro Street, Castro (861 6276); 1189 Potrero Avenue, Mission (647 1397); 5411 Geary Boulevard, Richmond (752 8370).

Spas & salons

International Orange
2044 Fillmore Street, between Pine & California Streets, Pacific Heights (563 5000/www. internationalorange.com). Bus 1, 3, 22. **Open** 11am-9pm Mon-Fri; 9am-7pm Sat, Sun. **Credit** AmEx, DC, MC, V. **Map** p313 H5.
Be sure you get an appointment: the secret is out about the refined treatments and professional facials here. Try the Red Flower Japan massage, a soothing mix of botanicals that awakens your senses (or, at least, leaves you smelling decent for 48 hours). *See p194.*

Kabuki Springs & Spa
Japan Center, 1750 Geary Boulevard, at Fillmore Street, Western Addition (922 6000/www.kabuki springs.com). Bus 22, 38. **Open** *Men only* 10am-10pm Mon, Thur, Sat. *Women only* 10am-10pm Wed, Fri, Sun. *Mixed* 10am-10pm Tue. **Admission** *Day pass* $15-$25. **Credit** AmEx, DC, Disc, MC, V. **Map** p314 H6.
This traditional Japanese bathhouse has communal tubs, a steam room, saunas, a cold plunge pool and a restful tatami room. Shiatsu, Swedish and prenatal massages, body wraps and scrubs, and other soothing services are available by appointment.

Osento
955 Valencia Street, at 21st Street, Mission (282 6333/www.osento.com). BART 24th Street/bus 14, 26, 48, 49, 67. **Open** noon-midnight daily. **Admission** *Day pass* $12-$20. **Credit** DC, MC, V. **Map** p318 K11.
Often thought of as catering to the city's lesbian community, Osento is simply a women-only bath-house. Walk into the peaceful surroundings, leave your clothes in a locker and relax in the whirlpool. After a cold plunge, choose between wet and dry saunas, or head for the outdoor deck. Massages by appointment only.

SenSpa
1161 Gorgas Avenue, off Presidio/Crissy Field exit, Presidio (441 1777/www.senspa.com). Bus 28, 29, 43, 76/PresidiGo shuttle. **Open** 10am-9pm Tue-Fri; 9am-7pm Sat, Sun. **Credit** AmEx, DC, MC, V. **Map** p313 E3.
Far from the madding crowd of Downtown – and somewhat challenging to locate – is this relatively new addition to the spa scene. But what an addition: the early 20th-century storage barracks that once catered to Letterman Hospital (now George Lucas's digital arts campus) has been transformed into a peaceful Asian-inspired oasis with walls of falling water, plants and skylights. The holistic treatments, massages and facials are delivered by expert aes-theticians; lymphatic detoxes, Ayurvedic facials and deep-tissue massages are among the specialities.

Shops

Fresh
301 Sutter Street, at Grant Avenue, Union Square & Around (248 0210/www.fresh.com). BART & Metro to Montgomery/bus 2, 3, 4, 15, 30, 38, 45, 76/cable

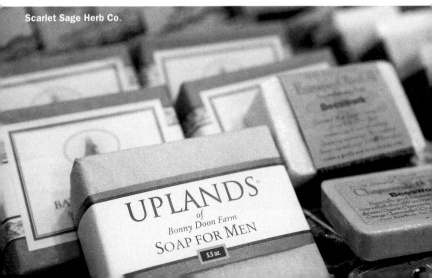

Scarlet Sage Herb Co.

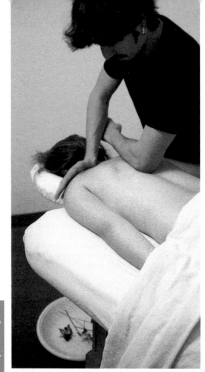

Eat, Drink, Shop

car Powell-Hyde or Powell-Mason. **Open** 10am-7pm Mon-Wed, Sat; 10am-8pm Thur; 10am-6pm Sun. **Credit** AmEx, DC, MC, V. **Map** p315 M5.

Ensconced in a Victorian corner spot, Fresh purveys its own inimitable soaps, perfumes, lotions, shower gels and make-up. As well as smelling good enough to eat (soy shampoo, pomegranate conditioner, brown sugar scrub), the products are excellent performers.

Kiehl's

2360 Fillmore Street, between Washington & Clay Streets, Pacific Heights (359 9260/www.kiehls.com). Bus 1, 3, 12, 22, 24. **Open** 11am-7pm Mon-Sat; 10am-6pm Sun. **Credit** AmEx, DC, MC, V. **Map** p313 H5.

The first Kiehl's botanical apothecary opened in New York's East Village in 1851; 150 years later the second one opened in Pacific Heights. The products are gentle and justifiably beloved, and include such perennial faves as the Creme de Corps. **Other locations** Westfield San Francisco Centre, 865 Market Street, Union Square & Around (644 0112).

Sephora

33 Powell Street, at Market Street, Union Square & Around (362 9360/www.sephora.com). BART & Metro to Powell/bus 27, 30, 31, 45 & Market Street routes/cable car Powell-Hyde or Powell-Mason. **Open** 10am-9pm Mon-Sat; 11am-7pm Sun. **Credit** AmEx, DC, Disc, MC, V. **Map** p315 M6.

Sephora's USP is its interactive floor plan: you can touch, smell and try on most of the premier perfumes and make-up brands without suffering the hard sell. **Other locations** 2083 Union Street, Cow Hollow (614 2704).

House & home

Jonathan Adler

2133 Fillmore Street, at Sacramento Street, Pacific Heights (563 9500/www.jonathanadler.com). Bus 2, 3, 4, 22, 38. **Open** 11am-7pm Mon-Wed; 10am-7pm Thur-Sat; noon-6pm Sun. **Credit** AmEx, DC, MC, V. **Map** p313 H5.

Everything NYC designer Jonathan Adler touches becomes utterly groovy in a very *Ice Storm* kind of way: his animal figurines, pillows, pottery and furnishings scream 'Let the key party begin!'

Monument

572 Valencia Street, at 19th Street, Mission (861 9800/www.monument.1stdibs.com). BART 16th Street/bus 14, 26, 33, 49. **Open** noon-6pm Mon-Thur, Sun; noon-7pm Fri, Sat. **Credit** DC, MC, V. **Map** p318 K11.

Mad glam mid-century modern makes its last glittery stand here. Take in the sensual lines of the sofas and the high drama of the mirrored cabinets.

Other Shop II

327 Divisadero Street, between Oak & Page Streets, Lower Haight (621 5424). Bus 6, 7, 22, 66, 71. **Open** noon-6pm daily. **Credit** DC, Disc, MC, V. **Map** p317 G8.

International Orange. See p193.

Come here for retro-mod home furnishings that revitalise the Space Age – or at least remind you why it was short-lived. Primary colours, burnished chrome and a plethora of cocktail accessories.

Sur La Table

77 Maiden Lane, at Stockton Street, Union Square & Around (732 7900/www.surlatable.com). BART & Metro to Powell/bus 2, 3, 4, 15, 30, 38, 45, 76 & Market Street routes/cable car Powell-Hyde or Powell-Mason. **Open** 10am-6pm Mon-Fri; 10am-7pm Sat; 11am-6pm Sun. **Credit** AmEx, DC, Disc, MC, V. **Map** p315 M5.

Nearly everything the passionate cook might desire can be found under these eaves, including high-end single-cup espresso makers and gingerbread house-making kits.

Other locations Ferry Building Marketplace No.37, Embarcadero (262 9970); 1806 4th Street, Berkeley (1-510 849 2252).

Zinc Details

1905 Fillmore Street, between Bush & Pine Streets, Pacific Heights (776 2100/www.zincdetails.com). Bus 2, 3, 4, 22, 38. **Open** 11am-7pm Mon-Sat; noon-6pm Sun. **Credit** AmEx, DC, Disc, MC, V. **Map** p314 H5.

Fun, funky and often fabulous contemporary design by Artemide, Le Klint, Marimekko, Vitra and other European and Japanese makers can be found in this forward-thinking, jam-packed emporium of rugs, lighting, tables, glassware, furniture, textiles and vases. Furniture is the focus of the branch at 2410 California Street (776 9002), just up Fillmore Street.

Music & entertainment

CDs, DVDs & records

Although the quality and variety of independent music shops means you needn't trouble yourself with the chain stores, there is at least one outlet in the city that's worth visiting: the sizeable **Virgin Megastore** (2 Stockton Street, at Market Street, Union Square & Around, 397 4525, www.virginmega.com).

We've listed the best generalists and genre specialists below, but those with a serious vocation for 180-gram will be more at home in the Lower Haight. On Haight Street, serious deck-heads have **Tweekin Records** (no.593, at Steiner Street, 626 6995, www.tweekin.com), while **Groove Merchant** (no.687, at Pierce Street, 252 5766) has bins of hard-to-find jazz, funk, soul and other dusty 12-inch delights. There are soul and funk 45s at chaotic **Rooky Ricardo's** (no.448, at Fillmore Street, 864 7526), but **Jack's Record Cellar** (254 Scott Street, between Haight & Page Streets, 431 3047) has the edge for hard-to-find jazz, R&B, pop and country. Experimental electronica is the speciality at **Open Mind Music** (2150 Market Street, near Church Street, Castro, 621 2244).

Amoeba Music

1855 Haight Street, between Shrader & Stanyan Streets, Haight-Ashbury (831 1200/www.amoeba.com). Metro to Carl & Cole/bus 6, 7, 33, 43, 66, 71. **Open** 10.30am-10pm Mon-Sat; 11am-9pm Sun. **Credit** AmEx, DC, Disc, MC, V. **Map** p317 E9.

Amoeba Music remains a mighty presence. It's partly a matter of scale – 25,000sq ft (2,325sq m) of former bowling alley, to be exact – but mainly a matter of breadth: there's every imaginable type of music, both new and used, the vast majority priced very fairly, as well as a massive DVD selection. The Berkeley branch used to be the stronger of the two, but the SF store now pips it. There are free gigs, too, with some surprisingly big names. The store also recently launched its own imprint: one of its first releases was a 1969 concert by Gram Parsons and the Flying Burrito Brothers at SF's Avalon Ballroom.

Other locations 2455 Telegraph Avenue, Berkeley (1-510 549 1125).

Aquarius Records

1055 Valencia Street, between 21st & 22nd Streets, Mission (647 2272/www.aquariusrecords.org). BART 24th Street/bus 14, 26, 48, 49, 67. **Open** 10am-9pm Mon-Wed; 10am-10pm Thur-Sun. **Credit** AmEx, DC, Disc, MC, V. **Map** p318 K12.

This splendid little neighbourhood record store could be classed as a boutique, were the staff not so wonderfully lacking in pretension (tiny hand-written notes attached to numerous CD covers reveal their enthusiasm). Expect carefully curated selections and rarities in everything from art rock to sludge metal.

Grooves Vinyl Attractions

1797 Market Street, between Pearl & McCoppin Streets, Hayes Valley (436 9933). Metro to Van Ness/bus 26. **Open** 11am-7pm daily. **Credit** AmEx, DC, Disc, MC, V. **Map** p318 J9.

Vinyl heaven – at least if your tastes don't run far beyond the 1970s. The store is packed with oddities and curios, including tons of old soundtracks, comedy records and sets by forgotten '70s crooners.

Medium Rare Records

2310 Market Street, at 16th Street, Castro (255 7273). Metro to Castro/bus 24, 33, 35, 37. **Open** 11am-9pm Mon-Thur, Sun; 11am-10pm Fri, Sat. **Credit** AmEx, DC, MC, V. **Map** p317 H10.

A lovingly assembled collection of CDs and DVDs is crammed into the tiny space here. The range meanders wildly across the decades and genres, with everything from disco to dance, vocal standards to show tunes. *See p196.*

Ritmo Latino

2401 Mission Street, at 20th Street, Mission (824 8556). BART 16th Street/bus 14, 26, 33, 49. **Open** 10am-9.30pm daily. **Credit** DC, Disc, MC, V. **Map** p318 K11.

If you look outside, you'll find handprints of Latin stars like Celia Cruz and Ricky Martin. Within, friendly staff can guide you to their recorded works, or to mariachi music, conjuntos or whatever rhythm you fancy. The store has expanded its wares of late into lifestyle products such as clothing.

Instruments & sheet music

Clarion Music

816 Sacramento Street, at Grant Àvenue, Chinatown (391 1317/www.clarionmusic.com). Bus 1, 12, 15, 30, 41, 45/cable car California. **Open** 11am-6pm Mon-Fri; 9am-5pm Sat. **Credit** AmEx, DC, Disc, MC, V. **Map** p315 M4.

It stocks didgeridoos and African drums, sure, but Clarion takes them as a starting point before heading into truly exotic waters: affordable H'mong jaw harps, say, or an impressively costly deluxe pipa.

Haight-Ashbury Music Center

1540 Haight Street, at Ashbury Street, Haight-Ashbury (863 7327/www.haight-ashbury-music.com). Metro to Carl & Cole/bus 6, 7, 33, 43, 66, 71. **Open** 11am-7pm Mon-Fri; 10am-6pm Sat; noon-6pm Sun. **Credit** AmEx, DC, Disc, MC, V. **Map** p317 F9.

A stop-off for local musos and visiting musicians, this shop sells new and second-hand instruments, microphones, mixers, amps and sheet music.

Sex shops

Eurotique Stormy Leather

1158 Howard Street, between 7th & 8th Streets, SoMa (626 1672/www.stormyleather.com). Bus 12, 14, 19, 26. **Open** noon-7pm daily. **Credit** AmEx, Disc, MC, V. **Map** p318 L7.

Medium Rare Records *See p195.*

Friendly female staff will help you select your leather corsetry or adult toys at this famous shop that has made corsets for the likes of Christina Aguilera. The shop showcases spanking skirts and a topless Equus ensemble (complete with horse's bridle), but those with more vanilla tastes can settle for a French maid outfit or a latex bustier.

Good Vibrations

603 Valencia Street, at 17th Street, Mission (522 5460/www.goodvibes.com). BART 16th Street/bus 14, 26, 33, 49. **Open** noon-7pm Mon-Wed; noon-8pm Thur; noon-9pm Fri; 11am-9pm Sat; 11am-7pm Sun. **Credit** AmEx, Disc, MC, V. **Map** p318 K10.

Buy a quality vibrator without suffering the seedy sex shop ambience. This 30-year-old shop caters to women with staff that pride themselves on providing a clean, safe environment for buying sex toys of every kind. Stock includes the popular Hitachi Magic Wand, I Rub My Duckie and the (in)famous Rabbit.

Other locations 1620 Polk Street, Polk Gulch (345 0400); 2504 San Pablo Avenue, Berkeley (1-510 841 8987).

Sports & fitness

For ski, snowboard, surf and in-line skate rentals, *see pp243-250.*

Lombardi Sports

1600 Jackson Street, at Polk Street, Polk Gulch (771 0600/www.lombardisports.com). Bus 12, 19, 27, 47, 49, 76. **Open** 10am-7pm Mon-Wed; 10am-8pm Thur, Fri; 10am-6pm Sat; 11am-6pm Sun. **Credit** DC, Disc, MC, V. **Map** p314 K4.

Although it does sell proper wilderness gear, affable Lombardi Sports also caters to those who weren't suckled by wolves. There's equipment and accessories for cycling, running, climbing and hiking, as well as snow-, water- and team sports, plus some fashion. The staff are knowledgeable.

See Jane Run Sports

3910 24th Street, at Sanchez Street, Noe Valley (401 8338/www.seejanerunsports.com). Metro to Church & 24th/bus 48. **Open** 11am-7pm Mon-Fri; 10am-6pm Sat; 10am-5pm Sun. **Credit** AmEx, DC, Disc, MC, V. **Map** p317 H12.

A shop for women who run, cycle, swim, hike or do yoga, with staff who are more than happy to spend time matching you to the right shoes.

Sports Basement

610 Mason Street, at Crissy Field, Presidio (437 0100/www.sportsbasement.com). **Open** 9am-8pm Mon-Fri; 8am-7pm Sat, Sun. **Credit** AmEx, DC, MC, V. **Map** p312 D2.

Size is everything at Sports Basement: this large branch includes end-of-line goods from top-tier brands (North Face, Teva, Pearl Izumi), offered at reductions of 30% to 60%.

Other locations 1590 Bryant Street, Potrero Hill (437 0100).

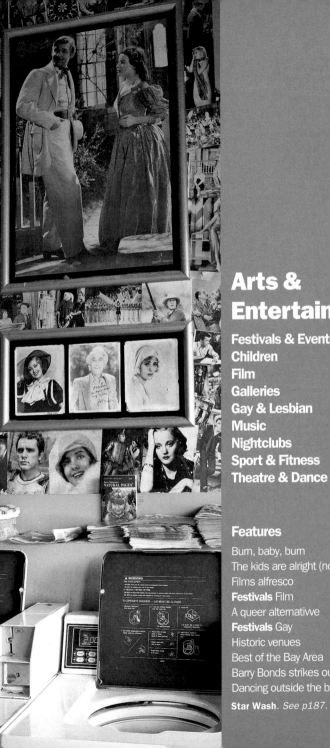

Arts & Entertainment

Features

Star Wash. *See p187*.

Festivals & Events

This city loves to party.

Food stalls, artists' stands and more: all the fun of **Union Street Festival**.

Events in a city as extrovert and dramatic as San Francisco are bound to be colourful, and sometimes a little fruity. Spring and summer are punctuated by weekly neighbourhood fairs and parades, the only drawback being the accompanying street closures and driving detours. When autumn and winter roll around, most events move indoors, but the activity barely lets up. There's always something going on here, whether it's a family fun run through the city or a transvestite beauty contest.

The dates listed below are as accurate as possible, but check before you make plans: festivals do occasionally shift dates. For up-to-date information, consult the San Francisco Visitor Information Center (*see p294*) or local papers, including the free alternative press.

Spring

St Patrick's Day Parade

From 2nd & Market Streets to Civic Center. **Date** Sun before 17 Mar. **Map** p314, p315 & p318.
The city has a sizeable Irish-American population, but everyone gets smiling Irish eyes in time for St Patrick's Day. The parade heads from 2nd and Market Streets to the Civic Center.

Sisters of Perpetual Indulgence Easter Celebrations

Mission Dolores Park, Dolores & 18th Streets, Mission (www.thesisters.org). BART 16th Street/ Metro to Church or Castro/bus 22. **Date** Easter weekend. **Map** p318 J11.
It was at this time of year in 1979 that a group of 'gay male nuns' (their words) took the habit – from a local production of *The Sound of Music*, that is – to begin their mission of 'spreading joy, absolving guilt and serving the community' through street theatre, charity events and political activism. Each Easter they head for Dolores Park to bestow sainthood on worthy persons and preside over Easter Bonnet and Hunky Jesus contests.

St Stupid's Day Parade

Transamerica Pyramid, 600 Montgomery Street, between Washington & Clay Streets, Financial District (www.saintstupid.com). BART & Metro to Embarcadero/bus 1, 2, 10, 14, 15, 31 & Market Street routes/cable car California. **Date** 1 Apr. **Map** p315 O4.
The riotous costumed procession winds its way through the Financial District every 1 April, stopping off at various 'Stations of the Stupid' (aka noted financial institutions) to pay tribute to the gods of commerce.

Cherry Blossom Festival
Japan Center, Geary Boulevard, between Fillmore & Laguna Streets, Japantown (563 2313/www.nccbf. org). Bus 2, 3, 4, 22, 38. **Date** Apr. **Map** p314 H6.
A joyous whirlwind engulfs the usually sleepy Japantown for two weekends in April. The Cherry Blossom Festival is a splendid celebration of Japanese cuisine, traditional arts and crafts, dance and martial arts. The Grand Parade starts at Civic Center and goes up Polk to Post ending in Japantown.

Cinco de Mayo
Around the city & Mission Dolores Park, Dolores & 18th Streets, Mission (www.thesisters.org). BART 16th Street/Metro to Church or Castro/bus 22. (www.sfcincodemayo.com). **Date** weekend before 5 May. **Map** p318 K7.
San Francisco's Latino residents and their friends celebrate General Ignacio Zaragoza's defeat of the French army at Puebla in 1862 with this raucous weekend of parades, fireworks and music. Think St Patrick's Day with tequila. There is also a free all-day festival in Dolores Park celebrating Mexican culture on the closest Saturday.

AIDS Candlelight Memorial March & Vigil
Castro & Market Streets, Castro (331 1500/ www.aidscandlelightvigil.org). Metro K, L, M to Castro/streetcar F/bus 24, 33, 35, 37. **Date** 3rd Sun in May. **Map** p317 H10.
This annual candlelit vigil begins at 8pm with a solemn procession from the Castro along Market Street, ending on the steps of the Main Library. There, crowds gather for speeches, an awards ceremony, celebrations and remembrances.

Bay to Breakers Foot Race
From Howard & Spear Streets, SoMa, to Ocean Beach, Golden Gate Park (359 2800/www.bayto breakers.com). **Date** 3rd Sun in May.
In an effort to raise spirits during the arduous and lengthy rebuilding process that followed the 1906 earthquake and fire, Randolph Hearst's *San Francisco Examiner* started this grandaddy of all San Francisco events in 1912. At the height of its popularity, the race attracted more than 110,000 participants. These days, weekend warriors dressed as salmon, jog-walkers pushing kegs of beer in shopping carts, and footloose nude zanies run, walk or stumble from the foot of Howard Street (bay), a distance of about 7.5 miles to Ocean Beach (breakers).

Carnaval
Harrison Street, between 16th & 23rd Streets, Mission (920 0125/www.carnavalsf.com). BART to 16th or 24th Streets/bus 12, 14, 22, 27, 33, 48, 49, 53. **Admission** $5. **Date** Memorial Day weekend. **Map** p318 L10/L11.
Organisers call it 'California's largest annual multi-cultural festival'. Locals call it the best place to eye-ball a dazzling parade of skimpily costumed samba dancers gyrating foxily to fizzing Latin music.

Summer

Union Street Festival
Union Street, between Gough & Steiner Streets, Cow Hollow (1-800 310 6563/www.unionstreet festival.com). Bus 22, 41, 45. **Date** early June. **Map** p313 H4.
This weekend-long street fair draws a six-figure crowd each June, with its artists' stands, food stalls, bands and assorted other entertainments.

Haight Ashbury Street Fair
Haight Street, between Masonic Avenue & Stanyan Street, Haight-Ashbury (www.haightashburystreet fair.org). Metro N to Cole/bus 6, 7, 33, 43, 66, 71. **Date** early June. **Map** p317 E9/F9.
It's the Summer of Love all over again, with more than 200 booths of greasy food, hippie craftwork and enough roach-clips, skins, bongs and hash pipes to fill out a Cheech and Chong script. Live music comes courtesy of local acts.

North Beach Festival
Grant Avenue, Green Street, Stockton Street & Washington Square, North Beach (989 2220/ www.sfnorthbeach.org). Bus 15, 30, 39, 41, 45/cable car Powell-Mason. **Date** June. **Map** p315 M3.
Whip out the beret and bang out a rhythm on the bongos, daddio – it's San Francisco's oldest street party, held in the birthplace of the beatniks. The North Beach Festival is heavy on art and crafts, but there's also live music, wine and, inevitably, plenty of top-notch Italian food.

North Beach Festival: SF's first street party.

Summer Solstice

Around the city. **Date** 21 June.
San Francisco's pagans, and the men and women who love them, meet on the year's longest day to drum, dance and celebrate. At sunset, pound along with a drum circle in Justin Herman Plaza at the Embarcadero or join the Baker Beach bonfires.

San Francisco LGBT Pride Celebration Parade

Market Street, between Embarcadero & 8th Street, Downtown (864 3733/www.sfpride.org). **Date** last Sun in June. **Map** p315 & p318.
A San Francisco institution – but a bit of a mouthful to say – the Lesbian, Gay, Bisexual and Transgender Pride Parade is every bit as campy as you'd expect. Local politicians cruising for the rainbow vote share the route with drag queens, leather daddies and dykes on bikes. It's the wildest, friendliest parade you'll ever witness. Arrive at least an hour early for a kerbside seat. The parade is the culmination of a weekend of Pride, with a celebration at Civic Center from noon until 6pm on Saturday.

Fourth of July Waterfront Festival

Between Aquatic Park & Pier 39, Fisherman's Wharf (San Francisco Visitor Information Center 981 1280). Streetcar F/bus 10, 15, 30, 39, 47/ cable car Powell-Hyde or Powell-Mason. **Date** 4 July. **Map** p314 K2.
You'll find plenty of live entertainment and food stalls here on the waterfront during the day, but be sure to stay for the spectacular fireworks display that gets under way around 9pm.

San Francisco Marathon

Around the city (1-888 958 6668/www.runsfm.com). **Date** usually 1st Sun in Aug.
The younger and more athletic cousin of Bay to Breakers Foot Race (*see p199*) has grown every year since its inception in 1977. The course starts at the Embarcadero and then heads round the entire city, through the Mission, the Haight, Fisherman's Wharf and the Marina.

Autumn

Ghirardelli Square Chocolate Festival

Ghirardelli Square, between North Point, Beach, Larkin & Polk Streets, Fisherman's Wharf (775 5500/www.ghirardellisq.com). Streetcar F/bus 10, 15, 30, 39, 47/cable car Powell-Hyde or Powell-Mason. **Date** early Sept. **Map** p314 J2.
Keep reminding yourself that doctors say a little chocolate is good for you, as you sample chocolate-covered strawberries, decadent brownies and chocolate cheesecake. Proceeds go to a local charity.

How Berkeley Can You Be?

Around Downtown Berkeley (www.howberkeley canyoube.com). BART Downtown Berkeley. **Date** late Sept.

Politicians and protestors, hippies and punks, Klingons and Stormtroopers make a show of civic pride with a procession of costumed (or naked) participants and 'art cars' – vehicles adorned with anything from organic fruit to cannabis – parading from the corner of California Street and University Avenue to Civic Center Park.

Folsom Street Fair

Folsom Street, between 7th & 12th Streets, SoMa (www.folsomstreetfair.org). Bus 9, 12, 14, 19, 27, 47. **Date** last Sun in Sept. **Map** p318 L8.
The Queen Mother of all leather street fairs, the Folsom Street Fair is a veritable gawkfest for visitors. Don your studded jockstrap and be prepared for masks, whips, chains and – that old favourite – public fellatio. Needless to say, this might not be suitable for the whole family.

ArtSpan Open Studios

Various venues (861 9838/www.artspan.org). **Date** Oct.
Get up close to San Francisco's creative visionaries throughout the month of October. More than 900 artists' studios open up to the public, with a different neighbourhood getting to show off its work every weekend. You'll find a free map detailing participating venues and the Directory of San Francisco Artists in city bookshops.

Castro Street Fair

Market & Castro Streets, from 16th to 19th Streets, Castro (841 1824/www.castrostreetfair.org). Metro K, L, M to Castro/streetcar F/bus 24, 33, 35, 37. **Date** early Oct. **Map** p317 H10.
A taste of the softer side of gay life in San Francisco, this one-day fair – started in 1974 by gay city official Harvey Milk – features food, crafts and community activists' stalls, along with plenty of rainbow merchandise.

Fleet Week

Fisherman's Wharf & Piers 30-32, Embarcadero (705 5500/www.military.com/fleetweek). Streetcar F/bus 10, 15, 30, 39, 47/cable car Powell-Hyde or Powell-Mason. **Date** Oct. **Map** p314 & p315.
Since the mid 1980s, the US Navy's acrobatic Blue Angels have rattled nerves and torn up the skies over San Francisco on Columbus Day weekend. The fleet sails into San Francisco Bay on Saturday morning; a spectacular air show and free battleship tours follow. A noisy couple of days.

Berkeley Unicycling & Juggling Festival

King Middle School, 1781 Rose Street, at Grant Street, Berkeley (www.berkeleyjuggling.org/festival). BART North Berkeley. **Date** early Oct.
In addition to unicycling and juggling, you can also see staff twirling, plate spinning, devil stick flipping, yo-yoing– in all, pretty much anything that requires a keen sense of balance and superhuman dexterity – at this Berkeley festival. Workshops allow you to get in on the fun.

Burn, baby, burn

Even if they aren't 'burners', most San Franciscans know about Burning Man. The festival has become a part of Bay Area culture – hardly surprising as this is where it all began.

In 1986 Larry Harvey and 20 friends burned an eight-foot wooden man at Baker Beach. The event caught people's imagination and as the annual beach party grew, the size of the man grew too. By 1990, with the man standing at 40 feet and the party 800-strong, local police intervened and put a stop to the revels.

Determined that Burning Man shouldn't die, Harvey and 80 others trekked to an ancient lake bed or *playa* in Nevada's Black Rock desert, 90 miles north of Reno. A new festival was born, its location as remote as it is stunning, with seemingly endless salt plains framed by mountains. Attendance doubled annually over the first few years in Nevada. By 2007, around 40,000 people made what became known as Black Rock City the third-largest city in the state for one week.

The early '90s pioneers were armed with little more than camping gear and high spirits, but over the years Burning Man has evolved into a highly organised event with daily newspapers, radio stations and an airport. From oyster shacks and whisky bars to steam baths and circus rings, burners set up theme camps offering everything imaginable and unimaginable. And it's all free: the only things you can officially buy are coffee and ice.

Another principle is 'leave no trace' or 'pack it in, pack it out'. The level of eco-consciousness is cheering: you won't see people littering. But, of course, the festival does leave a trace: it takes a lot

of energy to power the generators for a week, and 40,000 people consume a lot when they're partying in the desert.

Those thinking of attending should remember that for all its beauty, the desert can be unforgiving. Some years have seen white-outs (dust storms) with winds that blow tents away, freezing cold nights and blistering hot days. The elements make burners earn their good time. Participants are required to bring everything they could possibly need for a week in hardcore desert conditions: food and enough water (a gallon a day); a bicycle for getting around (preferably adorned with lights and decorations); and dust masks and goggles to brave the intense storms.

Lavish costumes, ingenious interactive sculptures and 'art cars' are optional. Theme camps spend weeks planning, days building and many hands working to create their art in their little section of the city, for the entertainment of their fellow burners, just to take it apart a week later.

So why do people go to so much effort to spend a week in such an extreme environment? According to burners, its down to the spirit of the occasion, which is unique and makes Burning Man far more than just a festival; many express an enthusiasm that verges on the religious. It's partly about a sense of belonging. Burners feel like a social group in West Coast society, if not across the US; the group Burners without Borders works year round on projects like building houses for Katrina victims or reconstruction following the earthquake in Peru. What started as a renegade beach party has developed into a community ethos and culture that extends well beyond that week in the desert.

Of course it's not everyone's cup of tea. Assuming you can handle the weather, if you don't love being surrounded by masses of dusty, costumed merrymakers off their heads after a week of excessive drug use, it might not be your scene. But whether you love it or hate it, it will certainly make an impression. The only way to find out is to go and see for yourself.

For almost everything you need to know go to www.burningman.com.

Arts & Entertainment

Exotic Erotic Ball

Cow Palace, 2600 Geneva Avenue, at Santos Street, Daly City (1-888 396 8426/www.exoticerotic ball.com). Bus 9, 9AX. **Tickets** $50-$150. **Credit** MC, V. **Date** late Oct.

It's obnoxious. It's exploitative. It's the bridge-and-tunnel crowd's annual excuse to pull on the latex and fishnets and party with other desperate housewives at the world's largest indoor masquerade ball.

Halloween San Francisco

Market Street, from 15th to Castro Streets; Castro Street, from Market to 19th Streets, Castro. Metro K, L, M to Castro/streetcar F/bus 24, 33, 35, 37. **Date** 31 Oct. **Map** p317 H10.

City Hall's doomed attempts to divert joyful Halloween revellers from the traditional fray in the Castro to the staid Civic Center have proved as unpopular as last year's pumpkin pie. So pop on your fright wig, head for the Castro, duck through the SFPD cordon and discover a land where dressed-up drag queens and half-naked pagans cavort. Leave the booze behind, though.

Día de los Muertos

24th & Bryant Streets, Mission (826 8009/www. dayofthedeadsf.org). Bus 27, 33, 48. **Date** 2 Nov. **Map** p319 M12.

Marchers gather at 24th and Bryant Streets to celebrate the Mexican Day of the Dead. After a traditional blessing, the music starts and the procession begins: Aztec dancers, children in papier-mâché skeleton masks and women clutching bouquets of dead flowers. Things wind up in Garfield Square, where people leave candles at a huge community altar. Dress code: dark but showy. If you really want to blend in, paint your face a ghoulish white and bring a noise-maker.

Miss Trannyshack Pageant

The Gift Center, 888 Brannan Street, at 8th Street, SOMA (www.trannyshack.com). Bus 10, 12, 19, 27, 47. **Admission** $35-$45. Date Nov. **Map** p314 K5.

An array of gender-bending beauties face off in a showdown for the coveted Miss Trannyshack tiara. Judges include local luminaries and minor celebrities.

Holiday Lighting Festivities

Union Square, between Geary, Powell, Post & Stockton Streets, Downtown; Ghirardelli Square, 900 North Point Street, at Polk Street, Fisherman's Wharf (http://gosanfrancisco.about.com). **Date** late Nov. **Map** p315 M5; p314 K2.

The lights go on all over town as the holidays approach, including at the above locations. At Union Square, a 67ft (20m) living white-fir tree is decorated with 2,000 lights, 400 ornaments and 500 bows. A 22ft wooden menorah is also lit as part of the Jewish Hanukkah celebrations.

Run to the Far Side

Golden Gate Park (759 2690/www.calacademy.org/ runwild). **Entrance** $24-$30. **Date** weekend after Thanksgiving. **Map** p316.

As the name suggests, participants in this annual foot race, a fundraiser for the California Academy of Sciences, dress up as their favourite Gary Larson character. They then walk or run either a three- or six-mile course around beautiful Golden Gate Park.

Winter

New Year's Eve

Around the city. **Date** 31 Dec.

For many years, San Franciscans have been gathering at Union Square or Ocean Beach to ring in the New Year. The city fathers have been discouraging such impromptu revelry in recent times, however, so check local newspapers. Other traditional festivities taking place around town include a cavalcade of bands performing in tents along the Embarcadero.

Martin Luther King Jr Birthday Celebration

1-510 268 3777/www.norcalmlk.org). BART & Metro to Montgomery. **Date** Mon after 15 Jan. **Map** p315 N6.

The parade celebrating Martin Luther King's birthday started off at the Caltrain station in 2008, with a specially chartered Freedom Train bringing in passengers from the surrounding area. It ended with a rally in Civic Center. Check the website for the route for other years.

Tet Festival

Around Civic Center & the Tenderloin (885 2743/ www.vietccsf.org). **Date** Jan-Feb.

San Francisco has a large population of Vietnamese-Americans who, along with Cambodian, Latino and African-American families, transform the city centre into a multicultural carnival.

San Francisco Tribal, Folk & Textile Arts Show

Fort Mason Center, Marina Boulevard, at Laguna Street, Marina (1-310 455 2886/www.caskeylees. com/shows/8/tribal/sf). Bus 10, 22, 28, 30, 47, 49. **Admission** $12; free under-16s. **No credit cards**. **Date** early Feb. **Map** p314 H2.

Part-show, part-sale: upwards of 100 folk and ethnic-art dealers sell all manner of pottery, baskets, textiles and jewellery.

Chinese New Year

Market Street, at 2nd Street, and around Chinatown (982 3071/www.chineseparade.com). **Date** Feb. **Map** p311 H3.

The start of the Chinese New Year offers the city's best parade that doesn't involve public nudity. With colourful beauty pageants, drumming, martial arts competitions, mountains of food on every street corner, endless firework displays and a huge procession of dancing dragons, acrobats and stilt-walkers, the party turns the city jubilant and upside down. It's also the occasion of the enormously popular Annual Treasure Hunt (www.sftreasurehunts.com), which gets nearly 1,600 people scurrying round Chinatown.

Children

There are plenty of thrills in them there hills.

Exploratorium. *See p205.*

Going *tête-à-tête* with belching sea lions, watching whales spout off the coast, running wild in Golden Gate Park, driving down crazy, twisting Lombard Street – the City by the Bay is like a 49-square-mile amusement park. Luckily, not only are there are enough attractions to keep children of all ages amused for weeks, but many of them will appeal to parents too.

Details of most special events and festivals can be found in the Sunday pink section of the *San Francisco Chronicle* (www.sfgate.com) or in *SF Weekly* (www.sfweekly.com). If you're itching to escape the city, hire a car or hop on a BART train and find a whole new range of activities and attractions over in the East Bay (*see pp124-29*), the best of which we also list in this chapter.

If you feel the need for a break from the children, many hotels have their own childcare service these days. Otherwise, get in touch with the **American ChildCare Service** (415 285 2300, www.americanchildcare.com). Adventurous youngsters will also enjoy the monthly **Kids' Night Out**, a safe overnight party for five- to 13-year-olds, supervised by the Presidio Community YMCA (447 9615, www.ymcasf.org/presidio).

San Francisco attractions & museums

In addition to the places reviewed below, San Francisco's gorgeous **Main Library** (100 Larkin Street, between Grove & Hyde Streets) has a Children's Center, which includes a storytelling room, a creative area for crafts and performances, and even a teenagers' drop-in section. If you're stuck for something to do, it's always worth contacting one of the 30 local libraries to see what events are being put on that week; full contact details can be found at www.sfpl.org. San Francisco museums of equal interest to kids and grown-ups include the **Cable Car Museum** (*see p83*) and the **San Francisco Maritime Museum** (*see p94*).

One of the city's major child-friendly sights, the **California Academy of Sciences** (321 8000, www.calacademy.org), along with its impressive Steinhart Aquarium, is relocating to a landmark new 'green' building at its former Golden Gate Park site, set to open in autumn 2008. Once reopened, the Academy will house 38,000 live animals, as well as the remodelled Morrison Planetarium.

The kids are alright (now)

... thanks to some super-snazzy playground updates.

In this city where adults outnumber children five to one and where the term 'swinging' is more often used to describe an adult 'lifestyle' rather than what kids do in the park, it's good to know that in one arena at least, children are having the last word. Playgrounds, for years the afterthought of park planners, are in the midst of a renaissance all around San Francisco. In the last several years, close to a dozen parks have been overhauled and renovated with innovative, artful and parent-pleasing features such as cushioned rubber mats, spider-web climbing nets, spinning bars, wave walls, water canals, and structures designed to promote motor-skill development, balance, strategy and co-ordination.

The biggest addition to the panoply is the **Koret Children's Quarter** in Golden Gate Park, which reopened in 2007 on the site of the Children's Playground, built in 1887 as America's first playground. The expansive park (across from Sharon Meadow, between Kezar Drive & Stanyan Street) is a whimsical tribute to the San Francisco Bay landscape, with a treehouse village, climbing wave walls, sea caves, tidepools and a huge climbing net with a lookout perch. Planners also restored the historic Herschell-Spillman Carousel at the west end of the playground, and the death-defying cement slides, which kids careen down using pieces of cardboard as sleds.

Another remarkable metamorphosis has taken place at the **Walter Haas Playground** in the Diamond Heights district in the south of the city (between Diamond Heights Boulevard and Addison Street). Once a desolate patch where empty swings rocked eerily in the fog like a scene from a Stanley Kubrick movie, it received a makeover that transformed it into a glorious grassy acre that now gives equal space to sand-sifting and tricycle-pedalling toddlers, monkey-bar-swinging preschoolers, and hoop-shooting teenagers. The views of the city skyline and the Bay are amazing too.

On a prime piece of real estate in the Presidio, **Julius Kahn Playground** (West Pacific Avenue, off Arguello Boulevard) attracts its fair share of posh nannies from surrounding Pacific Heights mansions, especially since its 2003 overhaul. The sunny, sheltered park offers a mini-climbing wall, spinning cups, a spiderweb dome and a sand canal fed by a slow-drip water spigot, as well as picnic tables and a clubhouse for arts and crafts.

Across town in the Sunset District, an area frequently shrouded in freezing fog, **Parkside Square** (Vicente Street & 26th Avenue) has become a surprisingly balmy oasis since its renovation a few years ago. The knoll above Stern Grove is surrounded by ball fields and basketball courts and features two colourful play structures for older and younger children that include running ramps, a pirate ship, tube slides, springy seesaws, and swinging bars. There's also a giant climbing dome, a sand area, and – bonus for parents – in the summer, you can hear music filtering up from the free Sunday Stern Grove concerts.

Koret Children's Quarter.

Aquarium of the Bay

Pier 39, Embarcadero at Beach Street, Fisherman's Wharf (1-888 732 3483/www.aquariumofthebay. com). Metro F to Pier 39/bus 10, 15, 30, 39, 47/ cable car Powell-Mason. **Open** *May-Sept* 9am-8pm daily. *Oct-Apr* 10am-6pm Mon-Thur; 10am-7pm Fri-Sun. **Admission** $13.95; $7.50 3-11s; $33.95 family. **Credit** MC, V. **Map** p314 L1.

Clear, acrylic underwater tunnels give visitors a diver's-eye view of the Bay, while moving walkways take you through 300ft (91m) of water, past more than 23,000 aquatic creatures. Upstairs, there are several touch-tide pools with urchins and bat rays. If you've got time, combine your visit with an island hop or Bay cruise. Blue & Gold Fleet (705 5555, www.blueandgoldfleet.com) offers hour-long Bay cruises, as well as trips to Angel Island, departing from Pier 39. Alcatraz Island Cruises (981 7625, www.alcatrazcruises.com) does two-and-a-half-hour and half-day tours of Alcatraz and Angel Islands, departing from nearby Pier 33; for details, *see pp92*.

Exploratorium

3601 Lyon Street, at Marina Boulevard, Marina (563 7337/www.exploratorium.edu). Bus 28, 30, 76. **Open** 10am-5pm Tue-Sun. **Admission** $13; $10 13-17s, discounts; $8 4-12s; free under-4s. Free 1st Wed of mth. **Credit** AmEx, MC, V. **Map** p313 E2.

Housed in the historic Palace of Fine Arts, the Exploratorium has over 600 interactive exhibits about science, art and human perception. A highlight is the Tactile Dome, a geodesic hemisphere of total blackness in which you try to identify various objects; book in advance (561 0362, $16). Another highlight is the Wave Organ, located nearby on the water's edge (*see p119*). Sea waves rush in underneath, pushing air up through the organ's tubes to create a symphony of eerie tones and sighs. *Photos p203*.

Jeremiah O'Brien Liberty Ship

Pier 45, Embarcadero, at Taylor Street, Fisherman's Wharf (544 0100/www.ssjeremiahobrien.com). Metro to Fisherman's Wharf/bus 10, 15, 30, 39, 47/cable car Powell-Mason. **Open** 10am-4pm daily. **Admission** $9; $5 discounts; $4 6-14s; free under-6s; $20 family. **No credit cards.** Map p314 K1.

There's plenty for history buffs big and small to explore aboard the *Jeremiah O'Brien*, a veteran of D-Day and the only original ship to sail under its own steam to the 50th anniversary of the Allied invasion at Normandy. From the faithfully restored engine room to the officers' bunk rooms, it's a fascinating bit of World War II arcana. It occasionally leaves dock for cruises, so be sure to call ahead. At Pier 43, between Hyde & Jefferson Streets, you'll also find a flotilla of turn-of-the-19th-century ships, including the three-mast, square-rigged *Balclutha* (*see p93*). The San Francisco Maritime Museum (*see p94*), closed for restoration until 2009, is nearby.

Randall Museum

199 Museum Street, off Roosevelt Way, Buena Vista (554 9600/www.randallmuseum.org). Bus 24, 37. **Open** 10am-5pm Tue-Sat. **Admission** free.

This small museum offers panoramic views of the city and hands-on fun for pre-teens, including an exhibit where they can create their own earthquake. Otherwise, visit the animal corral or drop in for Saturday arts-and-crafts classes.

San Francisco Zoo

Sloat Boulevard, at 47th Avenue, Sunset (753 7080/ www.sfzoo.org). Metro to SF Zoo/bus 18, 23. **Open** *Main zoo* 10am-5pm daily. *Children's zoo* Memorial Day-Labor Day 10.30am-4.30pm daily. Labor Day-Memorial Day 11am-4pm daily. **Admission** $11; $8 12-17s; $5 3-11s; free under-3s. Free 1st Wed of mth. **Credit** AmEx, MC, V.

The three-acre African Savanna, new Grizzly Gulch, and the expansive Lemur Forest are highlights of the zoo, where more than 1,000 species of mammals and birds make their home. Combine your visit with a walk along Ocean Beach and maybe lunch at the Beach Chalet or Louis' Diner. You can look out for whales in January and February.

Zeum

221 4th Street, at Howard Street, SoMa (777 2800/ www.zeum.org). Bus 12, 30, 45. **Open** 11am-5pm Wed-Sun. **Admission** $7; $6 discounts; $5 4-18s. **Credit** AmEx, MC, V. **Map** p315 N6.

Budding auteurs can direct their own videos at this lively art and technology centre. There are also workshops for creating sculptures and experimenting with computer-aided animation design. Nearby you'll find a bowling alley, a children's playground, an ice rink, a garden and a carousel.

Parks & beaches

There are many child-friendly attractions near **Fisherman's Wharf** (*see pp91-92*). The best are the historic ships at Hyde Street Pier and, at Pier 45, the **Musée Mécanique** (*see p94*), the submarine USS *Pampanito* (*see p94*) and the *Jeremiah O'Brien* (*see above*). There's a pack of rather boisterous sea lions in permanent residence on the docks at Pier 39, where you'll also find a carousel, a games arcade and street performers (*see p206*). The wharf is also the departure point for trips to Angel Island (*see p93*). Organised outings from here include the excellent Fire Engine Tour (*see p65*).

  Golden Gate Park attracts flocks of families at weekends, especially Sundays, when the main drive is closed to cars. Kids will want to head straight for Stow Lake, where they can hike out to Strawberry Hill or rent bicycles, paddle- and rowboats. Visit Spreckels Lake to marvel at the model boats (at Kennedy Drive & 35th Avenue), then wander down to the buffalo paddock to see the small herd of bison that have been residents in the park since 1892. The younger set will enjoy the Koret Children's Quarter playground (*see p204* **The kids are alright (now)**) and the nearby carousel. For more on Golden Gate Park, *see p109*. For a walk on the wilder side, head over to **Ocean Beach** (*see p117* **On the beach**). If it's cold, warm up with a hot chocolate in the Park Chalet.

Other Bay Area attractions & museums

In addition to the places featured below, several other East Bay attractions are great for kids. The **Chabot Space & Science Museum** (*see p126*) in Oakland is possibly the next best thing to space travel; Berkeley's **Lawrence Hall of Science** (*see p129*) is also terrific and very hands-on. The **Oakland Zoo** (*see p127*) is well worth a visit. And if you're heading south, don't miss the world-renowned **Monterey Bay Aquarium** (*see p278*).

Bay Area Discovery Museum

East Fort Baker, 557 McReynolds Road, Sausalito (339 3900/www.baykidsmuseum.org). Blue & Gold Fleet ferry from Pier 41, or Golden Gate ferry from Ferry Building. **Open** 9am-4pm Tue-Fri; 10am-5pm Sat, Sun. **Admission** $8.50 adults; $7.50 children; free under-1s. Free 2nd Sat of mth after 1pm. **No credit cards.**

This hands-on museum, located just below the north ramp of the Golden Gate Bridge and boasting spectacular skyline views, offers a load of hands-on activities for kids of ten and under. There's Lookout Cove, an expansive outdoor area with a sea cave, climbable shipwreck and miniature Golden Gate Bridge. Tot Spot gives toddlers their own indoor/outdoor nirvana, with a plastic trout-packed waterway, climbing structures and animal costumes.

Children's Fairyland

699 Bellevue Avenue, at Lake Merritt, Oakland (1-510 452 2259/www.fairyland.org). BART 19th Street/Oakland. **Open** times vary. **Admission** $6, incl unlimited rides. **Credit** MC, V.

Legend has it that Walt Disney was so taken with this whimsical theme park when he saw it in 1950 that he decided to build his own. Kids can follow Alice down the rabbit hole, ride a tiny Ferris wheel and catch daily puppet shows. There's also a pirate ship and toddler-sized houses to climb through.

Marine Mammal Center

1065 Fort Cronkhite, Sausalito (289 7325/www. tmmc.org). Visitor Centre 1049 Fort Cronkhite. Blue & Gold Fleet ferry from Pier 41, or Golden Gate ferry from Ferry Building. **Open** 10am-4pm daily. **Centre is closed until spring 2009; visitor centre remains open at times stated**. **Admission** free.

Visit the sea lions and sea otters at this non-profit centre, which rescues sick or stranded animals, nurtures them back to health and returns them to the Pacific. Spring is pupping season, and also the period when you can see most animals. Note that the centre reopens in spring 2009.

Parks & beaches

Toddlers will love the steam trains, farm animals and carousel ride at Berkeley's **Tilden Park** (1-510 562 7275, www.ebparks.org). Kids of all ages enjoy picnics at the park's Lake Anza, where the water is warm enough for a summer swim.

Shops & entertainment

826 Valencia

826 Valencia Street, between 19th & 20th Streets, Mission (642 5905/www.826valencia.org). BART 24th Street/bus 14, 26, 48, 49, 67. **Open** Drop-in tutoring 2.30-5.30pm Mon-Thur, Sun. *Pirate store* noon-6pm daily. **Admission** free. **Map** p318 K11.

Local literary lion Dave Eggers opened this non-profit kids' writing centre in 2002, an essential destination for those travelling with young aspiring scribes. In addition to offering workshops and free drop-in tutoring for children aged eight to 18, 826 is the Bay Area's only independent pirate supply store.

Metreon

4th Street, at Mission Street, SoMa (369 6000/www. metreon.com). BART or Metro to Powell/bus 14, 15, 30, 45 & Market Street routes. **Open** 10am-10pm daily. **Map** p315 N6.

Like it or not, pre-teens and teens will track down this mixed bag of shopping and entertainment. There's the Games Workshop (where you can paint your toy purchases for free), a high-tech arcade (complete with virtual bowling), an anime shop and a 15-screen Loews movie complex with an IMAX theatre. Parents can take infants to screenings at 11am on Mondays.

Pier 39

Beach Street & the Embarcadero, Fisherman's Wharf (705 5500/www.pier39.com). Metro to Pier 39/bus 10, 15, 30, 39, 47/cable car Powell-Mason. **Open** *Jan, Feb* 10.30am-7pm Mon-Thur, Sun; 10am-9pm Fri, Sat. *Mar-mid May, mid Sept-Oct* 10am-8pm Mon-Thur, Sun; 10am-9pm Fri, Sat. *Mid May-mid Sept* 10am-9pm Mon-Thur, Sun; 10am-10pm Fri, Sat. *Nov, Dec* 10.30am-8pm Mon-Thur, Sun; 10.30am-9pm Fri, Sat. **Map** p314 L1.

A bustling tourist trap, all T-shirt shops and traders flogging Celtic art and music boxes, plus street performers, restaurants, a games arcade, a carousel and kayak rentals. If you can handle the schlock, there are beautiful views and playful (or bickering) sea lions.

Circus skills

The **Circus Center** (755 Frederick Street, at Arguello Boulevard, 759 8123, www.circus center.org) offers courses in acrobatics, clowning and the trapeze. Most classes last several weeks, so call for details. **Acrosports** (639 Frederick Street, at Willard Street, 665 2276, www. acrosports.org) runs gymnastics, tumbling and circus classes for kids as young as two.

Film

Reel life in the City by the Bay.

The **Castro Theatre** is a glorious reminder of SF's neighbourhood film palaces. *See p209.*

With its distinctive neighbourhoods, impossibly steep streets and picture-postcard backdrop, San Francisco has long attracted film directors. The city has starred in many films, from vintage classics like *The Maltese Falcon* and *Vertigo* to modern offerings such as *Interview with the Vampire* and *The Hulk*. Cinema's fascination with Alcatraz (*see p93*) has been especially strong, with the former prison featuring in everything from *Escape from Alcatraz* and *The Rock* to *X-Men: The Last Stand*.

Of course, San Francisco's long-standing love affair with the movies goes far beyond its reputation as one of the world's finest locations. Its citizens' passion for cinema and its fertile creative environment have combined to foster everything from the digital-effects revolution of George Lucas's Industrial Light & Magic (ILM; *see p120* **Spatial effects**) and Pixar Studios to the birth of the Asian-American and gay and lesbian film movements in the Bay Area.

In addition to the city's many cinematic special events (*see p210* **Festivals**), the real draw for visiting film junkies is San Francisco's wealth of neighbourhood theatres. Constructed between 1910 and 1930 to serve the newly built residential districts that had sprouted up along the city's streetcar lines, the city's single-screen cinemas flourished through World War II, showing films after their initial run at the larger Market Street movie houses. While many have been lost over the years to land developers and competition from the multiscreens, several have survived thanks to the efforts of groups such as the **San Francisco Neighborhood Theater Foundation** (www.sfneighborhoodtheater. org). The jewel among these picture palaces is the **Castro Theatre** (*see p209*), a glamorous blend of Spanish, Italian and oriental decor with a glazed-tile foyer and a vertical neon sign that hark back to a time when a night at the movies was an enchanted evening.

Arts & Entertainment

My beautiful laundrette: **Star Wash**.

The screening of movies isn't just limited to conventional cinemas, however. You can spill soup all over yourself at movie restaurant **Foreign Cinema** (see p162) or catch a flick while you're working up a sweat on the treadmill: at the **Alhambra Crunch** gym (2330 Polk Street, between Green & Union Streets, Russian Hill, 292 5444, www.crunch.com), housed in what was once an art deco movie house, feature films play on a big screen in the main exercise area. You can even get a cinematic fix while washing your clothes: gaze upon stills of screen idols during the rinse cycle at **Star Wash** (see p187).

INFORMATION AND TICKETS

You can usually buy tickets direct from cinema box offices immediately before a screening. Many cinemas also run bargain-price matinées: contact the venue directly for details. For local listings, check any of the main print media outlets: the *Chronicle*, the *Examiner*, *SF Weekly* and the *Bay Guardian* all carry film listings, and the *Chronicle*'s website, www.sfgate.com, lists all local films online, along with a handy selection of critics' favourites. Showtimes, locations and tickets are also available by phone from **Moviefone** (777 3456, www.movietickets.com) or from **Fandango** (1-800 326 3264, www.fandango.com), but there's a $1 surcharge per ticket. A select few venues, including the Castro and the Roxie, also offer credit card bookings through **Ticketweb** (www.ticketweb.com).

Mainstream cinemas

As elsewhere, the steady decline of San Francisco's movie palaces was hastened by the rise of the massive modern multiplexes: with its gleaming escalators and long hallways, the **Sundance Kabuki** (1881 Post Street, at Fillmore Street, 929 4650, www.sundancecinemas.com) in Japantown, the 14-screen **AMC 1000 Van Ness** (1000 Van Ness Avenue, at O'Farrell Street, 1-800 231 3307, www.amctheatres.com) on the edge of the Tenderloin, and SoMa's 15-screen **AMC Metreon** (4th Street, at Mission Street, 369 6201, www.metreon.com) and new nine-screen **Century San Francisco Centre** (835 Market Street, between 4th & 5th Streets, 538 8422, www.cinemark.com), located in the city's swankiest shopping mall, have all the warm ambience, classy design and individuality of an airport lobby. Still, the screens are state of the art, the seats are very comfortable and the sound systems are beyond reproach. The Sundance Kabuki also serves as the main venue for the San Francisco International Film Festival (see p210 **Festivals**).

Other movie houses within easy reach of the centre of town include the Marina's funky **Presidio** (2340 Chestnut Street, between Scott & Divisadero Streets, 776 2388), the four-screen **Opera Plaza Cinema** (601 Van Ness Avenue, at Golden Gate Avenue, 267 4893) and the **Embarcadero Cinema** (Building 1, Embarcadero Center, Battery Street, between Sacramento & Clay Streets, 352 0835), the last two among five quality movie houses that make up the **Landmark Theaters** chain (for details of the others, contact 267 4893 or visit www.landmarktheater.com).

Tickets at all of the cinemas mentioned above cost around $10; credit cards are accepted.

Repertory cinemas

San Francisco's repertory theatres often owe their charm to a winning combination of independent ownership and unique buildings, as exemplified by the **Castro Theatre**, the **Roxie** and the **Red Vic**. A repertory film scene also thrives in the East Bay (see p211), and the **San Francisco Cinematheque** (see p211) is renowned for putting on avant-garde screenings at a variety of other venues.

Castro Theatre

*429 Castro Street, at Market Street, Castro
(621 6120/www.thecastrotheatre.com). Metro to
Castro/streetcar F/bus 24, 33, 35, 37.* **Tickets** $9;
$6 reductions. **No credit cards. Map** p317 H10.

One of San Francisco's finest and best-loved repertory cinemas, this movie palace was built in 1922. It
became a registered landmark 55 years later, affording it proper protection. These days it's a dream space
of classical murals and rare old film posters, with ceilings that shimmer with gold and films introduced to
the strains of a Mighty Wurlitzer organ. *Photo p207.*

Red Vic

*1727 Haight Street, at Cole Street, Haight-Ashbury
(668 3994/www.redvicmoviehouse.com). Bus 6, 7,
33, 43, 66, 71.* **Tickets** $8.50; $5-$6.50 reductions.
No credit cards. Map p317 E9.

Old sofas, popcorn in wooden bowls with butter and
brewer's yeast, and a choice of films ranging from
revivals to the best current movies make you feel
right at home here. Tickets for matinées are $6.50; a
'punch card' buys four pairs of tickets and costs $27.

Roxie New College Film Center
& Little Roxie

*3117 16th Street, between Valencia & Guerrero
Streets, Mission (863 1087/www.roxie.com). BART
16th Street/bus 14, 22, 26, 33, 49, 53.* **Tickets** $9;
$5-$6 reductions. **No credit cards. Map** p318 J10.

World premières of cutting-edge documentaries,
classic *films noirs* and '60s horror flicks are only a
taste of the impressive range of films staged at the
Roxie. Next door's Little Roxie has a great projection set-up, a terrific sound system and a programme
of stuff too weird even for its wacky parent to
show. Both theatres are a bit down at heel, but the
gritty atmosphere just adds to the funkiness.
Tickets cost $6 for the first show on Wednesday,
Saturday or Sunday; discount cards for $30 grant
admission to six screenings.

Off-mainstream cinemas

With the **Little Roxie** (*see above*) and
the new **Ninth Street Independent Film
Center** (*see p211*), times are improving for
off-mainstream cinema. Longer-established
venues to look out for include the 278-seat
cinema in **SFMOMA** (*see p81*) and the
96-seat media screening room in the **Yerba
Buena Center for the Arts** (*see p255*),
where the programmes of contemporary
and experimental work are often themed
with the exhibitions showing at the time.
However, it's the **SF Cinematheque** (*see
p211*) that remains the major driving force
for innovative film in the city.

Films alfresco

San Francisco is a town that truly loves its
cinema, hosting dozens of film festivals every
year from the mainstream to the fringe. But
particularly appealing are those that bring
viewers out of the theatre and into the fresh
air. Grab a picnic basket, a blanket and a
bottle of wine and you're set for a romantic
or family-friendly film experience like no other.

The largest of the outdoor film festivals is
Film Night in the Park (453 4333, www.film
night.org), which features classics and family-
friendly fare from *Casablanca* to *Cars* on
Friday and Saturday evenings from June to
October, with screenings taking place in Marin
County's public parks (suggested donation
$5). The festival also spills over into San
Francisco, with free screenings in Downtown's
Union Square, the Mission's Dolores Park
and North Beach's Washington Square Park
throughout the summer and early autumn.

Elsewhere, the neighbourhood-focused
Bernal Heights Outdoor Cinema (641 8417,
www.bhoutdoorcine.org) showcases the work
of indie filmmakers living in and around this
most bohemian of locales, with featured
screenings ranging from arty animated shorts

to cutting-edge documentaries. Films, most
of them no more than half an hour long,
are shown for free in local parks throughout
September, with various meet-the-filmmaker
events after the show.

If you're looking for more subversive
fare, the **Overcooked Cinema/Zeitgeist
International Film Festival** (www.overcooked
cinema.com; $5) offers short films and
videos (all under 15 minutes) every second
Monday in June, July and August (9pm), with
screenings taking place at beloved biker bar
Zeitgeist (199 Valencia Street, at Duboce
Avenue, Mission, 255 7505), which has
a huge outdoor patio. Across the Bay,
Old Oakland Outdoor Cinema (1-510 238
4734, www.filmoakland.com) screens four
mainstream classics between July and
October on a closed-off block of 9th Street
between Broadway and Washington (chairs
provided!) The **Brainwash Movie Festival**
(Alliance for West Oakland Development
car park, 1357 5th Street, 273 1545, www.
brainwashm.com) screens fringe shorts by
local and international filmmakers at 9pm
on the weekend following 4 July.

Arts & Entertainment

Festivals Film

The Bay Area's love affair with film is amply demonstrated by the volume and variety of its film festivals. Works by local movie-makers mingle with international productions, and the quality varies from high to horrific. We've listed the major festivals, but there are other smaller seasons throughout the year.

Noir City

www.noircity.com. **Venues** Palace of Fine Arts; Balboa Theatre. **Date** Jan.
Two weeks of classic *film noir* – some famous, some obscure – with talks and other special events to add further spice.

Spike & Mike's Festival of Animation

1-858 459 8707/www.spikeandmike.com. **Venues** Victoria Theatre, Mission. **Date** late Feb-Apr.
Mainstream animators such as Nick Park have shown early works at Spike & Mike's cultish festival, but it's the 'Sick and Twisted' segment that really raises the bar.

San Francisco International Asian American Film Festival

863 0814/www.festival.asianamerican media.org. **Venues** various theatres. **Date** mid Mar.
One of the longest-running Asian-American filmmaking showcases in the US provides a meeting ground for ethnic communities of all types from around the globe.

San Francisco International Film Festival

561 5000/www.sfiff.org. **Venues** various theatres. **Date** mid Apr-early May.
This is North America's longest-running film festival (it turned 50 in 2007), and one of its best. More than 200 films are screened; the 80,000 tickets sell like hot starlets.

San Francisco International LGBT Film Festival

703 8650/www.frameline.org. **Venues** various theatres. **Date** late June.
A crucial part of the month-long Gay Pride festivities: both a potent political statement and an unbridled celebration, with features, shorts, docs and experimental works.

San Francisco Silent Film Festival

777 4908/www.silentfilm.org. **Venue** Castro Theatre, Castro. **Date** early-mid July.

Screenings at this three-day event have musical accompaniment by a pianist, a Wurlitzer organist, or anything from Indian duos to avant-garde chamber groups.

Jewish Film Festival

621 0556/www.sfjff.org. **Venues** various theatres. **Date** late July-early Aug.
The world's largest Jewish film festival, the SFJFF spends two weeks presenting contemporary (and some archival) films on Jewish culture.

Festival ¡Cine Latino!

www.latinofilmfestival.org. **Venues** various theatres. **Date** Nov.
The best recent works from Central and South America, from obscure pieces to major works.

MadCat Women's International Film Festival

436 9523/www.madcatfilmfestival.org. **Venues** various theatres. **Date** mid Sept & early Oct.
This radical, alternative women's film festival happens over three weeks, squeezing in pioneering films that range from earnest feminist polemics to raunchy sexploitation.

Arab Film Festival

564 1100/www.aff.org. **Venues** various theatres. **Date** Oct.
This inclusive mix of features, documentaries and shorts, which turns 12 in 2008, provides a lively and involving survey of Arab cinema of every stripe and style.

Mill Valley Film Festival

383 5256/www.finc.org. **Venues** Cine Arts Sequoia, Mill Valley; Rafael Film Center, San Rafael. **Date** early Oct.
One of the state's best-known and most influential film events offers dozens of new movies over ten days. There's also a six-day Videofest, star guests and kids' events.

Film Arts Festival of Independent Cinema

552 8760/www.filmarts.org. **Venues** various theatres. **Date** early Nov.
The essential festival for a real snapshot of NorCal independents. Programming for the six-day fest is drawn from Bay Area filmmakers, featuring documentary, experimental and traditional narrative pieces in formats that range from Super-8 shorts to high-end DV.

Arts & Entertainment

Artists' Television Access

992 Valencia Street, at 21st Street, Mission (824 3890/www.atasite.org). BART 24th Street Mission/Metro to Church & 18th Street/bus 14, 26, 48, 49, 67. **Tickets** $5-$20. **No credit cards.** **Map** p318 K11.
Experimental and unusual programming, including open screenings, usually Thursday to Sunday.

Jewish Community Center

3200 California Street, at Presidio Avenue, Presidio Heights (292 1233/www.jccsf.org). Bus 1, 2, 3, 4, 43. **Tickets** free-$24; $10-$12 reductions. **Credit** AmEx, DC, MC, V. **Map** p313 F5.
This 468-seat theatre hosts cutting-edge international Jewish-themed films and videos, and features offerings from the Jewish Film Festival (*see p210*). Keep an eye out, too, for cinema events at the new Contemporary Jewish Museum (*see p81*).

Ninth Street Independent Film Center

145 Ninth Street, between Mission & Howard Streets, SoMa (no phone/www.ninthstreet.org). Bus 14, 19. **Tickets** vary. **No credit cards.** **Map** p318 L8.
Eight arts organisations banded together to bring the work of independent filmmakers to the public, resulting in this state-of-the-art facility. Look for screenings from San Francisco Cinematheque (*see below*), city-wide filmmakers group the Film Arts Foundation, LGBT film group Frameline, the Center for Asian American Media and more.

San Francisco Cinematheque

Various venues (522 1990/www.sfcinematheque.org). **Tickets** $6-$10. **Credit** varies.
For the stuff you simply can't see anywhere else, be it documentary, feature film, animation or whatever, this is the name to look for. The Cinematheque offers 50 events a year from October to December and February to June at venues including the Yerba Buena Center (*see p255*), the Roxie New College Film Center (*see p209*) and the Ninth Street Independent Film Center (*see above*).

East Bay cinemas

The East Bay has an embarrassment of cinematic riches. As well as Berkeley's **Fine Arts Cinema** and **Pacific Film Archive**, there's the **Parkway** in Oakland and a wealth of film festivals (*see p210*). Keep an eye on the historic, art deco **Paramount Theatre** (2025 Broadway, at 20th Street, Oakland, 1-510 465 6400, www.paramounttheatre.com), which hopes to revive its movie programming in 2008.

Cerrito Speakeasy Theater

10070 San Pablo Avenue, between Fairmount & Central Avenues, El Cerrito (1-510 814 2400/ www.picturepubpizza.com). BART El Cerrito. **Tickets** $7; $5 matinées. **No credit cards.**

The Cerrito is the newer offshoot of the Parkway (*see below*) and offers much the same fare, including pizza and beer with your film. The first two Tuesday shows are for the 'Baby Brigade' (parents and children under one year). Weekends are devoted to the Cerrito Classics screenings of cinema standards. Thrillville's B movies (www.thrillville.net) are also shown both here and at the Parkway venue. At weekends, patrons aged 18 and under must be accompanied by an adult.

Naz8

Gateway Plaza Shopping Center, 39160 Paseo Padre Parkway, at Walnut Avenue, Fremont (1-510 797 2000/www.naz8.com). BART Fremont. **Tickets** $9.50; $6.50 reductions. **Credit** AmEx, DC, MC, V.
This 3,000-seat Bollywood bonanza mainly features first-run movies from India and Pakistan, but also shows films from Afghanistan, China, Korea, the Philippines and Taiwan. You can even gorge on samosas or kulfi. On Tuesdays, tickets for all seats are just $5.

Pacific Film Archive

2575 Bancroft Way, between Telegraph Avenue & Bowditch Street, Berkeley (1-510 642 1124/ www.bampfa.berkeley.edu). BART Downtown Berkeley, then AC Transit bus 7, 51. **Tickets** $9.50; $5.50-$6.50 reductions. **Credit** AmEx, DC, MC, V.
Just off the university campus, the PFA has a collection of more than 7,000 titles, including Soviet, US avant-garde and Japanese cinema. Some 650 of them are screened annually to a clued-up audience.

Parkway Speakeasy Theater

1834 Park Boulevard, at E 18th Street, Oakland (1-510 814 2400/www.picturepubpizza.com). BART Lake Merritt, then AC Transit bus 14. **Tickets** $6; $4 matinées. **No credit cards.**
Two separate screens (one has comfy chairs, the other regulation seats), a dinner menu, a friendly atmosphere… what's not to like? Along with mainstream movies, the Parkway hosts the Thrillville cult movie cabaret (www.thrillville.net), plus a variety of day and evening events for different ages. Sundays are family night, and the first two Monday screenings are for the 'Baby Brigade'. Otherwise, it's 21 and over on weekdays.

Foreign-language films

Venues around town offer screenings of European films in their original languages: try the **Alliance Française** (1345 Bush Street, between Polk & Larkin Streets, 775 7755, www.afsf.com) in Polk Gulch, the **Goethe Institut** (530 Bush Street, between Grant Avenue & Stockton Street, 263 8760, www.goethe.de/ins/us) near Union Square, and the **Istituto Italiano di Cultura** (425 Washington Street, between Sansome & Battery Streets, 788 7142, www.iic sanfrancisco.esteri.it) in the Financial District.

Galleries

Art and soul.

Diversity and provocation are deep-rooted in the city's art scene. Over the last decade, a multitude of new galleries have sprung up throughout the city. These upstarts join an already strong collection of well-established, world-class galleries to create a dynamism reflecting the 'anything goes' attitude that has been the city's hallmark since the Gold Rush.

The best way to tour the scene is by neighbourhood, crawling through various adjacent venues in one go. Galleries will often co-ordinate their openings with one another, setting the cheap wine flowing on either the first Thursday or last Saturday of each month.

INFORMATION

Pick up a copy of either the *SF Bay Area Gallery Guide* or the West Coast edition of the *Art Now Gallery Guide* – both are handy for addresses and details of individual shows or special events. The *San Francisco Arts Monthly* (www.sfarts.org) has a more complete calendar of monthly exhibitions, as well as music, dance and theatre listings. Copies can be found in bookshops, hotels, galleries and museums. In addition, Gallery Crawl (www.kqed.org/gallery crawl), a podcast for local broadcaster KQED, has up-to-date information about the local scene.

Downtown

Most of San Francisco's upscale commercial galleries can be found in the Union Square district. Two buildings, just doors apart on Geary Street, house a few dozen galleries between them, so are a great place to start.

49 Geary Street

49 Geary Street, between Kearny Street & Grant Avenue, Union Square. BART & Metro to Powell/bus 2, 3, 4, 9X, 30, 38, 45, 76 & Market Street routes/ cable car Powell-Hyde or Powell-Mason. **Map** p315 M5.

Art Exchange

4th floor (956 5750). **Open** 11.30am-5.30pm Tue-Sat. **No credit cards.**
The Art Exchange specialises in secondary market art, meaning that it handles the resale of artworks from private collections. The gallery is wide open, with works large and small covering every square inch of wall space. If you are looking to learn more about purchasing art as an investment, the Art Exchange's Claire Carlevaro is the person to talk to.

Fraenkel Gallery

4th floor (981 2661/www.fraenkelgallery.com). **Open** 10.30am-5.30pm Tue-Fri; 11am-5pm Sat. **Credit** (books only) DC, MC, V.
There is a whiff of the official about the Fraenkel, a photography gallery established in 1979. Is it the warm space, inspiring quiet contemplation, or the gallery's impressive roster of photographers (Diane Arbus, Richard Avedon, Nan Goldin, Robert Frank) that elicits such reverence? You decide.

Jack Fischer Gallery

Suite 440 (956 1178/www.jackfischergallery.com). **Open** 11am-5.30pm Tue-Sat. **Credit** DC, MC, V.
Fischer says that the work he exhibits is 'from the heart and the gut'. His tiny gallery is devoted to 'outsider' and self-taught artists, and is so intelligently curated, stuffed with passionate work full of raw energy and surprise, that one hardly notices the confines of the space itself.

Mark Wolfe Contemporary Art

Suite 202 (369 9404/wolfecontemporary.com). **Open** 10.30am-5.30pm Tue-Fri; 11am-5.30pm Sat. **Credit** DC, MC, V.
Wolfe moved his former Urbis Artium Gallery here in 2005 and began pursuing a more formal direction. The large space is impressive; the art runs from high-tech and conceptual to crafty and fun.

Robert Koch Gallery

5th floor (421 0122/www.kochgallery.com). **Open** 10.30am-5.30pm Tue-Sat. **Credit** DC, MC, V.
Representing contemporary giants like Edward Burtynsky, Sally Mann, David Parker and Bill Owens, Robert Koch's gallery has a bit of a museum feel. Specialising in modernist and experimental photography from the early to mid 20th century, Koch's shows can feel revelatory.

Stephen Wirtz Gallery

3rd floor (433 6879/www.wirtzgallery.com). **Open** 9.30am-5.30pm Tue-Fri; 10.30am-5.30pm Sat. **No credit cards.**
From Todd Hido's spooky suburban landscapes to Melanie Pullen's fashion victims and the Starn Twins' multimedia extravaganzas, Stephen Wirtz's exhibitions invariably prompt discussion. The large gallery boasts five distinct spaces where any number of provocative works might be on display. The gallery often launches young artists.

Toomey Tourell

Suite 417 (989 6444/www.toomey-tourell.com). **Open** 11am-5.30pm Tue-Fri; 11am-5pm Sat. **Credit** AmEx, DC, MC, V.

John Berggruen Gallery.

If you like your art big, shiny and a bit in your face, then stop off here. Featuring the likes of map artist Matthew Picton and 'book coroner' Brian Dettmer, the gallery has a playful side beneath all the polish.

77 Geary Street

77 Geary Street, between Kearny Street & Grant Avenue, Union Square. BART & Metro to Powell/bus 2, 3, 4, 9X, 30, 38, 45, 76 & Market Street routes/ cable car Powell-Hyde or Powell-Mason. **Map** p315 M5.

Marx & Zavettero Gallery

2nd floor (627 9111/www.marxzav.com). **Open** 10.30am-5.30pm Tue-Fri; 11am-5pm Sat. **Credit** AmEx, DC, MC, V.
Whether it is exhibiting David Hevel's pop icon animal sculptures, Michael Arcega's conceptual constructions or Adam 5100's enormous stencil paintings, this gallery feels like it must have access to an extra dimension, expanding its frontiers to accommodate each new artist's vision.

Patricia Sweetow Gallery

Mezzanine (788 5126/www.patriciasweetowgallery. com). **Open** 10.30am-5.30pm Tue-Fri; 10.30am-5pm Sat. **No credit cards.**
Sweetow recently relocated to 77 Geary, where she shows painting, photography and sculpture from both established and emerging artists. To get a feel for the gallery, check out Jamie Vasta's glitter paintings, Jonathan Burstein's collage portraits or Christian Nguyen's architectural charcoals.

Rena Bransten Gallery

2nd floor (982 3292/www.renabranstengallery.com). **Open** 10.30am-5.30pm Tue-Fri; 11am-5pm Sat. **Credit** DC, MC, V.
In business since 1974, Rena Bransten originally focused on ceramic sculpture. Today the gallery's stable is more diverse, including sculptor Ruth Asawa, conceptual artist Vik Muniz, photographer Rebeca Bollinger and the late ceramicist Viola Frey.

Union Square & around

Dolby Chadwick

Suite 205, 210 Post Street, between Stockton Street & Grant Avenue (956 3560/www.dolbychadwick gallery.com). BART & Metro to Montgomery or Powell/bus 2, 3, 4, 9X, 30, 38, 45, 76 & Market Street routes/cable car Powell-Hyde or Powell-Mason. **Open** 10am-6pm Tue-Fri; 11am-5pm Sat. **Credit** AmEx, DC, MC, V. **Map** p315 M5.
Don't be intimidated by the creaky ride up in the old lift; this gallery couldn't be friendlier. Tall windows frame a view as compelling as the art. There are paintings, drawings and monotypes by emerging and mid-career artists, many priced under $1,000.

Gallery Paule Anglim

14 Geary Street, at Market Street (433 2710/ www.gallerypauleanglim.com). BART & Metro to Powell/bus 2, 3, 4, 9X, 30, 38, 45, 76 & Market Street routes/cable car Powell-Hyde or Powell-Mason. **Open** 10am-5.30pm Tue-Fri; 10am-5pm Sat. **No credit cards.** **Map** p315 M5.
An unimpressive façade gives no indication of the airy, light-filled interior at Gallery Paule Anglim, which simultaneously houses a major and a minor show at any given time. Expect everything from Bay Area innovators such as David Ireland and Barry McGee to international superstars like Louise Bourgeois and Robert Bechtle.

John Berggruen Gallery

228 Grant Avenue, between Post & Sutter Streets (781 4629/www.berggruen.com). BART & Metro to Montgomery/bus 2, 3, 4, 9X, 30, 38, 45, 76 & Market Street routes/cable car Powell-Hyde or Powell-Mason. **Open** 9.30am-5.30pm Mon-Fri; 10.30am-5pm Sat. **No credit cards.** **Map** p315 M5.
Founded in the mid '70s, Berggruen, with its smooth white walls and sleek blond floors, has played host to some of the biggest names in contemporary art, including Ellsworth Kelly, Alexander Calder, Robert Rauschenberg, Brice Marden and Frank Stella.

Arts & Entertainment

John Pence

750 Post Street, between Jones & Leavenworth Streets (441 1138/www.johnpence.com). Bus 2, 3, 4, 27, 38, 76. **Open** *10am-6pm Mon-Fri; 10am-5pm Sat.* **Credit** *AmEx, DC, MC, V.* **Map** *p314 L5.*

John Pence is the largest gallery in San Francisco, established in 1974 and offering an impressive 8,000sq ft (750 sq m) of exhibition space. It is home to a diverse stable of academic realists and features a rotating series of themed group exhibitions.

SoMa & South Beach

111 Minna Gallery

111 Minna Street, between 2nd & New Montgomery Streets (974 1719/www.111minnagallery.com). BART & Metro to Montgomery/bus 9, 9X, 10, 12, 14, 30, 45, 76 & Market Street routes. **Open** *Gallery noon-5pm Tue-Fri. Bar 5-10pm Tue, Wed; 5pm-2am Thur-Sat.* **Admission** *$3-$15.* **Credit** *AmEx, DC, MC, V.* **Map** *p315 N5.*

Smartly morphing into a happening hotspot most nights, 111 Minna is a laid-back urban hangout that features great art, drinking, dancing and a monthly indie film series. The gallery is home to an impressive roster of local and international artists, with tunes spun by a peerless collection of jet-set DJs.

Andrea Schwartz Gallery

525 2nd Street, between Bryant & Brannan Streets (495 2090/www.asgallery.com). Metro to 2nd & King/bus 9X, 10, 30, 45, 76. **Open** *9am-5pm Mon-Fri; 1-5pm Sat.* **Credit** *AmEx, DC, MC, V.* **Map** *p315 O6.*

This large space is aggressively modern, with steel girders, concrete floors and two walls of plate glass. The work is equally contemporary, featuring artists along the lines of Jorge Santos and Seamus Conley.

Braunstein/Quay

430 Clementina Street, between 5th & 6th Streets (278 9850/www.braunsteinquay.com). Bus 9X, 12, 14, 26, 27, 47. **Open** *11am-5.30pm Tue-Sat.* **No credit cards. Map** *p319 M7.*

Founded in the early 1960s, Braunstein/Quay made its reputation promoting Bay Area talents and launching several influential artists, among them the late ceramics master Peter Voulkos. Braunstein likes to mix things up, presenting various forms of sculpture, glass, furniture and fibre in a fine arts setting.

Catherine Clark Gallery

150 Minna Street, between 3rd & New Montgomery Streets (399 1439/www.cclarkgallery.com). BART & Metro to Montgomery/bus 9, 9X, 10, 12, 14, 30, 45, 76 & Market Street routes. **Open** *10.30am-5.30pm Tue-Fri; 11am-5.30pm Sat.* **Credit** *AmEx, DC, MC, V.* **Map** *p315 M5.*

Clark has a keen eye for modern art with legs: many works by her stable of sculptors, painters and mixed-media artists walk straight into regional museums. She recently moved here, behind SFMOMA, where she continues to provoke with a fun, slightly political bent. The gallery is one of few in town to specialise in video art, running a new one with each exhibition.

Crown Point Press

20 Hawthorne Street, between Howard & Folsom Streets, SoMa (974 6273/www.crownpoint.com). BART & Metro to Montgomery/bus 12, 15, 30, 45, 76. **Open** *10am-6pm Tue-Sat.* **Credit** *DC, MC, V.* **Map** *p315 N6.*

Crown Point is the world's leading publisher of etchings. Richard Tuttle, Laura Owens and other established artists work in print studios on the premises; their prints are then shown in the gallery's large, airy and inviting space.

Gallery 16

501 3rd Street, at Bryant Street (626 7495/www.gallery16.com). Metro to 2nd & King/bus 9X, 10, 30, 45, 47, 76. **Open** *9am-5pm Mon-Fri; 11am-5pm Sat.* **Credit** *AmEx, DC, Disc, MC, V.* **Map** *p319 O7.*

Gallery 16 publishes limited edition artist prints and books through its collaboration with Urban Digital Color. The gallery recently relocated to a huge space that features a wall of windows looking out on to 3rd Street, filling it with light.

MM Galleries

101 Townsend Street, Suite 207, at 2nd Street (543 1550/www.mmgalleries.com). Metro to 2nd & King/bus 9X, 10, 30, 45, 76. **Open** *11am-5pm Tue-Fri; noon-4pm Sat.* **Credit** *DC, Disc, MC, V.* **Map** *p319 O7.*

Marina and Kit, MM's co-owners and co-curators, may be more aptly described as co-conspirators. Seeing art as play, they bring a sense of mischief to every show. MM is a comfortable space, and each exhibition has a casual, accessible feel that belies the gallery's acumen for recognising serious talent.

Modernism

685 Market Street, between 3rd & New Montgomery Streets (541 0461/www.modernisminc.com). BART & Metro to Montgomery/bus 2, 3, 4, 31 & Market Street routes. **Open** *10am-5.30pm Tue-Sat.* **Credit** *AmEx, DC, MC, V.* **Map** *p315 N5.*

Modernism grapples with the age-old conundrum of how to show fine art that attracts high prices while maintaining a hospitable atmosphere. And loses. If you're not rich and conservatively dressed, there's a good chance you won't feel comfortable. A shame, as the art is amazing.

New Langton Arts

1246 Folsom Street, between 8th & 9th Streets (626 5416/www.newlangtonarts.org). Bus 9, 12, 19, 27, 47. **Open** *noon-6pm Tue-Sat.* **Credit** *DC, MC, V.* **Map** *p318 L8.*

At the forefront of the visual and media arts scene, this diminutive non-profit space is in a first-floor loft behind an unprepossessing black façade. Best known for installations and performance pieces, it also runs lively art and photography lectures.

SF Camerawork

2nd floor, 657 Mission Street, between New Montgomery & 3rd Streets (512 2020/www.sf camerawork.org). BART & Metro to Montgomery/ streetcar F/bus 9, 9X, 10, 14, 30, 45, 76 & Market

Street routes. **Open** noon-5pm Tue-Sat. **Admission** (suggested donation) $5; $2 reductions. **Credit** DC, MC, V. **Map** p315 N6.

This non-profit institution is devoted to supporting photographers. Founded in 1974, it recently relocated to a huge space around the corner from SFMOMA. The gallery still focuses on photography but has expanded its remit to include film, video, installation art and other related media.

Varnish Fine Art

77 Natoma Street, between 1st & 2nd Streets (222 6131/www.varnishfineart.com). BART & Metro to Montgomery/bus 9, 9X, 10, 12, 14, 30, 45, 76 & Market Street routes. **Open** 11am-11pm Tue-Fri; 1-5pm Sat. **Credit** AmEx, DC, MC, V. **Map** p315 N5.

Specialising in cast metal sculpture – and an excellent taste in wine – Varnish's core belief is that viewing art should be fun. This combination art gallery, library and wine bar is a great spot to meet for drinks before dinner and a good place to find new works by emerging artists.

The Mission & the Castro

Adobe Books

3166 16th Street, between Guerrero & Valencia Streets (864 3936). BART to 16th Street Mission/bus 14, 22, 26, 33, 49, 53. **Open** 11am-midnight daily. **Credit** DC, MC, V. **Map** p318 J10.

It may look like a used book store – which it is – but in the back of Adobe lies a tiny yet influential gallery run by a collective of Mission artists. Openings often feature in-store musical performances.

Creativity Explored

3245 16th Street, between Dolores & Guerrero Streets (863 2108/www.creativityexplored.org). BART to 16th Street Mission/Metro to Church/bus 14, 22, 26, 33, 49, 53. **Open** 10am-3pm Mon-Fri; 1-6pm Sat. **Credit** DC, MC, V. **Map** p318 J10.

The gallery at this non-profit space features the art of developmentally disabled artists who create, exhibit and sell their work on the premises. Be careful with your wallet, especially at the annual Halloween show, where some of the coolest portraits and abstracts in the city can be yours for under $100.

Eleanor Harwood Gallery

1295 Alabama Street, at 25th Street (282 4248/www.eleanorharwood.com). BART 24th Street Mission/bus 27, 33, 48. **Open** 1-5pm Thur-Sat & by appointment. **Credit** DC, Disc, MC, V. **Map** p318 L12.

The Eleanor Harwood Gallery, established in 2006 by one of the former curators at Adobe Books (*see above*), is devoted to young locals such as Spencer Mack, Alison Blickle and Jill Sylvia.

Galeria de la Raza

2857 24th Street, at Bryant Street (826 8009/www.galeriadelaraza.org). BART to 24th Street/bus 9, 27, 33, 48. **Open** noon-6pm Wed-Sat. **Credit** DC, MC, V. **Map** p319 M12.

This storefront gallery has celebrated contemporary Chicano/Latino culture since 1970 with bi-monthly exhibitions and the ongoing (Re)Generation project, designed to support young Latino artists.

Lab

2948 16th Street, at Capp Street (864 8855/www.thelab.org). BART to 16th Street Mission/bus 12, 14, 22, 33, 49, 53. **Open** 1-6pm Wed-Sat, during exhibitions. **Credit** DC, MC, V. **Map** p318 K10.

Located on a seedy corner, the Lab favours political and subversive photography, paintings and multimedia works. Its auctions, held several times a year, can be counted on for edgy pieces at decent prices.

Little Tree

3412 22nd Street, at Guerrero Street (643 4929/www.littletreegallery.com). BART to 24th Street Mission/Metro to Church & 24th Street/bus 14, 26, 48, 49, 67. **Open** noon-6pm Wed-Sat. **Credit** AmEx, DC, MC, V. **Map** p318 J12.

This intimate gallery mounts gorgeous, affordable art in a laid-back yet professional setting. Featuring witty and accomplished emerging artists, Little Tree crams a great deal of fun into its small space.

Needles & Pens

3523 16th Street, between Guerrero & Dolores Streets (255 1534/www.needles-pens.com). BART to 16th Street Mission/Metro to Church/bus 14, 22, 26, 33, 49, 53. **Open** noon-7pm daily. **Credit** AmEx, DC, MC, V. **Map** p318 J10.

Needles stocks a huge range of handmade gifts by local artists, including clothes, along with the latest in self-published 'zines and arty periodicals.

Receiver Gallery

1415 Valencia Street, at 25th Street (550 7287/www.receivergallery.com). BART 24th Street Mission/Metro to Church & 24th Street/bus 26, 27, 48, 67. **Open** 10am-6pm Mon-Fri; noon-4pm Sat. **Credit** AmEx, DC, Disc, MC, V. **Map** p318 K12.

Receiver is a combination interactive design studio and art gallery that also sells limited edition T-shirts. The emphasis is on graphics, cartoons and illustrations, and the roster features artists like Matt Furie, Jake Watling and Hannah Stouffer.

Southern Exposure

417 14th Street, at Valencia Street (863 2141/www.soex.org). BART to 16th Street Mission/Metro to Church/bus 14, 22, 26, 33, 49, 53. **Open** noon-5pm Tue-Sat. **Credit** DC, MC, V. **Map** p318 L10.

Large and inclusive, SoEx is the best non-profit in the city – many a young artist has been discovered here. The group exhibitions and parties are legendary; the juried art shows draw respected curators. *Photo p216.*

Triple Base

3041 24th Street, between Harrison & Folsom Streets (643 3943/www.basebasebase.com). BART 24th Street Mission/bus 12, 27, 48, 67. **Open** noon-5pm Thur-Sun. **No credit cards. Map** p318 L12.

The interest here is in site-specific and multidisciplinary works, but the limitations of the tiny

Southern Exposure. *See p215.*

gallery space can prevent those works from being overly ambitious. Triple Base is a hole in the wall deep in the Mission, but usually worth the detour.

The Haight & around

Giant Robot
618 Shrader Street, at Haight Street (876 4773/ www.giantrobot.com). Metro to Carl & Cole/bus 6, 7, 33, 37, 43, 71. **Open** noon-7pm Sun. **Credit** DC, MC, V. **Map** p317 E9.
It's a quarterly 'zine inspired by anime, punk rock and kung fu. It's also a shop on the far end of Haight that sells indie comics, Japanese goods, artist-designed T-shirts, and which regularly hosts small exhibitions by a local or international artist.

Park Life
220 Clement Street, at 3rd Avenue (386 7275/www. parklifestore.com). Bus 1, 2, 4, 33, 38. **Open** noon-8pm Mon-Thur, Sun; noon-9pm Sat. **Credit** AmEx, DC, MC, V. **Map** p312 D6.
Park Life is a store stocking all kinds of intriguing design items, many of them handmade by locals. The schedule of monthly art exhibitions is a bonus.

Upper Playground
252 Fillmore Street, at Haight Street (252 9144/ www.fifty24sf.com). Metro to Duboce & Church/ bus 6, 7, 22, 71. **Open** noon-7pm Tue-Sat. **Credit** AmEx, DC, MC, V. **Map** p317 H8.
The art gallery here, Fifty24SF, shares space with a clothing and record store (used soul and jazz vinyl a speciality). Monthly exhibits have a strong sense of the fantastic and a deep connection to pop culture.

Hayes Valley

Bucheon Gallery
389 Grove Street, at Gough Street (863 2891/www. bucheon.com). Bus 5, 21, 47, 49. **Open** 11am-6pm Tue-Sat. **Credit** DC, MC, V. **Map** p318 J7.
Committed to the contemporary, Bucheon puts its mid-sized space to the task of representing a diverse group of artists and challenging visitors' assumptions about modern art. Jake Watling, Bill Dunlap and Olive Ayhens are among the artists showed.

Jack Hanley Gallery
395 Valencia Street, at 15th Street (522 1623/www. jackhanley.com). BART to 16th Street Mission/Metro to Church/bus 14, 22, 26, 33, 49, 53. **Open** 11am-6pm Tue-Sat. **No credit cards. Map** p318 K9.
Considered the pre-eminent exhibition venue in San Francisco for young international artists, including many Europeans, Hanley has hosted many rising stars, among them Simon Evans and Chris Johanson.

Lincart
1632C Market Street, between Franklin & Gough Streets (503 1981/www.lincart.com). Metro to Van Ness/streetcar F/bus 6, 7, 26, 47, 49, 71. **Open** noon-6pm Tue-Sat. **Credit** AmEx, DC, MC, V. **Map** p318 K8.
Intimate and warm, this gallery quickly made a name for itself by showcasing playful works by young and emerging artists. It hosts events and art classes, and is one of the few places in the city where you'll find inexpensive rare art books.

San Francisco Arts Commission
401 Van Ness Avenue, at McAllister Street (554 6080/www.sfacgallery.org). Bus 5, 21, 47, 49. **Open** noon-5pm Wed-Sat, call for late hours. **Credit** AmEx, DC, Disc, MC, V. **Map** p318 K7.
This non-profit space focuses on contemporary art and the Bay Area's place in that field. In addition to regular programming at the War Memorial Building, SFAC maintains Grove Street Windows (155 Grove Street), where you can watch projections and other site-specific installations, and runs the Art at City Hall programme, a quarterly exhibition often curated in collaboration with local organisations.

On the street

You can find works of art all over the city without entering a gallery. San Francisco's well-established public art programme, largely funded by the SF Arts Commission (*see above*), is one of the most respected in the country. Additionally, locals have covered the walls of Balmy Alley (at 24th Street) and Clarion Alley (at Valencia) in the Mission district with some of the best murals you're likely to see anywhere; *see p96* **Walk**.

Finally, a fine way to sample a range of local artists' works is during the ArtSpan Open Studios weekends in October (*see p200*).

Gay & Lesbian

Where the out go out.

Meet and greet at the **Bar on Castro**. *See p221.*

A famous *New Yorker* cartoon depicts a couple reading a newspaper article about gay marriage. The punchline: 'Haven't these people suffered enough?' Nowhere is the subject of same-sex marriage more bittersweet than in San Francisco. In February 2004, more than 4,000 lesbian and gay couples made a dash for City Hall after new mayor Gavin Newsom proclaimed that the state statute prohibiting gay marriage violated California's constitution and directed officials to issue marriage licences to same-sex couples. But the Winter of Love – as it became known – was shortlived, as a rollercoaster of legislation was set in motion. First the marriages were nullified by the California Supreme Court, which ruled that the mayor had exceeded his authority. But then, in September 2004, the state became the first to legalise same-sex marriages. Less than a month later, however, Republican governor Arnold Schwarzenegger vetoed the same-sex marriage bill. Meanwhile, in the national arena, George W Bush was defeated in 2005 in his attempt to amend the US constitution to restrict marriage to 'one man, one woman'. At the time of writing, a ballot initiative supporting

same-sex marriage was gaining steam for a 2008 vote, in what some see as the most important civil rights battle of the era.

Armistead Maupin would be proud. According to the city's chronicler of gay life (*see p92* **Write on**), San Francisco 'was probably always destined to lead the century's last great fight for human rights'. From the excoriating energy of Ginsberg's *Howl* to the revolutionary Daughters of Bilitis, and from bar culture to the pre-Pride days of gay liberation, the city has long been a lightning rod for the upheavals associated with queer rights. After all, this was the place where, in 1977, Harvey Milk won a historic seat on the Board of Supervisors – a seat that proliferated into five in the 'Lavender Sweep' of the mid '90s.

NEIGHBOURHOODS

Polk Street, the Tenderloin, North Beach, Haight-Ashbury and SoMa were the neighbourhoods of choice for gays and lesbians in the 1970s, but the **Castro** – with its street fair, flourishing restaurants and bars, and talismanic **Castro Theatre** (*see p209*) – soon took over. Today, the area remains vibrant, with trendy, expensive houses and streets brimming with Pride flags, bars, eateries and shops.

Middle-class lesbians with kids and dogs have settled in cheery residential neighbourhoods such as **Bernal Heights** and **Glen Park**. Affluent queers thrive in villagey and ultra-gentrified **Noe Valley**, filled with chic shops and superb restaurants, while the **Mission**, the city's lively Latino birthplace, is home to scruffier queer types.

Gay men still gravitate towards **SoMa**, which is home to almost all of the gay clubs and many good gay bars, sex clubs and dance joints frequented by the brawny and well-toned. **Duboce Triangle** (between Market, Waller and Castro Streets), **Hayes Valley**, the **Haight** and **Potrero Hill** all also draw queer folk.

RESOURCES & INFORMATION

Queer San Francisco past and present can be explored at the Reading Room in the **Center** (1800 Market Street, at Octavia Boulevard, 865 5555, www.sfcenter.org), the **Eureka Valley/ Harvey Milk Memorial Branch Library** in the Castro (1 José Sarria Court, 16th Street, at Market Street, 355 5616), and at the **James C Hormel Gay & Lesbian Center** at the Main Library (see p76). **Cruisin' the Castro** (see p65) is a mazy walking tour, hosted by 'Leader of the Pack' Kathy Amendola and covering the history of SF's famous gay neighbourhood. SoMa is home to the **GLBT Historical Society** (Suite 300, 657 Mission Street, between New Montgomery & 3rd Streets, 777 5455, www.glbthistory.org, $4 suggested donation, closed Mon & Sun), which has riveting historical and cultural exhibits. For more pop-oriented gay fare, head to **A Different Light** (489 Castro Street, at 18th Street, 431 0891, www.adl books.com), SF's finest gay bookstore.

The best resources for up-to-date information are the free newspapers, notably the *San Francisco Bay Times* and the *BAR* (*Bay Area Reporter*). You'll find them in cafés, bookstores and street corner boxes. The **Center** (*see above*) organises meetings and events, as well as gathering information. The **Women's Building** (*see p98*) is a hub of resources and services. Queer-about-town Larry-bob Roberts regularly updates his voluminous website listings at www.sfqueer.com. The non gay-specific *Bay Guardian*, *SF Weekly* and *San Francisco Chronicle* are also worth a look.

Where to stay

For accommodation across the city, *see pp42-62*. Noteworthy gay-owned, gay-friendly or simply delightful places are listed below;

another particular favourite of ours is **Parker Guest House**, a lovely mini-mansion dating back to 1909.

Castro

Beck's Motor Lodge

2222 Market Street, at 15th Street, CA 94114 (621 8212/www.becksmotorlodgesf.com). Metro to Castro/streetcar F/bus 24, 33, 35, 37. **Rates** $93-$151 double. **Credit** AmEx, DC, Disc, MC, V. **Map** p318 H10.
Relatively cheap rates, a sun deck, private baths and, above all, a prime Castro location, help Beck's retain its popularity. Inside you'll find the tacky carpets and garish soft furnishings typical of a quintessential American motel. It has a reputation for being a very cruisey place to stay.

Inn on Castro

321 Castro Street, at Market Street, CA 94114 (861 0321/www.innoncastro.com). Metro to Castro/streetcar F/bus 24, 33, 35, 37. **Rates** $115-$160 double. **Credit** AmEx, DC, Disc, MC, V. **Map** p318 H10.
A beautifully restored Edwardian, with eight rooms and four apartments decorated with contemporary furnishings, original modern art and elaborate flower arrangements. The sumptuous breakfast includes delicious own-made muffins and fresh fruit.

24 Henry Guesthouse & Village House

24 Henry Street, between Sanchez & Noe Streets, CA 94114 (1-800 900 5686/864 5686/www.24 henry.com). Metro to Church & 18th or Castro/ streetcar F/bus 22, 37. **Rates** $75-$129 double. **Credit** AmEx, DC, MC, V. **Map** p318 H9.
All are welcome to this B&B, a handsome Victorian in the heart of the Castro. Of five furnished rooms, one has an en suite bathroom; the others share a double shower room with separate toilet. The Village House (4080 18th Street, between Castro & Hartford Streets), another Victorian, has five beautiful rooms.

Willows Inn

710 14th Street, at Church Streets, CA 94114 (431 4770/www.willowssf.com). Metro to Castro/streetcar F/bus 24, 33, 35, 37. **Rates** $115-$135 double. **Credit** AmEx, DC, Disc, MC, V. **Map** p318 H9.
This converted Edwardian has 12 comfy rooms with bentwood willow and antique furnishings. Baths are shared, but all rooms have vanity sinks. Soft kimono bathrobes are provided, and complimentary breakfast and cocktails are served daily.

Other neighbourhoods

Hayes Valley Inn

417 Gough Street, at Hayes Street, Hayes Valley, CA 94102 (431 9131/www.hayesvalleyinn.com). Bus 16, 21, 47, 49. **Rates** $73-$100 double. **Credit** AmEx, DC, Disc, MC, V. **Map** p318 J8.

A queer alternative

As one of the world's biggest gay meccas, San Francisco hosts the usual welcoming abundance of swanky lounges, pretty-boy cruise bars and all-night parties pumping an ecstatic mix of hard techno and diva-oriented tunes. But the city is also a vibrant enclave of queer rebels – colourful characters of all genders and persuasions whose tastes and styles go against the grain of mainstream gay and lesbian culture.

Rebellion against the norms of society, both gay and straight, has a long history here. Flamboyant patrons of San Francisco's (and thus the country's) original gay bars – including the Black Cat (which opened in 1933); lesbian bar Mona's (1936) and drag club Finocchio's (1933) – faced not only police harrassment, but also shunning by many of their homosexual peers, nervous about such openness.

This streak of celebratory revolt continued through the infamously dazzling 1970s antics of the Cockettes (a performance troupe known for its hallucinogenic breakdown of gender stereotypes and its peacocks on acid costumes) and into the early 1990s, when homocore bands like Pansy Division blended punk tunes with unabashed sexuality to highlight the rougher, rockier side of gay life. Things cooled off a bit at the height of the AIDS crisis, but they've warmed up again with the emergence of a new generation of young GLBT partiers, some now rebels against the norms of gay culture, and many with an affectionate regard for gay San Francisco's rock and bathhouse disco past as well as its electro and minimal techno present.

The city's alternaqueer scene is proudly underground – it takes a little digging to find it – but some good entry points, bar-wise, are the **Transfer** (*see p223*), **Aunt Charlie's Lounge** and the **Eagle Tavern** (for both, *see p224*), where you'll often find alluringly low-tech party flyers for future events and friendly alternative types who'll clue you in.

Prominent names to look out for are DJ Bus Station John, whose fabulously retro events offer pre-AIDS disco tunes in an old-school cruising environment; DJ Dirty Knees, who along with his partner Bill Picture hosts many of San Francisco's queer punk events; underground trash-drag princess Anna Conda; and the Honey Soundsystem (www.honey soundsystem.com, *pictured*), a roving gay DJ collective that showcases an array of rare dance music styles, including LA no-wave rock, acid house, early electro, Mexican banda and Balkan brass. The tunes may be a matter of individual taste, but the atmosphere at these alternative parties is gaily refreshing.

A European-style, 28-room pension in the centre of lively and lovely Hayes Valley. There's a bar, pets are welcome, and rooms have their own sinks. A kitchen and parlour are available to guests, but bathrooms are shared.

Metro
319 Divisadero Street, at Page Street, Haight, CA 94117 (861 5364/www.metrohotelsf.com). Bus 6, 7, 24, 71. **Rates** $86-$99 double. **Credit** AmEx, DC, Disc, MC, V. **Map** p317 G8.
The Metro is a gay-friendly establishment with a voluminous patio, and 24 well-appointed rooms with private baths in up-and-coming NoPa (North of Panhandle). Hip boutique shopping and unique eateries (the hotel's own restaurant serves some of the best Nepalese food in town) are little more than a stone's throw away.

Restaurants & cafés

GLBT diners are welcome throughout the city, but the following is a selection of our favourite places, some of which have a determinedly queer milieu. For the main restaurants and cafés section, *see pp132-61.*

The Castro

2223 Restaurant & Bar
2223 Market Street, between Noe & Sanchez Streets (431 0692/www.2223restaurant.com). Metro to Castro/streetcar F/bus 24, 33, 35, 37. **Open** 5-10pm Mon-Thur; 5-11pm Fri, Sat; 10am-2.30pm, 5-10pm Sun. **Main courses** $15-$32. **Credit** AmEx, DC, MC, V. **Map** p318 H10.

Mon-Thur; 11am-1am Fri; 10am-1am Sat; 10am-11pm Sun. **No credit cards. Map** p318 H11.
A great alternative to boozy nights, this club is home to clean and sober queers. There's a sitting room, a coffee bar and café, a room for board games, a video theatre and a backyard patio. The front steps are Castro's central gossip parlour and cruise lookout.

Catch
2362 Market Street, at Castro Street (431 5000/www.catchsf.com). Metro to Castro/streetcar F/bus 24, 33, 35, 37. **Open** 11.30am-3pm, 5.30-9.30pm Mon, Tue; 11.30am-3pm, 5.30-10pm Wed, Thur; 11.30am-3pm, 5.30-11pm Fri; 11am-3.30pm, 5.30-11pm Sat; 11am-3.30pm, 5.30-9.30pm Sun. **Main courses** $10-$25. **Credit** AmEx, DC, Disc, MC, V. **Map** p318 H10.
This seafood restaurant has an enclosed heated outdoor deck and live piano music. Dishes are well turned out, but not exceptional. No one seems to mind, though: the bar fills up with local yuppies on a date (or looking for one) and a broad selection of gym rats. You'll need to book at weekends.

Firewood Café
4248 18th Street, between Collingwood & Diamond Streets (252 0999/www.firewoodcafe.com). Metro to Castro/streetcar F/bus 24, 33, 35, 37. **Open** 11am-10.30pm Mon-Thur; 11am-11pm Fri, Sat; 11am-10pm Sun. **Main courses** $7-$14. **Credit** AmEx, DC, MC, V. **Map** p317 G11.
There's sometimes a queue outside the door for evening meals here, but the loyal customers are willing to wait. Menu standouts include melt-in-the-mouth roast chicken, pasta dishes and thin-crust pizzas. Eat in or phone to take out. Queer heaven.

Home
2100 Market Street, at Church Street (503 0333/www.home-sf.com). Metro to Church/streetcar F/bus 22, 37, 37. **Open** 5-10pm Mon-Thur; 5-11pm Fri; 10am-2pm, 5-11pm Sat, Sun. **Main courses** $10-$18. **Credit** AmEx, DC, MC, V. **Map** p318 H9.
True American comfort food – think meatloaf, collard greens, pot roast and banana bread pudding – is served (sometimes by drag queens) in an upscale atmosphere and accompanied by an impressive list of speciality cocktails. Sunday brunch is especially attractive, with a friendly crowd of regulars.

La Méditerranée
288 Noe Street, between Market & 16th Streets (431 7210/www.cafelamed.com). Metro to Castro/streetcar F/bus 24, 33, 35, 37. **Open** 11am-10pm Mon-Thur, Sun; 11am-11pm Fri, Sat. **Main courses** $9.50-$11.50. **Credit** AmEx, DC, MC, V. **Map** p318 H10.
A well-established success, due in no small part to the owners' brilliant use of fresh ingredients. Everything is keenly priced, with terrific houmous and baba ganoush, plus an excellent filo pastry combination plate. Feels like a genuine Mediterranean escape. **Other locations** 2210 Fillmore Street, Pacific Heights (921 2956); 2936 College Avenue, Berkeley (1-510 540 7773).

Mabel's Just For You Café.

Expect vibrant dishes that awaken the senses at this sleek restaurant. There are Med, Mexican and Caribbean influences on the menu, and excellent pizza, pasta and fish. It's one of the more popular places for the queer crowd, so the din may intrude on romantic tête-à-têtes. Sunday brunch is a winner.

Bagdad Café
2295 Market Street, at Noe Street (621 4434). Metro to Castro/streetcar F/bus 24, 33, 35, 37. **Open** 24hrs daily. **Main courses** $12-$23. **Credit** AmEx, DC, Disc, MC, V. **Map** p318 H10.
A bustling diner with a bird's-eye view of the busy Market-Noe intersection, this is a decent option for a sandwich, vegetarian lasagne or post-bar breakfast.

Café Flore
2298 Market Street, at Noe Street (621 8579/www.cafeflore.com). Metro to Castro/streetcar F/bus 24, 33, 35, 37. **Open** 7am-11pm Mon-Thur, Sun; 7am-midnight Fri, Sat. **Main courses** $7-$15. **Credit** AmEx, DC, MC, V. **Map** p318 H10.
Fresh-faced boys and girls crowd Flore's gorgeous patio day and night to check each other out and feast on local favourites (brunch is a must). Deep house and lounge tunes pump from the DJ booth when Brazilian and Hawaiian musicians aren't taking the stage.

Castro Country Club
4058 18th Street, at Hartford Street (552 6102/www.castrocountryclub.org). Metro to Castro/streetcar F/bus 24, 33, 35, 37. **Open** 11am-11pm

Samovar

498 Sanchez Street, at 18th Street (626 4700/ www.samovartea.com). Metro to Castro/streetcar F/bus 24, 33, 35, 37. **Open** 10am-10pm daily. **Main courses** $8-$18. **Credit** AmEx, DC, Disc, MC, V. **Map** p318 H10.

The Castro's only tearoom, this tranquil spot is a hit with locals searching out a quiet Zen-like refuge. There are more than 100 teas, plus, if you're peckish, healthy, Asian-inspired small plates. **Other locations** Yerba Buena Gardens, Upper Terrace, 730 Howard Street, SoMa (227 9400).

Other neighbourhoods

Asia SF

201 9th Street, at Howard Street, SoMa (255 2742/ www.asiasf.com). BART & Metro to Civic Center/ streetcar F/bus 12, 14, 19, 26, 47. **Open** Restaurant 6.30-10pm Tue, Wed; 6-10.30pm Thur, Sun; 7-11pm Fri; 5-11.15pm Sat. Club 7pm-3am Fri, Sat. **Main courses** $12.50-$20. **Credit** AmEx, DC, Disc, MC, V. **Map** p318 L8.

Those lovely ladies who serve you? They're not. Not women, that is, nor drag queens. The sexy creatures who bring the food and dance seductively atop the long red bar are 'gender illusionists'. The food is an inventive Cal-Asian, with small plates and shareable portions. A restaurant, lounge and club all in one, Asia SF's crowd is a compelling mix of local party-goers and wide-eyed businessmen. Very popular, so reservations are essential.

Emma's Coffee House

1901 Hayes Street, at Ashbury Street, Haight (221 3378). Bus 16, 21, 43. **Open** 6am-8pm Mon-Fri; 7am-8pm Sat, Sun. **No credit cards**. **Map** p317 F8.

Emma's is the real deal when it comes to the mighty bean, serving robustly strong Italian-style coffee made the right way. Two iMacs are available for customer use (first 15mins free with purchase; $2 for every 15mins thereafter). Saunter upstairs for a read in the tranquil lounge.

Liberty Café

410 Cortland Avenue, between Bennington & Wool Streets, Bernal Heights (695 8777/www.thelibertycafe.com). Bus 24, 67. **Open** 11.30am-3pm, 5.30-9.30pm Tue-Thur; 11am-3pm, 5.30-10pm Fri; 10am-2pm, 5.30-10pm Sat; 10am-2pm, 5.30-9.30pm Sun. **Main courses** $12.50-$19.50. **Credit** AmEx, DC, Disc, MC, V.

A neighbourhood gem that serves exquisite home-style American food. The chicken pot pie is a delight, while the desserts are among the best in the city, from the voluptuous banana cream pie to a luscious strawberry shortcake topped with whipped cream.

Mabel's Just for You Café

732 22nd Street, at 3rd Street, Potrero Hill (647 3033/www.justforyoucafe.com). Metro to 20th Street/bus 22, 48. **Open** 7.30am-3pm Mon-Fri; 8am-3pm Sat, Sun. **Main courses** $5-$11. **No credit cards**. **Map** p319 P11.

The popularity of the original version of this dyke-run café prompted the owners to move to these bigger quarters in Dogpatch, close to the Bay. The house speciality is a Cajun-style breakfast, with superb grits and fluffy pancakes.

PastaGina

741 Diamond Street, at 24th Street, Noe Valley (282 0738). Bus 24, 35, 48. **Open** 10am-9pm Mon-Fri; 10am-8.30pm Sat, Sun. **Main courses** $5-$10. **Credit** AmEx, DC, MC, V. **Map** p317 G12.

An exceptional gourmet take-out joint selling fresh pasta and classy salads, as well as Sonoma chicken, Thai vegetarian rolls, sauces, dips, cheeses from various countries, and European and Californian wines.

Regalito Rosticeria

3481 18th Street, at Valencia Street, Mission (503 0650/www.regalitosf.com). BART to 16th Street/bus 14, 33, 49. **Open** 5-10pm Tue-Fri; 11am-10pm Sat, Sun. **Main courses** $11-$16. **Credit** AmEx, DC, MC, V. **Map** p318 K10.

Opened in 2006 by chef Thomas Peña and his partner, Regalito offers Mexican-style cooking at its best. Hearty *enchiladas verdes*, delicately spiced chilli *relleno*, and the *pollo regalito* – roast chicken marinated in lemon or chilli-garlic sauce – represent an authentic taste of California's other native cuisine.

Bars

The Castro

Badlands

4121 18th Street, at Castro Street (626 9320/www. sfbadlands.com). Metro to Castro/streetcar F/bus 24, 33, 35, 37. **Open** 2pm-2am daily. **No credit cards**. **Map** p318 H11.

Young suburbanites drenched in scent and sporting the latest in designer label knock-offs flock to this flashy video bar, which boasts one of the few dancefloors in the Castro. The music ranges from popular hip hop to early 1990s diva favourites, and the queue outside on weekends is often a scene of its own.

Bar on Castro

456 Castro Street, between 18th & Market Streets (626 7220/www.thebarsf.com). Metro to Castro/ streetcar F/bus 24, 33, 35, 37. **Open** 4pm-2am Mon-Fri; 2pm-2am Sat, Sun. **No credit cards**. **Map** p318 H10.

A heaving sweatbox crammed with a multitude of pretty boys bumping and grinding to thumping dance tunes. After-work crowds tend to congregate during the week for the two-for-one happy hour (daily until 8pm). *Photo p217*.

440 Castro

440 Castro Street, at 18th Street (621 8732/www. daddysbar.com). Metro to Castro/streetcar F/bus 24, 33, 35, 37. **Open** noon-2am daily. **No credit cards**. **Map** p318 H11.

Formerly Daddy's, the Castro's reigning leather bar, 440 Castro has reinvented itself as a moderately

Festivals Gay

June's month-long **Gay Pride**, the largest gay carnival in the world, is the highlight of the year. It includes the spirit-buoying Trans March on Friday (www.transmarch.org), the boisterous Saturday night women-only **Dyke March** (241 8882,www.dyke march.org), both with onlookers of any gender cheering from the sidelines, and Sunday's **Pride Parade** (see p199). The crowds stream up Market Street to Civic Center Plaza to watch the leather-and-lace Dykes on Bikes leading the parade with their full-throttled Harley power and roar.

The centrepiece of Pride is Frameline's **San Francisco International Lesbian & Gay Film Festival** (see p210), a two-week festival of shorts, documentaries and features. Still racy, September's leather-besotted **Folsom Street Fair** (see p200) is the second largest gay event in SF; the **Up Your Alley Fair** (www.folsom streetfair.com/alley), a cruisey and risqué S&M festival in late July in SoMa, and the bear-oriented **Hairrison Street Fair** (summer dates vary, www.hairrison.org) also attract thousands. The Castro's other major street celebration is **Halloween** (see p200); if you're thinking of going, wear a costume or risk the scorn of patrolling homecoming queens.

On a more sombre note, there's the **AIDS Candlelight Vigil** (see p199) in May, with a walk along Market Street to the Main Library; the **AIDS Walk San Francisco** (www.aidswalk.net/sanfran) in July; and **World AIDS Day** on 1 December, which sees events throughout the city. You can also view portions of the **AIDS Memorial Quilt** (www.aidsquilt.org), founded in 1987.

swanky lounge but hasn't quite managed to shake off its preening he-man past. The crowd is an odd mix of old-school cruisers and youthful fans of hard techno, but the drinks specials are just right to smooth out the rougher edges.

Harvey's

500 Castro Street, at 18th Street (431 4278/ www.harveyssf.com). Metro to Castro/streetcar F/bus 24, 33, 35, 37. **Open** 11am-2am Mon-Fri; 9am-2am Sat, Sun. **Credit** AmEx, DC, MC, V. **Map** p318 H11.
The site of an infamous brawl with cops during the 1979 White Night riot that followed the lenient sentencing of Dan White, Harvey Milk's assassin,

this bar-restaurant – named after Harvey Milk – is usually pervaded by a spirit of bonhomie. Saturdays host a mixed bag of drag and musical performances, and a recent makeover highlights the colourful clientele.

Jet

2348 Market Street, between Castro & Noe Streets (www.jetsf.com). Metro to Castro/streetcar F/bus 24, 33, 35, 37. **Open** 5pm-2am Mon-Fri; 3pm-2am Sat, Sun. **No credit cards**. **Map** p318 H10.
Opulently appointed, complete with leather-padded walls, a mirrored bar and a pink double bed with pillows, this pricey new joint appeals to finely dressed Latin, hip hop and rock fans who like a little sparkle with their swizzle. A small dancefloor beckons with swaggering beats and raised go-go booths.

Midnight Sun

4067 18th Street, at Hartford Street (861 4186/ www.midnightsunsf.com). Metro to Castro/ streetcar F/bus 24, 33, 35, 37. **Open** 2pm-2am Mon-Fri; 1pm-2am Sat, Sun. **No credit cards**. **Map** p318 H11.
The big draw at Midnight Sun is video – that is, classic and contemporary music cross-cut with comedy clips, *The Sopranos* or *Sex and the City*. Two-for-one cocktails are on offer during the week (2-7pm), and weekends are a boy fest.

Mix

4086 18th Street, at Hartford Street (431 8616/ www.sfmixbar.com). Metro to Castro/streetcar F/ bus 24, 33, 35, 37. **Open** 6am-2am daily. **No credit cards**. **Map** p318 H11.
This rough-and-ready sports bar is a haven for queer jocks and those who adore them. Fervent fans pack the place to root for the San Francisco '49ers, and sunny weekends see the back patio grilling up burgers and hot dogs. The windows face 18th Street, which is perfect for ogling.

Moby Dick's

4049 18th Street, at Hartford Street (861 1199/ www.mobydicksf.com). Metro to Castro/streetcar F/bus 24, 33, 35, 37. **Open** 2pm-2am Mon-Fri; noon-2am Sat, Sun. **No credit cards**. **Map** p318 H11.
A true neighbourhood bar, Moby Dick's is exactly as it has been since the 1980s. It's popular with pool players (despite the fact that there's only one table) and pinball addicts (there are four machines at the back), but big windows and a prime Castro location afford ample cruising potential too. Daily drinks specials add to the attraction.

Orbit Room

1900 Market Street, at Laguna Street (252 9525). Metro to Van Ness or Church/streetcar F/bus 6, 7, 71. **Open** 2pm-2am daily. **No credit cards**. **Map** p318 J9.
This high-ceilinged art deco retreat with pedestal tables is a coffeehouse by day and a cocktail bar by night. The crowd is quite young, a mix of straights and queers, with some uptown lesbians thrown into

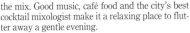

Empire Plush Room. *See p226.*

the mix. Good music, café food and the city's best cocktail mixologist make it a relaxing place to flutter away a gentle evening.

Pilsner Inn
225 Church Street, at Market Street (621 7058). Metro to Church/streetcar F/bus 22, 37. **Open** 10am-2am daily. **No credit cards**. **Map** p318 J9.
It all happens here, especially on the heated back patio. The Pilsner is a local favourite among youngish beauty boys, who play pool, pinball and computer games, or chat over the sounds of the retro jukebox. There's a wide choice of draft beers, and customers can wait at the front for opening tables at ever-popular Chow (*see p153*), serving American staples.

Transfer
198 Church Street, at Market Street (861 7499). Metro to Church/streetcar F/bus 22, 37. **Open** 5pm-2am daily. **No credit cards**. **Map** p318 J9.
An indie, electro and underground dance music fiesta for all orientations and sexual persuasions. Although relatively small, this former lesbian biker bar has become the top dancefloor hotspot for youthful scenemakers willing to get a few sweat stains on their unique apparel. Party programming changes nightly, but is always fun.

Twin Peaks Tavern
401 Castro Street, at Market Street (864 9470/ www.twinpeakstavern.com). Metro to Castro/streetcar F/bus 24, 33, 35, 37. **Open** noon-2am Mon-Wed; 8am-2am Thur-Sun. **No credit cards**. **Map** p318 H10.

Billing itself as 'the Gateway to the Castro', the snug Twin Peaks Tavern was one of the first gay bars in the US to brave the public gaze with street-level windows. Nowadays, habitués are mostly older, enjoying a quiet chat, good music and even a game of cards. The lovely antique bar serves everything except bottled beer.

The Mission

Although it's not strictly a gay bar, **El Rio** (3158 Mission Street, at Cesar Chavez Street, 282 3325, www.elriosf.com) draws queers to its riotous music nights. Among them are Mango, the monthly lesbian Saturday party, which has a huge following, and Sunday Salsa, also very queer.

Esta Noche
3079 16th Street, at Mission Street (861 5757/ www.estanochebar.com). BART to 16th Street Mission/bus 14, 22, 26, 33, 49, 53. **Open** noon-2am daily. **No credit cards**. **Map** p318 K10.
In business for decades, this gay-Latino-drag-sports bar attracts a gregarious, diverse clientele. There's a pool table for the daytime and animated drag shows and rousing lip-synching at night. Music mixes US and Latino pop, *cumbia* and merengue (DJs play nightly), and the place doubles as a welcome mat for Latino queens who are new to town. A word of warning, however: the street outside can be a bit on the menacing side.

Arts & Entertainment

Lexington Club
3464 19th Street, at Lexington Street (863 2052/
www.lexingtonclub.com). BART to 16th Street
Mission/bus 14, 26, 33, 49. **Open** 5pm-2am
Mon-Thur; 3pm-2am Fri-Sun. **No credit cards.**
Map p318 K11.
A legendary lesbian-owned, lesbian-operated bar,
where 'every night is ladies' night'. Primarily for the
younger set, the Lexington has a pool table (free on
Mondays) and full bar; crimson walls and church-
pew seating give the place a ready-for-anything
atmosphere. There's no dancing, but theme nights
include Sister Spit's rowdy performances, and Sunday
L Word parties. Frequent drinks specials too.

SoMa

Eagle Tavern
398 12th Street, at Harrison Street (626 0880/
www.sfeagle.com). Bus 9, 12, 27, 47. **Open** noon-
2am daily. **No credit cards. Map** p318 L9.
A venerable gay bar offering all-male leather action,
random mud-wrestling, goings-on in the beer garden and a chance to cosy up to gay (and straight)
indie rockers and punk outfits, including Pansy
Division, Erase Errata and Enorchestra. Sunday
afternoon beer busts (between 3.30pm and 5.30pm)
are ground zero for local alternaqueers (*see p219*
Alternaqueer explosion).

Hole in the Wall
289 8th Street, between Howard & Folsom Streets
(431 4695/www.holeinthewallsaloon.com). Bus 12,
19, 27, 47. **Open** noon-2am daily. **No credit cards.**
Map p318 L8.
This self-proclaimed 'nasty little biker bar', a veritable SoMa institution, is a magnet for the biker
crowd, although gay locals and tourists seem to love
it too. There's a beautifully re-felted pool table, video
games, pinball, rock 'n' roll oldies playing on repeat
and a bewildering array of gay memorabilia covering the walls and ceiling.

Lone Star Saloon
1354 Harrison Street, between 9th & 10th Streets
(863 9999/www.lonestarsaloon.com). Bus 12, 19,
27, 47. **Open** 2pm-2am Mon-Fri; noon-2am Sat, Sun.
No credit cards. Map p318 L8.
Once unabashed 'bear country', the Lone Star has of
late become more of a fashion show for beauty bears.
That said, it's still a jolly enough place, with pinball
machines, a pool table and a rear patio for smoking,
and authentic bear types can still be hunted here.

Powerhouse
1347 Folsom Street, between 9th & 10th Streets
(552 8689/www.powerhouse-sf.com). Bus 12, 19,
27, 47. **Open** 4pm-2am daily. **No credit cards.**
Map p318 L8.
White-hot and cruisey as hell, Powerhouse is one of
the city's most popular gay bars. Entertainment
includes buzz-cut nights, underwear or bare-chest
parties, wrestling, leather nights and S&M lessons.

Other neighbourhoods

Aunt Charlie's Lounge
133 Turk Street, at Taylor Street, Tenderloin
(441 2922/www.auntcharlieslounge.com). BART
& Metro to Powell/streetcar F/bus 27, 30, 45
& Market Street routes/cable car Powell-Hyde or
Powell-Mason. **Open** noon-midnight Mon, Wed;
noon-2am Tue, Thur, Fri; 10am-2am Sat; 10am-
midnight Sun. **No credit cards. Map** p314 L6.
Sports nights, stiff drinks, old-fashioned drag shows
and lip-synching on weekends, plus a long-standing
Tenderloin location all combine to make this a popular spot with loyal attendees.

Cinch
1723 Polk Street, between Clay & Washington
Streets, Polk Gulch (776 4162/www.thecinch.com).
Bus 1, 12, 19, 27, 47, 49, 76/cable car California.
Open 6am-2am daily. **No credit cards.**
Map p314 K4.
A double-shot of old-school San Francisco gay bar,
circa 1979. With an ostensible Western theme, this
comfortably ramshackle haunt harks back to the
days when this stretch of Polk Street was a more
rough-and-tumble area of hustlers, chasers and drag
queens with a broken heel or two. A tiered smoking
patio out back is perfect for slurred conversation.

Deco Lounge
510 Larkin Street, at Turk Street, Tenderloin
(346 2025/www.decosf.com). Bus 19, 31, 38.
Open 10am-2am Wed, Thur, Sun; 10am-4am
Fri, Sat. **No credit cards. Map** p314 K6.
Laid out like a spacious 1940s piano bar, complete
with plush decor and classic movie posters framed
and artfully lit on the walls, Deco somewhat incon-
gruously hosts many of the wildest gay parties in
the Tenderloin. Wet jockstrap contests, offbeat drag
shows and techno-driven bear parties can be found
here on many weekend nights; weekdays host a
crew of seen-it-all regulars.

Marlena's
488 Hayes Street, at Octavia Street, Hayes Valley
(864 6672/www.marlenasbarsf.com). Bus 16, 21,
47, 49. **Open** noon-2am daily. **No credit cards.**
Map p318 J8.
An eclectic crowd (including drag queens on the
weekends) shows up for the superb martinis at this
treasured former speakeasy. A fold-down Murphy
stage lends an eccentric, cosy ambience. There are
drag shows every second and fourth Saturday of the
month.

Martuni's
4 Valencia Street, at Market Street, Hayes Valley
(241 0205). BART or Metro to Van Ness/streetcar
F/bus 6, 7, 26, 71. **Open** 4pm-2am daily. **Credit**
DC, MC, V. **Map** p318 J8.
Martuni's is a warm, inviting piano bar with an open
mic. The martinis are enormous, the music mostly
show tunes, and the clientele extremely varied. The
only gay bar to have truly thrived in the vicinity.

Stray Bar

*309 Cortland Avenue, at Bocana Street, Bernal
Heights (821 9263/www.straybarsf.com). Bus
24.* **Open** 4pm-2am Mon-Fri; 2pm-2am Sat, Sun.
No credit cards.
Recently opened and beautifully renovated, this girl
bar attracts a heterogeneous clientele. The nightly
entertainment varies from live blues and jazz singers
to DJs spinning every kind of music, and there are
weekday happy hours from 5pm to 8pm.

Wild Side West

*424 Cortland Avenue, at Wool Street, Bernal
Heights (647 3099). Bus 24.* **Open** 1pm-2am daily.
No credit cards.
Probably the longest-lived lesbian hotspot in the city,
Wild Side West really sees itself as just another
neighbourhood bar. The walls are a shifting
art installation, the patio is perfect for live music or
poetry, and the clientele is happily mixed. The ace
jukebox plays Janis Joplin, Patsy Cline and – naturally – 'Walk on the Wild Side'.

Nightclubs

The dance scene changes with bewildering
rapidity, so call ahead, check websites or get
club-scene mags *Odyssey* and *Gloss* to make
sure a particular night is happening. Most
clubs are 21 and over, so bring valid photo
ID. For more nightclubs, *see pp238-42.*

The Castro

The Café

*2369 Market Street, at Castro Street (861 3846/
www.cafesf.com). Metro to Castro/streetcar F/bus
24, 33, 35, 37.* **Open** 3pm-2am daily. **Admission**
varies. **No credit cards. Map** p318 H10.
There's dancing every night at the Café, the Castro's
largest and most popular club. Once the area's only
women's bar, it now mainly attracts boys from outlying areas, but lasses show up during the day, on
weeknights and (especially) on Sunday afternoons.
The music blends house, hip hop and salsa. There
are two bars, a dancefloor and a patio, plus pinball,
pool and computer games.

SoMa

Mezzanine (444 Jessie Street, at 6th Street;
see p240) is also a big hit with the boys.

Eight

*1151 Folsom Street, between 7th & 8th Streets
(431 1151/www.eightsf.com). BART or Metro to
Civic Center/streetcar F/bus 12, 14, 19, 27.* **Open**
9pm-3am Fri; varies Thur, Sat, Sun. **No credit
cards. Map** p319 M8.
A solid, bi-level nightclub with a lovely lounge at
the top and a rolling programme of themed events,
Eight is also known for its attractive staff. Fridays

Outside the ever-popular **Café**.

host Dragon, a high-energy party for Asians and
friends; other nights see punk, disco, techno and
even Middle Eastern tunes pack the dancefloor.

Endup

*401 6th Street, at Harrison Street (646 0999/
www.theendup.com). Bus 12, 27, 47.* **Open** 10pm-
4am Thur; 10pm-6am Fri; 6am-1pm, 10pm-4am Sat;
6am-4am Sun.* **Admission** free-$20. **No credit
cards. Map** p319 M7.
A fixture since 1973, the Endup boasts all-night
house and techno madness on the weekends, plus a
Saturday morning club from 6am and the legendary
T-Dance from 6am on Sundays, which sees drag
queens and straight ravers revelling together.

Stud

*399 9th Street, at Harrison Street (252 7883/
www.studsf.com). Bus 12, 19, 27, 47.* **Open** from
5pm daily, closing varies. **Admission** free-$15.
No credit cards. Map p318 L8.
Now more than 40 years old, the Stud still has dancing all week. The crowd is mainly gay and male,
but the club prides itself on being 'omnisexual'.
Wondrous Heklina hosts the best drag in town on
Tuesdays at Trannyshack; other nights range from
queer punk and '80s disco to house. Saturdays offer
Nude Dude drinks specials and big dick contests.

Arts & Entertainment

Other neighbourhoods

Space 550

550 Barneveld Avenue, at Apparel Way, Bernal Heights (550 8286/www.space550.com). Bus 23, 24. **Open** varies. **Admission** varies. **No credit cards.**
Three ample dancefloors, live performances and seductive go-go dancers attract crowds of hip party-goers and sexy Latino queers to this warehouse club. Cream, every second Saturday, is for lusty lesbians.

Entertainment & culture

The Castro

The **Castro Theatre** at 429 Castro Street (*see p209*) hosts gay and camp screenings: you haven't lived until you've seen *Valley of the Dolls* or *All About Eve* here. It also holds frequent *Sound of Music* singalongs and, on Christmas Eve, the SF Gay Men's Chorus singing 'Home for the Holidays'.

The Mission

Brava! For Women in the Arts

Theatre Center, 2789 24th Street, at York Street (641 7657/box office 647 2822/www.brava.org). BART 24th Street/bus 9, 27, 33, 48. **Tickets** free-$50. **Credit** DC, Disc, MC, V. **Map** p319 M12.
Housed in an old vaudeville theatre, Brava is one of few theatres that specialise in work by women of colour and lesbian playwrights.

QComedy Showcase

Locations vary (www.qcomedy.com).
What's so funny about queers? QComedy Showcase will tell you at its many shows about town. The ebullient Nick Leonard hosts and performs regularly; top-flight comics Heather Gold, Charlie Ballard and Aundré the Wonderwoman also appear.

Theatre Rhinoceros

2926 16th Street, between Mission Street & South Van Ness Avenue (861 5079/www.therhino.org). BART to 16th Street Mission/bus 14, 22, 26, 33, 49, 53. **Tickets** $15-$30. **Credit** AmEx, DC, MC, V. **Map** p318 K10.
Billing itself as the 'world's oldest continually producing, professional queer theatre', Rhino creates theatre that is genuinely inviting rather than self-segregating. Its productions comprise comedy, reinterpreted classics, original drama and the occasional musical.

Other neighbourhoods

The **Magic Theatre** (Fort Mason, Marina Boulevard, at Buchanan Street; *see p252*) hosts a lesbian playwright festival every January and showcases queer plays through the year. Groundbreaking gay theatre is staged at the **New Conservatory Theatre** (25 Van Ness Avenue, between Fell & Oak Streets, Hayes Valley).

Empire Plush Room

York Hotel, 940 Sutter Street, between Leavenworth & Hyde Streets, Nob Hill (885 2800/www.theempireplushroom.com). Bus 2, 3, 4, 27, 38, 76. **Open** hours vary. **Admission** $20-$60. **Credit** AmEx, DC, Disc, MC, V. **Map** p314 K5.
Romantic and soul-stirring cabaret in a chic and jazzy setting. Shows are generally held Wednesdays to Sundays and often feature big names: recent performers include Lorna Luft. *Photo p223.*

Sports, health & fitness

All of San Francisco's workout spaces (*see p247*) are queer-friendly, but those listed below are especially gay-oriented. All offer daily (around $12-$20) and weekly ($40-$50) memberships.

Gold's Gym Castro

2301 Market Street, at Noe Street, Castro (626 4488/www.goldsgym.com). Metro to Castro/streetcar F/bus 24, 33, 35, 37. **Open** 5am-midnight Mon-Thur; 5am-11pm Fri; 7am-8pm Sun. **Credit** AmEx, DC, MC, V. **Map** p318 H10.
Cruisey, with a steam room that can only be described as steamy. Friendly staff and a fierce sound system make Gold's popular with both gay boys and lesbians.

Gym SF

2275 Market Street, between Sanchez & Noe Streets, Castro (863 4700/www.thegymsf.com). Metro to Castro/streetcar F/bus 24, 33, 35, 37. **Open** 5am-11pm Mon-Fri; 7am-10pm Sat; 8am-8pm Sun. **Credit** DC, MC, V. **Map** p318 H10.
The Castro's most notorious men-only sweat palace, well laid-out, seriously steamy and with enough weights for even the most ardent muscle man.

Magnet

4122 18th Street, at Castro Street, Castro (581 1600/www.magnetsf.org). Metro to Castro/streetcar F/bus 24, 33, 35, 37. **Open** noon-6pm Tue, Sat; 3-9pm Wed-Fri. **Map** p317 G11.
In response to rising HIV and STD rates among the city's queer men, community health groups have rallied to create Magnet. This welcoming space looks more like an upscale café than a health clinic. There are hangout areas, internet access, and free, anonymous HIV and STD testing and counselling.

World Gym

290 De Haro Street, at 16th Street, Potrero Hill (703 9650/www.worldgym.com). Bus 10, 19, 22. **Open** 5am-midnight Mon-Thur; 5am-11pm Fri; 6am-9pm Sat; 7am-8pm Sun. **Credit** AmEx, DC, Disc, MC, V. **Map** p319 M10.
The gym of gyms, where serious work is done. There are classes in almost everything, including yoga, boxing, Thai boxing, kickboxing and spin. The clientele takes in the whole of hetero San Francisco. Fabulous.

Music

SF pushes the musical boundaries.

If you're going to San Francisco, wear flowers in your hair, have plastic in your pocket and be fully prepared to hang with some of the most passionate, hip and adventurous artists and audiences in the country. Like its grande dame Victorians and rocked-out bike messengers, San Francisco's musical heritage endures, with the city managing to maintain its reputation as a hard-partying port in the storm of millennial change. Artists, writers and musicians have been coming here for decades, and both the rock and classical scenes reflect this: the city's cultural circuit is one of the most forward-thinking in the US. The inflated expectations of the turn-of-the-20th century venture capitalist-funded years have been tempered during the current tech boom – exemplified by the new-money arrivals of Wikipedia and YouTube and the biotech building explosion – and the brave new sensibilities that come with that business only feed the innovative musical climate. After all, the Bay Area still yields one of the highest levels of rock concert attendance in the country. Only New York and LA, both industry cities, attract more bands than SF, while few towns draw as many renowned classical musicians and international touring performers.

INFORMATION & TICKETS

The best overall sources of information are the *San Francisco Bay Guardian* (www.sfbg.com) and *SF Weekly* (www.sfweekly.com), both of which carry extensive listings. In addition, check www.sfgate.com, the *San Francisco Chronicle*'s website, and www.sfstation.com.

Classical & opera

The exploratory impulse that courses through much of the city's cultural landscape extends to its classical music scene. San Francisco's major orchestra and opera company are both renowned for their challenging projects, and a number of the city's smaller ensembles have built their reputations on contemporary music. However, there's plenty of familiar repertoire on offer at venues large and small. Area ensembles have also been making a concerted effort to reach new audiences, which means virtuosic performances are presented at fair prices in venues ranging from the modern (Louise M Davies Symphony Hall) to the historic (St Patrick's Church). Ticketing can

be complicated. Several of the larger ensembles sell tickets via subscription packages, and the most popular shows do sell out. However, individual tickets are available for most concerts; even on nights listed as sell-outs, there are usually a few seats available on the evening. A handful of the smaller venues don't sell tickets ahead of time, but try to book in advance (by phone or online) if possible.

Major companies & venues

San Francisco Opera

War Memorial Opera House, 301 Van Ness Avenue, at Grove Street, Civic Center (864 3330/www. sfopera.com). BART & Metro to Civic Center, Metro to Van Ness/bus 21, 47, 49 & Market Street routes. **Box office** 10am-5pm Mon; 10am-6pm Tue-Sat. **Tickets** $25-$235. **Credit** AmEx, DC, MC, V. **Map** p318 K7.

Inaugurated in 1923, the SF Opera achieved great renown between 2001 and 2005 under general director Pamela Rosenberg. After bringing the company into rude artistic health, overseeing triumphs such as the 2005 première of John Adams' *Doctor Atomic*, Rosenberg declined to renew her contract, and handed the reins to David Gockley in 2006. Gockley has since unveiled *Appomattox*, commissioned from composer Philip Glass and librettist Christopher Hampton. For 2008 the company also planned to present composer Stewart Wallace and local novelist Amy Tan's *The Bonesetter's Daughter* and a new co-production (with Washington National Opera) of Wagner's *Ring*, beginning with *Das Rheingold* in 2008 and culminating with the entire cycle in the 2010-11 season. The fall season runs early September to December; the summer season from May to July.

The SF Opera is based in the War Memorial Opera House, a grand Beaux Arts building designed by City Hall architect Arthur Brown Jr and built in 1932 as a memorial to the soldiers who fought in World War I. The 3,176-seat auditorium is modelled on European opera houses, with a vaulted ceiling, a huge art deco metal chandelier and a marble foyer. An $84-million revamp in 1997 not only restored the elegant building (restorers found clouds painted on the ceiling when they scraped away the grime), but installed up-to-date electronics and stage gear. The San Francisco Ballet (*see p256*) also performs here.

San Francisco Performances

Various venues (398 6449/www.performances.org). **Box office** 9.30am-5.30pm Mon-Fri. **Tickets** $20-$50. **Credit** DC, MC, V.

Directed with imagination and enthusiasm by Ruth Felt, this independent promoter puts on a programme of over 200 concerts each year in a wide variety of styles: the 2007-08 season included concerts by Philip Glass, Anne-Sophie Mutter, Dan Zanes and the Billy Childs Ensemble. Most performances are held at the Herbst Theatre (*see p252*), the Yerba Buena Center for the Arts Theater (*see below*), the Florence Gould Theater in the California Palace of the Legion of Honor (*see p115*), and Koret Auditorium at the de Young Museum (*see p113*), but there are also events at the likes of St John's Presbyterian Church in Berkeley (*see below*) and the Hotel Rex (*see p47*).

San Francisco Symphony

Louise M Davies Symphony Hall, 201 Van Ness Avenue, at Hayes Street, Civic Center (864 6000/ www.sfsymphony.org). BART & Metro to Civic Center, Metro to Van Ness/bus 21, 47, 49 & Market Street routes. **Box office** 10am-6pm Mon-Fri; noon-6pm Sat; 2hrs before concert Sun. **Tickets** $20-$125. **Credit** DC, MC, V. **Map** p318 K7.

Formed to boost public morale shortly after the 1906 earthquake and fire, the San Francisco Symphony performed its first concert in 1911. Today, under the dynamic direction of Michael Tilson Thomas, the orchestra is internationally recognised for its innovative work, winning several Grammy awards in the process. The symphony's series of Mahler concerts has garnered the ensemble particular acclaim.

The Symphony is based at the Louise M Davies Symphony Hall. Commonly known as the Davies, the striking, multi-tiered, curved-glass edifice has flawless acoustics and clear sightlines. There isn't a bad seat in the house, and that includes the 40 in the centre terrace section behind the orchestra that sell for just $20 and go on sale two hours before most performances (call for details). In addition to SF Symphony concerts, look out for events in the Great Performers series, which imports world-renowned soloists, conductors and ensembles for one-nighters.

Yerba Buena Center for the Arts Theater

701 Mission Street, at 3rd Street, SoMa (978 2787/ www.ybca.org). BART & Metro to Montgomery/bus 9, 9X, 10, 14, 30, 45, 71, 76. **Box office** noon-5pm Tue, Wed, Fri-Sun; noon-8pm Thur. **Tickets** $20-$100. **Credit** AmEx, DC, MC, V. **Map** p319 N6.

This 757-seat auditorium plays host to some of the most exciting contemporary music and dance companies in the country, among them Kronos Quartet and the San Francisco Contemporary Music Players (for both, *see below*). Designed by modernist architect James Stewart Polshek, the exterior of the cube-shaped theatre is covered in aluminium panels that catch the sparkling San Francisco light.

Church venues

A number of the city's churches host recitals and chamber concerts, often featuring local young musicians and often free of charge.

Among them are the **Old First Presbyterian Church** (1751 Sacramento Street, between Polk Street & Van Ness Avenue, 776 5552, www.oldfirst.org) on the edge of Pacific Heights; the **First Unitarian Universalist Church** (1187 Franklin Street, at Geary Street, 776 4580, www.uusf.org) near the Civic Center, famous for its Bartok birthday concert on the third Sunday in March; and Nob Hill's **Grace Cathedral** (*see p83*). **St Patrick's Church** (*see p79*) hosts concerts at 12.30pm every Wednesday, and **St Mary's Cathedral** (660 California Street) at 12.30pm every Tuesday (www.noontimeconcerts.org).

The intimate **St John's Presbyterian Church** in Berkeley (2727 College Avenue, between 1st & Garber Streets, 1-510 845 6830, www.stjohns.presbychurch.net) hosts numerous events throughout the year, with the popular **Chamber Music Sundaes** series (753 2792, www.chambermusicsundaes.org) among the highlights. Held over seven or eight Sunday afternoons from November to June, it features members of the SF Symphony playing varied programmes; tickets are around $25 each.

Other ensembles & venues

Aside from the players listed above, a number of groups call the city home. Among them are the **Philharmonia Baroque Orchestra** (252 1288, www.philharmonia.org), which performs baroque and classical repertoire on original instruments. The orchestra's season consists of about six programmes a year (September to April), which they 'tour' to the Herbst Theatre (*see p252*) and Berkeley's First Congregational Church (*see p229*), plus locations in Palo Alto and Contra Costa County. The 17-member **New Century Chamber Orchestra** (357 1111, www.ncco.org) has a similar set-up, playing roughly six times a year at the Florence Gould Theater in the California Palace of the Legion of Honor (*see p115*) as well as at St John's Presbyterian Church in Berkeley (*see above*) and beyond.

A few local ensembles are in demand across the world. **Kronos Quartet** (731 3533, www.kronosquartet.org) focuses on new works, many of them composed for the group. Founded in 1970, the **San Francisco Contemporary Music Players** (278 9566, www.sfcmp.org) is also in the vanguard of modern music, and commissions new works from both young and more established composers. The music performed by the all-male, Grammy-winning a cappella group **Chanticleer** (252 8589, www.chanticleer.org) is less challenging, but performed with no less skill. All three ensembles tour for much of the year but play in the Bay Area regularly: Kronos and the SFCMP at the Yerba Buena Center, and Chanticleer, whose Christmas programme is terrific, at a wide variety of local venues.

Two groups give the SF Opera some small measure of competition. Donald Pippin's **Pocket Opera** (972 8930, www.pocketopera. org) presents operas in English; performances are generally held at the Florence Gould Theater in the California Palace of the Legion of Honor (*see p115*). The **Lamplighters Musical Theatre** (227 4797, www.lamp lighters.org) has been presenting lighter works, including more Gilbert and Sullivan than strictly necessary, for half a century. The company performs at the Yerba Buena Center and the Herbst Theatre (*see p252*) as well as Napa and Antioch. Finally, look out for the **San Francisco Conservatory of Music** (864 7326, www.sfcm.edu), which showcases its young talent at a relatively new 400-seat Civic Center concert hall.

Berkeley & Oakland

Just over the Bay Bridge, the **Berkeley Symphony Orchestra** (1-510 841 2800, www.berkeleysymphony.org) plays half a dozen concerts a year at Zellerbach Hall on the UC Berkeley campus; Kent Nagano is their long-time director. Zellerbach Hall also offers concerts by everyone from John Adams to Cecilia Bartoli as part of **Cal Performances** (1-510 642 9988, www.calperfs.berkeley.edu). Nearby, the **Berkeley Opera** (1-510 841 1903,

www.berkeleyopera.org) stages three shows a year at the Julia Morgan Theatre (2640 College Avenue, 1-510 845 8542, www. juliamorgan.org). Other East Bay venues include the **First Congregational Church** in Berkeley (2345 Channing Way, 1-510 848 3696, www.fccb.org); Oakland's **Mills College** (5000 MacArthur Boulevard, 1-510 430 2296, www.mills.edu), where the Center for Contemporary Music has established a global reputation; and the **Paramount Theatre** (2025 Broadway, Oakland, 1-510 465 6400, www.paramounttheatre.com), which is home to the **Oakland East Bay Symphony** (1-510 444 0801, www.oebs.org) and the **Oakland Symphony Chorus** (1-510 207 4093, www.oaklandsymphonychorus.org).

Jazz & blues

West Coast jazz found a foothold here with the advent of Beat culture. Although the scene isn't as strong as it might be today, the Bay Area does continue to turn out musicians: the Berkeley High Jazz Ensemble, a high-school programme, has spawned the likes of Joshua Redman and David Murray, and 2007 saw the consolidation of the Fillmore Jazz Preservation District as **Yoshi's** (*see p231*) opened its flagship venue on Fillmore Street.

In addition, the **Fillmore Auditorium** (*see p232*), the **Hemlock Tavern** (*see p234*), the **Great American Music Hall** (*see p232*) and the **Intersection for the Arts** (*see p254*) stage sporadic jazz shows.

Elbo Room. See p230.

TICKETS

Booking ahead isn't always necessary at San Francisco's jazz and blues venues. However, at weekends and for big names, an advance reservation is always a good idea; Yoshi's is frequently busy, even during the week.

FESTIVALS

The free **Fillmore Street Jazz Festival** (1-800 731 0003, www.fillmorejazzfestival.com) in early July consists of two days of local acts; the end of the month sees the week-long **North Beach Jazz Festival** (www.nbjazzfest.com), which stages local musicians in a variety of locations. From June to October, **SF Jazz Summerfest** (www.sfjazz.org) runs around 25 free early evening and lunchtime shows in outdoor locations inside and outside the city. Then, from mid October to early November, come the big guns at the **San Francisco Jazz Festival** (www.sfjazz.org), a terrific series of shows throughout town. The **San Francisco Blues Festival** (www.sfblues.com), held over a weekend in late September at the Great Meadow by Fort Mason, is the oldest event of its type in the US.

Biscuits & Blues

401 Mason Street, at Geary Street, Union Square (292 2583/www.biscuitsandblues.com). Bus 2, 3, 4, 27, 38, 76/cable car Powell-Hyde or Powell-Mason. **Open** 6pm-midnight Tue-Sun. **Shows** 8pm and/or 10pm. **Admission** $10-$15. **Credit** AmEx, DC, MC, V. **Map** p318 L5.
This subterranean nightclub/restaurant is a pretty basic affair. Partly due to its location, it attracts a portion of middle-aged tourists and suburbanites, and can get fairly stuffy when crowded. However, it's still the best place in town to catch mainstream blues, played for genuinely excited crowds. The American food has a Southern accent.

Boom Boom Room

1601 Fillmore Street, at Geary Boulevard, Fillmore (673 8000/www.boomboomblues.com). Bus 2, 3, 4, 22, 38. **Open** 4pm-2am Tue-Sun. **Shows** 9pm Tue-Sun. **Admission** $5-$20. **Credit** DC, MC, V. **Map** p314 H6.
Formerly Jack's Bar, an SF fixture for more than 50 years, the Boom Boom Room has been remade as a classy version of a blues joint: John Lee Hooker named the club after his signature song and, until his death in 2001, held court up front. These days, the venue attracts solid blues, roots, funk, R&B and groove-oriented acts, with an occasional surprise rock star dropping in. *See also p235* **Historic venues**.

Elbo Room

647 Valencia Street, between 17th & 18th Streets, Mission (552 7788/www.elbo.com). BART 16th Street Mission/bus 14, 26, 33, 49. **Open** 5pm-2am daily. **Shows** 9pm or 10pm daily. **Admission** free-$10. **No credit cards. Map** p318 K10.

Although the Elbo has been commandeered by yuppies, it continues to be a place to hear good music on a lively stretch of Valencia Street. You're likely to hear jazz (usually with a beat-driven edge), pure funk, soul or Latin jazz in the open-raftered space upstairs, but also hip hop, hard rock, metal and random whacked-out experimentalism. On Sundays, it's the legendary Dub Mission DJ night. *Photo p229.*

Jazz at Pearl's

256 Columbus Avenue, between Broadway & Pacific Avenue, North Beach (291 8255/www.jazzatpearls.com). Bus 9X, 12, 30, 41, 45. **Open** from 7.30pm daily. **Shows** 8pm, 10pm daily. **Admission** $10-$25. **Credit** AmEx, DC, Disc, MC, V. **Map** p315 M3.
This intimate venue (just 25 tables) is the last jazz house left standing in North Beach, once the home for a hoppin' mid-century scene. However, it's a great little place. Singer Kim Nalley and husband Steve Sheraton bought the club from former owner Pearl Wong in 2003 and now book acts such as Pete Escovedo, Sonny Fortune and Marcus Shelby.

Rasselas Jazz

1534 Fillmore Street, at Geary Boulevard, Fillmore (346 8696/www.rasselasjazzclub.com). Bus 2, 3, 4, 22, 38. **Open** 6pm-midnight Mon-Thur, Sun; 5pm-2am Fri, Sat.* **Shows** usually 9pm Mon-Thur, Sun; 6pm, 9pm Fri, Sat. **Admission** usually 2 drink minimum. **Credit** AmEx, DC, MC, V. **Map** p314 H6.

Historic **Bimbo's 365 Club.** *See p232.*

Designed to be an anchor of the Fillmore Jazz Preservation District, Rasselas suffers from unadventurous programming, yet still manages to draw lively crowds at weekends. The decor – high ceilings, bachelor-pad furniture and a crackling fireplace behind the band – is suggestive of a 1960s playboy den, and combos usually get the weekend crowds of African-American revellers and white yuppies up on to their feet.

Saloon

1232 Grant Avenue, at Columbus Avenue, North Beach (989 7666). Bus 12, 15, 30, 41, 45. **Open** *noon-2am daily.* **Shows** *9pm Mon-Thur; 4pm Fri-Sun.* **Admission** *free-$5.* **No credit cards.** **Map** *p315 M3.*

A beer hall that scandalised the neighbourhood when it was established back in 1861 (it's now the oldest continuously operating bar in all of San Francisco), the Saloon has survived earthquakes and shifting musical tastes, and still remains a no-nonsense, rough-edged joint with a busy, bluesy calendar. Psychedelic-era rockers gracing the stage might include former members of Jefferson Airplane and Country Joe & the Fish.

Yoshi's

510 Embarcadero West, at Jack London Square, Oakland (1-510 238 9200/www.yoshis.com). Bus 58, 72, 301. **Open** *Box office 10am-10pm Mon-Fri; noon-9pm Sat, Sun. Lounge from 5pm daily.* **Shows** *8pm, 10pm Mon-Sat; 7pm, 9pm Sun.* **Admission** *$10-$50.* **Credit** *AmEx, DC, Disc, MC, V.*

The handsome, refined Jack London Square venue established Yoshi's as the best jazz joint in the Bay Area – possibly along the entire West Coast – and founder/co-owner Kaz Kajimura hopes to consolidate its reputation among artists and audiences alike with the new Fillmore Street branch in the Jazz Preservation District, which boasts a slightly larger live room and the same excellent acoustics as its predecessor. The Oakland club's separate dining room does good business on the strength of its Japanese food and Kajimura hopes to do the same in San Francisco, but the main attraction in both is the music, a cultured line-up of big names (working the weekend slots) and newcomers (earlier in the week). Book well in advance.

Other locations 1330 Fillmore Street, at Eddy Street, Western Addition (655 5600).

Rock, pop & hip hop

Public perception of the San Francisco sound is still stuck in the 1960s, when the likes of Jefferson Airplane drew young pilgrims; later, the Dead Kennedys, Metallica and Black Rebel Motorcycle Club added to the city's reputation for noisy guitar rock. These days, however, the Bay Area also has a potent hip hop scene, while Oakland is a hotbed of electronic and improvised noise experimentation informed by punk and indie-rock aesthetics.

The scene suffered a setback with the circa-Y2K tech-world bust. Though the city started to recover relatively quickly, music faced a longer hangover. Clubs and rehearsal spaces bit the dust, and musicians headed to Oakland and cheaper climes. Still, the scene has held on: well-renovated halls such as the **Independent** (*see p232*) sprang up; once-DJ-centred clubs such as the **Mezzanine** (*see p240*) built proper live music stages; and hotspots such as the **Rickshaw Stop** (*see p236*) and **12 Galaxies** (*see p233*) now draw trendies and serious listeners alike to once-quiet neighbourhoods.

The scene's continued success can be chalked up to a cross-genre cadre of youthful musicians and forward-thinking bookers and promoters that continue to form bands and fill stages all over: at clubs and other music events, sure, but also at galleries and warehouses. These days, SF boasts one of the most exciting underground scenes in the US. It has spawned international names like Devendra Banhart and Joanna Newsom (both of whom have since left the city limits); kicked off the clicks, whizzes and synths of E-40, the Federation, Turf Talk and the rest of the hyphy movement; nurtured rockers such as Wooden Shjips, Film School, Vetiver, Citay and Rogue Wave, who've all landed on respected indie labels; and inspired those – like hip hoppers Lyrics Born and Blackalicious, the rap experimentalists of Anticon and electronica terrorist Kid 606 – who are making it on their own imprints. The variety on that list is indicative of the eclecticism of the city's music today.

TICKETS

For larger concerts – pretty much anything at the 'Major venues' below – it's worth buying tickets in advance. Where possible, buy from the venue's own box office to avoid the booking fees levied by **Ticketmaster** (421 8497, www.ticketmaster.com). Advance purchase isn't always necessary for the venues listed under 'Bars & clubs' on *pp233-237* but it's never a bad idea if you want to be on the safe side. Always call ahead or look at venue websites before making a special trip.

FESTIVALS

There's everything from rock to opera at the **Stern Grove Festival** (www.sterngrove.org), on Sundays from June to August. Performances take place in an idyllic amphitheatre set in a grove of eucalyptus trees; admission is free. Probably the biggest rock festival of the year in SF is **Noise Pop** (www.noisepop.com), a week-long, city-wide series of indie shows in February. June's similarly spreadeagled **Mission Creek Music & Arts Festival**

Arts & Entertainment

(www.mcmf.org) likewise concentrates on alternative rock, albeit with a more local focus and a more experimental edge. And, speaking of experimental, lovers of the avant-garde ought to investigate August's **San Francisco Electronic Music Festival** (www.sfemf.org).

Major venues

The venues detailed below all host concerts on a regular basis. In addition, a handful of larger arenas stage the occasional show, among them **AT&T Park** (*see p245*), the **Nob Hill Masonic Center** (1111 California Street, at Taylor Street), the **Palace of Fine Arts** (*see p120*) the Concourse at **SF Design Center** (635 8th Street, at Brannan Street) and the cavernous **Bill Graham Civic Auditorium** (99 Grove Street, at Polk Street, 974 4060, www.billgrahamcivic.com) in San Francisco; the **Henry J Kaiser Arena** (10 10th Street) and **Oracle Arena** in Oakland (*see p245*); and the **Berkeley Community Theater** at Berkeley High School and **Greek Theatre** (1-510 642 9988, www.calperfs.berkeley.edu, www.another planetent.com) in Berkeley. A bit further out, the **Shoreline Amphitheatre** in Mountain View (1-650 967 3000, www.shorelineamp.com), the **Sleep Train Pavilion** in Concord (1-925 363 5701, www.chroniclepavilion.com), the **San José State University Event Center** (290 South 7th Street, San Jose, 1-408 924 6360) and **HP Pavilion** in San José (1-408 287 9200, www.hppsj.com) also stage big-name shows from time to time, especially during the summer months. Check venue websites or contact Ticketmaster (*see p231*) for tickets. *See also p235* **Historic venues**.

Bimbo's 365 Club

1025 Columbus Avenue, at Chestnut Street, North Beach (474 0365/www.bimbos365club.com). Bus 10, 20, 30/cable car Powell-Mason. **Box office** 10am-4pm Mon-Fri. **Tickets** $15-$50. **Credit** (advance bookings only) DC, MC, V. **Map** p314 L2.
Bimbo's began life as a Market Street speakeasy in 1931, moving to North Beach two decades later. The venue is still owned by the descendants of Agostino 'Bimbo' Giuntoli, one of its original owners, and has been nicely preserved, with a mermaid theme running throughout. Rita Hayworth once worked the boards as a dancer, but these days you're more likely to see Prefuse 73 spinning vinyl, or touring acts such as Sharon Jones & the Dap-Kings working up the crowd. *Photo p230.*

Fillmore Auditorium

1805 Geary Boulevard, at Fillmore Street, Fillmore (24hr hotline 346 6000/www.thefillmore.com). Bus 2, 3, 4, 22, 38. **Box office** 10am-4pm Sun; also 7.30-10pm show nights. **Tickets** $20-$50. **Credit** AmEx, DC, Disc, MC, V. **Map** p314 H6.

The 1,200-capacity Fillmore was built in 1912, but is better known as the venue in which Bill Graham launched his rock-promotion empire. The performers who play the gorgeous room tend to be on the verge of making it massive.

Grand at the Regency Center

1300 Van Ness Avenue, at Sutter Street, Tenderloin (673 5716). Bus 2, 3, 4, 19, 38, 47, 49, 76. **Box office** Ticketmaster only. **Tickets** prices vary. **Credit** AmEx, DC, MC, V. **Map** p314 K5.
Formerly a Masonic temple, a dance studio, a Polish arts foundation and a movie theatre, this gorgeous Beaux Arts-style ballroom, with its horseshoe-shaped balcony, hardwood floors and fin-de-siècle teardrop chandeliers, now stages everything from opera to rock and jazz gigs to dance events. The landmark 1909 building incorporates the legendary Avalon Ballroom, which once hosted shows by Janis Joplin and Country Joe & the Fish.

Great American Music Hall

859 O'Farrell Street, between Polk & Larkin Streets, Tenderloin (885 0750/www.musichallsf.com). Bus 2, 3, 4, 19, 38, 47, 49, 76. **Box office** 10.30am-6pm Mon-Fri; 1hr before show Sat, Sun. **Tickets** $10-$25. **Credit** DC, MC, V. **Map** p314 K6.
Originally a bordello, then a highfalutin nightclub operated by notorious fan dancer Sally Rand, the grande dame of the city's smaller venues is as beautiful today as at any point in its century-long history. The lavish room, done out with enormous mirrors, rococo woodwork and gold-leaf trim, is these days run by the owners of Slim's (*see below*), who present a cutting-edge roster of well-regarded local and touring musicians (many of the indie-rock ilk). Try to snag one of the coveted seats on the upper balcony.

Independent

628 Divisadero Street, at Hayes Street, Western Addition (771 1421/www.theindependentsf.com). Bus 21, 24. **Box office** 11am-6pm Mon-Fri; 1hr before show. **Tickets** $10-$25. **Credit** AmEx, DC, Disc, MC, V. **Map** p317 G8.
New owners have given this venerable black box the makeover it deserved, with work that included the installation of a stellar sound and light system. In accordance with the varied sounds in the club's storied past, the calendar is filled with a mix of touring rock, pop, metal, rap, jazz, Americana, jam and otherwise undefinable offerings such as Madlib, Sunn 0))), the Boredoms, Fiery Furnaces, High on Fire and Lyrics Born.

Slim's

333 11th Street, between Folsom & Harrison Streets, SoMa (255 0333/www.slims-sf.com). Bus 9, 12, 27, 47. **Box office** 10.30am-6pm Mon-Fri. **Tickets** $8-$35. **Credit** DC, MC, V. **Map** p318 L9.
It might be one of San Francisco's more important music venues, but the 550-capacity Slim's isn't one of its most comfortable: most patrons have to stand, sightlines are compromised by the floor-to-ceiling pillars and, on busy nights, it gets pretty steamy.

Music

The schedule is mostly made up of rock bands, who play alongside a smattering of hip hop acts, reggae groups and rootsy singer/songwriters.

The Warfield

982 Market Street, at Mason Street, Tenderloin (775 7722/www.livenation.com). BART & Metro to Powell/bus 27, 31 & Market Street routes/cable car Powell-Hyde or Powell-Mason. Box office 10am-4pm Sun; also 7.30-10pm show nights. **Tickets** $20-$50. **Credit** AmEx, DC, MC, V. **Map** p315 M6.
Another grand old theatre, this one dating back to 1922, that has been converted into a rock and pop venue in later life. A step up from the Fillmore in terms of capacity, the ornate, 2,100-seat room hosts major national and international acts, many making their last stop on the circuit before vaulting to arena-sized venues. It's very well designed: even the rear-most balcony seats have good views of the stage.

Bars & clubs

Several other bars and nightclubs around the city host worthwhile music nights. Among them are a number of gay venues (*see also* pp217-26), including the **Eagle Tavern** (*see* p224), which hosts punk and hardcore shows, and **Kimo's** (1351 Polk Street, Nob Hill, 885 4535), a landmark gay bar where rock acts of varying quality perform in its upstairs room.

Note that for all venues listed here, opening hours and showtimes can vary: 'usually 9pm' means the occasional show may begin at 8.30pm or 10pm. Always call or check online (most venues keep their websites bang up to date) before setting out.

12 Galaxies

2565 Mission Street, at 21st Street, Mission (970 9777/www.12galaxies.com). BART 24th Street Mission/bus 14, 26, 48, 49, 67. **Open** show nights only. **Shows** 9pm, nights vary. **Admission** $5-$25. **No credit cards. Map** p318 K11.
The sightlines are all swell at 12 Galaxies: check out the live music from the shining, retro-style bar, hunker down in a shadowy seat by the stage, or look down from the second-floor mezzanine. The likes of Alejandro Escovedo, DJ Logic, Railroad Earth, Lightning Bolt, Deerhunter and Black Dice have all graced the stage, though the line-up tends to be heavy on local talents such as Kelley Stoltz, the Oh Sees and the Sermon.

21 Grand

416 25th Street, at Broadway, Oakland (1-510 444 7263/www.21grand.org). BART 19th Street/ Oakland, then a short walk.
Shows were suspended at the time of writing at this white-box non-profit, due to 'compliance issues' with the city authorities. We hope these are successfully dealt with so 21 Grand can get back to hosting art shows as well as some of the more innovative musical programming in the East Bay: you're as likely to

Bottom of the Hill. *See p234.*

catch Sonic Youth complementing an SF arena slot opening for Pearl Jam with an intimate and experimental noise performance at this space as you are avant up-and-comers such as the Gowns, the High Places, Why? and Zeena Parkins.

Annie's Social Club

917 Folsom Street, at 5th Street, SoMa (974 1585/ www.anniessocialclub.com). Bus 9X, 12, 27, 30, 45, 76. **Open** 4pm-2am Mon-Fri; varies Sat, Sun. **Shows** times vary. **Admission** free-$15. **No credit cards. Map** p319 M7.
Once the venerable Covered Wagon Saloon and later the Cherry Bar, Annie's Social Club still proudly maintains its dive-joint roots. However, it's looking a little smarter these days, and runs a wider spectrum of entertainments: everything from metal to singer-songwriter shows, Britpop nights and punk rock karaoke.

Ashkenaz Music & Dance Community Center

1317 San Pablo Street, at Gilman Street, Berkeley (1-510 525 5054/www.ashkenaz.com). BART North Berkeley/AC Transit bus 9, 52, 72, 73. **Open**/**shows** times vary. **Admission** $6-$20. **No credit cards.**
Jam band groupies and folk fans will find plenty to love at this East Bay institution, which has been putting the groove into groovy since 1973. It's just steps away from the 924 Gilman Street Project (*see* p236), but music store aisles away in terms of genre. Known for its folk dance nights, Grateful Dead tributes and zydeco bands, the centre also serves up Western swing, African, Balkan and klezmer sounds. *See also p239* A different beat.

Arts & Entertainment

Bottom of the Hill

1233 17th Street, at Missouri Street, Potrero Hill (621 4455/www.bottomofthehill.com). Bus 10, 22, 53. **Open** *8.30pm-2am Mon, Tue, Sat, Sun; 4pm-2am Wed-Fri.* **Shows** *usually 9pm daily.* **Admission** *$5-$20.* **Credit** *AmEx, DC, MC, V.* **Map** p319 N10.

This little club, wedged among warehouses at the base of Potrero Hill, has long been a favourite with the indie-rock crowd. It features local and touring acts most nights, as well as occasional arena acts (Mars Volta, the Beastie Boys) hankering to play an intimate show. Underground bands that play here one year may become cult sensations or even major stars the next. The decor is classic dive, with quirky touches. *Photo p233.*

Café du Nord/
Swedish American Hall

2170 Market Street, between Church & Sanchez Streets, Castro (861 5016/www.cafedunord.com). Metro to Church/streetcar F/bus 22, 37. **Open** *1hr before show-2am.* **Shows** *times vary, daily.* **Admission** *$10-$35.* **Credit** *(bar only) AmEx, DC, MC, V.* **Map** p318 H9.

Several SF nightspots carry the feel of a Prohibition-era speakeasy, but none captures the spirit quite as well as the Café du Nord. Mind you, it does have a head start: it actually was one. The subterranean front room, which hosts cultured alternative acts, has red velvet walls and a 40ft (12m) mahogany bar that bustles with scenesters. Owner Guy Carson also books the likes of Cat Power, Joanna Newsom, Bert Jansch and Jenny Lewis to play the quaint, larger Swedish American Hall upstairs.

Edinburgh Castle Pub

950 Geary Street, at Polk Street, Tenderloin (885 4074/www.castlenews.com). Bus 2, 3, 4, 19, 38, 76. **Open** *Pub 5pm-2am daily. Venue from 9.30pm.* **Show** *times vary.* **Admission** *Pub free. Venue $5.* **Credit** *DC, MC, V.* **Map** p314 K6.

This oak-clad, beer-stained ode to Highland high times offers fish 'n' chips till 11pm and plenty of booths for loud conversation, but trip upstairs, past the pool table on the mezzanine, to catch the live punk, indie and metal shows, in addition to the occasional northern soul dance party and quiz night.

El Rio

3158 Mission Street, at Cesar Chavez Street, Mission (282 3325/www.elriosf.com). BART 24th Street Mission/bus 12, 14, 26, 49, 67. **Open** *Mar-Nov 5pm-2am Mon-Thur; 4pm-2am Fri; 3pm-2am Sat, Sun. Dec-Feb 5pm-2am Mon-Thur, Sat, Sun; 4pm-2am Fri.* **Shows** *times vary.* **Admission** *free-$10.* **No credit cards.** **Map** off p318 K12.

Head to the El Rio on a Sunday afternoon and make your way to the garden, where you'll find SF's most diverse and lively salsa party: a local tradition for more than 25 years and now taking place year-round. There's an outdoor barbecue, dancing lessons, decent margaritas and a friendly crowd of straights and queers. Other nights you might encounter experimental rock, DJs or the odd home-grown film festival.

Fat City

314 11th Street, at Folsom Street, SoMa (www.myspace.com/fatcitysf). Bus 9, 12, 27, 47. **Open/shows** *times vary.* **Admission** *free-$15.* **No credit cards.** **Map** p318 L8.

In keeping with the times, Fat City doesn't have a phone number but does have a MySpace page. The venue hosts everything from international DJ nights with the likes of Miss Kittin to live metal, rock and comedy. The new owners wisely retained the exposed red-brick walls and hardwood floors of the sizeable main room, making it the ideal blank slate for the city's more ambitious party organisers.

Freight & Salvage Coffee House

1111 Addison Street, at San Pablo Avenue, Berkeley (1-510 548 1761/www.thefreight.org). BART North Berkeley/bus 19, 51, 72. **Box office** *noon-7pm daily.* **Open** *from 7.30pm, days vary.* **Shows** *usually 8pm, days vary.* **Admission** *$16-$25.* **No credit cards.**

The venerable, booze-free Freight is a much-loved outpost of traditional music in all its incarnations, from folk to gospel. The monthly calendar might include sets from Iris Dement, Vasen, Lucy Kaplansky or the David Grisman Bluegrass Experience, plus Hawaiian slack-key players, Iraqi oud pluckers, Hungarian violinists or austere Appalachian mandolinists.

Hemlock Tavern

1131 Polk Street, at Post Street, Tenderloin (923 0923/www.hemlocktavern.com). Bus 2, 3, 4, 19, 38, 47, 49, 76. **Open** *4pm-2am daily.* **Shows** *9.30pm daily.* **Admission** *free-$10.* **No credit cards.** **Map** p314 K6.

Out front, the Hemlock looks like a capacious, matey watering hole, a lively mix of young tastemakers, art snobs and yuppies playing pool, yapping at the central bar or puffing in the open-air smoking 'room'. At the back, however, an intimate live room plays host to some of the more edgy and intelligent musical programming in the city. The roster is built around hipster-friendly artists such as Deerhoof and Wolf Eyes, with no knowing who will blow up next.

Hotel Utah

500 4th Street, at Bryant Street, SoMa (546 6300/www.thehotelutahsaloon.com). Bus 9X, 30, 45, 47, 76. **Open** *11.30am-2am Mon-Fri; 6pm-2am Sat, Sun.* **Shows** *usually 9pm daily.* **Admission** *$6-$10.* **Credit** *DC, MC, V.* **Map** p319 N7.

The down-and-dirty days of the Barbary Coast are ingrained in the timbers of this 1908 watering hole, which has welcomed the likes of Marilyn Monroe, Bing Crosby and an assortment of gangsters and beatniks. Now gaining a fresh lease of life, the Utah is both a characterful bar and a cosy music room, hosting indie rockers, singer-songwriters and the occasional more eclectic curiosity.

Knockout

3223 Mission Street, at Valencia Street, Mission (550 6994/www.theknockoutsf.com). Bus 12, 14, 26, 27, 49, 67. **Open** *5pm-2am daily.* **Shows** *usually 9pm or 10pm daily.* **Admission** *free-$8.* **No credit cards.**

Historic venues

Some accuse San Franciscans of being mired in musical nostalgia – fixated on 1950s Beat bohemia or stuck in a Summer of Love flashback. Perhaps they have a point, but in a city with a musical history this extraordinary, it would be harsh to criticise a music-lover for wanting to explore the iconic, still-raging hotspots where it all happened.

The town's grandest beauty – the **Great American Music Hall** (*see p232; pictured*) – is the perfect place to start: constructed in 1907, this erstwhile bordello has maintained its baroque, gilded beauty well, supported by marble columns and lined with ornate Barbary Coast-era mirrors. In the 1930s, it was owned by renowned fan-dancer/stripper Sally Rand, said to still haunt its corridors. Now the former jazz joint is known for its diverse rock and pop shows, plus special events such as a recent last-minute, one-night stand by Lauryn Hill.

Further east on Geary is the **Fillmore** (*see p232*), once a jazz-era big-band venue that went by the moniker the Majestic Ballroom. The elegant, chandeliered auditorium where rock impresario Bill Graham made his name has since ushered in memorable shows by the likes of the Who, Johnny Winter, Eric Clapton, Mike Bloomfield and Santana, as the posters lining the walls of the upstairs bar attest.

Just across the street lies the **Boom Boom Room** (*see p230*), in the same space that housed the once-jumping jazz joint Jack's, a linchpin of the district's lively African-American nightlife scene in the 1940s and '50s. John Lee Hooker gave the place its name and held court here until his death in 2001.

Less likely to be booming with cool sounds is the stately Beaux Arts-style **Grand** (*see p232*), which flings open its doors on a more irregular basis. Graham's down-home competitor and hippie king Chet Helms threw trippy rock shows in the hall during the '60s, when it was dubbed the Avalon Ballroom: there he unveiled his protégé Janis Joplin in 1966 and gathered the long-haired Love Generation for Moby Grape, the Steve Miller Blues Band and Bo Diddley, among others.

Further south in Downtown stands the ex-movie palace the **Warfield** (*see p233*), where Louis Armstrong once shared the bill with the talkies. More talent came to call when Graham announced the arrival of Bob Dylan's gospel shows here in 1979. Since then the cavernous hall has played host to such draws as the Grateful Dead, Elvis Costello, Nick Cave, Neil Young and Prince.

In North Beach, check into cellar comedy club the **Purple Onion** (140 Columbus Avenue, 956 1653, www.purpleonioncomedy.com), now suffering from a sad sports bar-style renovation. Back in its '50s and '60s heyday, the Kingston Trio, the Smothers Brothers, Rod McKuen and Maya Angelou whooped it up before tourists arrived looking for beatnik caricatures. And finally, towards Fisherman's Wharf, **Bimbo's 365 Club** (*see p232*) sets the scene for early '50s supper-club glamour with a parquet dancefloor, leather booths and kitsch-cool girl-in-a-fishbowl theme. Joey Bishop, Xavier Cugat and Louis Prima serenaded here years before the Strokes, Iggy Pop and Blonde Redhead worked its stage.

If you like small bands in intimate spaces, make tracks for the **Make-Out Room**.

Owned by 2007 mayoral candidate and Burning Man fan Chicken John back when it was called the Odeon, this shoebox of a club sports a small stage in the back, karaoke happy hours, late-night installments of beer-sodden bingo and other quirky diversions. Catch indie-rock combos like Imperial Teen spinoff Hey Willpower and Old Time Relijun.

Make-Out Room

3225 22nd Street, between Mission & Valencia Streets, Mission (647 2888/www.makeoutroom.com). BART 24th Street Mission/bus 14, 26, 48, 49, 67. **Open** 6pm-2am daily. **Shows** usually 9pm daily. **Admission** $5-$10. **No credit cards. Map** p318 K12.
One of the best places in town to see smallish bands, the Make-Out Room attracts a laid-back, alternative, youthful crowd on its weekend live music nights. The decor lives up to the name: there's a bearskin rug on one wall and a stag's head on another with a rainbow of bras strung from the antlers. The atmosphere, as with many Mission bars, is that of a cheery dive.

924 Gilman Street Project

924 Gilman Street, between 7th & 8th Streets, Berkeley (1-510 525 9926). BART Downtown Berkeley, then bus 9/bus 9, 72. **Open/shows** from 8pm Fri, Sat, sometimes Sun. **Admission** $5-$8, plus $2 annual membership. **No credit cards.**
This all-ages, alcohol-free institution, which is run by a collective, is internationally renowned among punks. Green Day started out playing here, but these days, you're more likely to catch the likes of Dr Know, MDC and This Bike Is a Pipe Bomb, along with committed locals such as Rock 'n' Roll Adventure Kids, Triclops! and La Plebe.

Red Devil Lounge

1695 Polk Street, at Clay Street, Polk Gulch (921 1695/www.reddevillounge.com). Bus 1, 19, 27, 47, 49, 76. **Open** usually 8pm-2am daily. **Shows** usually 9pm daily. **Admission** $3-$30. **Credit** AmEx, DC, Disc, MC, V. **Map** p314 K4.
This corner venue, done out with Gothic touches, has recently ramped up its music offerings, which sit alongside club nights in a fairly busy calendar. The line-ups aren't often cutting edge, but the venue does stage crowd-pulling acts such as the Misfits, the English Beat and KRS-One.

Rickshaw Stop

155 Fell Street, at Franklin Street, Hayes Valley (861 2011/www.rickshawstop.com). Metro to Van Ness/bus 21, 47, 49 & Market Street routes. **Open** 7pm-2am Wed-Sat. **Shows** times vary. **Admission** $5-$10. **No credit cards. Map** p318 K8.
Doing its best to fill a sparse strip near Civic Center, the Rickshaw taps a cool collegiate/rec-room vibe with its crash-pad decor of mod plastic loungers, foosball table and odalisque-via-Target lighting. Come for the laid-back hipster ambience and low-priced snack menu, but stay for hep local and touring bands and hot, hard-edged electro and mash-up DJs.

Starry Plough

3101 Shattuck Avenue, at Prince Street, Berkeley (1-510 841 2082/www.starryploughpub.com). BART Ashby. **Open** 4pm-2am daily. **Shows** usually 9.30pm Thur-Sat. **Admission** free-$12. **Credit** AmEx, MC, V.
Talented local indie-rock and folk acts, such as 20 Minute Loop and Sean Smith, and nationally famous cult singer-songwriters, among them Penelope

Houston and Vic Chesnutt, consort at this comfy, friendly pub that fronts on to a leafy, residential strip of Shattuck Avenue. There are also regular poetry slams and Irish sessions.

Stork Club

2330 Telegraph Avenue, between 23rd & 24th Streets, Oakland (1-510 444 6174/www.stork cluboakland.com). BART 19th Street/Oakland. **Open** 6pm-2am Tue-Sun. **Shows** usually 9pm. **Admission** usually $5. **No credit cards.**
Located on a slightly sketchy stretch of Telegraph Avenue, this quirky, two-room bar is the place in the East Bay to hear those edgy touring artists – who might also play at the Hemlock Tavern while they're in the area.

Thee Parkside

1600 17th Street, at Wisconsin Street, Potrero Hill (252 1330/www.theeparkside.com). Bus 10, 22, 53. **Open** 2pm-2am daily. **Shows** usually 9pm. **Admission** free-$15. **No credit cards.**
Map p319 N10.

This roadhouse started out as a lunch spot for dot-com cube farmers. When the pink slips began to flutter, Thee Parkside found new life as a rowdy joint specialising in roots, punk, country and garage rock. Things get sweaty in the main room, where the so-called 'stage' abuts the door. In the tiki patio out back, beer guzzlers heat up with a bit of ping-pong.

Uptown Night Club

1928 Telegraph Avenue, at 20th Street, Oakland (1-510 451 8100/www.uptownnightclub.com). BART 19th Street/Oakland. **Open** times vary. **Shows** usually 9pm. **Admission** free-$10. **No credit cards.**
Local punk magazine publisher Larry Trujillo recently took the helm at this promising, narrow space in a deco beauty of a downtown Oakland building. Since then he's booked punk vets like the Germs and the Adolescents, swingers Big Sandy and his Fly-Rite Boys, SF dance-poppers the Lovemakers and a raft of live burlesque, electro and new wave punk DJ nights.

Best of the Bay Area

Aided by a constant influx of talented newcomers and avid niche audiences, yet beset by high rents and a cultural insecurity complex regarding its existence off the NYC-LA grid, the Bay Area nonetheless has a rep in music circles for birthing intriguing bands and fostering musical movements of all stripes. Though dance-punk bands like the Rapture and !!! had to jump a jet to New York to make their fortunes, the scene continues to nurture newcomers. Now, decades after Metallica's garage days, metal is being revisited by a new generation of loud lads. Witness the formidable **High on Fire**, led by vocalist-guitarist Matt Pike of legendary sludge metal group Sleep and once boasting bassist Joe Preston of the Melvins; the droning art-metallists **Om**, with former Sleep bassist Al Cisneros and drummer Chris Hakius; political Oakland combo **Machine Head**, whose tour was recently banned from the Disney-owned House of Blues; pentagram fans **Saviours**; and veteran avant-riff instrumentalists the **Fucking Champs**, whose Tim Green records many an ear-bleeder at his Louder Studios.

Psychedelia in the harder, noisier and always electric vein of **Mammatus**, **Assemble Head in Sunburst Sound** and **Citay** builds on the acid rock legacy of SF's Blue Cheer. **Comets on Fire** work the Echoplex-enhanced noise levels most adeptly – and Comets side-projects like **Six Organs of Admittance**, **Howlin' Rain**, **NVH** and **Colossal Yes** fill local

clubs on a regular basis with everything from Fahey-like acoustics to pianoman melodicism.

The freakier breed of out-folk found its roots here in the form not only of **Six Organs** but also San Francisco Art Institute grad **Devendra Banhart**, his pal and one-time Aardvark Bookstore clerk Andy Cabic, who heads **Vetiver**, and former Mills College composition student and harpist **Joanna Newsom**. These days you're more likely to stumble over finger-picked shows by Nevada City's **Mariee Sioux** and the **Moore Brothers**, the East Bay's **Finches**, and SF musical theatre dabbler **Sonny Smith**. And check the websites of Fernwood Resort (www.fernwoodbigsur.com) and the **Henry Miller Library** (www.henry miller.org), both in Big Sur, for soft, sublime SF-LA sounds among the coastal redwoods, booked by organisers like Folk Yeah!.

On the hip hop front, hyphy – the minimalist, synth-driven, preternaturally catchy sound of Oakland – still rules 'Yay Area' streets, though hip hop powerhouse KMEL FM has distanced itself from the local scene of late. Still, with luck and an ear to the station, you might score a rare live hyphy performance by East Bay stalwarts like **E-40**, **Keak da Sneak**, **Mistah FAB**, the **Federation** or **Turf Talk**.

Finally, for a more electronic mash-up, keep an ear open for dubstep nights at **Anu** (43 6th Street, at Market Street, 543 3505, www.anu-bar.com) and the **Transfer** (198 Church Street, at Market Street, 861 7499).

Arts & Entertainment

Nightclubs

Calling all creatures of the night.

Like a lot of other things in San Francisco, the dotcom bubble sent the city's nightlife into a spin: dance clubs opened left, right and centre; dive bars started levying cover charges, and pubs were overtaken by dotcoms hosting IPO parties. These kids had money to spend, and needed places to spend it. If you had two turntables and a crate of vinyl, you could make a few hundred bucks a night, as long as you didn't mind pandering to the nouveaux riches' tastes. It wasn't to last. The bubble burst, and many of the once-thriving, overpriced venues closed, either because of excessive rents, noise violations or, more probably, the drastic exodus of young money when the tech party went pop.

Still, San Franciscans will never let their party spirit die. There was a turn towards smaller clubs (and prices). And when the underground techno and house scene was plagued by 'anti-rave' police crackdowns, activists set up groups such as the **San Francisco Late Night Coalition** (www. sflnc.com) to boost solidarity. The city council responded by creating a seven-member Entertainment Commission to regulate and promote nightlife, simultaneously taking the power to issue entertainment-related permits from the San Francisco Police Department.

Dancing isn't always central to a night out. The city's so-called 'cabaret laws' play havoc with promoters looking to license their venues for dancing. Up-and-up club owners try to secure Place of Entertainment licences, which allow dancing. That said, authorities tend to turn a blind eye to those without licences until more serious illegal activities draw their attention. If you're looking to shake it, **Milk**, **DNA Lounge** and **Mezzanine** are all good bets, and dancing has made a comeback at many smaller venues as well. The latest round of Silicon Valley successes has again filled the city with awkward techies eager to hit the floors – but this time good vibes, not vulgar displays of wealth, seem to rule the scene.

INFORMATION

Both print and online versions of *SF Weekly* and the *San Francisco Bay Guardian* have extensive clubs listings. It's also worth visiting Amoeba Music, Tweekin Records and Aquarius Records (for all, *see p195*) to pick up flyers and magazines advertising goings-on. Check online for details of under-the-radar events.

Ruby Skye.

The discussion boards at **Craigslist** (www.craigslist. org) and **SF Raves** (www.sfraves.org) are both useful; **Squid List** (www.laughingsquid.org) is the first place techno hippies look for multi-media extravaganzas. **Blasthaus** (www. blasthaus.com) lists major dance music events, while **SF Station** (www.sfstation.com) offers well-edited, succinctly written party listings with an updated calendar. However, the daddy of them all is **Flavorpill** (www.flavorpill.com/ sanfrancisco), its weekly dispatch outlining the best of the city's cultural happenings.

Admission prices depend on the night, but usually vary from nothing to $25. Many clubs stay open well past last orders, but by law they can't serve alcohol between 2am and 6am. Some clubs are strictly 21 and over; if you're under 21, check the club's policy before you go.

LATE-NIGHT TRANSPORT

The Muni Owl Service operates on the Muni Metro L and N lines and on the 5, 14, 22, 24, 38, 90, 91 and 108 bus lines from 1am until 5am. All other lines stop at 12.30am. BART runs roughly until midnight. For taxi companies, *see p285*.

Downtown

Union Square & around

Harry Denton's Starlight Room

Sir Francis Drake Hotel, 450 Powell Street,
between Post & Sutter Streets (395 8595/www.
harrydenton.com). BART & Metro to Powell/bus 2,
3, 4, 30, 45, 76 & Market Street routes/cable car
Powell-Hyde or Powell-Mason. **Open** 6pm-2am daily.
Admission free-$15 (free before 8.30pm). **Credit**
AmEx, DC, Disc, MC, V. **Map** p315 M5.
Both of Harry Denton's venues are a love 'em or
leave 'em affair. Block out the stunning 21st-floor
view over Union Square, the multiple mirrors and
the floral carpets, and you're left with a room of
dressed-up social and financial climbers dancing to
'Mustang Sally'. Meanwhile, Harry Denton's Rouge
(1500 Broadway, at Polk Street, 346 7683) offers the
delights of Vegas-style showgirls jiggling on the bar
and mingling with the starry-eyed punters.

Ruby Skye

420 Mason Street, between Geary & Post Streets
(693 0777/www.rubyskye.com). BART & Metro
to Powell/bus 2, 3, 4, 38, 76 & Market Street
routes/cable car Powell-Hyde or Powell-Mason.
Open 9pm-2am Thur; 9pm-3am Fri; 8pm-4am Sat.
Admission $10-$30. **Credit** AmEx, DC, Disc, MC,
V. **Map** p314 L5.
Converted from an elegant 1890s theatre, Ruby Skye
has retained a good many of its ornate Victorian
touches, while gaining thoroughly modern sound
and lighting systems in the translation. But with its

huge dancefloor and parade of surgically enhanced
women, the whole scene feels like it's been imported
from LA. Not surprisingly, it's a second home for
rave-circuit big names like Sasha and Digweed.

Vessel

85 Campton Place, off Stockton Street, between
Sutter & Post Streets (433 8585/www.vesselsf.com).
Bart & Metro to Montgomery/bus 2, 3, 4, 38, 76 &
Market Street routes/cable car Powell-Hyde or Powell-
Mason. **Open** 5pm-midnight Wed, Thur; 5pm-2am
Fri; 9pm-2am Sat. **Admission** free-$20. **Credit**
AmEx, DC, MC, V. **Map** p315 M5.
A blast from the city's ostentatious dotcom past –
a person could easily spend upwards of $1,000 here
on fancy champagne service to impress his or her
other half. Still, cruising through this incredibly
well-appointed bar early in the evening can be fun
(you're guaranteed a long wait in line and the often
disapproving scrutiny of the bouncers if you arrive
after 10pm), if only to revel in the screeching deca-
dence of San Francisco's monied class.

The Tenderloin

Bambuddha Lounge

Phoenix Hotel, 601 Eddy Street, at Larkin Street
(885 5088/www.bambuddhalounge.com). Bus 19,
31, 38. **Open** 5.30-10pm Wed, Thur; 5.30pm-2am
Fri, Sat. **Admission** $10 Fri, Sat from 10pm.
Credit AmEx, DC, MC, V. **Map** p314 K6.
This nouveau South-east Asian hangout is sleek
and minimal. Gentle lighting complements the
numerous conversation-promoting nooks and the

A different beat

The age of the world-travelling, superstar
San Francisco DJ may have come to a
bit of a close, but the city is still home to
globally renowned deck masters like Miguel
Migs, Mark Farina, David Harness and
acclaimed hip hop trio Triple Threat, whose
roving parties can be tracked through True
Skool (www.true-skool.org). Yet the city's
constant influx of tourists and immigrants
also lends itself to other dancefloor flavours,
reaching well beyond the mainstays of house,
hip hop and techno to embrace a thriving
international scene.

The Mission's **Café Cocomo** (www.cafe
cocomo.com) offers a nightly paradise of
authentic Latin musical styles – including
salsa, *cumbia* and tango – and also provides
lessons for beginners. Another touchstone of
Latin dance culture is the **Metronome Dance
Center** (www.metronomedancecenter.com),
which offers daily classes and several regular
parties at which to tap your every toe. If the

tabla-driven tunes of South Asia are more
your style, head to one of **NonStop Bhangra**'s
events (www.nonstopbhangra.com), or a party
hosted by the more electronic-oriented crew
Surya Dub (www.suryadub.com). Speaking
of dub, the long-running **Dub Mission** Sundays
at the Elbo Room (www.dubmission.com) will
scratch your stony Caribbean itch.

Lately, San Francisco also seems to have
taken a strong liking to Balkan and other
Central European musical vibes – **Amnesia**
(*see p241*) in the Mission and Berkeley's
Ashkenaz community centre (www.ashkenaz.
com) host several wild Balkan-themed parties
every month, often with live brass musical
accompaniment and a circus-like atmosphere.
Meanwhile, for a uniquely San Franciscan
take on Middle Eastern partying, don't miss
an opportunity to catch performance troupe
Fat Chance Belly Dance (www.fcbd.com)
at one of their several annual appearances.
You'll find yourself swaying along in no time.

performances, in a hipper-than-hip yet nonetheless eminently friendly atmosphere. This is the place to scope out the upper crust of the city's underground as they munch away on gourmet pizzas or sip their moderately priced cocktails.

SoMa & South Beach

For gay and lesbian bars and nightclubs in SoMa, among them the **Stud**, *see pp224-225*.

111 Minna

111 Minna Street, between 2nd & New Montgomery Streets (974 1719/www.111minnagallery.com). BART & Metro to Montgomery/bus 9, 9X, 10, 12, 14, 15, 30, 45, 76 & Market Street routes. **Open** *Gallery* noon-5pm Tue-Fri. *Bar* 5-10pm Wed; 5pm-2am Thur-Sat. **Admission** $3-$15. **Credit** AmEx, DC, MC, V. **Map** p315 N5.

This concrete box, located down an alley just south of Market Street, is an art gallery by day but a truly happening dance club by night. It draws an unusual hybrid clientele – serious rave yuppies – but is popular with all kinds of dance-music freaks thanks to a music policy that travels from garage to Afrobeat, stopping at all stations in between.

330 Ritch

330 Ritch Street, between Brannan & Townsend Streets (541 9574). Metro N to 2nd & King/bus 9X, 10, 30, 45, 47, 76. **Open** 5pm-2am Wed-Fri; 10pm-2am Sat, Sun. **Admission** free-$10. **Credit** AmEx, DC, MC, V. **Map** p319 O7.

The young crowd seems right at home in this spacious yet intimate spot, tucked away down an alley. The sounds include hip hop and classic soul, but Thursdays belong to long-running Popscene, a Britpop night (spot the scooters out front) that often features touring bands on the tiny stage – if you've got a British accent, you'll make friends easily.

DNA Lounge

375 11th Street, between Folson & Harrison Streets (626 1409/www.dnalounge.com). Bus 9, 12, 27, 47. **Open** 9pm-2am Tue-Thur; 9pm-4am Fri, Sat. **Admission** $5-$20. **No credit cards**. **Map** p318 L9.

Goth kids flock to SoMa for all manner of musical fetishes and countercultural indulgences. But none of their nights is complete without a stop in at the DNA Lounge. This long-time fixture has undergone massive remodelling over the years and now hosts DJ nights and concerts by the likes of Laibach. However, the wonderful stage set-up, viewable from both the dancefloor and the recessed mezzanine, has turned even hip hop acts on to this gem of a nightspot.

Mezzanine

444 Jessie Street, at 6th Street (820 9669/www.mezzaninesf.com). BART & Metro to Powell/bus 14, 26 & Market Street routes. **Open** 10pm-2am Fri; 10pm-7am Sat; other nights vary. **Admission** free-$30. **No credit cards**. **Map** p319 M7.

The Virgins in concert at **330 Ritch**.

bamboo daybeds alongside the cabaña-style pool, while the glittering bar and roaring fireplace area are inviting spots in which a see-and-be-seen crowd sits back and enjoys DJs spinning acid jazz, funky disco and other downtempo sounds. Club nights are Friday and Saturday.

Suite One8one

181 Eddy Street, at Taylor Street (345 9900/ www.suiteone8one.com). BART & Metro to Powell/ bus 27, 31, 38 & Market Street routes. **Open** 9pm-4am Thur-Sat. **Admission** $20. **Credit** AmEx, DC, MC, V. **Map** p314 K7.

The ultra-swank Suite One8one is one of SF's hottest spots, but it's not for everyone. Some cologne-soaked folks are suckers for a $20 cover, and that's potentially the appeal. Past the rather surly doormen, three floors boast a series of plush rooms and VIP areas. However, the pedestrian music, not to mention the rather snooty crowd, can leave one feeling a bit empty.

222 Club

222 Hyde Street, at Turk Street (440 0222/www. 222club.net). BART & Metro to Civic Center/bus 5, 16, 19, 31 & Market Street routes. **Open** 6pm-2am Tue-Sat. **Admission** varies. **Credit** AmEx, DC, MC, V. **Map** p314 K6.

One of the funkiest little clubs in San Francisco, the 222 Club hosts hip hop, house, techno and electro nights, alongside a smattering of experimental live

This 900-capacity club and art gallery has two long bars bordering the ample dancefloor and lofty space upstairs. Local DJs and even some live acts hold court on the weekends, while touring techno acts such as Richie Hawtin and Miss Kittin make it their sole stop in SF. Could it be that massive sound system, often thought of as the city's best?

6ix

60 6th Street, at Jessie Street (863 1221/www. clubsix1.com). BART & Metro to Powell/bus 14, 26 & Market Street routes. **Open** 9pm-2am Tue-Sat. **Admission** $5-$20. **Credit** AmEx, DC, MC, V. **Map** p318 L7.

Behind the doors of this venue, located on one of the city's grubbiest blocks (go in a group or avoid looking rich and/or touristy), you'll find a high-ceilinged chill-out room and bar with a low-ceilinged dancefloor below. DJs have been known to spin house, dub, dancehall and whatever else may be filling floors at the moment. The upstairs space features paintings and photography by local and international artists.

Temple

540 Howard Street, between 1st & 2nd Streets (978 9942/www.templesf.com). BART & Metro to Montgomery/bus 10, 14, 76 & Market Street routes. **Open** 10pm-4am Fri, Sat; other nights vary. **Credit** AmEx, DC, MC, V. **Map** p315 N5.

After a turn toward smaller clubs (and less expensive entry fees), many of the city's scenesters bemoaned a lack of larger venues that weren't overrun by obnoxious singles and clueless DJs. Enter Temple, a three-storey behemoth featuring an in-house Thai restaurant and several VIP enclaves, which opened in 2007 to great acclaim. While there are still a few bachelors-on-the-make in the mix, Temple's after-hours music programming includes some of the hottest house, techno and hip hop acts performing in a superclub environment.

1015 Folsom

1015 Folsom Street, at 6th Street (431 7444/www. 1015.com). Bus 12, 14X, 27. **Open** 10pm-7am Fri, Sat; other nights vary. **Admission** free-$20. **No credit cards. Map** p319 M7.

San Francisco's meat-and-potatoes dance club, 1015 is always a safe bet, whether you want to go dancing before, during or after hours. The three rooms each have their own vibe – move through space and time without changing venues. You'll find the same suburban crowd of pick-up artists and bimbos as in any big club, but they don't overwhelm the place.

Wish

1539 Folsom Street, between 11th & 12th Streets (431 1661/www.wishsf.com). Metro to Van Ness/ bus 9, 12, 27, 47. **Open** 5pm-2am Mon-Fri; 7pm-2am Sat. **Admission** varies. **Credit** AmEx, DC, MC, V. **Map** p318 L9.

A meat market on most nights, albeit a comfortable one, boasting some of the best downtempo and lounge music in the city and incredibly friendly staff. This is the place to hit on weeknights for a fancy cocktail with friends or to flirt with hot San Fran-citizens while soaking up the bubbly tunes on tap. On weekends, Wish is swarming with tipsy lookers eager to suck face and talk your ear off – perfect if that's what you're looking for.

The Mission & the Castro

The Mission

Amnesia

853 Valencia Street, between 19th & 20th Streets (970 0012). Bus 14, 26, 49. **Open** 6pm-2am daily. **Admission** free-$8. **No credit cards. Map** p318 K11.

Amnesia is still resisting the party-hearty armies that take over most of this stretch of the Mission at weekends. Instead, it draws a diverse, friendly, multi-ethnic crowd, and the DJ spins suitably eclectic sounds. With a nice selection of Belgian brews and friendly staff to boot, the patrons at the bar are as likely to be neighbourhood regulars as they are curious tourists checking out the action.

Mighty

119 Utah Street, at 15th Street (626 7001/ www.mighty119.com). Bus 9, 9X, 14X, 22, 53. **No credit cards. Map** p319 M9.

Open 10pm-4am Thur-Sat. **Admission** free-$15.

The slick interior and flawless sound system led *URB* magazine to name Mighty the 'Best New Club in America', but the place has also received plenty of accolades from San Franciscans. Indeed, it's such

DNA Lounge.

Arts & Entertainment

Milk DJ Bar & Lounge shakes up the scene.

a well-tuned space that Austin DJ D:Fuse recorded his *People_3* live set here. Rave it up at the main stage or take it easy in the chill-out room at the back.

Pink

2925 16th Street, between S Van Ness Avenue & Capp Street (431 8889/www.pinksf.com). BART 16th Street Mission/bus 14, 22, 33, 49. **Open** 10pm-2am Tue-Sun. **Admission** varies. **Credit** DC, MC, V. **Map** p318 K10.

A favourite spot for fans of DJ culture, Pink is a narrow bar with a small dancefloor, uncomfortably crowded during the weekend. Although the drinks prices might seem to cater to the upper echelon, music is still the club's focus; the venue frequently hosts international DJs with very little fanfare.

The Castro

For gay and lesbian bars and nightclubs in the Castro, *see pp221-225.*

Amber

718 14th Street, between Belcher & Church Streets (626 7827). Metro to Church/streetcar F/bus 22, 37. **Open** 6pm-2am Mon-Fri; 7pm-2am Sat, Sun. **Admission** varies. **No credit cards. Map** p318 H9.

Amber is known to locals as the unofficial straight bar of mostly gay Castro, but the real draw – apart from the diverse crowd, underground tunes and cosy atmosphere – is the lax smoking rules. Puffing in bars is illegal, but Amber slipped through a loophole in the law as it's owned by the staff. True, the fumes can be overwhelming, but they also draw an international patronage yearning for the smoky comforts of home.

The Haight & around

Haight-Ashbury

Milk DJ Bar & Lounge

1840 Haight Street, between Shrader & Stanyan Streets (387 6455/www.milksf.com). Bus 6, 7, 33, 43, 71. **Open** 9pm-2am daily. **Admission** free-$10. **Credit** (no credit cards at door) AmEx, DC, MC, V. **Map** p317 E9.

For years, the Haight-Ashbury district was ground zero for the city's rock scene, but these days hip hop is creeping in and proving itself a Haight Street mainstay, due in no small part to Milk's hip hop- and R&B-friendly bookers. Flash modern decor and a decent-sized dancefloor characterise the space, while big-name guests such as DJ Shadow have been known to drop in at events put on by True Skool and Future Primitive Sound.

Lower Haight

Underground SF

424 Haight Street, between Fillmore & Webster Streets (www.undergroundsf.com). Bus 6, 7, 22, 71. **Open** 9pm-2am daily. **Admission** free-$10. **Credit** DC, MC, V. **Map** p318 H8.

On a somewhat sketchy stretch of Lower Haight, the club formerly known as the Top is little more than a converted dive with a smallish dancefloor. But set the Underground's looks aside and pay attention with your ears instead: it has a deserved reputation as a centre for turntable culture, and is a favourite spot with more discerning queers who love disco-funk but hate ABBA.

The Western Addition

Madrone Lounge

500 Divisadero Street, at Fell Street (241 0202/ www.madronelounge.com). Bus 21, 24. **Open** 2pm-2am daily. **Admission** free-$5. **Credit** DC, MC, V. **Map** p317 G8.

This cosy room on the edge of the Lower Haight, which also functions as a cutting-edge art gallery, draws its share of students from the nearby USF and UCSF campuses for its regular happy hours and laid-back vibe. It's tiny, so when local bands notify USF's college radio station (KUSF 90.3 FM) of their concerts here, they have little trouble filling the joint.

Hayes Valley

The best bet for lively nightlife in the area is the **Rickshaw Stop** (*see p236*). On the edge of Hayes Valley, it supplements programmes of live music with hot club gatherings. Nights such as Fallout, Club ID and Blow-Up draw a heavy hipster contingent, and the venue always throws a great party. Arrive early for the authentic rickshaw-cart seating.

Arts & Entertainment

Sport & Fitness

With mountains and ocean to inspire, there's no excuse not to get out there.

Show off your ball control at the **Presidio Bowling Center**. *See p246.*

In a city where restaurant hopping can be considered a sport, you might not expect folks to understand the comparatively pedestrian pleasures of beer and a ballgame. Yet despite their well-earned reputation for culture and sophistication, San Franciscans are not above donning face paint and foam fingers and packing a stadium to cheer on their team.

The Bay Area is home to several professional sports teams, each of which inspires ferocious loyalty. San Francisco has the marquee teams – football's **49ers** (*see p245*) and baseball's **Giants** (*see p244*). Across the Bay Bridge are their scrappier Oakland counterparts, football's **Raiders** (*see p245*) and baseball's **Athletics** (*see p244*). Fiercer than these teams' on-field contests are the rivalries between their fans, for whom the stakes are no less than Bay Area bragging rights. Also in Oakland are basketball team the **Golden State Warriors** (*see p245*), who recently experienced a resurgence after more than a dozen dismal seasons. In San Jose, an hour's drive to the south, are the **Sharks** (*see p245*), who have the loudest and most devoted fan base in the National Hockey League.

San Franciscans aren't content to merely watch while others play, however, and there is a wealth of activities for the sporting. Thanks to its unique topography, San Francisco is ideal for outdoor athletes looking to challenge themselves. Whether navigating the plentiful trails of the Marin Headlands or braving treacherous urban traffic, cyclists are guaranteed a heart-pounding workout and world-class views. For runners, the city is home to two of northern California's largest foot races: **Bay to Breakers** (*see p199*) in May and the **San Francisco Marathon** in August. Despite the city's mild climate, skiers and snowboarders can still log time on the slopes by spending a weekend in the nearby Sierras. If you prefer to pursue your fitness away from the elements, health clubs and gyms are plentiful (*see p247*).

Spectator sports

For information on local events, head to the *San Francisco Chronicle*'s website at www.sfgate.com/sports, or check the paper's

'Sporting Green' section, which has a calendar of local sporting events and media broadcasts.

If you can stomach the phone-ins, KNBR (680 or 1050 AM, www.knbr.com) is good for news. If it's convenient, buy tickets in person from the team's stadium in order to avoid booking fees and surcharges. If that's not possible, call the team direct or buy tickets from its website. And if they're sold out, try **Tickets.com** (www.tickets.com) or **Ticketmaster** (421 8497, www.ticketmaster.com), both of which work with the major teams. Other brokers include **Premier Tickets** (1-800 376 6876, www.premiertickets.com), **Entertainment Ticketfinder** (1-800 523 1515, www.ticket finder.com) and **Mr Ticket** (1-800 424 7328, www.mrtix.com). Be warned, though: scams abound, especially with ticket touts (scalpers), so be on your guard.

Auto racing

Infineon Raceway
Intersection of Highways 37 & 121, Sonoma (1-800 870 7223/www.infineonraceway.com). **Open** *Box office* 8am-5pm Mon-Fri & race days. **Tickets** $10-$85. **Credit** AmEx, DC, Disc, MC, V.
Home to everything from NASCAR to monster-truck rallies, Infineon is a fun slice of Americana located just an hour away from the city.

Baseball

The two Bay Area teams could not be more different. While the National League's **San Francisco Giants** have a roster stacked with veterans, a middle-class following and a lovely Downtown stadium, the American League's **Oakland Athletics** favour youngsters, have

Barry Bonds strikes out

For 15 seasons, baseball player Barry Bonds was as important a local attraction as Fisherman's Wharf or the Golden Gate Bridge. So when the San Francisco Giants announced on 21 September 2007 that Bonds would not return to the team for the 2008 season, it was the end of an era.

From the moment Bonds was acquired in 1993 via a trade with the Pittsburgh Pirates, his tenure with the Giants carried mythological weight. Though he was already one of baseball's premier players, in San Francisco he inherited the legacy of two other legendary Giants – his father Bobby and godfather Willie Mays. In his first season with the team, the Giants – who had drawn below the league average each of the previous 15 years – came within two games of the play-offs, drawing 2.6 million fans and with Bonds winning his third of an eventual seven Most Valuable Player awards in the process.

For better or worse, Bonds continued to be the most potent force shaping the Giants' destiny for the following decade. Between 2000 and 2004, when he performed his most Herculean feats – including setting new single-season records for home runs, on-base percentage and walks – the Giants finished first or second in their division each year, and even scored a World Series appearance in 2000.

But Bonds' emergence as a central figure in Major League Baseball's steroid scandal eventually marked a tidal shift for the Giants. With the slugger's legal problems off the

field overshadowing the team's withering performance on it, the Giants posted three successive losing seasons between 2005 and 2007. The highlight of his controversial last few years with the Giants was his pursuit of Hank Aaron's all-time home run record. Though Bonds' quest guaranteed sell-out crowds game after game, his unwieldy salary precluded the team from signing superstar talent and forced them to rely on a corps of ageing veterans with declining skills. Fans lamented that the franchise was cashing in on Bonds' individual milestone at the expense of winning. Though Bonds finally succeeded in breaking Aaron's record on 7 August 2007, the Giants finished the season in last place, and didn't renew Bonds' contract.

But don't assume the post-Bonds era will be one of empty stands and Bush-league baseball. The Giants have a trio of talented young pitchers in Tim Lincecum, Matt Cain and Noah Lowry, as well as a promising offensive threat in outfielder Rajai Davis. And the team's management has made a commitment to give top prospects like second baseman Kevin Frandsen more playing time. Most importantly, with the burden of Bonds' salary gone, the Giants will be shopping for talent to complement their current core of players.

With the team's commitment to getting younger, faster and healthier, there is plenty to look forward to in the coming seasons. And who knows? Maybe somewhere on the roster is the next legend among Giants.

a more working-class fanbase and play in a concrete shell in the middle of nowhere.

At the Giants' AT&T Park, old-fashioned design and Bay views combine to create one of the most beautiful sports stadia in the country. However, though Oakland's McAfee Coliseum is no competition for its SF rival, the As have been the better team in recent years. The season runs April to September, play-offs in October.

Oakland Athletics *McAfee Coliseum, 7000 Coliseum Way, Nimitz Freeway, at Hegenberger Road, Oakland (1-510 568 5600/www.oakland athletics.com). BART Coliseum/Oakland Airport.* **Open** *Box office 9am-6pm Mon-Fri; 10am-4pm Sat; 2hrs before game.* **Tickets** $10-$50. **Credit** AmEx, DC, Disc, MC, V.

San Francisco Giants *AT&T Park, 24 Willie Mays Plaza, at 3rd & King Streets, South Beach (972 2000/www.sfgiants.com). Metro to 2nd & King/ bus 9X, 10, 30, 45.* **Open** *Box office 8.30am-5.30pm Mon-Fri; 2hrs before game Sat, Sun.* **Tickets** $10-$110. **Credit** DC, Disc, MC, V. **Map** p319 P7.

Basketball

San Francisco might not have a pro basketball team, but Oakland does: the **Golden State Warriors**, who play in the Oakland Arena behind the Coliseum. In 2007, the team made it to the play-offs for the first time in 13 years, igniting a wave of Warriors mania, so expect this to be a hot ticket. The NBA season runs November until mid April, play-offs in May. Rather more dramatic is the exciting college season, which runs from December through the 'March Madness' of the NCAA tournament. **Stanford** (1-800 782 6367, www.gostanford. com) and the **University of California at Berkeley** (1-800 462 3277, www.calbears.com) are both members of the Pac-10 and can usually be relied on to produce competitive teams.

In the summer, the **Kezar Pavilion** (Waller & Stanyan Streets, Haight) hosts a free Pro-Am league that showcases top local college talent and the occasional NBA star. If you think you've got game, check out the pick-up contests across the city: the best hoops are at **James Lick Middle School** (Clipper & Castro Streets, Noe Valley).

Golden State Warriors *Oracle Arena, 7000 Coliseum Way, Nimitz Freeway, at Hegenberger Road, Oakland (1-888 479 4667/www.warriors.com). BART Coliseum/Oakland Airport.* **Open** *Box office 10am-6pm Mon-Fri; 10am-4pm Sat.* **Tickets** $25-$1,700. **Credit** AmEx, DC, MC, V.

Football

The Bay separates the NFL's **San Francisco 49ers** from the **Oakland Raiders**, and their supporters remain fanatically opposed. The

49ers' record of selling out every home game for nearly 25 years (single-game seats are available if you're quick) was brought under threat in recent years: in 2006, the team disappointed fans with their fourth consecutive losing season.

Despite being a marginally more successful team in recent years (though it's all relative when you're this bad), the Raiders rarely sell out their home games in advance, and tickets can usually be obtained even minutes prior to kick-off. If you happen to find yourself in the 'Black Hole', home to Oakland's most rabid and creatively outfitted fans (think Darth Vader on a bad day), you'll be terrified. Possibly amused, but most likely terrified. The 'Big Game' between Stanford and Cal in November is the annual highlight of the college football season.

Oakland Raiders *McAfee Coliseum, 7000 Coliseum Way, Nimitz Freeway, at Hegenberger Road, Oakland (1-800 724 3377/www.raiders.com). BART Coliseum/Oakland Airport.* **Open** *Box office 8am-7pm Mon-Fri; 9am-4pm Sat; 2hrs before game Sun.* **Tickets** $26-$151. **Credit** AmEx, DC, Disc, MC, V.

San Francisco 49ers *Monster Park, 490 Jamestown Avenue, at Giants Drive, Bayview (656 4900/www.sf49ers.com). Ballpark Express 9X from Montgomery BART, 28X from Funston & California Streets, or 47X on Van Ness Avenue.* **Tickets** $64-$94. **Credit** V.

Horse racing

Golden Gate Fields *1100 Eastshore Highway, Albany (1-510 559 7300/www.goldengatefields.com). BART North Berkeley, then AC Transit shuttle bus.* **Open** *Race days varies. Box office varies.* **Tickets** $4-$15. **Credit** AmEx, DC, MC, V.

Ice hockey

Ice hockey came to the Bay Area more than a decade ago, courtesy of the National Hockey League's **San Jose Sharks**. Hockey is still a minority taste in the Bay Area compared to the other three major sports, but the Sharks are a perennial play-off contender and routinely sell out the 'Shark Tank'. The season runs October to April, followed by two months of play-offs.

San Jose Sharks *HP Pavilion, 525 West Santa Clara Street, at Autumn Street, San Jose (ticketmaster 421 8497/box office 1-408 287 9200/www.sj-sharks.com). CalTrain to San Jose Diridon Station.* **Open** *Box office 9.30am-5.30pm Mon-Fri; from 3hrs before game Sat, Sun.* **Tickets** $19-$150. **Credit** AmEx, DC, MC, V.

Active sports & fitness

Every Thursday, the *Chronicle* publishes a supplement called 'Outdoors', full of listings and information on open-air activities. For special events, it's also worth trying the Visitor Information Center (*see p294*). Competitor *Nor Cal Magazine* (www.citysportsmag.com), a regional magazine available in gyms and sports shops, carries information on participatory sports. Note: if you're hiring expensive equipment, photo ID or a credit card is usually required for the deposit.

Bowling

Presidio Bowling Center *Building 93, at Montgomery Street & Moraga Avenue, Presidio (561 2695/www.presidiobowl.com). Bus 29.* **Open** 9am-midnight Mon-Thur, Sun; 9am-2am Fri, Sat. **Rates** $3.75-$6.50/game. *Shoe rental $4.* **Credit** AmEx, DC, Disc, MC, V. **Map** p312 D3. *Photo p243.*

Yerba Buena Bowling Center *750 Folsom Street, between 3rd & 4th Streets, SoMa (820 3532/www.skatebowl.com). BART & Metro to Montgomery/bus 9X, 12, 30, 45, 76.* **Open** 10am-10pm Mon-Thur; 10am-midnight Fri, Sat; 10am-9pm Sun. **Rates** $3.50-$7/game. *Shoe rental $3.* **Credit** DC, MC, V. **Map** p315 N6.

Cycling

If you're looking to get around San Francisco quickly, hop on a bike. Hemmed in by the peninsula, the city is unable to sprawl like most conurbations, and while it's certainly hilly, the steepest inclines are easily avoided. Biking here is a memorable experience, taking in majestic sea views, the aroma of eucalyptus trees and the glorious Golden Gate Park.

Bike stores dot the centre of town, and bike lanes are widespread. Bicycles can be taken free of charge on BART, except for peak hours (7-9am and 4-6pm weekdays); the ferries will also take you and your bike. All major outdoor public events in San Francisco are required by law to offer free and secure bike parking.

The only downers are those typical of most major urban areas: theft, which is common, and traffic, which can be nasty. Always secure your bike with a U-lock when parking it, and don't leave it outside overnight (many hotels will be able to store it if you ask nicely). Back on the roads, SUVs, Hummers and other such monstrosities are notorious for disregarding anything smaller than they are; take care.

Many tourists head to Fisherman's Wharf and rent bikes for day-rides across the Golden Gate Bridge, but there's even more entrancing biking elsewhere in the Bay Area. The endless trails in the **Marin Headlands** (*see pp278-59*) offer unmatched sights and pulmonary exertions: the mountain bike was born on the paths of Bolinas Ridge in Marin County and Railroad Grade along Mount Tamalpais.

For more information, telephone the Marin Headlands Visitor Center (331 1540) or the Pantoll Ranger Station (388 2070).

For more on cycling in the city, contact the terrific **San Francisco Bicycle Coalition** (www.sfbike.org). Among other resources, it publishes an immeasurably useful map of the city with all gradients marked on it, so you can avoid the worst of the hills. You can download a PDF from its website, or purchase a printed copy online or from any bike store around town. Ray Hosler's *Bay Area Bike Rides* (Chronicle, $14.95) is another very worthwhile read.

Bike Hut
Pier 40, Embarcadero, at 1st Street, SoMa (543 4335/www.thebikehut.com). Metro to Brannan/bus 10. **Open** (unless raining) 10am-6pm daily. **Rates** (incl lock & helmet) $5/hr or $20/day. **Map** p319 P7.
This excellent little enterprise, staffed by volunteers (who train kids from deprived backgrounds in bike mechanics while on the job), rents and repairs bicycles from a location just south of the Bay Bridge.

Blazing Saddles
2715 Hyde Street, at North Point Street, Fisherman's Wharf (202 8888/www.blazingsaddles.com). Metro F to Fisherman's Wharf/bus 10, 19, 30, 47/cable car Powell-Hyde. **Open** from 8am daily. **Rates** $7-$9/hr or $28-$48/day. **Credit** AmEx, DC, Disc, MC, V. **Map** p314 K2.
Bikes are rented to those with a yen for cycling the 8 miles from Fisherman's Wharf over the Golden Gate Bridge to Sausalito. Guided tours are also offered. **Other locations** throughout the city.

Golden Gate Park Skate & Bike
3038 Fulton Street, between 6th & 7th Avenues, Richmond (668 1117). Bus 5, 21, 31, 44. **Open** 10am-5pm Mon-Fri; 10am-5.30pm Sat, Sun. **Rates** *Bikes* $5/hr or $25/day. *Skates* $5/hr or $20/day. **Credit** DC, MC, V. **Map** p316 C8.
Bikes, rollerskates and in-line skates are all available for rent (helmet and knee and elbow pads included), and you can take skateboarding lessons.

Mike's Bikes
1233 Howard Street, between 8th & 9th Streets, SoMa (241 2453/www.mikesbikes.com). Bus 9, 12, 27, 47. **Open** 11am-7pm Mon-Fri; 10am-6pm Sat, Sun. **Credit** AmEx, DC, Disc, MC, V. **Map** p318 L8.
Mike's doesn't offer rentals, but is an excellent one-stop shop for bikes, clothing and other accessories. **Other locations** 2161 University Avenue, Berkeley (1-510 549 8350).

Solano Avenue Cyclery
1554 Solano Avenue, Albany (1-510 524 1094/ www.solanoavenuecyclery.com). BART El Cerrito Plaza, then AC Transit bus 43. **Open** 11am-7pm Mon-Fri; 10am-6pm Sat. **Rates** $35-$40/day. **Credit** DC, Disc, MC, V.
Near Berkeley, this is a great place to launch into the East Bay trails. Ask about the Nimitz Bike Path.

Golf

Golden Gate Park Course

*John F Kennedy Drive, at 47th Avenue, Golden
Gate Park (751 8987/www.goldengateparkgolf.com).
Bus 5, 18, 31, 38.* **Open** dawn-dusk daily. **Rates**
Non-residents $14-$18. **Credit** DC, MC, V.
The Golden Gate Park Course is a handsome little
nine-hole par-three municipal number, reasonably
priced and located above Ocean Beach.

Harding Park Golf Course

*99 Harding Road, at Skyline Boulevard, Lake
Merced (information 664 4690/reservations 750
4653/www.harding-park.com). Bus 18, 88.* **Open**
dawn-dusk daily. **Rates** *Non-residents* $135-$155.
Credit AmEx, DC, MC, V.
Arguably one of the best municipal courses in the
country. Tee times are available up to 30 days
ahead with a $10 surcharge. Also here is the nine-
hole, par-30 Fleming Course (non-residents $25-$30).

Lincoln Park Golf Course

*300 34th Avenue, at Clement Street, Lincoln Park
(information 221 9911/reservations 750 4653/www.
lincolnparkgc.com). Bus 18.* **Open** dawn-dusk daily.
Rates *Non-residents* $34-$38. **Credit** DC, MC, V.
The wonderful view of the Golden Gate Bridge from
the 17th hole has made Lincoln Park one of the most
photographed courses in the US.

Presidio Golf Course

*300 Finley Road, at Arguello Gate, Presidio (561
4653/www.presidiogolf.com). Bus 28.* **Open** dawn-
dusk daily. **Rates** *Non-residents* $32-$108. **Credit**
AmEx, DC, MC, V. **Map** p312 C5.
Former presidents Roosevelt and Eisenhower both
played this 18-holer – the second oldest course west
of the Mississippi – when it was owned by the Army.
Built in 1885, it finally opened to the public in 1995
following a makeover by Arnold Palmer and co.

Gyms

San Franciscans love their corner gyms every
bit as much as their corner cafés and bars. Each
SF neighbourhood seems to have at least one.

24 Hour Fitness Center

*1200 Van Ness Avenue, at Post Street, Cathedral Hill
(776 2200/www.24hourfitness.com). Bus 2, 3, 4, 19,
38, 47, 49, 76.* **Open** 24hrs daily. **Rates** $15/day.
Credit AmEx, DC, Disc, MC, V. **Map** p314 K6.
This chain has several branches around the city, all
offering a variety of facilities and classes. For other
locations, check online or call 1-800 249 6756.

Embarcadero YMCA

*169 Steuart Street, between Mission & Howard
Streets, Financial District (957 9622/www.ymcasf.
org). BART & Metro to Embarcadero/streetcar F/
bus 1, 14, 21, 31, 71 & Market Street routes.* **Open**
5.30am-9.45pm Mon-Fri; 8am-7.45pm Sat; 9am-5.45pm
Sun. **Rates** $15/day. **Credit** DC, MC, V. **Map** p315 O4.

Above par: **Golden Gate Park Course.**

San Francisco has plenty of YMCAs, but this is the only one that boasts a waterfront view. A day pass will give you access to aerobics classes, free weights, Cybex and Nautilus machines, racquetball and basketball courts, and the 25m swimming pool. For the pass, you'll need photo ID.

Koret Health & Recreation Center

University of San Francisco, Parker Avenue & Turk Boulevard, Richmond (422 6821/www.usfca.edu/ koret). Bus 5, 21, 31, 33. **Open** 6am-10pm (pool closes at 9pm) Mon-Fri; 8am-8pm (pool closes at 6pm) Sat, Sun. **Rates** $15/day. **Credit** DC, MC, V. **Map** p317 E8.
Koret has an Olympic-sized pool, a gym and six racquetball courts, though for the latter you'll need to bring your own equipment.

Hiking

Walking San Francisco's splendid hills is a delight, and both the Presidio and Golden Gate Park offer decent walking. Less than a half-hour outside the city lie trails with stunning views and fragrant paths. Just across the Golden Gate Bridge, the short and easy **Morning Sun Trail** rises from a parking lot at Spencer Avenue (exit off US 101 north). The trail offers lovely views east towards the city over the Bay and Angel Island, and west to the thundering Pacific. Alternatively, take Golden Gate Transit bus 10 to Mill Valley for the day-long **Dipsea Trail** to Stinson Beach. The **Bootjack Trail** to the summit of Mount Tamalpais is popular too. Call the Pantoll Ranger Station (388 2070) for trail information or visit www.mttam.net. The **Bay Area Sierra Club** (1-510 848 0800, www.sanfranciscobay.sierraclub.org) in Berkeley has a wealth of hiking knowledge.

Horse riding

If you want equestrian action, horses and tours are offered at the **Sea Horse & Friendly Acres Ranch** (1-650 726 2362, www.horse rentals.com/seahorse.html), near Half Moon Bay, and the **Chanslor Stables** (1-707 875 3333, www.chanslor.com) next to Bodega Bay.

In-line skating

Sunday skating in **Golden Gate Park** is hard to beat: the beach at one end, sunny meadows along the way and no motor vehicles anywhere to be seen. For wide smiles – without the wide polyester collars – join the mix of in-line skating, disco twirling and breakdancing near 6th Avenue on JFK Drive. Skates are available for rent at **Golden Gate Park Skate & Bike** (*see p246*), or for purchase from **Skates on Haight**. On Fridays, join the **Midnight**

Get in shape for Yosemite at **Mission Cliffs**.

Rollers night-time skate, which leaves Ferry Plaza opposite the Ferry Building at 9.15pm sharp; for information, see www.cora.org.

Skates on Haight

1818 Haight Street, at Stanyan Street, Haight-Ashbury (752 8375/www.skatesonhaight.com). Metro to Cole & Carl/bus 7, 33, 66, 71. **Open** 10am-6pm daily. **Credit** AmEx, DC, Disc, MC, V. **Map** p317 E9.
Skates on Haight was at least partly responsible for launching the worldwide skateboarding craze during the 1970s. Stock these days includes in-line skates, roller skates and snowboards.

Rock climbing

Devoted climbers travel to **Lake Tahoe** and **Mount Shasta**, but **Yosemite** is the state's climbing mecca, with lessons available year-round. *See pp273-74.* While you're still in the city, warm up at Mission Cliffs.

Mission Cliffs

2295 Harrison Street, at 19th Street, Mission (550 0515/www.mission-cliffs.com). Bus 12, 27. **Open** 6.30am-10pm Mon-Fri; 9am-7pm Sat, Sun. **Rates** $10-$18/day. **Credit** AmEx, DC, Disc, MC, V. **Map** p318 L11.
This 14,000sq ft (4,300sq m) of urban wilderness and polished jungle gym runs beginner's lessons from noon until 7.30pm on weekdays.

Arts & Entertainment

Running

Crissy Field is highly popular with runners, and it's easy to see why. Each step of the route from Fort Mason past Marina Green along the Golden Gate Promenade is a postcard, leading all the way to historic Fort Point beneath the bridge. The **Embarcadero** offers another lovely path beneath the city's other beautiful bridge, and **Golden Gate Park** offers a third option, with the track at Kezar Stadium on the eastern edge providing a good spot for sprints.

For something more sociable, the **San Francisco Dolphin South End Runners** has group runs at 9.30am every Sunday, in which non-members can take part for $5. Call 978 0837 or check out www.dserunners.com for more details. Annual races include the **Bay to Breakers** (*see p199*) in May and the **San Francisco Marathon** (*see p200*) in July.

Sailing, kayaking & rowing

There are numerous boating and kayaking outfits in the Bay Area and along the Pacific coastline; all offer equipment, lessons and trips. Rowing opportunities range from single sculls to whale-boat racing; for details call **Open Water Rowing** (332 1091, www.owrc.com) in Sausalito or **South End Rowing Club** (776 7372, www.south-end.org) in San Francisco. Pedalos and rowing boats are available for rent at **Stow Lake** in Golden Gate Park.

Cal Adventures
UC Aquatic Center, 112 University Avenue, at Shorebird Park, Berkeley Marina (1-510 642 4000/ www.oski.org). BART Downtown Berkeley, then AC Transit bus 9. **Open** *Mar-Nov* noon-sunset Wed-Fri; 7.30am-sunset Sat, Sun. **Rates** *Kayaks* $15/hr. *Sailboats* $15/hr.
Cal Adventures rents out 15ft (4.5m) Coronados on the South Sailing Basin. Those without proper certification must be accompanied by an instructor.

California Canoe & Kayak
409 Water Street, at Franklin Street, Jack London Square, Oakland (1-510 893 7833/www.calkayak. com). BART 12th Street Oakland. **Open** 11am-6pm Mon-Fri; 10am-6pm Sat, Sun. **Rates** *Kayaks* $15/hr. *Canoes* $25/hr. **Credit** AmEx, DC, Disc, MC, V.
One of the Bay Area's best locations for hiring and buying kayaks and seagoing gear. Lessons and day trips navigate the nearby Oakland Estuary.

Sea Trek
Schoonmaker Point Marina, at Libertyship Way, Sausalito (weekdays 332 8494/weekends 332 4465/ www.seatrekkayak.com). Blue & Gold Fleet ferry from Pier 41, or Golden Gate ferry from Ferry Building. **Open** 9am-4pm daily. **Rates** *Kayak rental* $15-$25/hr. *Tours* $65-$135. **Credit** AmEx, DC, Disc, MC, V.

Sea Trek hosts summer camps for kids, books expeditions to Alaska and Baja, and supports waterway conservation. Beginners' classes in kayaking, guided tours and moonlight paddles are available; rental covers everything from pro gear to wave-rider kayaks suitable for novices.

Spinnaker Sailing
Pier 40, South Beach Harbor, Embarcadero, at Townsend Street, South Beach (543 7333/www. spinnaker-sailing.com). **Open** 9am-5pm daily (10am-4pm Wed-Sun in winter). **Rates** *Boat rental* $382-$865/day. **Credit** AmEx, DC, MC, V. **Map** p319 P7.
Professional instruction, boats from 22ft (7m) to 80ft (24m), and a great location near the ballpark.

Skateboarding

The police have done a pretty thorough job of eliminating skate rats from once-favourite sites such as Justin Herman Plaza and Pier 7 on the Embarcadero, though you'll be able to sniff out a Safeway parking lot or two and any number of downtown concrete ramps. If you're posing or want to learn, invest in helmet, gloves, knee and elbow pads at DLX. Dusting up on the slang won't hurt either.

DLX
1831 Market Street, between Guerrero & Octavia Streets, Upper Market (626 5588/www.dlxsf.com). Metro to Church or Van Ness/streetcar F/bus 6, 7, 26, 66. **Open** 11am-7pm Mon-Sat; 11am-6pm Sun. **Credit** AmEx, DC, MC, V. **Map** p318 J9.
DLX is the mother of all skateboarding shops in SF, and has a comprehensive range of clothes, boards, accessories and stickers.

Skiing & snowboarding

You can hit the slopes on a day trip, but most people prefer to spend at least a weekend in the Sierras. For leading resorts around **Lake Tahoe**, *see pp271-72*. During the season (Nov-Apr), most ski shops offer package deals. Check www.goski.com for listings of all the major California resorts.

SFO Snowboarding
1630 Haight Street, at Ashbury Street, Haight-Ashbury (626 1141/www.sfosnow.com). Bus 6, 7, 33, 43, 66, 71. **Open** 11am-7pm Mon-Sat; 11am-6pm Sun. **Credit** AmEx, DC, Disc, MC, V. **Map** p317 E9.
Boards, boots, bindings and more for rent, plus an array of cold-weather clothes for sale.

Mountain West
290 Division Street, Suite 101, between 10th & Brannan Streets, SoMa (www.mountainwest online.com/552 7055). Bus 27, 47. **Open** 10am-7pm Mon-Fri; 10am-6pm Sat; 11am-5pm Sun. **Credit** DC, MC, V. **Map** p319 M9.

Arts & Entertainment

Staffed by knowledgeable enthusiasts, Mountain West is the place to buy or rent the latest skiing and snowboarding equipment with brand names like Nordica and Burton. Boot fitting, and ski and snowboard tuning and repairs are also offered.

Surfing

Here are the facts: the waves around San Francisco are dangerous and shark infested – not a good place to learn. An hour north of San Francisco on Highway 1, **Stinson Beach** has gentler waves and fewer surfers, while the experts head to **Mavericks** in Santa Cruz. But whether you're a pro headed to Ocean Beach and beyond or a newbie boogie-boarding the black-sand beaches of Marin County, Wise Surfboards is the first choice for gear.

Wise Surfboards

800 Great Highway, at Cabrillo Street, Ocean Beach (750 9473/www.wisesurfboards.com). Bus 5, 18, 31, 38. **Open** 9am-6pm daily. **Credit** AmEx, DC, MC, V.
Located right on Ocean Beach, this shop sells boards, wetsuits and various accessories, and hosts a 24-hour surf report phoneline (273 1618), updated several times daily.

Swimming

The ocean is usually too chilly and turbulent for a proper swim, but there are plenty of pools in town, including those at the **Embarcadero YMCA** (*see p247*) and the **Koret Center** (*see p248*). The most central pools can be found at **Hamilton Recreation Center** (Geary Boulevard & Steiner Street, 292 2001, closed for renovations until early 2009) and the **North Beach Pool** (661 Lombard Street, at Mason Street, 391 0407). For your nearest municipal pool, check the White Pages under 'City Government Offices: Recreation and Parks'.

Tennis

Indoor tennis is almost exclusively a members-only affair, but there are plenty of outdoor courts. **Golden Gate Park** has several (near the Stanyan Street entrance, 753 7001), and there are busy courts at **Mission Dolores Park** (*see p98*). Both locations are free and open from sunrise to sunset. You can find a full list of tennis facilities in the SBC Yellow Pages under 'Neighbourhood Parks'.

Whale-watching

Whale-watching happens during the migration season (Nov-Dec and late Mar/early Apr), and occurs primarily just north and south of San Francisco. On occasion, it can be as easy as

taking a pair of binoculars to the shore and having a look. Mendocino and Monterey are popular viewing spots, but we recommend the tip of **Point Reyes** (*see p263*), an hour's drive north of the city. You might see glorious humpback and blue whales, as well as sea lions.

Oceanic Society Expeditions

Quarters 35N, Fort Mason, at Franklin & Bay Streets, Marina (1-800 326 7491/www.oceanic-society. org). Bus 10, 19, 28, 30, 47, 49. **Open** 9am-5pm Mon-Fri. **Rates** *Voyages* (reservations required) $85-$105. **Credit** AmEx, DC, Disc, MC, V. **Map** p314 H2.
A cut above most tourist trips – the staff are experts in natural history and marine life. At weekends from June to November, a full-day trip heads 26 miles west to the Farallon Islands, home of the largest seabird rookery in the continental US. Along the way, humpback whales can often be seen. Trips to see grey whales take place the rest of the year.

Windsurfing

San Francisco is a popular windsurfing centre; the 30-plus launch sites include **Candlestick** and **Coyote Points**, as well as **Crissy Field**, the site of several international competitions.

Yoga

For many San Franciscans, yoga is as vital as coffee at work and drinks afterwards. The city's myriad yoga schools offer a variety of styles for students of all levels.

Bikram's Yoga College of India

910 Columbus Avenue, at Lombard Street, North Beach (346 5400/www.bikramyoga.com). Bus 15, 30, 39/cable car Powell-Mason. **Open** *Classes* 9am, 4.30pm, 6.30pm Mon-Fri; 9am, 4.30pm Sat, Sun. **Rates** $15/class. **Credit** DC, MC, V. **Map** p314 L2.
Yogic exercises based on the 'hot yoga' techniques of Bikram Choudhury. Bring a towel, though: the classes take place in a sweltering room.

Mindful Body

2876 California Street, at Broderick Street, Pacific Heights (931 2639/www.themindfulbody.com). Bus 1, 24. **Rates** 7am-9pm Mon-Fri; 8am-7pm Sat, Sun. **Rates** $11-$15/class. **Credit** DC, MC, V. **Map** p313 G5.
The popular Ashtanga class here builds endurance, strength and flexibility.

Yoga Tree

1234 Valencia Street, between 23rd & 24th Streets, Mission (647 9707/www.yogatreesf.com). BART 24th Street/bus 14, 26, 48, 49, 67. **Open** call for class schedule. **Rates** $16/class. **Credit** AmEx, DC, MC, V. **Map** p318 K12.
Popular with beginners and good for drop-ins, Yoga Tree has four locations around town and offers daily classes as well as workshops, massage and retreats. **Other locations** throughout the city.

Theatre & Dance

From reimagined classics to experimental multimedia work, anything goes.

The **Magic Theatre** has been conjuring up quality plays for four decades. *See p252.*

While inevitably overshadowed by some larger cities, San Francisco's theatre and dance scenes prove time and again that they can more than hold their own against such contenders as New York and Chicago almost any night of the week. In fact, from Broadway-bound mega-budget musicals like *Wicked* and extraordinary solo works such as actor-playwright Sarah Jones's Tony Award-winning *Bridge and Tunnel*, all the way up to avant-garde shows like *The Black Rider*, Robert Wilson's collaboration with William Burroughs and local boy Tom Waits, San Francisco's discriminating audiences, excellent venues and fine pool of artistic talent make it an ideal launch pad for the rest of the country.

The city's vibrant and eclectic modern dance scene, meanwhile, takes in the entire spectrum, from the world-class **San Francisco Ballet** (*see p256*) to ethnic dance ensembles and a thriving hybrid dance-theatre movement.

INFORMATION AND TICKETS

The *Chronicle*'s Sunday 'Datebook' section, accessible online at www.sfgate.com, has extensive listings. *San Francisco Weekly* and the *San Francisco Bay Guardian*, two weekly free sheets, also run reviews and listings. For online listings, check www.bayinsider.com, www.sfarts.org and www.laughingsquid.org.

Prices vary wildly: tickets for some leftfield shows are just $5, but you could pay 30 times that for a blockbuster. To avoid booking fees, call the theatre's own box office or book online at its website. If you're willing to take a chance, the **TIX Bay Area** booth in Union Square (433 7827, www.tixbayarea.org) sells half-price tickets for many shows on the day of the performance. It opens at 11am from Tuesday to Friday, and at 10am at weekends. Some venues sell through **Ticketmaster** (512 7770, www.ticketmaster.com); other agencies, some of which charge quite hefty fees, include **Mr Ticket** (775 3031, www. mrticket.com) and **City Box Office** (392 4400, www.cityboxoffice.com). Some theatres run 'pay what you can' schemes on Thursdays (or, at the Magic Theatre, Tuesdays).

Mainstream theatres

A handful of San Francisco's theatres host major touring shows. **Best of Broadway** (www.shnsf.com) offers imports from the Great

White Way in three beautiful old houses: the grand **Orpheum** (1192 Market Street, at Hyde Street, Civic Center) and the 2,300-seat art deco **Golden Gate Theatre** (1 Taylor Street, at Golden Gate Avenue, Tenderloin), which both specialise in musicals, and the elegant, intimate **Curran Theatre** (445 Geary Street, between Mason & Taylor Streets, Tenderloin), which stages both non-musical Broadway and pre-Broadway fare. For further information on all three, call 551 2000; to purchase tickets, which typically run from $20 to around $95, call Ticketmaster (*see p251*).

The **Herbst Theatre** (401 Van Ness Avenue, at Grove Street, Civic Center, 392 4400) hosts local and out-of-town guests, many as part of the **San Francisco Performances** series (*see p227*). Finally, both the 80-year-old **Marines' Memorial Theatre** (609 Sutter Street, at Mason Street, Tenderloin, 771 6900, www.marinesmemorialtheatre.com) and the **Post Street Theatre** (450 Post Street, between Powell & Mason Streets, Union Square & Around, 771 6900, www.poststreet theatre.com) present off-Broadway, regional and local productions.

Regional theatres

American Conservatory Theater

Geary Theater, 415 Geary Street, between Mason & Taylor Streets, Tenderloin (information 834 3200/ box office 749 2228/www.act-sfbay.org). Bus 2, 3, 4, 27, 38/cable car Powell-Hyde or Powell-Mason. **Tickets** $12-$80. **Credit** AmEx, DC, MC, V. **Map** p314 L6.

Since opening in 1967, the ACT has been staging modern classics and new works by the likes of David Mamet, earning it a solid reputation. It is also known for its fine conservatory, whose alumni include Annette Bening and Denzel Washington. In addition to ACT shows, the exquisite Geary Theater usually hosts one or two touring productions per season (recently, John Doyle's much-lauded reimagining of *Sweeney Todd*), and stages the always popular *A Christmas Carol* every year.

Magic Theatre

Building D, Fort Mason, Marina Boulevard, at Buchanan Street, Marina (441 8822/www.magic theatre.org). Bus 10, 20, 22, 28, 30, 47, 49/cable car Powell-Hyde. **Tickets** $20-$50. **Credit** AmEx, DC, Disc, MC, V. **Map** p314 H2.

Drawing its name from a line in Herman Hesse's *Steppenwolf*, the Magic Theatre has impressed locals throughout its 40-year history with stagings of groundbreaking works by the likes of former resident playwright Sam Shepard. The two 150-seat houses, in premises overlooking the Golden Gate Bridge, offer an intriguing mix of new works by both emerging playwrights and leading lights. *Photo p251.*

Fringe theatres & companies

For gay theatre and cabaret, *see p226*.

Asian American Theater Company

Various venues (tickets 1-800 838 3006/www.asian americantheater.org). **Tickets** $10-$25. **Credit** AmEx, DC, MC, V. **Map** p318 L8.

Started by ACT (*see above*) in 1973, AATC fosters work that speaks to the experience of Americans of Asian and Pacific Island descent. Phillip Kan Gotanda and David Henry Hwang are among the exceptional talents nurtured in its first 30 years; both have recently returned to collaborate with the next generation. The emphasis is on new work, and the quality can vary wildly.

Beach Blanket Babylon

Club Fugazi, 678 Green Street, between Columbus Avenue & Powell Street, North Beach (421 4222/ www.beachblanketbabylon.com). Bus 9X, 12, 20, 30, 41, 45/cable car Powell-Mason. **Tickets** $25-$78. **Credit** DC, Disc, MC, V. **Map** p314 L3.

The longest-running musical revue in theatrical history, *Beach Blanket Babylon* sells its formulaic blend of songs, puns and outrageous headgear with such irresistible conviction that it's become an institution. Featuring an array of tabloid-friendly 'guest stars' from popular culture and the news, this queer eye on the straight world will celebrate its 35th year in 2009. Evening performances are for over-21s only.

Dark Room

2263 Mission Street, between 18th & 19th Streets, Mission (401 7987/tickets 1-800 838 3006/www. darkroomsf.com). BART 16th Street Mission/ bus 14, 22, 33, 49, 53. **Tickets** $5-$20. **Credit** DC, Disc, MC, V. **Map** p318 K11.

Operated by the buoyant team of Jim Fourniadis and Erin Ohanneson, this funky black box theatre space in the heart of the Mission knows what it likes. And if you revel in an unabashed embrace of pop culture detritus, then chances are you'll like it too. Recent programming included a revival of *Clue: The Play* and *Creepshow Live* (a Halloween treat). Additionally a comedy showcase and music venue, the Dark Room also sports a regular bad movie night (free popcorn provided), with audiences encouraged to yell back at the screen.

EXIT Theatre

156 Eddy Street, between Mason & Taylor Streets, Tenderloin (673 3847/tickets 1-800 838 3006/ www.theexit.org). BART & Metro to Powell/bus 27, 30, 45 & Market Street routes/cable car Powell-Hyde or Powell-Mason. **Tickets** $10-$20. **Credit** DC, Disc, MC, V. **Map** p314 L6.

This three-stage set-up offers eclectic, provocative shows, from new one-acts to work by well-known authors. The Exit also hosts the annual San Francisco Fringe Festival every autumn, the largest in the US. The main location has the added attraction of a refreshment lounge; a fourth stage (Exit on Taylor) lies just around the corner at 277 Taylor Street.

Arts & Entertainment

Dancing outside the box

Eric Kupers doesn't look like a typical dancer: he's not the 'right' shape. And therein lies the crux of his message: dance is about expression, movement and stepping outside the restrictions that body image conceptions place on us.

After years of maintaining a traditional dancer's physique, Kupers decided to allow his body to relax into its natural state and started developing new work from there. The work of Kupers' company, **Dandelion Dancetheater** (www.dandeliondancetheater. org; *pictured*), is a classic example of a non-classical approach to multi-disciplinary dance. Kupers likes to push the boundaries of what people expect from dance, most notoriously with Dandelion's Undressed Project, which he describes as 'a vehicle for examining body diversity in dance'. To Kupers, the nudity was less of a concern than the exploration of the human form and how it moves; the press and public were, perhaps unsurprisingly, gripped by the eclectic mixture of naked bodies on stage, with performers ranging from an obese middle-aged woman to a man with a prosthetic leg.

It's work like Dandelion's that makes the Bay Area dance scene so interesting and innovative. Known for presenting raw and groundbreaking work, San Francisco has an attitude towards life and expression that is mirrored in its acceptance of work that pushes the boat far out into the Bay. The seeds of this vibrant arts and dance scene were sown back in the 1970s, when Anna Halprin founded the **Tamalpa Institute** (www.tamalpa.org), which introduced dance and movement as a healing and therapeutic art. Some 30 years on, the institute still thrives, offering training programmes and workshops. Another early trailblazer was Krissy Keefer, whose **Wallflower Order** presented radical work featuring all-women troupes addressing political and women's issues. In the '80s, Keefer went on to found **Dance Brigade** (www.dancebrigade.org), which continues to explore issue-oriented dance theatre. Other companies in the area that have broken the mould of mainstream dance include **Contraband** (www.sara sheltonmann.org) and the **Joe Goode Performance Group** (www.joegoode.org; *see p256*), both of which were formative in merging dance and theatre with their multidisciplinary work. Meanwhile, the award-winning **AXIS Dance Company** (www.axis dance.org) presents original, physically integrated dance, with able-bodied dancers performing duets with those in wheelchairs.

Visitors looking for a taster of what's on offer should check out www.dancersgroup. org, which lists all the upcoming dance events in the area. If you're in the Bay in July, the **WestWave Dance Festival** (www. westwavedancefestival.org) showcases the work of over 50 local choreographers. You can also look at specific venues – such as **CounterPULSE** (*see p256*), Dance Brigade's **Dance Mission** (3316 24th Street, 826 4441, www.dancemission.com) and **Malonga Casquelourd Arts Center** (formerly Alice Arts; 1428 Alice Street, Oakland, 1-510 238 7219) – all of which continue to offer a safe haven for dancers looking to present alternative and original work. Mama Calizo's **Voice Factory** (1519 Mission Street, 368 1244, www.voicefactorysf.org), meanwhile, provides a forum specifically for queer artists.

Arts & Entertainment

Intersection for the Arts

446 Valencia Street, between 15th & 16th Streets, Mission (information 626 2787/box office 626 3311/ www.theintersection.org). BART 16th Street/bus 14, 22, 26, 33, 49, 53. **Tickets** *$9-$25.* **Credit** *DC, MC, V.* **Map** *p318 K10.*

The oldest alternative space in San Francisco, Intersection offers a community-conscious array of artistic undertakings including powerhouse theatre, combining the talents of resident company Campo Santo with visiting playwrights such as Naomi Iizuka and John Steppling. The small theatre isn't hugely comfortable – there are only folding chairs – but performances are intense. There's also a great art gallery upstairs.

Last Planet

351 Turk Street, at Hyde Street, Tenderloin (440 3505/www.lastplanettheatre.com). BART & Metro to Civic Center/bus 21, 47, 49 & Market Street routes. **Tickets** *$10-$18.* **Credit** *DC, MC, V.* **Map** *p314 L6.*

Last Planet occupies a high-ceilinged corner of an old, decorative 1928 YMCA building. The 100-seat house has been comfortably renovated, with good sightlines and an exceptionally large stage. Edgy modern pieces by established playwrights, including many an overlooked gem from the dreamier fringes of contemporary drama, are filtered through the company's audacious and rather arch sensibility.

Lorraine Hansberry Theatre

345 3980/www.lorrainehansberrytheatre.com. **Tickets** *$16-$35.* **Credit** *AmEx, DC, Disc, MC, V.*

The foremost African-American theatre in the Bay Area produces four or five plays each year, either by black playwrights or dealing with issues affecting African-Americans. They usually include a musical Christmas offering, such as Langston Hughes's *Black Nativity*. Note that the theatre will be relocating from its Nob Hill location to an as-yet undetermined new home after the 2007-08 season.

Marsh

1062 Valencia Street, at 22nd Street, Mission (information 826 5750/tickets 1-800 838 3006/ www.themarsh.org). BART 24th Street/bus 14, 26, 49, 67. **Tickets** *$8-$35.* **Credit** *(advance bookings only)* *DC, Disc, MC, V.* **Map** *p318 K12.*

The Marsh works hard to present new works, especially solo fare, priding itself on allowing performers to take risks. At the same time, the atmosphere around its two stages and adjacent café is mellow and inviting. Emerging acts such as Josh Kornbluth often move on to larger venues in the Bay Area or countrywide, while seasoned pros like Merle Kessler (aka Ian Shoales) and John O'Keefe alight here as well.

Off-Market Theatres

965 Mission Street, between 5th & 6th Streets, SoMa (820 1656/www.offmarketsf.com). BART & Metro to Powell/bus 14, 27, 30, 45 & Market Street routes/cable car Powell-Hyde or Powell-Mason. **Tickets** *$10-$20.* **Credit** *varies.* **Map** *p319 M7.*

Versatile: **Yerba Buena Center for the Arts**.

This SoMa theatre/gallery complex hosts a variety of smaller companies and troupes, but the main stage and the 50-seat studio are now respectively run by the Custom Made Theatre Company (262 0477, www.custommade.org) and the improvisational Lila Theatre (820 1467, www.lilatheatre.org). The ambience is often upbeat but the quality is erratic.

Project Artaud Theater

450 Florida Street, between 17th & Mariposa Streets, Mission (626 4370/www.artaud.org). Bus 22, 27, 33, 53. **Tickets** *$5-$30.* **Credit** *DC, MC, V.* **Map** *p318 L10.*

The non-profit Project Artaud Theater offers a variety of new works, often boundary-pushing and hybrid in character, and including everything from one-person plays and modern dance to outspoken aerial circus theatre like local artist-activist Keith Hennessey's recent *Sol Niger*. Two other member theatres share parts of the block-long structure: the Traveling Jewish Theatre (*see p255*) and the Theater of Yugen/Noh Space (www.theatreof yugen.org), which specialises in Eastern-influenced theatre, Butoh and performance art.

SF Mime Troupe

Various venues (285 1717/www.sfmt.org).

No, it's not that kind of mime. This is the city's premier political satirist company, offering free summer shows in various Bay Area parks for the past 40-plus years. Decidedly left wing and always

Arts & Entertainment

painfully contemporary, the SF Mime Troupe is a constant source of wonder and a perennial thorn in the side of the civic authorities.

SF Playhouse

533 Sutter Street, between Powell & Mason Streets, Nob Hill (677 9596/www.sfplayhouse.org). Bus 2, 3, 4, 9X, 27, 38, 76/cable car Powell-Hyde or Powell-Mason. **Tickets** $20-$38. **Credit** AmEx, DC, MC, V. **Map** p315 M5.

A modest-sized repertory house known for its sophistication, the Playhouse consistently attracts prime local talent for its mix of revivals and edgy premières (a recent Bay Area debut of Stephen Adly Guirgis's *Jesus Hopped the 'A' Train* being a notable example). There's also an end-of-season musical, but you are likely to do well with anything on the programme.

Thick House

1695 18th Street, at Carolina Street, Potrero Hill (401 8081/www.thickhouse.org). Bus 19, 53. **Tickets** vary. **No credit cards**. **Map** p319 N10.

Home of Thick Description, a leading producer of multiracial theatre, this black box theatre also hosts other worthwhile companies, with an output geared towards contemporary and cutting-edge drama.

Traveling Jewish Theatre

Various venues (522 0786/www.atjt.com).

Aesthetically sophisticated and ensemble-driven, TJT's work ranges from the classics (recently, *Death of a Salesman*) to boldly contemporary drama.

Word for Word

Various venues (437 6775/www.zspace.org/wordforword.htm).

Well suited to a famously literary city, this professional theatre company 'brings literature to its feet' by staging short stories by acclaimed authors such as Michael Chabon and Tobias Wolff. The thrilling inventiveness and talent brought to bear on such pop-up book productions has earned the company acclaim from both literature-lovers and lazy readers.

Yerba Buena Center for the Arts

701 Mission Street, at 3rd Street, SoMa (978 2787/www.ybca.org). BART & Metro to Montgomery/bus 9, 9X, 12, 30, 45, 76. **Tickets** $5-$100. **Credit** AmEx, DC, MC, V. **Map** p315 N6.

This angled, blue-tiled box, one of the city's most striking performance spaces, boasts a wide variety of events, ranging from the Afro Solo Festival to holiday season must-see *The Velveteen Rabbit. See also p82 and p228.*

East Bay theatres & companies

Aurora Theatre Company

2081 Addison Street, at Shattuck Avenue, Berkeley (1-510 843 4822/www.auroratheatre.org). BART Downtown Berkeley. **Tickets** $28-$45. **Credit** AmEx, DC, MC, V.

Based in a custom-designed 150-seat theatre, Aurora produces a top-notch five-play season running the gamut from Shakespeare to LaBute via new translations of Ibsen. Meticulously crafted small theatre.

Berkeley Repertory Theater

2025 Addison Street, between Shattuck Avenue & Milvia Street, Berkeley (information 1-510 647 2900/tickets 1-510 647 2949/www.berkeleyrep.org). BART Downtown Berkeley. **Tickets** $22-$60. **Credit** AmEx, DC, Disc, MC, V.

The acclaimed Berkeley Rep comprises a 400-seat thrust-stage auditorium and a 600-seat proscenium space. Seasons usually cover a classic drama and several new works by contemporary writers. East Bay resident Rita Moreno recently continued her association with the theatre in a critically acclaimed production of *The Glass Menagerie.*

California Shakespeare Theater

Bruns Amphitheatre, 100 Gateway Boulevard, off Cal State 24, Orinda (1-510 548 9666/www.cal shakes.org). BART Orinda, then free shuttle bus. **Tickets** $32-$60. **Credit** AmEx, DC, MC, V.

Cal Shakes regularly draws on the best Bay Area and national talent in its inventive presentations of Shakespeare and other classic writers, such as Shaw and Marivaux (whose *Triumph of Love* recently enjoyed an adaptation here). The superb 545-seat Bruns Amphitheatre, set amid rolling hills and the picnic-ready grounds of a eucalyptus grove, is beautiful, but be sure to pack a warm coat for the foggy night air.

Shotgun Players

Ashby Stage, 1901 Ashby Avenue, at Martin Luther King Jr Way, Berkeley (1-510 841 6500/www. shotgunplayers.org). BART Ashby. **Tickets** $15-$30. **Credit** DC, MC, V.

Now ensconced in its own spiffy space (except during its annual free summer show in Berkeley's John Hinkle Park), Shotgun began as an 'underground' theatre but grew into one of the more popular mid-sized companies in the Bay Area, staging everything from reimagined Greek tragedies to works by David Mamet and local premières like the Pulitzer Prize finalist *Bulrusher* by Eisa Davis.

Dance

In addition to the companies listed below, there is a strong tradition of ethnic dance in SF. The **Lily Cai Chinese Dance Company** (474 4829, www.ccpsf.org) has been blending ancient forms with modern dance since 1988; **Chitresh Das Dance Company** (333 9000, www.kathak. org) performs narrative-driven Kathak dance, one of the six main Indian classical dance forms; and Carolena Nericcio's **Fat Chance Belly Dance** (431 4322, www.fcbd.com; *see also p239* **A different beat**) has been performing an 'American Tribal' style of traditional Middle Eastern dancing since 1987.

Alonzo King's Lines

Yerba Buena Center for the Arts; see p255 (information 863 3040/tickets 978 2787/ www.linesballet.org). **Tickets** $20-$50.
This excellent contemporary and eclectic ballet company stages mainly new works and tours extensively, both at home and abroad. A staple of the SF dance scene, it performs twice a year at Yerba Buena.

Cal Performances

Zellerbach Hall, UC Berkeley campus, Berkeley (1-510 642 9988/www.calperfs.berkeley.edu). BART Downtown Berkeley. **Tickets** $10-$250. **Credit** AmEx, DC, Disc, MC, V.
An adjunct of UC Berkeley, Cal Performances offers a smattering of everything: dance, music and drama. In the former category, it regularly presents companies from around the country and the globe, such as Alvin Ailey, Twyla Tharp and Mark Morris.

Capacitor

Various venues (345 7575/www.capacitor.org).
This unique company fuses modern dance with original prop designs and interactive media to produce science-themed performances, with subjects ranging from the origin of the universe to the future of our species and everything in between.

CounterPULSE

1310 Mission Street, at 9th Street, SoMa (626 2060/ tickets 1-800 838 3006/www.counterpulse.org). BART or Metro to Civic Center/bus 14, 19, 26 & Market Street routes. **Tickets** free-$20. **Credit** DC, Disc, MC, V. **Map** p318 L8.
In 2005, 848 Community Space, the tiny but prolific breeding ground for improvisational and cutting-edge dance and performance throughout most of the 1990s, moved to this newly equipped, larger location and assumed a new name. Nonetheless, you'll still find experimental and innovative work in dance and performance here, as well as puppet activism, pagan festivals, healing circles and more.

Erika Chong Shuch Performance (ESP) Project

www.espproject.org.
Dancer and choreographer Erika Shuch's ESP Project is, along with artists like Deborah Slater and Jess Curtis, at the forefront of a strong dance-theatre movement in the Bay Area. In residency at Intersection for the Arts (*see p254*), the ESP Project recently premièred a wonderfully intimate and idiosyncratic anthropology of UFO obsession, *ORBIT (notes from the edge of forever)*.

Footloose

Shotwell Studios, 3252-A 19th Street, at Shotwell Street, Mission (920 2223/tickets 1-800 838 3006/ www.ftloose.org). BART 16th Street/bus 14, 22, 33, 49, 53. **Tickets** $10-$40. **Credit** (advance bookings only) DC, Disc, MC, V. **Map** p318 K11.
Not far from the established modern dance centre at ODC (*see below*) is this eclectic mix of emerging and seasoned dancers and choreographers operating under the Footloose banner. The emphasis here is on work by women, culminating in an annual Women on the Way Festival of up-and-coming artists.

Joe Goode Performance Group

Yerba Buena Center for the Arts; see p255 (information 561 6565/tickets 978 2787/ www.joegoode.org). **Tickets** $20-$38.
The JGPG has pushed modern dance to new theatrical heights, pursuing with gusto its founder's mission to explore contemporary issues, from gender to AIDS. The company also holds workshops for community groups, including at-risk youth and battered women. It performs at the Yerba Buena Center every June.

ODC Dance

3153 17th Street, between Shotwell Street & Van Ness Avenue, Mission (863 9834/www.odcdance.org). BART 16th Street/bus 14, 22, 33, 49, 53. $10-$40. **Credit** AmEx, DC, MC, V. **Map** p318 K10.
Founded in 1971, the Oberlin Dance Collective has garnered an international reputation for its physically and intellectually vigorous modern dance. It has its own school, gallery and theatre, which hosts a variety of works all year round, while ODC itself also performs twice a year at the Yerba Buena Center. ODC recently expanded into an adjacent 23,000sq ft (2,100sq m) performance space on Shotwell Street (ODC Dance Commons), and also began renovations on its 17th Street theatre in late 2007.

San Francisco Ballet

War Memorial Opera House, 301 Van Ness Avenue, between Grove & McAllister Streets, Civic Center (information 861 5600/tickets 865 2000/www.sf ballet.org). BART & Metro to Civic Center/bus 21, 47, 49 & Market Street routes. **Tickets** $12-$135. **Credit** AmEx, DC, MC, V. **Map** p318 K7.
Founded in 1933, the San Francisco Ballet is the longest-running professional ballet company in the US. In 1939, it presented the first full-length US production of *Coppélia*, followed in 1940 by the country's first complete *Swan Lake*. The company is based in the War Memorial Opera House (*see p227*), and its annual season (Feb-May) is typically an even blend of traditional pieces and new works.

Smuin Ballet

Yerba Buena Center for the Arts; see p255 (information 495 2234/tickets 978 2787/www. smuinballet.org). **Tickets** $18-$50.
The sudden death of dancer and choreographer Michael Smuin in 2007 left many wondering if the company he founded in 1994 would carry on, but carry on it did, to the continuing delight of audiences in the Bay Area and beyond. A former principal dancer and director of SF Ballet, who also worked on Broadway and in film and television, Smuin left a national legacy of bold dancer-driven work melding classical and modern techniques. Often audacious, always technically rigorous and inventive, Smuin Ballet offers winter, spring and holiday programmes of Smuin classics along with premières by other choreographers influenced by his vision.

Trips Out of Town

Sausalito. *See p258*.

Heading North

Over the Golden Gate Bridge and into lush Marin County.

The Golden Gate Bridge sometimes seems the only link between bustling San Francisco and languid **Marin County**. The city's wealthy northern neighbour, Marin extends from **Sausalito**, a quarter-hour by car from San Francisco, to **Bodega Bay** and inland to **Novato**; the protected parkland that sprawls across the county leaves it virtually immune to overpopulation. Of the county's towns, those on the east side (**Tiburon**, Sausalito, **Mill Valley**) tend to be well heeled and staid, while those on the western coast (**Stinson Beach**, **Point Reyes Station** and, notoriously, **Bolinas**) are more bohemian.

Sausalito to Larkspur

The first exit north of the Golden Gate Bridge, **Vista Point**, offers amazing views. Pull off at the following exit, Alexander Avenue, for the **Bay Area Discovery Museum** (*see p206*), an interactive museum geared towards youngsters that's snuggled in **Fort Baker**, at the northern foot of the bridge. Just north, the **Marin Headlands** offer plenty of opportunities for outdoor activity, as well as breathtaking views of the city and the wide-open Pacific Ocean. Here, too, is the **Marine Mammal Center**, a sanctuary for injured seals and sea lions. The main facility is being rebuilt and won't reopen to the public until 2009, but you can still stop at the Visitor Center (289 7355, www.tmmc.org).

Sausalito, the southernmost Marin County town, is not as quaint as its reputation suggests, but it is picturesque, with a maze of tiny streets stretching from the shoreline all the way up to US 101. Originally a fishing village, the town is now home to prosperous artists and yacht owners, and well-off businessfolk. The ferry from San Francisco's Pier 41 or Ferry Building, which provides great views of the Golden Gate Bridge and Alcatraz from the top deck, docks downtown, which is all manicured gardens and pretty bungalows. Along North Bridgeway, opposite Spring Street, is the turn-off for the **San Francisco Bay Model Visitor Center** (*see below*). Across Richardson Bay is tiny downtown **Tiburon**. Again, there are no real sights, just the temptation to enjoy a lingering meal at one of the harbour-view restaurants on

Main Street. However, it's also notable as the departure point for the ferry to **Angel Island**.

Marin County lacks a real centre: though sizeable, Marin City, Corte Madera and Fairfax aren't very interesting unless you're shopping for a BMW or a hot tub. It is, however, worth taking the North San Pedro Road exit off US 101 towards **San Rafael**. On the north side of the city is Frank Lloyd Wright's grand **Marin Civic Center** (Avenue of the Flags, 499 6400, www.marincenter.org), fondly nicknamed 'Big Pink', while a post-war **replica of Mission San Rafael Arcangel** sits on 5th Avenue. Smaller than the 1817 original, the mission has a cemetery that contains the mortal remains of Chief Marin, the rebellious Native American leader who waged battle against Spanish explorers and after whom the county is probably named.

From there, head to **Mill Valley**, at the bottom of Mount Tamalpais, where yuppies enjoy charming boutiques and restaurants, as well as a prestigious film festival. You'll also find picnic-friendly **Tennessee Beach**, accessible from Highway 101. Take the Mill Valley/Shoreline Highway exit towards Stinson Beach, then turn left on Tennessee Valley Road, which ends in the parking area a mile from the beach. The **Miwok Livery Stables** (701 Tennessee Valley Road, 383 8048, www.miwokstables.com) are also around here, catering for riders of all levels of experience. Quaint **Larkspur** is little frequented by tourists, though it's still visited by them more often than is the nearby **San Quentin Prison** (*see p262 San Quentin blues*).

San Francisco Bay Model Visitor Center

2100 Bridgeway, at Olive Street, Sausalito (332 3870/www.spn.usace.army.mil/bmvc). **Open** *Labor Day-Memorial Day* 9am-4pm Tue-Sat. *Memorial Day-Labor Day* 9am-4pm Tue-Fri; 10am-5pm Sat, Sun. **Admission** free.

This two-acre, 1:5-scale hydraulic model of San Francisco Bay and delta was built in 1957 as a means of demonstrating how navigation, recreation and ecology interact. As such, it prevented the construction of various dams that would have disastrously altered the Bay's tidal range. There are walkways over the model, from which you can watch a complete lunar day in under 15 minutes.

Sausalito.

Where to eat, drink & stay

On Bridgeway, Sausalito's main drag, there is excellent regional Italian food at **Poggio** (no.777, 332 7771, www.poggiotrattoria.com). In **Tiburon**, try Main Street: most come to eat, drink Margaritas and take in the views from **Guaymas** (no.5, 435 6300, www.guaymas restaurant.com, mains $17-$25), or for the excellent weekend brunch at **Sam's Anchor Café** (no.27, 435 4527, www.samscafe.com, mains $17-$27), which invites you to accompany some hard liquor on to the waterfront deck. Larkspur's highly regarded **Lark Creek Inn** (234 Magnolia Avenue, 924 7766, www.lark creek.com, mains $25-$32) is a lovely Victorian house with giant sloping skylights, half hidden in a grove of redwoods. Its organic salads and vegetables come from the farmers' market. **Left Bank** (507 Magnolia Avenue, 927 3331, www.leftbank.com, mains $10-$32) is a quasi-Parisian bistro. The first-rate **Marin Brewing Company** (1809 Larkspur Landing Circle, 461 4677, www.marinbrewing.com, mains $12-$17) is a good spot for a brew and some bar food.

In Mill Valley, visit ski-lodge-style **Buckeye Roadhouse** (15 Shoreline Highway, 331 2600, www.buckeyeroadhouse.com, mains $16-$30), for upscale all-American food and great martinis.

If you're in this part of the world, you're probably day-tripping. However, one great alternative to lodging in San Francisco is to stay at the **Inn Above Tide** in Sausalito (30 El Portal, 1-800 893 8433, 332 9535, www.inn abovetide.com, $295-$565 double), where all the peaceful and well-appointed balcony rooms – with balconies literally over the bay – offer wonderful views of San Francisco.

Getting there

By car

Take US 101 across the Golden Gate Bridge. For Sausalito (8 miles from San Francisco), take the Alexander Avenue or Spencer Avenue exit. For Mill Valley (10 miles) and Larkspur, take the East Blithedale exit; you can also reach Larkspur by the Paradise Drive or Lucky Drive exits. For Tiburon, turn off here but follow the signs to Highway 131.

By bus

Golden Gate Transit runs bus services from San Francisco to Sausalito (route 10), Tiburon and Mill Valley (routes 10, 70 or 80 to Marin City, then route 15) and for Larkspur (routes 70 or 80 to Corte Madera, then routes 18 or 22), but taking the ferry and connecting to a bus there is usually far quicker. See schedules at www.goldengate.org.

By ferry

Golden Gate Transit ferries run daily from the Ferry Building on the Embarcadero to Sausalito and Larkspur; the Blue & Gold Fleet sails to Tiburon from the Ferry Building, and to Sausalito and Angel Island from Pier 41, Fisherman's Wharf.

Tourist information

Mill Valley *Mill Valley Chamber of Commerce, 85 Throckmorton Avenue (388 9700/www.millvalley. org).* **Open** 9am-noon Tue-Fri, or by appointment.
Sausalito *Historical Exhibit & Visitor Center, 780 Bridgeway (331 1093/www.sausalito.org).* **Open** 11.30am-4pm Tue-Sun.

Angel Island

The largest island in the San Francisco Bay is a delightful, wild place with a fascinating history. Camp Reynolds, in the east of the island, was established in 1863 by Union troops to protect the Bay against a Confederate attack; later, from 1910 to 1940, the west of the island became the site of a US government immigration station set to screen immigrants under the terms of the 1882 Chinese Exclusion Act. Known as 'the Ellis Island of the West', Angel Island was notorious. Boatloads of Chinese immigrants were detained for months so officials could interrogate them; many were eventually sent home, never having touched the mainland. During World War II, Angel Island was an equally unwelcome home to German and Japanese POWs. The military remained in control through the '50s, when the island served as a missile base, but in 1963 the land was ceded to the government as a state park.

Ayala Cove, where the ferry docks, has a visitors' centre (435 3522) and also marks the beginning of the five-mile Perimeter Trail, which will take you past the immigration station, wooden Civil War barracks and other military remnants hidden among the trees. At 797 feet (243 metres), the peak of **Mount Livermore** affords a panoramic view of the Bay from the island's centre. There's a wonderful diversity of bird and animal species on the island, from deer to seals, pelicans to hummingbirds. You'll also find **Quarry Beach**, a sheltered sunbathing strip popular with kayakers. Those who don't want to walk can take the tram tour and anyone who wants to stay overnight can pitch up at the campsite. For details of camping, guided tours, and bike or kayak rental, see www.angelisland.org; if you do want to camp, book well in advance.

Getting there

By ferry
The Angel Island ferry (435 2131, $3.50 return) runs from Tiburon, daily in summer and weekends only in winter. Schedule information can be found at www.angelislandferry.com.

Mount Tamalpais & Muir Woods

Mount Tamalpais State Park covers ten square miles on the western and southern slopes of the peak. Visible from as far away as Sonoma, the mountain itself soars to nearly 2,600 feet (almost 800 metres), but its rise is so steep it seems far taller. Beautiful at any time of day, it's magnificent at sunset. The roads that snake over Mount Tam, while challenging, are great for hiking and for bicycling; indeed, the mountain bike was invented here. The **Mount Tamalpais Interpretive Association** (258 2410, www.mttam.net) offers organised group hikes. If you're feeling adventurous, call the **San Francisco Hanggliding Center** (1-510 528 2300, www.sfhanggliding.com).

Nearby **Muir Woods National Monument** (388 2595, www.visitmuirwoods.com, $5) contains majestic groves of towering coastal redwoods, many over 500 years old. You'll find several miles of trails here, of which one, the mile-long Main Trail Loop, is accessible to the disabled. Redwood Creek is lined with madrone and big-leaf maple trees, wild flowers (even in winter), ferns and wild berry bushes. Deer,

chipmunks and a variety of birds live peacefully among the redwoods, while the creek is a migratory route for steelhead trout and silver salmon. To avoid crowds, visit on weekday mornings and late afternoons.

Where to eat, drink & stay

The restaurant at the English-styled **Pelican Inn** (10 Pacific Way, 383 6000, mains $15-$29) is not great, but it's the best eating option near the beach. It's also a fine hotel (from $200 double): quaint rooms have canopied beds, balconies and private bathrooms. Rugged travellers should try the 100-year-old **West Point Inn** (646 0702, www.westpointinn.com, $35/adult, $17.50/child), a collection of five rustic cabins that's a two-mile hike up Mount Tam from **Pantoll Ranger Station** (388 2070). Guests bring their own sleeping bags and cook grub in a communal kitchen. There's no electricity, but nothing beats the views.

Getting there

By car
Take US 101 across the Golden Gate Bridge, then turn on to Highway 1. Muir Woods is 15 miles from San Francisco.

By bus
Launched in 2005, a free shuttle bus, no.66, runs from Marin City to Muir Woods on weekends and holidays from Memorial Day to Labor Day. Otherwise, Golden Gate Transit bus 63 goes from Marin City to Stinson Beach and local trailheads from mid Mar to mid Dec, and to Audubon Canyon Ranch from Mar to July.

Tourist information

Mount Tamalpais *Mount Tamalpais State Park (388 2070/www.parks.ca.gov).* **Open** 7am-sunset daily.
Muir Woods *Muir Woods Visitor Center (388 2595/www.visitmuirwoods.com).* **Open** 8am-sunset daily. **Admission** $5.

Stinson Beach & Bolinas Beach

The drive from Mill Valley to **Stinson Beach** along **Panoramic Highway** is long and filled with dangerous hairpin bends and sheer drops of hundreds of feet. Deer are apt to make appearances frighteningly close to the road. Nonetheless, the route is gorgeous, with spectacular views of the ocean, redwoods casting shadows on to the road and ferns dotting the ground along the way.

Stinson was only connected to Sausalito by a dirt road in 1870; prior to that, sole access

Muir Woods.

San Quentin blues

Located on 432 acres of prime real estate in Marin County and with breathtaking views of the Bay, **San Quentin State Prison** is the oldest jail in California. Opened in July 1852, it was built in response to the rampant lawlessness of California's Gold Rush by convicts who spent their nights on a prison ship and their days constructing the penitentiary.

The hulking prison and its sprawling grounds are easily viewed from the ferries travelling between San Francisco and Larkspur, with the installation looking quite benevolent from the outside. However, a slew of famous and infamous prisoners have called the maximum security San Quentin home during its century and a half of history, including legendary 19th-century stagecoach robber Black Bart; Helter Skelter psycho Charles Manson; country singer Merle Haggard; Wallace Fard Muhammad, the founder of the Nation of Islam; Bobby Kennedy's assassin Sirhan Sirhan; and serial killer Richard Ramirez, known as the 'Night Stalker', who terrorised Los Angeles for two years in the 1980s and still sits on San Quentin's Death Row, the only one in the state.

The final destination for those on Death Row, the San Quentin gas chamber, first saw use in 1938. In recent years the space has been adapted for execution by lethal injection, first adopted as a more 'humane' method. However, lethal injection is currently facing legal challenge on the grounds that it constitutes 'cruel and unusual punishment', largely thanks to cases in which death has been lingering rather than instantaneous. There has thus been a moratorium on such executions in California since 2006.

Johnny Cash brought more fame to St Quentin. In 1969, he ticked off prison authorities behind his legendary live concert here (taped and re-released in 2006 as *At San Quentin – the Legacy Edition*), where he debuted the song 'San Quentin', to thundering applause, with its opening line, 'San Quentin, you've been livin' hell to me'. He wasn't the only musician to be attracted by the prison's notoriety: in 2003, metalheads Metallica filmed their video for 'St Anger' here.

Today, more than 5,222 men sport prison blues at San Quentin. Life is undeniably tough, but during female warden Jeanne Woodford's tenure, San Quentin has developed rehabilitation programmes galore. It's the only California prison with a fully accredited college programme, where inmates can take classes in critical thinking, literature or physics, many taught by graduate students from the University of California at Berkeley.

Just inside the prison's east gate is a small museum. It includes a model of a prison cell, and such morbid exhibits as a miniature gas chamber and artefacts from the original gallows. Visits are by appointment only (454 1460).

---

was by boat, and there's still a delicious sense of isolation. A good reason to visit is the beach itself, prettier and much warmer than San Francisco's Ocean Beach. Lifeguards are on duty May through October, and there's a 50-acre park with more than 100 picnic tables. All-nude **Red Rock Beach** is a bare half mile south of downtown. Just north of Stinson Beach is the pristine **Bolinas Lagoon Preserve** (4900 Highway 1, 868 9244, www.egret.org). The Alice Kent Trail leads to an observation point, from which you can see egrets and great blue herons.

Between the lagoon and the Pacific is **Bolinas**, a beachside hamlet far enough off the beaten track for locals to find it worthwhile binning road signs to dissuade outsiders. But if you can, navigate your way into town and to the beach, which has small enough waves to be a great spot for novice surfers: try **Bolinas Surf Lessons** (2 Mile Surf Shop, 22 Brighton Avenue, 868 0264,

www.surfbolinas.com). The water is also good for kayaking and fishing; camping, campfires and dogs are allowed on the beach. The town is a haven for writers and artists, as the **Bolinas Museum** (48 Wharf Road, 868 0330, www.bolinasmuseum.org, closed Mon-Thur) makes clear. At the Palomarin field station of nearby **Point Reyes Bird Observatory** (900 Mesa Road, 868 0655, www.prbo.org), the public can watch biologists catch and release birds, using special 'mist' nets, every day except Mondays from May to late November, and on Wednesday, Saturday and Sunday mornings in winter.

Where to eat, drink & stay

The thing to eat in Stinson is, of course, seafood: try the **Stinson Beach Grill** (3465 Highway 1, 868 2002, mains $10-$25), or the **Sand Dollar Restaurant** (3458 Shoreline Highway, 868 0434, mains $9-$32). Both are pleasant, casual, rather pricey beachside restaurants serving typical American seafood dishes.

Bolinas has only a few choice spots: on Wharf Road, try the **Coast Café** (no.46, 868 2298, www.bolinashotel.com, closed Mon, mains $8-$28). For a pint, the **Saloon at Smiley's** (41 Wharf Road, 868-1311) has been in the business for more than 150 years, and claims to be the second oldest bar in California.

Accommodation-wise, Stinson's cute and simple **Sandpiper** (1 Marine Way, 1-877 557 4737, 868 1632, www.sandpiperstinsonbeach. com, $95-$195 double) has rooms and cabins within walking distance of the waves, while the funky **Stinson Beach Motel** (3416 Highway 1, 868 1712, www.stinsonbeachmotel.com, $85-$200 double) is in 868 1311, $92-$104 double).

Getting there

By car
Take US 101 across the Golden Gate Bridge and then, at Marin City, pick up Highway 1. This will lead you to Stinson Beach and (follow the signs) to Bolinas.

By bus
Golden Gate Transit's 63 service runs from Marin City to Stinson Beach. The West Marin Stagecoach (www.marin-stagecoach.org) operates four buses a day from Marin City to Stinson Beach and Bolinas.

Point Reyes National Seashore

If you head north from Stinson Beach on Highway 1, you'll come to the **Bear Valley Visitor Center** (*see below*) near Olema. The centre acts as the entry point for the most famous parcel of land in these parts: the vast wilderness of **Point Reyes National Seashore**. This protected peninsula is an extraordinary wildlife refuge, with sea mammals, waterfalls and miles of unspoilt beaches. From the visitor centre, you can either head west towards the coast for **Drake's Beach**, or go north via Inverness to the tip of the peninsula: **Point Reyes Lighthouse** (669 1534, closed Tue & Wed) is a perfect lookout for whale-watching. Several trails also start here, including the popular **Chimney Rock**. Nearby **Inverness** is picturesque, with many homes still owned by the families that built them, while tiny **Point Reyes Station** bustles with energy along its three-block Downtown; both are hubs for organic farmers and ranchers, as well as artisanal cheesemakers. Make a note to check in at the **Cowgirl Creamery** (80 4th Street, 663 9335, www.cowgirlcreamery.com), where you can try a bounty of fine local cheeses.

Natural historians and those with more energy than is good for them should press on along Highway 1 to **Tomales Bay**. There, **Blue Waters Kayaking** (12938 Sir Francis Drake Boulevard, at the Golden Hinde Inn, 669 2600, www.bwkayak.com) offers half- or full-day paddle trips, and (by appointment) romantic full-moon tours.

Where to eat, drink & stay

In Point Reyes Station, the **Station House Café** (Main Street, 663 1515, www.stationhouse cafe.com, closed Wed, mains $9-$30) is a mellow place that serves California cuisine, while the **Pine Cone Diner** (60 4th Street, 663 1536, www.thepineconediner.com, mains $6-$10) is a much-treasured retro spot for breakfast or lunch.

In Inverness, **Manka's Inverness Lodge** (30 Callender Way, 669 1034, www.mankas. com, $215-$615 double) has eight rooms, a suite, two cabins and a dramatic 1911 boathouse over the water. The Lodge's main house burned down in January 2007; at the time of writing the restaurant remains closed.

In nearby Marshall is **Nick's Cove** (23240 State Route 1, 663 1033, www.nickscove.com, mains $12-$32, $295-$395 double). Here, former fishing cabins built over Tomales Bay have been transformed into rustic but luxurious cottages. The restaurant is top-notch, majoring in locally sourced seafood, meat and other produce, and with cooking by Mark Franz of Farallion in San Francisco.

Since 1876, Olema has been home to the charming **Olema Inn** (10000 Sir Francis Drake Boulevard, 663 9559, www.theolemainn.com, $145-$185 double). In Point Reyes, try art-heavy **Abalone Inn** (12355 Sir Francis Drake Boulevard, 663 9149, 1-877 416 0458, www.abaloneinn.com, $110-$150 double) or **Knob Hill** (40 Knob Hill Road, 663 1784, www.knobhill.com, $75-$160 double).

Getting there

By car
Take US 101 across the Golden Gate Bridge, then Highway 1. Point Reyes is 32 miles from San Francisco.

By bus
There is no direct public transport to Point Reyes.

Tourist information

Point Reyes *National Seashore Bear Valley Visitor Center (464 5100/www.nps.gov/pore).* **Open** 9am-5pm Mon-Fri; 8am-5pm Sat, Sun.
Lighthouse Visitor Center Point (669 1534/www.nps. gov/pore). **Open** 10am-4.30pm Mon, Thur-Sun, weather permitting.

Trips Out of Town

Napa Valley.

Wine Country

Drink in the scenery.

Everything you've heard about California's Wine Country is true – rolling hills planted with lush rows of tangled vines, refreshing country air, destination restaurants, upscale resorts: the attractions are endless. It may only take an hour to drive from San Francisco to Napa and Sonoma Counties, but it really is another world.

Since pioneering Hungarian farmer Agoston Haraszthy de Mokcsa planted his 500-acre Buena Vista wine estate in the middle of the 19th century, the Wine Country has changed hugely. From modest beginnings, the area has become masterful at marketing not only its product, but itself; it has sold an image of an idyllic, cultured and rather romantic place, where the local fine wines are an integral part of a sophisticated yet laid-back way of life.

It's a lifestyle to which five million visitors a year aspire. Summer here is ridiculously busy, so the best times to visit are spring, when the hills are verdant and the vineyards carpeted with mustard flowers, and autumn, when the burnished light and auburn vine leaves lend the place a calming ambience.

NAPA AND SONOMA

The region is separated into the Napa and Sonoma Valleys, located on either side of a low-lying mountain range. Of the two, Napa is the largest, the most famous and the most popular. Sonoma is far smaller and slower. No town in either valley is more than a stone's throw from countryside dotted with vines and cows. Most of the higher-priced wineries are in Napa, but alongside industry behemoths are smaller wineries, many family-owned. Even in Napa you'll find 'crossroads wineries', off the main route, that do not charge for tastings, a practice that's now pretty much standard at the majority of tasting rooms. Wining here is as important as dining. Many wineries have picnic areas, but it's courteous to buy a bottle to enjoy with your feast. Plenty of restaurants allow BYOB: check the corkage fee when booking, and do purchase something from the wine list if you're planning to consume more than one bottle.

Most wineries are open daily. The fee, which covers tasting several wines and, in some cases, a tour, can be anything up to $10, which can sometimes be put towards purchases. For a guide to the region's labels and grapes, *see p269* **Grape expectations**.

The classic Wine Country route winds through both valleys. Drive up Highway 29 to **Calistoga**, hitting the towns of **Napa**, **Yountville**, **Oakville**, **Rutherford** and **St Helena** on the way. From Calistoga, head west on Petrified Forest Road for 12 miles towards **Fulton**, then drive a few miles south on Highway 101 to **Santa Rosa**, where you can pick up Route 12, which takes you south through the Sonoma Valley.

If you'd rather take in the scenery in a more sedate fashion, tourist offices (*see p268 & p270*) can provide information on bike hire and chauffeur-driven tours, as well as activities such as hot-air ballooning. They also distribute a booklet offering discounts at wineries (see also www.passport2winecountry.com).

Napa Valley

The 30-mile-long Napa Valley, on the east side of the Mayacamas Mountains, was originally settled by the Wappo Indian tribe several centuries ago. The Gold Rush of the 1850s saw its population grow, with Europeans as well as Californians; Prussian immigrant Charles Krug introduced grapes here in 1861.

The valley, bisected by the Napa River, runs from the San Pablo Bay's fertile Carneros region north to Calistoga. There are now 250 commercial vineyards here, along with smaller 'custom crush' wineries. Many are situated on the often-busy Highway 29 (aka the St Helena Highway), which runs up the centre of the valley; along the way, towns and villages have plenty of shopping and dining opportunities. Boutique wineries are found mostly on the **Silverado Trail**, a more scenic and less cramped artery to the east, or on the lanes that criss-cross the valley. Alternatively, take the **Wine Train** (1-800 427 4124, 1-707 253 2111, www.winetrain.com), which runs between Napa and St Helena or Rutherford. Rides on restored pre-1950s Pullman coaches start at $49.50.

Towns & attractions

Once a blue-collar town, **Napa** has grown increasingly tourist-oriented over the last few years, although it's still largely nondescript. Most of the changes have centred on its historic Downtown, where the media attention paid to the opening of **COPIA** (*see below*) in 2001 helped stimulate investment. Next door is the Oxbow Public Market complex (610 First Street), set to house food and wine vendors and restaurants when it opens in late 2008.

North of here, things get more genteel. **Yountville** is white-collar territory, with posh restaurants, immaculate hotels and upscale shops. The tidy towns of **Rutherford** and **Oakville** are both dominated by the wineries that surround them, but **St Helena**, further north, has real charm, and can be enjoyed in a more modest way than its shiny veneer suggests. It's home to the **Robert Louis Stevenson Silverado Museum** (1490 Library Lane, 1-707 963 3757, www.silveradomuseum.org, noon-4pm Tue-Sun, admission free), a collection of Stevenson's manuscripts, plus his wedding ring and marriage licence. But the town is best known for its slew of chic boutiques, upscale eateries and gourmet food shops: on Main Street, don't miss **Woodhouse Chocolate** (no.1367, 1-800 966 3468, 1-707 963 8413, www.woodhousechocolate.com), or, for olive oils, condiments and more, **Olivier Napa Valley** (no.1375, 1-707 967 8777, www.oliviernapavalley.com). Just south of town, on Highway 29, is the West Coast's only outpost of posh deli and wine store **Dean & Deluca**, complete with coffee and pastry bar (607 South St Helena Highway, 1-707 967 9980, www.deandeluca.com).

In **Calistoga**, it's geothermal springs, not wineries, that bring in the visitors. The town is awash with spas offering treatments, from dips in mineral pools to baths in volcanic ash. Among them are the charming, 55-year-old **Dr Wilkinson's Hot Springs Resort** (1507 Lincoln Avenue, 1-707 942 4102, www.drwilkinson.com, $109-$199 double) and the **Golden Haven Hot Springs Spa & Resort** (1713 Lake Street, 1-707 942 6793, www.goldenhaven.com, $79-$199 double); at the high end of the scale is the breathtaking **Calistoga Ranch**, with 46 deluxe lodges and a splendid spa (580 Lommel Road, 1-707 254 2800, www.calistogaranch.com, $550-$3,850 per lodge). The town's other draw is the **Old Faithful Geyser** (www.oldfaithfulgeyser.com), one of only three geysers on earth that blast out water and steam at regular intervals – around every 30 to 40 minutes – to heights from 60 to 100 feet (18 to 30 metres).

COPIA: The American Center for Wine, Food & the Arts

500 First Street, Napa (1-707 259 1600/ www.copia.org). **Open** 10am-5pm Mon, Wed-Sun. **Admission** $5; $4 reductions; free under-12s. **Credit** AmEx, DC, Disc, MC, V.

A vast $50-million facility, COPIA puts an interesting spin on the museum concept in its celebrations of eating, drinking and living well. Art and interactive exhibits line the walls; cooking demonstrations and concerts crop up frequently on the calendar. Daily events include wine tastings and tours of the garden, and there's also a well-stocked gift shop and a couple of good eating options, such as Julia's Kitchen (1-707 265 5700). Check the website for full details, and book in advance for popular events. A farmers' market is held in COPIA's car park on Tuesday and Saturday mornings from May to October (1-707 252 7142).

Wineries

Depending on the traffic, which can get pretty bad at peak times, you're rarely more than a ten-minute drive from a winery in the Napa Valley. Though Napa itself doesn't have any, it does have a number of fine tasting rooms, led by the **Vintner's Collective** (1245 Main Street, 1-707 255 7150, www.vintnerscollective.com). Notable wineries south-west of the town, along or off the Carneros Highway towards Sonoma, include **Domaine Carneros** (1240 Duhig Road, 1-707 257 0101, www.domaine.com), where the pinot you'll be sipping is sparkling: the winery is owned by Taittinger. The views are spectacular, as they are from the terrace at off-the-beaten-track **Artesa Vineyards & Winery** (1345 Henry Road, 1-707 224 1668, www.artesawinery.com).

North of Napa on the Silverado Trail is newcomer **Black Stallion** (no.4089, 1-707 253 1400, www.blackstallionwinery.com), which opened in summer 2007 on the site of a former equestrian centre.

The leading winery near Yountville is **Domaine Chandon** (1 California Drive, 1-707 944 2280, www.chandon.com), which offers an excellent tour ($7) introducing visitors to its interpretation of *méthode champenoise*. Oakville is home to the **Robert Mondavi Winery** (7801 St Helena Highway, 1-888 766 6328, www.robertmondaviwinery.com, reservations recommended), a good bet for first-timers, and the unstuffy **PlumpJack** (620 Oakville Crossroad, 1-707 945 1220, www.plumpjack.com). Also here, at Oakville Cross Road and St Helena Highway, is the original, branch of the **Oakville Grocery** (*see p270*).

Another cluster of wineries draws oenophiles to Rutherford. **Mumm** (8445 Silverado Trail, 1-707 967 7700, www.mummcuveenapa.com) has a collection of Ansel Adams photographs, while Francis Ford Coppola's **Rubicon Estate** (formerly Niebaum-Coppola Winery; 1991 St Helena Highway, 1-707 968 1100, www.niebaum-coppola.com) has memorabilia from the great man's movies. **St Supéry** (8440 St Helena Highway, 1-707 963 4507, www.stsupery.com) encourages novices with tastings suitable for first-timers.

The list of wineries in St Helena is led by historic **Beringer** (2000 Main Street, 1-707 967 4412, www.beringer.com), where events run from a $15 half-hour tour to a $110 vineyard tour with lunch. **Charles Krug** (2800 Main Street, 1-800 682 5784, www.charleskrug.com), founded in 1861, enhances its wines with summer chocolate tastings; **Burgess Cellars** (1108 Deer Park Road, 1-707 963 4766, www. burgesscellars.com, tastings by appointment only) is a beautiful mountainside winery. Two relative curiosities are **Prager** (1281 Lewelling Lane, 1-707 963 7678, www.pragerport.com), where the speciality is port, and the **Silverado Brewing Company** (3020A St Helena Highway, 1-707 967 9876, www.silverado brewingcompany.com), for those more keen on the grain than the grape. Up the road in Calistoga, try **Clos Pegase** (1060 Dunaweal Lane, 1-707 942 4981, www.clospegase.com); for the wines, sure, but also for the architecture (by Michael Graves) and the sculpture garden.

Where to eat & drink

As well as a chic hotel (the Napa River Inn, *see below*), a pastry shop and a day spa, the restored Napa Mill in Napa houses several fine restaurants. 'Global comfort food' is no oxymoron at **Celadon** (500 Main Street, 1-707 254 9690, www.celadonnapa.com, mains $16-$30), with the likes of flash-fried calamari with a spicy chipotle chilli glaze, while Greg Cole's **Angèle** (540 Main Street, 1-707 252 8115, www.angelerestaurant.com, mains $18-$30) is a favourite spot for terrace drinks and French country cooking. The river patio of the **Napa General Store** (540 Main Street, 1-707 259 0762, mains $7-$14) is good for sandwiches, salads and thin pizzas. In town, **ZuZu** (829 Main Street, 1-707 224 8555, www.zuzunapa. com, tapas $3-$14) is a reliable tapas bar.

Yountville is renowned around the world as the home of the **French Laundry** (6640 Washington Street, 1-707 944 2380, set menu $240), regularly identified as one of the world's great restaurants. Prices are high to say the least, and you'll have to book two months in advance, but you'll get a world-class meal. Thomas Keller, lord of the Laundry, also runs urbane **Bouchon** (6534 Washington Street, 1-707 944 8037, mains $16-$30), where the French menu is priced more moderately. Its chic next-door bakery offers posh picnic fare. Philippe Jeanty is the other big name around these parts, with the casual **Bistro Jeanty**

(6510 Washington Street, 1-707 944 0103, www.bistrojeanty.com, mains $16-$30) being his signature spot. Well worth tying in with a wine tasting is **étoile**, the excellent California-French restaurant at Domaine Chandon (*see p266*, mains $34-$42).

St Helena options are plentiful: for breakfast, try the **Model Bakery** (1357 Main Street, 1-707 963 8192, www.themodelbakery.com); for lunch, there's **Ana's Cantina** (1205 Main Street, 1-707 963 4921, mains $8-$12) or the 1949-vintage **Taylor's Refresher** (933 Main Street, 1-707 963 3486, www.taylorsrefresher. com, mains $6-$14), offering terrific 1950s-style burgers and shakes. For dinner, **Martini House** (1245 Spring Street, 1-707 963 2233, www.martini house.com, mains $32-$42) celebrates Napa's bounty with top-quality cooking and, at the downstairs Wine Cellar bar, a huge list of wines.

Calistoga's restaurants are concentrated mainly on Lincoln Avenue: sturdy American classics dominate at **Brannan's** (no.1374, 1-707 942 2233, www.brannansgrill.com, mains $16-$35) and the **Flatiron Grill** (no.1440, 1-707 942 1220, www.flatirongrill.com, mains $12-$26).

Where to stay

Lodgings around Napa run the gamut from quaint Queen Anne-style B&Bs to full resorts. The sleek, luxurious **Carneros Inn** (4048 Carneros Highway, 1-707 299 4900, www.the carnerosinn.com, $480-$655 double), just south-west of Napa, fits into the latter category: its 86 ultra-modern cottages have fireplaces, flat-panel televisions and outdoor showers. In the Napa Mill, you'll find the deluxe, 66-room **Napa River Inn** (500 Main Street, 1-877 251 8500, 1-707 251 8500, www.napariverinn.com, $190-$230 double). The **Oak Knoll Inn** (2200 E Oak Knoll Avenue, 1-707 255 2200, www.oak knollinn.com, $350-$750 double) is one of the valley's most quaint B&Bs; and if you've had enough of all things quaint, the **John Muir Inn** (1998 Trower Avenue, 1-800 522 8999, 1-707 257 7220, www.johnmuirnapa.com, $125-$203 double) is an above-par motel.

There are fewer budget options in Yountville; the high-class **Villagio Inn & Spa** (6481 Washington Street, 1-800 351 1133, 1-707 944 8877, www.villagio.com, $207-$585 double/suite) is one of several deluxe hotels. In Rutherford, you'll need to spend a lot of cash for a night at the **Auberge du Soleil** (180 Rutherford Hill Road, 1-800 348 5406, 1-707 963 1211, www.aubergedusoleil.com, $550-$3,500 double/suite), one for special occasions. Along St Helena's Main Street, try the luxurious **Inn at Southbridge** (no.1020, 1-800 520 6800, 1-707 967 9400, www.innatsouthbridge.com,

$280-$570 double), or the delightful **El Bonita Motel** (no.195, 1-800 541 3284, 1-707 963 3216, www.elbonita.com, $120-$235 double), an aesthetic mix of art deco and French colonial that's something of a bargain by St Helena standards. Outside town, the **Meadowood** complex (900 Meadowood Lane, 1-800 458 8080, 1-707 963 3646, www.meadowood.com, $475-$1,600 double) comprises a hotel, separate cottages and restaurants, as well as a golf course, swanky fitness centre and spa. For Calistoga lodgings, *see p266*.

Wherever you want to stay in the area, be certain to book well in advance, especially in summer. If you do get stuck, try Napa Valley Reservations Unlimited (1-800 251 6272, www.napavalleyreservations.com).

Tourist information

Calistoga *Calistoga Chamber of Commerce & Visitor Center, 1506 Lincoln Avenue (1-707 942 6333/www.calistogachamber.com).* **Open** 8am-5pm Mon-Sat; 8am-4pm Sun.

Napa *Napa Valley Conference & Visitor Center, 1310 Napa Town Center (1-707 226 7459/ www.napavalley.com).* **Open** 9am-5pm daily.

St Helena *St Helena Chamber of Commerce, 1010 Main Street (1-800 799 6456/www.sthelena. com).* **Open** 10am-5pm Mon-Fri; 11am-3pm Sat.

Yountville *Yountville Chamber of Commerce, 6484 Washington Street (1-707 944 0904/www. yountville.com).* **Open** 10am-5pm daily.

Sonoma Valley

The Sonoma Valley, which runs about 23 miles north from San Pablo Bay, is home to around 200 wineries. However, the main attraction of a Sonoma tour is the landscape. The county's topography is diverse, from beaches to redwood forests and rolling hills. It's also agriculturally rich, and the areas around towns such as Glen Ellen and Sebastopol brim with farms.

Towns & attractions

Although its central plaza is now ringed by restaurants, bookshops, wine tasting rooms, food shops and a cinema (the delightful 75-year-old Sebastiani Theatre), the town of **Sonoma** retains the feel of old California. The town was founded in 1823 as the **Mission San Francisco Solano** (114 East Spain Street, 1-707 938 9560, 10am-5pm daily); today, the mission is part of the loose affiliation of humbly atmospheric sites known as Sonoma State Historic Park. The town hall and Bear Flag Monument on the plaza mark the site where the Californian Bear Flag first flew: for the 25 days of the riotous Bear Flag Revolt

in 1846, this was the capital of the independent Republic of California. Fast-forward more than 160 years and the plaza is home to the town's Tuesday evening farmers' market (Apr-Oct; 1-707 538 7023). Just north of Sonoma, the small town of **Glen Ellen** was once the home of Jack London, adventurer, farmer, autodidact and author; **Jack London Historic State Park** contains the charred remains of Wolf House, the author's home.

Its population is twice that of the city of Napa, but **Santa Rosa** manages to retain a low-key appeal. Historic Railroad Square is the city's busy downtown area, but the real visitor attraction is the park on the corner of Santa Rosa and Sonoma Avenues: **Luther Burbank Home & Gardens**. Also here is the **Charles M Schulz Museum** (2301 Hardies Lane, 1-707 579 4452, www.schulzmuseum.org), commemorating the man who created Snoopy, Charlie Brown and the whole *Peanuts* gang.

Further north is **Healdsburg**, a highfalutin boutique town where Bay Area boomers come to drop some serious cash. Gourmet food stores, artisan bakeries and sleek eateries bring in the herds – as does the annual ten-day jazz fest, held in June (1-707 433 4644) – but the **Healdsburg Museum** (221 Matheson Street, 1-707 431 3325, www.healdsburgmuseum.org), with Pomo Indian baskets and other cultural artefacts, is pretty authentic. The town's central plaza is a lovely place to stroll, and hosts a Tuesday evening farmers' market (June-Oct; 1-707 431 1956).

Luther Burbank Home & Gardens

Santa Rosa Avenue, at Sonoma Avenue (1-707 524 5445/www.lutherburbank.org). **Open** *Apr-Oct* 10am-3.30pm Tue-Sun. **Admission** $4; $3 discounts; free under-12s. **No credit cards**.

America's most renowned horticulturist, Burbank developed more than 800 new varieties of plant during his life. His former house and grounds are now a national historic landmark. Guided tours (booking isn't necessary) and themed gardens explain and demonstrate this botanical pioneer's work.

Wineries

Sonoma County's quaint, family-owned wineries are more secluded than many of their Napa neighbours. Its history is intertwined with that of the California wine industry, which began at what is now the **Buena Vista Carneros Winery** (18000 Old Winery Road, 1-800 926 1266, www.buenavistawinery.com). Of the nearly 40 wineries in the valley, several are near the city's main plaza. **Bartholomew Park Winery** (1000 Vineyard Lane, 1-707 935 9511, www.bartholomewparkwinery.com) is great for picnics; **Sebastiani Vineyards**

Grape expectations

Not all Californian wines are widely available outside the state, so here's a guide to which label does what. A huge volume of fruit and flavour is the hallmark of today's Californian wines; common varieties include crisp chardonnays, big cabernet sauvignons, soft merlots, sauvignon blancs, pinot noirs, rieslings and the versatile zinfandel.

Napa labels

Bouchon (pinot, chardonnay); **Carneros Creek** (pinot noir); **Chimney Rock** (chardonnay, cabernet); **Clos Pégase** (cabernet, chardonnay, merlot, petite syrah, port); **Cuvaison** (cabernet, chardonnay); **Joseph Phelps** (chardonnay); **Opus One** (cabernet); **Pine Ridge** (chardonnay, cabernet, merlot); **Robert Sinskey** (pinot noir); **Silver Oak** (cabernet); **Stag's Leap** (cabernet, chardonnay, sauvignon blanc).

Sonoma labels

Cline (zinfandel); **Dry Creek** (chardonnay); **Field Stone** (cabernet, petite syrah); **Foppiano** (petite syrah, zinfandel); **Geyser Peak** (chardonnay); **Gundlach Bundschu** (merlot, pinot noir, chardonnay, cabernet, zinfandel); **Lambert Bridge** (fumé blanc, pinot noir, zinfandel); **Matanzas Creek** (chardonnay); **Pezzi King** (pinot noir, zinfandel, cabernet); **Roche** (chardonnay, pinot noir); **Shug** (pinot noir).

(389 Fourth Street East, 1-707 938 5532, www.sebastiani.com) may not be the region's most charming winery, but it gives another perspective on the ubiquitous family.

The **Carneros** area includes southern Sonoma as well as Napa; wineries take advantage of the cooler climate to produce excellent pinot noir grapes and sparkling wines. Fans of sparkling wines should try a tasting at **Gloria Ferrer Champagne Caves** (23555 Arnold Drive, 1-707 996 7256, www.gloriaferrer.com). Further south, the **Viansa Winery** (25200 Arnold Drive, 1-707 935 4700, www.viansa.com), a Tuscan-style winery situated on a knoll, offers informal tastings, and has a large Italian-style deli.

The pick of the viticulture in and around Glen Ellen includes the **Arrowood Vineyards & Winery** (14347 Sonoma Highway, 1-707 935

2600, www.arrowoodvineyards.com) and the **Benziger Family Winery** (1883 London Ranch Road, 1-888 490 2739, 1-707 935 3000, www.benziger.com), which makes its wines using bio-dynamic farming methods devised in the 1920s by Rudolf Steiner. Nearby **Kenwood** is synonymous with the **Kenwood Vineyards** (9592 Sonoma Highway, 1-707 833 5891, www.kenwoodvineyards.com), known for wine made from grapes grown on Jack London's former ranch (novelist Haruki Murakami drinks a bottle from here on his birthday each year). The original barn, now the tasting room and shop, dates from before Prohibition.

The area around Santa Rosa boasts several fine vineyards. **Kendall-Jackson Wine Center** (5007 Fulton Road, 1-866 287 9818, 1-707 571 8100, www.kj.com) has a state of the art tasting room and education centre.

Trips Out of Town

Where to eat & drink

In Sonoma, the **girl & the fig** (110 West Spain Street, 1-707 938 3634, www.thegirland thefig.com, mains $17-$25), inside the landmark Sonoma Hotel (*see below*), has a reputation for garden-fresh French dishes including salads, steaks and cheese plates. Small but characterful **Café La Haye** (140 E Napa Street, 1-707 935 5994, www.cafelahaye.com, mains $16-$24) is another winner, although it's open for dinner only (Tue-Sat). Picnickers get supplies from **Artisan Bakers** (750 W Napa Street, 1-707 939 1765, www.artisanbakers.com), the **Vella Cheese Company** (315 Second Street East, 1-707 938 3232, www.vellacheese. com) and **Sonoma Market** (500 W Napa Street, 1-707 996 3411).

In Santa Rosa, try **Willi's Wine Bar** (4404 Old Redwood Highway, 1-707 526 3096, www.williswinebar.net) for superior small plates and decent wines by the glass.

Healdsburg has plenty of appealing options, from pricey to wallet-friendly. Among the latter is **Manzanita** (336 Healdsburg Avenue, 1-707 433 8111, www.manzanita336.com, mains $26-$30), with its excellent Mediterranean menu. The Hotel Healdsburg (*see below*) is home to award-winning chef Charlie Palmer's **Dry Creek Kitchen** (no.317, 1-707 431 0330, www.charliepalmer.com/dry_creek, mains $26-$38), where the changing menus are based on fresh seasonal ingredients. Within the Les Mars hotel (*see below*), Douglas Keane's Cal-French cuisine at **Cyrus** (1-707 433 3311, www.cyrusrestaurant.com, 3 courses $75, 4 courses $87, 5 courses $99) continues to make waves. DIY options include the gourmet **Oakville Grocery** (24 Matheson Street, 1-707 433 3200, www.oakvillegrocery.com), whose patio is a popular spot to eat goodies purchased locally. For a sugar rush, don't miss **Powell's**, a delightfully nostalgic sweet shop/ice-cream parlour on the corner of the main plaza (322 Center Street, 1-707 431 2784, www.powellsweetshoppe.com).

Where to stay

In Sonoma, try the **Sonoma Hotel** (110 West Spain Street, 1-800 468 6016, 1-707 996 2996, www.sonomahotel.com, $99-$198 double) and the comfy **El Dorado Inn** (405 First Street West, 1-707 996 3030, www.hotel eldorado.com, $155-$195 double). To spoil yourself, the **Ledson Hotel** (480 First Street East, 1-707 996 9779, www.ledsonhotel.com, $350-$395 double) has six ultra-deluxe rooms, but for pampering to the max it has to be the stunning **Fairmont Sonoma Mission Inn**

& Spa (100 Boyes Boulevard, 1-707 938 9000, www.fairmont.com/sonoma, $229-$375 double), a few miles out of town in Boyes Hot Springs.

In Kenwood, you'll likely be tempted by the historic, luxurious **Kenwood Inn & Spa** (10400 Sonoma Highway, 1-800 353 6966, 1-707 833 1293, www.kenwoodinn.com, $250-$750 double/suite). Glen Ellen, meanwhile, is home to the **Jack London Lodge** (13740 Arnold Drive, 1-707 938 8510, www.jacklondon lodge.com, $90-$170 double), a straight-ahead motel, and **Gaige House** (13540 Arnold Drive, 1-800 935 0237, 1-707 935 0237, www.gaige.com, $200-$695 double/suite), a sleek, chic B&B complete with spa, pool and hot tubs.

Santa Rosa's nicest option is the 44-room **Vintners Inn** (4350 Barnes Road, 1-707 575 7350, www.vintnersinn.com, $165-$295 double), a prime place to stay for some proper Wine Country relaxation. The **Gables** (4257 Petaluma Hill Road, 1-800 422 5376, 1-707 585 7777, www.thegablesinn.com, $175-$195 double) is a lovely old Victorian Gothic inn, spread across several secluded acres.

In Healdsburg, a number of decent motels off the freeway will serve as a good base if you don't want to blow your entire budget on accommodation, but for high-flyers, the trendy **Hotel Healdsburg** (25 Matheson Street, 1-800 889 7188, 1-707 431 2800, www. hotelhealdsburg.com, $260-$790 double), and the posh French-style **Les Mars** (27 North Street, 1-877 431 1700, www.lesmarshotel.com, $475-$1,025 double), are pure luxury.

A good resource for B&B bookings is the Bed & Breakfast Association of the Sonoma Valley (1-800 969 4667, www.sonomabb.com), which shows availability and has links to the B&Bs' own websites.

Tourist information

Healdsburg *Healdsburg Chamber of Commerce & Visitors Bureau, 217 Healdsburg Avenue (1-707 433 6935/www.healdsburg.org).* **Open** 9am-5pm Mon-Fri; 9am-3pm Sat; 10am-2pm Sun.

Santa Rosa *Santa Rosa CVB, 9 Fourth Street (1-800 404 7673, 1-707 577 8674/www.visitsanta rosa.com).* **Open** 9am-5pm Mon-Sat; 10am-5pm Sun.

Sonoma *Sonoma Valley Visitors Bureau, 453 First Street East (1-707 996 1090/www.sonomavalley. com).* **Open** 9am-5pm Mon-Sat; 10am-5pm Sun.

Getting there

By car

Wine Country is an hour (44 miles) by car from San Francisco, over the Golden Gate along US 101. Head east at Ignacio to Highway 37 and take Highway 121 north. From here, Highway 12 follows the Sonoma Valley, while Highway 29 leads along Napa Valley.

Heading East

Northern California's natural world.

Lake Tahoe

Reaching a maximum depth of 1,636 feet (500 metres), 22-mile-long **Lake Tahoe** is the tenth deepest lake in the world and the second deepest in the US. It is blessed with remarkable water clarity, a result of the pure High Sierra streams and snow melt that drain into it. Much of the lake's 72 miles of shoreline – two-thirds of which lie inside California's boundary line, with one-third in Nevada – have been divvied up into exclusive parcels of private property, but there's still plenty here to enjoy.

From March to early November, it's easy to drive the perimeter of the lake, much of it served by public transport. The **Tahoe Rim Trail** (information 1-775 298 0012) provides extensive trails to explore on foot, horse or by bike. On the California side you'll find such attractions as the **Sugar Pine Point State Park** (1-530 525 7982), near Meeks Bay, and further south the **Emerald Bay State Park** (1-530 541 3030), which overlooks the bay of the same name. There are plenty of beaches around the lake, among them **Sand Harbor**, **Zephyr Cove** and **Camp Richardson**, though only during August and September is the water, fed by snow melt, warm enough for swimming – and even then it's extremely cold. For a bird's-eye view of the area, take a trip with **Lake Tahoe Hot Air Balloons** (1-530 544 1221, www.laketahoe balloons.com) from South Lake Tahoe, or in the sightseeing cable cars operated by **Heavenly Valley** (1-775 586 7000, www.skiheavenly.com).

The north end of Lake Tahoe is roughly a three-and-a-half-hour drive from San Francisco via Sacramento on I-80. The other route, via US 50, leads to the south shore. The two shores are geographically close, but culturally far apart. At **Tahoe City**, the main settlement on the north shore, the lodgings and restaurants are casual and mellow. However, down in **South Lake Tahoe**, on the California–Nevada border, things are very different, thanks to the presence of some looming, all-hours hotel-casinos. Drive from one to the other along the lake's west side, and you'll pass three state parks: **Sugar Pine Point**, **DL Bliss** and **Emerald Bay**. Hikers, bikers and cross-country skiers come here to enjoy miles of trails, and campers toast marshmallows under starry skies. For more information on all, see www.parks.ca.gov.

Lake Tahoe.

Truckee, an Old West railroad town about 12 miles north of the lake, is worth a visit for its wooden sidewalks, historic station and wooden-framed shopfronts. While you're there, head over to **Donner Memorial State Park**, a few miles west of Truckee off Highway 80. It's named after a doomed group of pioneers, who suffered mulitple misfortunes as they attempted to cross the pass here in the viciously cold winter of 1842; starvation drove some of them to cannibalism.

Skiing

The ski season varies each year, but is usually December to late April. Two of the most popular ski areas are **Squaw Valley** (1-530 583 6955, www.squaw.com), site of the 1960 Winter Olympics, and **Alpine Meadows** (1-800 441 4423, 1-530 583 4232, www.skialpine.com). Alpine Meadows is more family-oriented and has better snowboarding, while Squaw Valley is glitzier, with more exciting runs. Other options include **Boreal** (1-530 426 3666, www.borealski.com), whose lower prices attract snowboarders; **Northstar-at-Tahoe** (1-530 562 1010, www.skinorthstar.com), which has excellent beginners' slopes; and **Sugar Bowl** (1-530 426 9000, www.sugarbowl.com), which is also adjacent to the area's largest cross-country (Nordic) ski area, Royal Gorge. Lift passes tend to be expensive, but most resorts offer half-day passes for the afternoon and, sometimes, mid-week specials. If you're not confident about your ability, invest in a lesson; a lift pass for the day is generally included in the price.

If you're driving and are not tied to a particular schedule, avoid heading to the slopes on Friday afternoons: San Franciscans tend to leave work early to get a head start. Likewise, Sunday evenings can be a nightmare if you're trying to get back into the city. You can even get some skiing in as a day trip: it means leaving town at 6am, but you'll be among the first to experience the day's fresh powder snow when the lifts open at 9am.

Where to eat & drink

Haute cuisine is rare in Tahoe, but you'll find loads of unpretentious, friendly restaurants. The bigger restaurant chains are in the casinos, along with Vegas-style 'all-you-can-eat' buffets. In north Tahoe, try the historic **River Ranch Lodge** near Alpine Meadows (1-530 583 4264, www.riverranchlodge.com, closed lunch Mon-Fri except summer, mains $17-$30). Diners can choose between sitting indoors or taking a spot on the patio by the Truckee River's white water. The **Bridge Tender Tavern** (65 W Lake Boulevard, 1-530 583 3342, mains $7-$11) has delectable burgers and a great river view.

On the south shore, the intimate **Café Fiore** (1169 Ski Run Boulevard, 1-530 541 2908, closed lunch, mains $15-$30) is the spot for special occasions, with fabulous Italian cuisine (reservations required). Those on a more modest budget should try the non-trad Mexican food at the **Cantina** (763 Emerald Bay Road, 1-530 544 1233, mains $9-$15) and wash it down with one of the restaurant's celebrated Margaritas.

In Truckee, try **Moody's Bistro**, beneath the Truckee Hotel (10007 Bridge Street, 1-530 587 8688, mains $22-$34), which has a louche, live jazz-driven atmosphere and an impeccably sourced Californian menu.

Where to stay

On the north shore, Tahoe City overflows with condo complexes offering vacation lodging. For something more interesting, try the cosy **River Ranch Lodge** (1-530 583 4264, www.riverranchlodge.com, $80-$200 double); the 19 river-view rooms are hard to come by but worth the effort. The same goes for the lakeside rooms at **Sunnyside Lodge** outside Tahoe

City (1850 W Lake Boulevard, 1-530 583 7200, www.sunnysideresort.com, $100-$285 double).

On the west shore, **Tahoma Meadows B&B** (6821 W Lake Boulevard, 1-530 525 1553, www.tahomameadows.com, $95-$245 double) gets plenty of repeat business at its 14 cabins. For lakefront lodging, stay at the **Shore House B&B** (7170 N Lake Boulevard, Tahoe Vista, 1-530 546 7270, www.shorehouselake tahoe.com, $190-$275 double), legendary for its gourmet breakfasts.

South Lake Tahoe's big spot is the former Caesar's Tahoe, now **MontBleu Resort Casino & Spa** (1-775 588 3515, www.mont bleuresort.com, $89-$350 double). Many south shore lodgings offer free shuttle buses to the casinos: try the **Inn by the Lake** (1-800 877 1466, 1-530 542 0330, www.innbythelake.com, $108-$238 double) for good-value rooms and easy transport. At the higher end, book a stay at one of five rooms or three cabins at the **Black Bear Inn** (1-877 232 7466, 1-530 544 4451, www.tahoe blackbear.com, $215-$255 double), a luxurious B&B built in the 1990s with an old-style Tahoe look. South of Tahoe, **Kirkwood Ski & Summer Resort** (off Highway 88, 1-800 967 7500, www.kirkwood.com, $170-$270 double) is a family-oriented ski resort with both hotel- and condo-style lodging.

Truckee has some decent mid-range B&B options, notably the eight-room **Richardson House** (10154 High Street, 1-530 587 5388, www.richardsonhouse.com, $100-$225 double), high above Truckee's historic district, and **River Street Inn** (10009 E River Street, 1-530 550 9290, www.riverstreetinntruckee.com, $115-$180 double), a historic B&B that's been renovated to a comfortable and chintz-free standard.

Tourist information

Donner Memorial State Park Visitors' Centre *12593 Donner Pass Road, Truckee (1-530 582 7892/www.parks.ca.gov). Open* 9am-4pm daily.

North Lake Tahoe Chamber of Commerce *380 North Lake Boulevard, Tahoe City (1-530 581 6900, www.gotahoenorth.com). Open* 9am-5pm daily.

South Lake Tahoe Visitor Center *3066 Lake Tahoe Boulevard, South Lake Tahoe (1-530 541 5255/www.tahoeinfo.com). Open* 9am-5pm daily.

Getting there

By car

A car is your best means of transport for exploring Lake Tahoe, especially if you're skiing. It takes 3.5hrs to drive here from San Francisco, traffic and weather permitting. To reach the north shore, follow I-80 east over the Bay Bridge all the way to Truckee, then take Highway 89 to Tahoe City. To reach the south shore, take I-80 to Sacramento, then turn off on to US 50.

24,
uckee and Reno and
nd $69 return; buses
a day; Reno buses are

amtrak.com) leaves
ar Oakland, at
st after 1.30pm and
one way). There are
n Sacramento.

By air

Reno-Tahoe International Airport, 58 miles north-east of the lake, is served by several airlines. Fares are around $200 from SFO. The South Tahoe Express (1-866 898 2463, www.southtahoe express.com) offers a regular daily shuttle bus and limo service to South Lake Tahoe from the airport for around $43 return.

Yosemite

The most enchanting, intoxicating, stunning, breathtaking... it's natural to talk about **Yosemite National Park** in superlatives. The park covers some 1,200 square miles of forest, alpine meadows, sheer granite cliffs, lush waterfalls and undisturbed wildlife. Park elevations range from 2,000 feet to over 13,000 feet (600 to nearly 4,000 metres). Highway 120 runs east–west for the entire length of the park, climbing to 9,945 feet (3,031 metres) at **Tioga Pass**, the highest automobile pass in California.

Visit in the less crowded off-season, if possible, from October to May. In spring, the wild flowers are in bloom, and in winter, snowcapped peaks are majestic (though parts of the park are inaccessible). If you must visit in high season, try to avoid the perpetually packed Yosemite Valley. You don't need reservations to visit the park (although you should certainly book lodgings in advance): you can drive in at any time. The $20 entrance fee per vehicle is good for seven days. However, be aware that Yosemite is massive, with more than 250 miles of roads criss-crossing the park. To see even a respectable chunk, you'll need a few days.

Most people head straight for seven-mile-long **Yosemite Valley**, where most of the park services and places to stay are located. It's both touristy and more of a proper town than first-timers expect; indeed, it's estimated that more than half of Yosemite's visitors see only Yosemite Valley, even though the Valley makes up less than one per cent of the park.

Yosemite is all about views: as you drive into the valley, **El Capitan** is the first dramatic sight, a sheer rock wall 3,000 feet (914 metres)

high. Look out for tiny, ant-like figures slowly crawling up its grey granite face: it's one of the most popular climbing spots in the US.

For non-Valley sites, head for **Crane Flat** and **Tuolumne Meadows** (via Highway 120), **Glacier Point** (near Badger Pass), the **Hetch Hetchy Reservoir** (north of Big Oak Flat) and **Tunnel View** at the eastern end of the Wawona tunnel on Highway 41. You'll get a bird's-eye view from Glacier Point and a spectacular view of the Sierras from Tunnel View.

Hiking

Though the roads are engineered as scenic drives, the best way to experience the park and properly commune with nature is on foot. There are hiking trails throughout the park. **Mist Trail** is the most popular: it's three miles from Happy Isles to Vernal Falls and back, or a seven-mile round trip to Nevada Falls. Standing beneath the pounding water of Yosemite Falls is a heart-stopping start to an ambitious hike to the top of **Yosemite Point** (a round trip of just under seven miles). The hike to **Glacier Point** is just as challenging, but you can cheat by driving there instead. Then there's the hike to **Half Dome** (16-mile round trip), which is strictly for the hardcore, as you have to cling to cables anchored into a sheer rockface for the last half mile. Allow ten to 12 hours. For more information on trails, see www.nps.gov/yose/planyourvisit/valleyhikes.htm.

Backpacking and camping in the wilderness is the best way to avoid the crowds and get the most out of the park: there are unofficial campsites set up by other backpackers, but no facilities. However, the park has a visitor quota for backpackers, so make sure you plan ahead. The **Yosemite Mountaineering School** (1-209 372 8344, www.yosemite mountaineering.com) offers excellent classes for beginners (from $120 per day), as well as five-day climbs. Alternatively, the **Activities Desk** (1-209 372 4386) can direct you to a number of fun things to do; you can rent rafts to float down the Valley's winding **Merced River** (available from Curry Village in Yosemite Valley, near the put-in point), rent bicycles and explore the Valley or hire horses from summer stables at Yosemite Valley (1-209 372 8348), Tuolumne Meadows (1-209 372 8427) and Wawona (1-209 375 6502).

Between November to March you can take advantage of the terrific winter sports. Practise figures-of-eight with a head-on view of Half Dome at Curry Village's outdoor ice rink (1-209 372 8341). Rent downhill or cross-country skis, or a snowboard, and carve a few S-turns down the slopes at family-oriented **Badger Pass**

Trips Out of Town

Ski Area (1-209 372 1114, www.badgerpass.
com, closed early spring-late autumn).

Some safety advice. Stay away from cliff
edges and watch for storm clouds: injuries and
fatalities are regularly caused by people taking
nosedives over the falls or getting hit by
lightning while climbing. Take a decent map,
compass and sensible shoes. Heed the warnings
about bears and lock food and cosmetics in bear-
safe boxes. And fill up your car before arriving;
filling stations are few and far between (there's
one at Crane Flat, and one at Wawona).

Where to eat & drink

Three main areas of the Valley can satisfy your
stomach's cravings: Yosemite Lodge (*see below*),
Yosemite Village and Curry Village. **Mountain
Room** is the best of the handful of restaurants
at Yosemite Lodge (*see below*), serving grills
and other hearty main courses. Try to get a
table near the windows for a memorable view
of Yosemite Falls. The neighbouring Food
Court is a good option if you are in a hurry.

In Yosemite Village, **Degnan's Deli** is busy
at lunchtime, with made-to-order sandwiches,
salads and soups. **Degnan's Café** serves ice-
cream and coffee, while upstairs is the **Loft**,
a pizza joint that only opens in summer. And
Curry Village also has a variety of options, from
cheap-and-easy burritos and pizza to the grand,
jacket-and-tie required **Ahwahnee Hotel** (*see
below*), whose Sunday brunches are legendary.
Reservations are a must (1-209 372 1489).

Where to stay

The seven lodgings available inside the park
run the gamut from slum-like to extravagant. In
Yosemite Valley, try to avoid **Housekeeping
Camp** ($76 for up to 4 people), a collection of
duplex units that are a strange hybrid of cabin
and campsite. A more civilised choice is the
260-room **Yosemite Lodge** ($98-$177 double),
which has all the charm (and facilities) of a
chain motel but is unbeatable for its central
location. Those with money to blow should
consider the **Ahwahnee Hotel** ($426 double),
a National Historic Landmark built in 1927 of
huge timbers and river rock.

Outside Yosemite Valley, near the south
entrance, is the whitewashed, Victorian-style
Wawona Hotel ($119-$183 double), housed in
six buildings, and the modern, fairly upscale
Tenaya Lodge (1-888 514 2167, 1-877 322
5492, www.tenayalodge.com).

Reservations for lodgings are all made at
Yosemite Reservations (1-559 252 4848,
www.yosemitepark.com). For rooms from May
to September, make reservations six months to

Yosemite. *See p273.*

a year in advance. At other times, it's not
hard to book a room in the Valley, especially
midweek. Rates drop outside peak season.

Tourist information

General information is available from the
National Park Service on 1-209 372 0200
and at www.nps.gov/yose. Another useful
website is www.yosemitepark.com.

There are four visitor centres in the park. The
Valley Visitor Center, in Yosemite Valley, is
the largest. The **Big Oak Flat Information
Station**, **Wawona Information Station** and
Tuolumne Meadows Visitor Center are
open on a more limited basis.

Getting there

By car

Highway 41 leads in from the south, Highway 140 from
the west (the best entrance) and Highway 120 from the
north-west. Highway 120 (the Tioga Road) is the only
road across the park, but closes in winter (approx Nov-
May) due to snow. Allow 4hrs from San Francisco.

By bus

Gray Line (1-888 428 6937, 558 9400, www.grayline
sanfrancisco.com) runs one-day tours from $115,
while Green Tortoise (1-800 867 8647, www.green
tortoise.com) runs 2- and 3-day camping tours (from
$170, includes food and park fees).

By train

Each morning, Amtrak trains 712 and 714 from
Oakland to Merced (1-800 872 7245, www.amtrak.
com, $30 one way, 3hrs) connect with a Via
Adventures (1-209 384 1315) bus to Yosemite.

Heading South

Miles of gorgeous California coast.

The romantically named **Half Moon Bay**.

Half Moon Bay & the coast

Half Moon Bay is a small, easygoing seaside town with a rural feel to it. Quaint Main Street is good for a wander, with bookshops, florists and antiques shops, but the town is most famous for its pumpkins at Halloween and Christmas trees.

At Half Moon Bay and Highway 1, the **Sea Horse & Friendly Acres Ranch** (*see p248*) offers beach horseback rides for a range of levels. Then there's **Mavericks**: right in the middle of Half Moon Bay and about half a mile offshore, it's one of the gnarliest big-wave surf spots in the world. A big date in the diary is the **Mavericks Surfing Contest**, held every January, when the world's best wave riders coverge to battle it out against huge Pacific swells.

Travel eight miles further down Highway 1 where it crosses Highway 84 and drop in on the **San Gregorio General Store** (1-650 726 0565, www.sangregoriostore.com). Serving the local community since 1889, it's a hybrid bar, music hall, all-purpose store and gathering place.

Continuing south from San Gregorio, you'll find probably the best of the region's beaches: **San Gregorio State Beach**, a strip of white sand distinguished by sedimentary cliffs. Another 15 miles down the coast are the historic buildings and rolling farmlands of **Pescadero**, with locals still tending their artichoke fields and strawberry patches.

Where to eat, drink & stay

In Half Moon Bay, cosy **Pasta Moon** (315 Main Street, 1-650 726 5126, www.pastamoon.com, mains $18-$23) serves elegant own-made pasta dishes. Old-school **Main Street Grill** (547 Main Street, 1-650 726 5300, http://mainstgrill hmb.com, closed dinner, mains $5.75-$9.50) and the bistro fare at **Rogue Chefs** (no.730, 1-650 712 2000, www.roguechefs.com, open Fri and Sat dinner 5.30-9.30pm only, , menus $45 3 courses, $65 5 courses) are both excellent. **Half Moon Bay Brewing Company** (390 Capistrano Avenue, Princeton-by-the-Sea, 1-650 728 2739, www.hmbbrewingco.com, $10-$21) boasts views of the harbour, plus excellent burgers. With spectacular ocean views and an outdoor deck is **Sam's Chowder House** (4210 North Cabrillo Highway, Half Moon Bay, 1-650 712 0245, www.samschowderhouse.com, mains $15-$28), delivering up platters of good seafood. For more variety and excellent Mediterranean cuisine don't drive by **Cetrella** (845 Main Street, 1-650-726-4090, www.cetrella.com, closed Mon and lunch except Sun, mains $18-$35).

There's no shortage of places to stay in and around Half Moon Bay. The grandest is the **Ritz-Carlton** (1 Miramontes Point Road, 1-800 241 3333, 1-650 712 7000, www.ritzcarlton.com, $299-$419 double), on a bluff overlooking the rugged coastline. About 25 miles south of here, the **Costanoa Coastal Lodge & Camp** (2001 Rossi Road, 1-877 262 7848, 1-650 879 1100, www.costanoa.com) is more rustic resort than campground: there are individual wooden cabins ($95-$195 double) and a 40-room lodge ($165-$365 double), but you can also pitch a tent ($40-$65).

Getting there

By car

Half Moon Bay is 30 miles south of San Francisco on Highway 1, about a 45min drive.

Trips Out of Town

By train & bus

Take a BART train to Daly City (15min journey), pick up SamTrans bus 110 to Linda Mar and transfer to bus 294 for Half Moon Bay.

Tourist information

Half Moon Bay *Half Moon Bay Coastside Chamber of Commerce, 235 Main Street Half Moon Bay (1-650 726 8380/www.hmbchamber.com).* **Open** 9am-5pm Mon-Fri.

Silicon Valley

Silicon Valley runs south from the base of San Francisco Bay. Routinely dismissed as mere sprawl, it actually offers fine strolling in the pretty downtowns of upscale Los Altos, Los Gatos and Saratoga. More substantial pleasures are found in Palo Alto, the site of Stanford University. Here the 20 bronzes that comprise the on-campus **Rodin Sculpture Garden**, associated with the Cantor Arts Center (328 Lomita Drive, 1-650 723 3469, tours 2pm Wed, 11.30am Sat, 2pm Sun), make a neat diversion.

Despite all the concrete, **San Jose** is the most appealing Silicon Valley town for visitors. Attractions include the interactive **Children's Discovery Museum** (180 Woz Way, 1-408 298 5437, www.cdm.org, closed Mon, $8); the **Tech Museum of Innovation**, a new interactive science and technology centre and IMAX theatre (201 South Market Street, 1-408 795 6105, www.thetech.org, $8) and nearby **Monopoly in the Park** (Guadalupe River Park, West Fernando Street, 1-408 995 6487, www.monopolyinthe park.com). The latter, a 930-square-foot (86-square-metre) board game, is the closest ordinary people get to buying property in Silicon Valley; you'll have to reserve a game in advance. The **San Jose Museum of Art** (110 S Market Street, 1-408 271 6840, http://sjmusart.org, closed Mon, $8) has a collection of nearly 1,400 pieces, most from the latter part of the 20th century. There's good shopping, too, with S Bascom Avenue boasting **Streetlight Records** (no.980, 1-888 330 7776) and, for pop-culture collectibles, **Time Tunnel Toys** (no.532, 1-408 298 1709, closed Mon & Sun).

Rosicrucian Egyptian Museum & Planetarium

1342 Naglee Avenue, at Park Avenue, San Jose (1-408 947 3636/www.egyptianmuseum.org). **Open** 10am-5pm Mon-Fri; 11am-6pm Sat, Sun. *Planetarium shows* 2pm Mon-Fri; 2pm, 3.30pm Sat, Sun. **Admission** $9; $5-$7 reductions. **Credit** AmEx, MC, V.

Located in Rosicrucian Park, this museum has the biggest Egyptian collection on the West Coast. There are six real mummies, a collection of more than 4,000 ancient artefacts and full-scale replica tombs. The planetarium's free 35-minute show explores 'The Mithraic Mysteries', connecting the Roman cult to modern astronomy.

Silicon Valley.

Trips Out of Town

Winchester Mystery House

525 South Winchester Boulevard, San Jose
(1-408 247 2101/www.winchestermysteryhouse.com).
Open from 9am daily; tour times vary by season.
Admission free. **Tours** $20.95-$28.95; $17.95-
$25.95 reductions. **Credit** Disc, MC, V.
Haunted by the ghosts of those killed by the namesake rifle, widow-heiress Sarah Winchester spent
38 years continuously building this 160-room mansion to placate the malevolent spirits. Flashlight
tours on Friday the 13th and Halloween are extra
creepy, but at any time the oddity of the place (a
staircase heads into a bare ceiling, a window is set
in the floor) is impressive. Still, the small museum
celebrating the gun might be seen, given the
widow's fears, to be a little insensitive.

Where to eat, drink & stay

Given all the expense accounts, it's no
surprise to find quality restaurants here.
Palo Alto offers new American cuisine at
Zibibbo (430 Kipling Street, 1-650 328 6722,
mains $14-$30) and Californian-Indian at *SF
Chronicle*-favoured **Mantra** (632 Emerson
Street, 1-650 322 3500, www.mantrap
aloalto.com, closed Sat-Mon lunch, mains
$15-$26); in San Jose, try highly regarded
chop house **AP Stumps** (163 W Santa Clara
Street, 1-408 292 9928, www.apstumps.com,
mains $15-$40).

If you want to stay, downtown San Jose
has a **Ramada Inn** (455 S 2nd Street, 1-408
298 3500, www.ramada.com, $105-$147 double)
and the classy **Hotel De Anza** (233 W Santa
Clara Street, 1-408 286 1000, www.hotel
deanza.com, $129-$249 double), with its Hedley
Club Lounge where you can sit by the fire and
take in some jazz piano. If you are looking for
chic luxury, try the **Hotel Valencia** on
Santana Row (355 Santana Row, 1-408 551
0010, http://sanjose.hotelvalencia.com, $200-
$460 double).

Getting there

By car
San Jose is about 50 miles south of San Francisco
on Highway 101.

By train
CalTrain travels every 30mins from San Francisco
to San Jose, making several stops along the way,
including Palo Alto. CalTrain also runs the Baby
Bullet commuter train from SF to San Jose.

Tourist information

San Jose *San Jose CVB, 408 Almaden Boulevard
(1-408 295 9600/1-800 726 5673/www.sanjose.org).*
Open 9am-5pm Mon-Fri.

Santa Cruz

Established as a mission at the end of the 18th
century, Santa Cruz is now a beach town well
known for being easygoing and politically
progressive. The University of California at
Santa Cruz takes the lead; its students can
often be found down at robustly independent
Bookshop Santa Cruz (1520 Pacific Avenue,
1-831 423 0900, www.bookshopsantacruz.com).

All that remains of Misión la Exaltación de
la Santa Cruz is the Neary-Rodriguez Adobe in
Santa Cruz Mission State Historic Park;
commonly known as **Mission Adobe** (1-831
425 5849, closed Mon-Wed in winter, $1-$2) it
once housed the mission's Native American
population. Down the street is **Mission Plaza**
(1-831 426 5686, closed Mon), a complete 1930s
replica. The Santa Cruz Museum of Natural
History (1305 East Cliff Drive, 1-831 420 6115,
www.santacruzmuseums.org, closed Mon,
$1.50-$2.50) contains info about the Ohlone
people who once populated the area. The
culturally inclined can visit the **Santa Cruz
Museum of Art & History** (*see p278*), while
pop-culture fans will be unable to resist the
Mystery Spot (465 Mystery Spot Road, 1-831
423 8897, $5), a few miles north of the city in the
woods off Highway 17. It's a 150-foot (46-metre),
in diameter, patch of earth that has been
confounding the laws of physics and gravity
since its discovery in 1939. Kitsch nonsense.

Bang on the beach, the **Santa Cruz Beach
Boardwalk** (400 Beach Street, 1-831 423 5590,
closed Mon-Fri Sept-May, unlimited rides
$26.95) is an amusement park that hails back
to the city's 19th-century heyday and contains,
among other things, a vintage carousel and a
classic wooden rollercoaster.

The Boardwalk's **Cocoanut Grove
Ballroom** (1-831 423 2053) is another remnant,
with live music for weekends and holidays
bringing it back to life. Continuing the beach
theme, the engaging
Surfing Museum (West Cliff Drive, 1-831
420 6289, www.santacruzsurfingmuseum.org,
closed Tue & Wed, hours vary in winter), while
right outside the lighthouse is **Steamer Lane**,
one of the best surfing spots in the state.

Fans of towering redwoods should head
north into the Santa Cruz Mountains to **Big
Basin Redwoods State Park** (21600 Big
Basin Way, Boulder Creek, 1-831 338 8860,
www.bigbasin.org) or **Henry Cowell
Redwoods State Park** (101 North Big Trees
Park Road, Felton, 1-831 335 4598), which has
a tree you can drive through. Also to the north,
a mile past Western Drive on Highway 1, you'll
find the 4,500 acres (1,820 hectares) of former
dairy farm **Wilder Ranch State Park**

(1-831 423 9703). Centred on a quaint compound of historic Victorian houses and gardens, the park also has 34 miles of trails.

Some 50 wineries are scattered across the area, most open to the public but free of the crowds that put some off Wine Country (see pp264-70). Two of the best of the Santa Cruz-based wineries are **Bonny Doon** (10 Pine Flat Road, 1-831 425 3625, www.bonnydoonvineyard.com) and award-winning **Storrs** (303 Potrero Street, 1-831 458 5030, www.storrswine.com).

Santa Cruz Museum of Art & History

McPherson Center, 705 Front Street, at Cooper Street (1-831 429 1964/www.santacruzmah.org). Open 11am-5pm Tue-Sun. **Admission** $5; $3 students, seniors; $2 12-17s; free under-12s. Free 1st Fri of mth. **Credit** MC, V.
This fair art museum features rotating exhibitions, as well as a permanent display of early Santa Cruz artefacts and a library. The museum also offers tours of the Evergreen Cemetery, one of the region's first Protestant burial grounds.

Where to eat, drink & stay

High above Santa Cruz Yacht Harbor, the **Crow's Nest** (2218 East Cliff Drive, 1-831 476 4560, mains $14-$24) offers magnificent views and great seafood. Downtown has a whole world of options, among them the hip **Mobo Sushi** (105 S River Street, 1-831 425 1700, www.mobosushirestaurant.com, sushi $3-$6) and premier Mexican **El Palomar** (1336 Pacific Avenue, 1-831 425 7575, mains $8-$20). On the Eastside, there's fabulous wood-fired pizza to be had at **Engfer Pizza Works** (537 Seabright Avenue, 1-831 429 1856, closed Mon, pizzas $8-$15), as well as a ping pong table and an exotic array of old-time sodas.

And you're spoilt for cheap choices. One of the best is the **Saturn Café** (145 Laurel Street, 1-831 429 8505, mains $6-$8), the kind of vegetarian spot even meat-eaters are impressed with.

Santa Cruz has many dreary motels, but there are some charming spots. The **Babbling Brook Inn** (1025 Laurel Street, 1-831 427 2437, www.babblingbrookinn.com, $142-$317 double) is surrounded by an acre of leafy gardens with tall redwood trees and, naturally, a garrulous watercourse. Overlooking the sea, the **Pleasure Point Inn** (2-3665 East Cliff Drive, 1-831 469 6161, www.pleasurepointinn.com, $225-$295 double) is modern, upscale and well appointed. The Gothic Victorian **Compassion Flower Inn** (216 Laurel Street, 1-831 466 0420, www.compassionflowerinn.com, $115-$175 double) is a handsome old B&B also notable for being one of the first medical-marijuana-friendly hotels in the US.

Getting there

By car

Santa Cruz is 74 miles south of San Francisco on I-280 (take Highway 17 to I-85 to get to I-280).

By train & bus

Amtrak shuttle buses link San Jose and Santa Cruz. Greyhound buses leave San Francisco for Santa Cruz about four times a day.

Tourist information

Santa Cruz *Santa Cruz County CVB, 1211 Ocean Street, nr Washburn Avenue (1-831 425 1234/1-800 833 3494/www.scccvc.org).* Open 9am-5pm Mon-Fri; 10am-4pm Sat, Sun.

The Monterey Peninsula

Monterey's rise to fame was gradual. It was first settled by Spanish explorer Sebastián Vizcaino in 1602, although it wasn't actually colonised until 168 years later, when Junipero Serra arrived, setting up the second of his 23 missions here. For the Spanish, the town was a crucial settlement, and remained important when the Mexicans seceded from Spain in 1822 and assumed stewardship over California; it was at **Custom House** (*see below*) 24 years later that the American flag was raised in California for the first time with any degree of permanency.

Monterey's unlikely journey from capital of Alta California to sardine capital of the world took several generations, during which the town and neighbouring **Pacific Grove** briefly became popular resorts. The fishing industry drove the economy for the first part of the 20th century; when the fish and the money both ran out, the fishermen left the place to the tourists, and Monterey is now one of the most popular towns for visitors on the West Coast, especially during its celebrated jazz festival, held every September (1-831 373 3366, www.monterey jazzfestival.org).

Monterey

All of downtown Monterey's low-key attractions are scattered around its fringes, meaning that **Alvarado Street**, its main drag, is populated chiefly with restaurants and shops. Stroll south and you'll come to the **Monterey Museum of Art** (559 Pacific Street, 1-831 372 5477, www.montereyart.org, closed Mon & Tue, $5), which has an august permanent collection containing photography by Ansel Adams and Edward Weston. Continuing north along Alvarado Street, meanwhile, leads you towards the water and the spreadeagled

Wildlife at home off the coast at **Monterey**.

Monterey State Historic Park (1-831 649 7118, www.parks.ca.gov). The self-guided **Path of History tour** takes in some of the park's historic buildings (as well as others around town), including the **Custom House**, an adobe building dating back around 175 years. For further information, ask at the tourist office.

Adjoining **Fisherman's Wharf** is smaller than the version in San Francisco, but is just like it in one regard: it fails to live up to its name. The fishermen who once drove the town's economy long ago drew in their nets for the final time, leaving their former base to the tourists. Fisherman's Wharf is now merely a collection of shops and restaurants, working a tired spell on a steady stream of easily impressed visitors.

Thought Fisherman's Wharf was touristy? You're going to be in for a shock when you get to **Cannery Row**. This stretch of waterside road was once home to the robust fishing industry immortalised by John Steinbeck in his 1945 novel. Steinbeck would be appalled to see it now, its old buildings converted into bars, gift shops and hokey attractions that trade off his name in a variety of inventively crass ways. The one redeeming feature is the celebrated **Monterey Bay Aquarium**.

Monterey Bay Aquarium

*886 Cannery Row (1-831 648 4800/www.mbay aq.org). **Open** Memorial Day-Labor Day 9.30am-6pm daily. Labor Day-Memorial Day 10am-6pm daily. **Admission** $24.95; $15.95-$22.95 reductionss; free under-3s. **Credit** AmEx, MC, V.*
The centrepiece of the museum is still the vast Kelp Forest exhibit, crammed with marine life both prosaic and exotic. Over in the Outer Bay Wing is the Outer Bay, a breathtaking collection of fish and sharks in a tank that holds a cool million gallons of water. Get here to see feeding time. Also in this wing

is Jellies: Living Art, showcasing the staggering beauty of jellyfish. Among the other inhabitants of the building are the perennially cute sea otters (also popular at feeding time), while newer exhibits include Wild About Otters (freshwater otters), a revamped Splash Zone (penguins) and the self-explanatory Mission to the Deep. The Portola Café, with its bay views and surprisingly good food, is way above your average museum eatery.

Pacific Grove & Carmel

Just down the road from Monterey lies the sweet little town of **Pacific Grove**, a more moneyed settlement than its neighbour and a far less touristy one to boot. Its downtown (around the junction of Lighthouse Avenue and Forest Street) is largely unencumbered by gift shops and galleries; its restaurants are no more expensive than they need to be. Pick up a walking tour leaflet from the Chamber of Commerce (*see p280*) for details on the histories of the town's century-old private residences.

The **Pacific Grove Museum of Natural History** (165 Forest Avenue, 1-831 648 5716, www.pgmuseum.org, closed Mon & Sun) is home to an interesting exhibition on the Monarch butterflies that spend winters here (ask at the visitor centre for details of where to see them). The town wears its nickname, Butterfly Town USA, with pride. However, its main attraction is its craggy coastline. Catch it on a grey day, and the coast hugging **Ocean View Boulevard** is awesome, waves beating furiously against the rocks. On bluer days, it's more serene; several parks and viewpoints offer the chance to picnic while watching sea lions laze the day away.

Just south of Pacific Grove is the **17-Mile Drive**, a privately owned road, established in 1881, that takes drivers alongside some breathtaking coastal scenery. So breathtaking, in fact, that the road's owners charge drivers around $10 just to see it. Also here is **Pebble Beach Golf Links** (1-800 654 9300, www. pebblebeach.com); regarded by many as one of the world's finest courses, it's also, at $475 a round, one of the most expensive.

The southern point of the 17-Mile Drive is the infuriating town of **Carmel-by-the-Sea**. If this formerly charming but now merely cutesy idyll proves anything, it's that money doesn't buy taste. The shops in the centre hawk chintzy souvenirs and frumpy clothes; the restaurants serve generally mediocre food at inflated prices; and the galleries deal only in art of the most preternaturally ghastly kind; and its undeniable aesthetic charm is excised by the pomposity of its residents. However, the town does have two splendid beaches: **Carmel Beach**, at the western end of Ocean Avenue, and, down the coast, the less crowded and more pleasant **Carmel River State Beach** (1-831 649 2836), which also includes a bird sanctuary. A word of warning: both beaches might look idyllic, but tides can be lethal. Swimming is a bad idea.

Where to eat & drink

Your best bet in downtown Monterey is chic **Montrio** (414 Calle Principal, 1-831 648 8880, www.montrio.com, closed lunch, mains $9-$30), where the California cuisine lives up to the stylish room in which it's served. It's an egalitarian place, too, popular with the Gold Card crew but also with local couples and tourists. **Stokes** (500 Hartnell Street, 1-831 373 1110, www.stokesrestaurant.com, closed lunch Mon-Fri, mains $14-$24) has retained its favoured status with locals for two reasons: one, it's off the beaten path for tourists, despite being housed in a gorgeously converted 170-year-old adobe house, and two, the Mediterranean cuisine is flavourful.

There's a high hit-rate of quality to quantity in Pacific Grove. You'll find daisy-fresh fish creations at smart-casual **Passionfish** (701 Lighthouse Avenue, 1-831 655 3311, www. passionfish.net, closed lunch, mains $17-$24) and some fair Mediterranean-influenced food at **Fandango** (223 17th Street, 1-831 372 3456, www.fandangorestaurant.com, mains $17-$34). In Carmel, the best of a mixed bunch is the **Flying Fish Grill** (Carmel Plaza, Mission Street, 1-831 625 1962, closed lunch, mains $18-$39).

Where to stay

There are a number of individualistic lodgings closer to downtown Monterey. The most appealing of these is the **Old Monterey Inn**

(500 Martin Street, 1-800 350 2344, www.old montereyinn.com, $240-$480 double), an immaculate B&B set on a quiet street. Also worth a look is the elegant **Spindrift Inn** (475 Cannery Row, 1-800 841 1879, 1-831 646 8900, www.spindriftinn.com, $159-$489 double), which bears nary a trace of its former incarnation as a whorehouse. But the best bargain is the century-old **Monterey Hotel** (406 Alvarado Street, 1-800 966 6490, 1-831 375 3184, www.montereyhotel.com, $89-$299 double), good value given its central location. Bear in mind that it's nigh-on impossible to find spur-of-the-moment accommodation during the annual jazz fest.

Over in Pacific Grove, try the **Martine Inn** (255 Ocean View Boulevard, 1-831 373 3388, 1-800 852 5588, www.martineinn.com, $159-$425 double). Owned by Don Martine, who spends his spare time restoring classic cars (he's happy to show them off), the hotel has 24 rooms with unique antique fixtures. Also here is the **Jabberwock Inn** (598 Laine Street, 1-888 428 7253, 1-831 372 4777, www.jabberwock inn.com, $165-$295 double), a fab B&B in a century-old mansion that's gently themed around the works of Lewis Carroll. A good bet in Carmel is the **Mission Ranch** (26270 Dolores Street, 1-800 538 8221, 1-831 624 6436, www.missionranchcarmel.com, $110-$290 double), where the tastefully decorated rustic rooms look out over handsome countryside. If money's no object, head for the award-winning **Inn at Spanish Bay** (2700 17-Mile Drive, 1-800 654 9300, www.pebblebeach.com, $565-$775 double).

Tourist information

Carmel *Carmel Chamber of Commerce, San Carlos Street, between 5th & 6th Streets (1-800 550 4333/1-831 624 2522/www.carmelcalifornia.org).* **Open** 9am-5pm daily.

Monterey *Monterey Visitor Center, 401 Camino El Estero, at Franklin & Camino El Estero (1-888 221 1010/1-831 649 1770/www.montereyinfo.org).* **Open** 9am-5pm daily.

Pacific Grove *Pacific Grove Chamber of Commerce, corner of Central & Forest Avenues (1-800 656 6650/1-831 373 3304/www.pacific grove.org).* **Open** 9.30am-5pm Mon-Fri; 10am-3pm Sat.

Getting there

By car

Monterey is 110 miles from San Francisco if you take US 101 to CA-17 to Highway 1, and a bit further if you take Highway 1 all the way. Plan on a 2-3hr drive. It's 5 miles to Monterey from Carmel, and 6 miles to Pacific Grove.

Directory

Features

OUR CLIMATE NEEDS
A HELPING HAND TODAY

Be a smart traveller. Help to offset your carbon emissions
from your trip by pledging Carbon Trees with Trees for Cities.

All the Carbon Trees that you donate through Trees for Cities
are genuinely planted as additional trees in our projects.

Trees for Cities is an independent charity working with local
communities on tree planting projects.

www.treesforcities.org   Tel 020 7587 1320

Trees for Cities
Charity registration number 1032154

Directory

Getting Around

San Francisco International Airport (SFO)

1-650 821 8211/www.flysfo.com.
SFO lies 14 miles south of the city, near US101.

If you're staying downtown, take the **train** from the BART station in the International terminal (accessible from all terminals via SFO's free Airtrain). The journey to town costs $5.15 and takes 30mins; trains leave SFO from 4am to 10.15pm. BART is a far better bet than the three SamTrans **bus** routes – the KX, the 292 and the 24-hour 397 – that serve SFO (fares vary from $1.50 to $4); the buses can take ages to make the journey from the airport to the city.

Shuttle vans, which hold 8-12 people and offer door-to-door service, are a more direct option. Shuttles operate on a walk-up basis at the airport, though you must book for your return journey. Firms running shuttle vans include **Bay Shuttle** (564 3400), **SuperShuttle** (558 8500) and **American Airporter Shuttle** (202 0733); the airport's website has a full list. The fare into San Francisco will be $10-$17; ask about discounted rates for two or more travellers in the same party. Vans leave regularly from the upper level of the terminal: follow the red 'passenger vans' signs outside the baggage-claim area.

Taxis run to and from SFO, though they're pricey: expect to pay around $50 plus tip, though you might be able to haggle a flat rate.

For a **limousine**, use the toll-free white courtesy phones located in the terminal to summon a car (walk-up service isn't permitted). The fare will likely be at least $60 plus tip.

Mineta San Jose International Airport (SJC)

1-408 501 7600/www.sjc.org.
Efficient SJC is the airport of choice for many Silicon Valley travellers. However, those without cars but with San Francisco lodgings face a lengthy and/or pricey journey to the city.

Without a car, the best way to get to San Francisco from SJC is by **train**. Ride the Airport Flyer bus (20mins) from the airport to Santa Clara

station, then take the Caltrain service to San Francisco station (4th & King Streets, $7.50, 90mins). Door-to-door **shuttle vans**, available on a walk-up basis, are quicker, but cost up to $90. A **taxi** will set you back $130 plus tip.

Oakland International Airport (OAK)

1-510 563 3300/www.flyoakland.com.
The ride into San Francisco from Oakland Airport is simple by train. The AirBART bus shuttle links the airport to the Coliseum/Oakland Airport BART station; the ride costs $3 and takes 20-30mins. From the station, take the next Daly City or Millbrae train to San Francisco ($3.35; about 25mins to Downtown). Note: this is generally not a safe option for lone passengers at night. Instead, take one of the myriad **shuttle vans**, available on a walk-up basis, or a very expensive taxi/limo ride.

Airlines

Air Canada *1-888 247 2262/ www.aircanada.com.*

American Airlines *1-800 433 7300/www.aa.com.*

British Airways *1-800 247 9297/ www.britishairways.com.*

Continental *domestic 1-800 523 3273/international 1-800 231 0856www.continental.com.*

Delta *domestic 1-800 221 1212/ international 1-800 241 4141/ www.delta.com.*

Northwest *domestic 1-800 225 2525/international 1-800 447 4747/ www.nwa.com.*

Southwest *1-800 435 9792/ www.southwest.com.*

United Airlines *domestic 1-800 864 8331/international 1-800 538 2929/www.united.com.*

US Airways *domestic 1-800 428 4322/international 1-800 622 1015/ www.usairways.com.*

Virgin Atlantic *1-800 862 8621/ www.virginatlantic.com.*

Virgin America *1.877.359.8474/ www.virginamerica.com.*

San Francisco's mass-transit network is comprehensive and efficient. Buses, streetcars and

cable cars are run by the San Francisco Municipal Railway, aka **Muni** (www.sfmuni.com, 701-2311 (San Fran 3-1-1 Customer Service Centre)) while the Bay Area Rapid Transit rail network, aka **BART** (989 2278, www.bart. gov) connects San Francisco to Oakland, Berkeley and beyond. Maps and timetables are available online, and free leaflets available at stations offer details on popular routes and services. However, Muni's system-wide *Street & Transit Map*, costing $3 and available from bookshops, drugstores and the SFVIC (*see p295*), is a sound investment. Further details on Bay Area transit, including route guidance, can be found at **www.511.org** or **www.transit.511.org**, or by calling 511 from a local phone.

For information about single fares on the modes of transport in San Francisco, *see p284*. However, if you plan to travel often in the Bay Area, the **TransLink** card may help: the reuseable ticket is valid on all major transit networks, including Muni, BART and Caltrain. Tag the TransLink card when you start your journey (and, on BART, when you exit). The cost of the ride will be deducted, and any remaining value can be used on your next trip. When the card runs low, add funds at machines around the transit network. TransLink cards are available online and at shops displaying the Translink logo; for more information, see www.translink.org.

Alternatively, the **Passport**, valid for unlimited travel on all Muni vehicles (but not BART

Directory

trains), is aimed at tourists. Passports are valid for one day ($11), three days ($18) and seven days ($24), and are sold at the Visitor Center or the cable car ticket booths, both downtown at Powell and Market, Ghirardelli Square at Hyde and Beach Streets, and in Fisherman's Wharf at Bay and Taylor Streets, Montgomery metro station, the TIX booth in Union Square, the SFMTA Customer Service Centre and SFO.

At $15, the **weekly Muni pass** is cheaper than the equivalent Passport, but comes with two caveats: one, the pass only runs Monday to Sunday (seven-day Passports begin on any day of the week), and two, there's a $1 surcharge for each cable car ride. **The monthly Muni pass** ($45), valid from the first of the month until three days into the following month, is also valid on the eight BART stations within the city of San Francisco, but not beyond (so you'll have to pay extra to get to Oakland, Berkeley and SFO). Weekly and monthly passes are available at the locations listed above, with the exception of TIX.

BART

Bay Area Rapid Transit is a $5-billion network of five high-speed rail lines serving San Francisco, Daly City, Colma and the East Bay. It's modern and efficient, run by computers at Oakland's Lake Merritt station, with announcements, trains, ticket dispensers, exit and entry gates all automated. BART is of minor use for getting around San Francisco – it only has eight stops in the city – four on Market Street, two on Mission Street and two further south – but it's the best way to get to Berkeley and Oakland.

Fares vary by destination, from $1.50 to $6.60. Machines at each station dispense reusable tickets encoded with the amount of money you entered (cash and credit cards are both valid). Your fare will be deducted from this total when you end your journey, and any remaining value will be valid for future trips. You can add value to the card at all ticket machines.

Stations are marked with blue and white signs at street level. Trains run from 4am on weekdays, 6am on Saturday and 8am on Sunday, and shut down around midnight. As of January 2008, new scheduling has brought minor change to the running times of BART trains – for further information see www.bart.gov.

Buses

Muni's orange and white buses are the top mode of public transport in SF. Relatively cheap, they can get you to within a block or two of almost anywhere in town. Bus stops are marked by a large white rectangle on a street with a red kerb; a yellow marking on a telephone or lamp post; a bus shelter; and/or a brown and orange sign listing buses that serve that route.

A single journey on a Muni bus is $1.50; seniors, 4-17s and the disabled pay 50¢, while under-4s travel free. Exact change is required. Free transfers, which let passengers connect with a second Muni bus or streetcar route at no extra charge, are valid for 90 minutes after the original fare was paid. (The transfer tokens serve as your ticket/receipt; always ask for one when you board.)

Major bus routes

San Francisco's bus network is comprehensive but complicated, especially to newcomers to the city. The Muni maps are very useful, but for quick reference, here are some key routes.

5, 6, 7, 9, 21, 71 These six routes run down Market Street from the Financial District to Civic Center; for ease of use, we've used the shorthand '**Market Street routes**' for them in our Downtown listings. Route **5** continues through the Western Addition to the northern edge of Golden Gate Park; routes **6**, **7** and **71** head into the Haight, with the **6** then running into the Sunset and the **71** taking the southern edge of Golden Gate Park; route **9** runs south down Potrero Avenue in the Mission and all the way to the edge of the city; and route **21** cuts through the Hayes Valley to the north-east corner of Golden Gate Park.

14 Runs the length of Mission Street; good for riding between the Mission and Downtown.

38 Apart from a stretch in central San Francisco, where the one-way system means it's forced east down O'Farrell Street, this route runs the length of Geary Street/Boulevard.

45 After stopping at SBC Park, SFMOMA, Union Square, Chinatown and North Beach, this useful route then heads west along Union Street through Cow Hollow to the Presidio.

49 Links Fort Mason, Polk Gulch, the Tenderloin, Civic Center and the Mission along Van Ness Avenue, before heading further south.

Directory

Buses run 5am-1am during the week, 6am-1am on Saturdays and 8am-1am on Sundays. From 1am to 5am, a skeleton crew runs the Owl, nine lines on which buses run every half-hour.

Cable cars

There are 44 cable cars in San Francisco, 27 in use at peak hours, moving at top speeds of 9.5mph on three lines: California (California Street, from the Financial District to Van Ness Avenue), Powell-Mason and Powell-Hyde (both from Market Street to Fisherman's Wharf).

Lines operate from 6am to midnight daily. If you don't have a Muni pass, buy a $5 one-way ticket from the conductor (under-5s go free). Transfers are not valid. The stops are marked by pole-mounted brown signs with a cable car symbol; routes are marked on Muni bus maps.

Ferries

Ferries are used mainly by suits during peak hours, but they double as an inexpensive tourist excursion across the Bay to Sausalito, Tiburon or Larkspur. There are also ferries from San Francisco to Alcatraz and Angel Island in San Francisco Bay.

Blue & Gold Fleet (705 8200, www.blueandgold fleet.com) runs boats to Sausalito and Angel Island from Pier 41 at Fisherman's Wharf. Commuter services to Alameda, Oakland (both $6 one way), Tiburon and Vallejo ($9 and $12.50 respectively) leave from the Ferry Building on the Embarcadero. The competing **Golden Gate Transit Ferry Service** (455 2000, www.goldengate. org), meanwhile, runs services from the Ferry Building to Sausalito and Larkspur (both $7.10 one way).

Streetcars

The Muni Metro streetcar – or tram - is used rarely by tourists, though it's a very useful service. Five lines (J, K, L, M and N) run under Market Street in Downtown and above ground elsewhere, while the F line runs beautiful vintage streetcars on Market Street and along the Embarcadero as far as Fisherman's Wharf. Fares are the same as on Muni's buses, and transfers are valid.

Along Market, Muni makes the same stops as BART; past the Civic Center, routes branch out towards the Mission, the Castro, Sunset and beyond. Lines run 5am-1am Mon-Sat; 8am-1am Sun.

Taxis

Taxi travel in San Francisco is relatively cheap, since the city is relatively small. The base fare is $3.10, with an additional charge of 45¢ per one-fifth of a mile ($2.25 a mile); there's a $2 surcharge »for all rides starting at SFO.

The problem is that there simply aren't enough cabs in San Francisco, especially during morning and evening rush hours and sometimes late at night. If you're downtown, your best bet is to head for one of the bigger hotels; or, if you're shopping or at dinner, to ask the shop or restaurant to call a cab for you. If you're in an outlying area, phone early to request one and ask how long you'll need to wait.
City Wide Dispatch 920 0700.
Luxor 282 4141/www.luxorcab.com.
National 648 4444.
Veteran's 552 1300.
Yellow 333 3333/626 2345/www.yellowcabsf.com.

Outside San Francisco

The **CalTrain** commuter line (1-800 660 4287, www.caltrain.com) connects San Francisco with San Jose and ultimately Gilroy. Fares are

calculated by the number of zones through which the train travels; fares range from $2.25 to $11 one way; discounts, ten-ride tickets, and daily and monthly passes are all available.

Several companies run bus services around the rest of the Bay Area. AC Transit (817 1717, quoting 'AC Transit', www.actransit.org) runs buses trans-bay and to Alameda and Contra Costa Counties; buses A to Z go across the Bay Bridge to Berkeley and Oakland. Golden Gate Transit (455 2000, www.goldengate.org) serves Marin and Sonoma Counties from Sausalito to Santa Rosa. And SamTrans (1-800 660 4287, www.samtrans.org) looks after San Mateo County, with a service to downtown San Francisco.

Driving

Three words: don't do it. It's not so much that the traffic in San Francisco is bad – it's no worse (and, it should be added, not much better) than any average US city. However, the hills are hellish (remember, you're not Steve McQueen and this isn't Bullitt), the streetcars are a bitch and the parking is horrendous. There's very little street parking, and private garages charge can charge as much as $15 to $30 day.

However, if you must drive, be aware of a few things. The speed limit is 25mph; seatbelts are compulsory. Cable cars always have the right of way. When parking on hills, set the handbrake and 'kerb' the front wheels (towards the kerb if facing downhill, away if facing uphill). Always park in the direction of the traffic, and never block driveways. Don't park at kerbs coloured white (passenger drop-off zones), blue (drivers with disabilities only), yellow (loading and unloading commercial vehicles only) or red (bus stops or fire

Directory

hydrants). Green kerbs allow only ten-minute parking. And if you venture across the water, make sure you have enough cash to pay the toll ($5 for the Golden Gate Bridge and $4 for the Bay Bridge), levied on the return trip.

For information on the latest highway conditions, call the 24-hour CalTrans Highway Information Service on 511, or check online at www.dot.ca.gov.

Breakdown services

Members of the American Automobile Association (AAA; 1-800 222 4357, www.aaa.com), and members of affiliated clubs such as the British AA, receive free towing and roadside service.

Fuel stations

There aren't a huge number of stations in the city limits. However, if you're running low, there's an Arco at Mission and 14th Streets; Divisadero and Fell, a Union 76 on Harrison Street just before the Bay Bridge on-ramp, and a Shell at Fell and Steiner Streets.

Parking

There are garages around town, but you'll pay for the privilege of parking in them. Inquire about discounted (or 'validated') rates, but before you park, always ask your hotel: few have their own lots, but many have an arrangement with a nearby garage.

If you're parking during the day, look out for the few large city lots where you can plug a parking meter by the hour (keep your quarters handy). Otherwise, there are garages at the following locations; with the exception of the Mission garage, closed midnight to 6am, all are open 24 hours.

Financial District *Between Battery, Drumm, Clay & Sacramento Streets.* **Map** p315 N4.

Union Square *333 Post Street (enter on Geary Street), between Stockton & Powell Streets.* **Map** p3315 M5.

SoMa *833 Mission Street, between 4th & 5th Streets.* **Map** p315 M6.

North Beach *735 Vallejo Street, between Stockton & Powell Streets.* **Map** p314 L3.

Chinatown *651 California Street, at Kearny Street.* **Map** p315 M4.

Mission *3255 21st Street, between Bartlett & Valencia Streets.* **Map** p318 K11.

Western Addition *1610 Geary Boulevard, between Webster & Laguna Streets.* **Map** p314 H6.

Marina *2055 Lombard Street, between Webster & Fillmore Streets.* **Map** p313 H3.

Vehicle hire

Most car-hire agencies are at or near the airport, though some have satellite locations Downtown. Call around for the best rate, and book well ahead if you're planning to visit at a holiday weekend. Every firm requires a credit card and matching driver's licence; few will rent to under-25s. Prices won't include tax, liability insurance or collision damage waiver (CDW); US residents may be covered on their home policy, but foreign residents will need to buy insurance.

Alamo *US: 1-800 462 5266/www. goalamo.com. UK: 0870 400 4562/www.alamo.co.uk.*

Avis *US: 1-800 230 4898/331 1212/www.avis.com. UK: 0844 581 0147/www.avis.co.uk.*

Budget *US: 1-800 527 0700/www. budget.com. UK: 0844 581 2231/ www.budget.co.uk.*

Dollar *US: 1-800-800-5252/1-800 800 3665/www.dollar.com. UK: 0808 234 7524/www.dollar.co.uk.*

Enterprise *US: 1-800 261 7331/ www.enterprise.com. UK: 0870 350 3000/www.enterprise.com/uk.*

Hertz *US: 1-800 654 3131/www. hertz.com. UK: 0870 844 8844/ www.hertz.co.uk.*

National *US: 1-800 227 7368/ www.nationalcar.com.*

Thrifty *US: 1-800 847 4389/ www.thrifty.com. UK: 01494 751600/0808 234 7642/ www.thrifty.co.uk.*

Cycling

San Francisco is a real cycling city. A grid of major cycle routes across the town is marked by oval-shaped bike-and-bridge markers. North–south routes use odd numbers; east–west routes even; full-colour signs indicate primary cross-town routes; neighbourhood routes appear in green and white. The *Yellow Pages* has a map of the routes, but you can also call the **Bicycle Information Line** on 585 2453 for details. Daunted by the hills? Pick up the *San Francisco Bike Map & Walking Guide*, which indicates the gradients of the city's streets. There are also two scenic cycle routes: one from Golden Gate Park south to Lake Merced, the other heading north from the southern end of Golden Gate Bridge into Marin County.

You can take bicycles on BART free of charge (except in rush hour). Bike racks on the front of certain Muni buses take up to two bikes. On CalTrain, cyclists can take their bikes on cars that display yellow bike symbols. You can also stow bikes in lockers at CalTrain stations. For more on cycling in San Francisco, including other tips for riding in town and a list of shops offering bike rentals, *see p246*.

Walking

Exploring on foot is the most enjoyable and insightful way to see San Francisco. In a city where road rage is frequent, pedestrians walk unimpeded, often arriving sooner than their petrol-consuming counterparts. For walking tours of the city, covering everything from the shops of Chinatown to old Victorian houses, *see p65*.

Resources A-Z

Addresses

Addresses follow the standard US format. The room and/or suite number usually appears after the street address, followed on the next line by the city name and the zip code.

Age restrictions

Buying alcohol 21
Drinking alcohol 21
Driving 16
Sex (heterosexual couples) 18
Sex (homosexual couples) 18
Smoking 18

Attitude & etiquette

If you're here on banking business, a suit may be in order, but otherwise, dressing down is fine. Few restaurants in town operate a dress code, though some bars forbid jeans, sneakers and/or tank tops.

Business

San Francisco is a world-class vacation and business city. Around 1.5 million people a year come for conventions; plenty of others arrive here on day-to-day business. Many banking companies are based here (Wells Fargo, Charles Schwab); other big industries include bio-medical technology, telecommunications, law, shipping and some of the giants in new technology.

Conventions

Big conventions are held at the Moscone Convention Center (747 Howard Street, between 3rd & 4th Streets, SoMa, 974 4000, www.moscone.com), situated on two SoMa blocks. The busiest times are usually mid January (when the city hosts the MacWorld Expo), May and September.

Courier services

DHL 1-800 225 5345/www.dhl.com. Credit AmEx, DC, Disc, MC, V.
Federal Express 1-800 463 3339/www.federalexpress.com. Credit AmEx, DC, Disc, MC, V.
UPS 1-800 742 5877/www.ups.com. Credit AmEx, MC, V.

Office services

Copy Central *705 Market Street, at 3rd Street, Financial District (882 7377/www.copycentral.com). BART & Metro to Montgomery/bus 2, 3, 4, 31 & Market Street routes.* **Open** 7.30am-10pm Mon-Thur; 7.30am-7pm Fri; 10am-6pm Sat; noon-6pm Sun. **Credit** AmEx, DC, Disc, MC, V. **Map** p315 M5.
Other locations: 2336 Market Street, Castro, 431 6725.

Kinko's *369 Pine Street, at Montgomery Street, Financial District (834 1053/www.fedex kinkos.com). BART & Metro to Montgomery/bus 1,9X, 10, 12, 20, 41/cable car California.* **Open** 7am-11pm Mon-Fri; 10am-6pm Sat, Sun. **Credit** AmEx, DC, Disc, MC, V. **Map** p315 N5.
Other locations: 1967 Market Street, Mission, 252 0864; 1 Daniel Burnham Court, Nob Hill, 292 2500 & locations throughout the city.

Mail Boxes Etc *268 Bush Street, between Montgomery & Sansome Streets, Financial District (765 1515/www.mbe.com). Bus 1, 9X, 10, 12, 20, 41/cable car California.* **Open** 8am-5.30pm Mon-Fri. **Credit** AmEx, DC, Disc, MC, V. **Map** p315 N5.

Office Depot *33 3rd Street, at Market Street, Financial District (777 1728/www.officedepot.com). BART & Metro to Montgomery/bus 2, 3, 4, 31 & Market Street routes.* **Open** 8am-7pm Mon-Fri; 10am-5pm Sat. **Credit** AmEx, Disc, MC, V. **Map** p315 M5.
Other locations: City Shopping Center, 2675 Geary Boulevard, Western Addition, 441 3044; Potrero Center, 2300 16th Street, Potrero Hill, 252 8280.

Useful organisations

The San Francisco Main Library (*see p77*) has access to vast amounts of business-related information. You don't need a library card for in-house print research or to read back-dated newspapers. The research desk staff are terrific; phone 557 4400 for assistance.

Law Library

401 Van Ness Avenue, at McAllister Street, Civic Center (554 6821/ www.ci.sf.ca.us/sfll). BART & Metro to Civic Center/bus 5, 21, 47, 49, & Market Street routes. **Open** 8.30am-5pm Mon-Fri. **Map** p318 K7. Open to the public for research, but only San Francisco-based lawyers can borrow books and materials.

Mechanic' Institute Library

57 Post Street, between Montgomery & Kearny Streets, Financial District (393 0101/www.milibrary.org). BART & Metro to Montgomery/bus

---

Travel advice

For current information on travel to a specific country— including the latest news on health issues, safety and security, local laws and customs – contact your home country's government department of foreign affairs. Most have websites with useful advice for would-be travellers.

Australia
www.smartraveller.gov.au

Canada
www.voyage.gc.ca

New Zealand
www.mft.govt.nz/travel

Republic of Ireland
http://foreignaffairs.gov.ie

UK
www.fco.gov.uk/travel

USA
www.state.gov/travel

Directory

2, 3, 4, 76 & Market Street routes.
Open 9am-9pm Mon-Thur; 9am-6pm
Fri; 10am-5pm Sat; 1-5pm Sun.
Admission Non-members $10/
day; $35/wk. Membership $95/yr.
Map p315 N5.
Many of the same data sources as the
Main Library but in only a fraction
of the space. Its true source of fame,
however, lies in its chess room (421
2258, www.chessclub.org), the best
place in town for a quiet game.

Consulates

For a complete list, consult the
Yellow Pages.
Australian Consulate-General
Suite 1800, 575 Market Street, at
Sansome Street, CA 94105 (536
1970/www.austemb.org). BART
& Metro to Montgomery/bus 2,
3, 4, 76 & Market Street routes.
Map p315 N5.
British Consulate-General Suite
850, 1 Sansome Street, at Market
Street, CA 94104 (617 1300/www.
britainusa.com/sf). BART & Metro
to Montgomery/bus 2, 3, 4, 76 &
Market Street routes. **Map** p315 N5.
Consulate-General of Canada
Suite 1288, 580 California Street, at
Kearny Street, CA 94104 (834
3180/www.dfait-maeci.gc.ca). Bus 1,
9X,10, 12, 20, 41/cable car
California. **Map** p314 N4.
Consulate-General of Ireland
Suite 3350, 100 Pine Street, at Front
Street, CA 94111 (392 4214/www.
irelandemb.org). BART & Metro to
Embarcadero/bus 1, 2, 9X,10, 14,
20, 41 & Market Street routes.
Map p315 N4.
New Zealand Consulate Suite
700, 1 Maritime Plaza, Front Street,
at Clay Street, CA 94111 (399 1255/
www.mfat.govt.nz). BART & Metro
to Embarcadero/bus 1, 2, 9X,10, 14,
20, 41 & Market Street routes/cable
car California. **Map** p314 N4.

Consumer

Attorney General: Public Inquiry Unit
1-800 952 5225/http://ag.ca.gov/
consumers.
Call to complain about consumer law
enforcement or any other agency.

Better Business Bureau
1-866 411 2221/1-510 844 2000/
www.goldengatebbb.org.
The BBB provides information
on the reliability of a company
and a list of companies with good
business records. It's also the
place to call to file a complaint
about a company.

Customs

International travellers go
through US Customs directly
after Immigration. Give the
official the filled-in white form
you were given on the plane.
    Foreign visitors can import
the following goods duty free:
200 cigarettes or 50 cigars (not
Cuban; over-18s) or 2kg of
smoking tobacco; one litre of
wine or spirits (over-21s); and
up to $100 in gifts ($800 for
returning Americans). You
must declare and maybe forfeit
plants or foodstuffs. Check US
Customs online for details
(www.cbp.gov/xp/cgov/travel).
UK Customs & Excise allows
returning travellers to bring in
£145 worth of goods.

Disabled

Despite its topography, San
Francisco is disabled-friendly;
California is the national leader
in providing facilities for the
disabled. All public buildings
are required by law to be
wheelchair-accessible; most
city buses can 'kneel' to make
access easier; the majority of
city street corners have
ramped kerbs; and most
restaurants and hotels can
accommodate wheelchairs.
Privileges include free parking
in designated (blue) areas
and in most metered spaces;
display a blue and white
'parking placard' for both.
Still, what a building is
supposed to have and what it
actually has can be different;
wheelchair-bound travellers
should call the Independent
Living Resource Center (543
6222, www.ilrcsf.org).
Braille Institute 1-800 272
4553/www.brailleinstitute.org.
Volunteers can connect anyone who
has sight difficulties with services for
the blind throughout the US.
California Relay Service 711 or
TTY to voice 1-800 735 2929/voice
to TTY 1-800 735 2922./ www.ddtp.
org/california_relay_service. **Open**
24hrs daily.
Relays calls between TTD and
voice callers.

Crisis Line for the Handicapped
1-800 426 4263. Open 24hrs daily.
Phoneline/referral service with
advice on many issues.

Electricity

US electricity voltage is 110-
120V 60-cycle AC. Except for
dual-voltage, flat-pin plug
shavers, foreign appliances
will usually need an adaptor.

Emergencies

Ambulance, fire or police 911.
Coast Guard 399 3547.
Poison Control Center 1-800 222
1222, www.calpoison.org

Gay & lesbian

**Community United Against
Violence** 333 4357/www.cuav.org.
A group assisting GLBT victims of
domestic violence or hate crimes.
New Leaf 626 7000/www.newleaf
services.org. **Open** 9am-8pm Mon-
Thur; 9am-7pm Fri.
A GLBT counselling service that
deals with a variety of issues.

Health & medical

For opticians, see p192; for
pharmacies, see p193.

Accident & emergency

Foreign visitors should always
ensure they have full travel
insurance: health treatment
can be pricey. Call the
emergency number on your
insurance before seeking
treatment; they'll direct you to
a hospital that deals with your
insurance company. There are
24hr emergency rooms at the
locations listed below.

California Pacific Medical Center
Castro Street, at Duboce Avenue,
Lower Haight (600 6000). Metro to
Duboce & Church/bus 24, 37. **Map**
p318 H9.

St Francis Memorial Hospital
900 Hyde Street, between Bush &
Pine Streets, Nob Hill (353 6000).
Bus 1, 2, 3, 4, 27, 38, 76.
Map p314 K5.

San Francisco General Hospital

1001 Potrero Avenue, between 22nd & 23rd Streets, Potrero Hill (206 8000). Bus 9, 33, 48. **Map** p319 M12.

UCSF Medical Center

505 Parnassus Avenue, between 3rd & Hillway Avenues, Sunset (476 1000). Metro to UCSF/bus 6, 43. **Map** p316 D10.

Clinics

Haight-Ashbury Free Clinics, Inc *558 Clayton Street, at Haight Street, Haight-Ashbury (746 1950/ www.hafci.org). Metro to Cole & Carl/bus 6, 7, 33, 43, 71.* **Open** Appointments call for details. *Drop-in clinic* from 4.45pm Mon, Tue; *acupuncture drop-in* 8.45am Mon. **Map** p317 E9.
Health care, including a variety of speciality clinics, is provided to the uninsured on a sliding-scale basis; most patients pay little or nothing.
Lyon-Martin Women's Health Services *1748 Market Street, between Octavia & Gough Streets, Upper Market (565 7667/*

www.lyon-martin.org). Metro to Van Ness/streetcar F/bus 6, 7, 47, 49, 71. **Open** *Appointments* call for details. **Credit** MC, V. **Map** p318 J8.
Named after two founders of the modern lesbian movement in the US, this clinic offers affordable health care for women and transgender patients.

St Anthony Free Medical Clinic *121 Golden Gate Avenue, at Jones Street, Tenderloin (241 2600/www. stanthonysf.org). BART & Metro to Civic Center/bus 5, 31 & Market Street routes.* **Open** *Drop-in clinic* 8am-noon, 1-4.30pm Mon-Fri. **Map** p314 L6.
Free medical services for those with or without insurance. Arrive early.

Contraception & abortion

Planned Parenthood Clinics *815 Eddy Street, between Van Ness Avenue & Franklin Street, Tenderloin (1-800 967 7526/www. plannedparenthood.org). BART & Metro to Civic Center/bus 31, 42, 47, 49.* **Open** 9am-5pm Mon, Tue, Thur, Fri; 11am-7pm Wed; 9am-1pm Sat. **Sat. Credit** MC, V. **Map** p314 K6.

In addition to contraception, Planned Parenthood's multilingual staff provides low-cost general health-care services, HIV testing and gynaecological exams; with the exception of the morning-after pill, all are by appointment only.

Dentists

1-800 Dentist

1-800 336 8478/www.1800 dentist.com. **Open** 24hrs daily. Dental referrals.

University of the Pacific School of Dentistry

2155 Webster Street, at Sacramento Street, Pacific Heights (929 6400). Bus 1, 3, 12, 22. Open 8am-5pm Mon-Fri. **Map** p313 H5.
Supervised dentists-in-training provide a low-cost service.

HIV & AIDS

AIDS-HIV Nightline *434 2437.* **Open** 5pm-5am daily.
Hotline offering emotional support.
California AIDS Foundation *1-800 367 2437.* **Open** 9am-5pm Mon, Wed-Fri; 9am-9pm Tue.
Information and advice.

Helplines

Alcoholics Anonymous *674 1821/www.alcoholics-anonymous.org.* **Open** 24hrs daily.
Drug Crisis Information *362 3400/hearing-impaired 781 2224.* **Open** 24hrs daily.
Narcotics Anonymous *621 8600/www.na.org.* **Open** 24hrs daily.
SF General Hospital Psychiatric Helpline *206 8125.* **Open** 24hrs daily.
SF Rape Treatment Center *206 3222.* **Open** 8am-5pm Mon, Tue, Thur, Fri; 8am-7pm Wed.
Suicide Prevention *781 0500/ www.sfsuicide.org.* **Open** 24hrs daily.
Talk Line Family Support 441 5437/www.sfcapc.org. Open 24hrs daily.
Women Against Rape Crisis Hotline 647 7273. Open 24hrs daily.

ID

Even if you look 30, you'll need photo ID (preferably a driver's licence with a photo) to get into the city's bars, or to buy alcohol in a restaurant or shop.

Passport update

People of all ages who enter the US on the Visa Waiver Progam (VWP; *see p295*) are now required to carry their own machine-readable passport, or MRP. MRPs are recognisable by the double row of characters along the foot of the data page. All burgundy EU and EU-lookalike passports issued in the UK since 1991 (and still valid) should be machine readable. Some of those issued outside the country may not be, however; in this case, holders should apply for a replacement even if the passport has not expired. Check at your local passport-issuing post office if in any doubt at all.

The US requirement for passports to contain a 'biometric' chip applies only to those issued from 26 October 2006. Since then, all new and replacement UK passports should be compliant, following a gradual phase-in. The biometric chip contains a facial scan and biographical data.

There is no current requirement for UK passports to contain fingerprint or iris data. The application process remains as it was, except for new guidelines that ensure the photograph you submit can be used to generate the facial scan in the chip.

Further information for UK citizens is available at www. passport.gov.uk or 0870 521 0410. Nationals of other countries should check well in advance of their trip whether their passport meets the requirements for the time of their trip, at http://travel.state.gov/visa and with the issuing authorities of their home country.

Directory

Immigration

Immigration regulations apply to all visitors to the US. During the flight, you will be issued with an immigration form to present to an official on the ground. You'll have your fingerprints and photograph taken as you pass through. If you have a foreign passport, expect close questioning. For more on passports, *see p289*. Passport update; for visas, *see p295*.

Insurance

Non-nationals should arrange comprehensive baggage, trip-cancellation and medical insurance before they leave. US citizens should consider doing the same. Read the small print: consequences of security scares, including cancelled flights, may not be covered.

Internet

Getting online here is very easy these days. Most hotels offer some form of in-room high-speed access for travellers with laptops; a number of hotels also provide at least one public computer.

In addition, a number of cafés and even a few bars across the city offer 'free' wireless access (you pay for your drink, but not the connection), and the city has a handful of wireless 'hotspots'; the best known is in Union Square. If you don't have a laptop, head to the Main Library (*see p77*), which has several terminals available for free, or an internet café. For more on getting online in the city, see www.bawug.org, www.wifinder.com or www.wififreespot.com/ca.html.

Left luggage

Leaving luggage has got trickier since 9/11. However, larger hotels should allow you to leave bags, while at SFO, you can store everything from bags to bicycles at the Airport Travel Agency (1-650 877 0422, 7am-11pm daily), on the Departures level of the International Terminal.

Legal help

Lawyer Referral Service
989 1616/www.sfbar.org. **Open** 8.30am-5.30pm Mon-Fri.
Callers are referred to attorneys and mediators for all legal problems.

Libraries

For San Francisco Main Library, *see p78*; for business libraries, *see p287*.

Lost property

Property Control
850 Bryant Street, between 6th & 7th Streets, SoMa (553 1377). Bus 12, 19, 27, 47. **Open** 8.30am-4pm Mon-Fri. **Map** p319 M8.
Make a police report - then hope.

Airports
For items lost en route, contact the specific airline. If you leave a bag at the airport, it may get destroyed, but it's worth calling the numbers below.
San Francisco International Airport *Terminal 1, 1-650 821 7014.* **Open** 8am-8pm Mon-Fri.
Mineta San Jose International Airport *Terminal A, Baggage Claim, 1-408 277 5419.* **Open** 8am-4pm Mon-Fri.
Oakland International Airport *1-510 563 3982.* **Open** 8.30am-5pm Mon-Fri.

Public transport
The Muni lost-and-found office is on 923 6372. For BART, phone 1-510 464 7090; for AC Transit, try 1-510 891 4706; call 257 4476 for Golden Gate Transit; and for SamTrans, dial 1-800 660 4287.

Media

The San Francisco media exists not only to report what's going on, but to confirm the inhabitants' collective belief that they're living in the most trend-setting quadrant of the globe. The city supports only one major newspaper, the *San Francisco Chronicle*, as well as a faltering tabloid, the *Examiner*. Livelier are the alternative weekly tabloids, the *San Francisco Bay Guardian* and *SF Weekly*. The best media, though, are based out of town. The *San Jose Mercury News* remains the best read, and Oakland's KTVU (channel 2) gets the best news ratings.

Newspapers

Local papers are listed below. For broader coverage, try the regional edition of the *New York Times* ($1.25) or the national edition of the *Los Angeles Times* ($1). *USA Today* (75¢) makes good fishwrap; it's distributed free in many hotels.

San Francisco Chronicle
www.sfgate.com/chronicle.
Complaining about the Chron (50¢) has become a San Francisco cliché. The region's largest circulation paper, it's the only real choice for local news since the Hearst Corporation bought it for $660 million in 2000 and closed down the *Examiner*, its only rival (it's since re-emerged as a tabloid, but it's hardly a rival). The sports writing is generally engaging, and both the 'Datebook' culture section and the presence of a few good columnists make it a decent Sunday read, but the Chron still lacks the punch and vigour of a big-city newspaper.

San Francisco Examine
www.examiner.com.
This free tabloid is sometimes good for a laugh or a sensational story.

San Jose Mercury News
www.mercurynews.com.
If you're thirsting for news outside San Francisco, this paper (50¢) offers the Bay Area's best overall news reporting, business and sport; its business coverage of Silicon Valley and internet commerce is first-rate.

Alternative weeklies

San Francisco Bay Guardian
www.sfbg.com.
One of a pair of free weekly arts tabloids that battle for supremacy in San Francisco, this thick, lively rag mixes a progressive stance – it eagerly annoys the conservative local establishment by exposing cronyism, graft, fraud and double standards –

with arts coverage. Available free from newspaper boxes and in bars, restaurants, cafés and coffeeshops.

SF Weekly *www.sfweekly.com.*
Lighter on politics and issue-oriented pieces than the BG, the *Weekly* betters it with its arts coverage, more comprehensive than that of its rival. In common with many alternative weeklies, some of the pieces could stand to lose 1,000 words here or there, but the writing is generally strong. Highlights include a personal ads section so steamy it would make an exhibitionist blush. Available in the same places that carry the BG.

San Francisco Bay Times
www.sfbaytimes.com.
A free fortnightly tabloid directed at the gay and lesbian community. It features listings, commentary, classified advertisements and personals. Find it in coffeeshops and bookstores in the Castro.

BAR (Bay Area Reporter)
www.ebar.com.
Similar to the *Bay Times*, the free weekly BAR features listings and news that affects the gay community. Copies can be found in most of the same places as the Bay Times.

Street Sheet
Written by the homeless and sold by them for $1. No need to look for it: it will come looking for you.

Magazines

San Francisco Magazine
(www.sanfran.com) is a lively glossy monthly covering everything from local politics to the dining scene. Literary periodical **Zyzzyva** (www.zyzzyva.org), produced three times a year, offers short stories, poetry, creative non-fiction and original art. Francis Ford Coppola's quarterly **Zoetrope: All-Story Magazine** (www.all-story.com) publishes short fiction and one-act plays. The quarterly **Juxtapoz** (www.juxtapoz.com) preaches to the alt-arts crowd. **The Believer** (www.believer mag.com) is a literary and culture monthly associated with McSweeney's and Dave Eggers.

Television

The Bay Area has affiliates of all three major networks: ABC (local station is KGO, found on channel 7), NBC (KNTV,

channel 11) and CBS (KPIX, channel 5). KRON (channel 4) is devoted to Bay Area news and syndicated sitcoms; KTVU (channel 2) is part of the Fox TV network. PBS, the Public Broadcasting Service, has stations in San Francisco (KQED, on channel 9), in San Jose (KTEH, channel 54) and in San Mateo (KCSM, channel 60).

Radio

San Francisco's constantly changing radio profile reflects a number of ongoing difficulties: attracting enough listeners in a competitive market, and outsmarting weather and geography, which combine to undermine reliable radio signals. But Bay Area radio is still spectacular.

The weaker, non-commercial stations lie to the left of the FM dial; the powerhouses with the loudest ads cluster on the right. AM is mostly reserved for talk, news and sports broadcasts, with a few foreign-language, oldie and Christian stations peppering the mix.

News & talk

For news, KGO-AM (810 AM; www.kgoam810.com), NPR-affiliated KQED (88.5 FM; www.kqed.org) and KALW (91.7 FM; www.kalw.org) remain your best bets. KCBS (740 AM; www.kcbs.com) runs solid news and priceless traffic reports (every 10mins). Berkeley-based KPFA (94.1 FM; www.kpfa.org) offers a jumble of talk programming during the day. A welcome recent addition is left-wing Green 960 on KQKE (960 AM; www.quakeradio.com). For sports, try KNBR (680 AM; www.knbr.com)

Classical & jazz

KDFC (102.1 FM; www.kdfc.com) is the best classical station in the city, but its programming is conservative. There's less choice for jazz fans: the most popular 'jazz' station in the city is KKSF (103.7 FM; www.kksf.com), which deals only in elevator-friendly smooth jazz.

Dance, hip hop & soul

KMEL (106.1 FM; www.106k mel.com) is the Bay Area's foremost station for hip hop. KYLD (94.9 FM; www.wild949.com) is a party station. For something different, tune in to

non-profit KPOO (89.5 FM, www. kpoo.com), where innovative hip hop and hardcore rap alternate with cool blues shows on weekend nights.

Rock & pop

KLLC (97.3 FM; www.radioalice.com) dominates the airwaves with its mix of mid-1990s comfort-rock and endless plays of the latest Maroon 5 KITS (105.3 FM; www.live105.com), offers a more alternative mix; KFOG (104.5 FM; www.kfog.com) plays the classic-rock card. Those in search of more eclectic listening tune in to college and independent stations such as KFJC (89.7 FM; www.kfjc.org), UC Berkeley's KALX (90.7 FM; http:// kalx.berkeley.edu) and KUSF (90.3 FM; http://kusf.org).

Money

The US dollar ($) is divided into 100 cents (¢). Coin denominations run from the copper penny (1¢) to the silver nickel (5¢), dime (10¢), quarter (25¢) and less-common half-dollar (50¢). There are also two $1 coins: the silver Susan B Anthony and the gold Sacagawea. Notes or 'bills' are the same green colour and size; they come in denominations of $1, $5, $10, $20, $50 and $100. The $20 and $50 have recently been redesigned with features that make them hard to forge, including, for the first time, some subtle colours other than green and black. Old-style bills remain legal currency.

ATMs

There are ATMs throughout the city: in banks, stores and even bars. ATMs accept Visa, MasterCard and American Express, as well as other cards, but almost all charge a usage fee. If you don't remember your PIN, most banks will dispense cash to cardholders. Wells Fargo offers cash advances at all of its branches.

Banks & bureaux de change

The easiest way to change money is simply use the ATM

Directory

machines. Your bank will give you the current rate of exchange and the fee is usually no more than you would pay in commission anywhere else anyway. Most banks are open from 9am to 6pm Monday to Friday and from 9am to 3pm on Saturday. Photo ID is required to cash travellers' cheques. Many banks don't exchange foreign currency, so arrive with some US dollars. If you arrive after 6pm, change money at the airport. If you want to cash travellers' cheques at a shop, note that some require a minimum purchase. You can also obtain cash with a credit card from certain banks, but be prepared to pay interest rates that vary daily.

American Express Travel Services

455 Market Street, at 1st Street, Financial District (536 2600/www. americanexpress.com/travel). BART & Metro to Montgomery/bus 2, 3, 4, 10 & Market Street routes. **Open** 9am-5.30pm Mon-Fri; 10am-2pm Sat. **Map** p315 N5.
AmEx will change travellers' cheques and money, and also offers (for AmEx cardholders only) poste restante.

Western Union

1-800 325 6000/www.western union.com. **Open** 24hrs daily.
The old standby for bailing travellers out of trouble. Get advice on how to get money wired to you and where to pick it up. You can also wire money to anyone outside the state over the phone, using your MasterCard or Visa. You'll pay a huge commission when sending money.

Credit cards

Bring at least one major credit card: they are accepted – often required – at nearly all hotels, restaurants and shops. The cards most accepted in the US are American Express, Diners Club, Discover, MasterCard and Visa.

Lost or stolen cards

American Express *Cards* 1-800 992 3404. *Travellers' cheques* 1-800 221 7282.
Diners Club 1-800 234 6377.

Discover 1-800 347 2683.
MasterCard 1-800 622 7747.
Visa Cards 1-800 847 2911.
Travellers' cheques 1-800 227 6811.

Police stations

Central Station *766 Vallejo Street, between Stockton & Powell Streets, North Beach (315 2400). Bus 9X, 12, 20, 30, 41, 45/cable car Powell-Mason.* **Map** p315 M3.
Southern Station *850 Bryant Street, between 6th & 7th Streets, SoMa (553 1373). Bus 9X, 12, 19, 27, 47.* **Map** p319 M8.

Postal services

Post offices mostly open from 9am to 5.30pm Monday to Friday, 9am to 2pm Saturday. All close on Sundays. Phone 1-800 275 8777 for information on your nearest branch. Stamps can be bought at any post office and also at some hotel receptions, vending machines and ATMs. Stamps for postcards within the US cost 26¢; for Europe, the charge is 90¢. For couriers and shippers, *see p287.*

Poste Restante (General Delivery)

Main Post Office, 101 Hyde Street, at Golden Gate Avenue, Civic Center (1-800 275 8777). BART & Metro to Civic Center/bus 5, 19, 21, 47, 49 & Market Street routes. **Open** 10am-2pm Mon-Sat. **Map** p318 L7.
If you need to receive mail in SF and you're not sure where you'll be staying, have the envelope addressed with your name, c/o General Delivery, San Francisco, CA 94102, USA. Mail is only kept for ten days from receipt, and you must present some photo ID to retrieve it.

Religion

Calvary Presbyterian *2515 Fillmore Street, at Washington Street, Pacific Heights (346 3832/www.calvarypresbyterian.org). Bus 3, 12, 24.* **Map** p309 E3.
Cathedral of St Mary of the Assumption *1111 Gough Street, at Geary Boulevard, Western Addition (567 2020/www.stmarycathedral sf.org). Bus 2, 3, 4, 38.* **Map** p314 J6. Catholic.
Glide Memorial *330 Ellis Street, at Taylor Street, Tenderloin (674 6000/ www.glide.org). Bus 27, 31, 38/cable

car Powell-Hyde & Powell-Mason.* **Map** p314 L6. Methodist.
Grace Cathedral *1100 California Street, at Taylor Street, Nob Hill (749 6300/www.gracecathedral.org). Bus 1, 27/cable car California.* **Map** p314 L5. Episcopalian.
Masjid Darussalam (Islamic Society of San Francisco) *20 Jones Street, at Market Street, Tenderloin (863 7997/www.islam sf.net). BART & Metro to Civic Center/streetcar F/bus 5, 31 & Market Street routes.* **Map** p318 L7.
Old St Mary's Cathedral *660 California Street, at Grant Avenue, Chinatown (288 3800/www.oldsaint marys.org). Bus 1, 9X, 30, 45/cable car California.* **Map** p315 M5. Catholic.
St Paul's Lutheran Church *950 McAllister Street, between Buchanan & Laguna Streets, Western Addition (673 8088). Bus 5, 21.* **Map** p314 J6.
Temple Emanu-el *2 Lake Street, at Arguello Boulevard, Presidio Heights (751 2535/www.emanuelsf.org). Bus 1, 2, 3, 4, 33.* **Map** p312 D6. Synagogue.
Zen Center *300 Page Street, at Laguna Street, Lower Haight (863 3136/www.sfzc.org). Bus 6, 7, 71.* **Map** p318 J8.

Safety & security

Crime is a reality in all big cities, but San Franciscans generally feel secure in their town. There is really just one basic rule of thumb you need to follow: use your common sense. If a neighbourhood doesn't feel safe to you, it probably isn't. Only a few areas warrant caution during daylight hours and are of particular concern at night. These include the Tenderloin (north and east of Civic Center); SoMa (near the Mission/6th Street corner); Mission Street between 13th and 18th Streets; and the Hunter's Point neighbourhood near 3Com Park. Golden Gate Parkshould be avoided at night. Many tourist areas, most notably around Union Square, are sprinkled with homeless people who beg for change but are basically pretty harmless.

If you're unlucky enough to be mugged, your best bet is to give your attackers whatever they want, then call the police from the nearest pay phone by dialling 911. (Don't forget to get the reference number on the claim report for insurance purposes and to get travellers' cheque refunds.) If you are the victim of a sexual assault and wish to make a report, call the police, who will escort you to the hospital for treatment. For helplines that serve victims of rape or other crimes, *see p289.*

Smoking

Smokers may rank as the only group of people who are not especially welcome in San Francisco. Smoking is banned in all public places, including banks, sporting arenas, theatres, offices, the lobbies of buildings, shops, restaurants, bars, and any and every form of public transport. There are many small hotels and B&Bs that don't allow you to light up anywhere inside. On the other hand, a select few bars cheerfully ignore the law.

Study

California's higher education system is a hierarchy that starts with publicly funded community colleges and city colleges at the lower end of the scale, followed by California State Universities, which cater primarily to undergraduates and do not grant doctorates, and then, at the top of the pile, the University of California system, which includes formal, research-oriented universities with rigorous entry demands (increasingly so, given recent funding cuts). There are also many private -- and pricey – universities, among them Stanford and the University of San Francisco.

In general, universities in the United States are much more flexible about part-time studying than their European

counterparts. Stipulations for non-English-speaking students might include passing the TOEFL (Test of English as a Foreign Language); most students also have to give proof of financial support.

Visas & ID cards

To study in the Bay Area (or, for that matter, anywhere in the United States), exchange students should apply for a J-1 visa, while full-time students enrolled in a degree programme must apply for an F-1 visa. Both are valid for the duration of the course and for a limited period thereafter.

Foreign students need an International Student Identity Card (ISIC) as proof of student status. This can be bought from your local travel agent or student travel office. In San Francisco, an ISIC can be bought at either of the two STA Travel offices (530 Bush Street, between Grant Avenue and Stockton Street, 421 3473; 36 Geary Street, between Kearny Street and Grant Avenue, 391 8407). You'll need proof you're a student, ID and a passport-size photo.

Tax

Sales tax of 8.5 per cent is added on to the label price in shops within city limits, and 8.25 per cent in surrounding cities. Hotels charge a 14 per cent room tax and the same percentage on hotel parking.

Telephones

Dialling & codes

The phone system is reliable and, for local calls, cheap. Long-distance, particularly overseas, calls are best paid for with a rechargeable, pre-paid phonecard ($6-$35) available from vending machines and many shops. You can use your MasterCard with AT&T

(1-800 225 5288) or Sprint (1-800 877 4646).

Direct dial calls

If you are dialling outside your area code, dial 1 + area code + phone number; on pay phones an operator or recording will tell you how much money to add. All phone numbers in this guide are given as if dialled from San Francisco; hence, Berkeley numbers have the 1-510 prefix, while Marin County numbers have no prefix.

Collect calls

For collect or when using a phone card, dial 0 + area code + phone number and listen for the operator/recorded instructions. If you're completely befuddled, dial 0 and plead your case with the operator.

Area codes
San Francisco & Marin County 415
Oakland & Berkeley 510
The peninsula cities 650
San Jose 408
Napa, Sonoma & Mendocino Counties 707

International calls
Dial 011 followed by the country code. If you need operator assistance with international calls, dial 00.
Australia 61
Germany 49
Japan 81
New Zealand 64
UK 44

Public phones

Public pay phones only accept nickels, dimes and quarters, but check for a dialling tone before you start feeding in your change. Local calls usually cost 50¢, though some companies operate pay phones that charge exorbitant prices, The rate also rises steeply as the distance between callers increases (an operator or recorded message will tell you how much to add).

Operator services

Operator assistance 0
Emergency (police, ambulance and fire) 911
Local and long-distance directory enquiries 411
Toll-free numbers generally start with 1-800, 1-888 or 1-877, while pricey pay-per-call lines (usually phone-sex numbers) start with 1-900.

Telephone directories

Directories in San Francisco are divided into Yellow Pages (classified) and White Pages (business and residential), and are available at many public phones, in hotels and at libraries around the city. They contain a wealth of travel information, including area codes, event calendars, park facilities, post office addresses and city zip codes. If you can't find a directory in the phone booth you're using, dial 411 (for directory assistance) and ask for your listing by name (and, if you have it, the address).

Mobile phones

San Francisco, like most of the continental US, operates on the 1900 GSM frequency. Travellers from Europe with tri-band phones will be able to connect to one or more of the networks here with no problems, assuming their service provider at home has an arrangement with a local network; always check before travelling. European travellers with dual-band phones, however, will need to rent a handset upon arrival. Check the price of calls before you go. Rates may be hefty and, unlike in the UK, you'll probably be charged for receiving as well as making calls. It might be cheaper to rent or buy a mobile phone while you're in town – try the agency below, or check the Yellow Pages. Alternatively, you can simply get a pre-paid SIM card when you arrive.

AllCell Rentals

1-877 724 2355/www.allcellrentals. com. **Open** 24hrs daily. **Credit** AmEx, DC, Disc, MC, V.
Rentals of mobile, GSM and satellite phones and pagers. You pay for daily, weekly or monthly rental ($19.95/$69.95), plus the airtime (99¢ per minute). There also may be a delivery fee, depending on the product you rent.

Time & dates

San Francisco is on Pacific Standard Time, which is three hours behind Eastern Standard Time (New York) and eight hours behind Greenwich Mean Time (UK). Daylight Savings Time, which is almost concurrent with British Summer Time, runs from the first Sunday in April, when the clocks are rolled ahead one hour, to the last Sunday in October. Going from the west to east coast, Pacific Time is one hour behind Mountain Time and two hours behind Central Time, three hours behind Eastern Time.

British readers should note that in the US, dates are written in the order month, day, year: 2.5.98 is February 5, not May 2.

Tipping

Unlike in Europe, tipping is a way of life in the US: many locals in service industries rely on gratuities as part of their income, so you should tip accordingly. In general, tip bellhops and baggage handlers $1-$2 a bag; tip cab drivers, waiters and waitresses, hairdressers and food delivery people 15-20 per cent of the total tab; tip valets $2-$3; and tip counter staff 25¢ to 10 per cent of the order, depending on its size. In restaurants, you should tip at least 15 per cent of the total bill and usually nearer 20 per cent; most restaurants will add this to the bill automatically for a table of six or more. In bars, bank on tipping around a buck a drink, especially if you want to hang around for a while. If you look after the bartender, they'll look after you; tipping pocket change may leave you dry for a while.

If you get good service, leave a good tip; if you get bad service, leave little and tip the management with words.

Toilets/restrooms

Restrooms can be found in prime tourist areas such as Fisherman's Wharf and Golden Gate Park, as well as in shopping malls. If you're caught short, don't hesitate to enter a restaurant or a bar and ask to use its facilities.

In keeping with its cosmopolitan standing, San Francisco has installed 20 of the French-designed, self-cleaning JC Decaux lavatories throughout the high-traffic areas of the city. Keep an eye out for these forest-green commodes (they're usually

Climate

	Average high	Average low	Average rain
Jan	56°F (13°C)	46°F (8°C)	4.5in (11.4cm)
Feb	60°F (15°C)	48°F (9°C)	2.8in (7.1cm)
Mar	61°F (16°C)	49°F (9°C)	2.6in (6.6cm)
Apr	63°F (17°C)	50°F (10°C)	1.5in (3.8cm)
May	64°F (17°C)	51°F (10°C)	0.4in (1cm)
June	66°F (19°C)	53°F (11°C)	0.2in (0.5cm)
July	66°F (19°C)	54°F (12°C)	0.1in (0.25cm)
Aug	66°F (19°C)	54°F (12°C)	0.1in (0.25cm)
Sept	70°F (21°C)	56°F (13°C)	0.2in (0.5cm)
Oct	69°F (20°C)	55°F (13°C)	1.1in (2.8cm)
Nov	64°F (18°C)	51°F (10°C)	2.5in (6.4cm)
Dec	57°F (14°C)	47°F (8°C)	3.5in (8.9cm)

plastered with high-profile advertising). Admission is 25¢ for 20min; after that, you may be fined for indecent exposure, because the door pings open automatically. Be aware that some people use the toilets for purposes other than those for which they were designed.

Tourist information

One of the attractions of San Francisco is that there are many wonderful places to visit beyond the city itself. For full listings of the best of these options, including details on tourist offices, *see pp258-80*.

San Francisco Visitor Information Center
Lower level of Hallidie Plaza, 900 Marke t Street, at Powell Street (391 2000/http://onlysf.sfvisitor.org). BART & Metro to Powell/bus 27, 30, 45 & Market Street routes/cable car Powell-Hyde or Powell-Mason. **Open** 9am-5pm Mon-Fri; 9am-3pm Sat, Sun. **Map** p315 M6.
Located in Downtown, this is the visitor centre for the efficient and helpful San Francisco Convention & Visitor Bureau. You won't find any parking, but you will find tons of free maps, brochures, coupons and advice. The number above gives access to a 24hr recorded message listing daily events and activities; you can also use it to request free information about hotels, restaurants and shopping.

Berkeley Convention & Visitors Bureau
2015 Center Street, between Shattuck & Milvia Streets, Berkeley, CA 94704 (1-800 847 4823/1-510 549 7040 /www.visitberkeley.com). BART Downtown Berkeley. **Open** 9am-5pm Mon-Fri.
A block from the Downtown Berkeley BART station. Staff can post a visitors' guide on request.

Oakland Convention & Visitors Bureau
463 11th Street, between Broadway & Washington Streets, Oakland, CA 94609 (1-510 839 9000/www. oaklandcvb.com). BART 12th Street/City Center. **Open** 8.30am-5pm Mon-Fri.
Located in opposite the City Hall in downtown Oakland. Phone if you would like to be sent a visitors' guide to Oakland.

Visas

Under the current Visa Waiver Scheme, citizens of 27 countries, including the UK, Ireland, Australia and New Zealand, do not need a visa for stays of less than 90 days (for business or pleasure). Visitors are required to have a machine-readable passport that's valid for the full 90-day period and a return or open standby ticket. Mexicans and Canadians don't usually need visas but must have legal proof of their citizenship.

All other travellers must have visas. However, given current security fears, it's advisable to double-check requirements before you set out. For more, *see p288* **Travel advice**, *p290* Immigration and *p289* **Passport update**; *see also below* Work.

Visa application forms and complete information can be obtained from the nearest US embassy or consulate. It's wise to send in your application at least three weeks before you plan to travel. If you require a visa more urgently you should apply via the travel agent who is booking your ticket.

For further information on visa requirements, see http://travel.state.gov. UK citizens can call the Visa Information Line: 09042 450100 (£1.20/min) or look online at www.usembassy.org.uk.

When to go

Climate

San Francisco may be in California, but its climate, like its politics, is all its own. When planning a trip, don't anticipate the normal seasons, climatically, at least. Spring and autumn are relatively predictable, with warm days and cool nights. During the summer, however, days are often chilly, but the nights are usually mild. In midwinter,

what seems like months of rain will break for a week of sun. In general, temperatures rarely stray above 80°F (27°C) or below 45°F (7°C). San Francisco is small, but the weather varies wildly between neighbourhoods. The city's western terrain is flat, and so fog often covers Golden Gate Park and the Sunset and Richmond areas. However, the fog is often too heavy to climb further east, so the areas east of Twin Peaks - the Mission, the Castro, Noe Valley - are often sunny just as Golden Gate Park is shrouded in fog. Add in the wind that whips in to Fisherman's Wharf, and you may experience four seasons in one day.

Public holidays
New Year's Day 1 Jan
Martin Luther King Jr Day 3rd Mon in Jan
President's Day 3rd Mon in Feb
Memorial Day last Mon in May
Independence Day 4 July
Labor Day 1st Mon in Sept
Columbus Day 2nd Mon in Oct
Veterans' Day 11 Nov
Thanksgiving Day 4th Thur in Nov
Christmas Day 25 Dec

Work

For foreigners to work legally in the US, a US company must sponsor your application for an H-1 visa, which enables you to work in the country for up to five years. For the H-1 visa to be approved, your prospective employer must convince the Immigration Department that there is no American citizen qualified to do the job as well as you. Students have a much easier time. UK students can contact the British Universities North America Club (BUNAC) for help in arranging a temporary job and the requisite visa (16 Bowling Green Lane, London, EC1R 0QH; 020 7251 3472, www.bunac.org/uk).

Directory

Further Reference

Fiction & poetry

Isabel Allende
Daughters of Fortune
A delightfully written piece centred on the Gold Rush and one young woman's search for love in a tumultous city.

James Dalessandro *1906 A Novel*
A fictionalised, though grippingly researched, account of San Francisco's catastrophic year of earthquake and fire.

Dave Eggers *A Heartbreaking Work of Staggering Genius*
A beautiful memoir of bringing up a younger brother, wrapped in fun postmodern flim-flam.

Jim Fadiman
The Other Side of Haight
This enjoyable book details the early psychedelic experiments in the Haight-Ashbury neighbourhood.

Allen Ginsberg
Howl and Other Poems
Grab your chance to read the rant that caused all the fuss way back in the 1950s.

Glen David Gold
Carter Beats the Devil
A sleight-of-hand comedy thriller set in 1920s San Francisco.

Dashiell Hammett
The Maltese Falcon
One of the greatest detective writers and one of the world's best detective novels, set in a dark and dangerous San Francisco.

Jack Kerouac *On the Road; The Subterraneans; Desolation Angels; The Dharma Bums*
Famous for a reason: bittersweet tales of drugs and sex in San Francisco and around the world, from the best Beat of them all.

Jack London *Tales of the Fish Patrol; John Barleycorn*
Early works from London, set in the writer's native city. For his musings on the Sonoma Valley, pick up *Valley of the Moon*.

Armistead Maupin
Tales of the City (6 volumes)
This witty soap opera, later a very successful TV series, follows the lives and loves of a group of San Francisco friends.

Frank Norris *McTeague*
Working-class life and loss set in unromanticised Barbary Coast days. A cult classic of the 1890s.

James Patterson *1st to Die*
A detective, diagnosed with a terminal illness, struggles to catch a serial killer in San Francisco.

Domenic Stansberry
The Last Days of Il Duce
A fearsome, authentic piece of *noir* fiction, set in North Beach.

John Steinbeck
The Grapes of Wrath
Grim tales of California in the Great Depression by the master of American fiction.

Amy Tan *The Joy Luck Club*
A moving story of the lives and loves of two generations of Chinese-American women living in San Francisco.

Alfredo Vea *Gods Go Begging*
A San Francisco murder trial has ties to the Vietnam War.

William T Vollmann
Whores for Gloria
The boozy story of a middle-aged alcoholic whose fall into decrepitude occurs in the seamy underbelly of the Tenderloin.

Tom Wolfe *The Electric Kool-Aid Acid Test; The Pump House Gang*
Alternative lifestyles in trippy, hippy, 1960s California.

Non-fiction

Walton Bean
California: An Interpretive History
An anecdotal account of California's shady past.

Po Bronson
The Nudist on the Late Shift
An unblinking treatise on the Silicon Valley scene.

Herb Caen *Baghdad by the Bay*
Local gossip and lightly poetic insight from the much-missed *Chronicle* columnist.

Carolyn Cassady
Off the Road: My Years with Cassady, Kerouac and Ginsberg
Not enlightened feminism, but an interesting alternative examination of the Beats.

Joan Didion
Slouching Towards Bethlehem; The White Album
Brilliant essays examining California in the past couple of decades by one of America's most respected authors.

Timothy W Drescher
San Francisco Bay Area Murals
A well-resourced book with plenty of maps and 140 photos.

Lawrence Ferlinghetti & Nancy J Peters *Literary San Francisco*
The city's literary pedigree examined by the founder of City Lights books.

Robert Greenfield *Dark Star: An Oral Biography of Jerry Garcia*
The life and (high) times of the Grateful Dead's late frontman.

Emmett Grogan
Ringolevio: A Life Played for Keeps
Part-memoir, part-social history, part-fable, *Ringolevio* traces the story of Grogan, one of the founders of the Diggers, from New York to 1960s Haight-Ashbury. Fantastic.

Michael Lewis *Moneyball: The Art of Winning an Unfair Game*
Oakland A's GM Billy Beane may go down as one of the most influential baseball executives of the last half-century. This vital book profiles Beane and his team.

Beth Lisick
Everybody into the Pool
A tremendously enjoyable and occasionally laugh-out-loud funny collection of essays about Lisick's journey from child to adult in the Bay Area.

Malcolm Margolin
The Ohlone Way
How the Bay Area's original inhabitants lived, researched from oral histories.

John Miller (ed) *San Francisco Stories: Great Writers on the City*
Contributions by Herb Caen, Anne Lamott, Amy Tan, Ishmael Reed and many others.

Ray Mungo
San Francisco Confidential
A gossipy look behind the city's closed doors.

John Plunkett & Barbara Traub (eds) *Burning Man*
Photo-heavy manual to the the annual insanity that is the Burning Man Festival.

Marc Reisner *Cadillac Desert: A Dangerous State*
The role of water in California's history and future; a projection of apocalypse founded on shifting tectonics and hairtrigger irrigation.

Nathaniel Rich *San Francisco Noir*
San Francisco's cinematic history gets re-examined in this beautifully written piece, which falls somewhere between guidebook, cultural criticism and academic tract.

Richard Schwartz *Berkeley 1900*
An in-depth account of the early origins of complex and controversial Berkeley.

Joel Selvin *San Francisco: The Magical History*
Tour of the sights and sounds of the city's pop music history by the *Chronicle*'s music critic.

Randy Shilts
And the Band Played On
Shilts' crucial work is still the most important account of the AIDS epidemic in San Francisco.

John Snyder *San Francisco Secrets: Fascinating Facts About the City by the Bay*
This amusing collection of city trivia comes complete with facts and figures galore.

Gertrude Stein
The Making of Americans
This autobiographical work includes an account of Stein's early childhood in Oakland.

Tom Stienstra & Ann Marie Brown *California Hiking*
What it says: an outstanding guide to over 1,000 hikes all over the state. Stienstra is the outdoors columnist for the *San Francisco Chronicle*. Other books in the excellent Fogohorn Outdoors series on California cover camping, hiking, biking and fishing.
Robert Louis Stevenson *An Inland Voyage; The Silverado Squatters*
Autobiographical narratives describing the journey from Europe to western America.
Bonnie Wach *San Francisco As You Like It*
City tours to suit pretty much all personalities and moods, from Ivy League shoppers to cheapskate fitness-freak vegetarians.

Film

Birdman of Alctraz (1961)
Hopelessly overlong and laughably inaccurate, but, thanks largely to Burt Lancaster's likeable title turn, a decent film regardless.
Bullitt (1968)
This Steve McQueen film boasts the all-time greatest San Francisco car chase.
Chan Is Missing (1982)
Two cab drivers search for a man who stole their life savings in this movie, which gives an authentic, insider's look at Chinatown.
The Conversation (1974)
Gene Hackman's loner surveillance expert gets in a little deeper than he planned in Coppola's classic. The opening scene, shot in Union Square, is a cinematic *tour de force*.
Crumb (1994)
An award-winning film about the comic book master and misanthrope Robert Crumb.
Dark Passage (1947)
This classic thriller starts in Marin County, where Bogart escapes from San Quentin Prison, and ends up in Lauren Bacall's SF apartment.
Dirty Harry (1971)
Do you feel lucky?
The Graduate (1967)
Hoffman at his best, with shots of Berkeley as well as a a cool wrong-direction shot on the Bay Bridge.
Harold and Maude (1971)
Bay Area scenery abounds in this bittersweet cult classic about an unbalanced boy who falls in love with an elderly woman.
Jimi Plays Berkeley (1970)
Stirring footage of the town during its radical days, plus Hendrix at his very best.
The Maltese Falcon (1941)
Hammett's classic made into a glorious 1940s thriller, full of great street scenes.

Mrs Doubtfire (1993)
Relentlessly hammy Robin Williams plays a divorcee posing as a nanny to be near his kids.
Pacific Heights (1990)
Pity the poor landlord: Michael Keaton preys on doting yuppie parents-to-be.
San Francisco (1936)
Ignore the first 90 minutes of moralising and sit back to enjoy the Great Quake.
So I Married An Axe Murderer (1993)
This San Francisco-set romantic comedy features Mike Meyers giving an immensely funny send-up of 1950s beat culture.
The Sweetest Thing (2002)
Gross-out movie meets chick flick, with Cameron Diaz.
The Times of Harvey Milk (1984)
This Oscar-winning documentary focuses on the first 'out' gay politician in the United States.
Vertigo (1958)
A veteran cop becomes obsessed with a mysterious blonde. A die-cast San Francisco classic.
The Voyage Home: Star Trek IV (1986)
The gang come to SF to to save some whales in this flick, the best of the series.
The Wedding Planner (2000)
This update of the classic screwball comedy is a bit clunky, but J-Lo is immaculately cast.
The Wild Parrots of Telegraph Hill (2000)
A delightful documentary about Mark Bittner and the North Beach birds who love him dearly.

Music

Big Brother and the Holding Company *Cheap Thrills* (1968)
Classic Janis Joplin, housed in a classic Robert Crumb sleeve. Tracks include 'Ball and Chain' and 'Piece of My Heart'.
Black Rebel Motorcycle Club *Take Them On, On Your Own* (2003)
They smoke, they wear leather jackets. Rebels, huh?
Chris Isaak *Heart Shaped World* (1989)
What a 'Wicked Game' to be so good-looking, with a voice like that.
Creedence Clearwater Revival *Willie and the Poor Boys* (1969)
Classic southern rock with a San Francisco touch.
The Dead Kennedys *Fresh Fruit for Rotting Vegetables* (1980)
Excellent, angry SF punk.
Deerhoof *The Runners Four* (2005)
A surprisingly straightforwward set from the local critics' darlings. For something a little more out-there, try 1999's *Holdy Paws*.

Digital Underground *Sex Packets* (1990)
Terrific, if slightly dated, hip hop.
Erase Errata *At Crystal Palace* (2003)
Angular, uplifting rock from the queens of the underground.
Gold Chains *Young Miss America* (2003)
Bay Area hip hop, 21st-century style.
The Grateful Dead *Dick's Picks Vol.4* (1996)
Jerry Garcia and the boys in their 1970 prime at the Fillmore East.
Jefferson Airplane *Surrealistic Pillow* (1967)
Folk, blues and psychedelia. Grace Slick helps define the SF sound.
Joshua Redman *Wish* (1993)
Quality jazz from the Bay Area tenor saxophonist.
Kid 606 *The Action Packed Mentallist Brings You the Fucking Jams* (2003)
This demented set of cut-ups and samples is as close as this sonic terrorist has ever come to accessible.
Primus *Pork Soda* (1993)
Wryly intelligent punk-funk in the Zappa tradition.
Sly and the Family Stone *Stand!* (1969)
Funk-rock masters. If you haven't heard this, you haven't really heard the 1960s.

Websites

www.craigslist.org
How San Franciscans hook up. Hilarious and enlightening.
http://onlysf.sfvisitor.org
The CVB's site is packed with information on the town.
www.mistersf.com
A delicious collection of local oddballs, notorious history and contemporary culture.
www.oaklandhistory.com
Pretty much what the title suggests, and pretty interesting to boot.
www.sanfranciscomemories.com
Wonderful photographs of the city in days gone by.
www.sfbg.com
The online edition of the *San Francisco Bay Guardian*.
www.sfgate.com
The *San Francisco Chronicle* online.
www.sfheritage.org
This site focuses on the city's architectural heritage.
www.sfstation.com
Upcoming events, clubs, parties, film and restaurant reviews and more.
www.sfweekly.com
Listings, reviews and features.
www.streetcar.org
The past and present of SF's classic streetcars, now on the F line.
www.transitinfo.org
Very useful for all forms of Bay Area public transport.

Directory

Index

Advertisers' Index

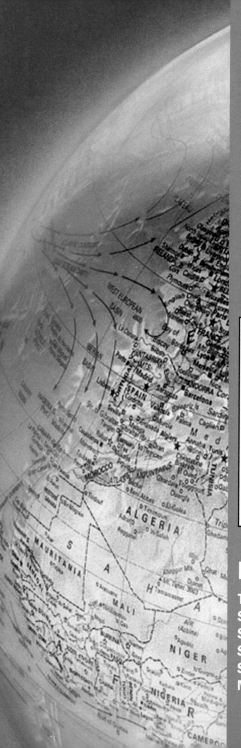

Major sight or landmark	■
Hospital or college	■
Railway station	■
Parks	■
River	■
Interstate Highway	🛡80
US Highway	(101)
State or Provincial Highway	①
Main road	—
Airport	✈
Church	✚
Area name	CASTRO

Maps

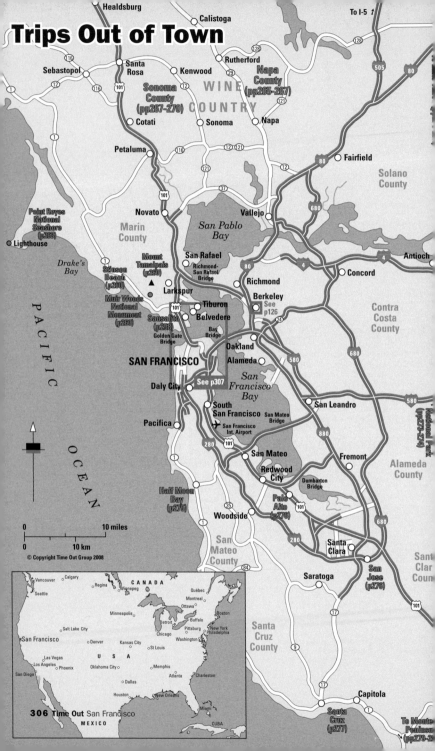

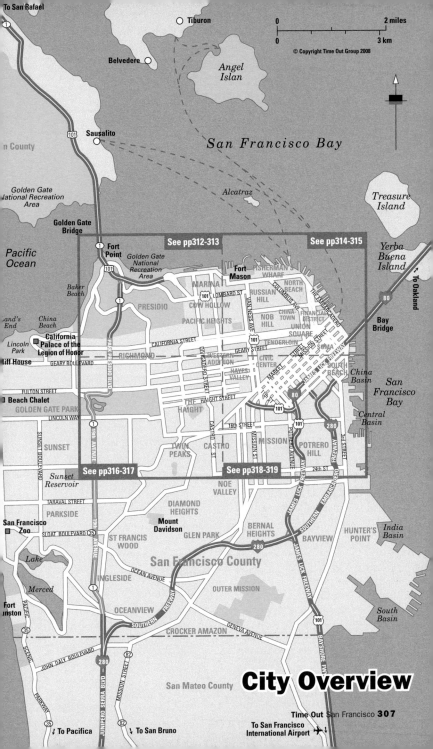

To San Rafael

Tiburon

Belvedere

Angel
Islan

San Francisco Bay

Sausalito

n County

Alcatraz

Treasure
Island

Golden Gate
National Recreation
Area

Golden Gate
Bridge

Yerba
Buena
Island

Pacific
Ocean

Fort
Point

See pp312-313

See pp314-315

To Oakland

Golden Gate
National
Recreation
Area

Fort
Mason

FISHERMAN'S
WHARF

Baker
Beach

MARINA

NORTH
BEACH

Bay
Bridge

RUSSIAN
HILL

COLUMBUS AVE

THE EMBARCADERO

LOMBARD ST

COW HOLLOW

PRESIDIO

CHINA
TOWN

FINAN-
CIAL
DISTRICT

land's
End

China
Beach

PACIFIC HEIGHTS

NOB
HILL

VAN NESS AVE

Lincoln
Park

California
Palace of the
Legion of Honor

CALIFORNIA STREET

UNION
SQUARE

TENDERLOIN

San
Francisco
Bay

WESTERN
ADDITION

GEARY STREET

liff House

RICHMOND

GEARY BOULEVARD

CIVIC
CENTER

SOMA

SOUTH
BEACH

China
Basin

HAYES
VALLEY

MARKET STREET

MISSION STREET

JAMES LICK FREEWAY

FULTON STREET

THE
HAIGHT

HAIGHT STREET

Beach Chalet

GOLDEN GATE PARK

LINCOLN WAY

Central
Basin

CASTRO ST

16th STREET

MISSION STREET

POTRERO AVENUE

19th AVENUE

See pp316-317

TWIN
PEAKS

CASTRO

MISSION

POTRERO
HILL

See pp318-319

3rd STREET

Sunset
Reservoir

24th ST.

SUNSET

NOE
VALLEY

TARAVAL STREET

DIAMOND
HEIGHTS

SUNSET BOULEVARD

PARKSIDE

San Francisco
Zoo

SLOAT BOULEVARD

Mount
Davidson

GLEN PARK

BERNAL
HEIGHTS

BAYVIEW

HUNTER'S
POINT

India
Basin

ST FRANCIS
WOOD

Lake

280

Merced

INGLESIDE

OCEAN AVENUE

San Francisco County

JAMES LICK FREEWAY

SOUTHERN EMBARCADERO FREEWAY

Fort
unston

OCEANVIEW

SCENIC

SOUTHERN

FREEWAY

GENEVA AVENUE

CROCKER AMAZON

South
Basin

BAYSHORE FWY

JOHN DALY BOULEVARD

JUNIPERO SERRA BLVD

MISSION STREET

San Mateo County

San Francisco County

City Overview

To Pacifica

To San Bruno

To San Francisco
International Airport

SCENIC PARKWAY

© Copyright Time Out Group 2008

2 miles

3 km

San Francisco by Area

San Francisco
Bay

Marina Green

MARINA   BOULEVARD

Crissy Field

Palace of
Fine Arts &
Exploratorium

MARINA

Moscone
Playground

101

LOMBARD   STREET

DIVISADERO   STREET

COW HOLLOW

Cow Hollow
Playground

PRESIDIO

VALLEJO   STREET

PACIFIC
HEIGHTS

Presidio
Golf Course

WEST PACIFIC AVENUE

Alta Plaza
Park

PRESIDIO HEIGHTS

California Pacific
Medical Center

Mountain Lake
Park

CALIFORNIA   STREET

PINE   STREET

BUSH   STREET

UCSF Medical
Center

Japan Ce

CLEMENT   STREET

GEARY   EXPRESSWAY

ARGUELLO   BOULEVARD

Kaiser
Medical
Center

PARK   PRESIDIO   BOULEVARD

CALIFORNIA   STREET

GEARY   BOULEVARD

GEARY   BOULEVARD

RICHMOND

University
of
San Francisco

WESTERN
ADDITION

TURK   STREET

GOLDEN   GATE   AVENUE

BALBOA   STREET

FULTON   STREET

Alamo
Square

Painte
Ladie

University of
San Francisco

MASONIC   AVENUE

DIVISADERO   STREET

FELL   STREET

OAK   STREET

FULTON   STREET

St Mary's
Medical Center

FELL   STREET

Panhandle

OAK   STREET

Golden Gate Park

Sharon
Meadow

HAIGHT-
ASHBURY

Buena Vista
Park

Duboce
Park

Muni Metro
Duboce & N

STANYAN   STREET

ASHBURY   STREET

BUENA VISTA TERRACE EAST

UCSF Davies

CASTRO   STREET

MARKET STREET

LINCOLN   WAY

Muni
Metro
Carl & Cole

Corona Heights
Park

Muni
Metro
UCSF Parnassus

PARNASSUS   AVENUE

COLE
VALLEY

SUNSET

Muni
Metro
Judah & 9th Ave

University of California
San Francisco

17th   STREET

Muni
Metro
Castro

CASTRO

DIAMOND   STREET

0   ¼   ½ mile

0   1 km

© Copyright Time Out Group 2008

San Francisco Bay

Aquatic Park

Pier 39

FISHERMAN'S WHARF

JEFFERSON STREET

THE EMBARCADERO

NORTH POINT STREET

BAY STREET

Russian Hill Park

San Francisco Art Institute

NORTH BEACH

Coit Tower

Lombard Street

COLUMBUS

RUSSIAN HILL

Washington Square

BROADWAY

VALLEJO STREET

BROADWAY

PACIFIC AVENUE

Jackson Square

JACKSON STREET

Portsmouth Square

CHINATOWN

Transamerica Pyramid

FINANCIAL DISTRICT

Ferry Building

EMBARCADERO

Muni Metro BART Embarcadero

STEUART STREET

Muni Metro Folsom

Bay Bridge

101

VAN NESS AVENUE

FRANKLIN STREET

LARKIN STREET

POLK STREET

POLK GULCH

NOB HILL

Huntington Park

St Francis Memorial Hospital

PINE STREET

BUSH STREET

SUTTER STREET

GEARY STREET

MARKET

FREMONT STREET

BEALE STREET

1st STREET

UNION SQUARE & AROUND

BART Montgomery

SFMOMA

Yerba Buena Gardens

Muni Metro BART Powell

HOWARD STREET

FOLSOM STREET

HARRISON STREET

2nd STREET

3rd STREET

Muni Metro Brannan

THE EMBARCADERO

TENDERLOIN

GEARY STREET

GOLDEN GATE AVENUE

TAYLOR STREET

LEAVENWORTH STREET

HYDE STREET

5th STREET

4th STREET

SOMA

80

BRYANT STREET

South Park

BRANNAN STREET

SOUTH BEACH

Muni Metro 2nd & King

St Mary's Cathedral

GEARY STREET

GOUGH STREET

FRANKLIN STREET

Jefferson Square

Asian Art Museum

CIVIC CENTER

City Hall

BART Civic Center

6th STREET

7th STREET

8th STREET

9th STREET

CalTrain Depot

Muni 4th & King

AT & T Park

BERRY ST

China Basin

HAYES VALLEY

Muni Van Ness

HOWARD STREET

FOLSOM STREET

VAN NESS AVENUE

10th STREET

BRYANT STREET

BRANNAN STREET

8th STREET

6th STREET

3rd STREET

Muni Metro Mission Rock

UPPER MARKET

101

16th STREET

Muni Metro UCSF Mission Bay

16th STREET

280

Muni Metro Mariposa

GUERRERO STREET

SOUTH VAN NESS AVENUE

POTRERO AVENUE

16th STREET

16th St BART

Franklin Square

Jackson Park

MISSION

POTRERO HILL

3rd STREET

Central Basin

Muni Metro 20th St

Street Index

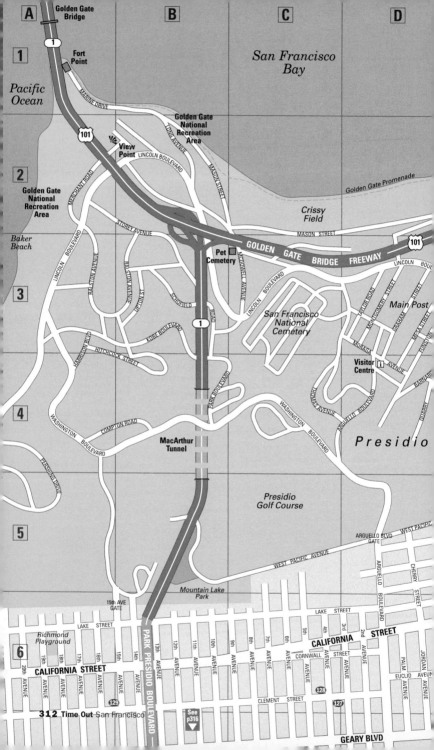

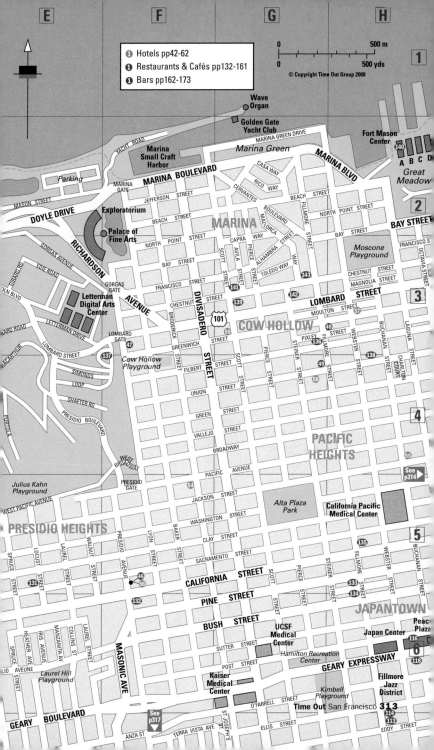

Ferries to
North Bay

Pier
39

1

Municipal
Pier

Aquatic
Park

Hyde Street
Pier

Fisherman's
Wharf

THE EMBARCADERO

STREET

The
Cannery

The
Anchorage

JEFFERSON STREET

BEACH STREET

Cable
Car

NORTH POINT STREET

FISHERMAN'S
WHARF

Fort Mason
Center

National Maritime
Museum

Cable
Car

BAY STREET

FRANCISCO

A B C D

Hostel

Ghirardelli
Square

San Francisco
Art Institute

COLUMBUS AVE

North
Beach
Playground

CHESTNUT STREET

NORTH
BEACH

2

Great
Meadow

MACARTHUR AVENUE

BEACH STREET

Russian
Hill Park

NORTH POINT ST

Moscone
Playground

BAY STREET

FRANCISCO STREET

BAY STREET

RUSSIAN
HILL

Lombard
Street

GREENWICH STREET

Washing
Squa

CHESTNUT STREET

MAGNOLIA STREET

LOMBARD STREET

FILBERT STREET

UNION STREET

GREEN STREET

POWELL STREET

3

MOULTON ST

GREENWICH STREET

PIXLEY ST

FILBERT STREET

LAGUNA STREET

OCTAVIA STREET

GOUGH STREET

FRANKLIN STREET

POLK STREET

LARKIN STREET

HYDE STREET

LEAVENWORTH STREET

JONES STREET

TAYLOR STREET

UNION STREET

GREEN STREET

VALLEJO STREET

Ina Coolbrith
Park

BROADW

WEBSTER STREET

BUCHANAN STREET

CHARLTON COURT

UNION STREET

Octagon
House

BROADWAY

Haas-Lilienthal
House

GREEN STREET

VALLEJO STREET

BROADWAY

PACIFIC AVENUE

Cable
Muse

JACKSON STREET

WASHINGTON STREET

4

POLK
GULCH

NOB
HILL

CLAY STREET

PACIFIC AVENUE

JACKSON STREET

California Pacific
Medical Center

WASHINGTON STREET

Lafayette
Park

SACRAMENTO STREET

Grace
Cathedral

Huntington
Park

SACRAMENTO STREET

CALIFORNIA STREET

VAN NESS AVENUE

Cable
Car

PINE STREET

5

CALIFORNIA STREET

FILLMORE STREET

PINE STREET

BUSH STREET

AUSTIN STREET

FERN STREET

HEMLOCK STREET

St Francis
Memorial Hospital

BUSH STREET

POST STREET

GEARY STREET

SUTTER STREET

JAPANTOWN

POST STREET

O'FARRELL STREET

TENDERLOIN

GEARY STREET

6

SUTTER STREET

Peace
Plaza

Japan Center

GEARY
EXPRESSWAY

STEINER STREET

WEBSTER STREET

BUCHANAN STREET

LAGUNA STREET

Cathedral of St Mary
of the Assumption

CEDAR STREET

MYRTLE STREET

OLIVE STREET

WILLOW STREET

ELLIS STREET

EDDY STREET

LARKIN STREET

LEAVENWORTH STREET

Glide
Memorial
Church

Hallidie Plaza
Visitor Informa

JONES STREET

TURK STREET

Kimball
Playground

Fillmore
Jazz
District

314 Time Out San Francisco

Jefferson
Square

GOUGH STREET

See
p318

ELM STREET

GOLDEN GATE AVENUE

HYDE STREET

St Boniface
Catholic Church

EDDY STREET

THE WESTERN
ADDITION

Kimbell
Playground

ELLIS STREET

Fillmore Jazz
District

EDDY STREET

TURK ST

GOLDEN GATE AVENUE

ALLISTER STREET

Alamo
Square

Painted
Ladies

HAYES STREET

FELL STREET

OAK STREET

PAGE STREET

HAIGHT STREET

WALLER STREET

LOWER HAIGHT

HERMANN STREET

Duboce Park

Muni
Metro
Duboce & Noe

UCSF
Davies

HENRY STREET

See
p317

Muni
Metro
Castro

Jefferson
Square

California
State
Building

Veterans
Building

Opera
House

Symphony
Hall

HAYES
VALLEY

FULTON STREET

BIRCH STREET

GROVE STREET

LINDEN STREET

HICKORY STREET

LILY STREET

ROSE STREET

See
p314

McALLISTER STREET

Asian Art
Museum

St Boniface
Catholic Church

Civic
Center
Plaza

UN
Plaza

City
Hall

CIVIC
CENTER

Main
Library

Muni Metro
Civic Center

BART
Civic Center

Bill Graham
Civic
Auditorium

FRANKLIN ST

MARKET STREET

STEVENSON STREET

SOMA

VAN

HOWARD STREET

FOLSOM STREET

HARRISON STREET

101 CENTRAL SKYWAY

DUBOCE AVENUE

CLINTON PARK

BROSNAN STREET

14th STREET

Muni
Metro
Church

GUERRERO STREET

Mission
Dolores

16th STREET

BART
16th St

17th STREET

Muni
Metro
Church & 18th St

Mission
Dolores
Park

Mission
Playground

Coronado
Playground

MISSION

18th STREET

19th STREET

20th STREET

21st STREET

22nd STREET

23rd STREET

Precita Eyes Mural
Arts & Visitors Cen

BART
24th St

Muni
Metro
Church & 24th St

❶ Hotels pp42-62
❶ Restaurants & Cafés pp132-161
❶ Bars pp161-173

0 ————— 500 m
0 ————— 500 yds

© Copyright Time Out Group 2008

Muni Metro

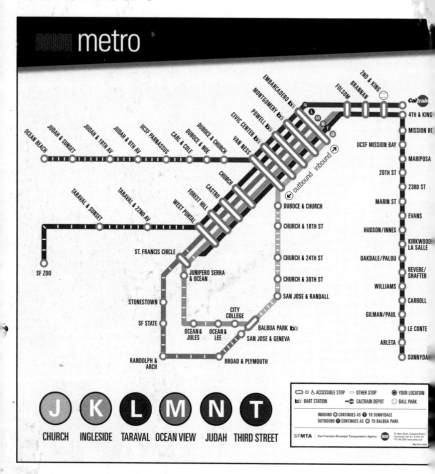